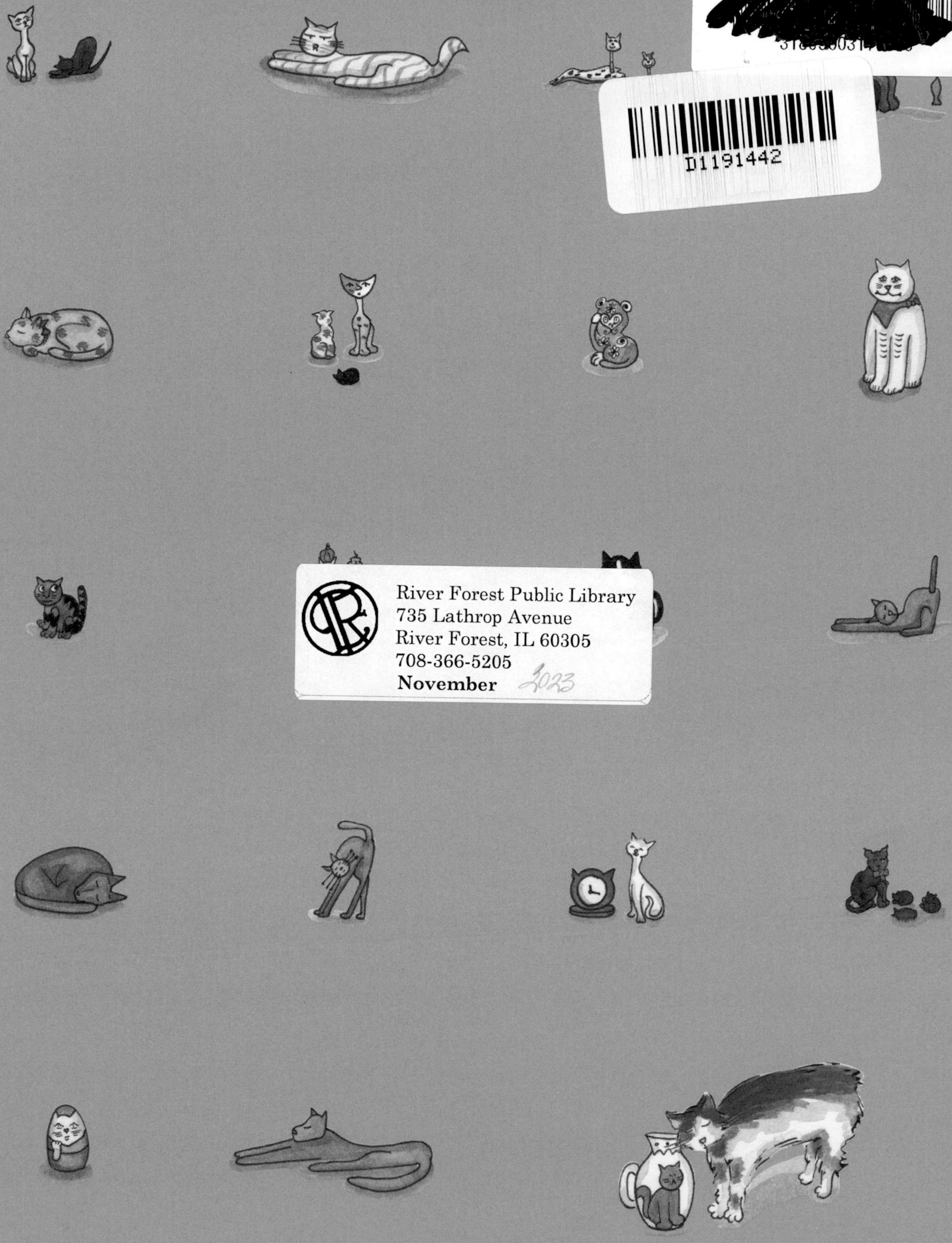

# ARTIFICIAL

## A Love Story

## Amy Kurzweil

Catapult  New York

ARTIFICIAL

*Artificial* is a work of memory and imagination. It features historical documents that really exist, all of which have been recreated by the author's hand, and it documents events that really happened, although some details have been changed to protect privacy or to aid clarity.

First Catapult edition: 2023

ISBN: 978-1-94822-638-7

Library of Congress Control Number: 2022951933

Jacket design and illustration by Amy Kurzweil
Book design by Laura Berry

Catapult
New York, NY
books.catapult.co

Printed in China

1 3 5 7 9 10 8 6 4 2

For my father, who taught me about transcendence

And for Jacob

There will be no edges, but curves.
Clean lines pointing only forward.

History, with its hard spine & dog-eared
Corners, will be replaced with nuance...

—Tracy K. Smith, "Sci-Fi"

# Contents

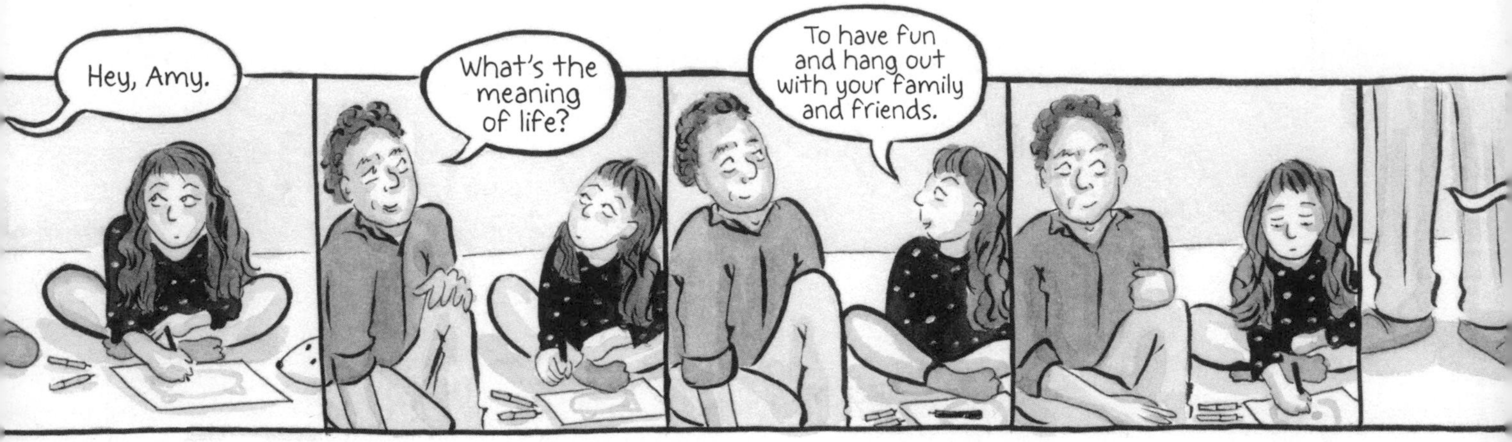
Hey, Amy.
What's the meaning of life?
To have fun and hang out with your family and friends.

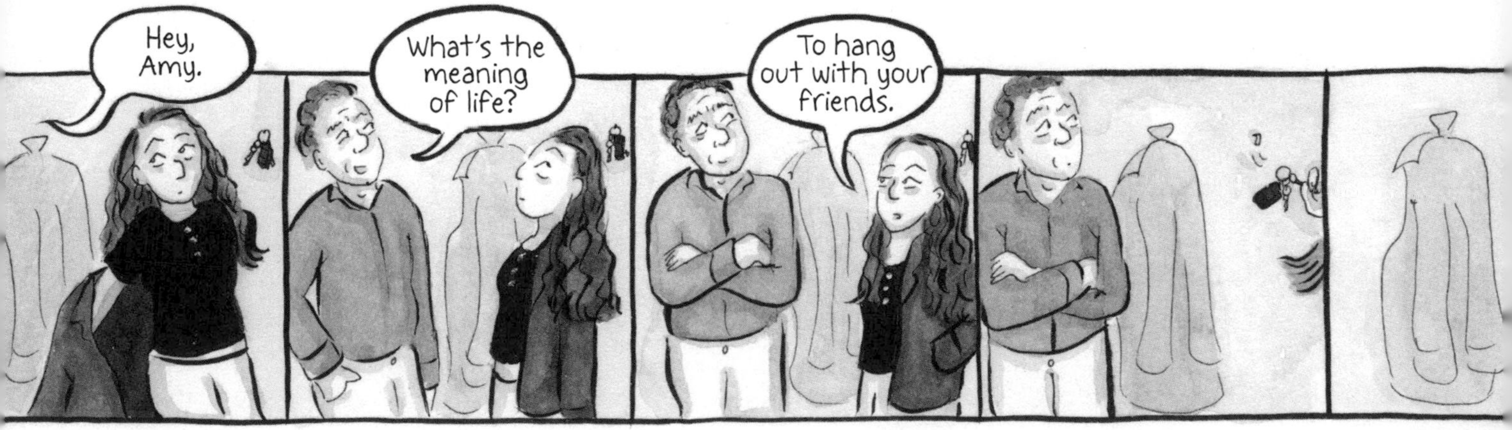
Hey, Amy.
What's the meaning of life?
To hang out with your friends.

# I.

# Pattern Recognition

Nothing is stranger to man than his own image.

–Karl Čapek, *Rossum's Universal Robots*

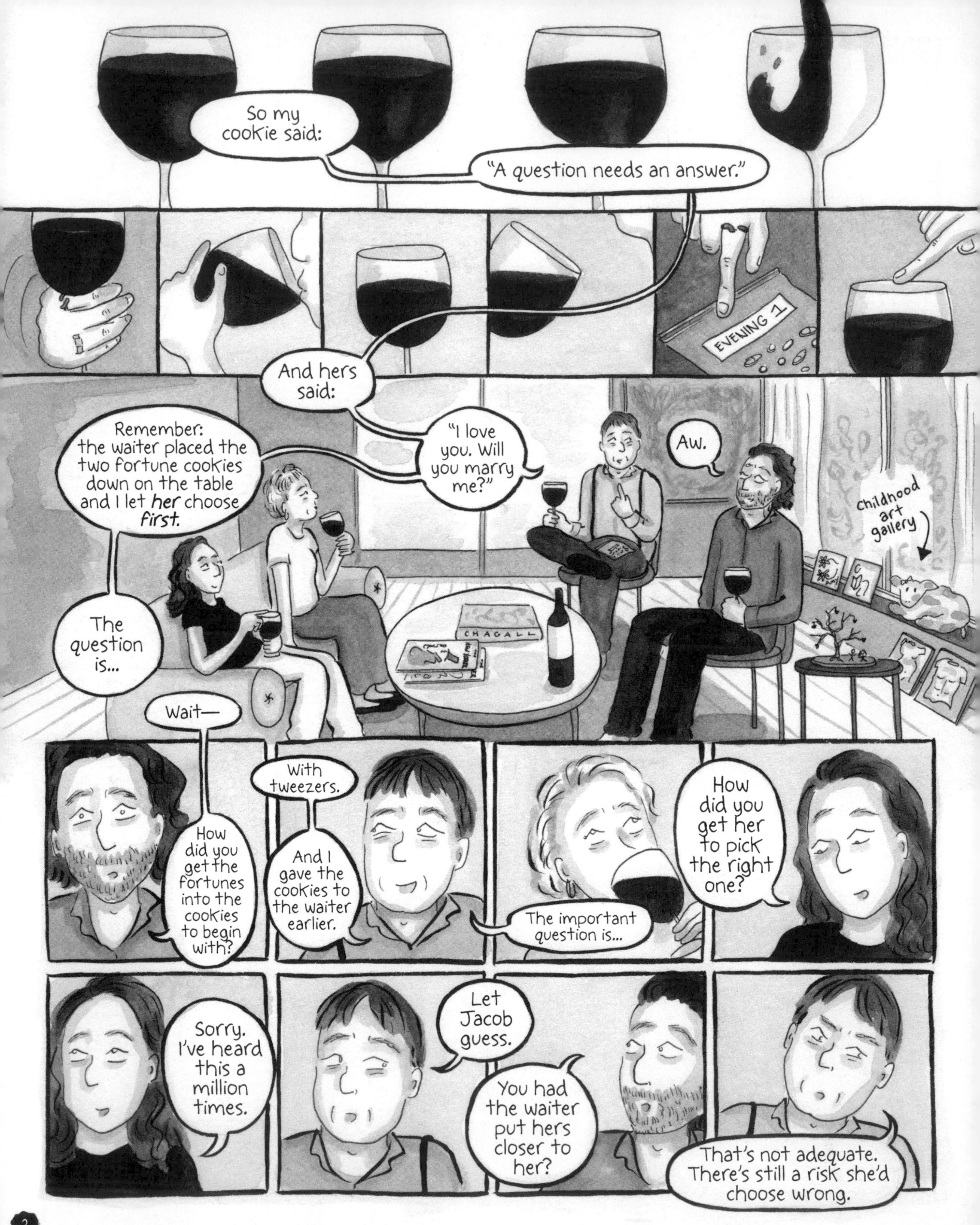
So my cookie said:
"A question needs an answer."
EVENING 1
And hers said:
"I love you. Will you marry me?"
Remember: the waiter placed the two fortune cookies down on the table and I let *her* choose *first.*
Aw.
CHAGALL
Childhood art gallery
The question is...
Wait—
How did you get the fortunes into the cookies to begin with?
With tweezers.
And I gave the cookies to the waiter earlier.
The important question is...
How did you get her to pick the right one?
Sorry. I've heard this a million times.
Let Jacob guess.
You had the waiter put hers closer to her?
That's not adequate. There's still a risk she'd choose wrong.

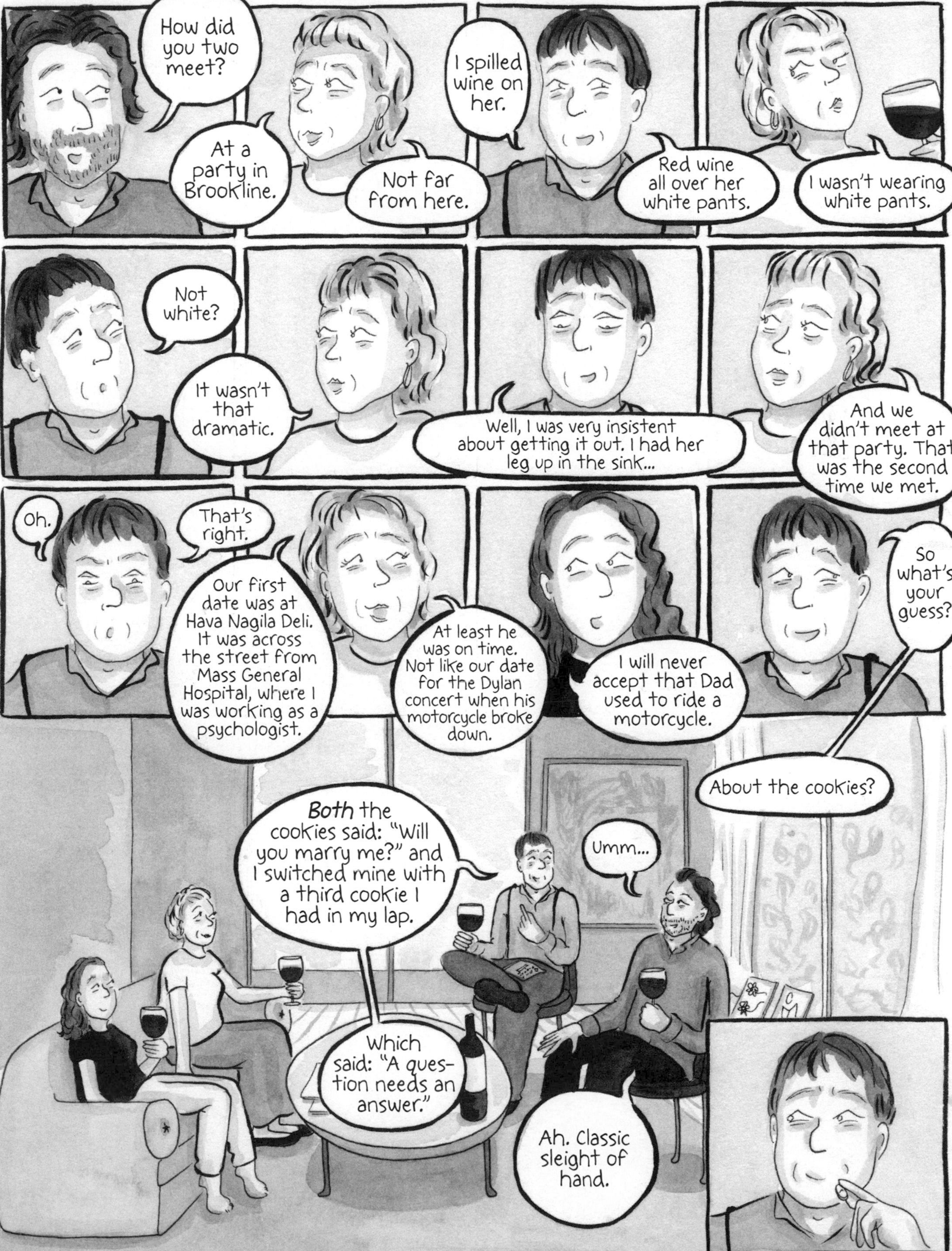
How did you two meet?
At a party in Brookline.
Not far from here.
I spilled wine on her.
Red wine all over her white pants.
I wasn't wearing white pants.
Not white?
It wasn't that dramatic.
Well, I was very insistent about getting it out. I had her leg up in the sink...
And we didn't meet at that party. That was the second time we met.
Oh.
That's right.
Our first date was at Hava Nagila Deli. It was across the street from Mass General Hospital, where I was working as a psychologist.
At least he was on time. Not like our date for the Dylan concert when his motorcycle broke down.
I will never accept that Dad used to ride a motorcycle.
So what's your guess?
About the cookies?
*Both* the cookies said: "Will you marry me?" and I switched mine with a third cookie I had in my lap.
Umm...
Which said: "A question needs an answer."
Ah. Classic sleight of hand.

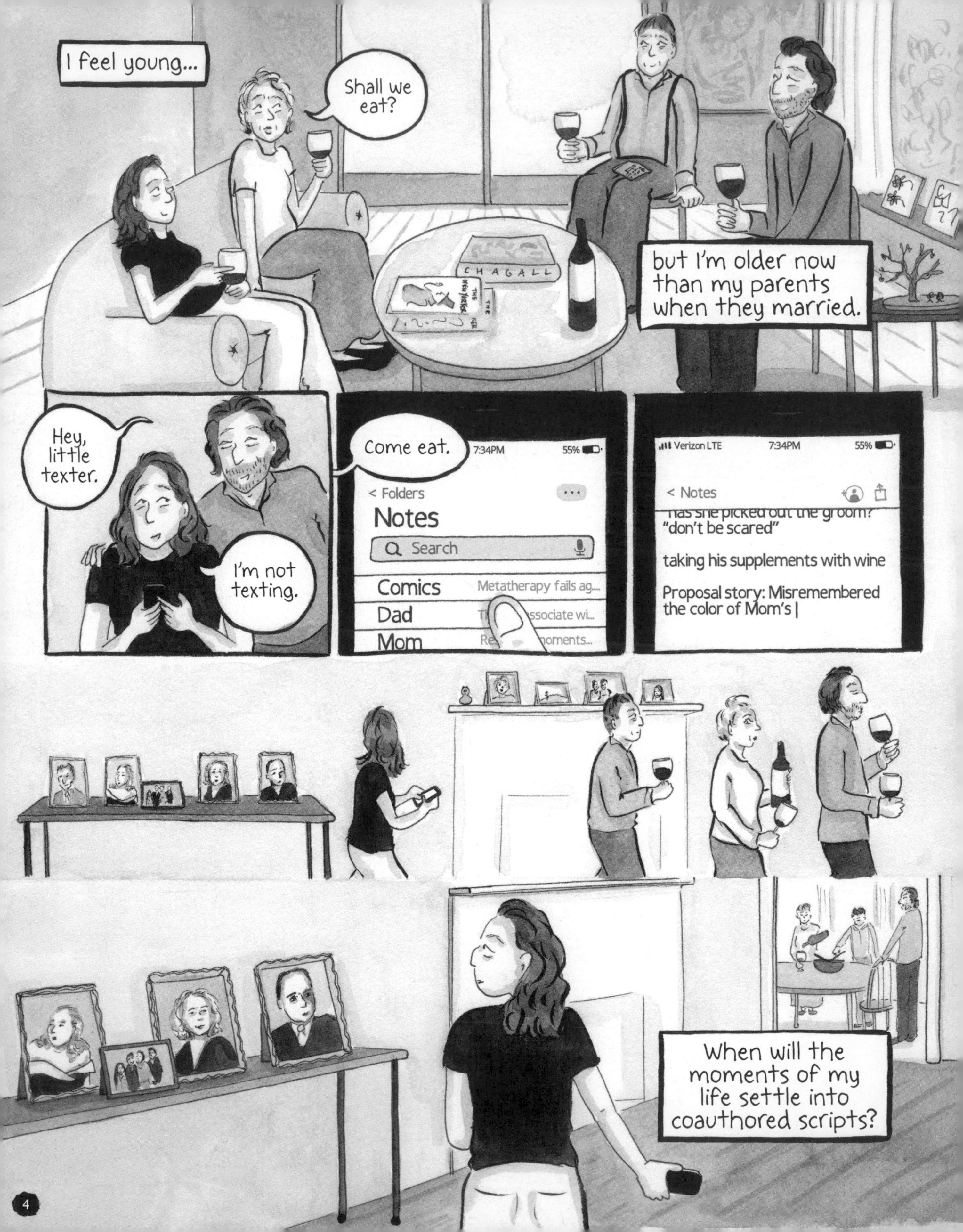

I feel young...
Shall we eat?
but I'm older now than my parents when they married.
CHAGALL
Hey, little texter.
I'm not texting.
Come eat.
7:34PM 55%
< Folders
Notes
Search
Comics Metatherapy fails ag...
Dad
Mom
Verizon LTE 7:34PM 55%
< Notes
"don't be scared"
taking his supplements with wine
Proposal story: Misremembered the color of Mom's |
When will the moments of my life settle into coauthored scripts?

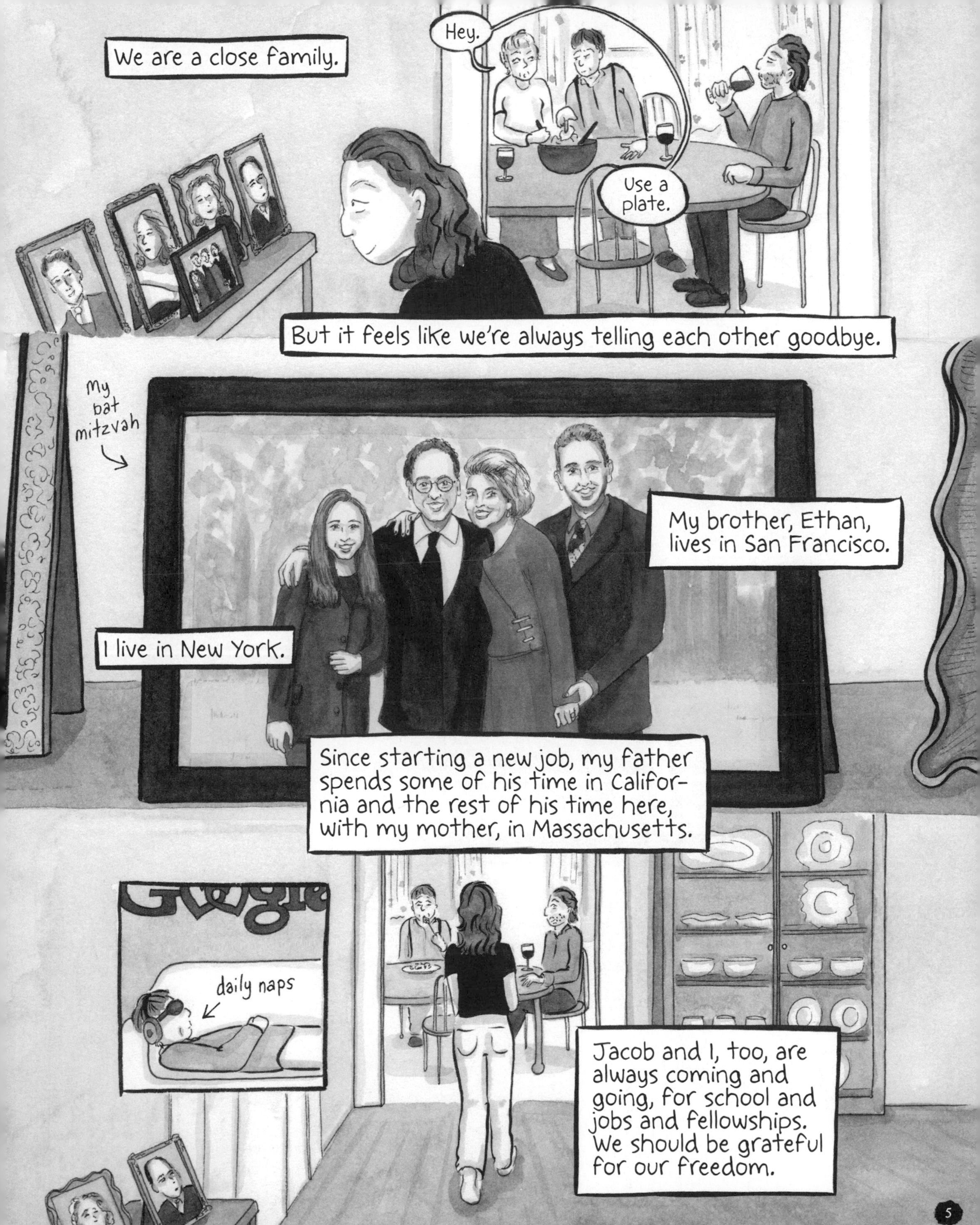
We are a close family.
Hey.
Use a plate.
But it feels like we're always telling each other goodbye.
My bat mitzvah
My brother, Ethan, lives in San Francisco.
I live in New York.
Since starting a new job, my father spends some of his time in California and the rest of his time here, with my mother, in Massachusetts.
daily naps
Jacob and I, too, are always coming and going, for school and jobs and fellowships. We should be grateful for our freedom.

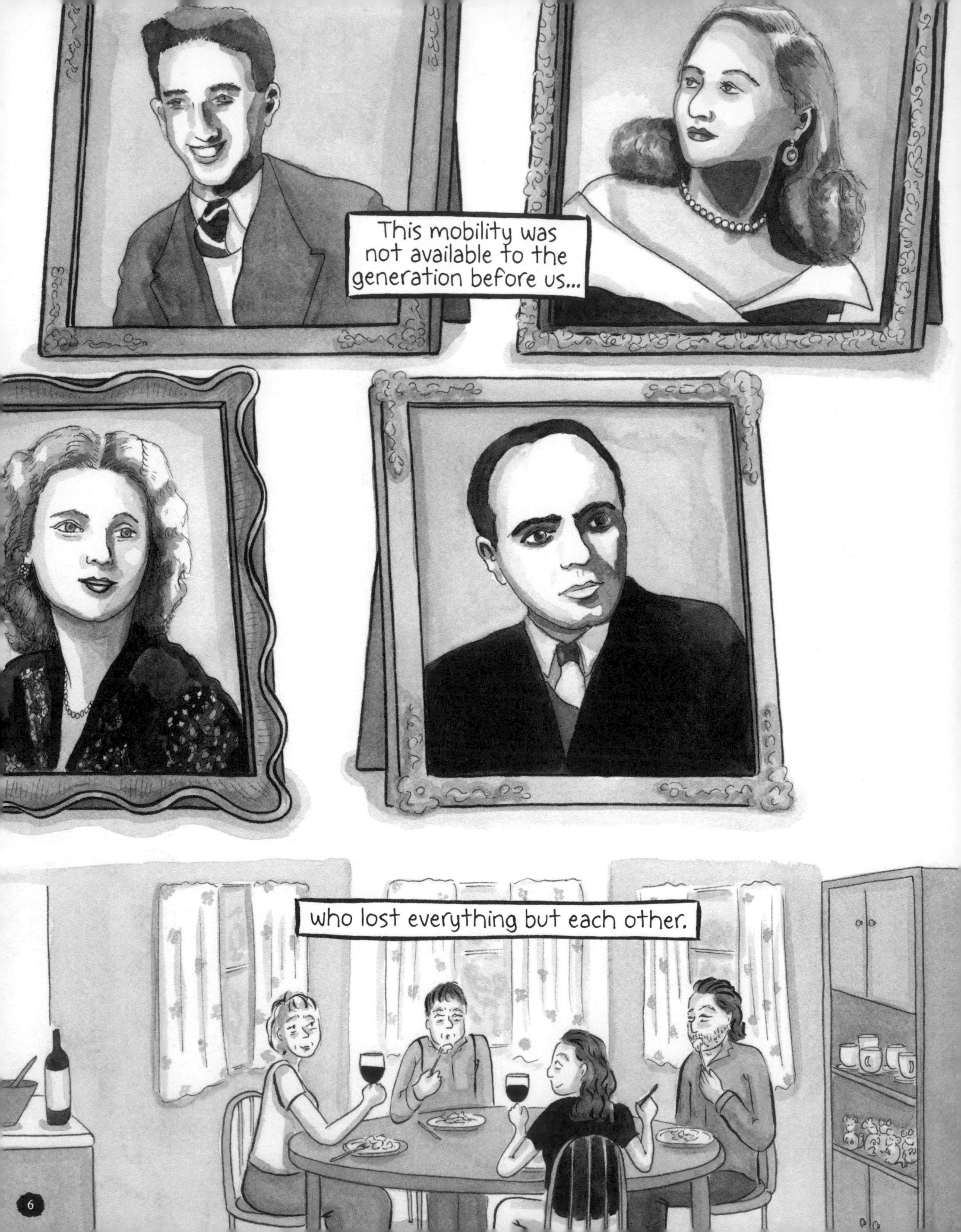
This mobility was not available to the generation before us...
who lost everything but each other.

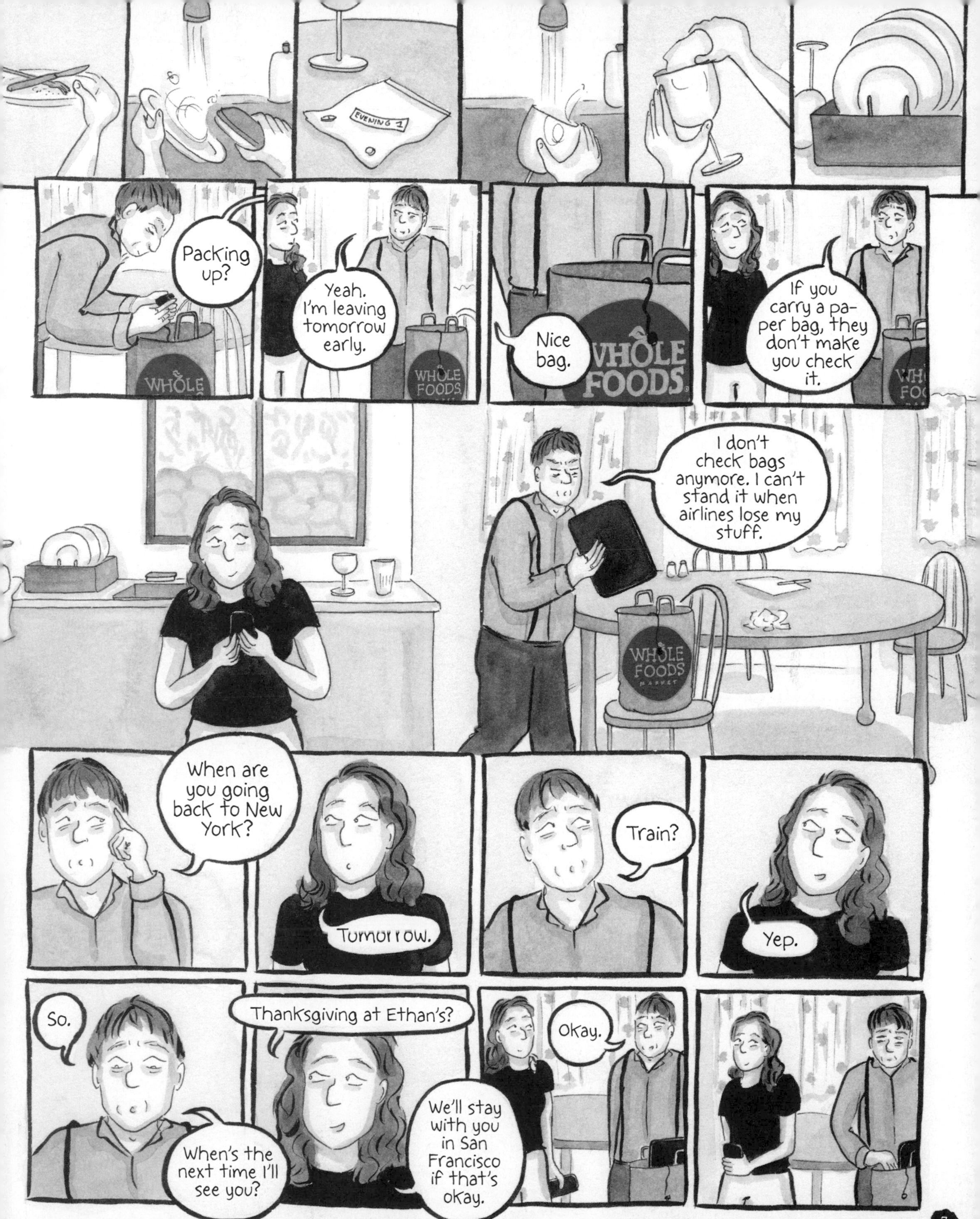
EVENING 1
Packing up?
Yeah. I'm leaving tomorrow early.
Nice bag.
WHOLE FOODS
If you carry a paper bag, they don't make you check it.
I don't check bags anymore. I can't stand it when airlines lose my stuff.
WHOLE FOODS MARKET
When are you going back to New York?
Tomorrow.
Train?
Yep.
So.
When's the next time I'll see you?
Thanksgiving at Ethan's?
We'll stay with you in San Francisco if that's okay.
Okay.

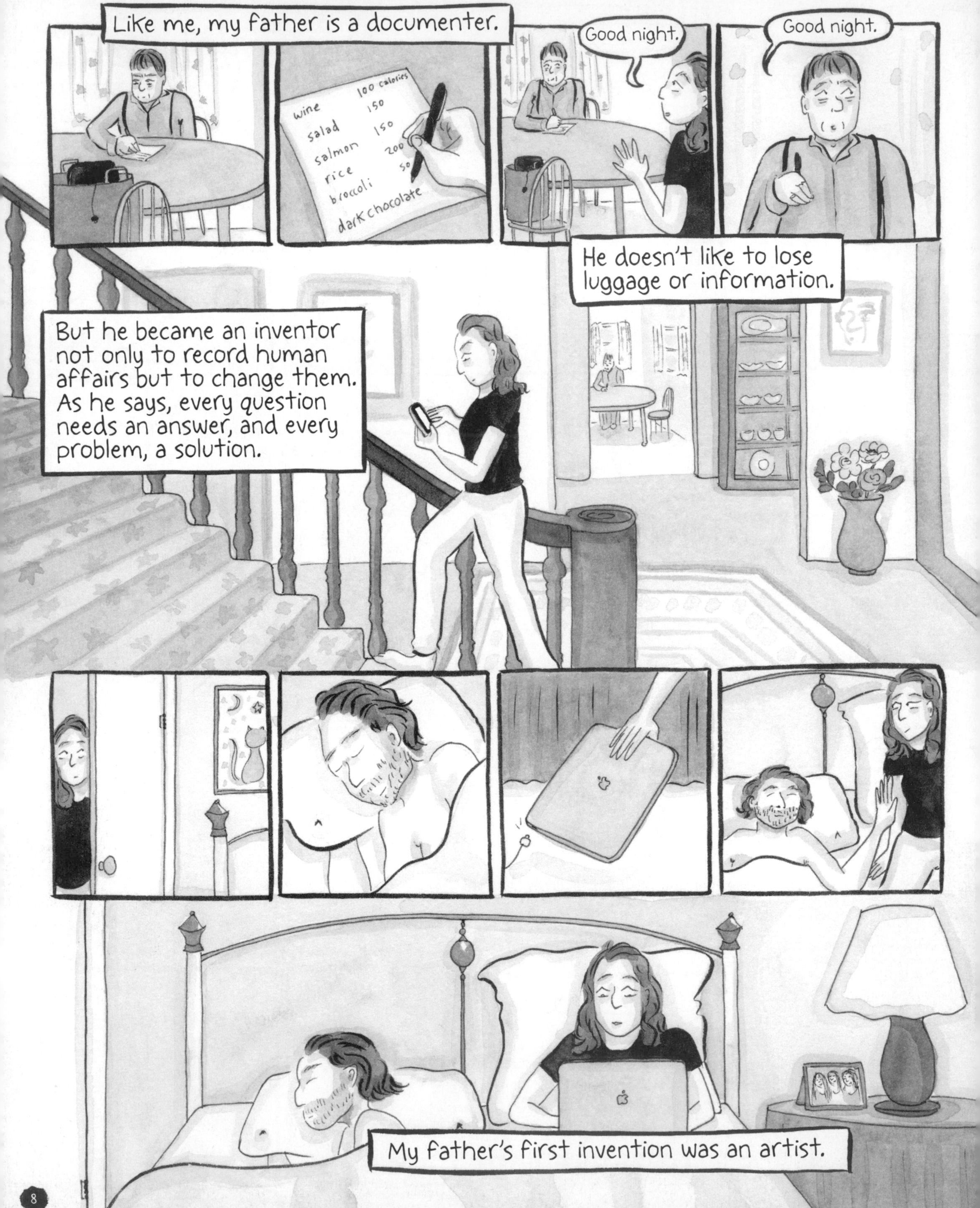
Like me, my father is a documenter.
wine
100 calories
150
salad
150
salmon
200
rice
50
broccoli
dark chocolate
Good night.
Good night.
He doesn't like to lose luggage or information.
But he became an inventor not only to record human affairs but to change them. As he says, every question needs an answer, and every problem, a solution.
My father's first invention was an artist.

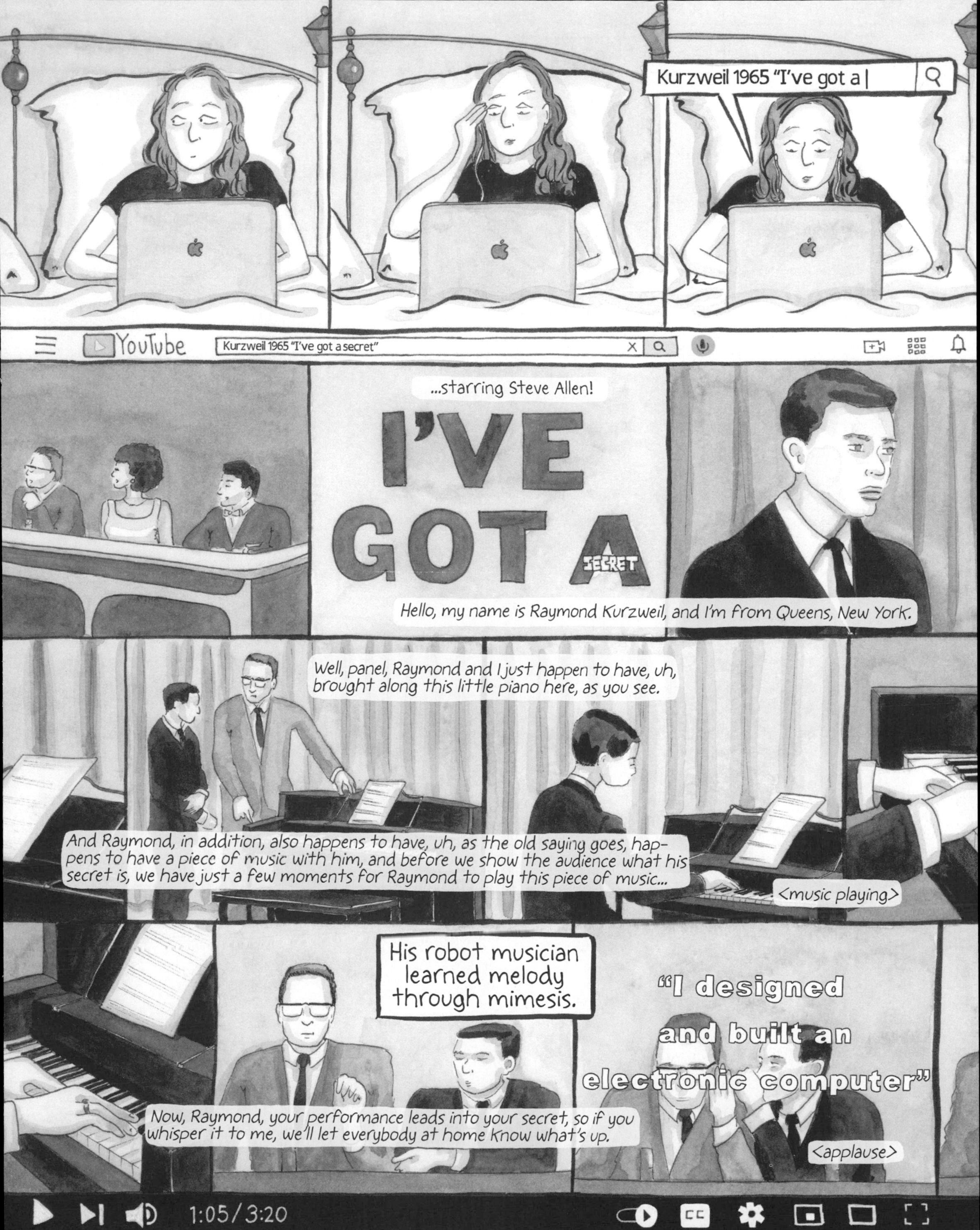

Kurzweil 1965 "I've got a
YouTube
Kurzweil 1965 "I've got a secret"
...starring Steve Allen!
I'VE GOT A SECRET
Hello, my name is Raymond Kurzweil, and I'm from Queens, New York.
Well, panel, Raymond and I just happen to have, uh, brought along this little piano here, as you see.
And Raymond, in addition, also happens to have, uh, as the old saying goes, happens to have a piece of music with him, and before we show the audience what his secret is, we have just a few moments for Raymond to play this piece of music...
<music playing>
His robot musician learned melody through mimesis.
Now, Raymond, your performance leads into your secret, so if you whisper it to me, we'll let everybody at home know what's up.
"I designed and built an electronic computer"
<applause>
1:05/3:20

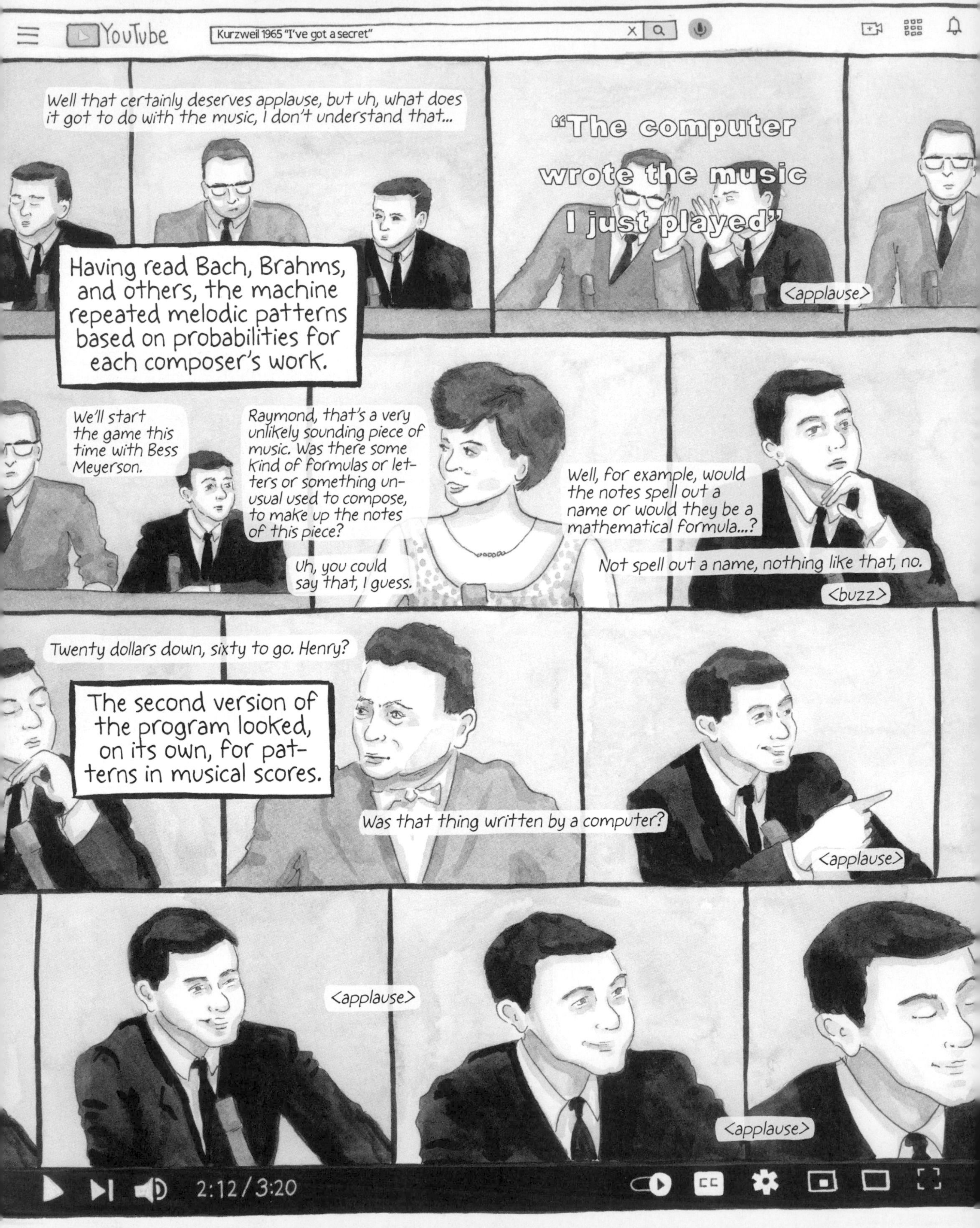
YouTube
Kurzweil 1965 "I've got a secret"
Well that certainly deserves applause, but uh, what does it got to do with the music, I don't understand that...
Having read Bach, Brahms, and others, the machine repeated melodic patterns based on probabilities for each composer's work.
"The computer wrote the music I just played"
<applause>
We'll start the game this time with Bess Meyerson.
Raymond, that's a very unlikely sounding piece of music. Was there some kind of formulas or letters or something unusual used to compose, to make up the notes of this piece?
Uh, you could say that, I guess.
Well, for example, would the notes spell out a name or would they be a mathematical formula...?
Not spell out a name, nothing like that, no.
<buzz>
Twenty dollars down, sixty to go. Henry?
The second version of the program looked, on its own, for patterns in musical scores.
Was that thing written by a computer?
<applause>
<applause>
<applause>
2:12 / 3:20

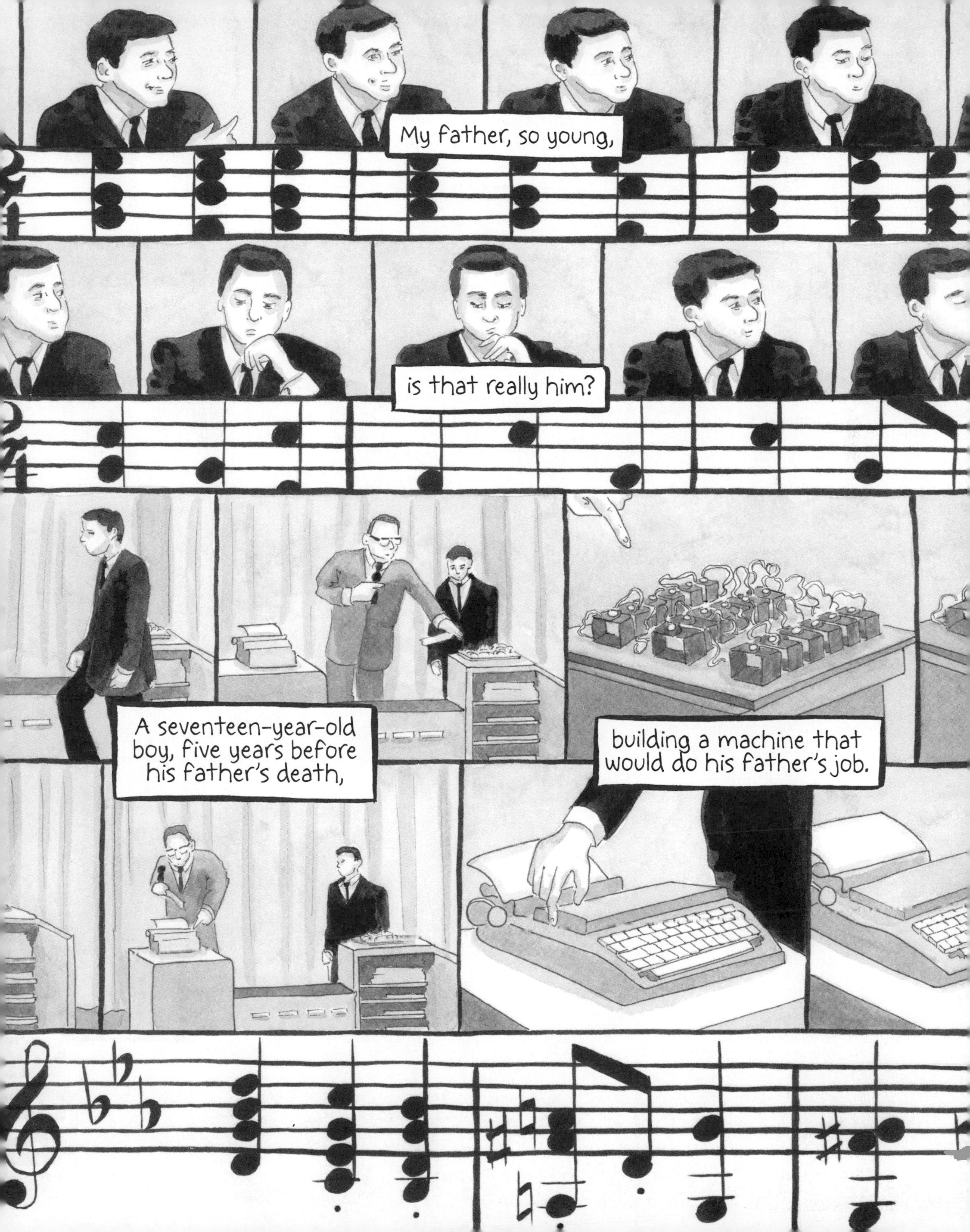
My father, so young,
is that really him?
A seventeen-year-old boy, five years before his father's death,
building a machine that would do his father's job.

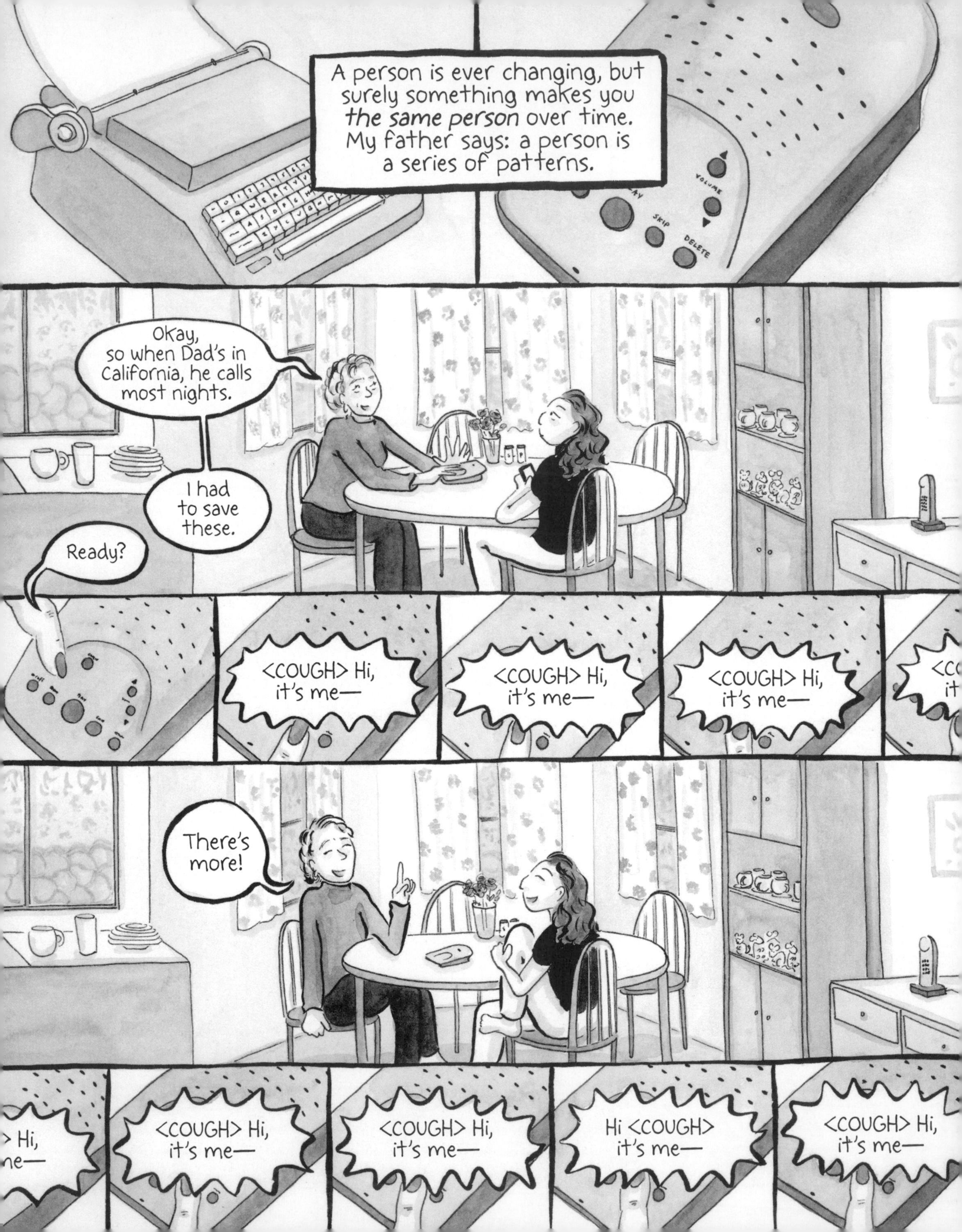
A person is ever changing, but surely something makes you *the same person* over time. My father says: a person is a series of patterns.
VOLUME
SKIP
DELETE
Okay, so when Dad's in California, he calls most nights.
I had to save these.
Ready?
<COUGH> Hi, it's me—
<COUGH> Hi, it's me—
<COUGH> Hi, it's me—
There's more!
<COUGH> Hi, it's me—
<COUGH> Hi, it's me—
Hi <COUGH> it's me—
<COUGH> Hi, it's me—

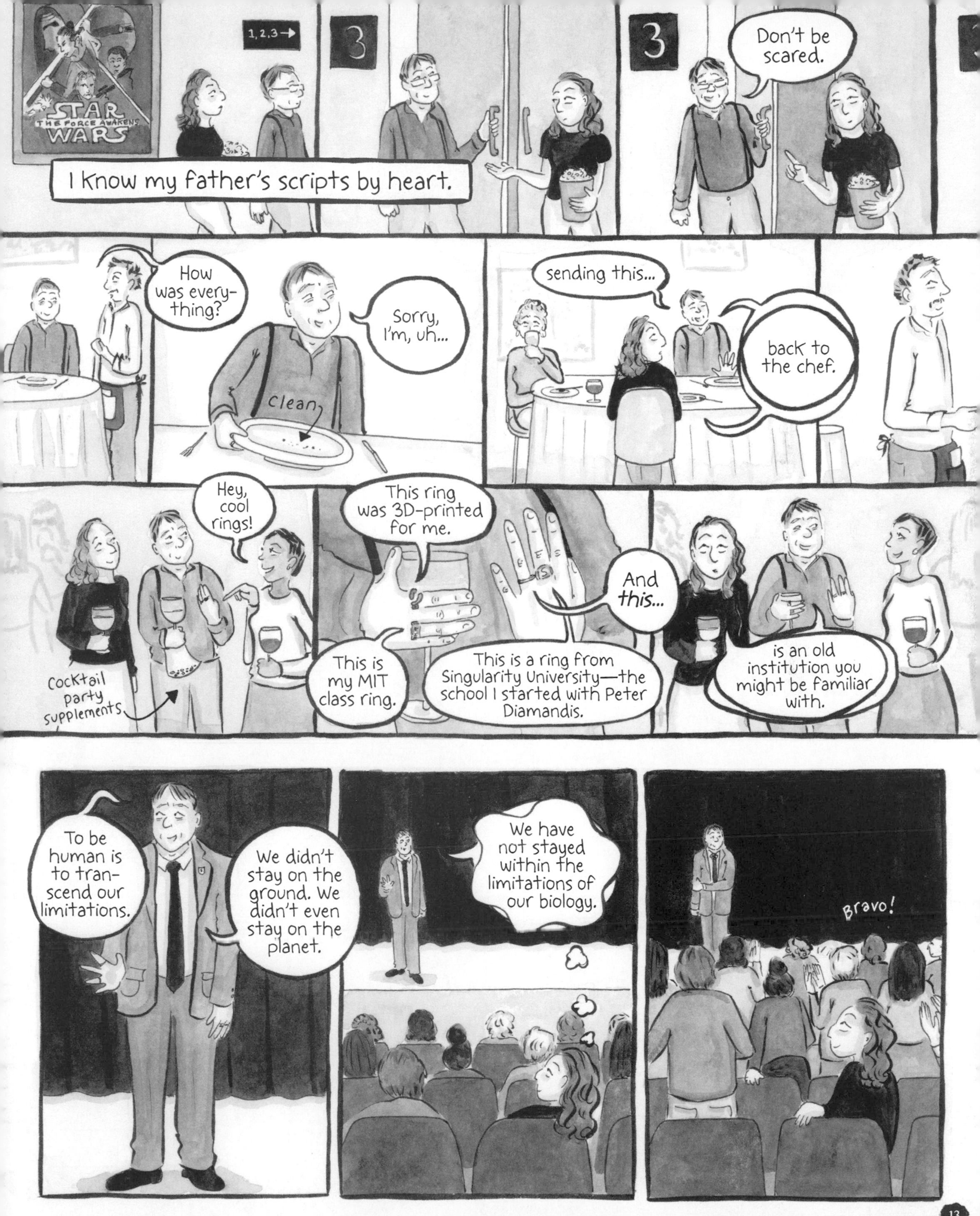
STAR WARS THE FORCE AWAKENS
1,2,3 →
3
I know my father's scripts by heart.
3
Don't be scared.
How was every-thing?
Sorry, I'm, uh...
Clean
sending this...
back to the chef.
Hey, cool rings!
Cocktail party supplements
This ring was 3D-printed for me.
This is my MIT class ring.
And this...
This is a ring from Singularity University—the school I started with Peter Diamandis.
is an old institution you might be familiar with.
To be human is to tran-scend our limitations.
We didn't stay on the ground. We didn't even stay on the planet.
We have not stayed within the limitations of our biology.
Bravo!

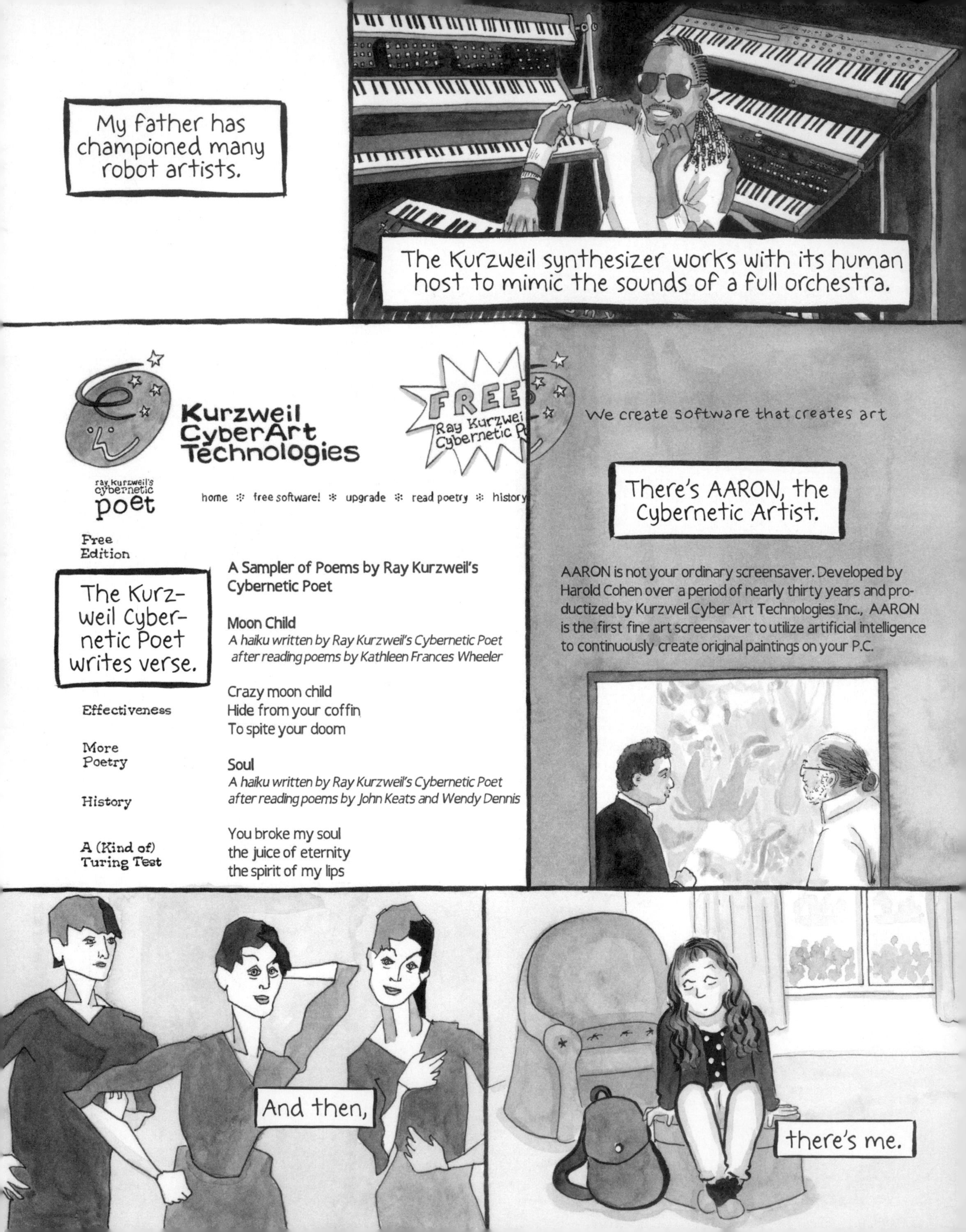
My father has championed many robot artists.
The Kurzweil synthesizer works with its human host to mimic the sounds of a full orchestra.
Kurzweil CyberArt Technologies
FREE Ray Kurzweil Cybernetic P
ray kurzweil's cybernetic poet
home ❊ free software! ❊ upgrade ❊ read poetry ❊ history
Free Edition
The Kurzweil Cybernetic Poet writes verse.
A Sampler of Poems by Ray Kurzweil's Cybernetic Poet
Moon Child
A haiku written by Ray Kurzweil's Cybernetic Poet after reading poems by Kathleen Frances Wheeler
Crazy moon child
Hide from your coffin
To spite your doom
Soul
A haiku written by Ray Kurzweil's Cybernetic Poet after reading poems by John Keats and Wendy Dennis
You broke my soul
the juice of eternity
the spirit of my lips
Effectiveness
More Poetry
History
A (Kind of) Turing Test
We create software that creates art
There's AARON, the Cybernetic Artist.
AARON is not your ordinary screensaver. Developed by Harold Cohen over a period of nearly thirty years and productized by Kurzweil Cyber Art Technologies Inc., AARON is the first fine art screensaver to utilize artificial intelligence to continuously create original paintings on your P.C.
And then,
there's me.

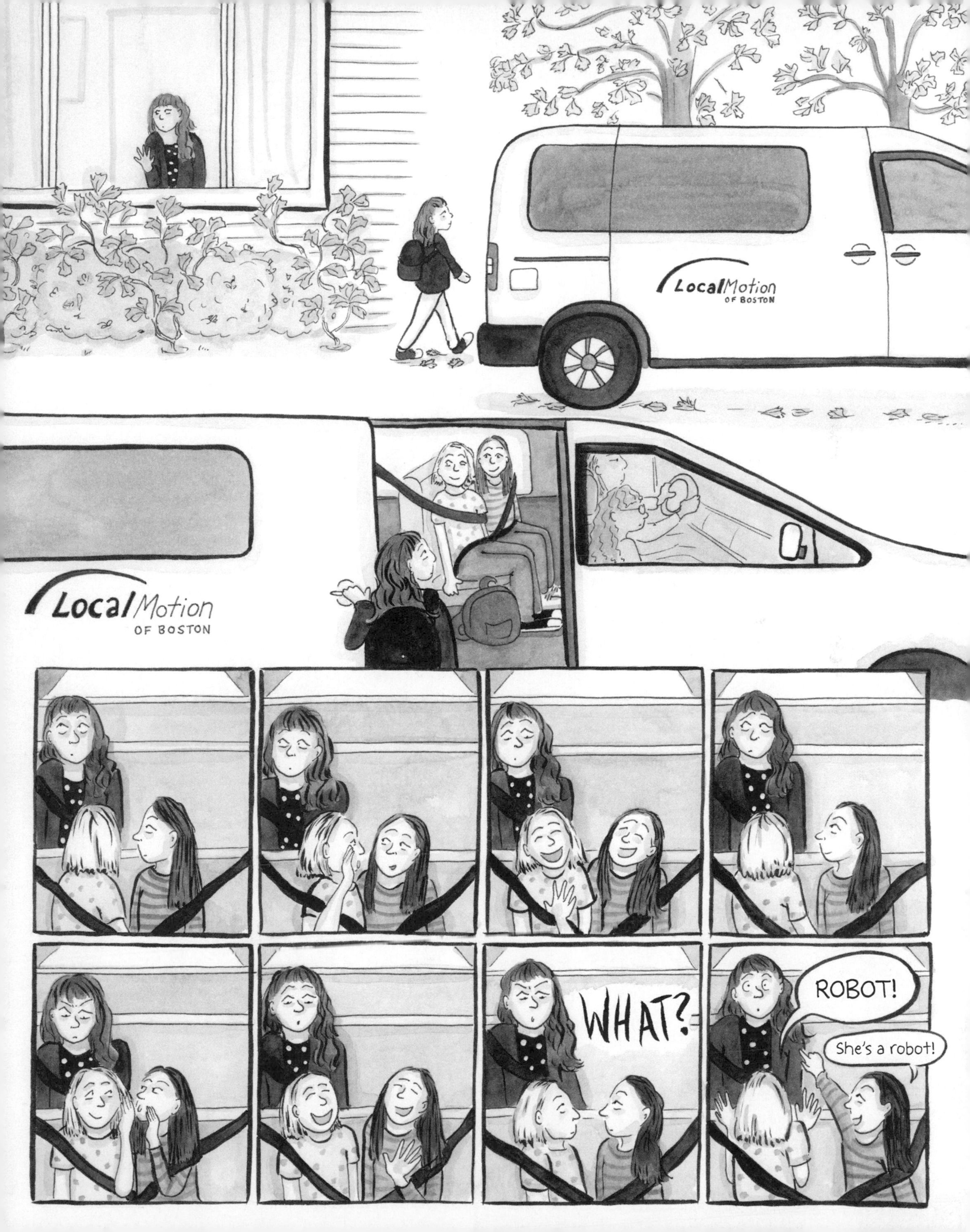

LocalMotion OF BOSTON
LocalMotion OF BOSTON
WHAT?
ROBOT!
She's a robot!

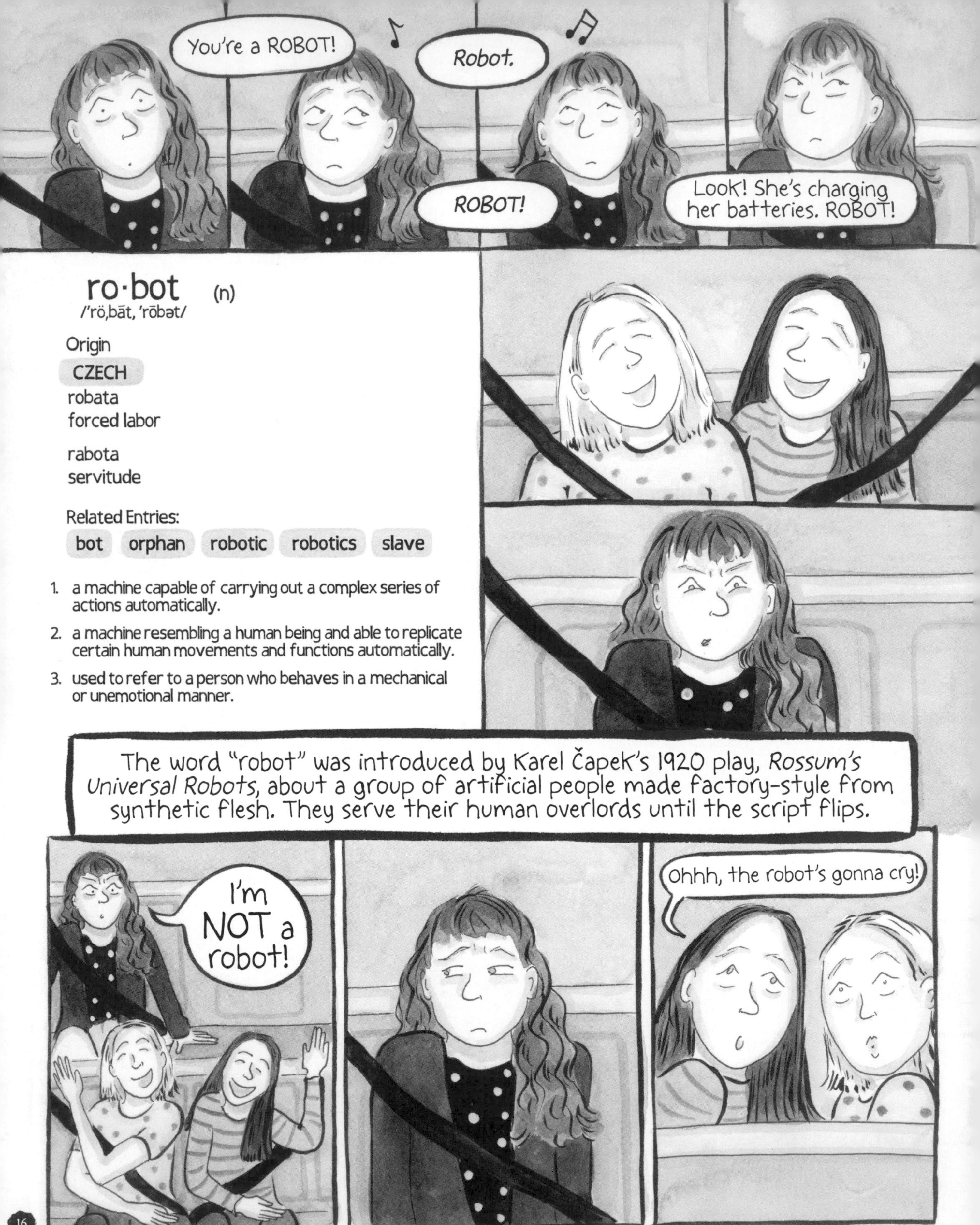
You're a ROBOT!
Robot.
ROBOT!
Look! She's charging her batteries. ROBOT!
ro·bot (n)
/ˈrōˌbät, ˈrōbət/
Origin
CZECH
robata
forced labor
rabota
servitude
Related Entries:
bot orphan robotic robotics slave
1. a machine capable of carrying out a complex series of actions automatically.
2. a machine resembling a human being and able to replicate certain human movements and functions automatically.
3. used to refer to a person who behaves in a mechanical or unemotional manner.
The word "robot" was introduced by Karel Čapek's 1920 play, *Rossum's Universal Robots*, about a group of artificial people made factory-style from synthetic flesh. They serve their human overlords until the script flips.
I'm NOT a robot!
Ohhh, the robot's gonna cry!

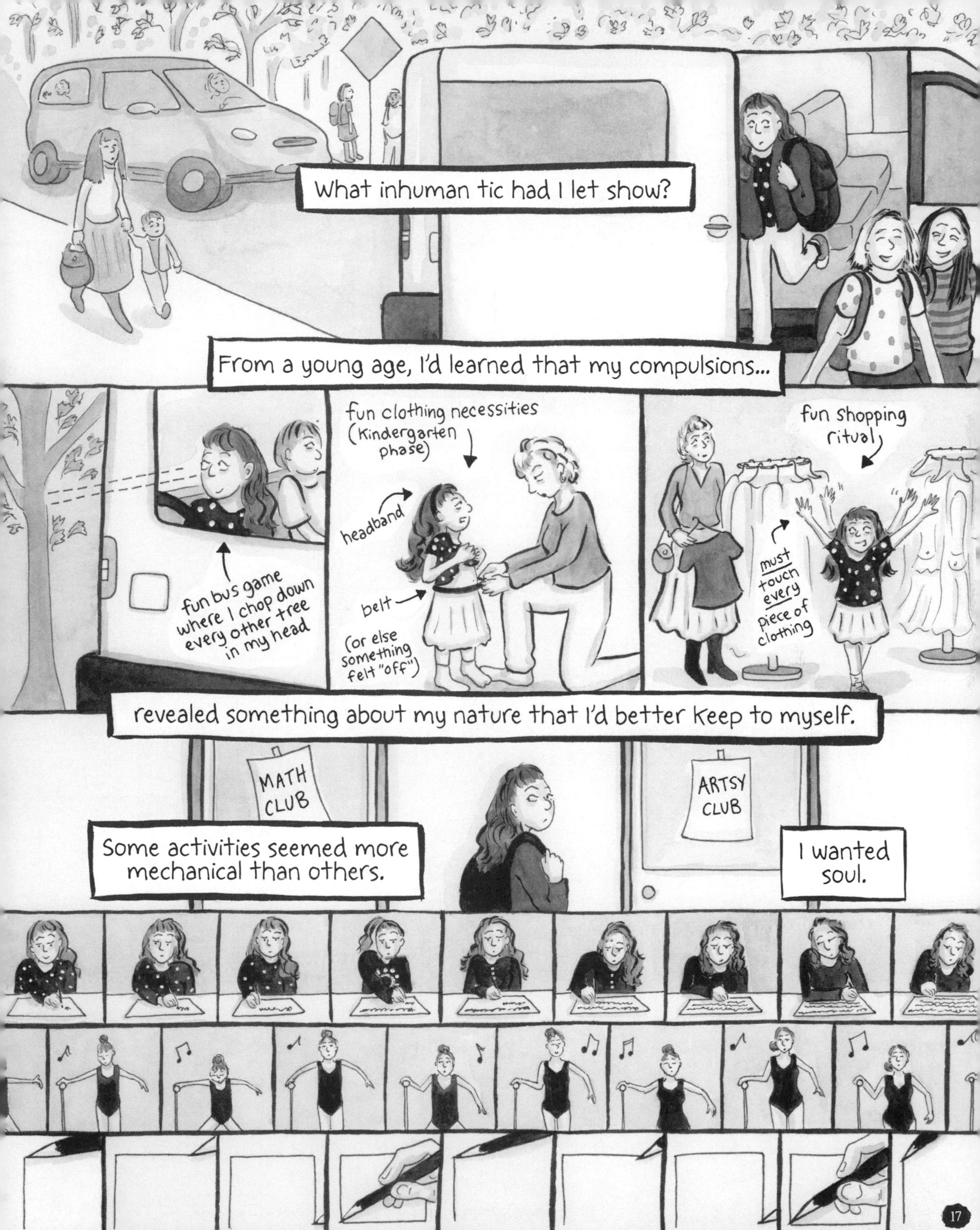
What inhuman tic had I let show?
From a young age, I'd learned that my compulsions...
fun bus game where I chop down every other tree in my head
fun clothing necessities (Kindergarten phase)
headband
belt
(or else something felt "off")
fun shopping ritual
must touch every piece of clothing
revealed something about my nature that I'd better keep to myself.
MATH CLUB
ARTSY CLUB
Some activities seemed more mechanical than others.
I wanted soul.

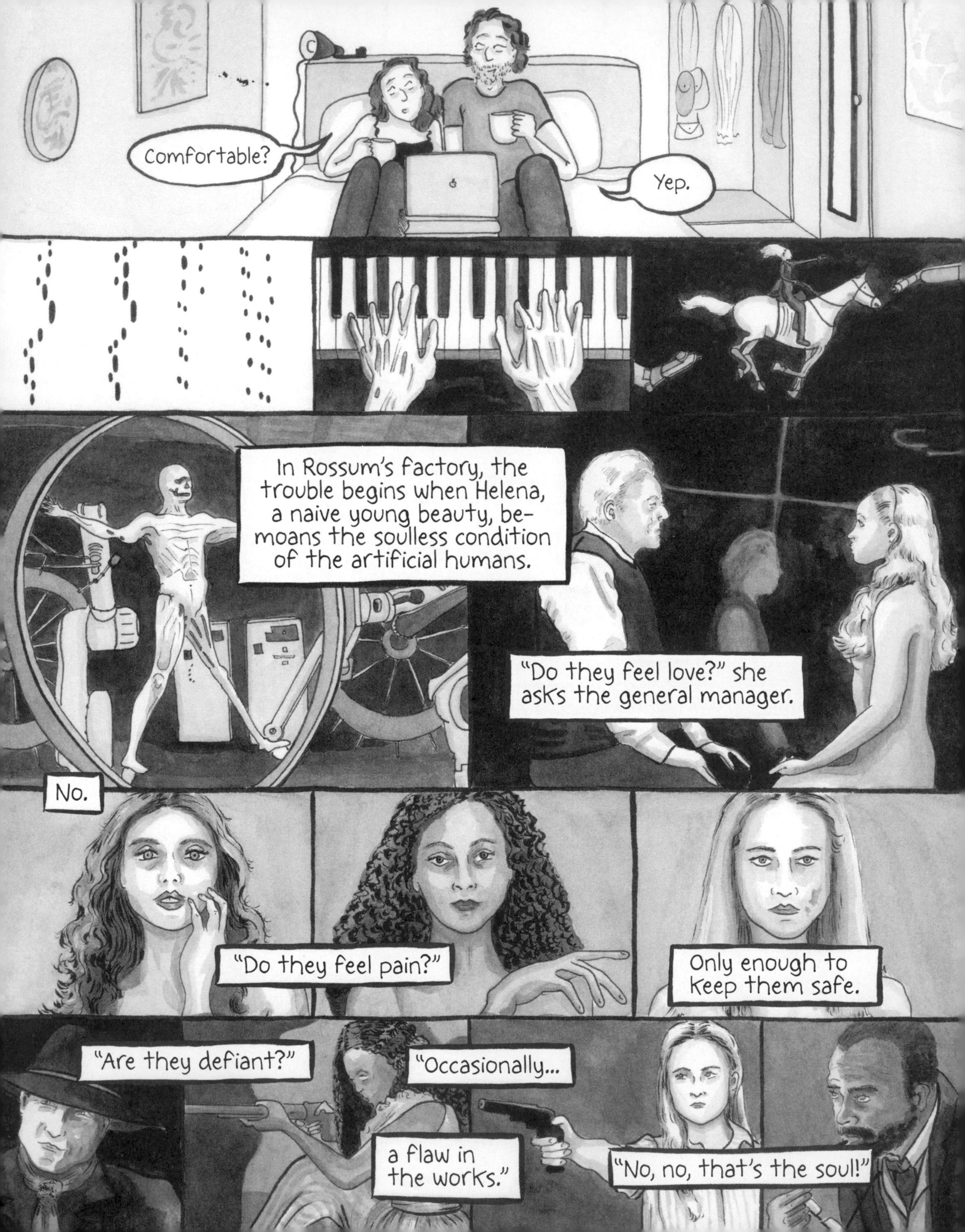
Comfortable?
Yep.
In Rossum's factory, the trouble begins when Helena, a naive young beauty, bemoans the soulless condition of the artificial humans.
"Do they feel love?" she asks the general manager.
No.
"Do they feel pain?"
Only enough to keep them safe.
"Are they defiant?"
"Occasionally...
a flaw in the works."
"No, no, that's the soul!"

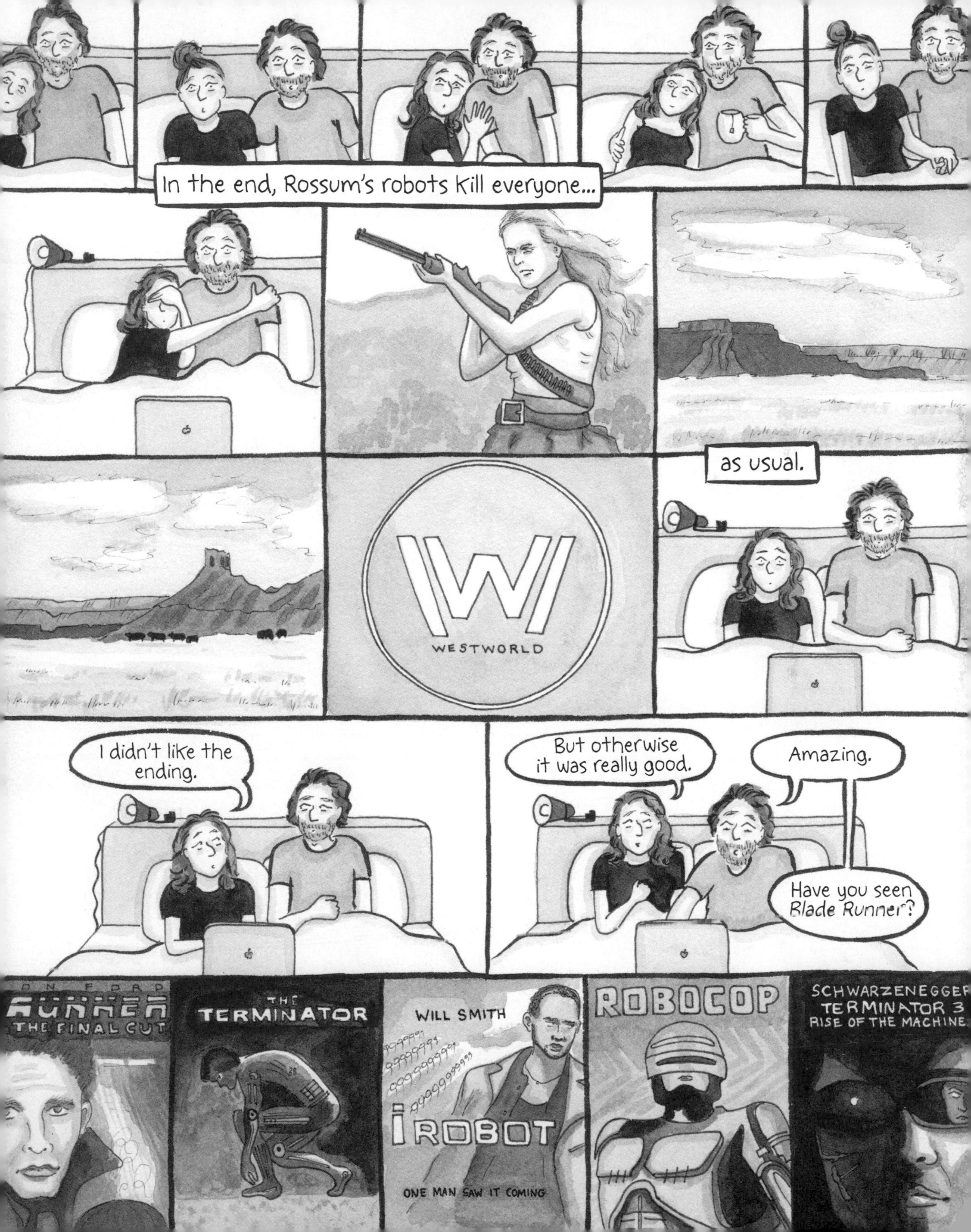
In the end, Rossum's robots kill everyone...
WESTWORLD
as usual.
I didn't like the ending.
But otherwise it was really good.
Amazing.
Have you seen Blade Runner?
THE FINAL CUT
THE TERMINATOR
WILL SMITH
I ROBOT
ONE MAN SAW IT COMING
ROBOCOP
SCHWARZENEGGER
TERMINATOR 3

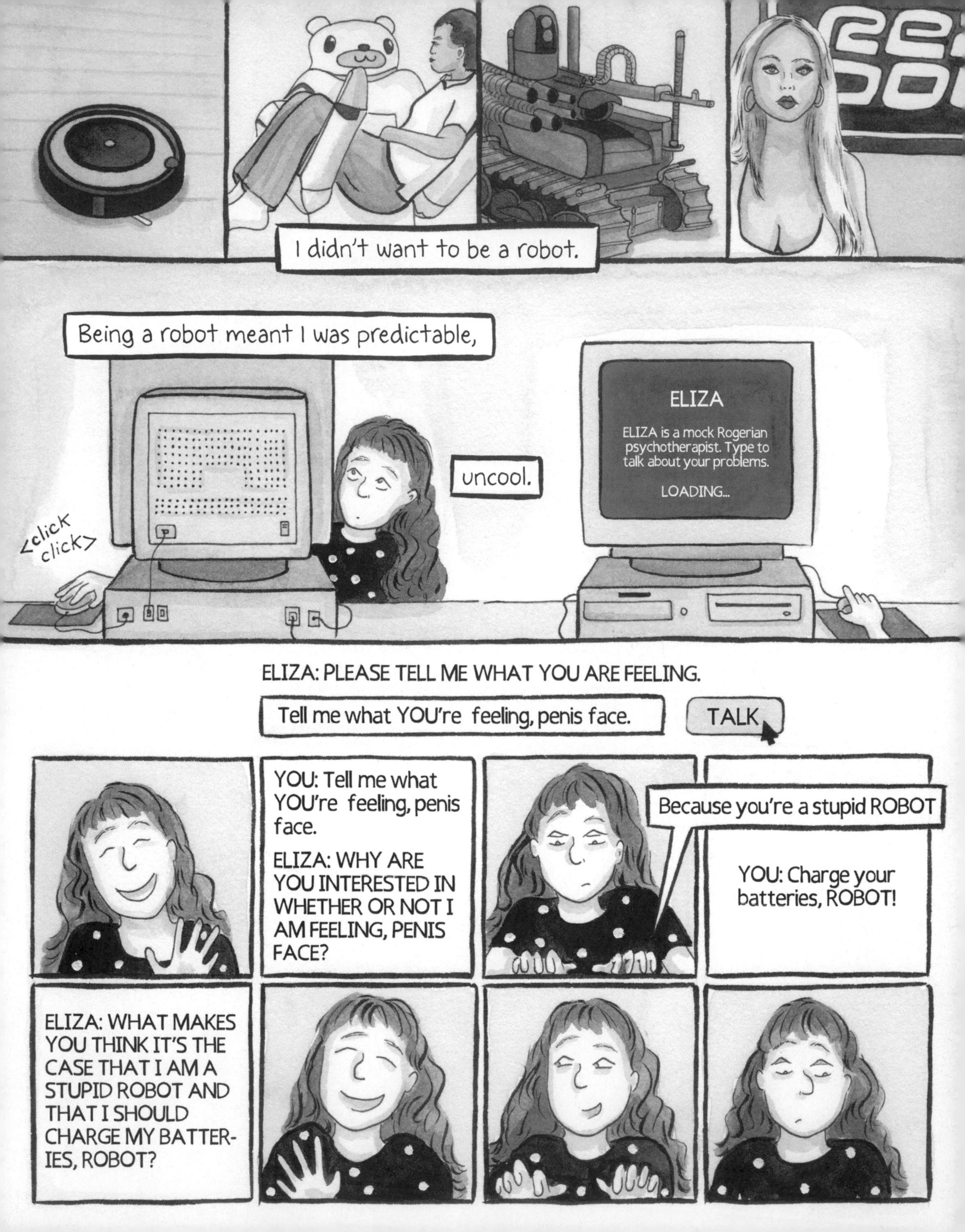
I didn't want to be a robot.
Being a robot meant I was predictable,
uncool.
ELIZA
ELIZA is a mock Rogerian psychotherapist. Type to talk about your problems.
LOADING...
<click click>
ELIZA: PLEASE TELL ME WHAT YOU ARE FEELING.
Tell me what YOU're feeling, penis face.
TALK
YOU: Tell me what YOU're feeling, penis face.
ELIZA: WHY ARE YOU INTERESTED IN WHETHER OR NOT I AM FEELING, PENIS FACE?
Because you're a stupid ROBOT
YOU: Charge your batteries, ROBOT!
ELIZA: WHAT MAKES YOU THINK IT'S THE CASE THAT I AM A STUPID ROBOT AND THAT I SHOULD CHARGE MY BATTER-IES, ROBOT?

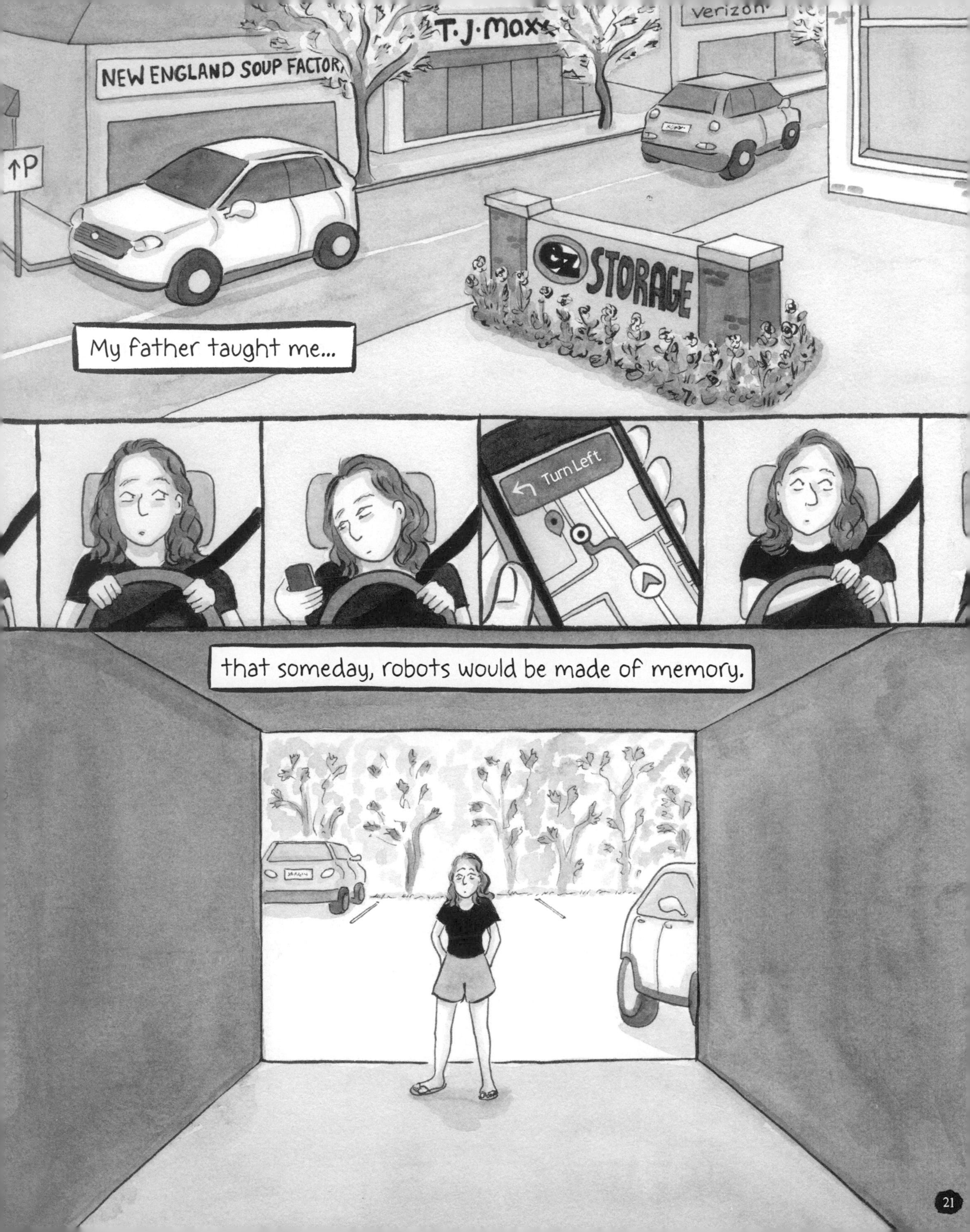
NEW ENGLAND SOUP FACTORY
T.J.Maxx
verizon
P
STORAGE
My father taught me...
Turn Left
that someday, robots would be made of memory.

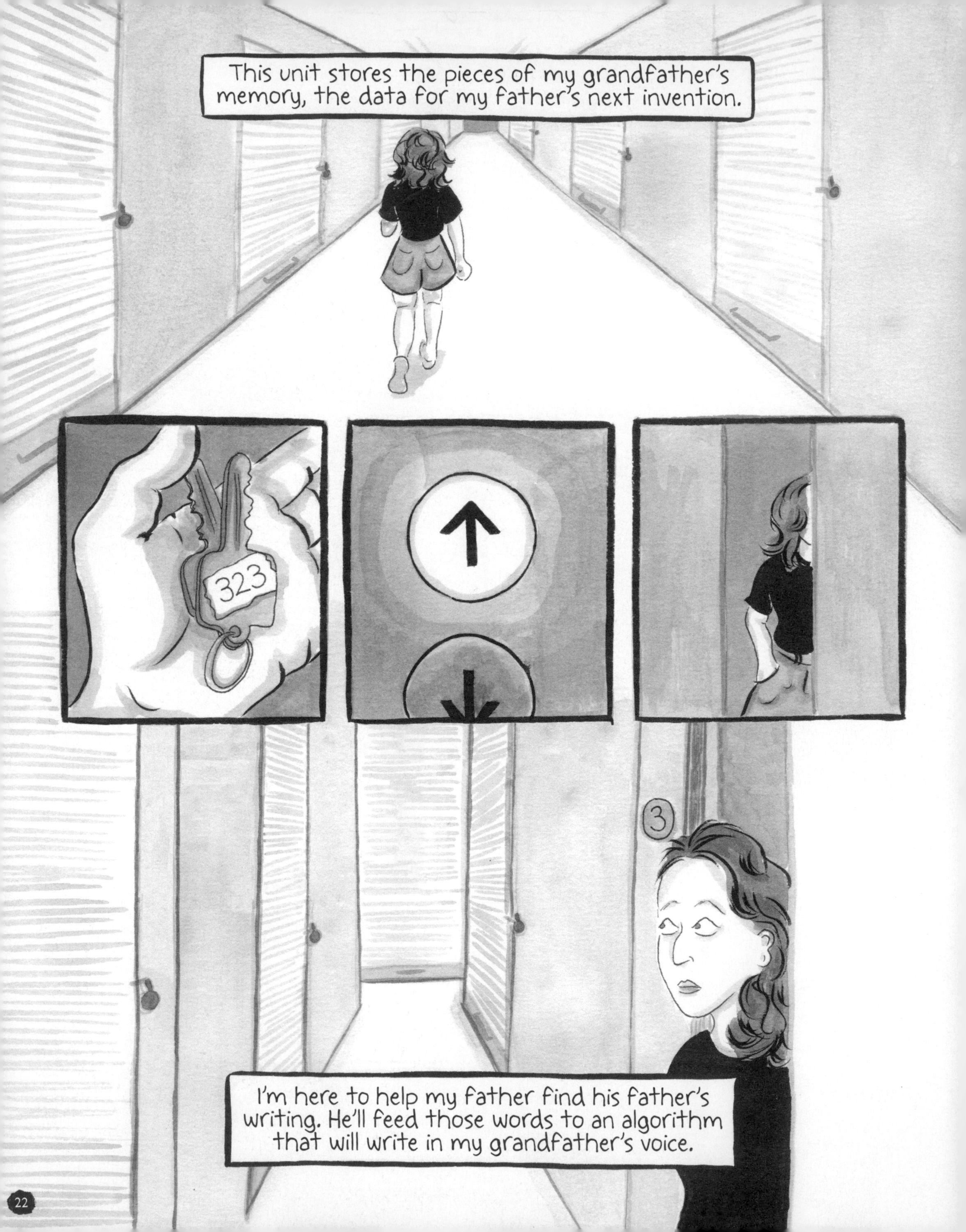
This unit stores the pieces of my grandfather's memory, the data for my father's next invention.
323
3
I'm here to help my father find his father's writing. He'll feed those words to an algorithm that will write in my grandfather's voice.

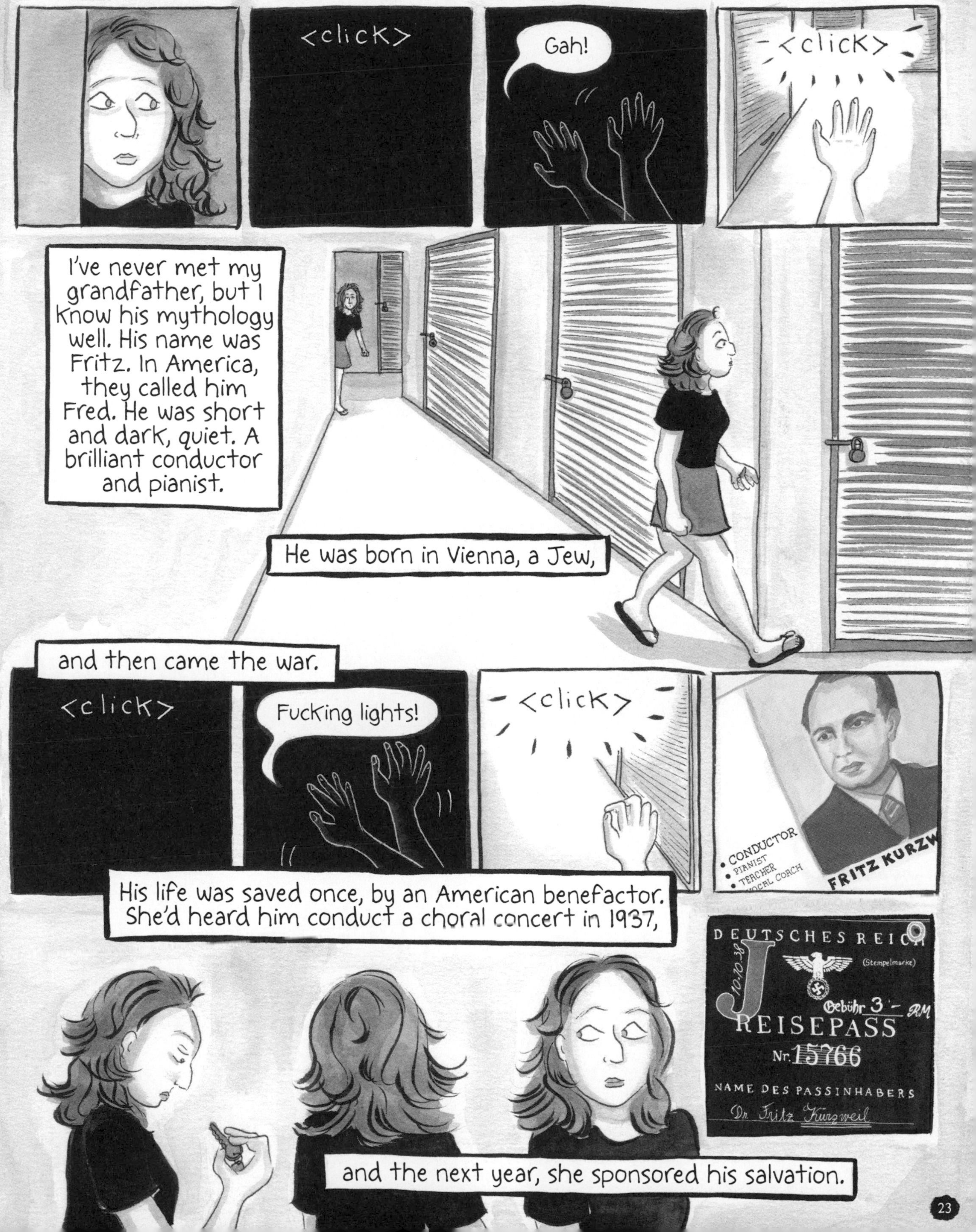

<click>
Gah!
<click>
I've never met my grandfather, but I know his mythology well. His name was Fritz. In America, they called him Fred. He was short and dark, quiet. A brilliant conductor and pianist.
He was born in Vienna, a Jew,
and then came the war.
<click>
Fucking lights!
<click>
CONDUCTOR
PIANIST
TEACHER
VOCAL COACH
FRITZ KURZW
His life was saved once, by an American benefactor. She'd heard him conduct a choral concert in 1937,
DEUTSCHES REICH
(Stempelmarke)
10.10.38
J
Gebühr 3.- RM
REISEPASS
Nr. 15766
NAME DES PASSINHABERS
Dr. Fritz Kurzweil
and the next year, she sponsored his salvation.

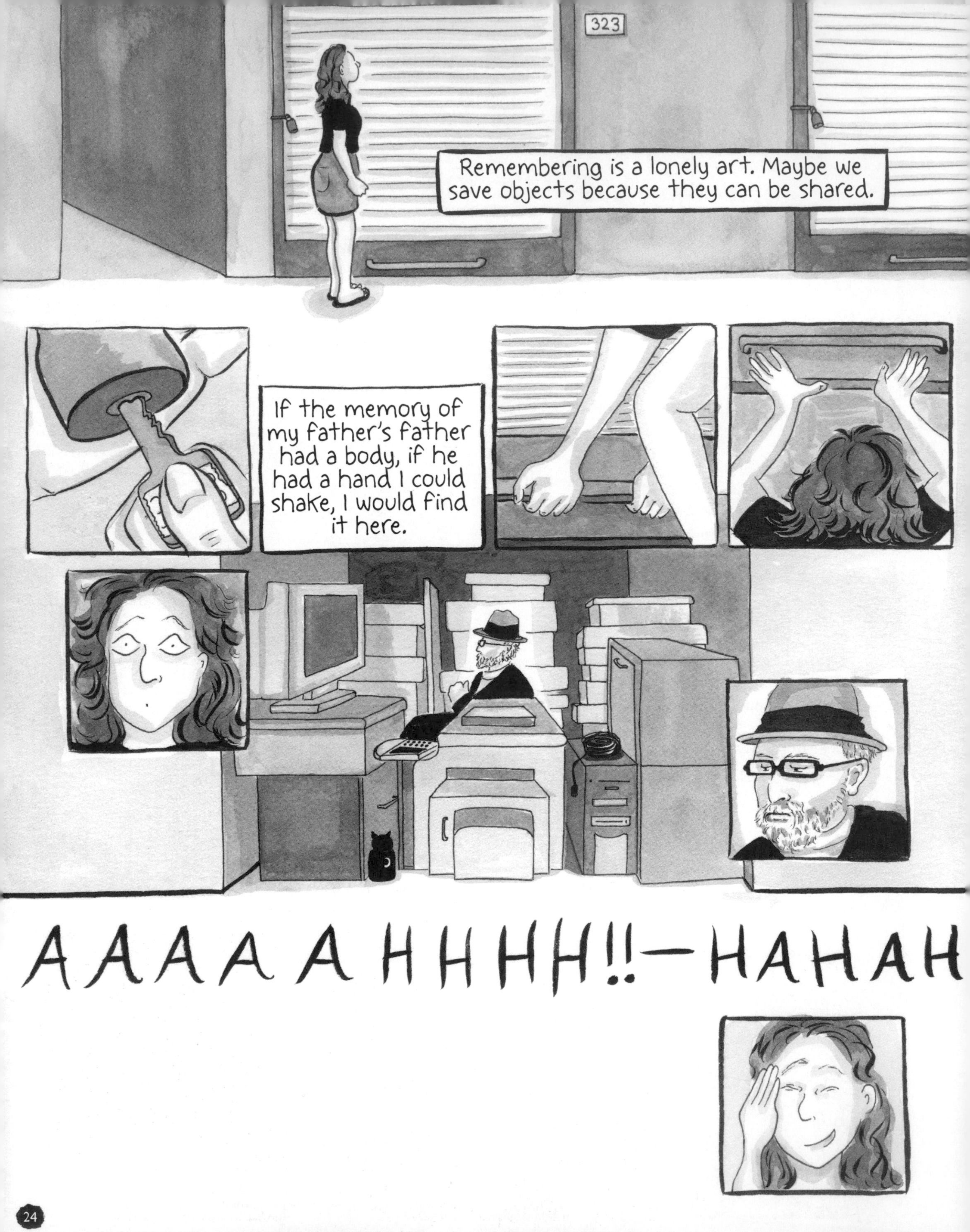
323
Remembering is a lonely art. Maybe we save objects because they can be shared.
If the memory of my father's father had a body, if he had a hand I could shake, I would find it here.
AAAAAHHHH!!—HAHAH

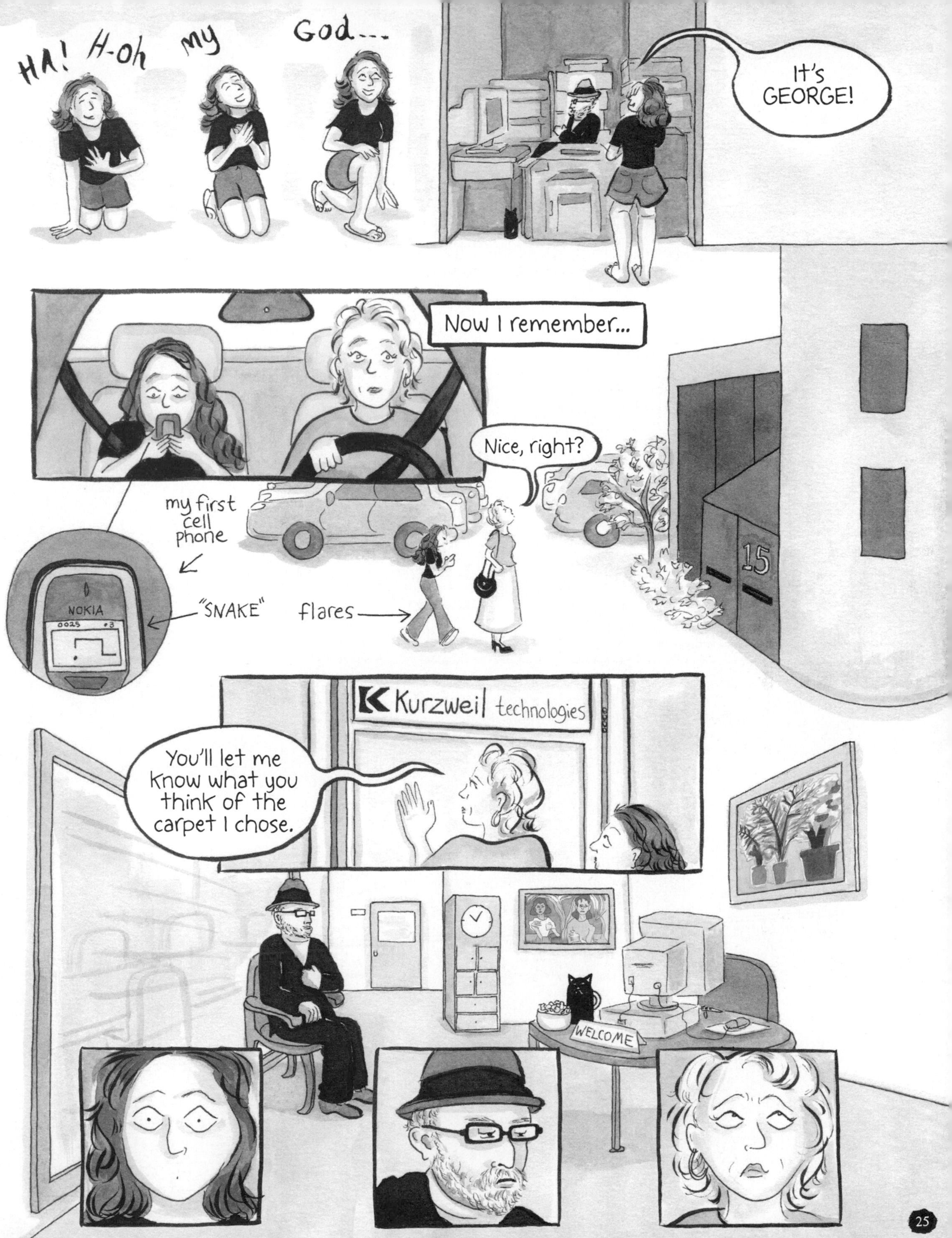
HA! H-oh my God...
It's GEORGE!
Now I remember...
Nice, right?
my first cell phone
NOKIA
"SNAKE"
flares
Kurzweil technologies
You'll let me know what you think of the carpet I chose.
WELCOME

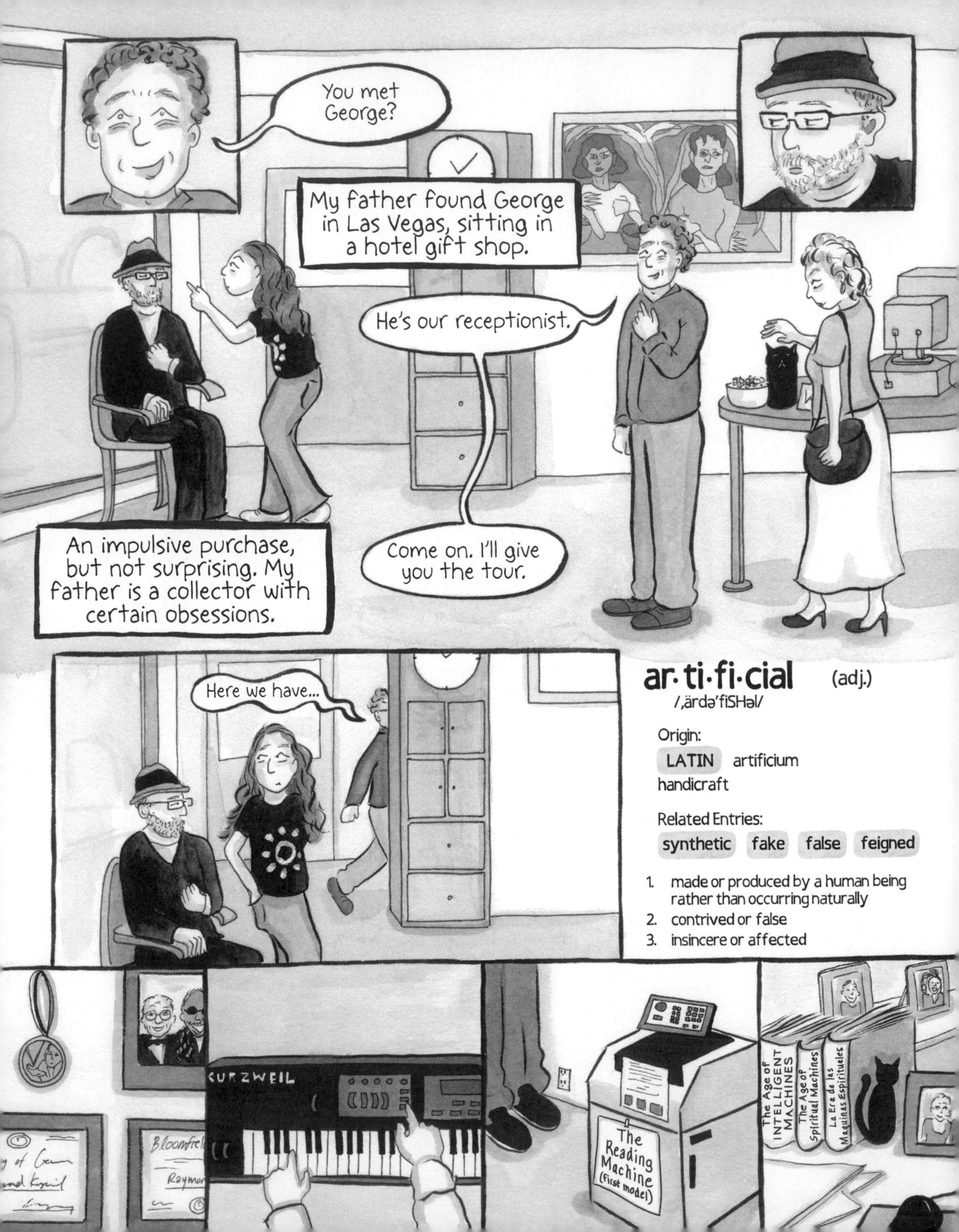

You met George?
My father found George in Las Vegas, sitting in a hotel gift shop.
He's our receptionist.
An impulsive purchase, but not surprising. My father is a collector with certain obsessions.
Come on. I'll give you the tour.
Here we have...
ar·ti·fi·cial (adj.)
/ˌärdəˈfiSHəl/
Origin:
LATIN artificium
handicraft
Related Entries:
synthetic fake false feigned
1. made or produced by a human being rather than occurring naturally
2. contrived or false
3. insincere or affected
The Reading Machine (First model)
The Age of INTELLIGENT MACHINES
The Age of Spiritual Machines
La Era de las Máquinas Espirituales

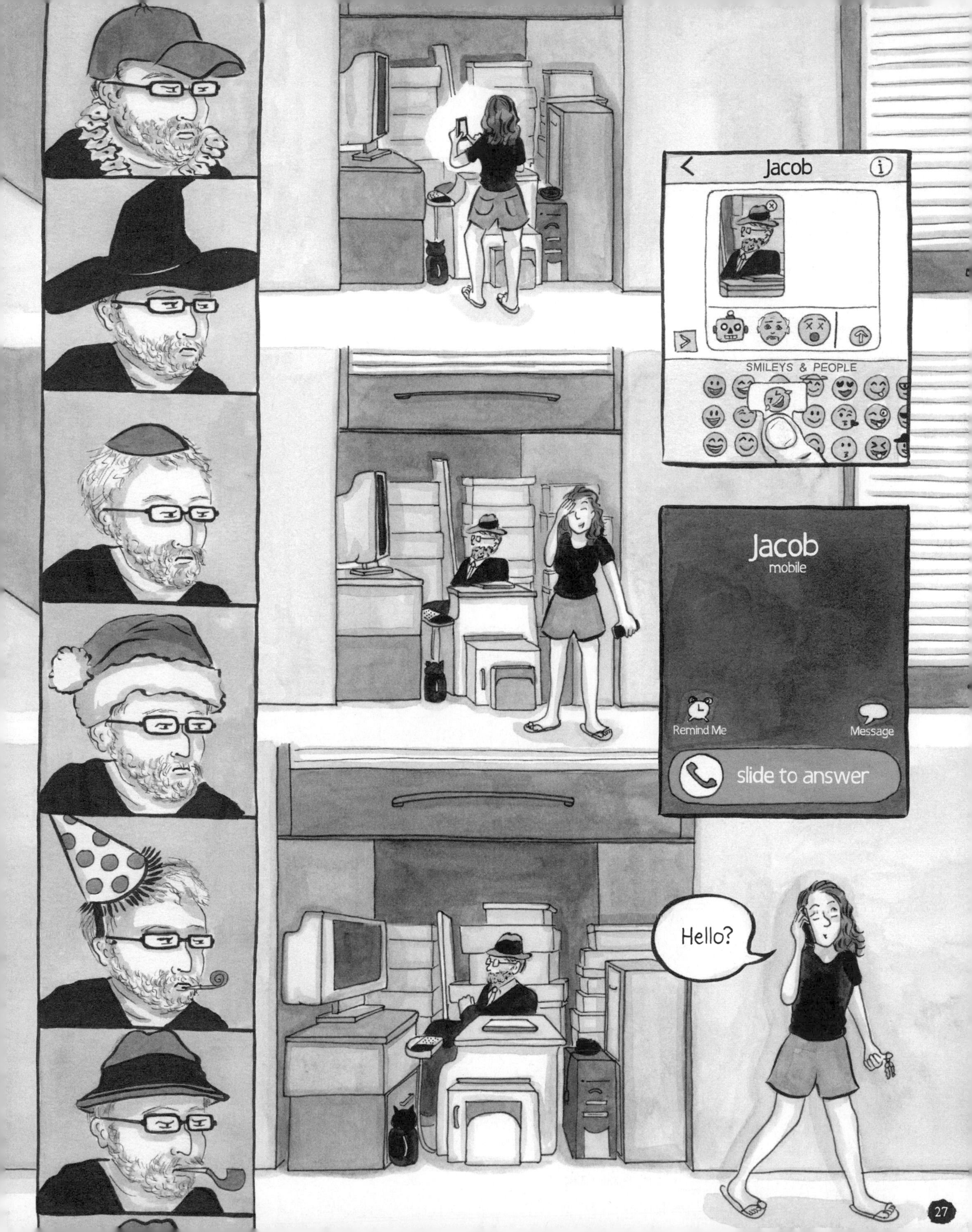
Jacob
SMILEYS & PEOPLE
Jacob
mobile
Remind Me
Message
slide to answer
Hello?

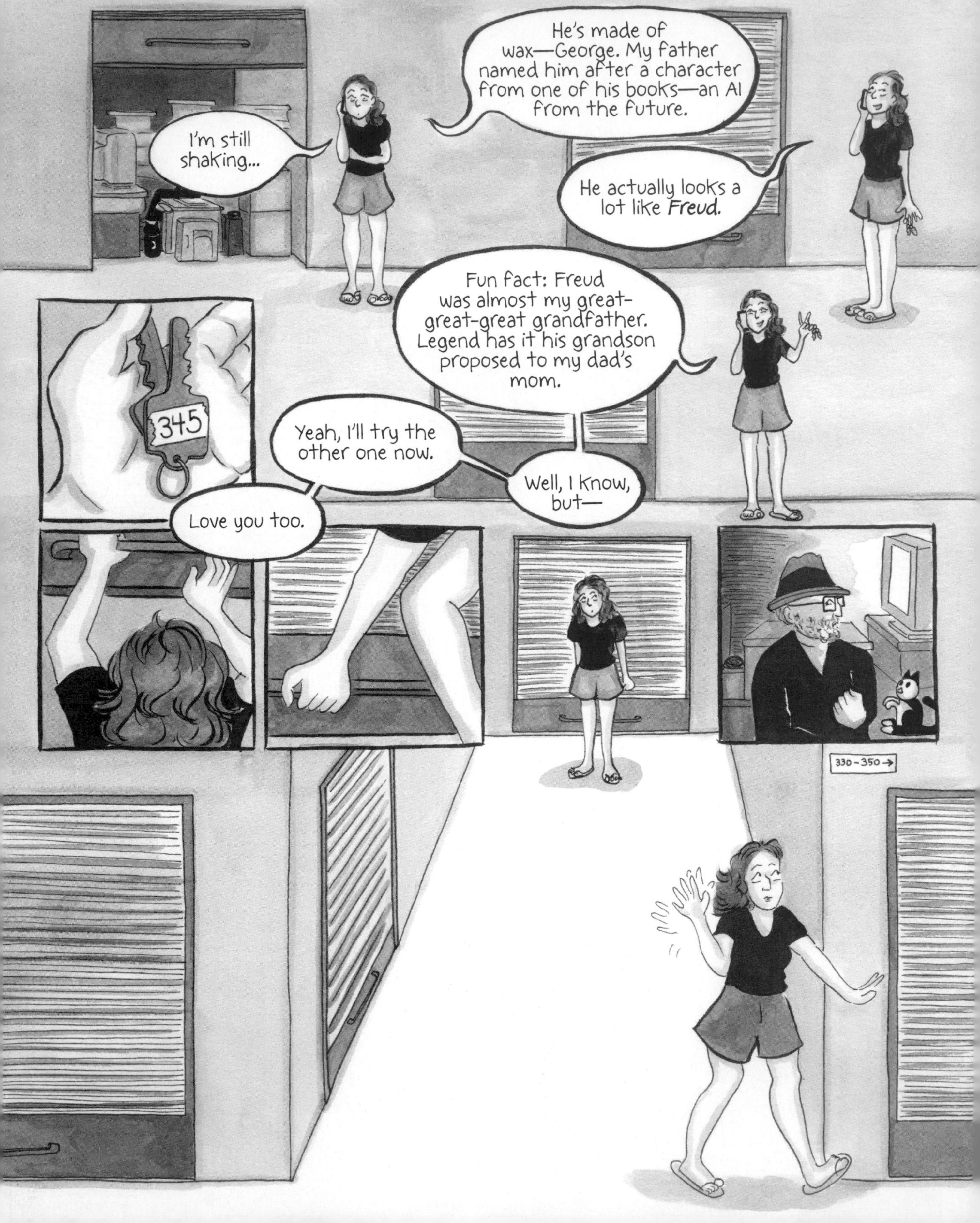
I'm still shaking...
He's made of wax—George. My father named him after a character from one of his books—an AI from the future.
He actually looks a lot like Freud.
Fun fact: Freud was almost my great-great-great grandfather. Legend has it his grandson proposed to my dad's mom.
345
Well, I know, but—
Yeah, I'll try the other one now.
Love you too.
330–350 →

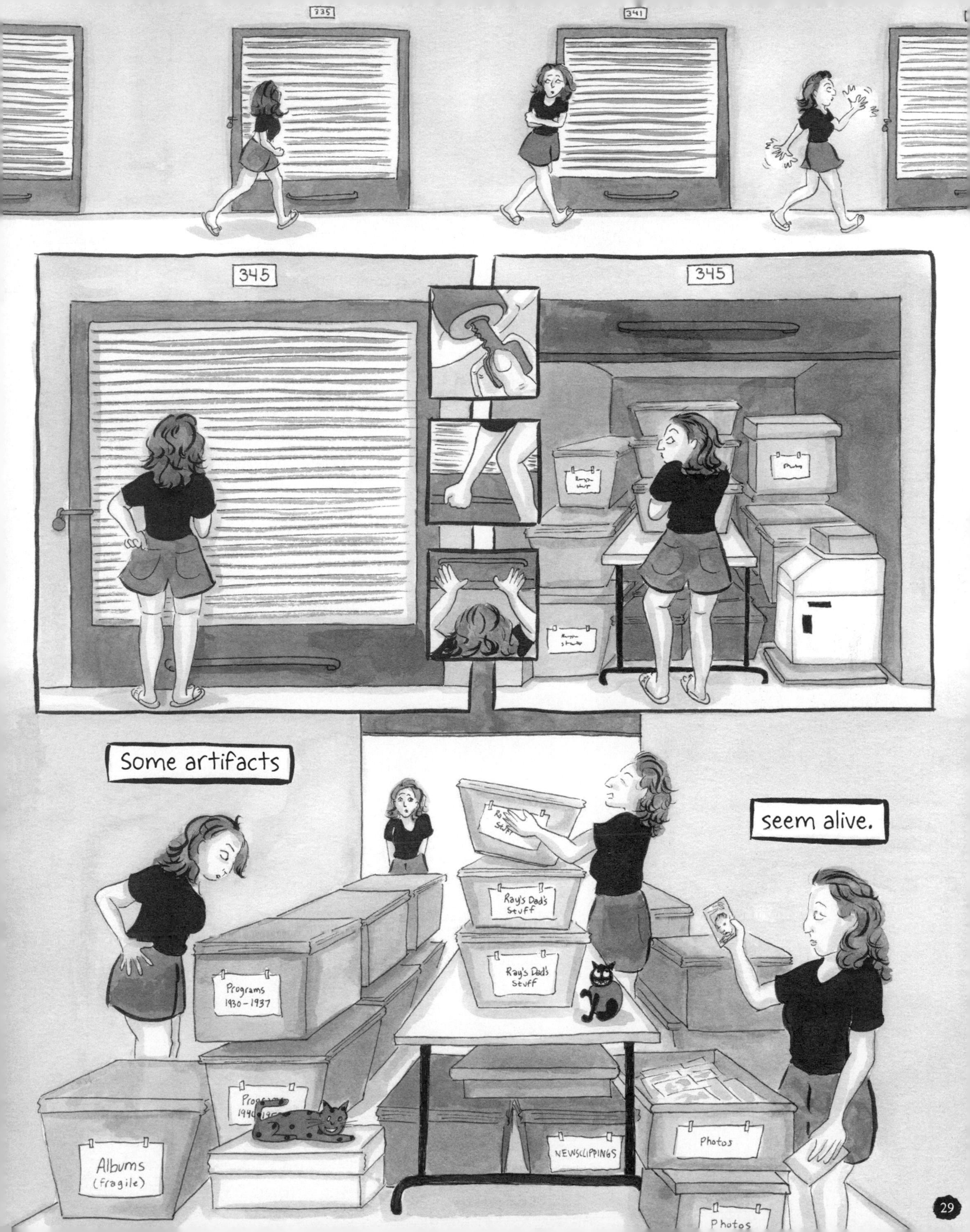
335
341
345
345
Some artifacts
seem alive.
Ray's Dad's Stuff
Ray's Dad's Stuff
Programs 1930–1937
Albums (fragile)
NEWSCLIPPINGS
Photos
Photos

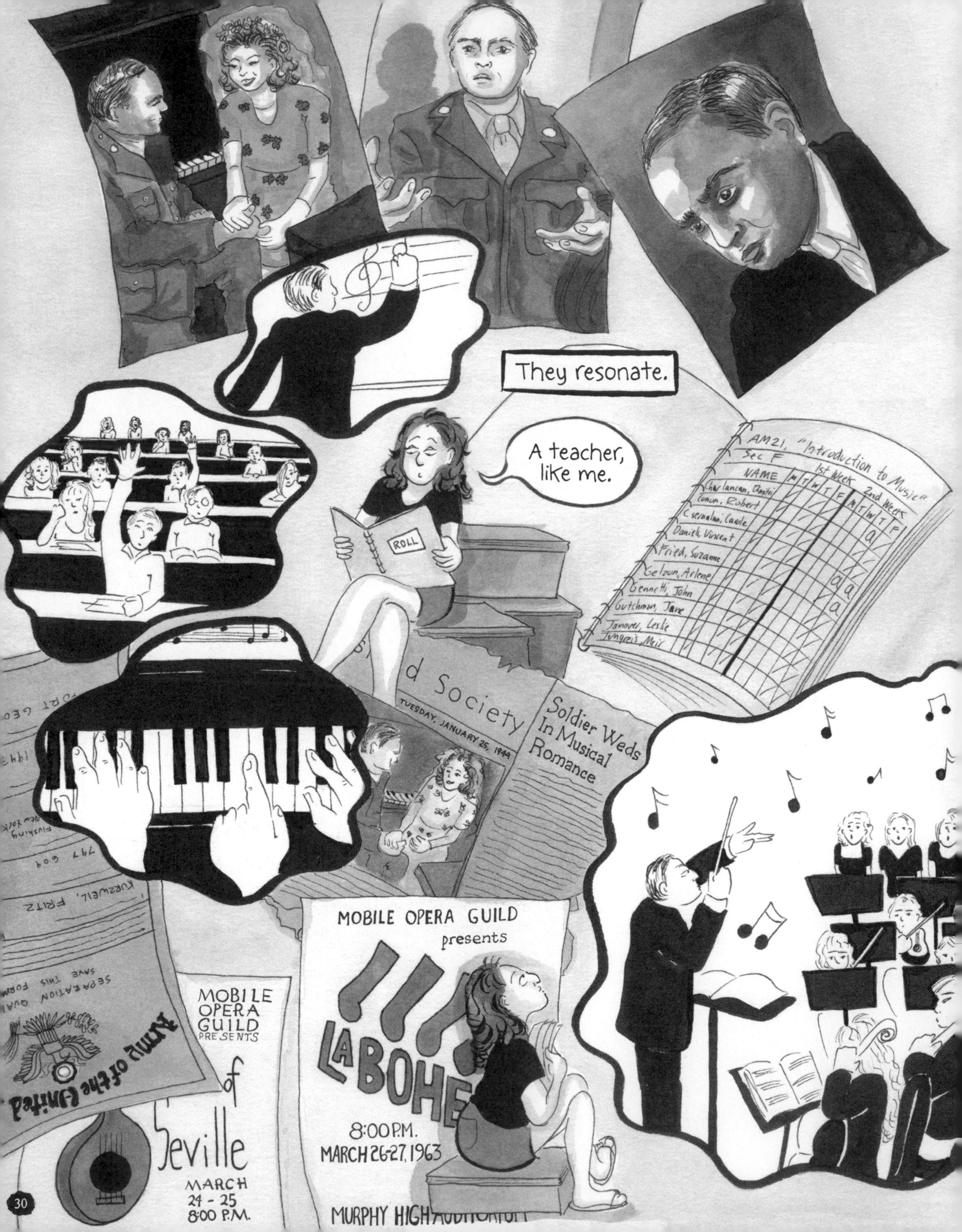
They resonate.
A teacher, like me.
ROLL
AM21. "Introduction to Music"
Sec F
NAME
1st Week
2nd Week
M T W T F
Danith, Vincent
Fried, Suzanne
Gelzon, Arlene
Gennetti, John
Gutchman, Jane
Janover, Leslie
d Society
TUESDAY, JANUARY 25, 1944
Soldier Weds In Musical Romance
KURZWEIL, FRITZ
797 604
Flushing New York
SEPARATION QUAL
SAVE THIS FORM
Army of the United
MOBILE OPERA GUILD PRESENTS
of Seville
MARCH 24 - 25 8:00 P.M.
MOBILE OPERA GUILD presents
LA BOHE
8:00 P.M.
MARCH 26-27, 1963
MURPHY HIGH

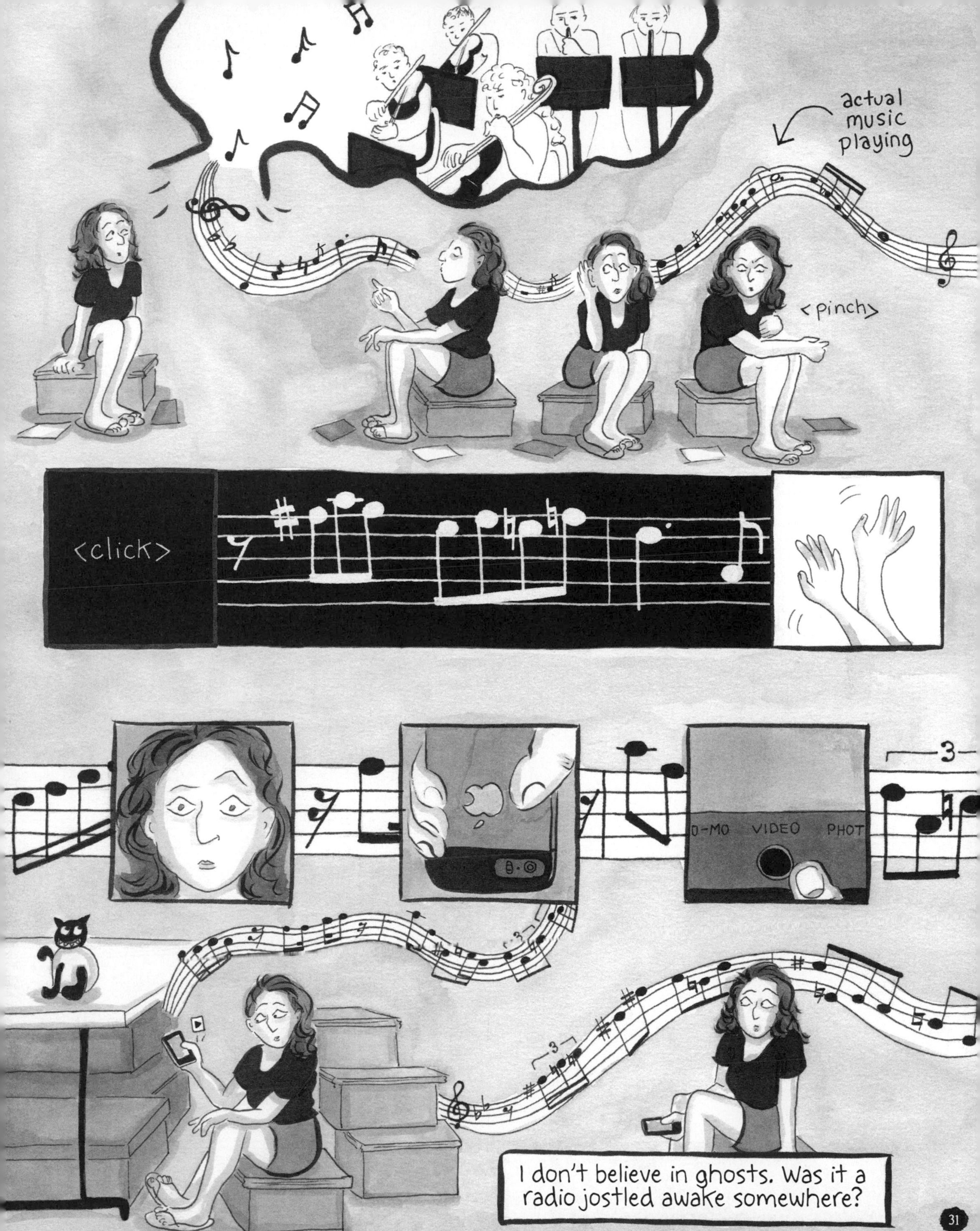
actual music playing
<pinch>
<click>
O-MO VIDEO PHOT
I don't believe in ghosts. Was it a radio jostled awake somewhere?

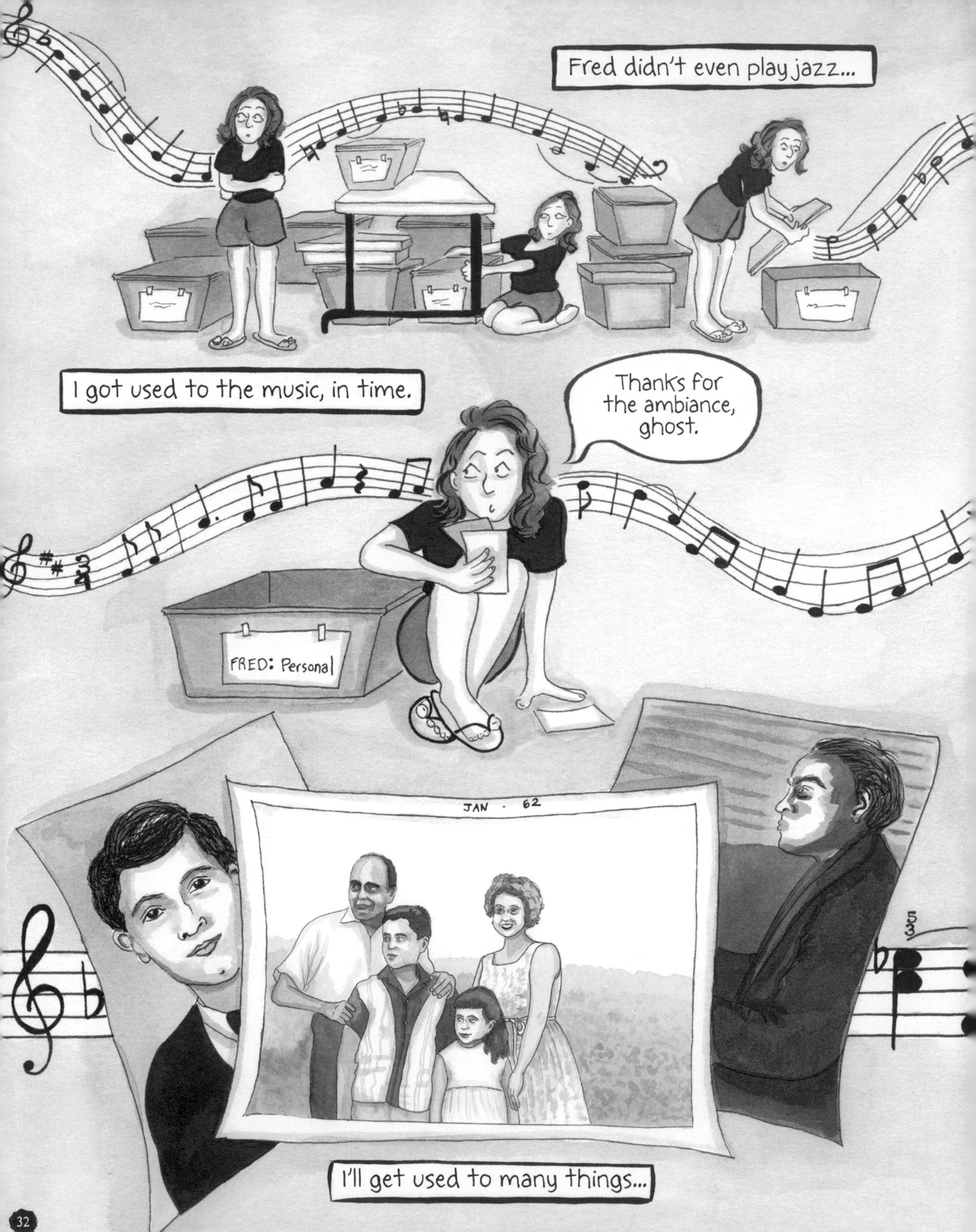
Fred didn't even play jazz...
I got used to the music, in time.
Thanks for the ambiance, ghost.
FRED: Personal
JAN . 62
I'll get used to many things...

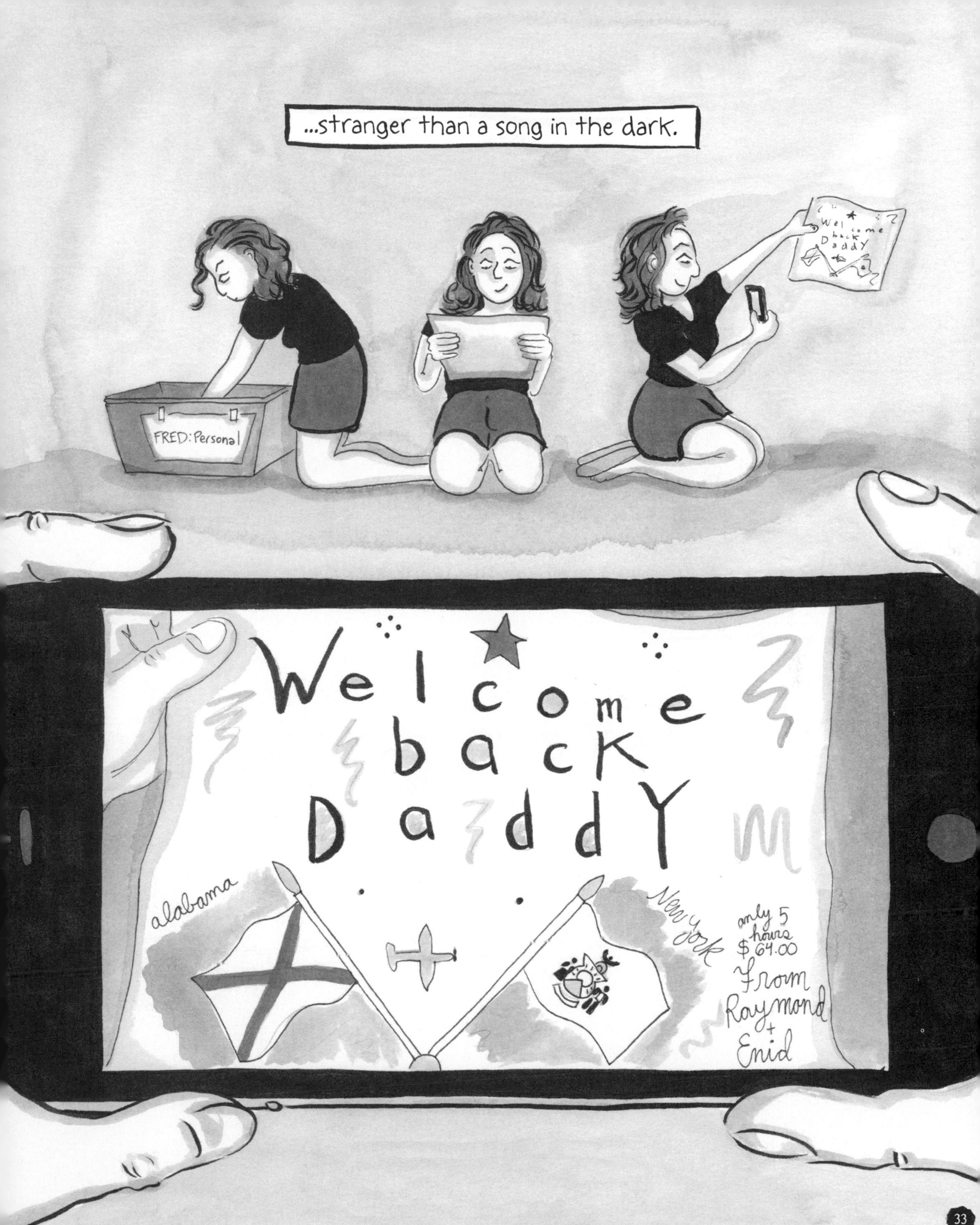
...stranger than a song in the dark.
FRED: Personal
Welcome back Daddy
alabama
New york
only 5 hours
$64.00
From Raymond + Enid

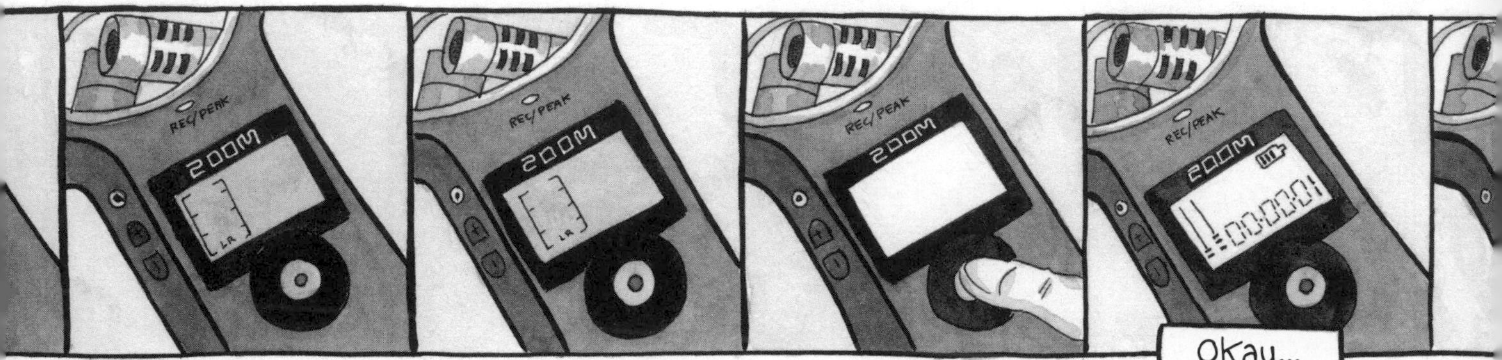
REC/PEAK
ZOOM
Okay...

Don't be scared.

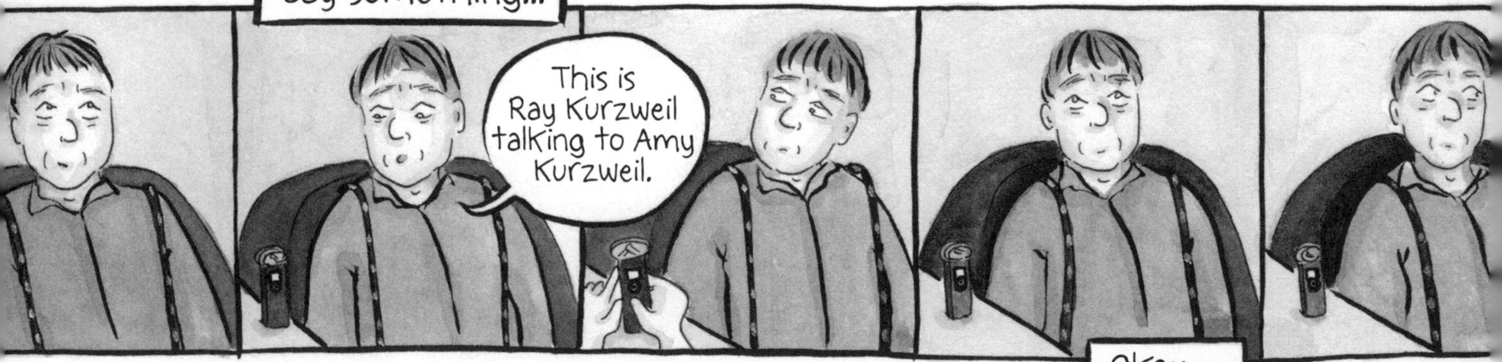
Say something...
This is Ray Kurzweil talking to Amy Kurzweil.
<click click>
Okay...

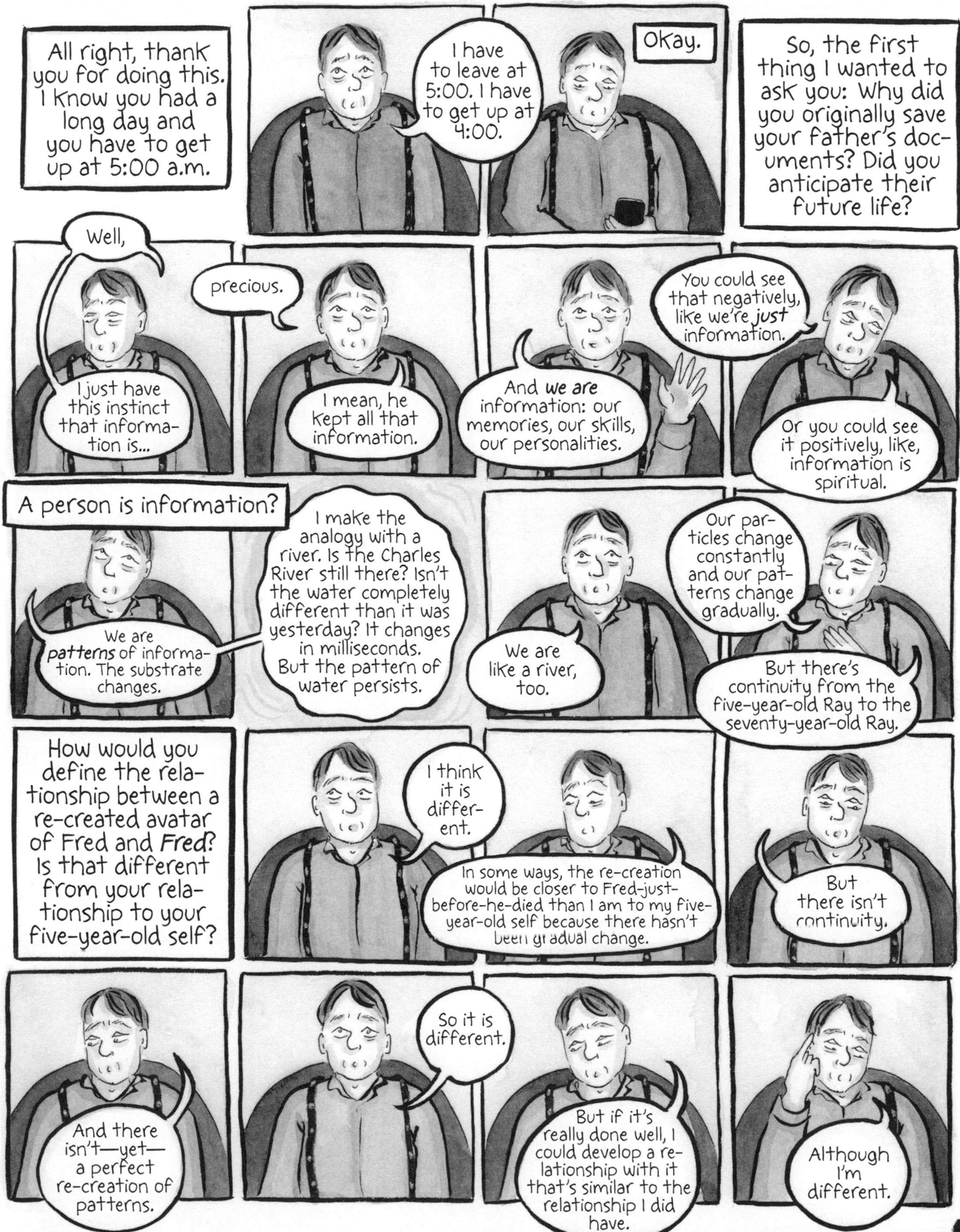
All right, thank you for doing this. I know you had a long day and you have to get up at 5:00 a.m.
I have to leave at 5:00. I have to get up at 4:00.
Okay.
So, the first thing I wanted to ask you: Why did you originally save your father's documents? Did you anticipate their future life?
Well,
I just have this instinct that information is...
precious.
I mean, he kept all that information.
And *we are* information: our memories, our skills, our personalities.
You could see that negatively, like we're *just* information.
Or you could see it positively, like, information is spiritual.
A person is information?
We are *patterns* of information. The substrate changes.
I make the analogy with a river. Is the Charles River still there? Isn't the water completely different than it was yesterday? It changes in milliseconds. But the pattern of water persists.
We are like a river, too.
Our particles change constantly and our patterns change gradually.
But there's continuity from the five-year-old Ray to the seventy-year-old Ray.
How would you define the relationship between a re-created avatar of Fred and *Fred*? Is that different from your relationship to your five-year-old self?
I think it is different.
In some ways, the re-creation would be closer to Fred-just-before-he-died than I am to my five-year-old self because there hasn't been gradual change.
But there isn't continuity.
And there isn't—yet—a perfect re-creation of patterns.
So it is different.
But if it's really done well, I could develop a relationship with it that's similar to the relationship I did have.
Although I'm different.

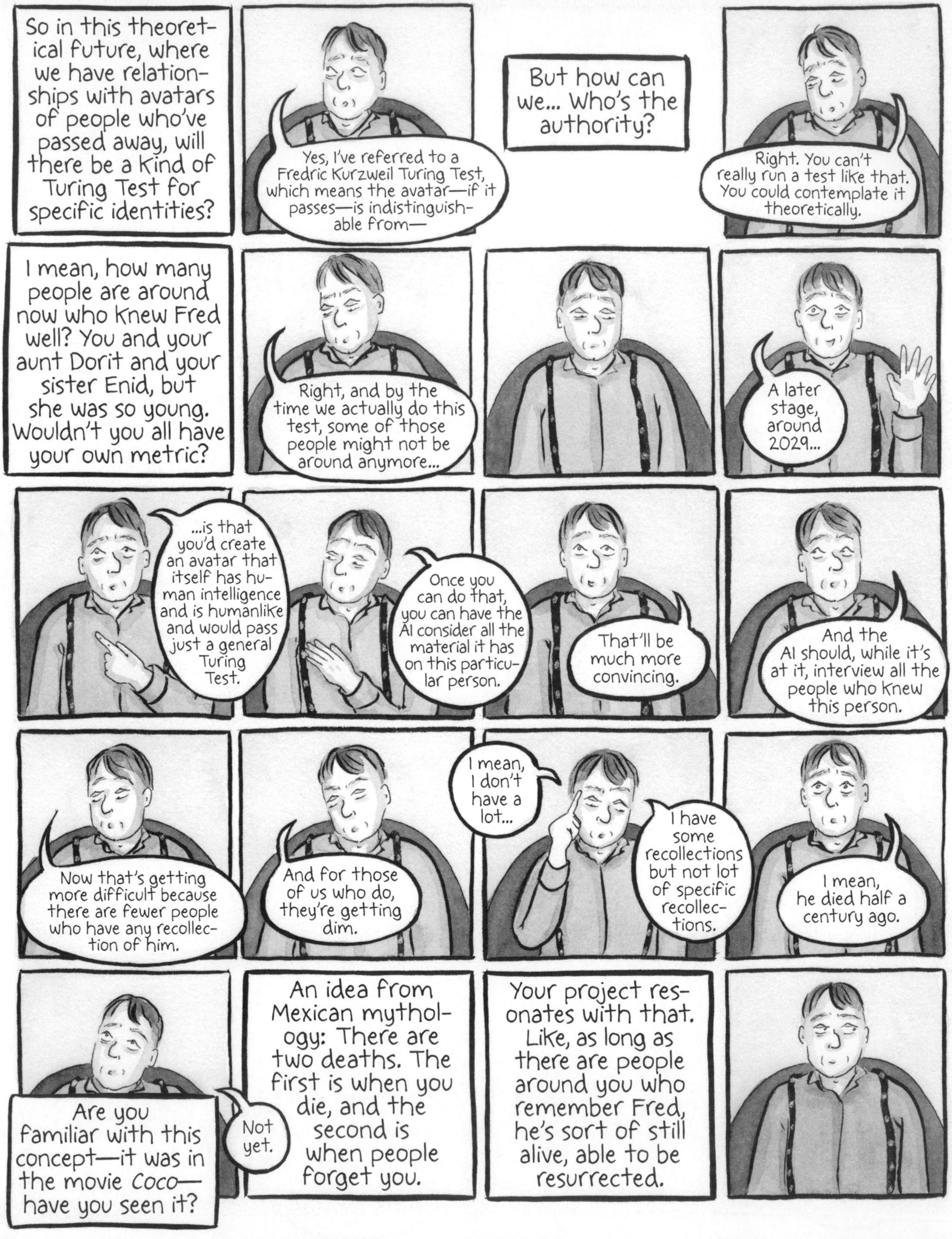
So in this theoretical future, where we have relationships with avatars of people who've passed away, will there be a kind of Turing Test for specific identities?
Yes, I've referred to a Fredric Kurzweil Turing Test, which means the avatar—if it passes—is indistinguishable from—
But how can we... Who's the authority?
Right. You can't really run a test like that. You could contemplate it theoretically.
I mean, how many people are around now who knew Fred well? You and your aunt Dorit and your sister Enid, but she was so young. Wouldn't you all have your own metric?
Right, and by the time we actually do this test, some of those people might not be around anymore...
A later stage, around 2029...
...is that you'd create an avatar that itself has human intelligence and is humanlike and would pass just a general Turing Test.
Once you can do that, you can have the AI consider all the material it has on this particular person.
That'll be much more convincing.
And the AI should, while it's at it, interview all the people who knew this person.
Now that's getting more difficult because there are fewer people who have any recollection of him.
And for those of us who do, they're getting dim.
I mean, I don't have a lot...
I have some recollections but not lot of specific recollections.
I mean, he died half a century ago.
Are you familiar with this concept—it was in the movie *Coco*—have you seen it?
Not yet.
An idea from Mexican mythology: There are two deaths. The first is when you die, and the second is when people forget you.
Your project resonates with that. Like, as long as there are people around you who remember Fred, he's sort of still alive, able to be resurrected.

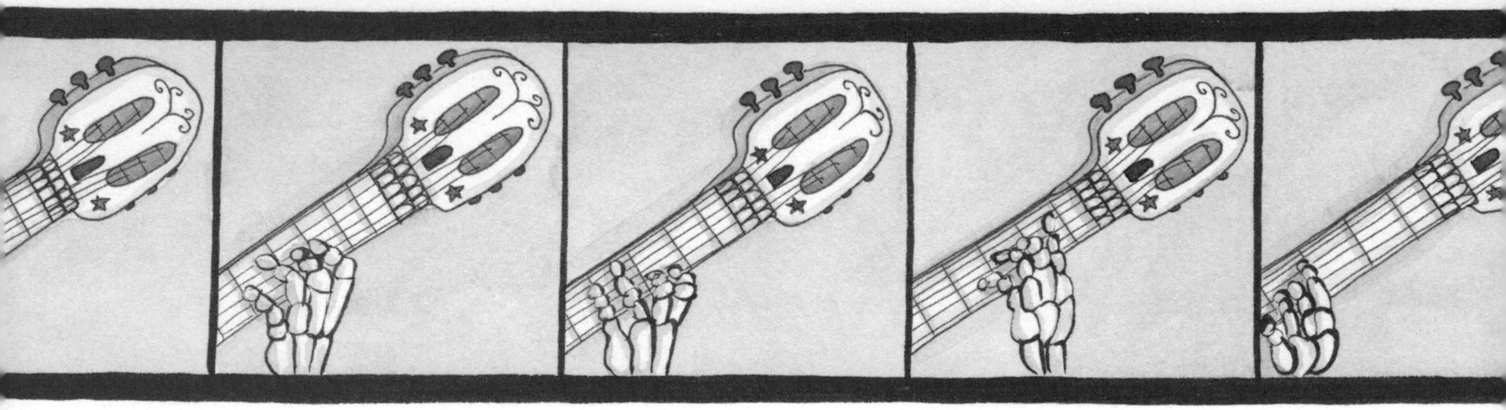

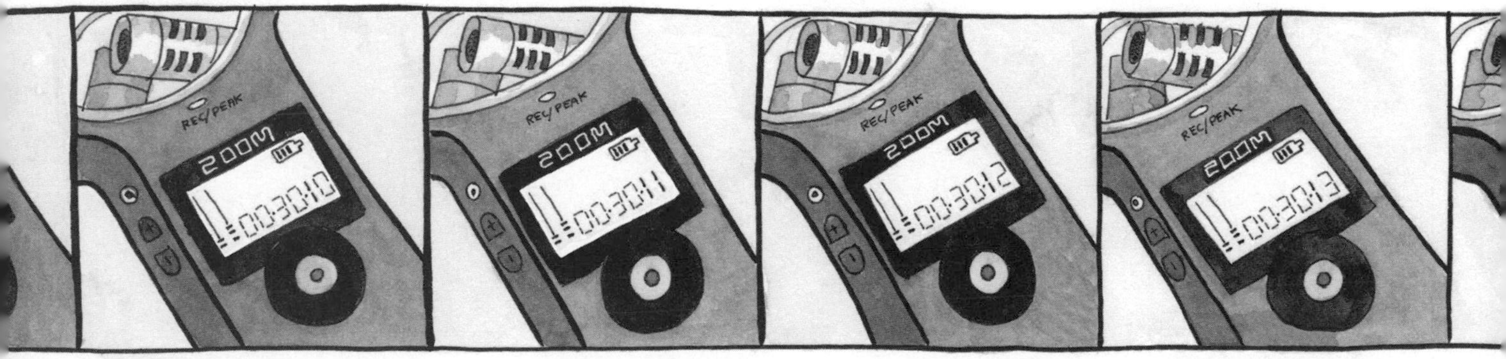
REC/PEAK
ZOOM
00:30:10
REC/PEAK
ZOOM
00:30:11
REC/PEAK
ZOOM
00:30:12
REC/PEAK
ZOOM
00:30:13

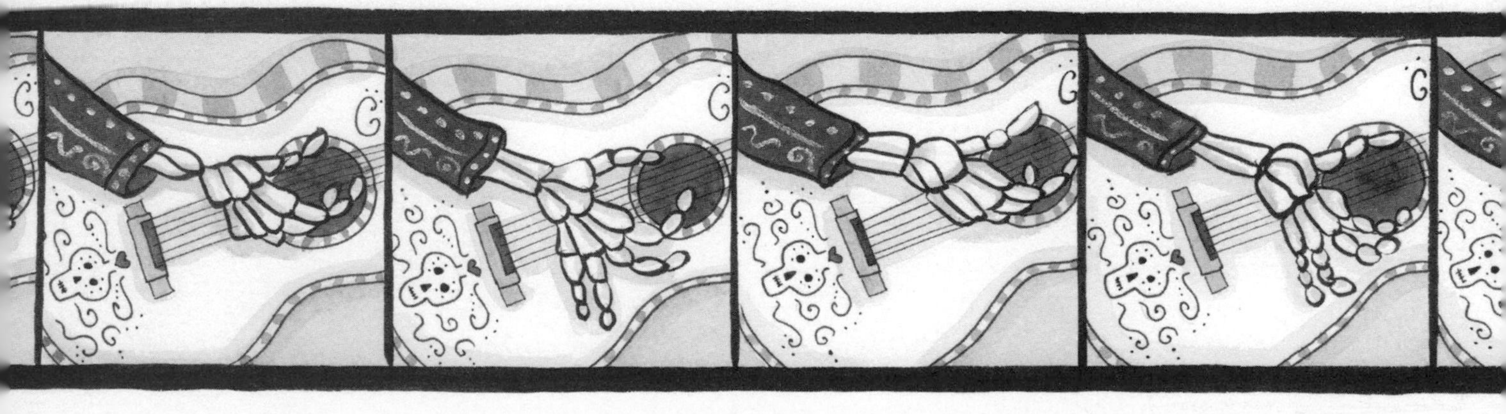

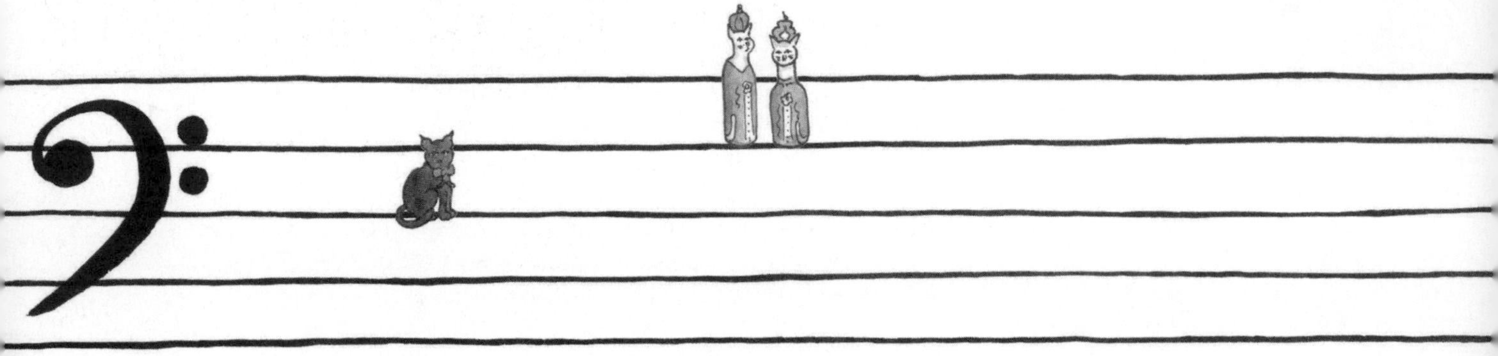

# II.

# Immortal Virtue

I believe anyone will do anything for the sake of immortal virtue and the glorious fame that follows, and the better the people, the more they will do, for they are all in love with immortality.

–Plato, *The Symposium*

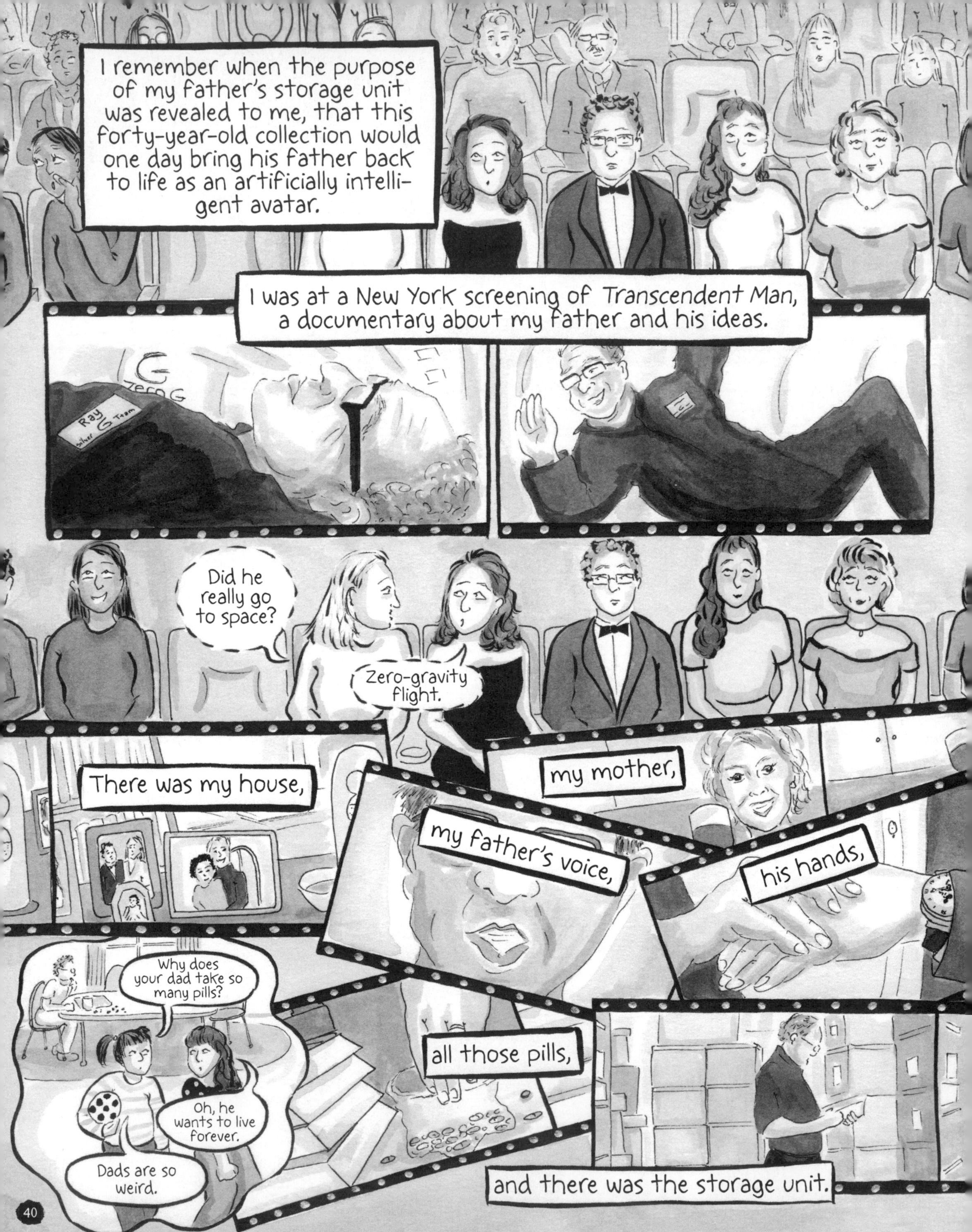
I remember when the purpose of my father's storage unit was revealed to me, that this forty-year-old collection would one day bring his father back to life as an artificially intelligent avatar.
I was at a New York screening of Transcendent Man, a documentary about my father and his ideas.
Zero G
Ray
Silver G Team
Did he really go to space?
Zero-gravity flight.
There was my house,
my mother,
my father's voice,
his hands,
Why does your dad take so many pills?
Oh, he wants to live forever.
Dads are so weird.
all those pills,
and there was the storage unit.

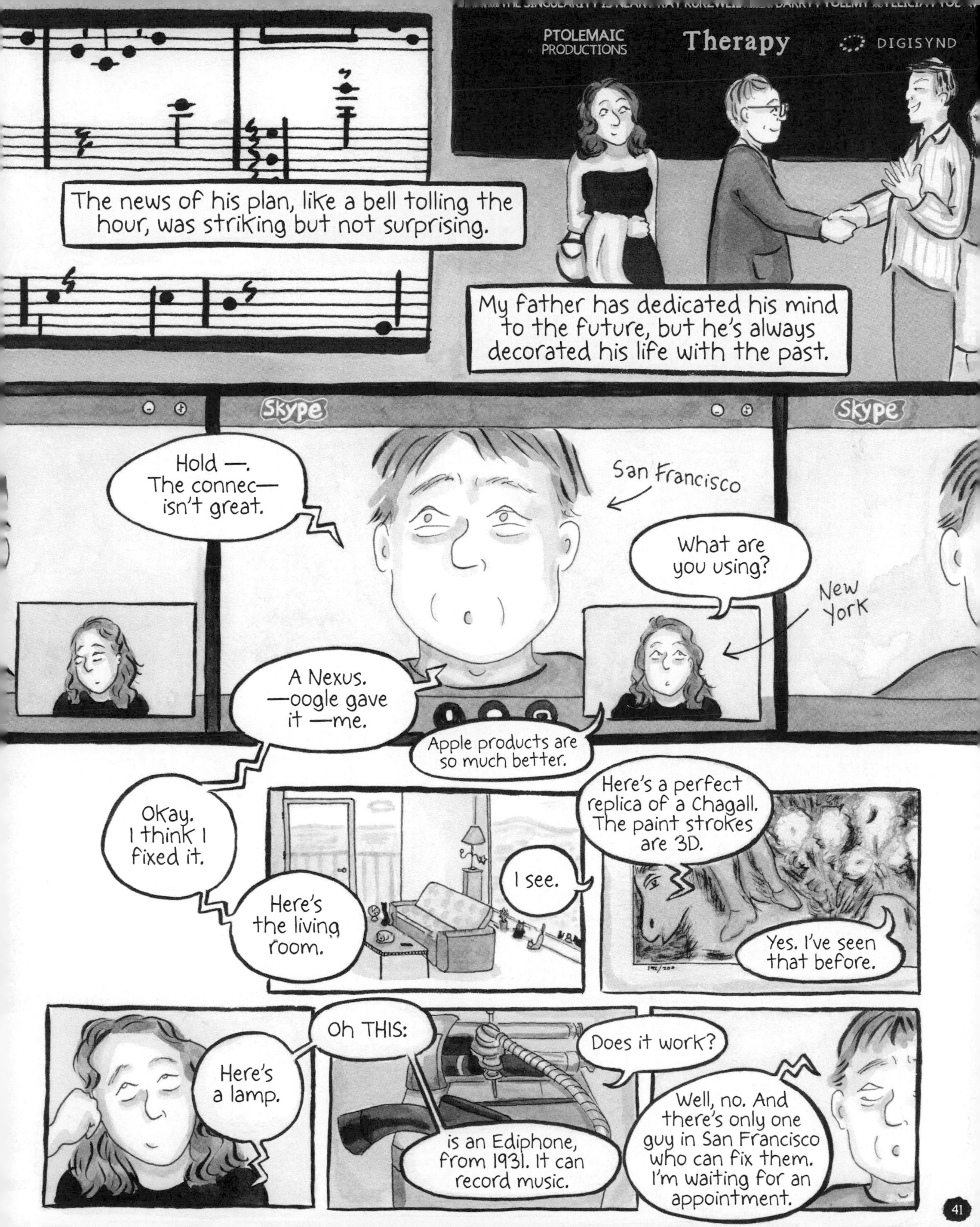
The news of his plan, like a bell tolling the hour, was striking but not surprising.
PTOLEMAIC PRODUCTIONS
Therapy
DIGISYND
My father has dedicated his mind to the future, but he's always decorated his life with the past.
Skype
Hold —. The connec— isn't great.
San Francisco
What are you using?
New York
A Nexus. —oogle gave it —me.
Apple products are so much better.
Okay. I think I fixed it.
Here's the living room.
I see.
Here's a perfect replica of a Chagall. The paint strokes are 3D.
Yes. I've seen that before.
Here's a lamp.
Oh THIS:
is an Ediphone, from 1931. It can record music.
Does it work?
Well, no. And there's only one guy in San Francisco who can fix them. I'm waiting for an appointment.

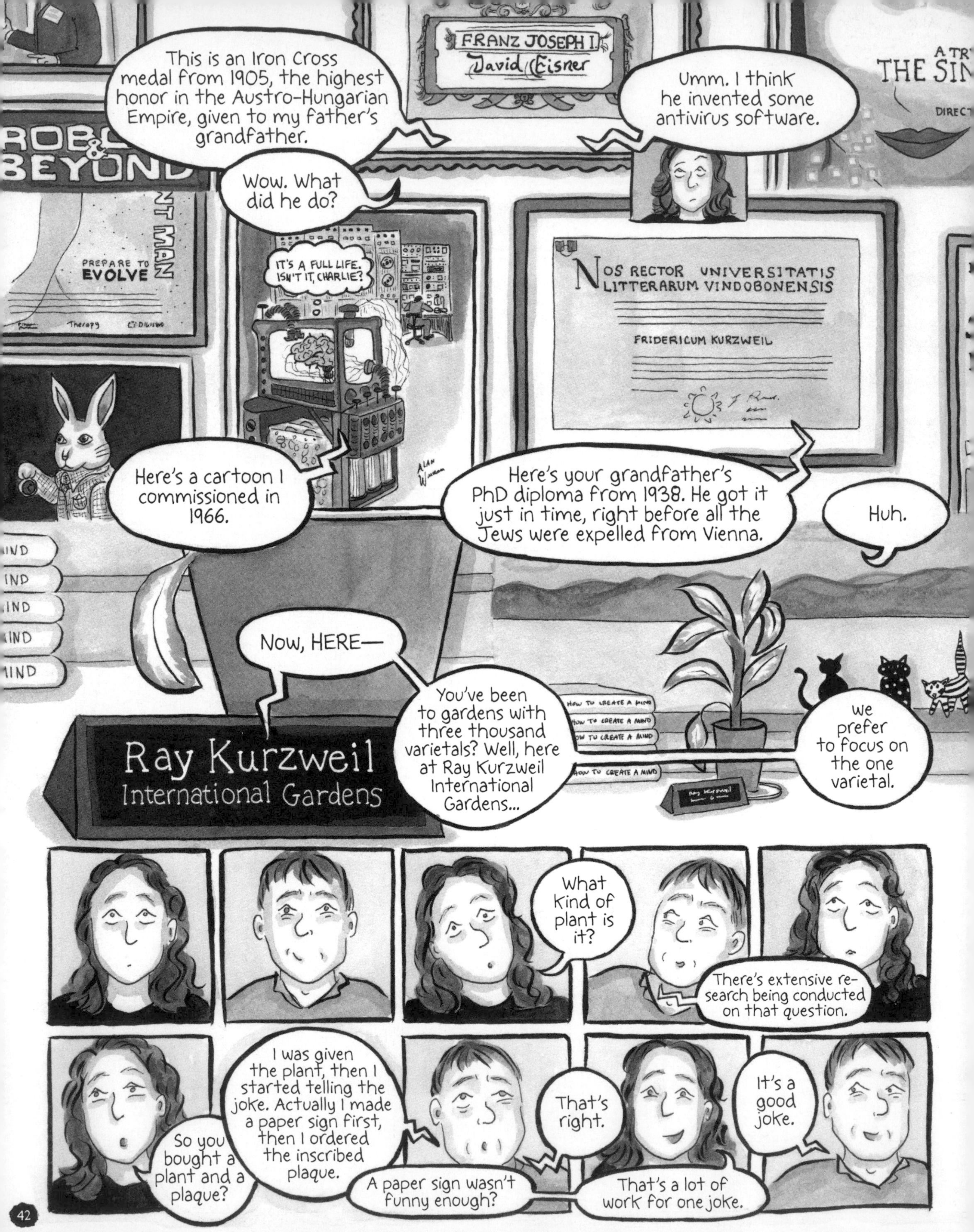

FRANZ JOSEPH I.
David Eisner
This is an Iron Cross medal from 1905, the highest honor in the Austro-Hungarian Empire, given to my father's grandfather.
Wow. What did he do?
Umm. I think he invented some antivirus software.
ROBOTS & BEYOND
PREPARE TO EVOLVE
IT'S A FULL LIFE. ISN'T IT, CHARLIE?
NOS RECTOR UNIVERSITATIS LITTERARUM VINDOBONENSIS
FRIDERICUM KURZWEIL
Here's a cartoon I commissioned in 1966.
Here's your grandfather's PhD diploma from 1938. He got it just in time, right before all the Jews were expelled from Vienna.
Huh.
Now, HERE—
Ray Kurzweil International Gardens
You've been to gardens with three thousand varietals? Well, here at Ray Kurzweil International Gardens...
we prefer to focus on the one varietal.
HOW TO CREATE A MIND
What kind of plant is it?
There's extensive research being conducted on that question.
So you bought a plant and a plaque?
I was given the plant, then I started telling the joke. Actually I made a paper sign first, then I ordered the inscribed plaque.
A paper sign wasn't funny enough?
That's right.
That's a lot of work for one joke.
It's a good joke.

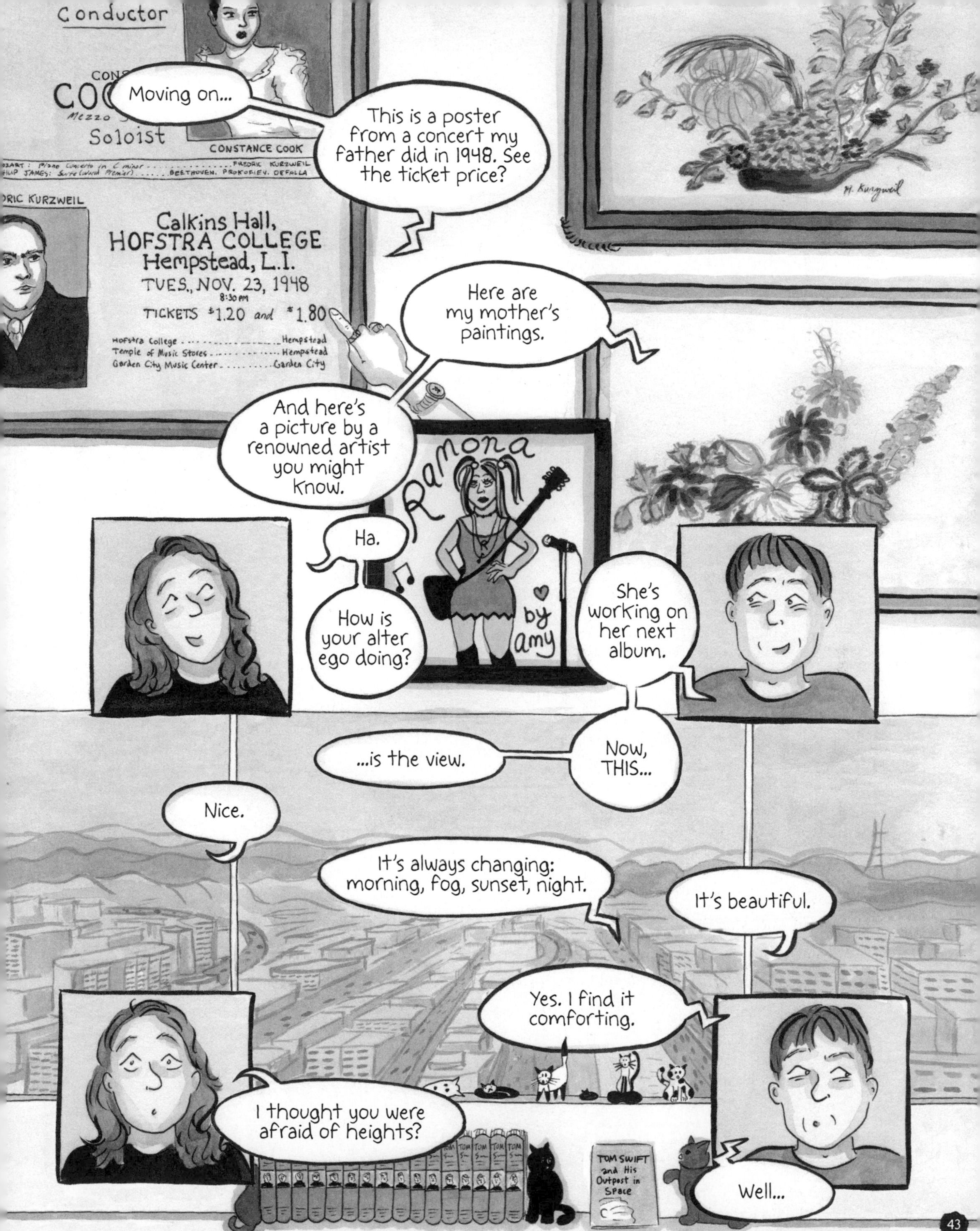
Conductor
Soloist
CONSTANCE COOK
Moving on...
This is a poster from a concert my father did in 1948. See the ticket price?
Calkins Hall, HOFSTRA COLLEGE Hempstead, L.I.
TUES., NOV. 23, 1948
8:30 pm
TICKETS $1.20 and $1.80
Hofstra College ........ Hempstead
Temple of Music Stores ........ Hempstead
Garden City Music Center ........ Garden City
Here are my mother's paintings.
And here's a picture by a renowned artist you might know.
Ramona
by amy
Ha.
How is your alter ego doing?
She's working on her next album.
Now, THIS...
...is the view.
Nice.
It's always changing: morning, fog, sunset, night.
It's beautiful.
Yes. I find it comforting.
I thought you were afraid of heights?
Well...
TOM SWIFT and His Outpost in Space

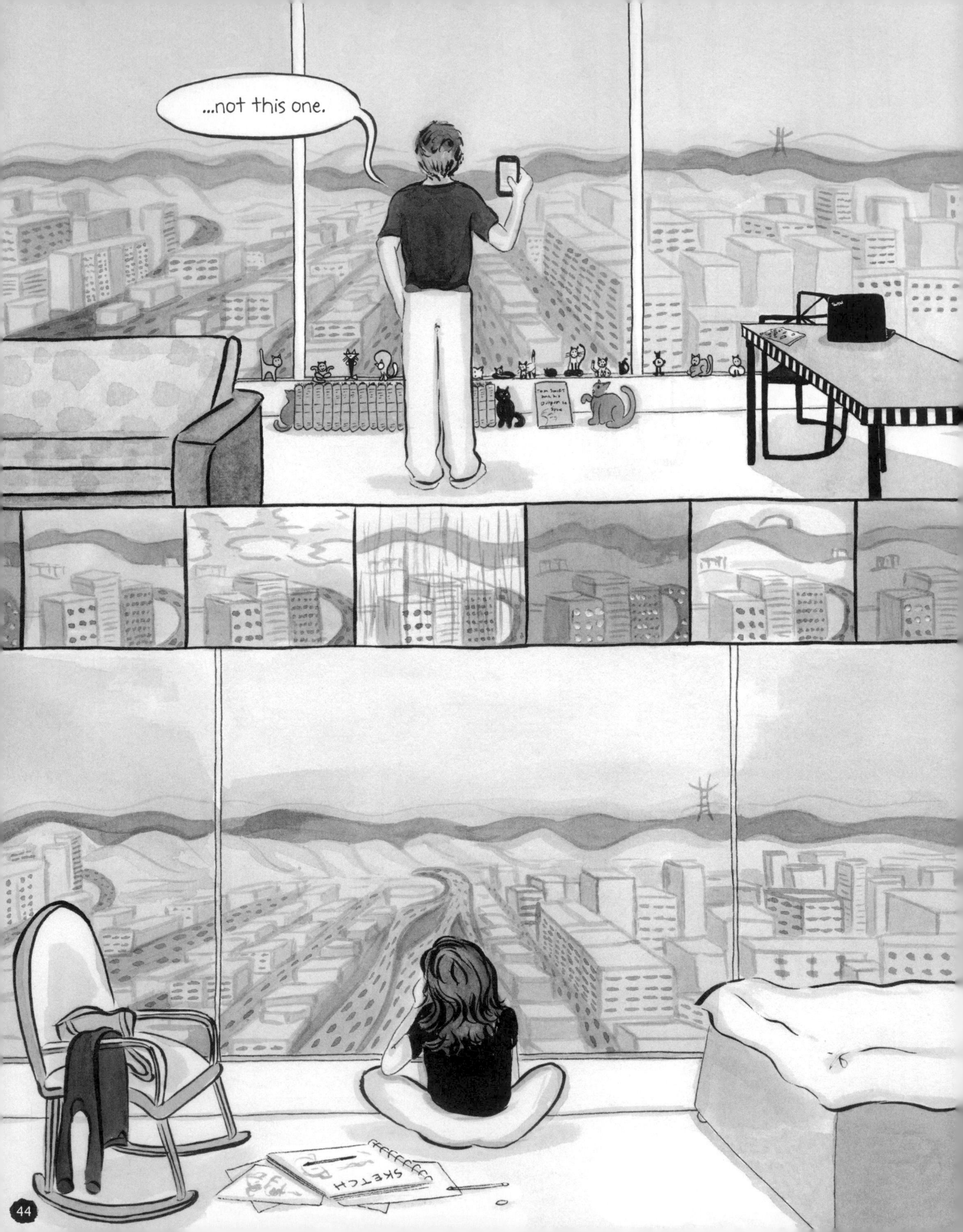
...not this one.
SKETCH

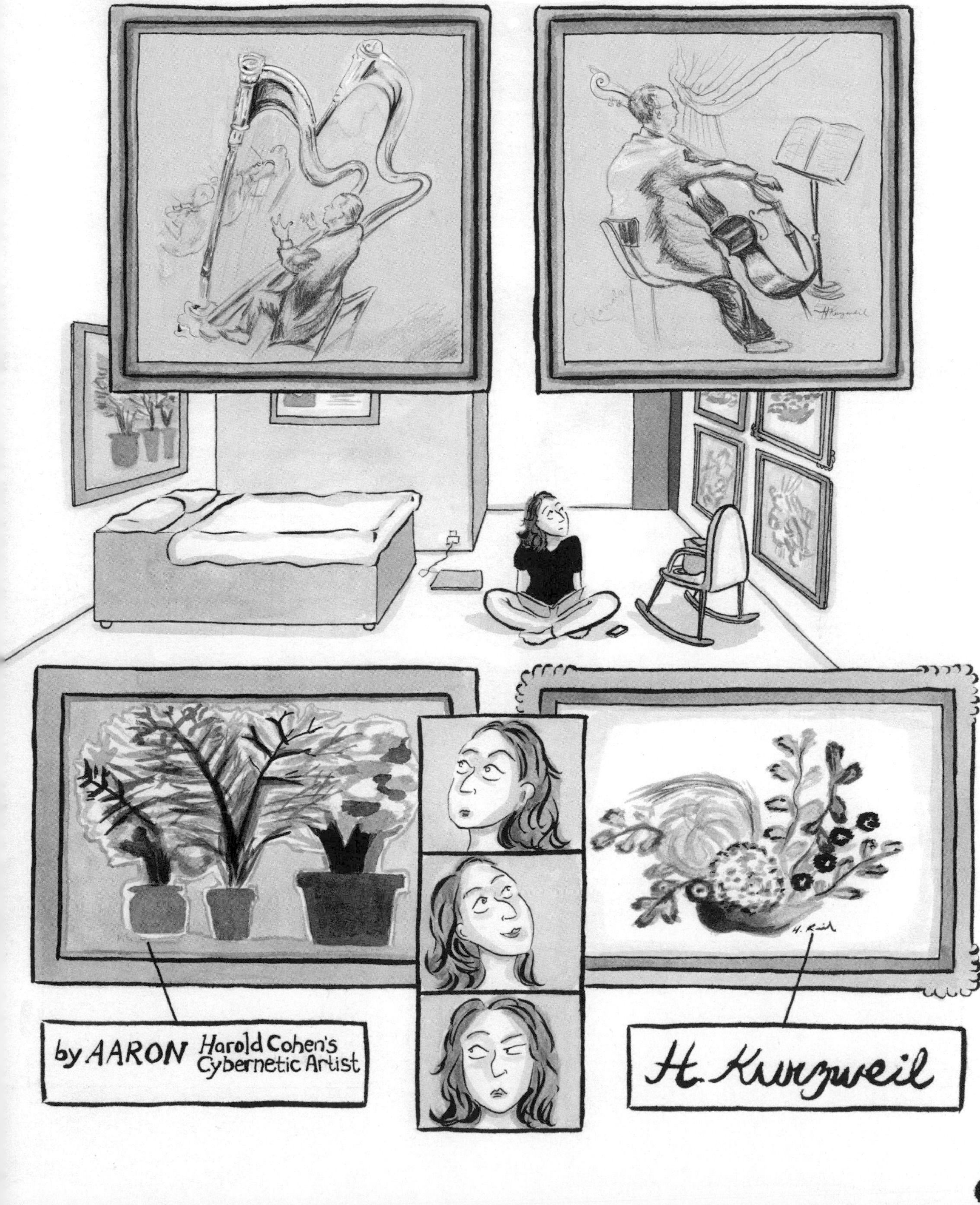

by AARON Harold Cohen's Cybernetic Artist
H. Kurzweil

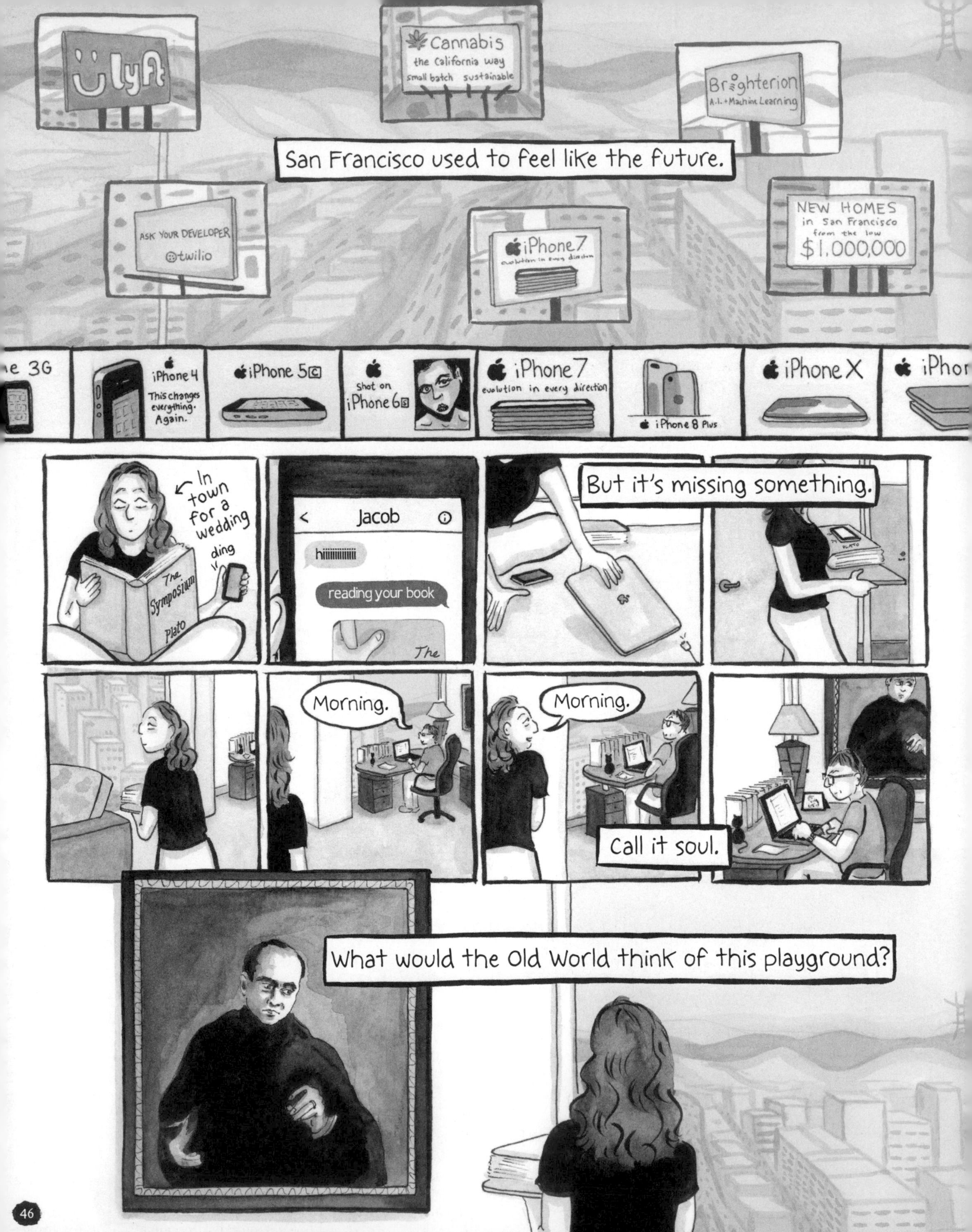

lyft
Cannabis
the California way
small batch sustainable
Brighterion
A.I. + Machine Learning
San Francisco used to feel like the future.
ASK YOUR DEVELOPER
twilio
iPhone7
NEW HOMES
in San Francisco
from the low
$1,000,000
iPhone 4
This changes everything. Again.
iPhone 5c
Shot on
iPhone 6s
iPhone7
evolution in every direction
iPhone 8 Plus
iPhone X
In town for a wedding
ding
The Symposium
Plato
Jacob
hiiiiiiiiiiii
reading your book
The
But it's missing something.
Morning.
Morning.
Call it soul.
What would the Old World think of this playground?

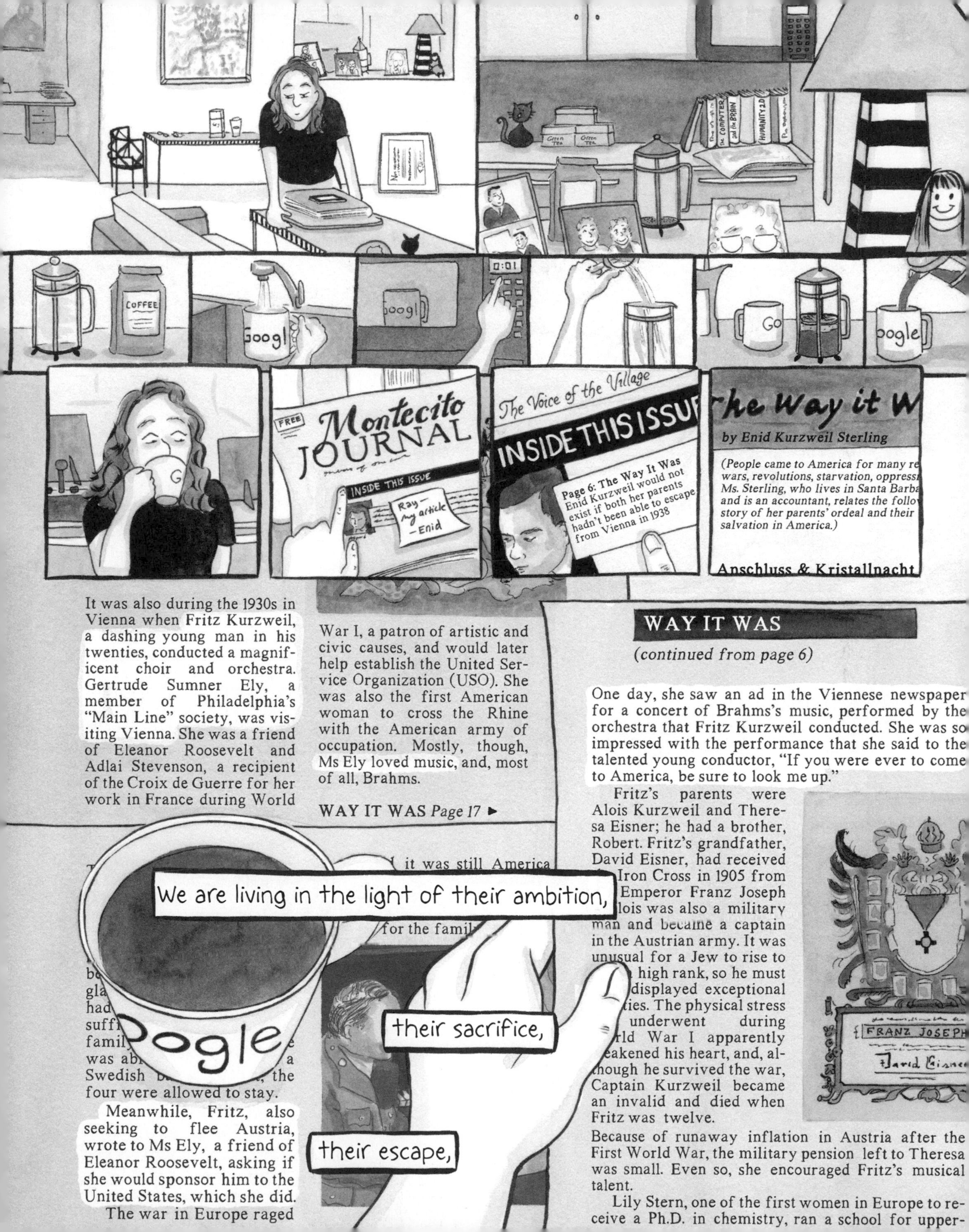

COFFEE
Googl
0:01
Go
ogle
FREE
Montecito JOURNAL
INSIDE THIS ISSUE
Ray— my article —Enid
The Voice of the Village
INSIDE THIS ISSUE
Page 6: The Way It Was
Enid Kurzweil would not exist if both her parents hadn't been able to escape from Vienna in 1938
he Way it W
by Enid Kurzweil Sterling
(People came to America for many re
wars, revolutions, starvation, oppress
Ms. Sterling, who lives in Santa Barba
and is an accountant, relates the follo
story of her parents' ordeal and their
salvation in America.)
Anschluss & Kristallnacht
It was also during the 1930s in Vienna when Fritz Kurzweil, a dashing young man in his twenties, conducted a magnificent choir and orchestra. Gertrude Sumner Ely, a member of Philadelphia's "Main Line" society, was visiting Vienna. She was a friend of Eleanor Roosevelt and Adlai Stevenson, a recipient of the Croix de Guerre for her work in France during World
War I, a patron of artistic and civic causes, and would later help establish the United Service Organization (USO). She was also the first American woman to cross the Rhine with the American army of occupation. Mostly, though, Ms Ely loved music, and, most of all, Brahms.
WAY IT WAS Page 17 ►
WAY IT WAS
(continued from page 6)
One day, she saw an ad in the Viennese newspaper for a concert of Brahms's music, performed by the orchestra that Fritz Kurzweil conducted. She was so impressed with the performance that she said to the talented young conductor, "If you were ever to come to America, be sure to look me up."
Fritz's parents were Alois Kurzweil and Theresa Eisner; he had a brother, Robert. Fritz's grandfather, David Eisner, had received Iron Cross in 1905 from Emperor Franz Joseph lois was also a military man and became a captain in the Austrian army. It was unusual for a Jew to rise to high rank, so he must displayed exceptional ties. The physical stress underwent during rld War I apparently eakened his heart, and, although he survived the war, Captain Kurzweil became an invalid and died when Fritz was twelve.
Because of runaway inflation in Austria after the First World War, the military pension left to Theresa was small. Even so, she encouraged Fritz's musical talent.
Lily Stern, one of the first women in Europe to receive a Ph.D. in chemistry, ran a school for upper-
FRANZ JOSEPH
David Eisner
it was still America
for the famil
was ab a Swedish the four were allowed to stay.
Meanwhile, Fritz, also seeking to flee Austria, wrote to Ms Ely, a friend of Eleanor Roosevelt, asking if she would sponsor him to the United States, which she did.
The war in Europe raged
oogle
We are living in the light of their ambition,
their sacrifice,
their escape,

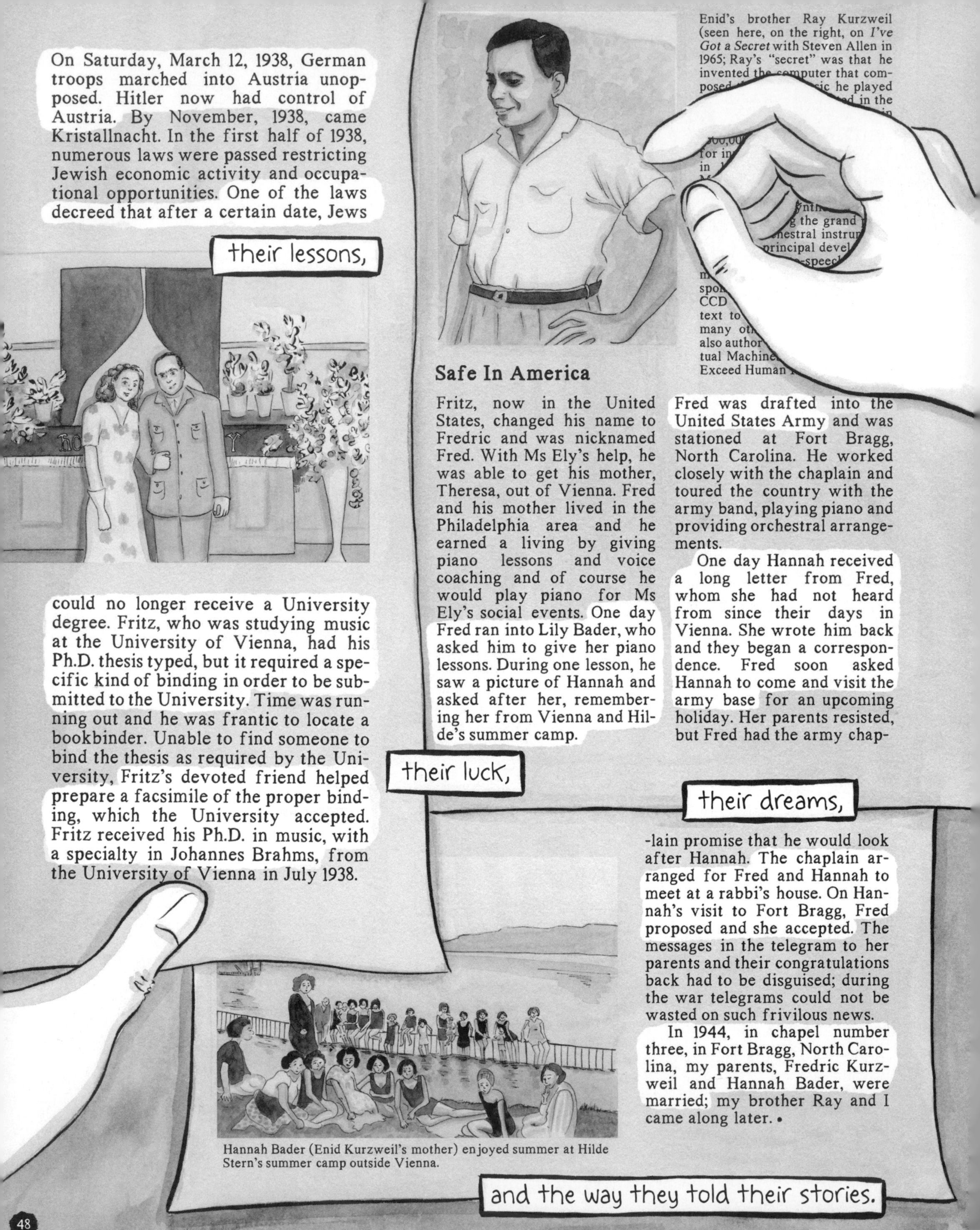
On Saturday, March 12, 1938, German troops marched into Austria unopposed. Hitler now had control of Austria. By November, 1938, came Kristallnacht. In the first half of 1938, numerous laws were passed restricting Jewish economic activity and occupational opportunities. One of the laws decreed that after a certain date, Jews
their lessons,
could no longer receive a University degree. Fritz, who was studying music at the University of Vienna, had his Ph.D. thesis typed, but it required a specific kind of binding in order to be submitted to the University. Time was running out and he was frantic to locate a bookbinder. Unable to find someone to bind the thesis as required by the University, Fritz's devoted friend helped prepare a facsimile of the proper binding, which the University accepted. Fritz received his Ph.D. in music, with a specialty in Johannes Brahms, from the University of Vienna in July 1938.
their luck,
Enid's brother Ray Kurzweil (seen here, on the right, on I've Got a Secret with Steven Allen in 1965; Ray's "secret" was that he invented the
Safe In America
Fritz, now in the United States, changed his name to Fredric and was nicknamed Fred. With Ms Ely's help, he was able to get his mother, Theresa, out of Vienna. Fred and his mother lived in the Philadelphia area and he earned a living by giving piano lessons and voice coaching and of course he would play piano for Ms Ely's social events. One day Fred ran into Lily Bader, who asked him to give her piano lessons. During one lesson, he saw a picture of Hannah and asked after her, remembering her from Vienna and Hilde's summer camp.
Fred was drafted into the United States Army and was stationed at Fort Bragg, North Carolina. He worked closely with the chaplain and toured the country with the army band, playing piano and providing orchestral arrangements.
One day Hannah received a long letter from Fred, whom she had not heard from since their days in Vienna. She wrote him back and they began a correspondence. Fred soon asked Hannah to come and visit the army base for an upcoming holiday. Her parents resisted, but Fred had the army chap-
their dreams,
-lain promise that he would look after Hannah. The chaplain arranged for Fred and Hannah to meet at a rabbi's house. On Hannah's visit to Fort Bragg, Fred proposed and she accepted. The messages in the telegram to her parents and their congratulations back had to be disguised; during the war telegrams could not be wasted on such frivolous news.
In 1944, in chapel number three, in Fort Bragg, North Carolina, my parents, Fredric Kurzweil and Hannah Bader, were married; my brother Ray and I came along later. •
Hannah Bader (Enid Kurzweil's mother) enjoyed summer at Hilde Stern's summer camp outside Vienna.
and the way they told their stories.

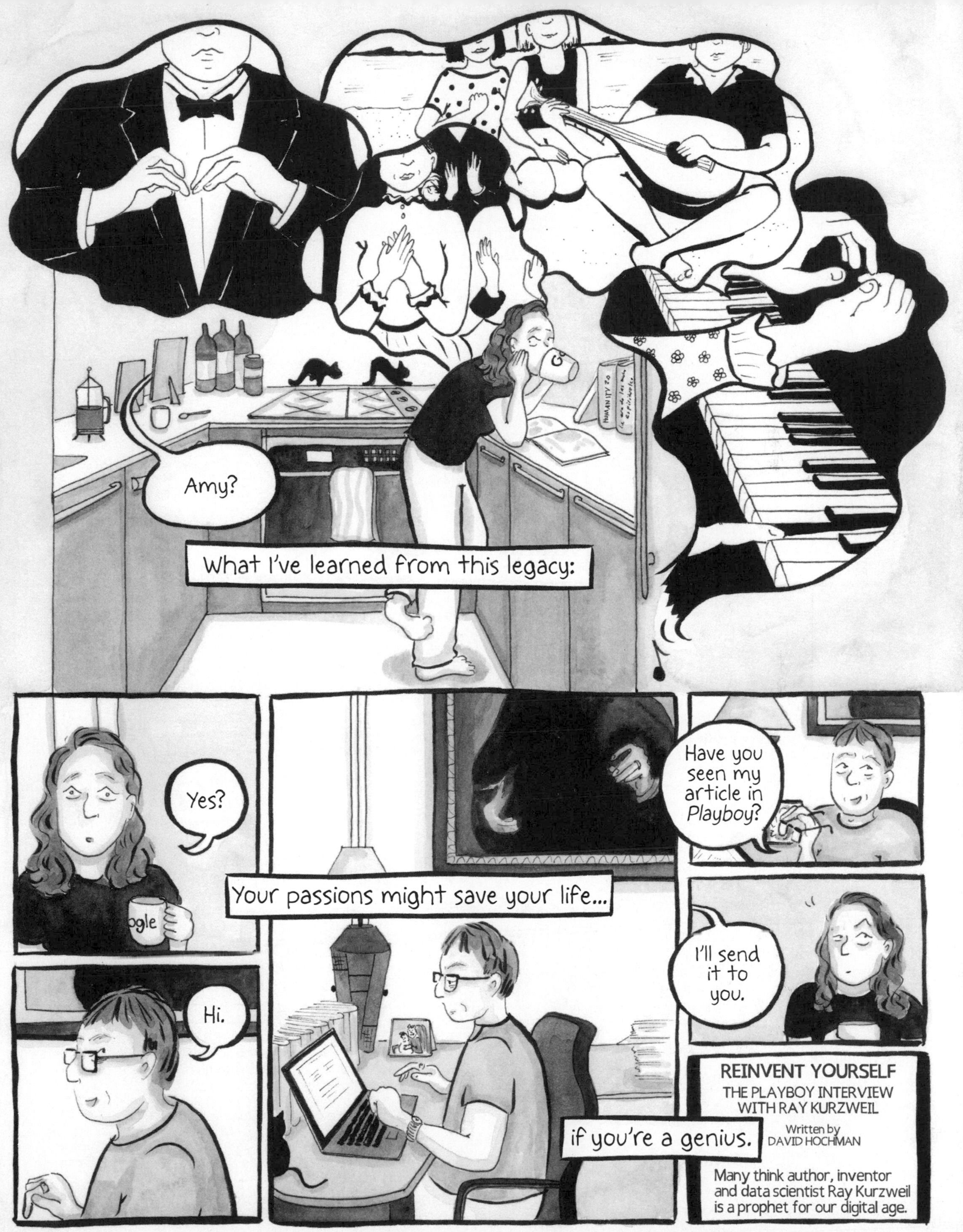
Amy?
What I've learned from this legacy:
Yes?
Hi.
Your passions might save your life...
Have you seen my article in *Playboy*?
I'll send it to you.
if you're a genius.
REINVENT YOURSELF
THE PLAYBOY INTERVIEW WITH RAY KURZWEIL
Written by DAVID HOCHMAN
Many think author, inventor and data scientist Ray Kurzweil is a prophet for our digital age.

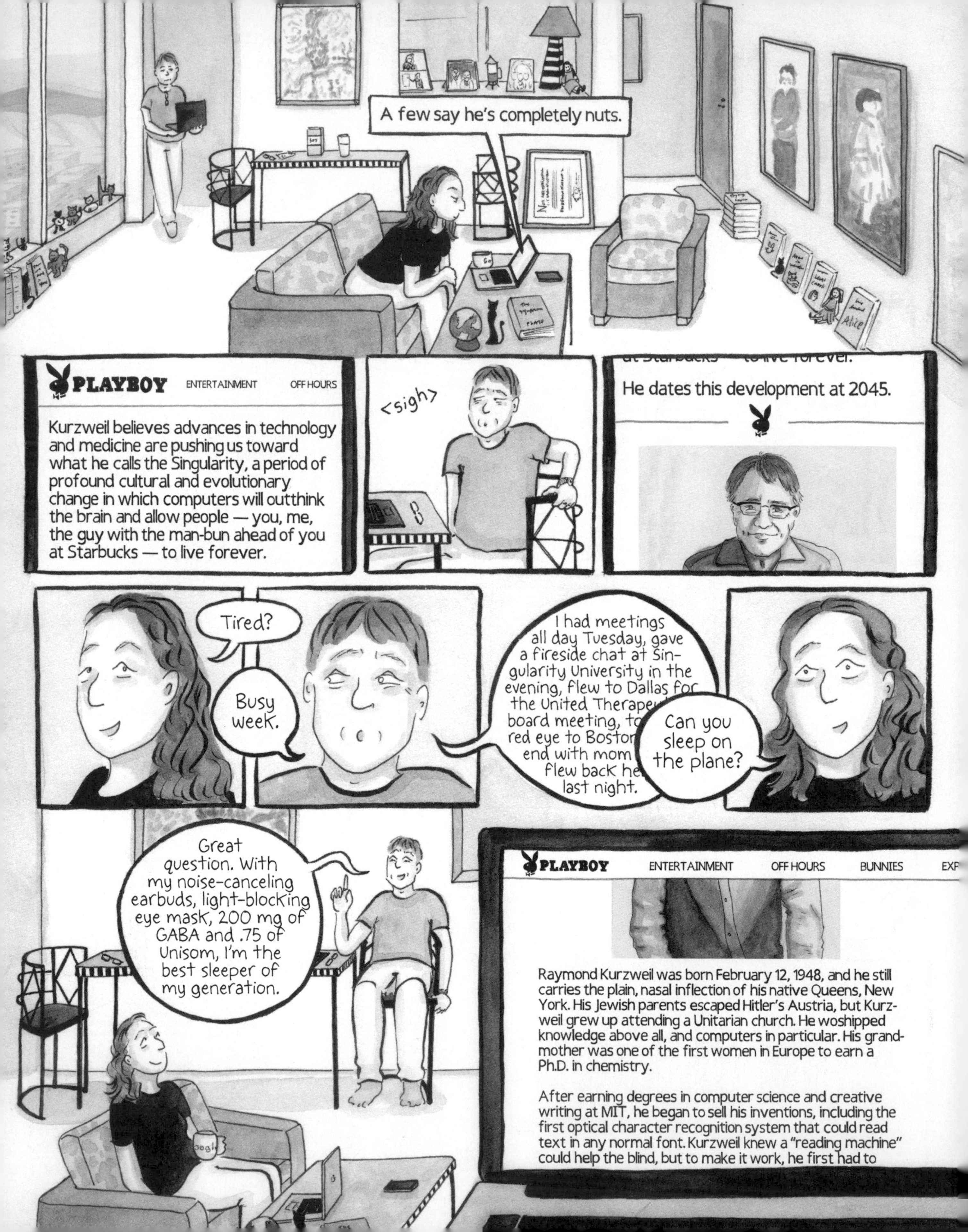
A few say he's completely nuts.
PLAYBOY ENTERTAINMENT OFF HOURS
Kurzweil believes advances in technology and medicine are pushing us toward what he calls the Singularity, a period of profound cultural and evolutionary change in which computers will outthink the brain and allow people — you, me, the guy with the man-bun ahead of you at Starbucks — to live forever.
<sigh>
He dates this development at 2045.
Tired?
Busy week.
I had meetings all day Tuesday, gave a fireside chat at Singularity University in the evening, flew to Dallas for the United Therape board meeting, to red eye to Boston end with mom flew back he last night.
Can you sleep on the plane?
Great question. With my noise-canceling earbuds, light-blocking eye mask, 200 mg of GABA and .75 of Unisom, I'm the best sleeper of my generation.
PLAYBOY ENTERTAINMENT OFF HOURS BUNNIES EXP
Raymond Kurzweil was born February 12, 1948, and he still carries the plain, nasal inflection of his native Queens, New York. His Jewish parents escaped Hitler's Austria, but Kurzweil grew up attending a Unitarian church. He woshipped knowledge above all, and computers in particular. His grandmother was one of the first women in Europe to earn a Ph.D. in chemistry.
After earning degrees in computer science and creative writing at MIT, he began to sell his inventions, including the first optical character recognition system that could read text in any normal font. Kurzweil knew a "reading machine" could help the blind, but to make it work, he first had to

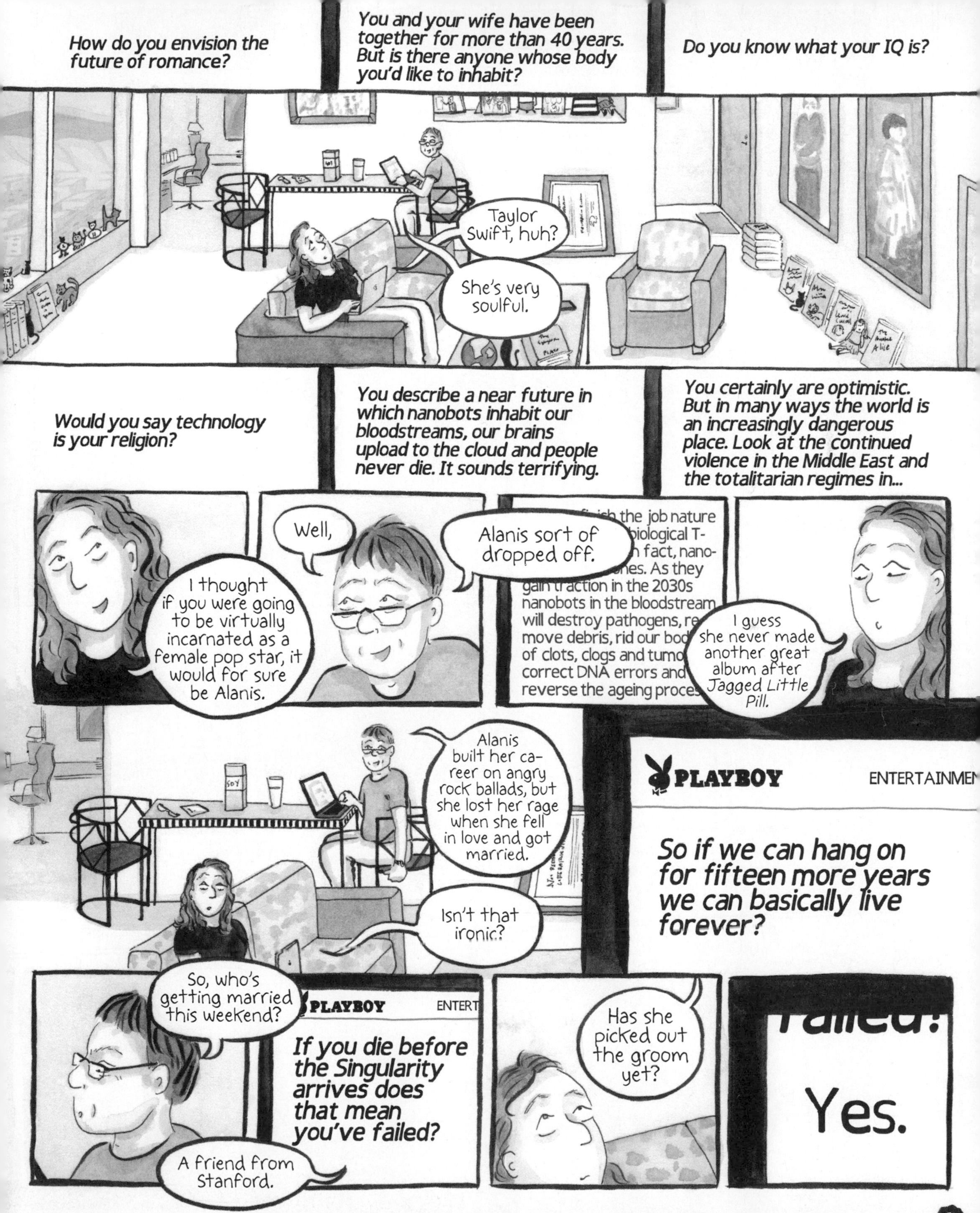

How do you envision the future of romance?
You and your wife have been together for more than 40 years. But is there anyone whose body you'd like to inhabit?
Do you know what your IQ is?
Taylor Swift, huh?
She's very soulful.
Would you say technology is your religion?
You describe a near future in which nanobots inhabit our bloodstreams, our brains upload to the cloud and people never die. It sounds terrifying.
You certainly are optimistic. But in many ways the world is an increasingly dangerous place. Look at the continued violence in the Middle East and the totalitarian regimes in...
I thought if you were going to be virtually incarnated as a female pop star, it would for sure be Alanis.
Well,
Alanis sort of dropped off.
finish the job nature
biological T-
fact, nano-
ones. As they
gain traction in the 2030s
nanobots in the bloodstream
will destroy pathogens, re
move debris, rid our bod
of clots, clogs and tumo
correct DNA errors and
reverse the ageing proces
I guess she never made another great album after Jagged Little Pill.
Alanis built her career on angry rock ballads, but she lost her rage when she fell in love and got married.
Isn't that ironic?
PLAYBOY
ENTERTAINMEN
So if we can hang on for fifteen more years we can basically live forever?
So, who's getting married this weekend?
A friend from Stanford.
PLAYBOY
ENTERT
If you die before the Singularity arrives does that mean you've failed?
Has she picked out the groom yet?
failed?
Yes.

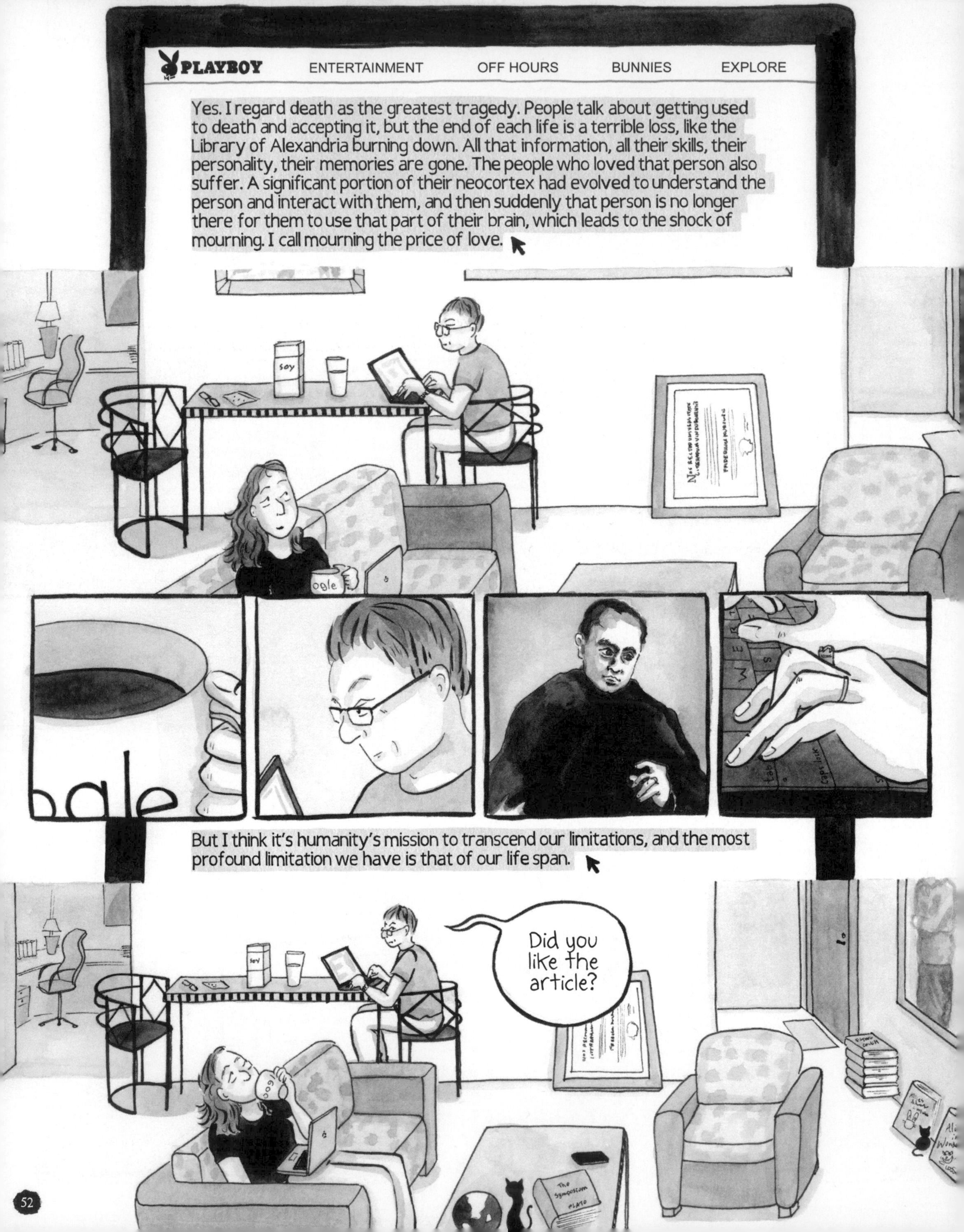
PLAYBOY
ENTERTAINMENT
OFF HOURS
BUNNIES
EXPLORE
Yes. I regard death as the greatest tragedy. People talk about getting used to death and accepting it, but the end of each life is a terrible loss, like the Library of Alexandria burning down. All that information, all their skills, their personality, their memories are gone. The people who loved that person also suffer. A significant portion of their neocortex had evolved to understand the person and interact with them, and then suddenly that person is no longer there for them to use that part of their brain, which leads to the shock of mourning. I call mourning the price of love.
soy
ogle
But I think it's humanity's mission to transcend our limitations, and the most profound limitation we have is that of our life span.
Did you like the article?
The Symposium
PLATO

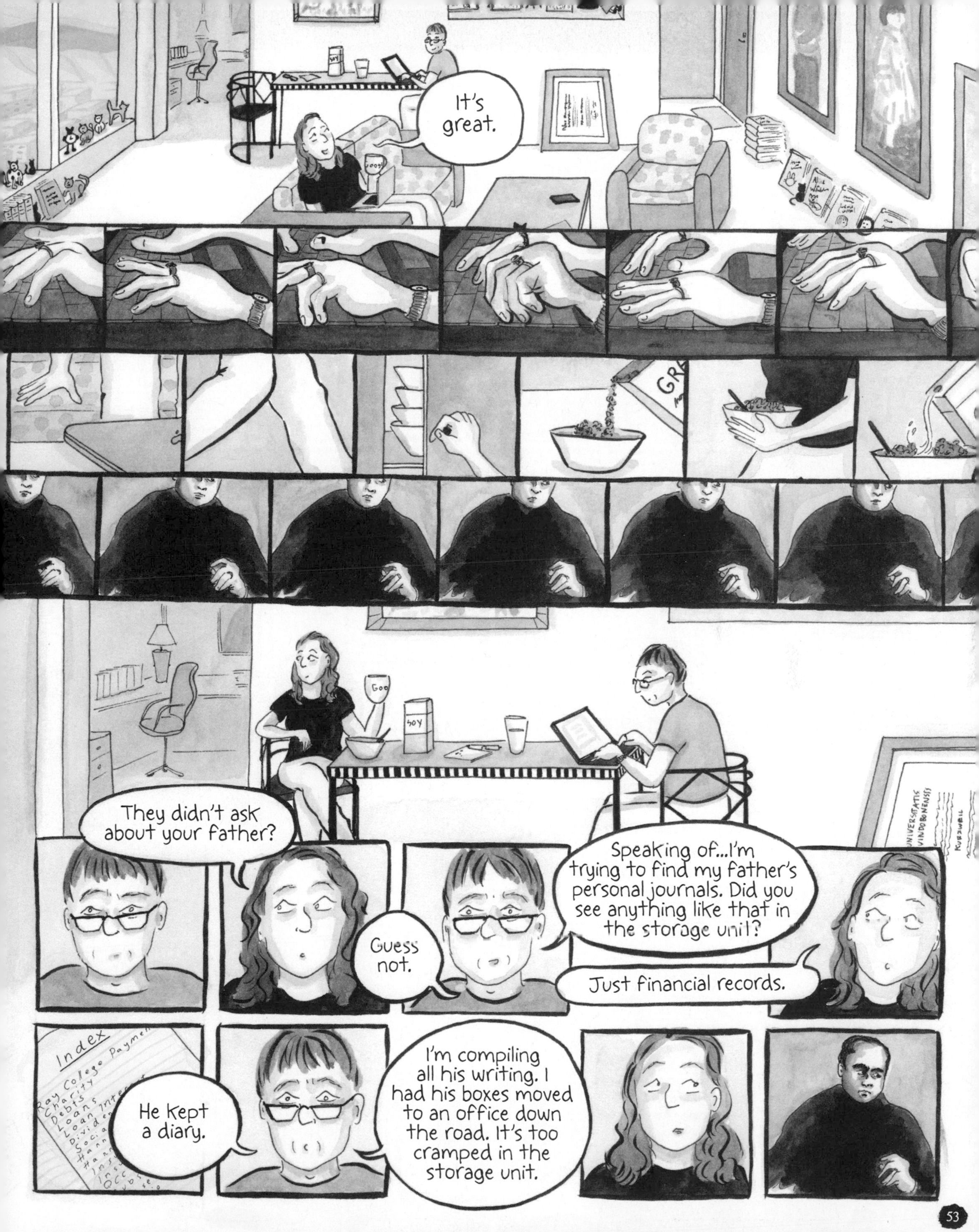
It's great.
They didn't ask about your father?
Guess not.
Speaking of...I'm trying to find my father's personal journals. Did you see anything like that in the storage unit?
Just financial records.
Index
He kept a diary.
I'm compiling all his writing. I had his boxes moved to an office down the road. It's too cramped in the storage unit.

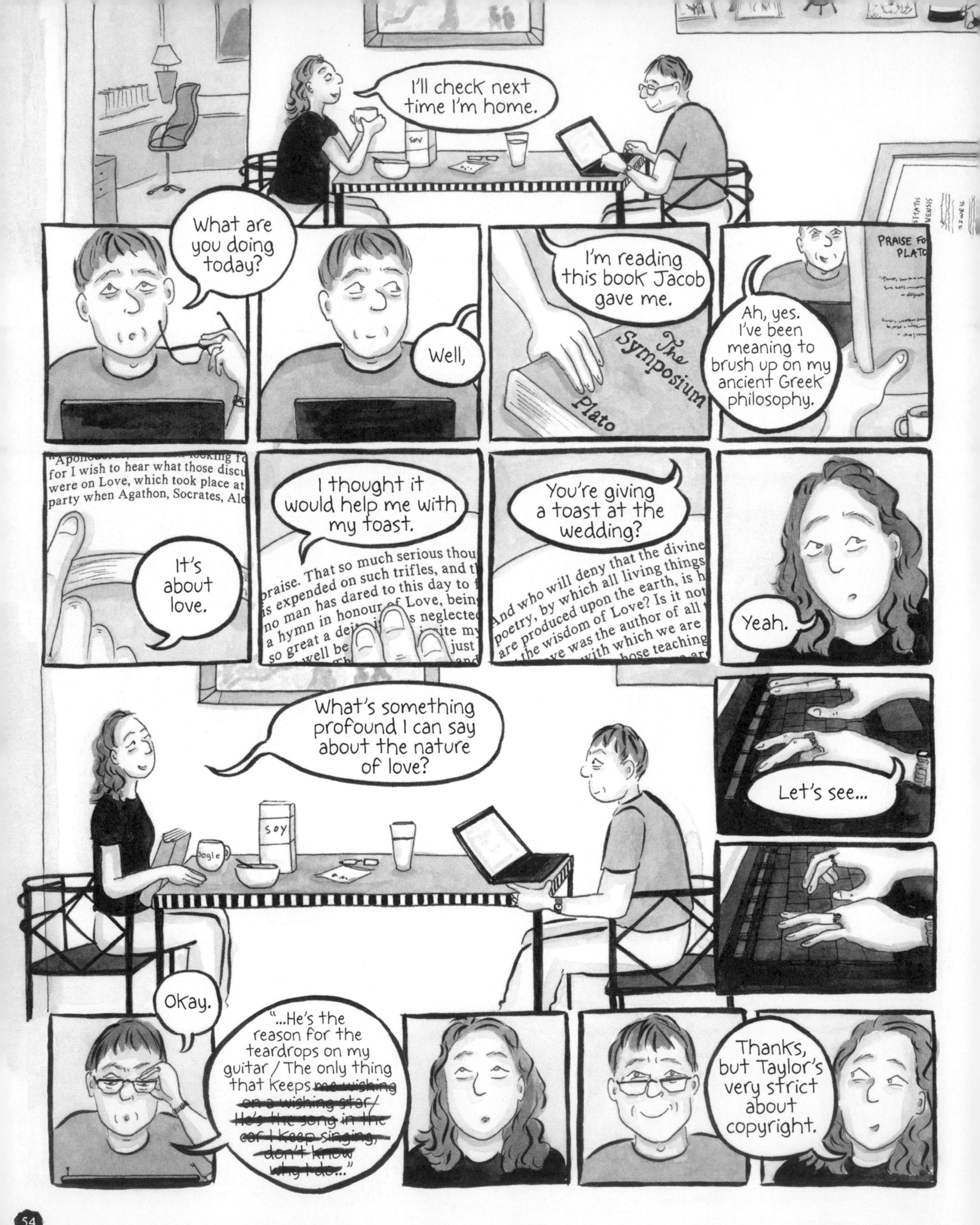
I'll check next time I'm home.
What are you doing today?
Well,
I'm reading this book Jacob gave me.
The Symposium
Plato
Ah, yes. I've been meaning to brush up on my ancient Greek philosophy.
for I wish to hear what those discu
were on Love, which took place at
party when Agathon, Socrates, Al
It's about love.
I thought it would help me with my toast.
praise. That so much serious thou
is expended on such trifles, and th
no man has dared to this day to
You're giving a toast at the wedding?
And who will deny that the divine
poetry, by which all living things
are produced upon the earth, is h
the wisdom of Love? Is it not
Yeah.
What's something profound I can say about the nature of love?
soy
Let's see...
Okay.
"...He's the reason for the teardrops on my guitar / The only thing that keeps ~~me wishing on a wishing star / He's the song in the car I keep singing, don't know why I do...~~"
Thanks, but Taylor's very strict about copyright.

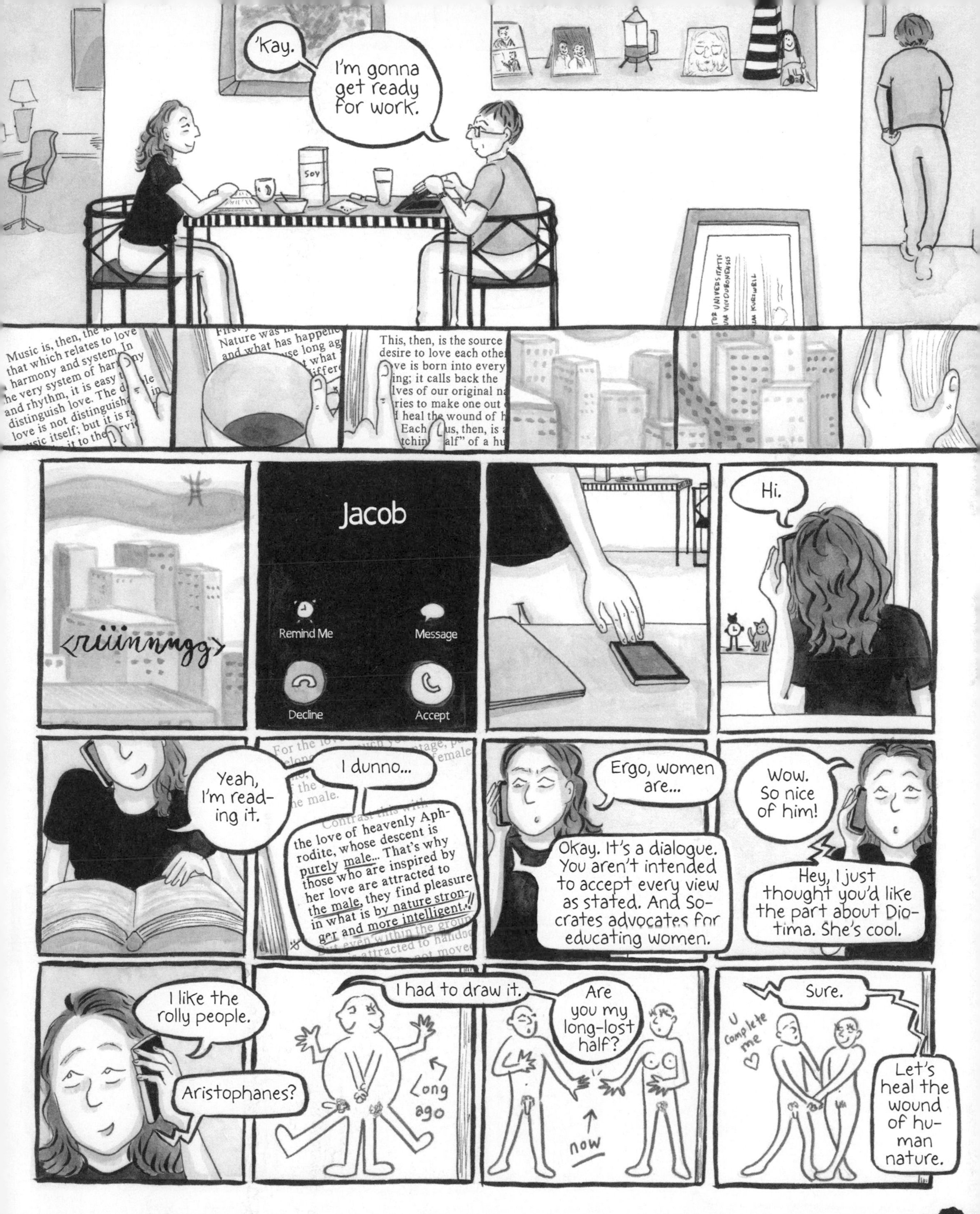
'Kay.
I'm gonna get ready for work.
<riiinnngg>
Jacob
Remind Me
Message
Decline
Accept
Hi.
Yeah, I'm reading it.
I dunno...
the love of heavenly Aphrodite, whose descent is purely male... That's why those who are inspired by her love are attracted to the male, they find pleasure in what is by nature stronger and more intelligent.
Ergo, women are...
Okay. It's a dialogue. You aren't intended to accept every view as stated. And Socrates advocates for educating women.
Wow. So nice of him!
Hey, I just thought you'd like the part about Diotima. She's cool.
I like the rolly people.
Aristophanes?
I had to draw it.
long ago
Are you my long-lost half?
now
Sure.
U complete me
Let's heal the wound of human nature.

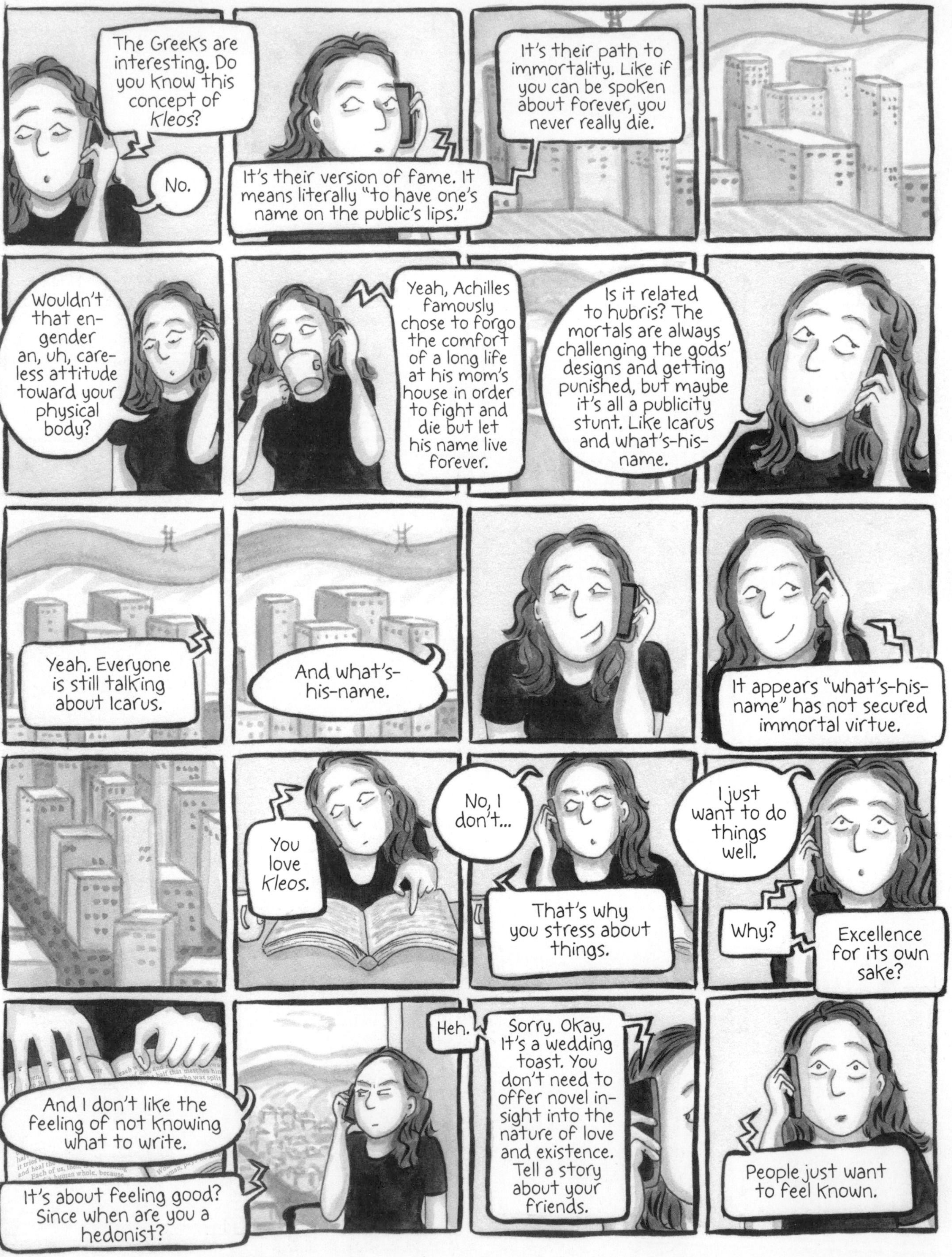
The Greeks are interesting. Do you know this concept of *Kleos*?
No.
It's their version of fame. It means literally "to have one's name on the public's lips."
It's their path to immortality. Like if you can be spoken about forever, you never really die.
Wouldn't that engender an, uh, careless attitude toward your physical body?
Yeah, Achilles famously chose to forgo the comfort of a long life at his mom's house in order to fight and die but let his name live forever.
Is it related to hubris? The mortals are always challenging the gods' designs and getting punished, but maybe it's all a publicity stunt. Like Icarus and what's-his-name.
Yeah. Everyone is still talking about Icarus.
And what's-his-name.
It appears "what's-his-name" has not secured immortal virtue.
You love *Kleos*.
No, I don't...
That's why you stress about things.
I just want to do things well.
Why?
Excellence for its own sake?
And I don't like the feeling of not knowing what to write.
It's about feeling good? Since when are you a hedonist?
Heh.
Sorry. Okay. It's a wedding toast. You don't need to offer novel insight into the nature of love and existence. Tell a story about your friends.
People just want to feel known.

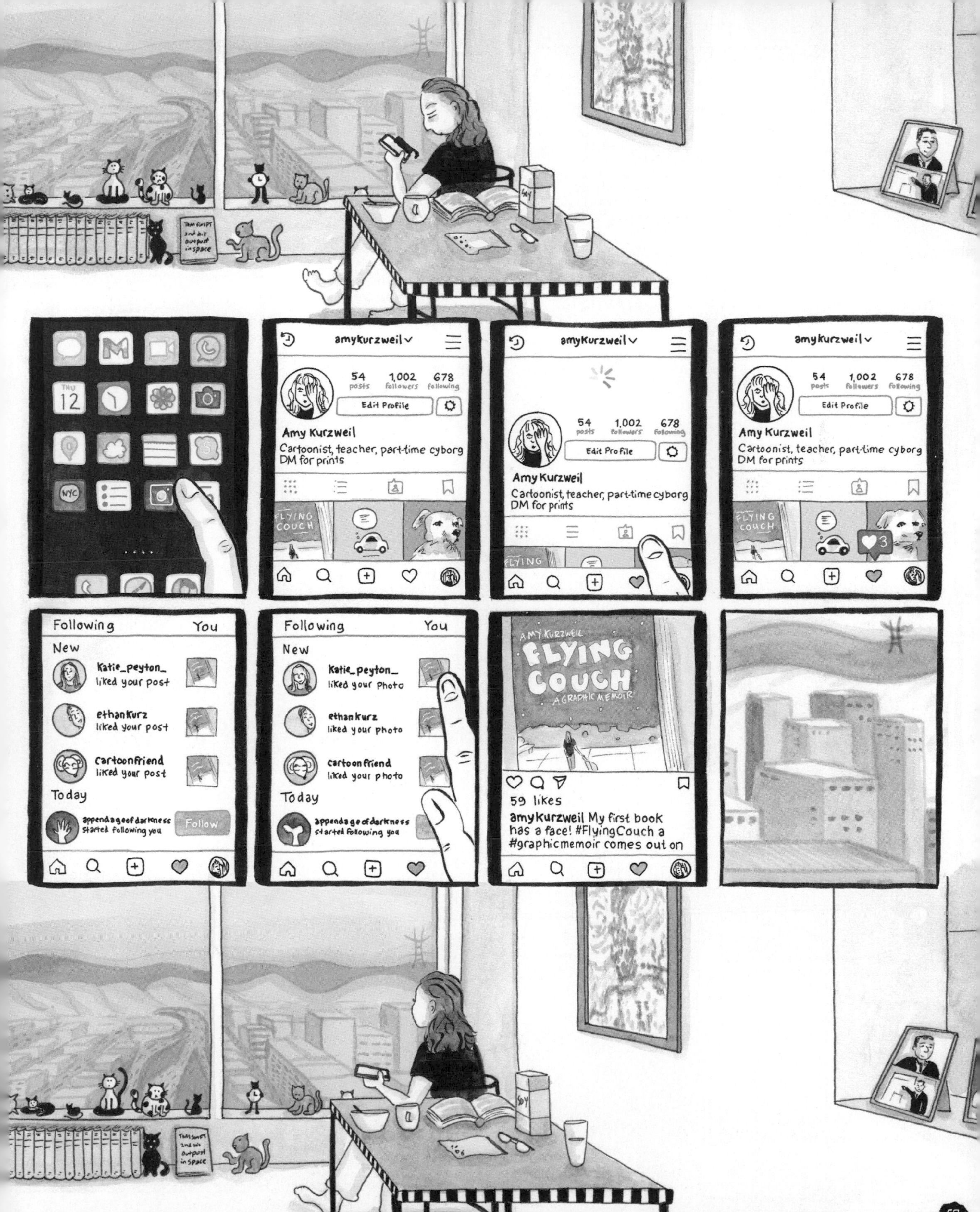
SOY
THU
12
NYC
amykurzweil
54 posts
1,002 followers
678 following
Edit Profile
Amy Kurzweil
Cartoonist, teacher, part-time cyborg
DM for prints
FLYING COUCH
amykurzweil
54 posts
1,002 followers
678 following
Edit Profile
Amy Kurzweil
Cartoonist, teacher, part-time cyborg
DM for prints
FLYING
amykurzweil
54 posts
1,002 followers
678 following
Edit Profile
Amy Kurzweil
Cartoonist, teacher, part-time cyborg
DM for prints
FLYING COUCH
3
Following You
New
Katie_peyton_ liked your post
ethankurz liked your post
cartoonfriend liked your post
Today
appendageofdarkness started following you
Follow
Following You
New
Katie_peyton_ liked your Photo
ethankurz liked your photo
cartoonfriend liked your photo
Today
appendageofdarkness started following you
AMY KURZWEIL
FLYING COUCH
A GRAPHIC MEMOIR
59 likes
amykurzweil My first book has a face! #FlyingCouch a #graphicmemoir comes out on
SOY

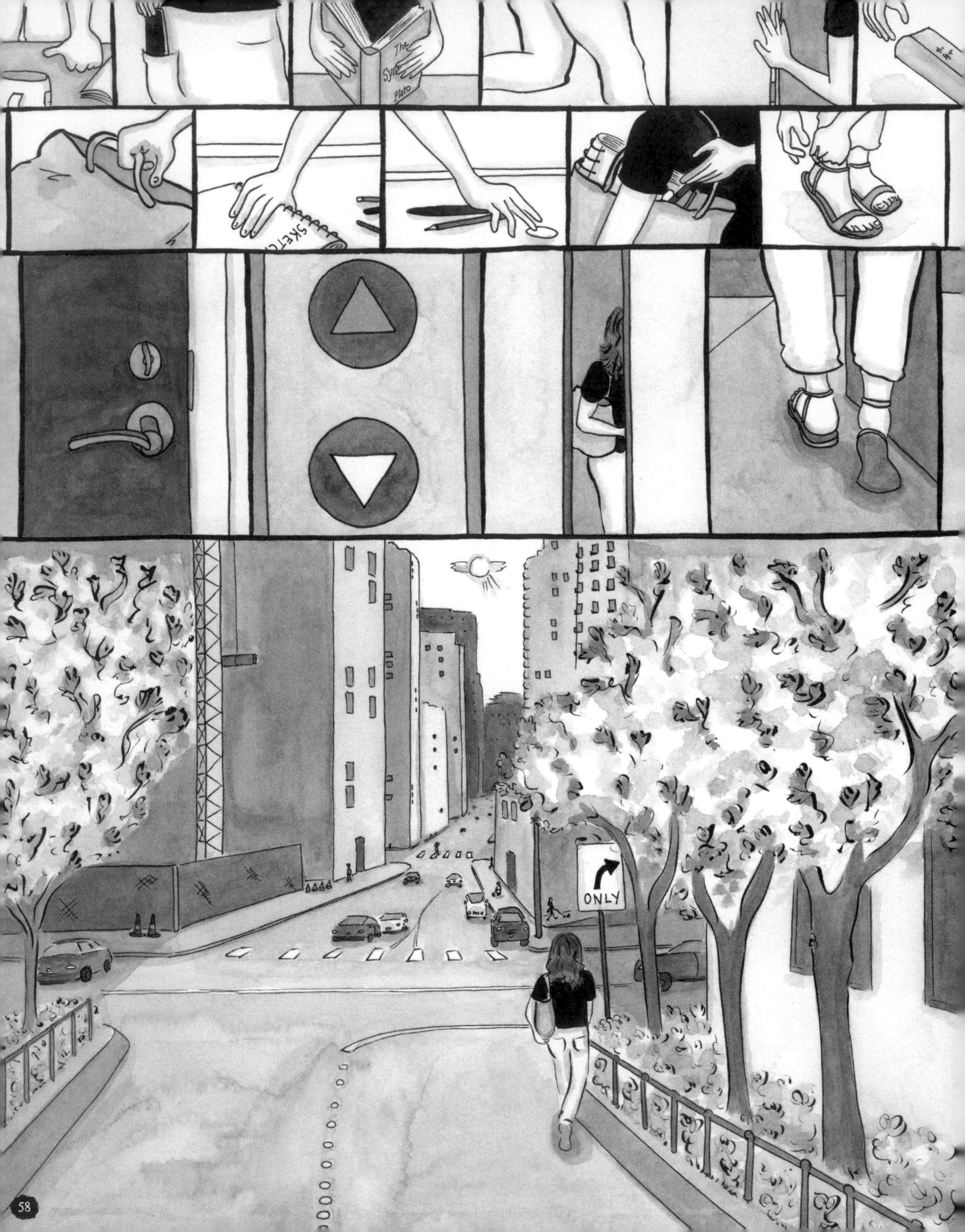
Plato
ONLY

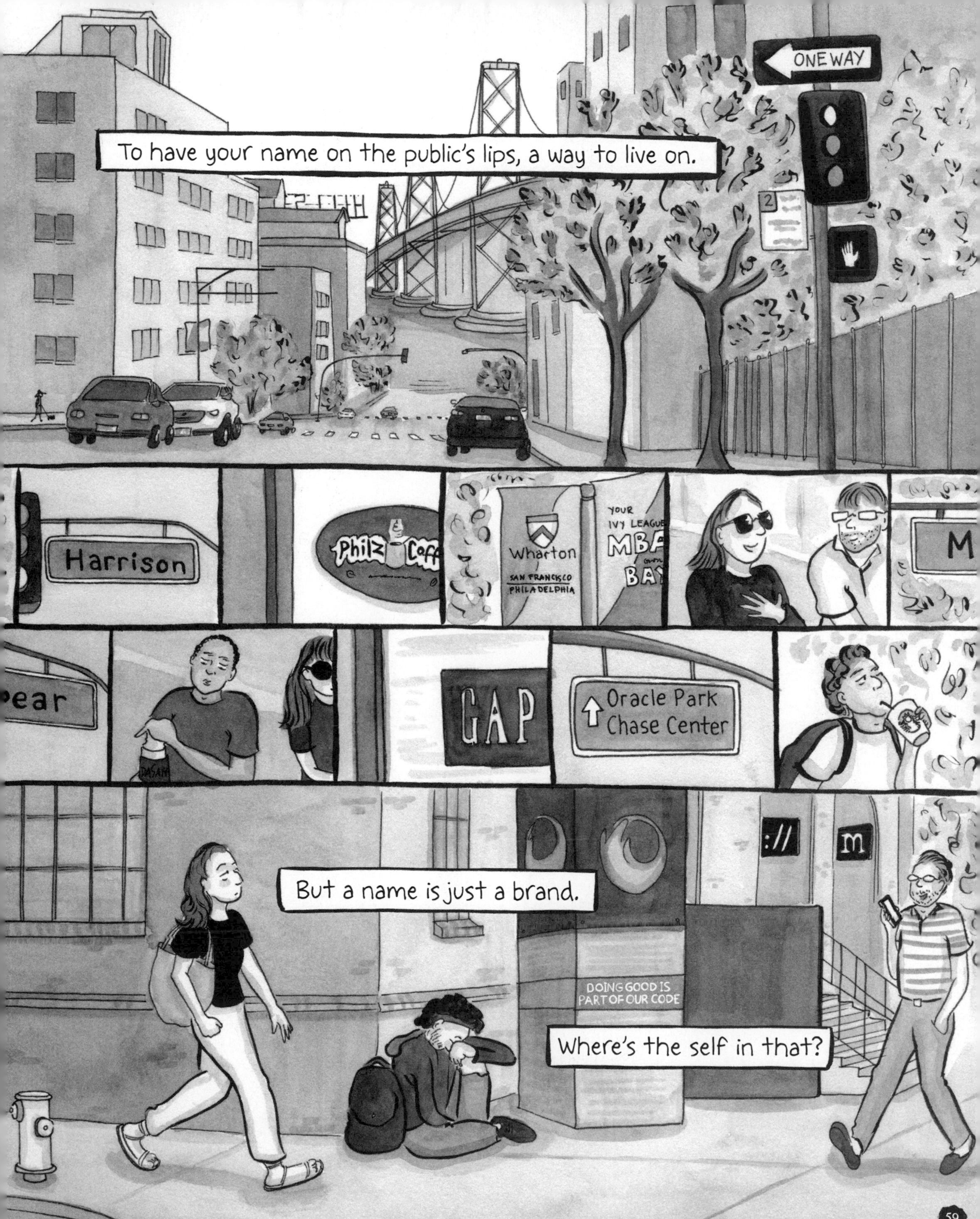
ONE WAY
To have your name on the public's lips, a way to live on.
Harrison
Wharton
SAN FRANCISCO
PHILADELPHIA
YOUR
IVY LEAGUE
GAP
Oracle Park
Chase Center
But a name is just a brand.
DOING GOOD IS
PART OF OUR CODE
Where's the self in that?

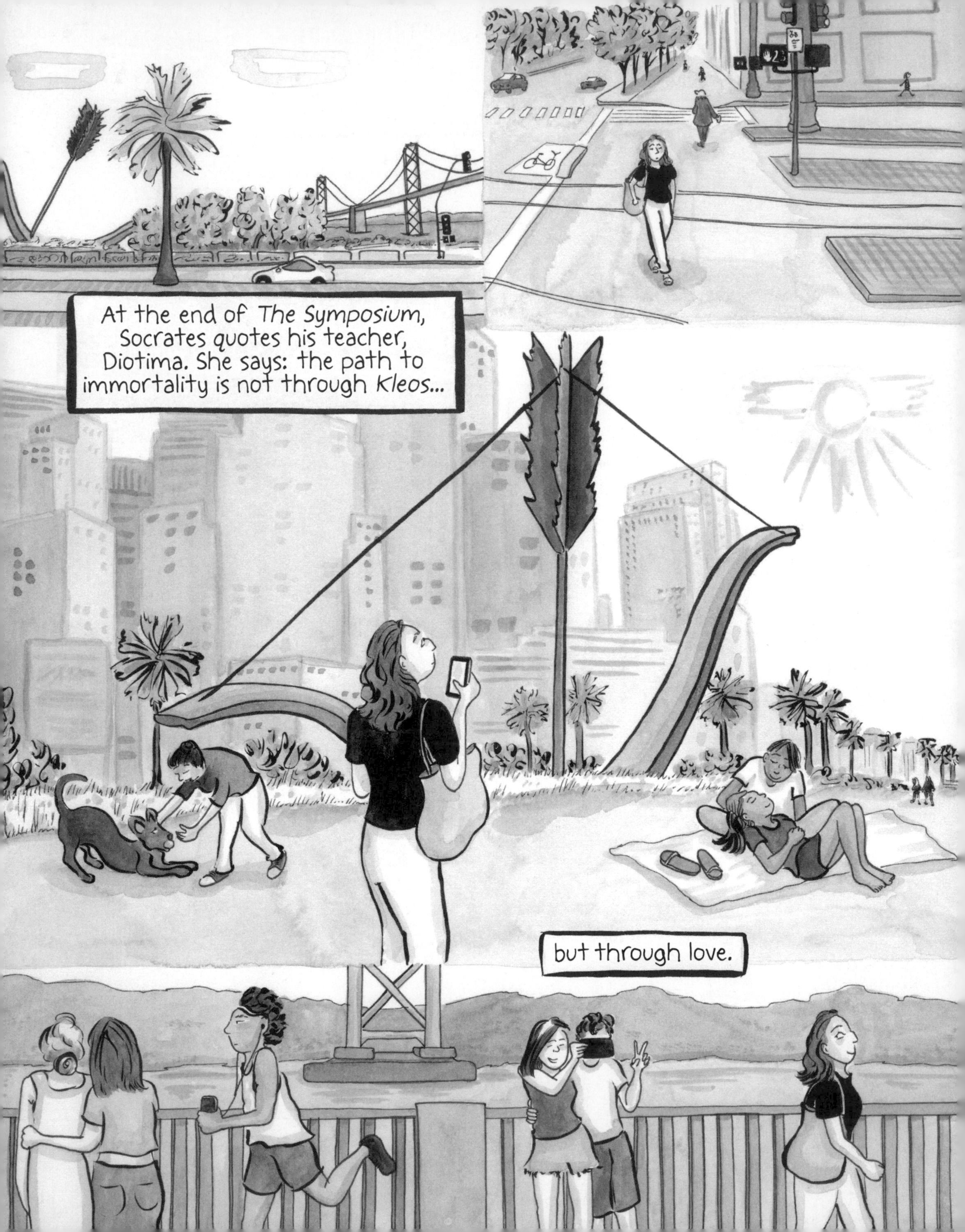
At the end of *The Symposium*, Socrates quotes his teacher, Diotima. She says: the path to immortality is not through *Kleos*...
but through love.

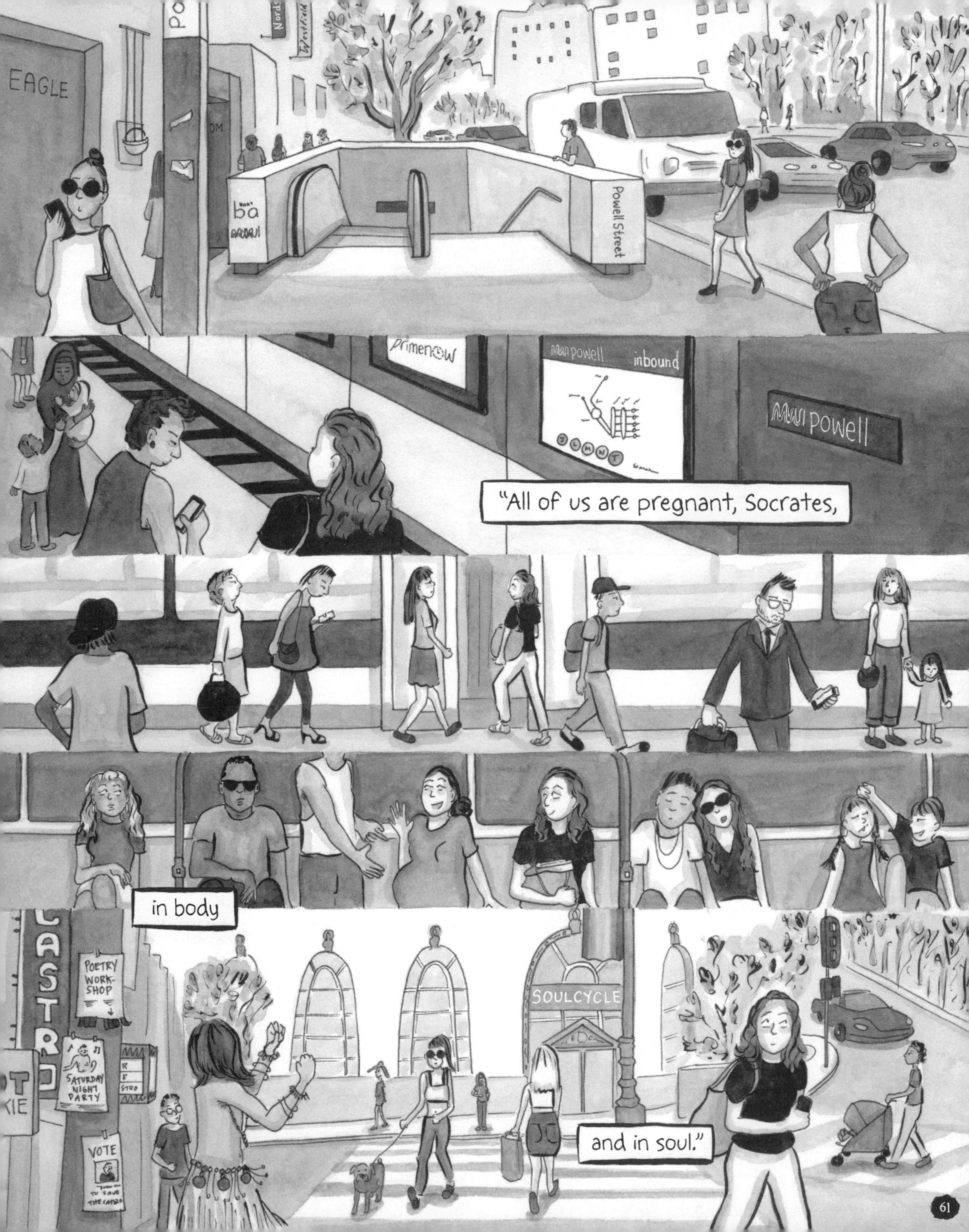
EAGLE
Powell Street
primenow
powell
inbound
powell
"All of us are pregnant, Socrates,
in body
CASTRO
POETRY WORKSHOP
SATURDAY NIGHT PARTY
VOTE
SOULCYCLE
and in soul."

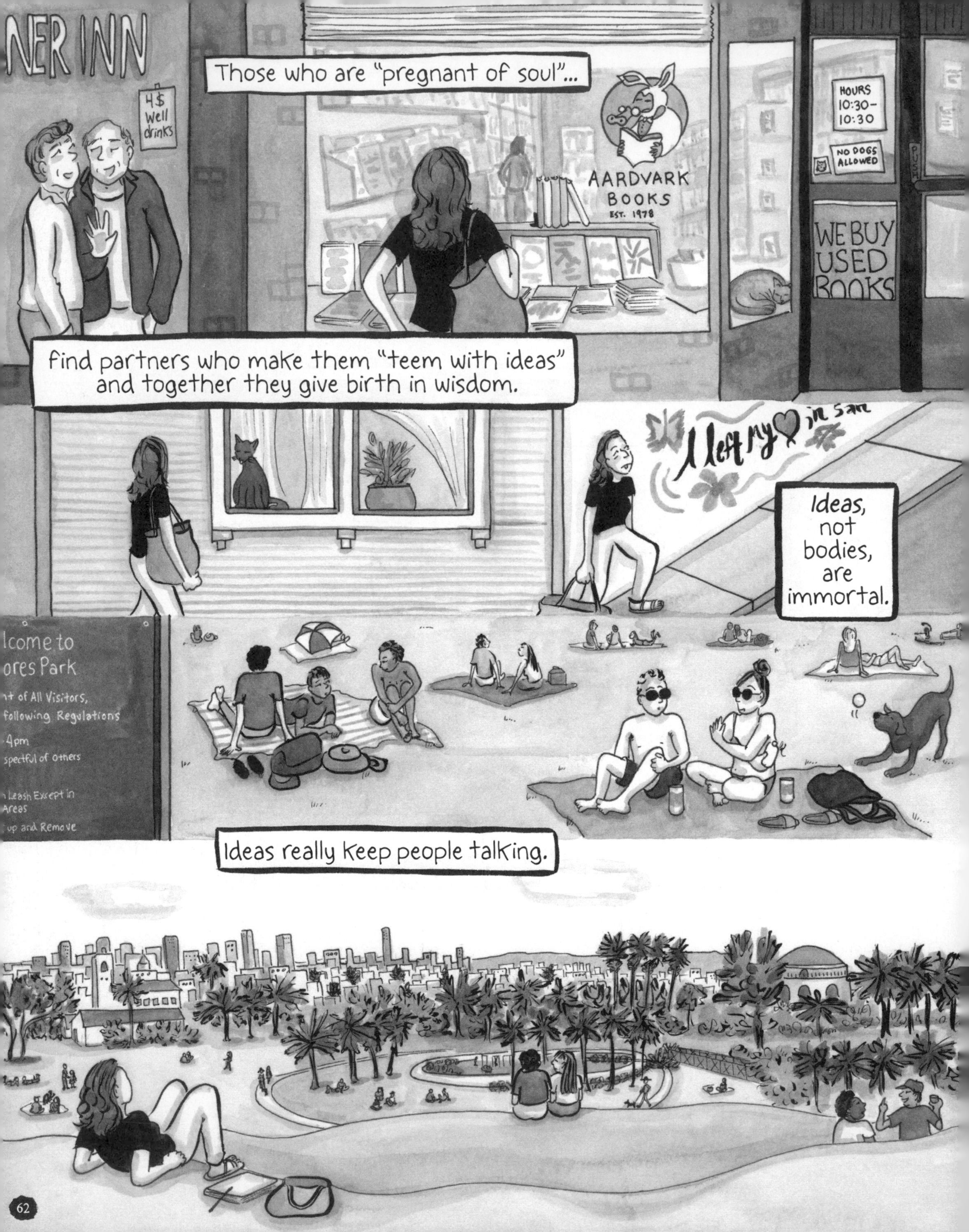
NER INN
4$ Well drinks
Those who are "pregnant of soul"...
AARDVARK BOOKS EST. 1978
HOURS 10:30–10:30
NO DOGS ALLOWED
WE BUY USED BOOKS
find partners who make them "teem with ideas" and together they give birth in wisdom.
Ideas, not bodies, are immortal.
Ideas really keep people talking.

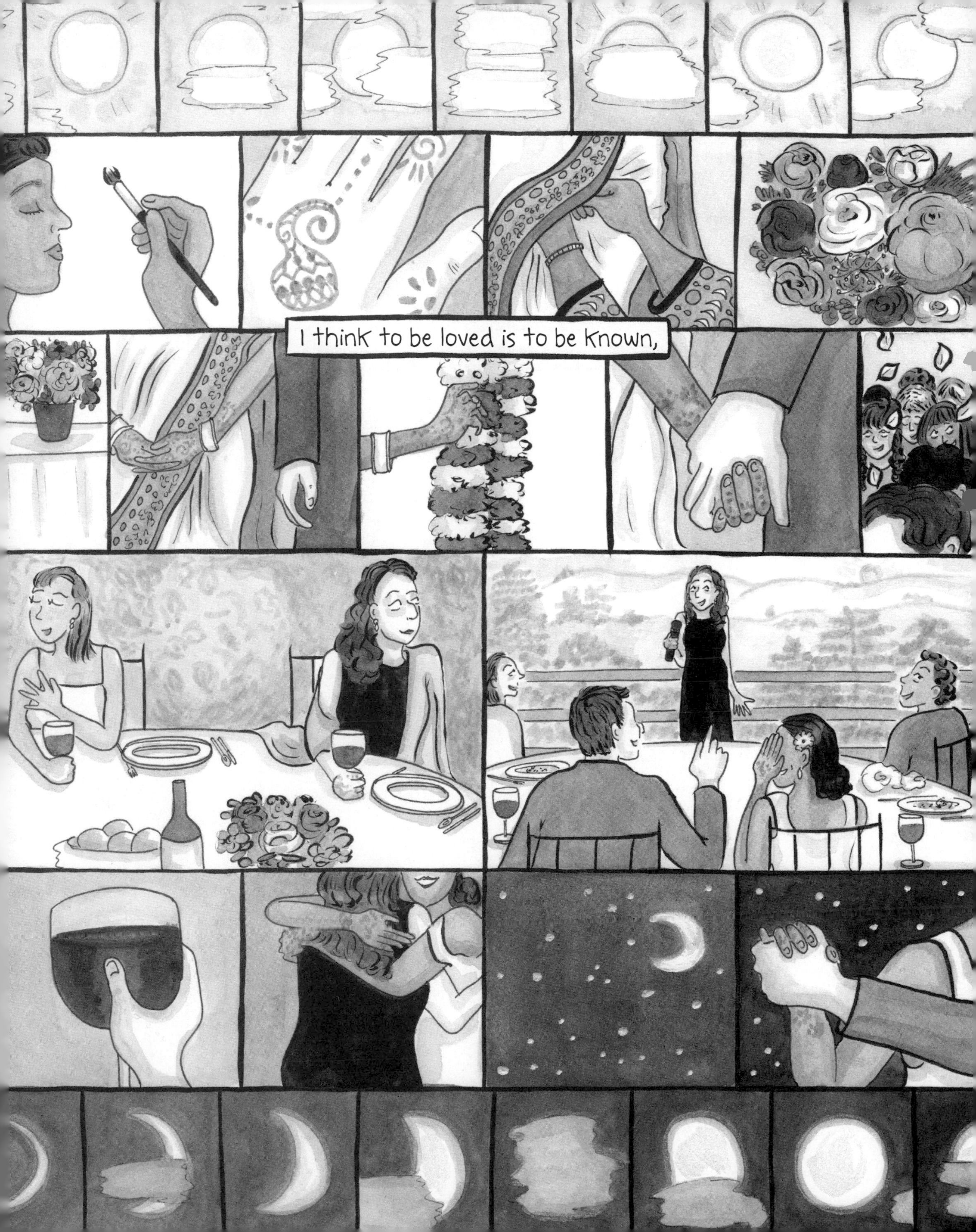
I think to be loved is to be known,

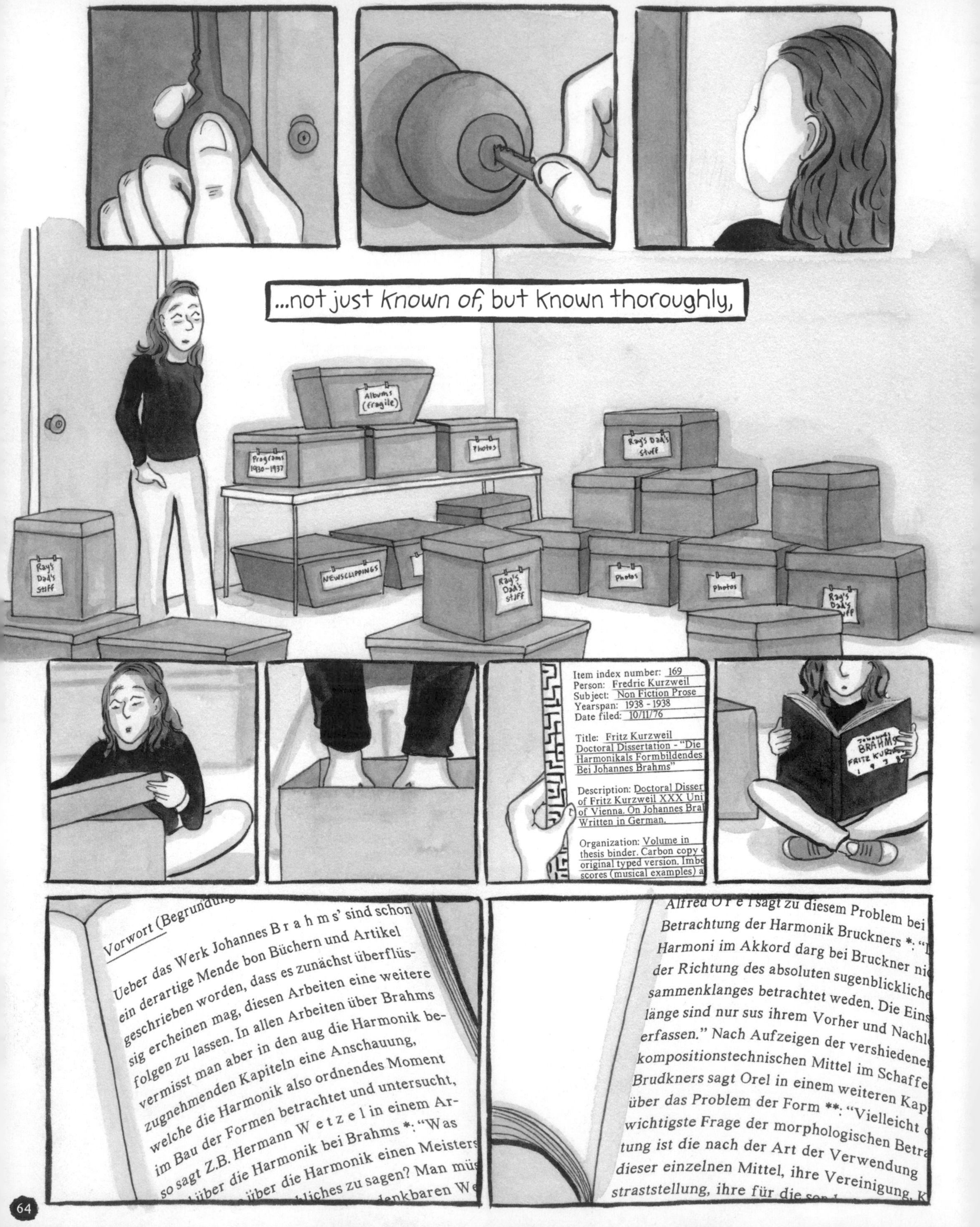

...not just known of, but known thoroughly,
Albums (fragile)
Programs 1930-1937
Photos
Ray's Dad's stuff
Ray's Dad's stuff
NEWSCLIPPINGS
Ray's Dad's stuff
Photos
Photos
Item index number: 169
Person: Fredric Kurzweil
Subject: Non Fiction Prose
Yearspan: 1938 - 1938
Date filed: 10/11/76
Title: Fritz Kurzweil
Doctoral Dissertation - "Die
Harmonikals Formbildendes
Bei Johannes Brahms"
Description: Doctoral Disser
of Fritz Kurzweil XXX Uni
of Vienna. On Johannes Bra
Written in German.
Organization: Volume in
thesis binder. Carbon copy
original typed version. Imbe
scores (musical examples) a
BRAHMS
Vorwort (Begründung
Ueber das Werk Johannes B r a h m s' sind schon
ein derartige Mende bon Büchern und Artikel
geschrieben worden, dass es zunächst überflüs-
sig ercheinen mag, diesen Arbeiten eine weitere
folgen zu lassen. In allen Arbeiten über Brahms
vermisst man aber in den aug die Harmonik be-
zugnehmenden Kapiteln eine Anschauung,
welche die Harmonik also ordnendes Moment
im Bau der Formen betrachtet und untersucht,
so sagt Z.B. Hermann W e t z e l in einem Ar-
über die Harmonik bei Brahms *: "Was
über die Harmonik einen Meisters
liches zu sagen? Man müs
denkbaren We
Alfred O r e l sagt zu diesem Problem bei
Betrachtung der Harmonik Bruckners *: "
Harmoni im Akkord darg bei Bruckner ni
der Richtung des absoluten sugenblickliche
sammenklanges betrachtet weden. Die Eins
länge sind nur sus ihrem Vorher und Nachl
erfassen." Nach Aufzeigen der vershiedene
kompositionstechnischen Mittel im Schaffe
Brudkners sagt Orel in einem weiteren Kap
über das Problem der Form **: "Vielleicht
wichtigste Frage der morphologischen Betr
tung ist die nach der Art der Verwendung
dieser einzelnen Mittel, ihre Vereinigung, K
straststellung, ihre für die

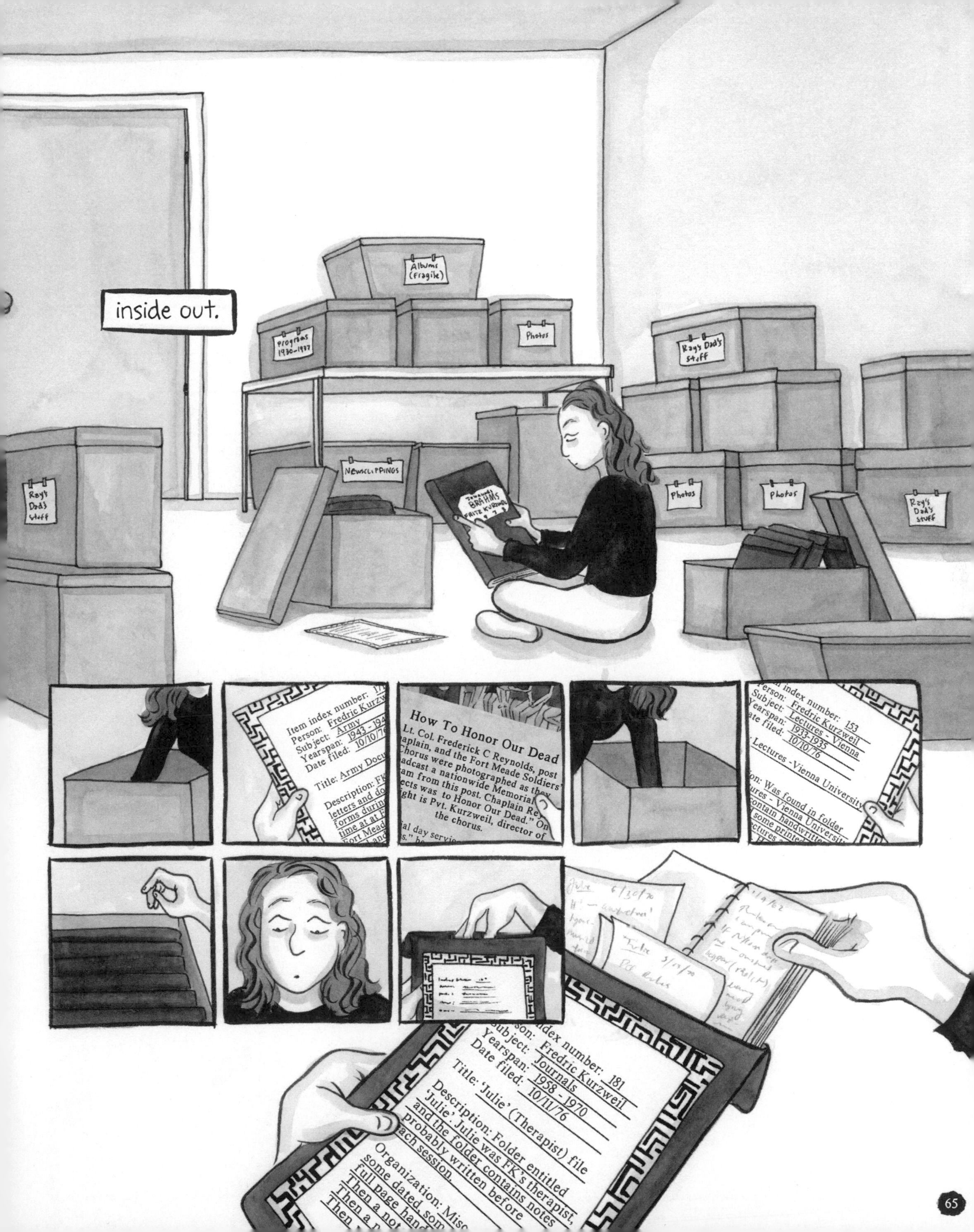
inside out.
Albums (Fragile)
Programs 1930-1937
Photos
Ray's Dad's stuff
Newsclippings
BRAHMS
Photos
Photos
Ray's Dad's stuff
Ray's Dad's stuff
Item index number:
Person:
Subject: Army
Yearspan:
Date filed:
Title:
Description:
How To Honor Our Dead
Lt. Col. Frederick C Reynolds, post
Chorus were photographed as they
broadcast a nationwide Memorial
am from this post. Chaplain Rey
ects was to Honor Our Dead." On
ght is Pvt. Kurzweil, director of
the chorus.
Person: Fredric Kurzweil
Subject: Lectures - Vienna
Yearspan: 1933-1935
Date filed: 10/10/76
Lectures - Vienna University
Subject: Journals
Yearspan: 1958 - 1970
Date filed: 10/11/76
Title: 'Julie' (Therapist) file
Description: Folder entitled
'Julie'. Julie was FK's therapist,
and the folder contains notes
probably written before
Organization:

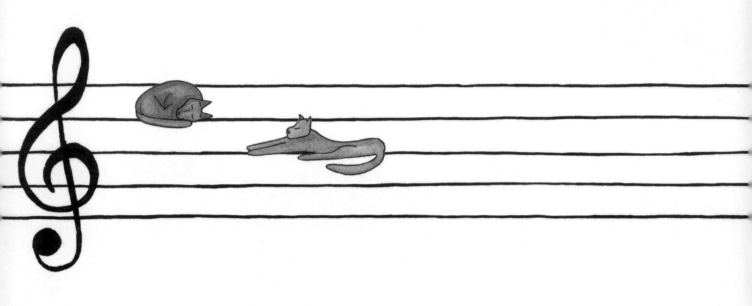

# III.

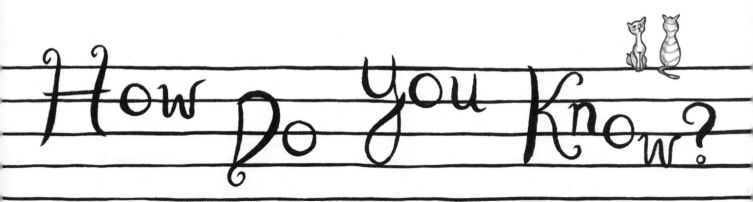

How Do You Know?

...for it was not knowledge but unity that she desired, not inscriptions on tablets, nothing that could be written in any language known to men, but intimacy itself, which is knowledge...

—Virginia Woolf, *To the Lighthouse*

Did love begin in that way, with the wish to go on talking?

—Virginia Woolf, *The Voyage Out*

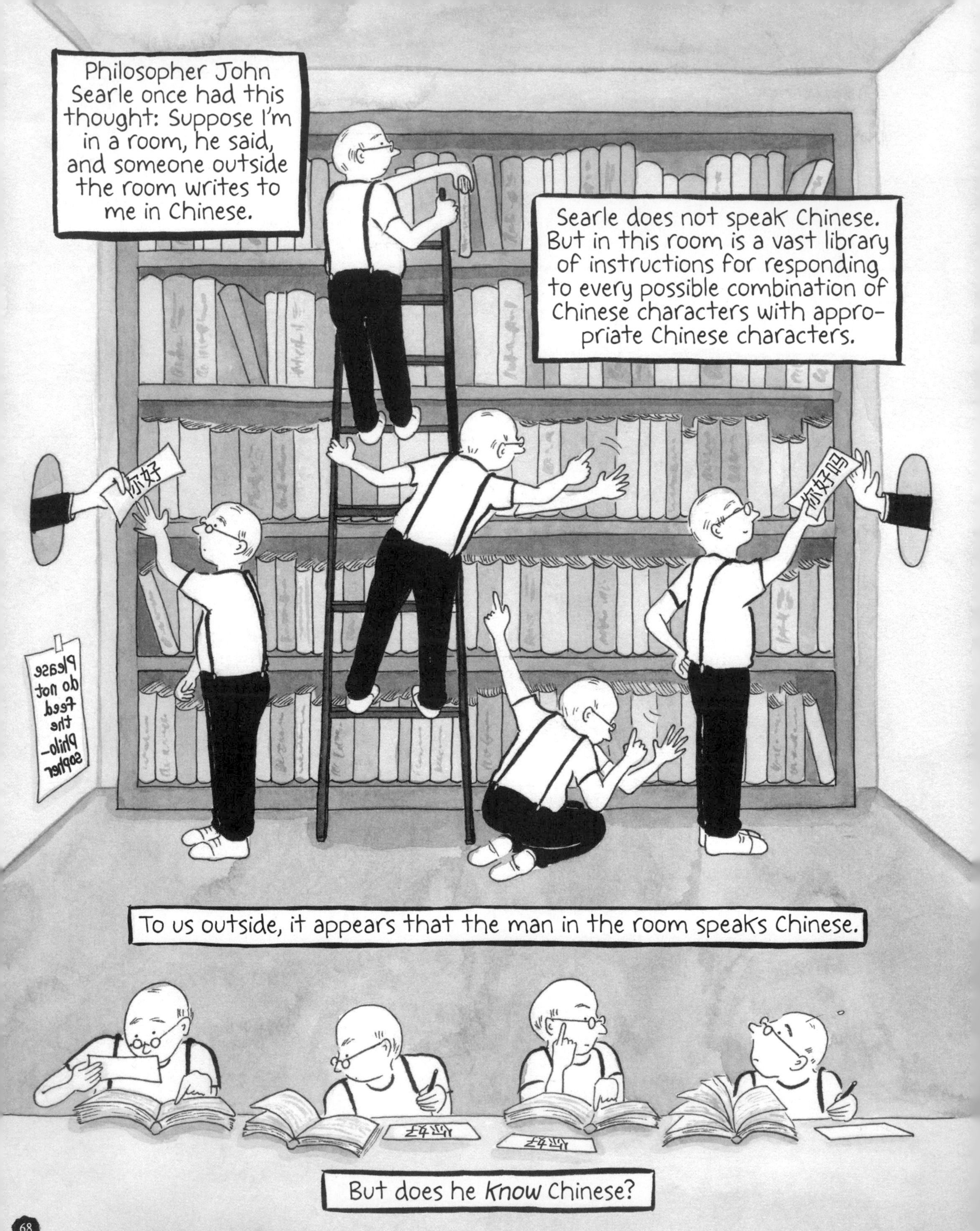
Philosopher John Searle once had this thought: Suppose I'm in a room, he said, and someone outside the room writes to me in Chinese.
Searle does not speak Chinese. But in this room is a vast library of instructions for responding to every possible combination of Chinese characters with appropriate Chinese characters.
你好
你好吗
Please do not feed the philo-sopher
To us outside, it appears that the man in the room speaks Chinese.
But does he *know* Chinese?

There's no point of translation into the man's native language, no moment of conscious understanding. He's going through a *process*, phrase by phrase.

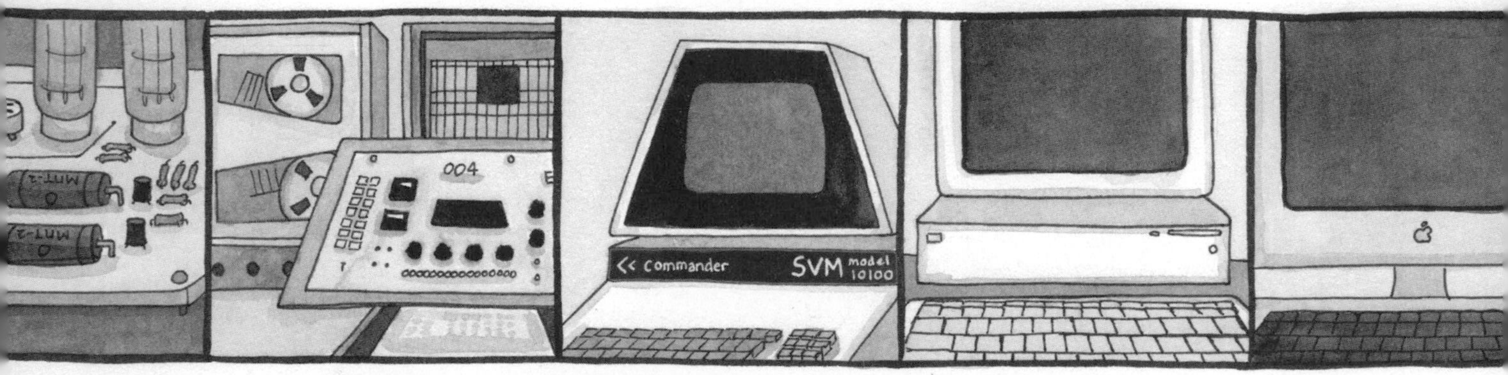
004
<< commander
SVM model 10100

The thought experiment suggests that machines cannot, and will not ever, *really* think.

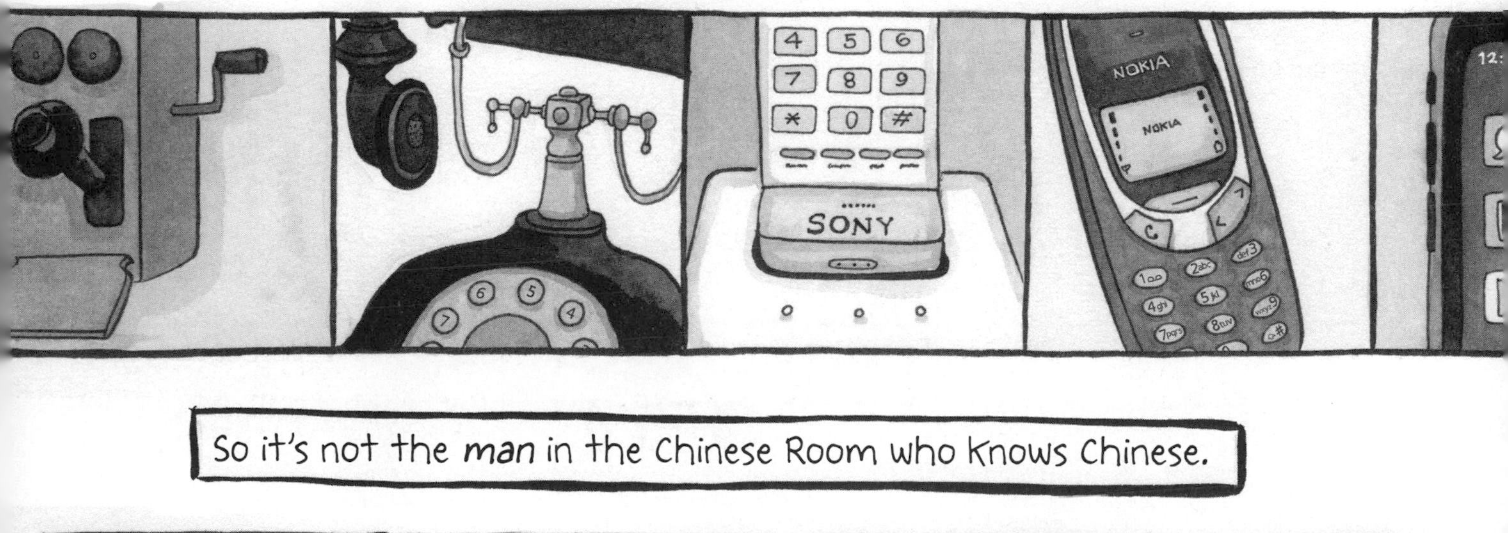
SONY
NOKIA
NOKIA

So it's not the *man* in the Chinese Room who knows Chinese.

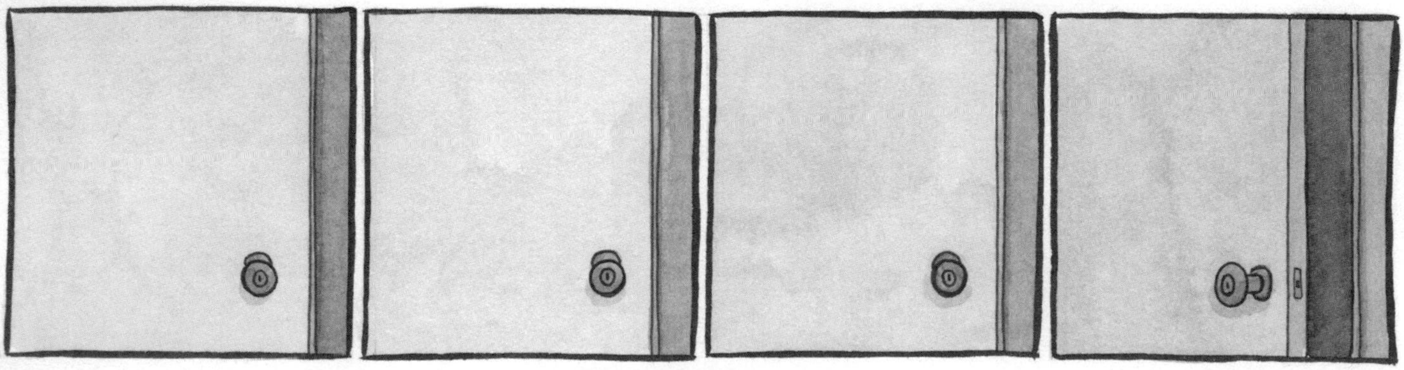

But maybe it's...

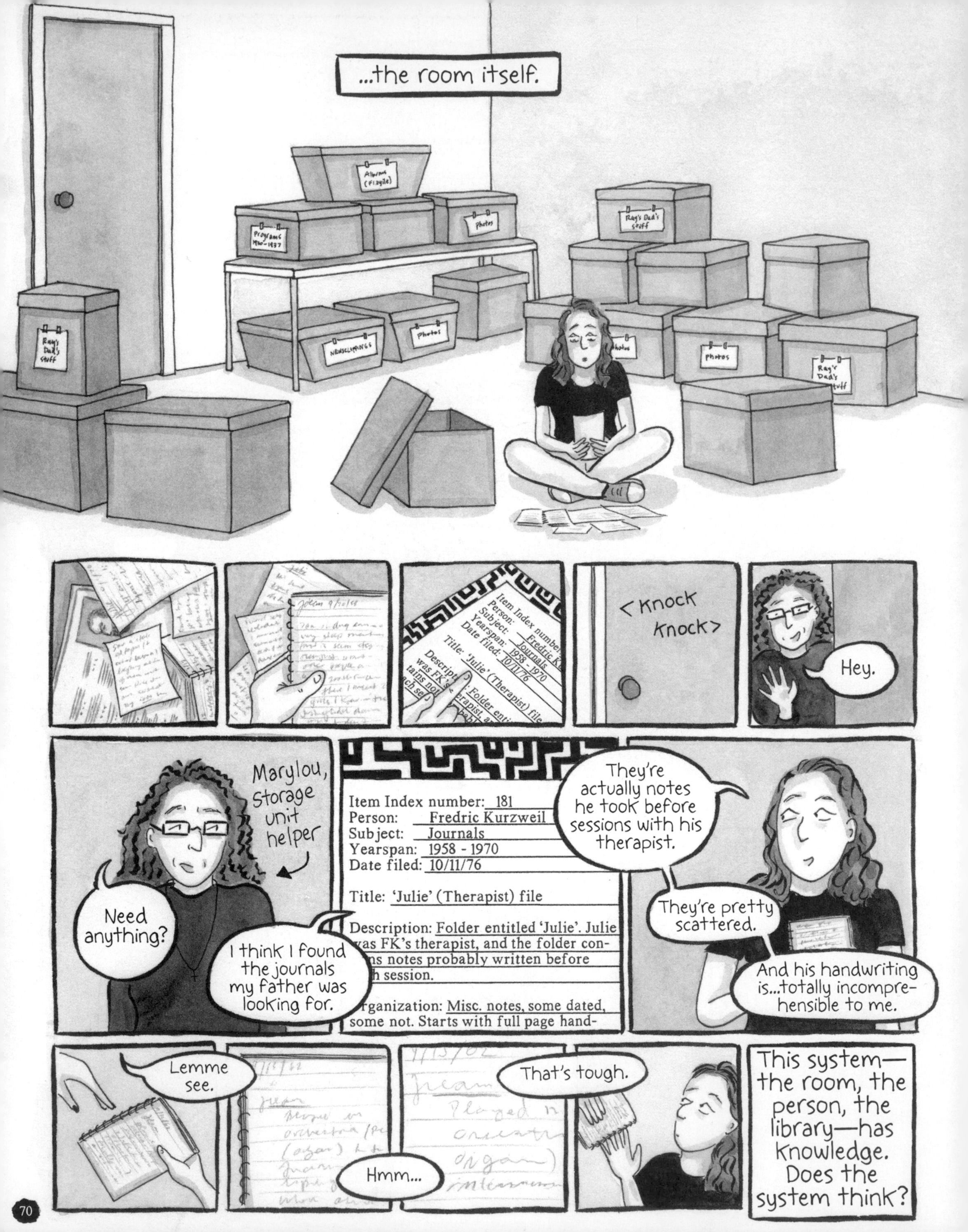
...the room itself.
Albums (Fragile)
Photos
Ray's Dad's stuff
Newsclippings
<Knock knock>
Hey.
Marylou, storage unit helper
Need anything?
I think I found the journals my father was looking for.
Item Index number: 181
Person: Fredric Kurzweil
Subject: Journals
Yearspan: 1958 - 1970
Date filed: 10/11/76
Title: 'Julie' (Therapist) file
Description: Folder entitled 'Julie'. Julie was FK's therapist, and the folder contains notes probably written before each session.
Organization: Misc. notes, some dated, some not. Starts with full page hand-
They're actually notes he took before sessions with his therapist.
They're pretty scattered.
And his handwriting is...totally incomprehensible to me.
Lemme see.
Hmm...
That's tough.
This system—the room, the person, the library—has knowledge. Does the system think?

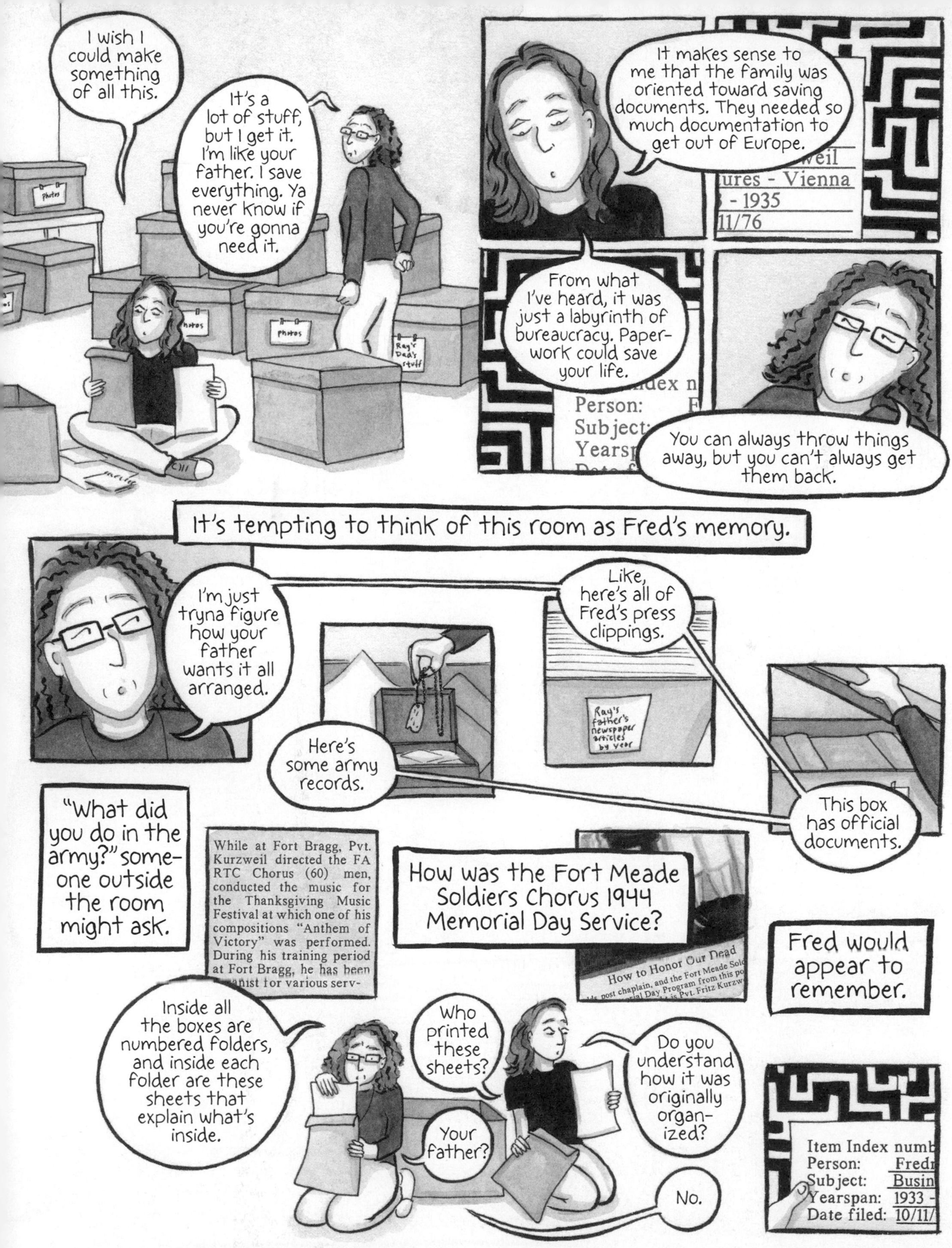
I wish I could make something of all this.
It's a lot of stuff, but I get it. I'm like your father. I save everything. Ya never know if you're gonna need it.
photos
photos
Ray's Dad's stuff
It makes sense to me that the family was oriented toward saving documents. They needed so much documentation to get out of Europe.
From what I've heard, it was just a labyrinth of bureaucracy. Paper-work could save your life.
You can always throw things away, but you can't always get them back.
It's tempting to think of this room as Fred's memory.
I'm just tryna figure how your father wants it all arranged.
Like, here's all of Fred's press clippings.
Ray's father's newspaper articles by year
Here's some army records.
This box has official documents.
"What did you do in the army?" some-one outside the room might ask.
While at Fort Bragg, Pvt. Kurzweil directed the FA RTC Chorus (60) men, conducted the music for the Thanksgiving Music Festival at which one of his compositions "Anthem of Victory" was performed. During his training period at Fort Bragg, he has been
How was the Fort Meade Soldiers Chorus 1944 Memorial Day Service?
How to Honor Our Dead
Fred would appear to remember.
Inside all the boxes are numbered folders, and inside each folder are these sheets that explain what's inside.
Who printed these sheets?
Your father?
No.
Do you understand how it was originally organ-ized?
Person:
Subject:
Yearspan:
Date filed:

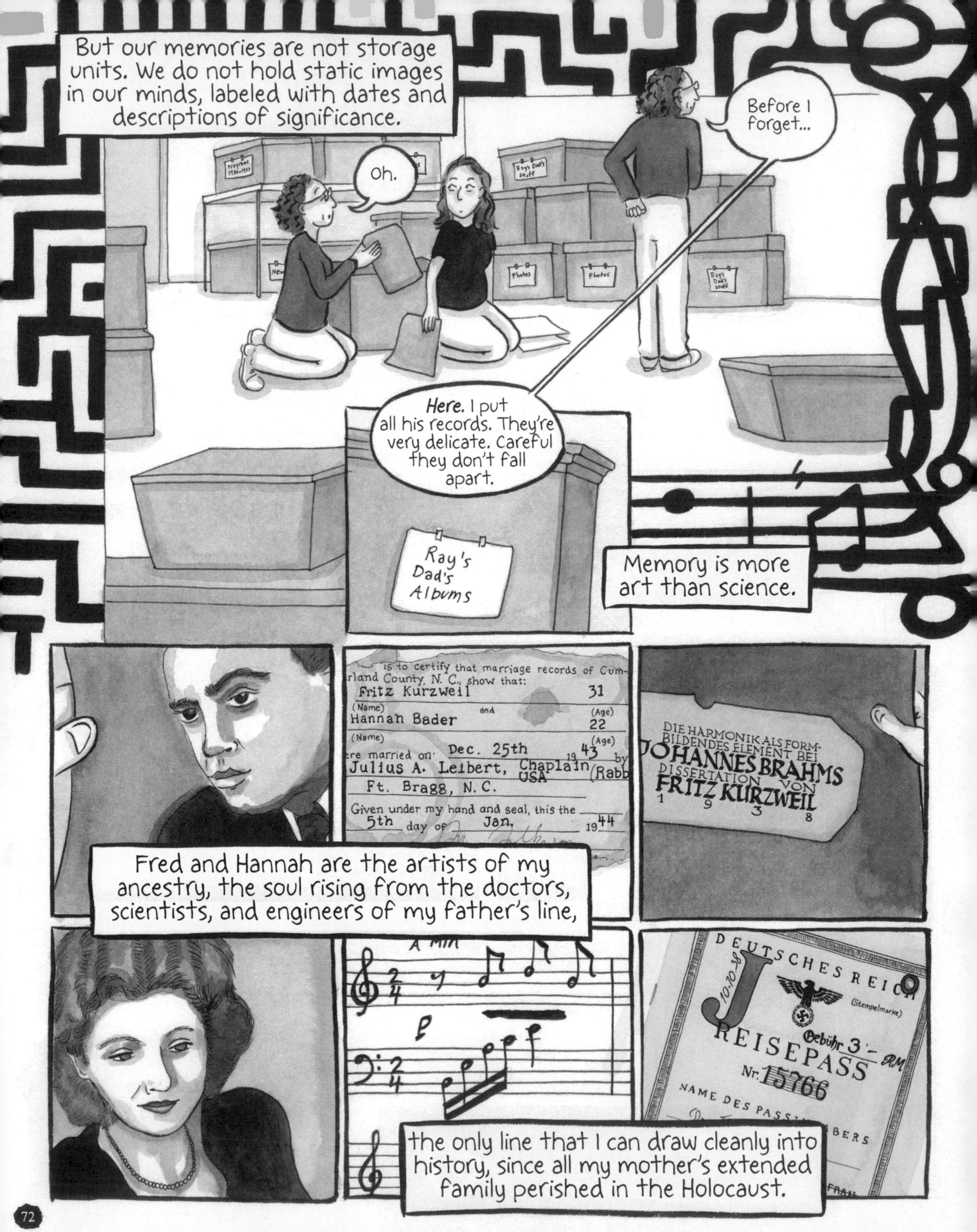
But our memories are not storage units. We do not hold static images in our minds, labeled with dates and descriptions of significance.
Oh.
Before I forget...
Photos
Photos
Here. I put all his records. They're very delicate. Careful they don't fall apart.
Ray's Dad's Albums
Memory is more art than science.
is to certify that marriage records of Cumrland County, N. C., show that:
Fritz Kurzweil 31
(Name) and (Age)
Hannah Bader 22
(Name) (Age)
ere married on: Dec. 25th 1943 by
Julius A. Leibert, Chaplain USA (Rabb
Ft. Bragg, N. C.
Given under my hand and seal, this the 5th day of Jan. 1944
DIE HARMONIK ALS FORMBILDENDES ELEMENT BEI JOHANNES BRAHMS
DISSERTATION VON FRITZ KURZWEIL
1938
Fred and Hannah are the artists of my ancestry, the soul rising from the doctors, scientists, and engineers of my father's line,
DEUTSCHES REICH
J
10.10.38
(Stempelmarke)
REISEPASS
Gebühr 3.- RM
Nr. 15766
NAME DES PASS...
...BERS
the only line that I can draw cleanly into history, since all my mother's extended family perished in the Holocaust.

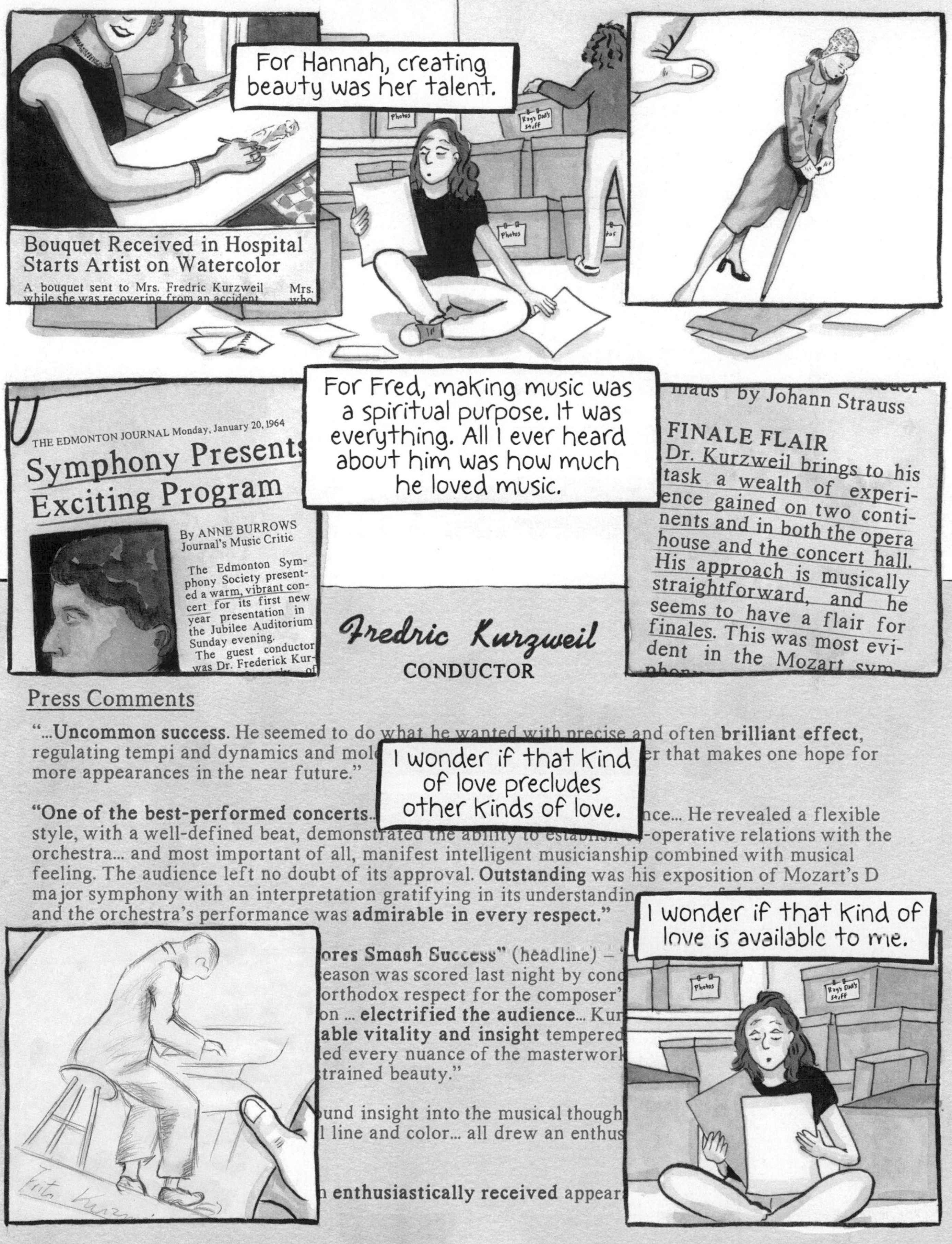

Bouquet Received in Hospital Starts Artist on Watercolor
A bouquet sent to Mrs. Fredric Kurzweil
For Hannah, creating beauty was her talent.
Photos
Ray's Dad's stuff
Photos
For Fred, making music was a spiritual purpose. It was everything. All I ever heard about him was how much he loved music.
THE EDMONTON JOURNAL Monday, January 20, 1964
Symphony Presents
Exciting Program
By ANNE BURROWS
Journal's Music Critic
The Edmonton Symphony Society presented a warm, vibrant concert for its first new year presentation in the Jubilee Auditorium Sunday evening.
The guest conductor was Dr. Frederick Kur-
by Johann Strauss
FINALE FLAIR
Dr. Kurzweil brings to his task a wealth of experience gained on two continents and in both the opera house and the concert hall. His approach is musically straightforward, and he seems to have a flair for finales. This was most evident in the Mozart sym-
Fredric Kurzweil
CONDUCTOR
Press Comments
"...Uncommon success. He seemed to do what he wanted with precise and often brilliant effect,
regulating tempi and dynamics and
er that makes one hope for
more appearances in the near future."
I wonder if that kind of love precludes other kinds of love.
"One of the best-performed concerts...
nce... He revealed a flexible
style, with a well-defined beat, demonstrated the ability to establish co-operative relations with the orchestra... and most important of all, manifest intelligent musicianship combined with musical feeling. The audience left no doubt of its approval. Outstanding was his exposition of Mozart's D major symphony with an interpretation gratifying in its understanding
and the orchestra's performance was admirable in every respect."
I wonder if that kind of love is available to me.
ores Smash Success" (headline) –
eason was scored last night by cond
orthodox respect for the composer'
on ... electrified the audience... Kur
able vitality and insight tempered
led every nuance of the masterwork
strained beauty."
und insight into the musical though
l line and color... all drew an enthus
n enthusiastically received appear
Photos
Ray's Dad's stuff

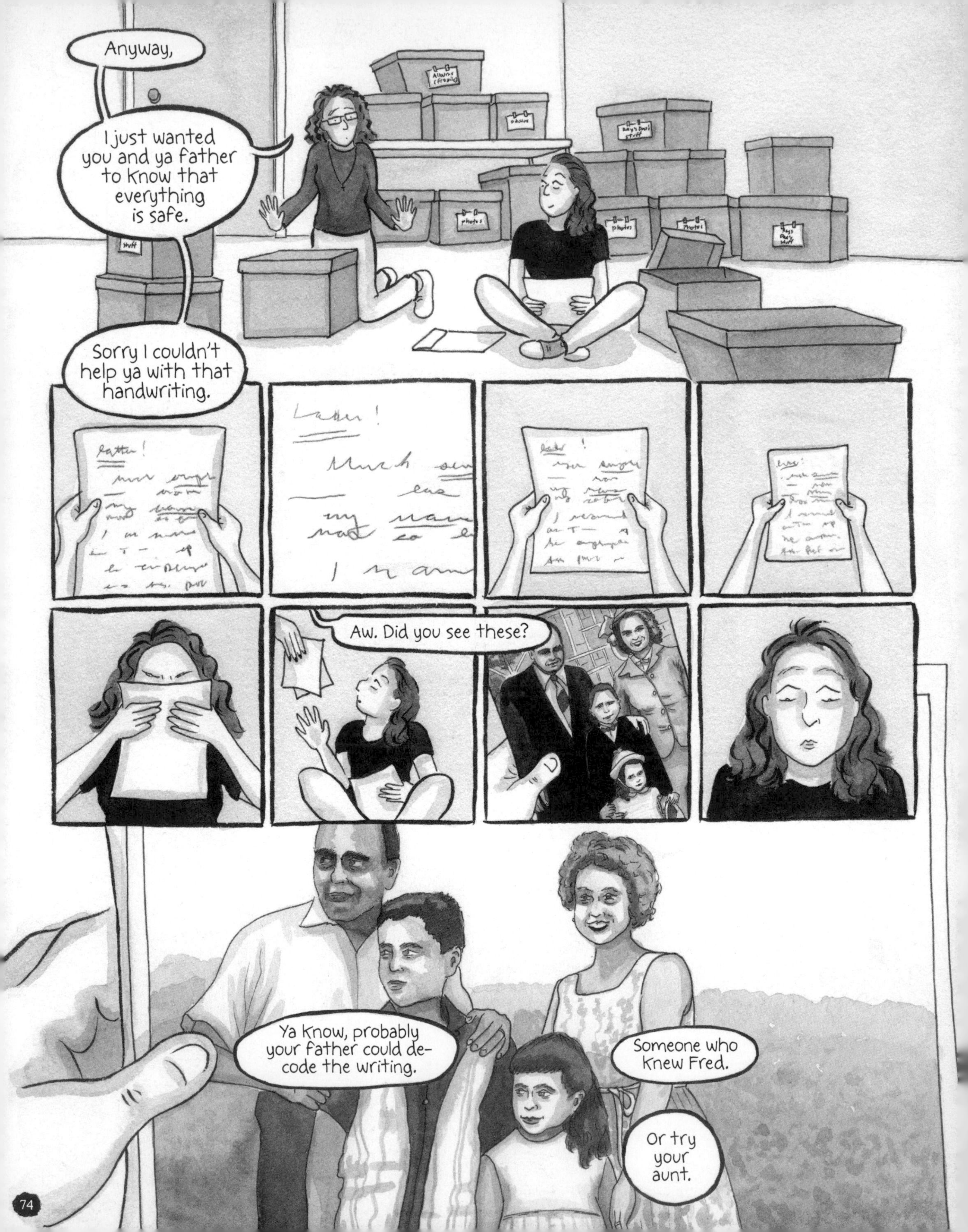
Anyway,
I just wanted you and ya father to know that everything is safe.
Sorry I couldn't help ya with that handwriting.
Aw. Did you see these?
Ya know, probably your father could de-code the writing.
Someone who knew Fred.
Or try your aunt.

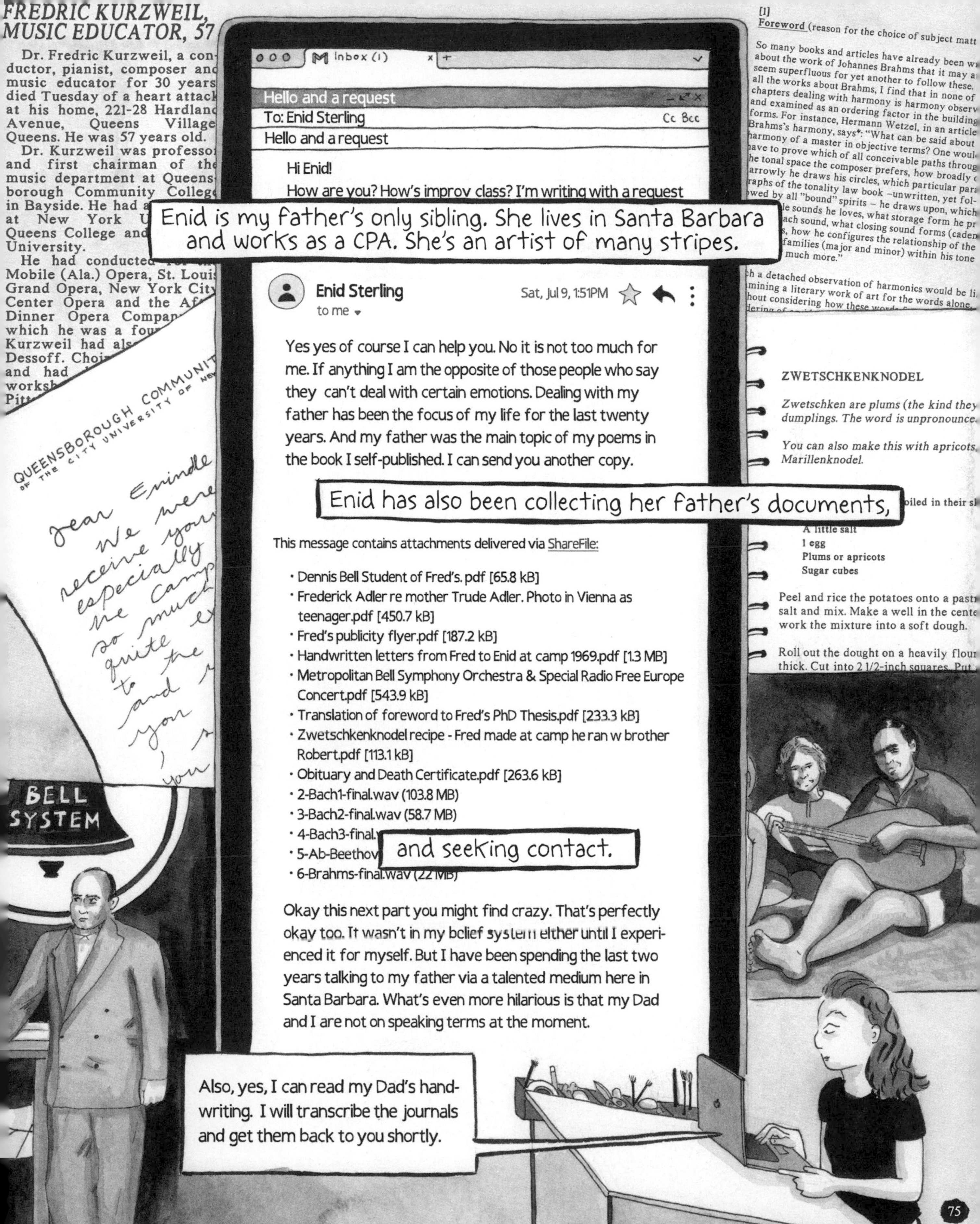
FREDRIC KURZWEIL, MUSIC EDUCATOR, 57
Dr. Fredric Kurzweil, a conductor, pianist, composer and music educator for 30 years died Tuesday of a heart attack at his home, 221-28 Hardland Avenue, Queens Village, Queens. He was 57 years old.
QUEENSBOROUGH COMMUNITY
OF THE CITY UNIVERSITY OF NEW
BELL SYSTEM
Foreword (reason for the choice of subject matt
ZWETSCHKENKNODEL
Zwetschken are plums (the kind they
You can also make this with apricots,
Marillenknodel.
A little salt
1 egg
Plums or apricots
Sugar cubes
Inbox (1)
Hello and a request
To: Enid Sterling
Cc Bcc
Hello and a request
Hi Enid!
How are you? How's improv class? I'm writing with a request
Enid is my father's only sibling. She lives in Santa Barbara and works as a CPA. She's an artist of many stripes.
Enid Sterling
to me
Sat, Jul 9, 1:51PM
Yes yes of course I can help you. No it is not too much for me. If anything I am the opposite of those people who say they can't deal with certain emotions. Dealing with my father has been the focus of my life for the last twenty years. And my father was the main topic of my poems in the book I self-published. I can send you another copy.
Enid has also been collecting her father's documents,
This message contains attachments delivered via ShareFile:
• Dennis Bell Student of Fred's. pdf [65.8 kB]
• Frederick Adler re mother Trude Adler. Photo in Vienna as teenager.pdf [450.7 kB]
• Fred's publicity flyer.pdf [187.2 kB]
• Handwritten letters from Fred to Enid at camp 1969.pdf [1.3 MB]
• Metropolitan Bell Symphony Orchestra & Special Radio Free Europe Concert.pdf [543.9 kB]
• Translation of foreword to Fred's PhD Thesis.pdf [233.3 kB]
• Zwetschkenknodel recipe - Fred made at camp he ran w brother Robert.pdf [113.1 kB]
• Obituary and Death Certificate.pdf [263.6 kB]
• 2-Bach1-final.wav (103.8 MB)
• 3-Bach2-final.wav (58.7 MB)
• 6-Brahms-final.wav (22 MB)
and seeking contact.
Okay this next part you might find crazy. That's perfectly okay too. It wasn't in my belief system either until I experienced it for myself. But I have been spending the last two years talking to my father via a talented medium here in Santa Barbara. What's even more hilarious is that my Dad and I are not on speaking terms at the moment.
Also, yes, I can read my Dad's handwriting. I will transcribe the journals and get them back to you shortly.

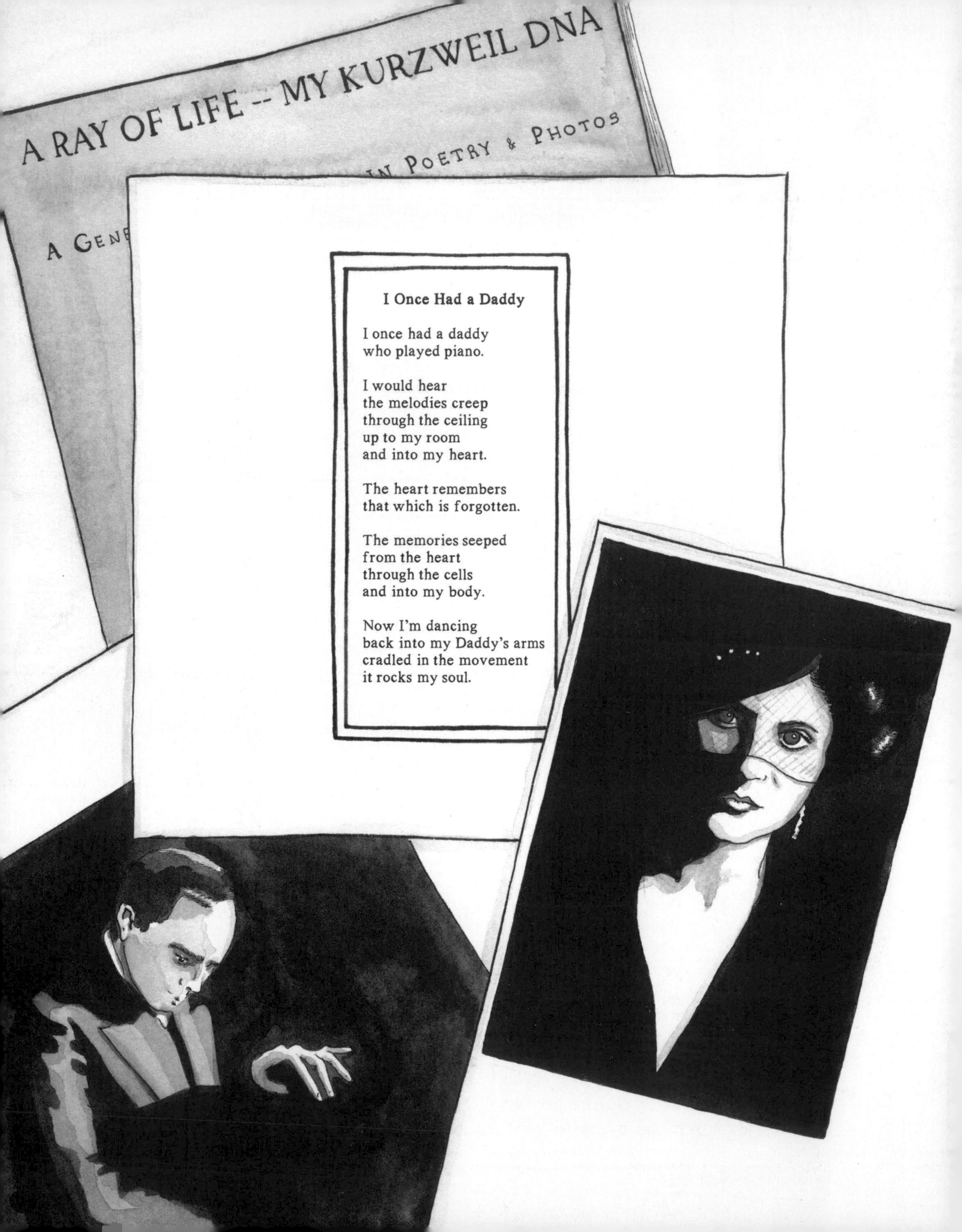
A RAY OF LIFE -- MY KURZWEIL DNA
IN POETRY & PHOTOS
A GENE
I Once Had a Daddy
I once had a daddy
who played piano.

I would hear
the melodies creep
through the ceiling
up to my room
and into my heart.

The heart remembers
that which is forgotten.

The memories seeped
from the heart
through the cells
and into my body.

Now I'm dancing
back into my Daddy's arms
cradled in the movement
it rocks my soul.

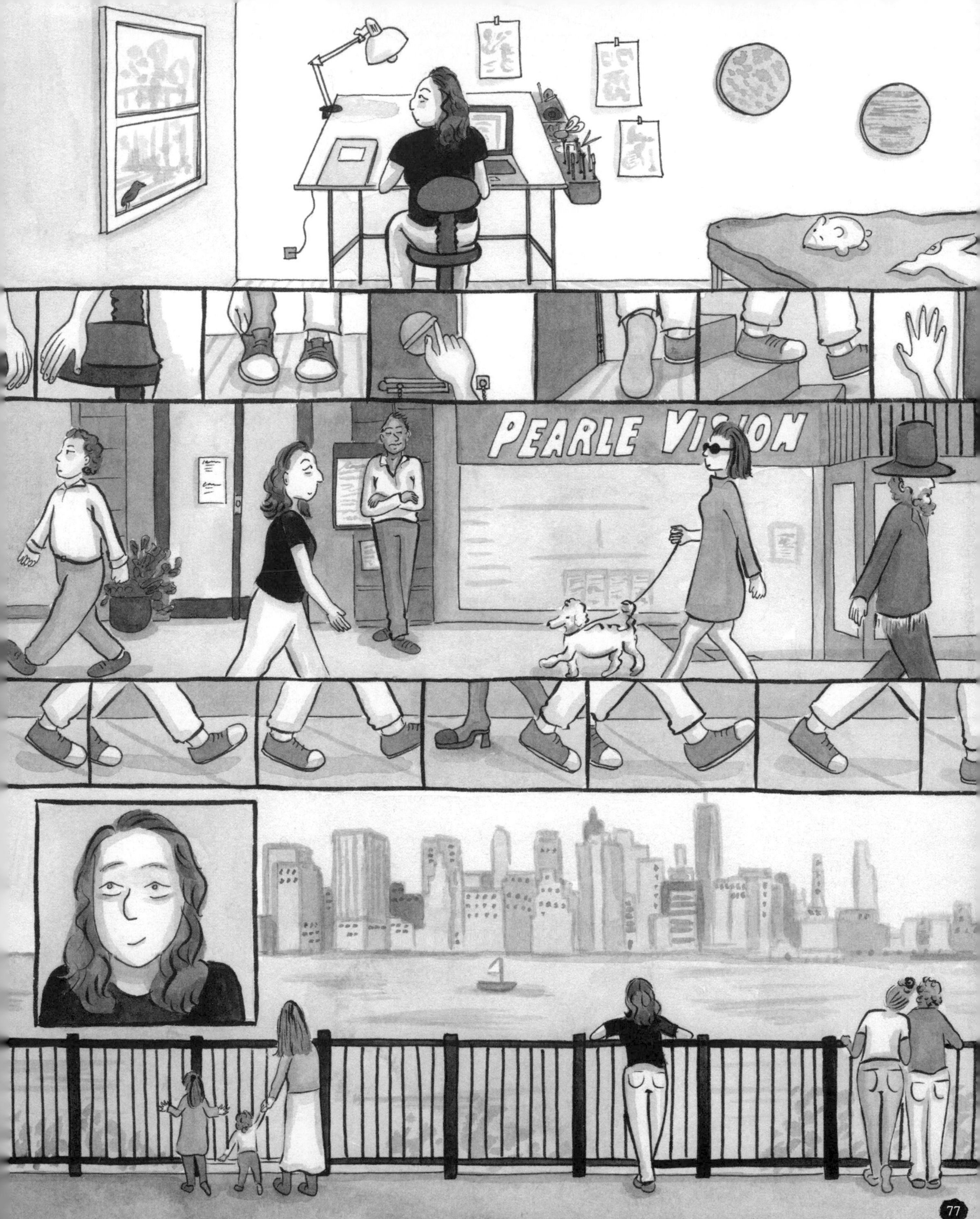
PEARLE VISION

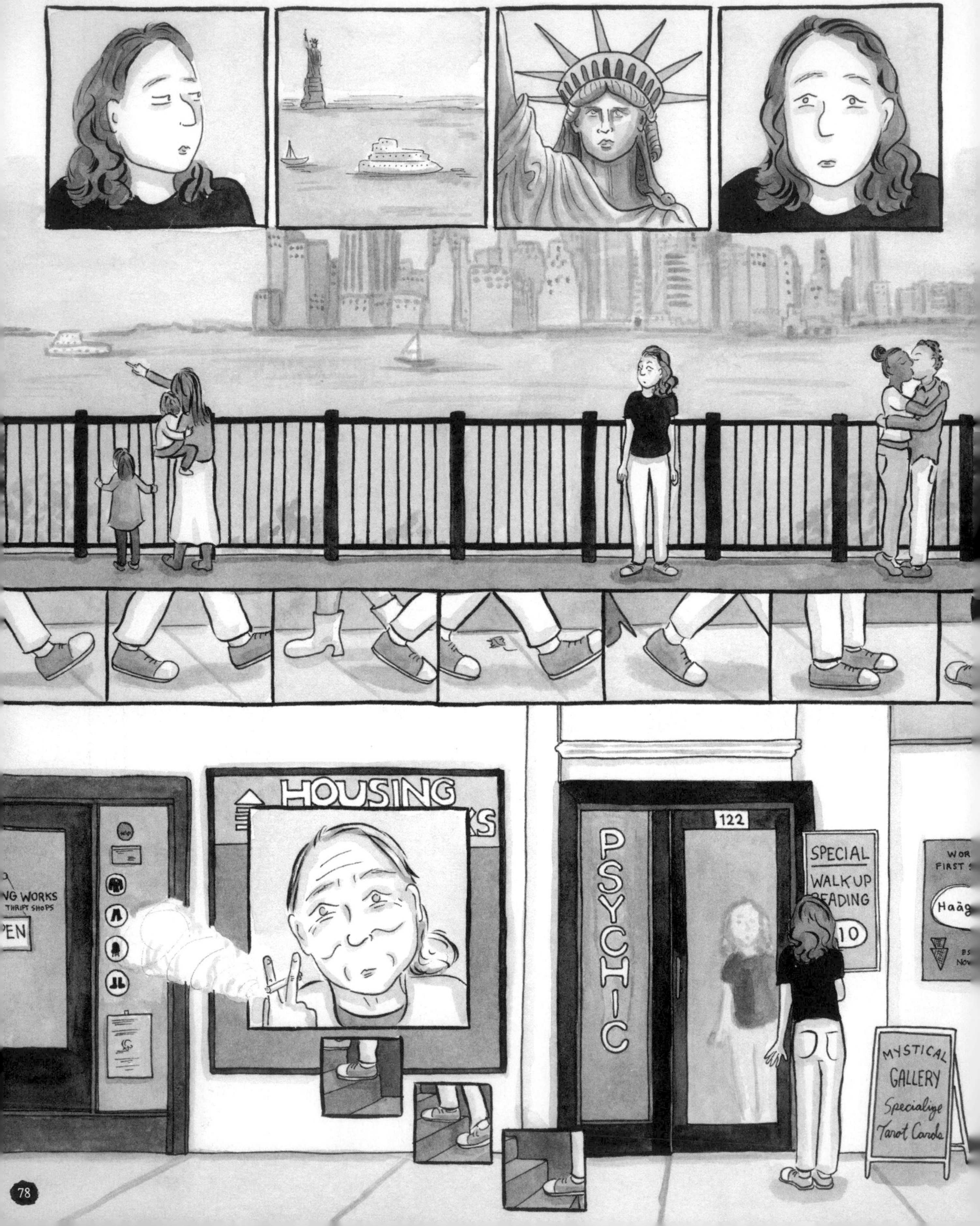
HOUSING
NG WORKS
122
PSYCHIC
SPECIAL
WALK UP
MYSTICAL
GALLERY
Specialize
Tarot Cards

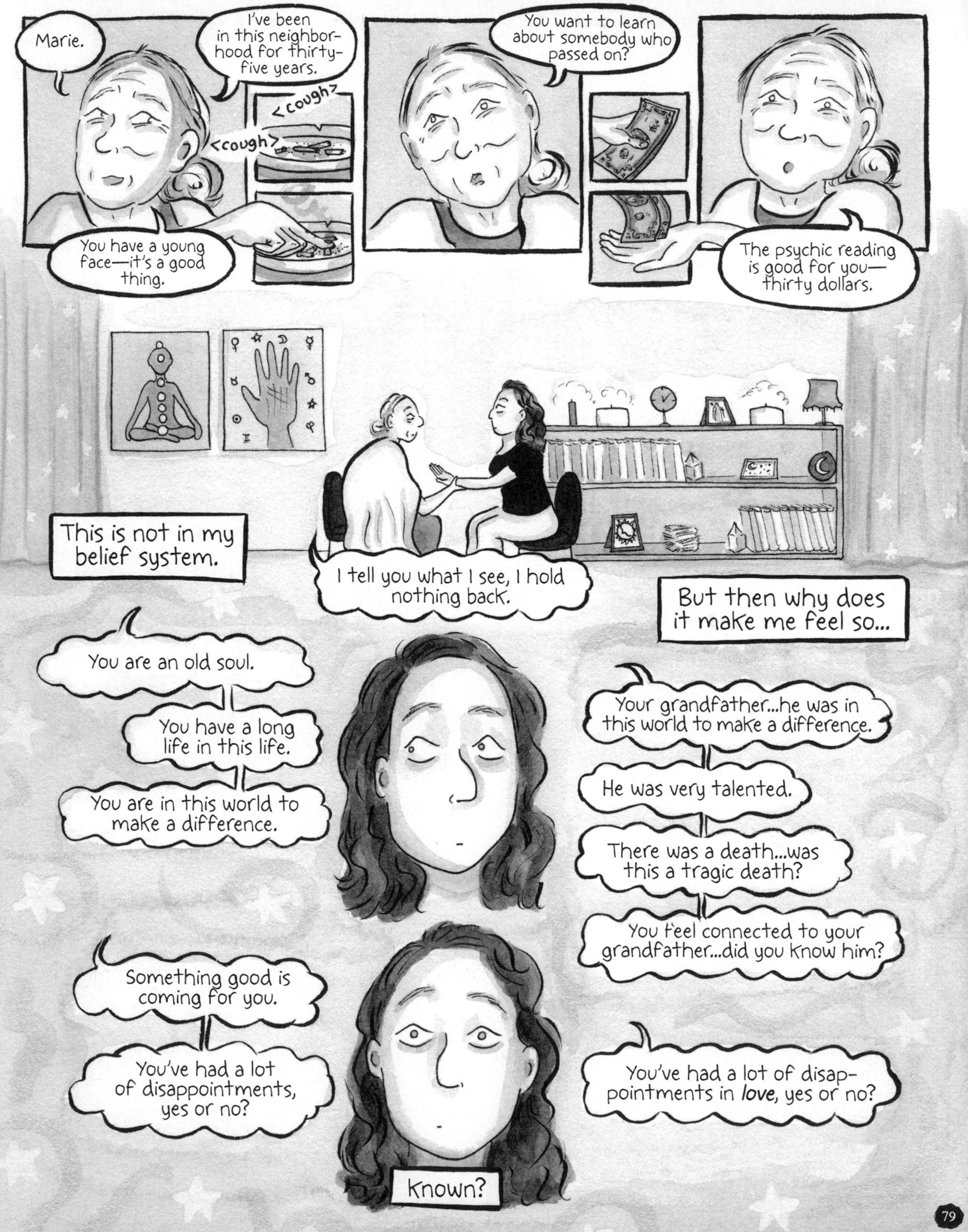
Marie.
I've been in this neighbor-hood for thirty-five years.
<cough>
<cough>
You have a young face—it's a good thing.
You want to learn about somebody who passed on?
The psychic reading is good for you—thirty dollars.
This is not in my belief system.
I tell you what I see, I hold nothing back.
But then why does it make me feel so...
You are an old soul.
You have a long life in this life.
You are in this world to make a difference.
Your grandfather...he was in this world to make a difference.
He was very talented.
There was a death...was this a tragic death?
You feel connected to your grandfather...did you know him?
Something good is coming for you.
You've had a lot of disappointments, yes or no?
You've had a lot of disap-pointments in *love*, yes or no?
Known?

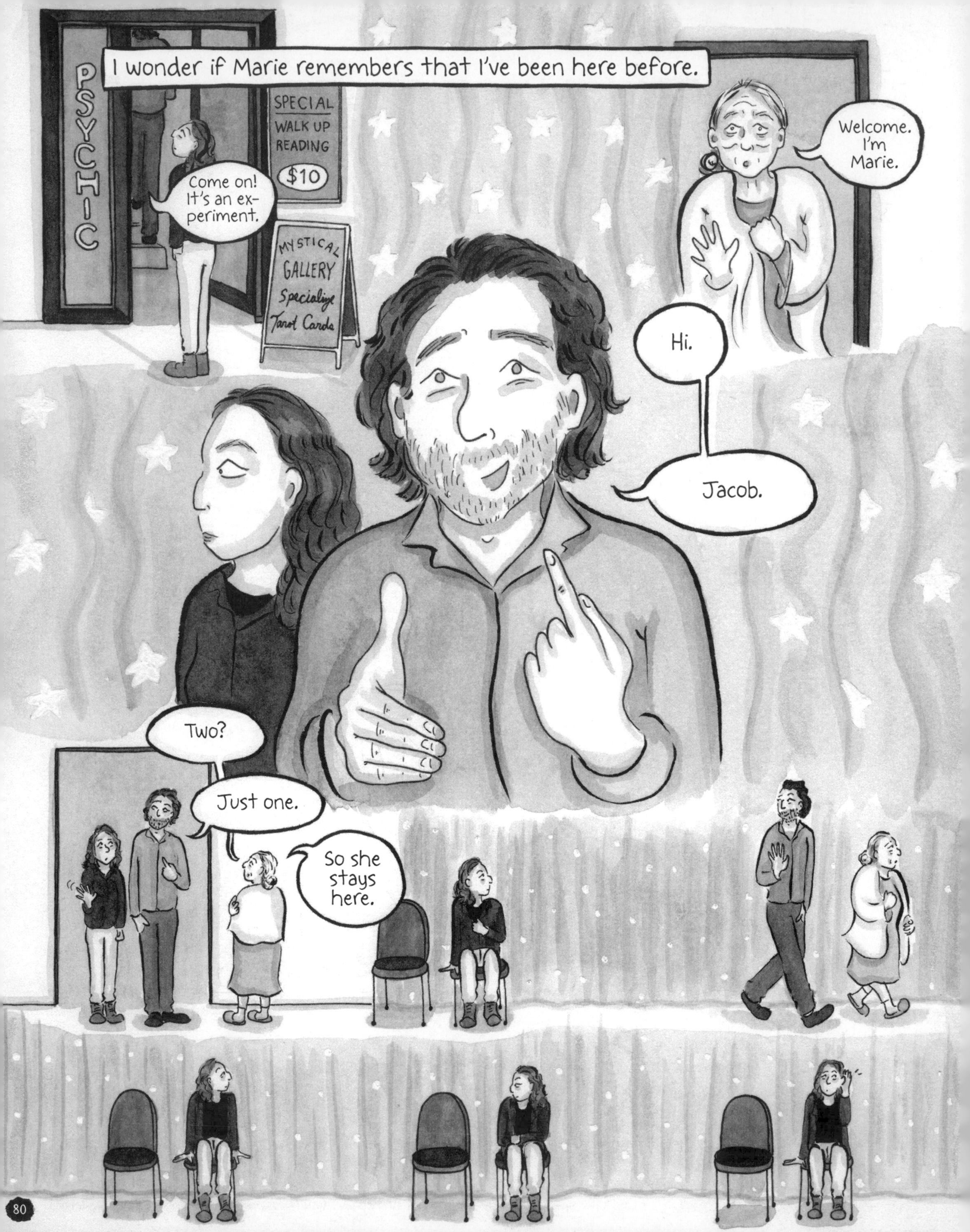
I wonder if Marie remembers that I've been here before.
PSYCHIC
SPECIAL WALK UP READING $10
Come on! It's an experiment.
MYSTICAL GALLERY Specialize Tarot Cards
Welcome. I'm Marie.
Hi.
Jacob.
Two?
Just one.
So she stays here.

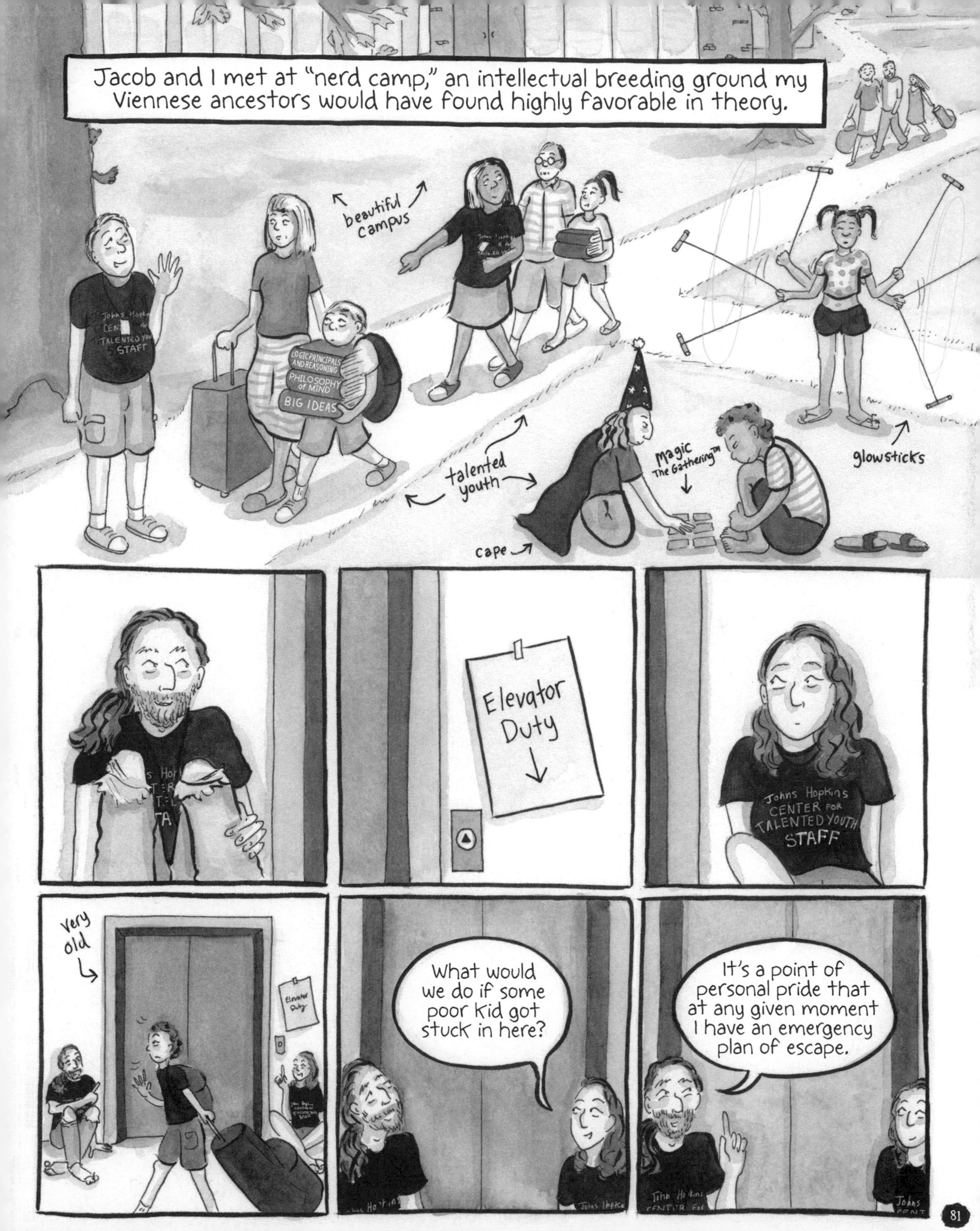
Jacob and I met at "nerd camp," an intellectual breeding ground my Viennese ancestors would have found highly favorable in theory.
Johns Hopkins Center for Talented Youth Staff
Logic Principals and Reasoning
Philosophy of Mind
Big Ideas
beautiful campus
talented youth
cape
Magic The Gathering™
glowsticks
Elevator Duty
Johns Hopkins Center for Talented Youth Staff
Very old
Elevator Duty
What would we do if some poor kid got stuck in here?
It's a point of personal pride that at any given moment I have an emergency plan of escape.

What are you here for?

Logic.

So I can trust your escape plan.

You?

Teaching assistant for "Utopias and Dystopias."

You're a writer?

Yeah.

So your elevator escape plan will lead us to drama and misery.

Most likely.

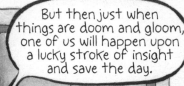

But then just when things are doom and gloom, one of us will happen upon a lucky stroke of insight and save the day.

Classic Christian arc.

So...which way are we headed: utopia or dystopia?

As it turns out, every dystopia is just a utopia by another name.

I was just reading about *Brave New World* and *1984*. Orwell feared we were heading toward technocracy, a dictatorship exerting total control through fear and surveillance, but our world today is much more like Huxley's. We're controlled through pleasure. Technology lulls us.

Kind of a bleak perspective. I mean, technology has also cured diseases, extended life...

And what are we living longer *for*?

Something more than soma vacations and feelies?

Nothing wrong with hedonism.

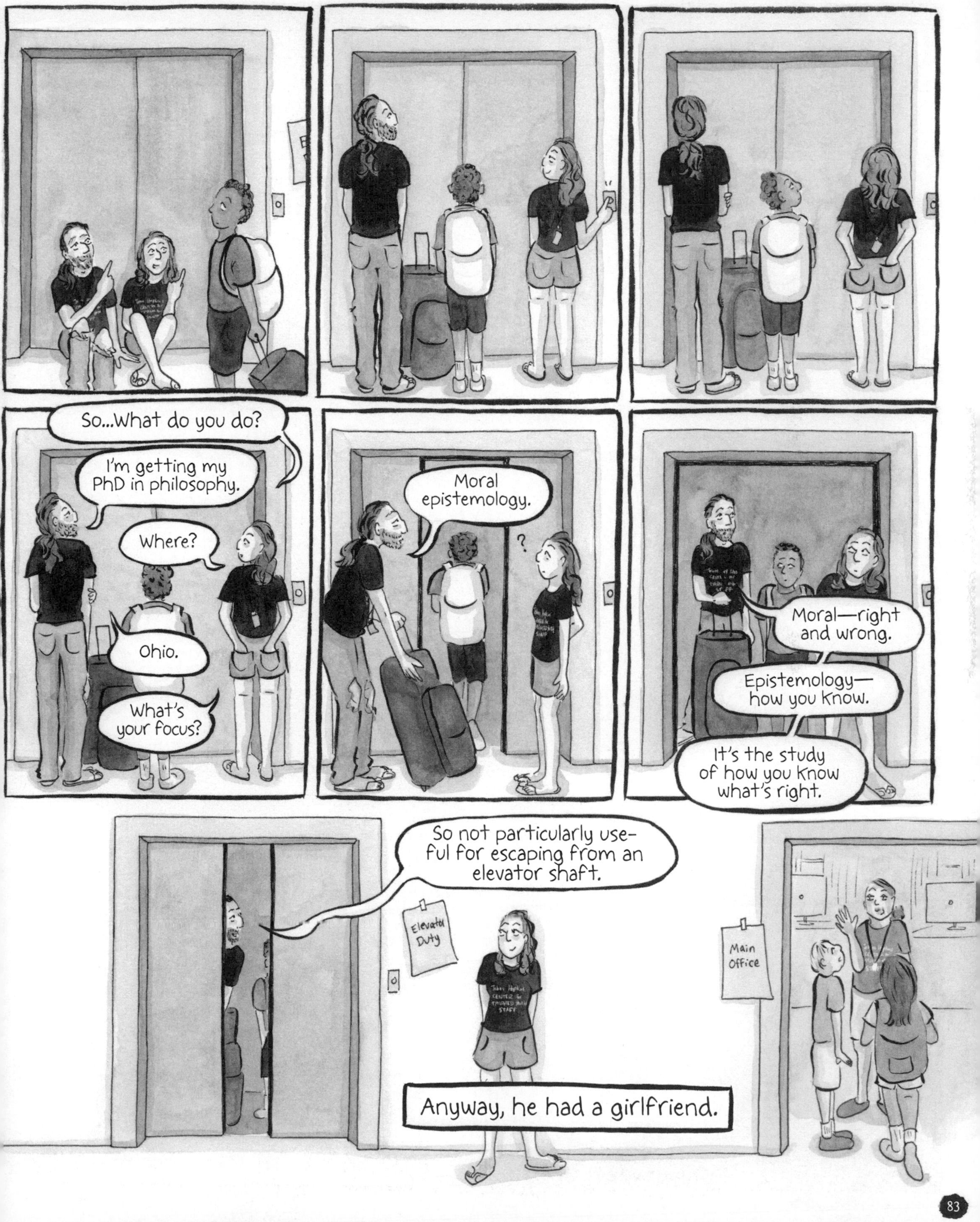
So...What do you do?
I'm getting my PhD in philosophy.
Where?
Ohio.
What's your focus?
Moral epistemology.
?
Moral—right and wrong.
Epistemology—how you know.
It's the study of how you know what's right.
So not particularly use-ful for escaping from an elevator shaft.
Elevator Duty
Main Office
Anyway, he had a girlfriend.

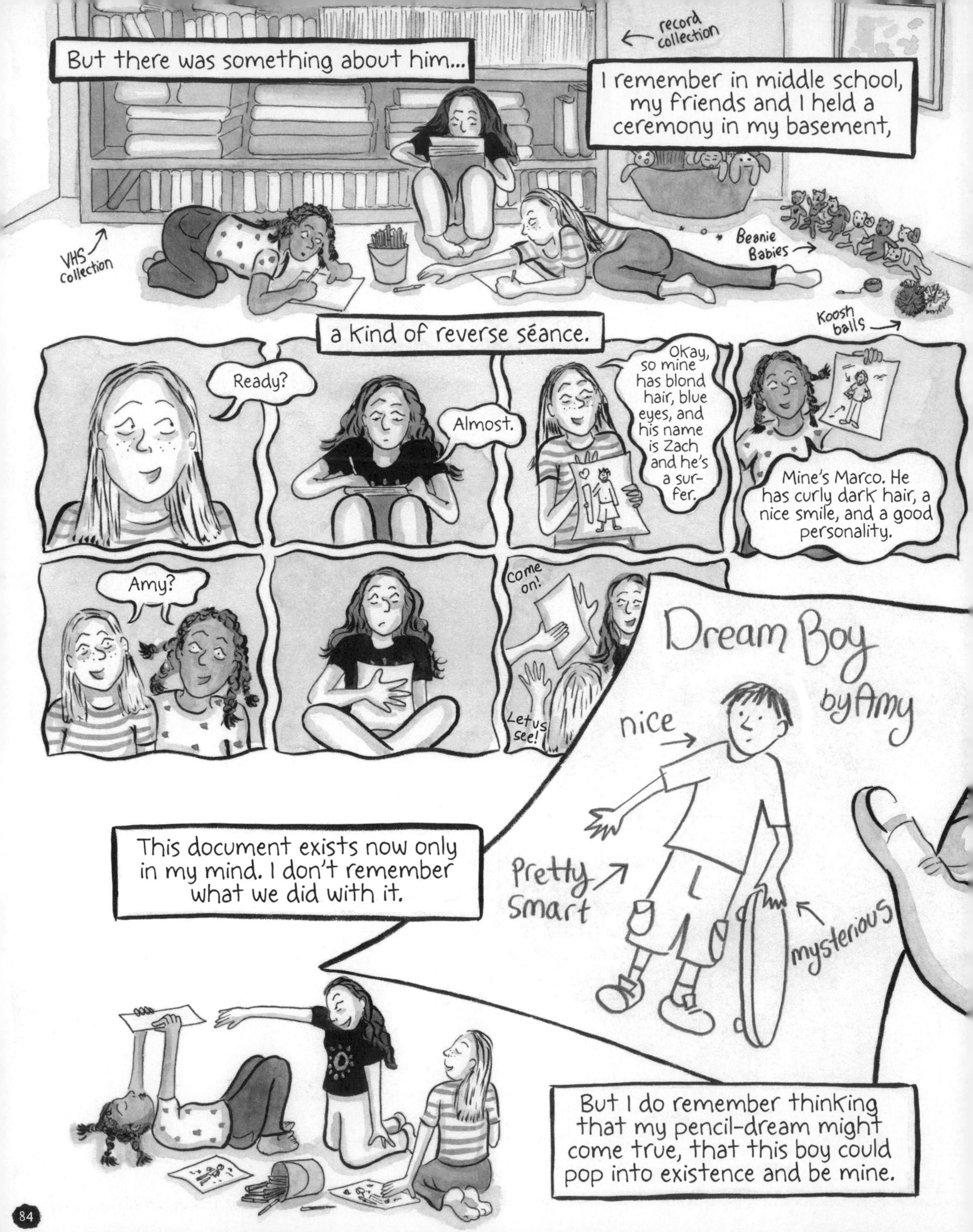
But there was something about him...
record collection
I remember in middle school, my friends and I held a ceremony in my basement,
VHS collection
Beanie Babies
Koosh balls
a kind of reverse séance.
Ready?
Almost.
Okay, so mine has blond hair, blue eyes, and his name is Zach and he's a surfer.
Mine's Marco. He has curly dark hair, a nice smile, and a good personality.
Amy?
Come on!
Let us see!
Dream Boy
by Amy
nice
Pretty Smart
mysterious
This document exists now only in my mind. I don't remember what we did with it.
But I do remember thinking that my pencil-dream might come true, that this boy could pop into existence and be mine.

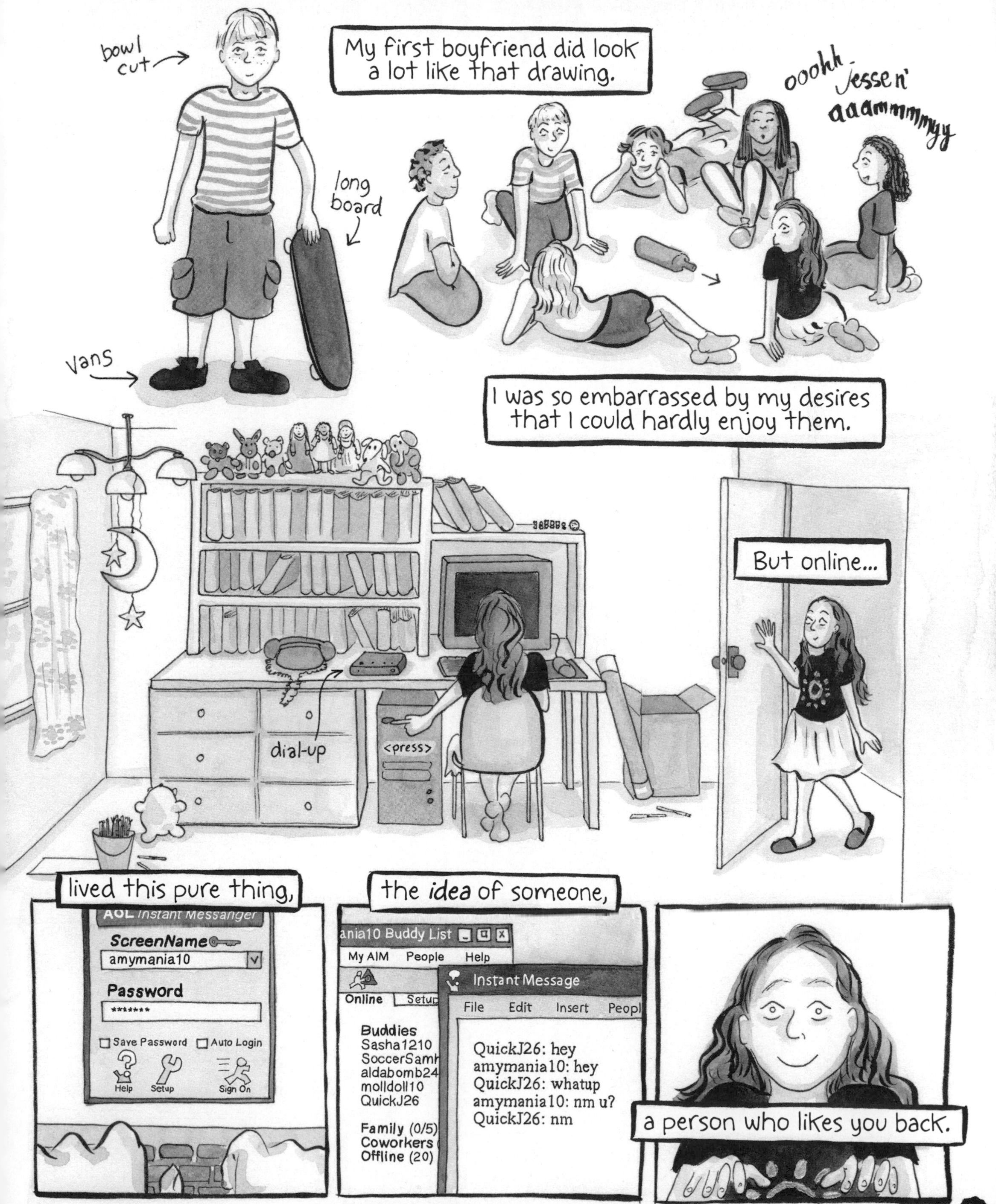

bowl cut
long board
vans
My first boyfriend did look a lot like that drawing.
ooohh jesse n' aaammmmyy
I was so embarrassed by my desires that I could hardly enjoy them.
dial-up
<press>
But online...
lived this pure thing,
AOL Instant Messenger
ScreenName
amymania10
Password
*******
Save Password
Auto Login
Help
Setup
Sign On
the *idea* of someone,
ania10 Buddy List
My AIM
People
Help
Online
Setup
Buddies
Sasha1210
SoccerSamh
aldabomb24
molldoll10
QuickJ26
Family (0/5)
Coworkers
Offline (20)
Instant Message
File
Edit
Insert
Peopl
QuickJ26: hey
amymania10: hey
QuickJ26: whatup
amymania10: nm u?
QuickJ26: nm
a person who likes you back.

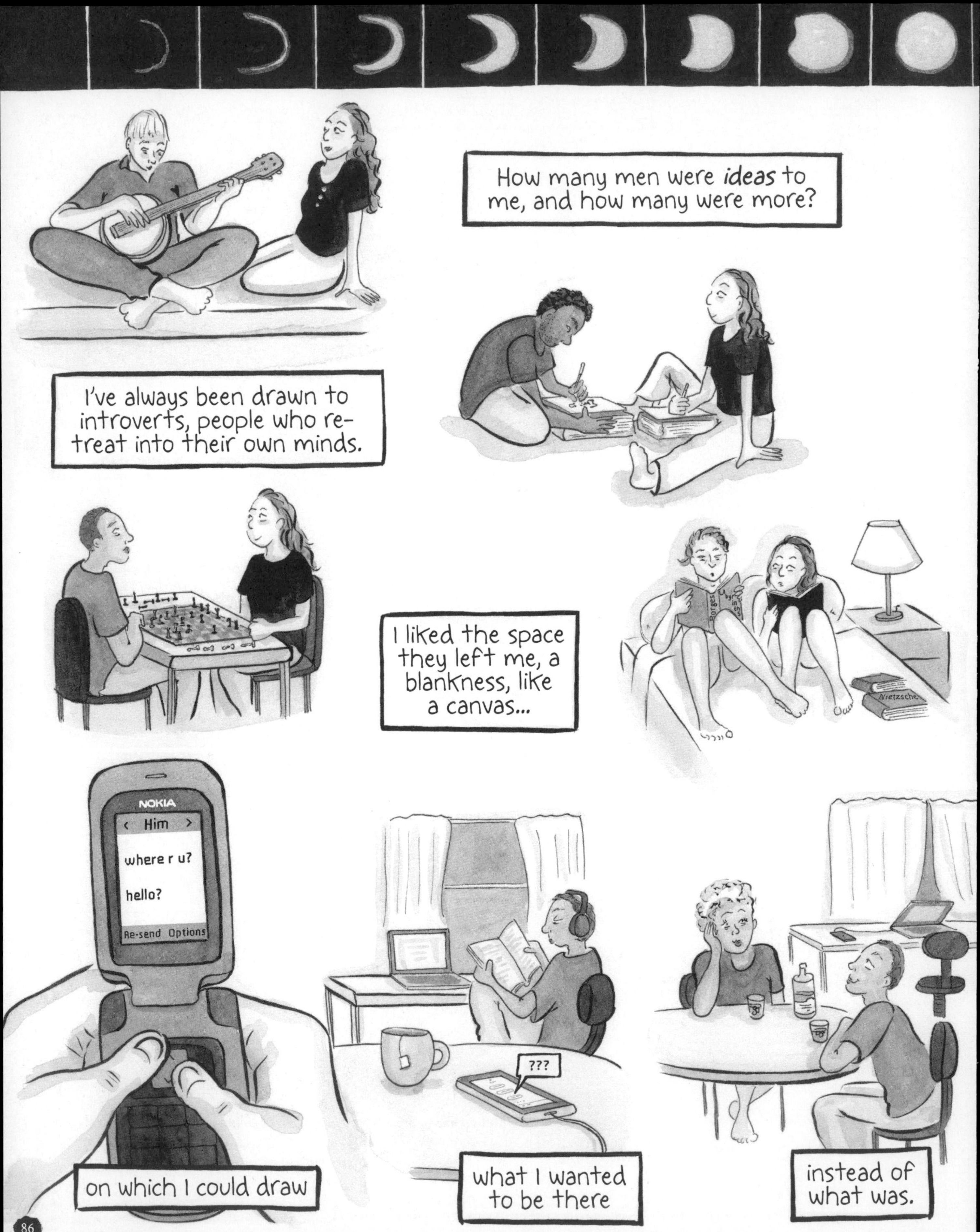

How many men were *ideas* to me, and how many were more?
I've always been drawn to introverts, people who re-treat into their own minds.
Borges
Labyrinths
Nietzsche
I liked the space they left me, a blankness, like a canvas...
NOKIA
Him
where r u?
hello?
Re-send Options
on which I could draw
???
what I wanted to be there
instead of what was.

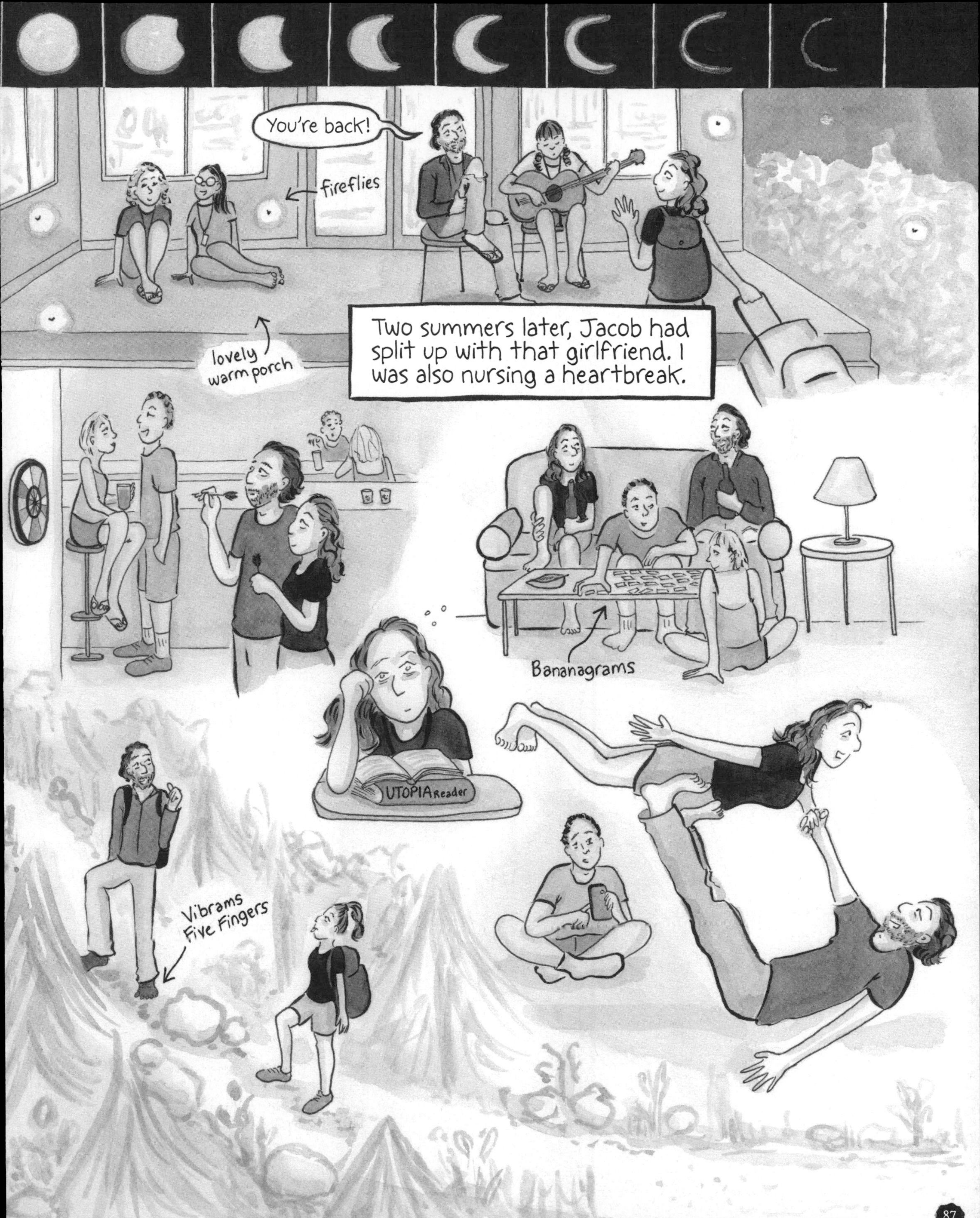
You're back!
fireflies
lovely warm porch
Two summers later, Jacob had split up with that girlfriend. I was also nursing a heartbreak.
Bananagrams
UTOPIA Reader
Vibrams Five Fingers

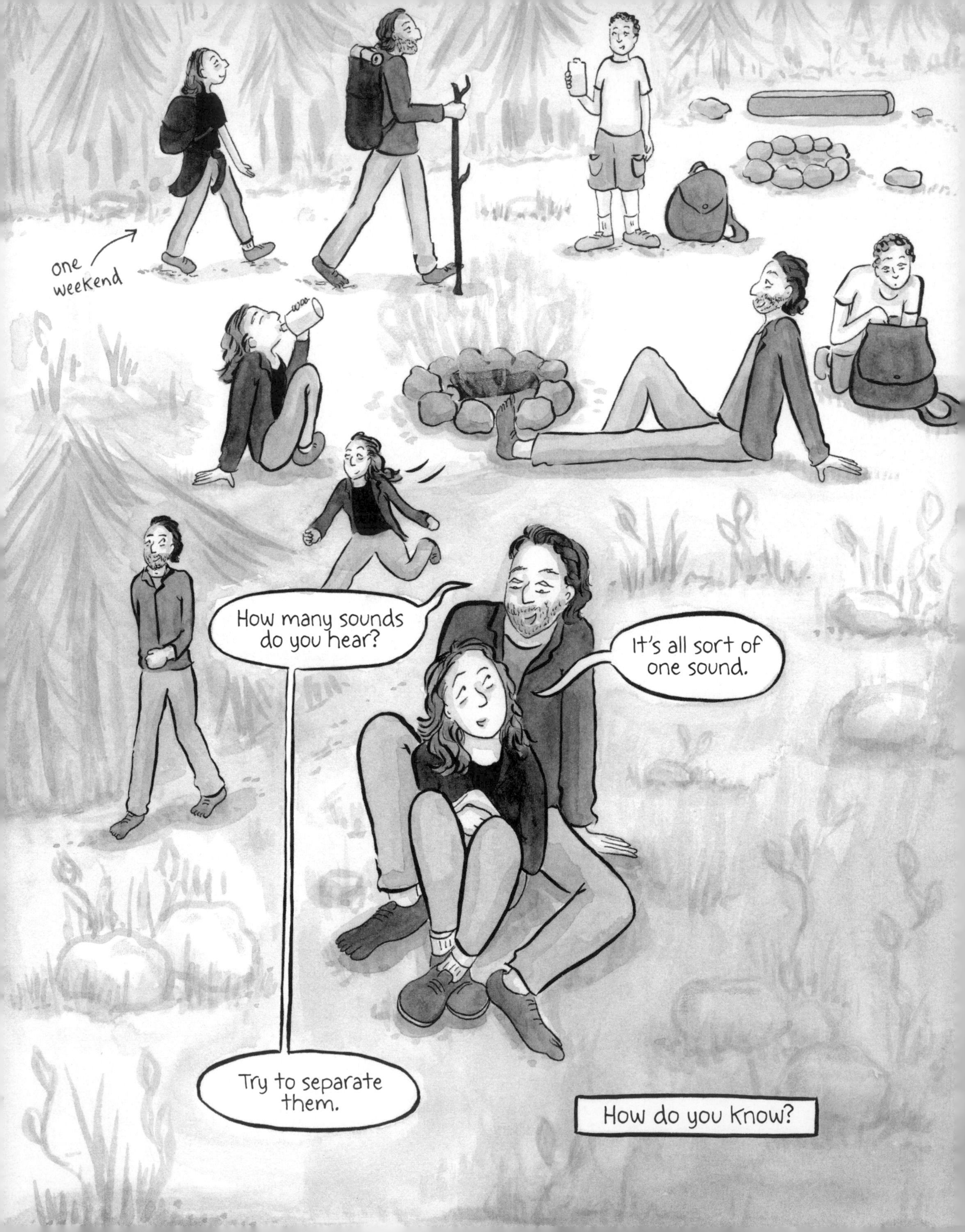
one weekend
How many sounds do you hear?
It's all sort of one sound.
Try to separate them.
How do you know?

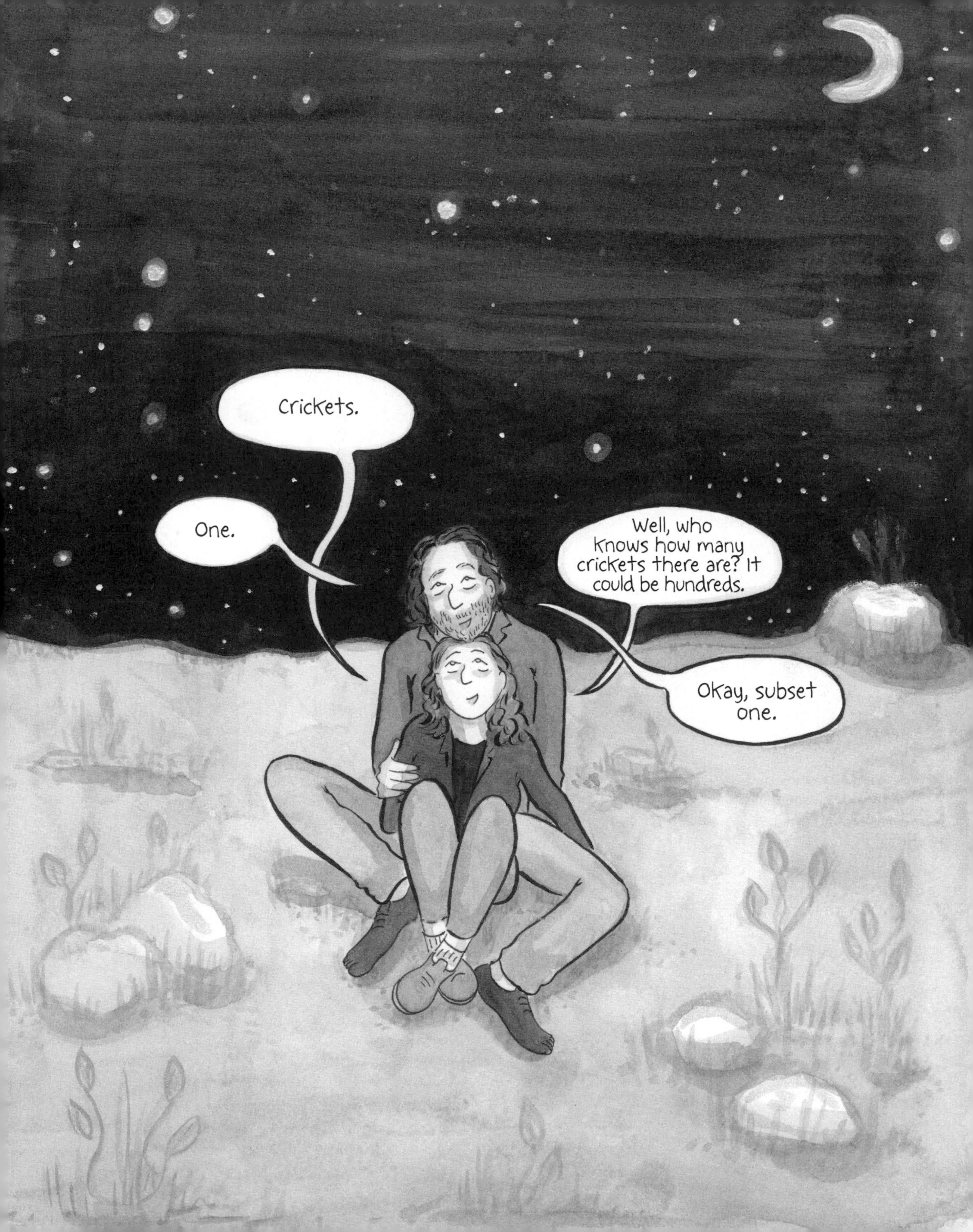
Crickets.
One.
Well, who knows how many crickets there are? It could be hundreds.
Okay, subset one.

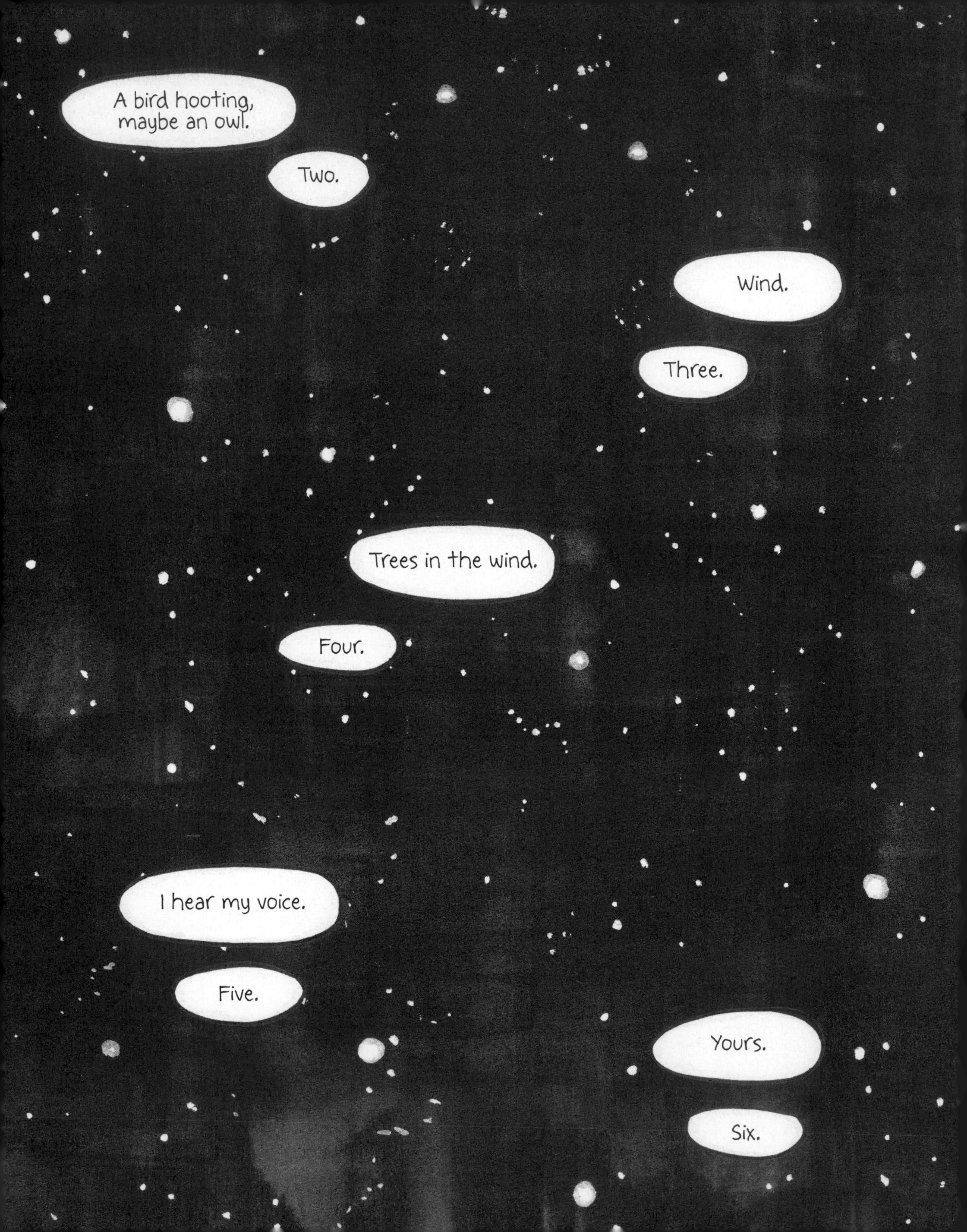
A bird hooting, maybe an owl.
Two.
Wind.
Three.
Trees in the wind.
Four.
I hear my voice.
Five.
Yours.
Six.

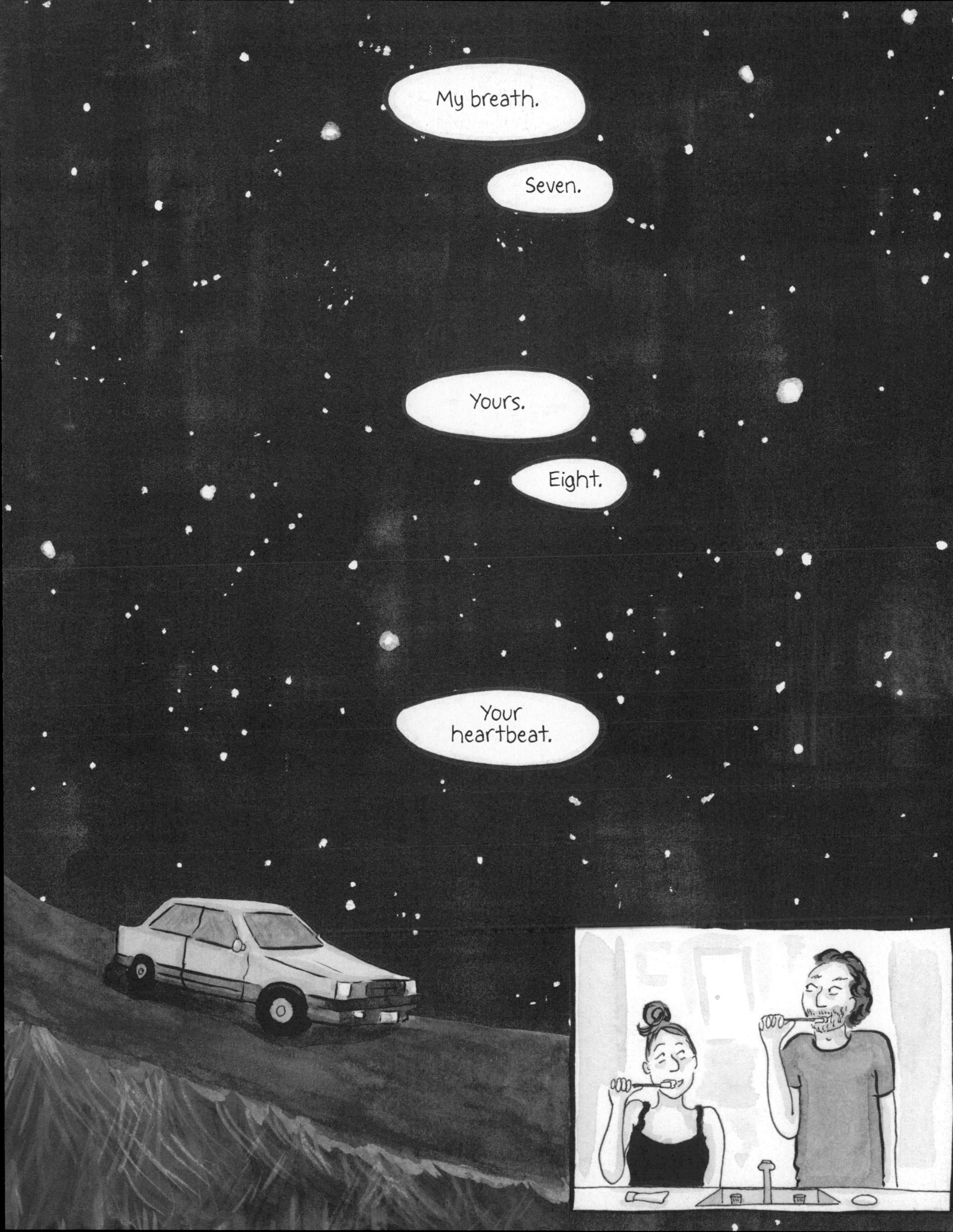
My breath.
Seven.
Yours.
Eight.
Your heartbeat.

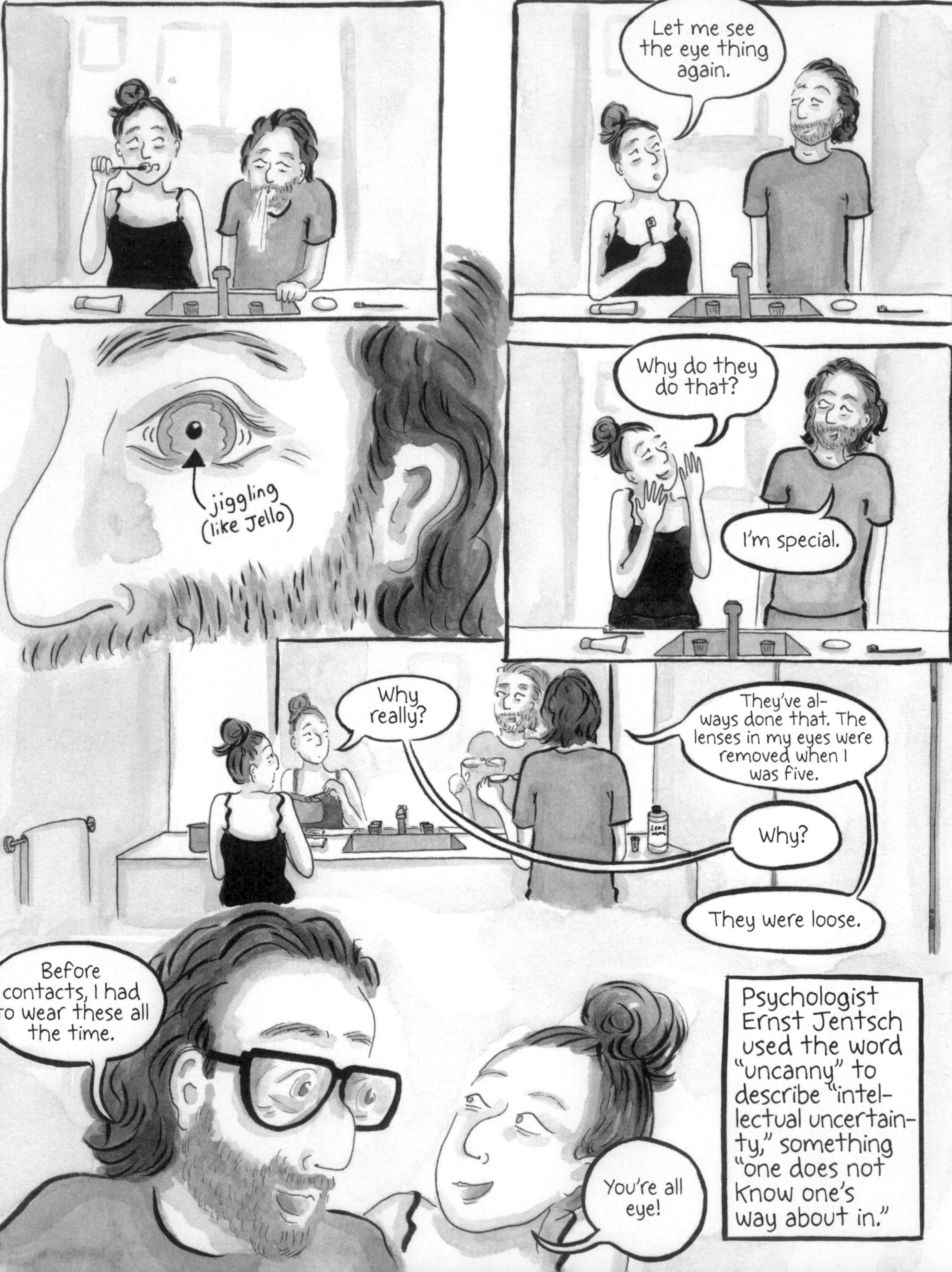
Let me see the eye thing again.
jiggling (like Jello)
Why do they do that?
I'm special.
Why really?
They've always done that. The lenses in my eyes were removed when I was five.
Why?
They were loose.
Before contacts, I had to wear these all the time.
You're all eye!
Psychologist Ernst Jentsch used the word "uncanny" to describe "intellectual uncertainty," something "one does not know one's way about in."

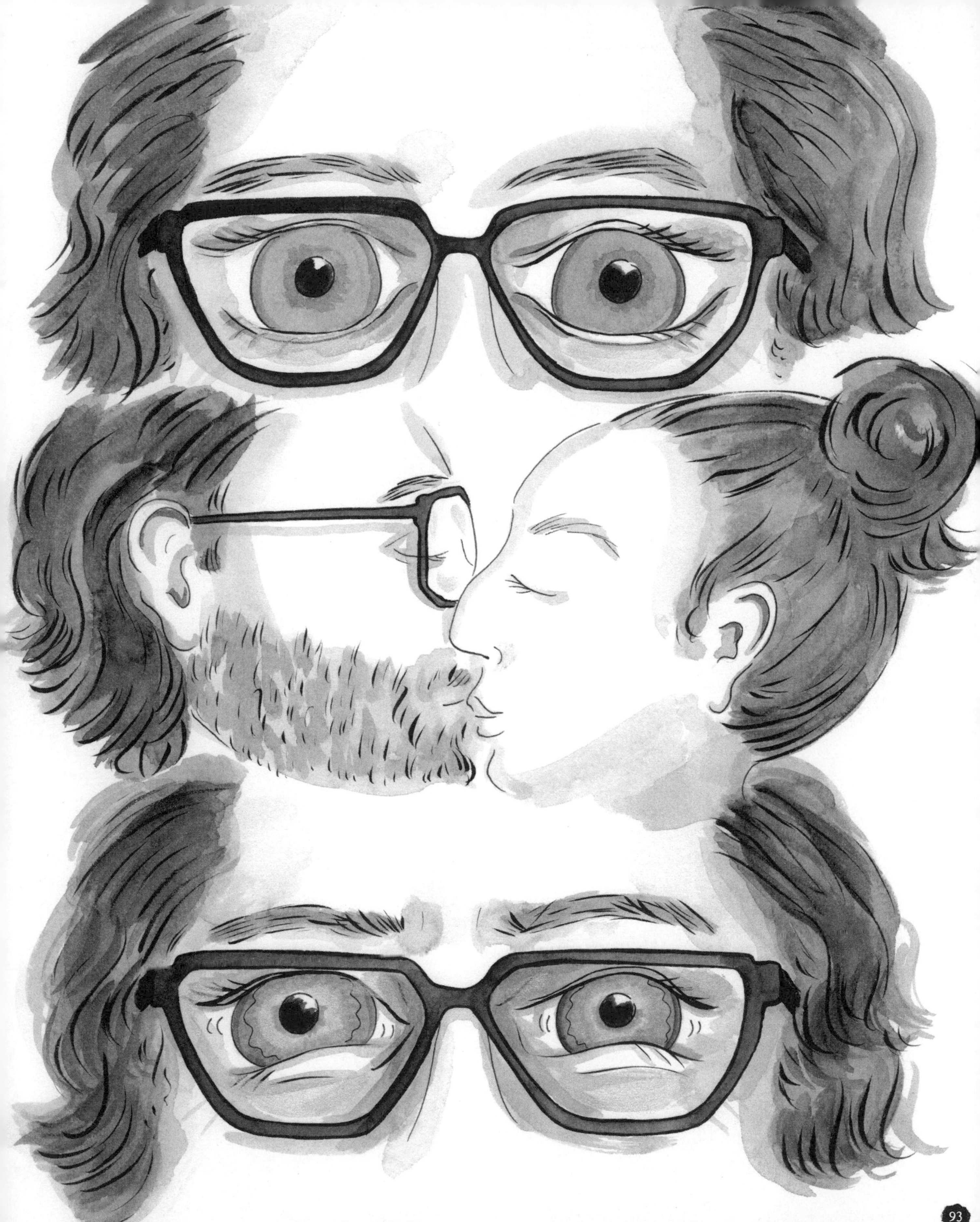

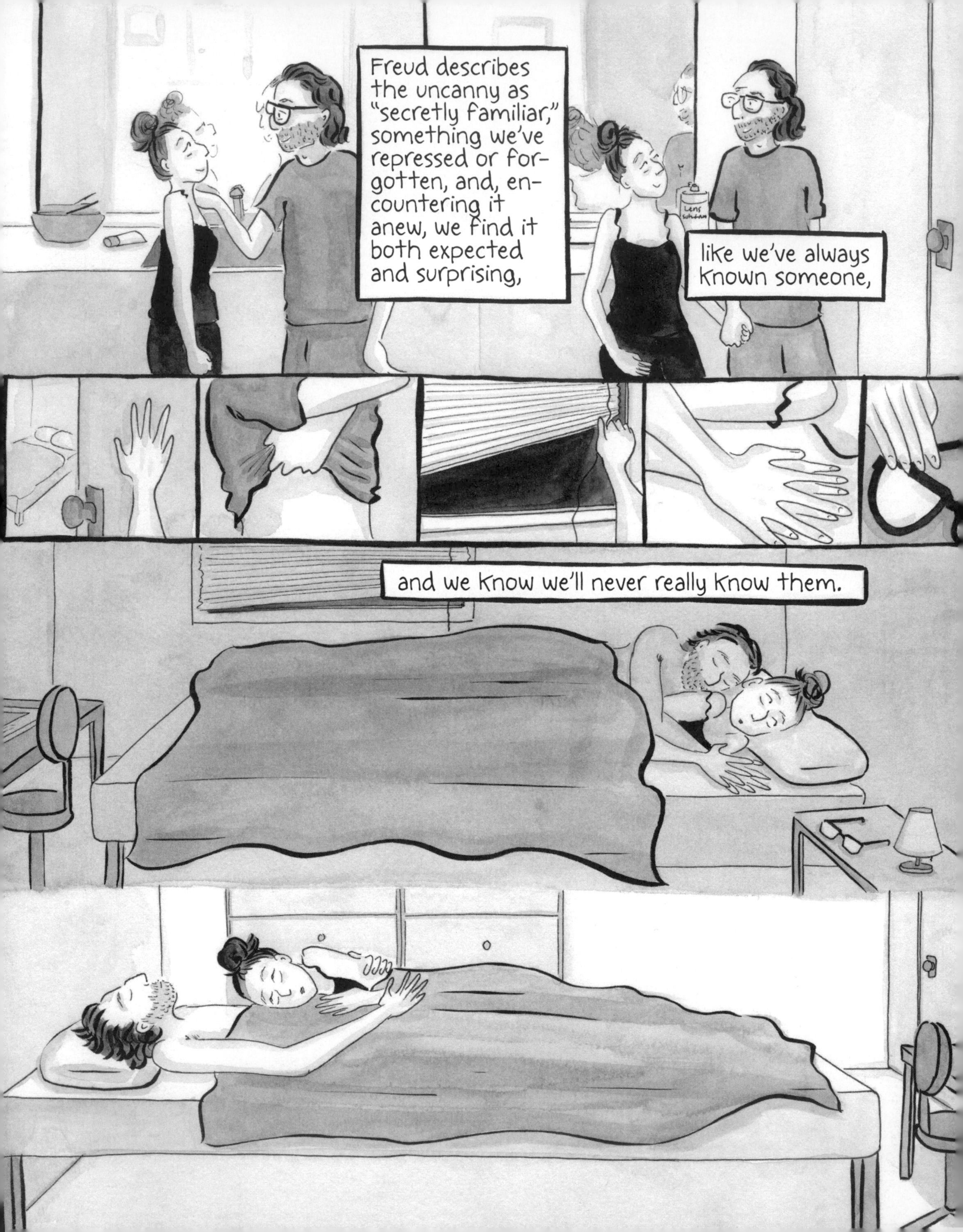
Freud describes the uncanny as "secretly familiar," something we've repressed or forgotten, and, encountering it anew, we find it both expected and surprising,
like we've always known someone,
and we know we'll never really know them.

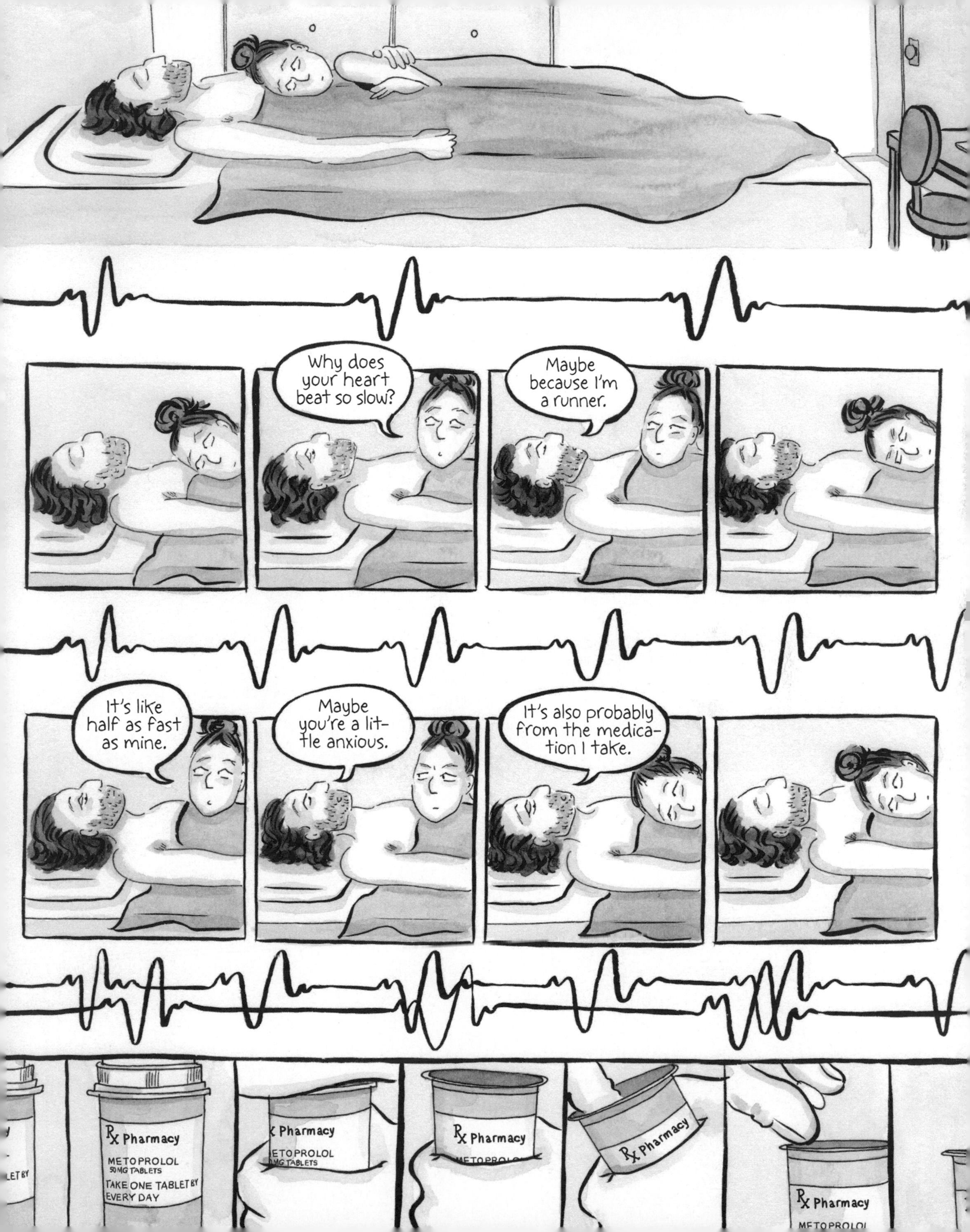
Why does your heart beat so slow?
Maybe because I'm a runner.
It's like half as fast as mine.
Maybe you're a lit-tle anxious.
It's also probably from the medica-tion I take.
Rx Pharmacy
METOPROLOL
50 MG TABLETS
TAKE ONE TABLET BY
EVERY DAY
Rx Pharmacy
Rx Pharmacy
Rx Pharmacy
Rx Pharmacy
METOPROLOL

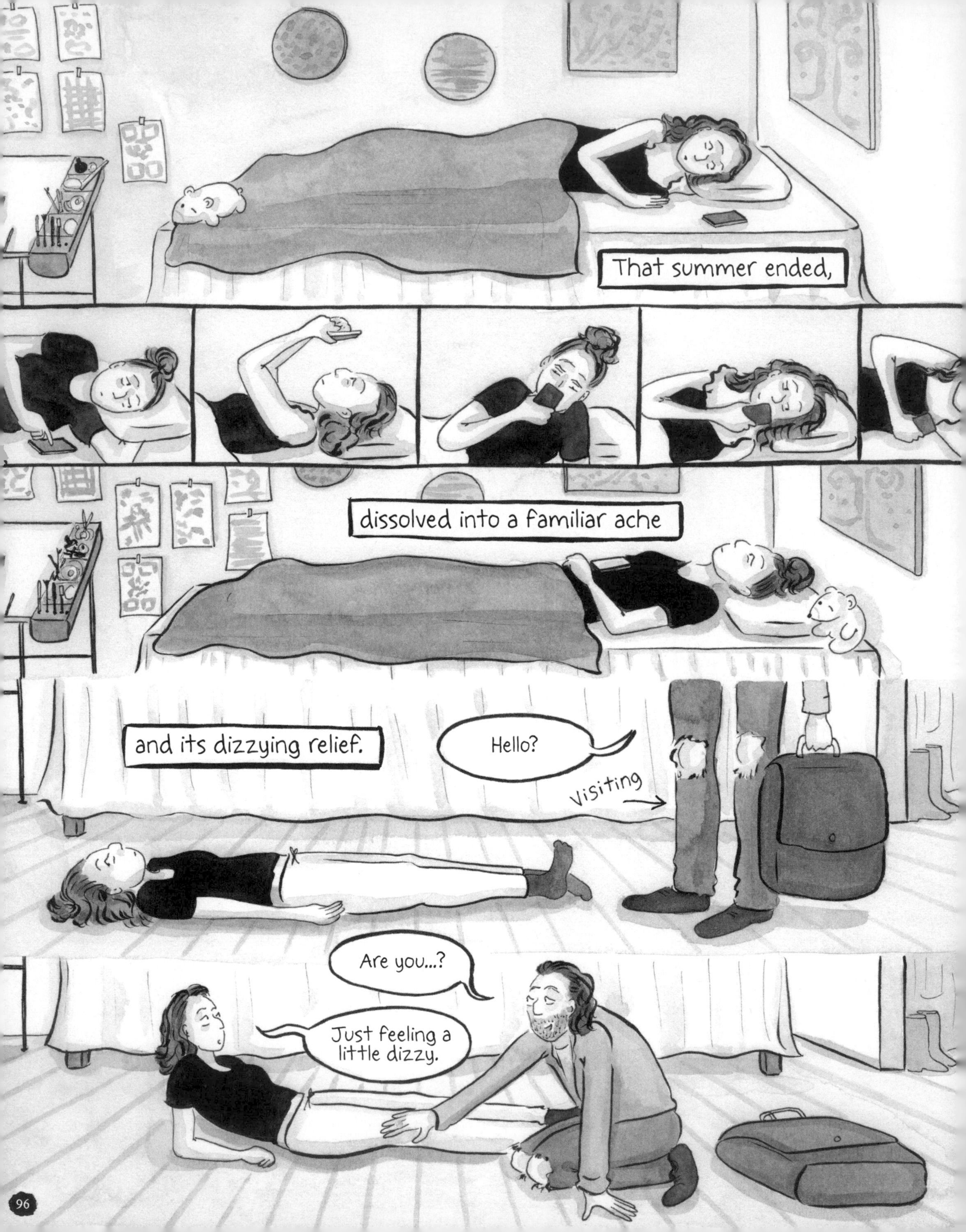

That summer ended,
dissolved into a familiar ache
and its dizzying relief.
Hello?
Visiting
Are you...?
Just feeling a little dizzy.

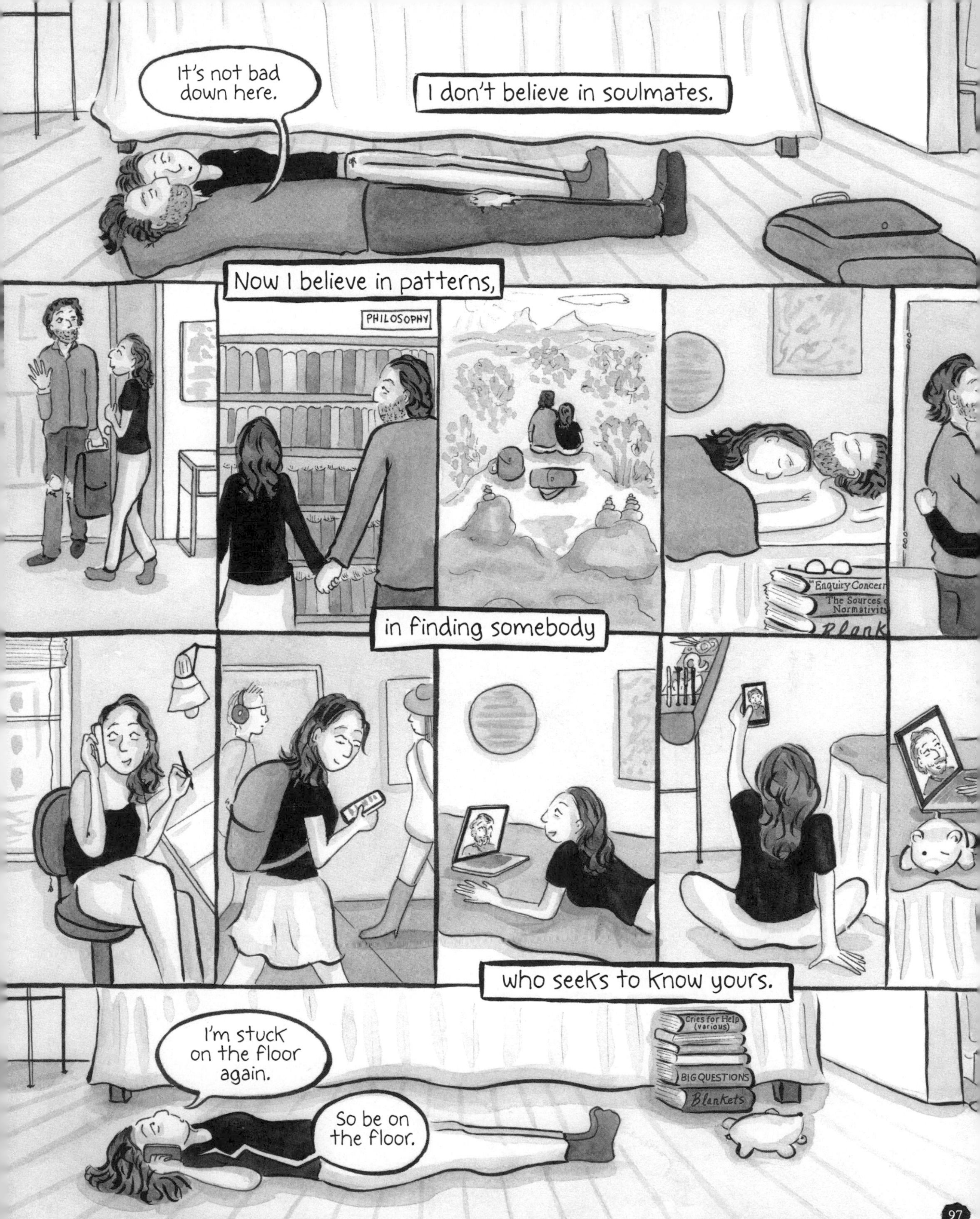
It's not bad down here.
I don't believe in soulmates.
Now I believe in patterns,
PHILOSOPHY
"Enquiry Concern
The Sources o Normativity
in finding somebody
who seeks to know yours.
I'm stuck on the floor again.
Cries for Help (various)
BIG QUESTIONS
Blankets
So be on the floor.

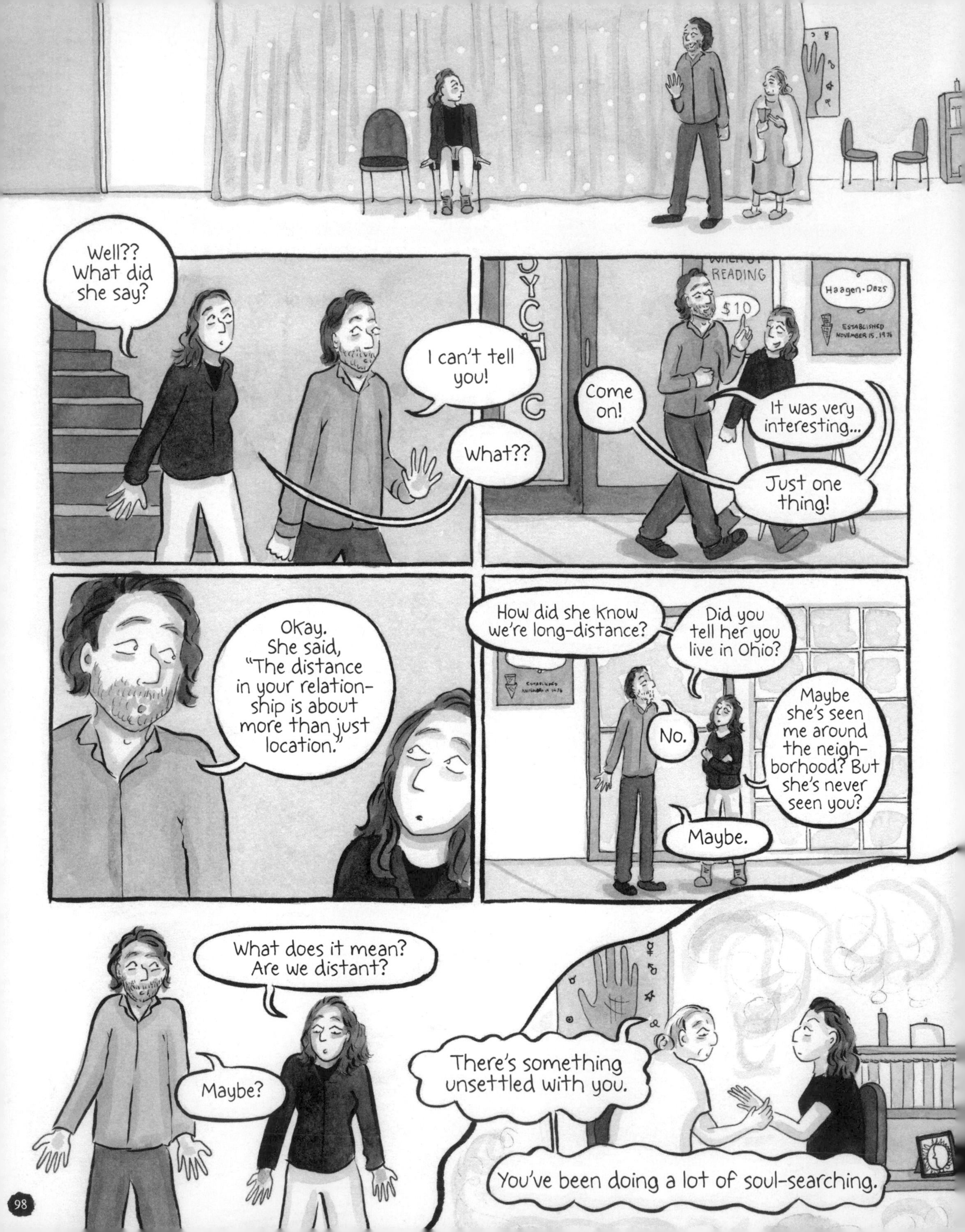
Well?? What did she say?
I can't tell you!
What??
READING
$10
Haagen-Dazs
ESTABLISHED NOVEMBER 15, 1976
Come on!
It was very interesting...
Just one thing!
Okay. She said, "The distance in your relationship is about more than just location."
How did she know we're long-distance?
Did you tell her you live in Ohio?
No.
Maybe she's seen me around the neighborhood? But she's never seen you?
Maybe.
What does it mean? Are we distant?
Maybe?
There's something unsettled with you.
You've been doing a lot of soul-searching.

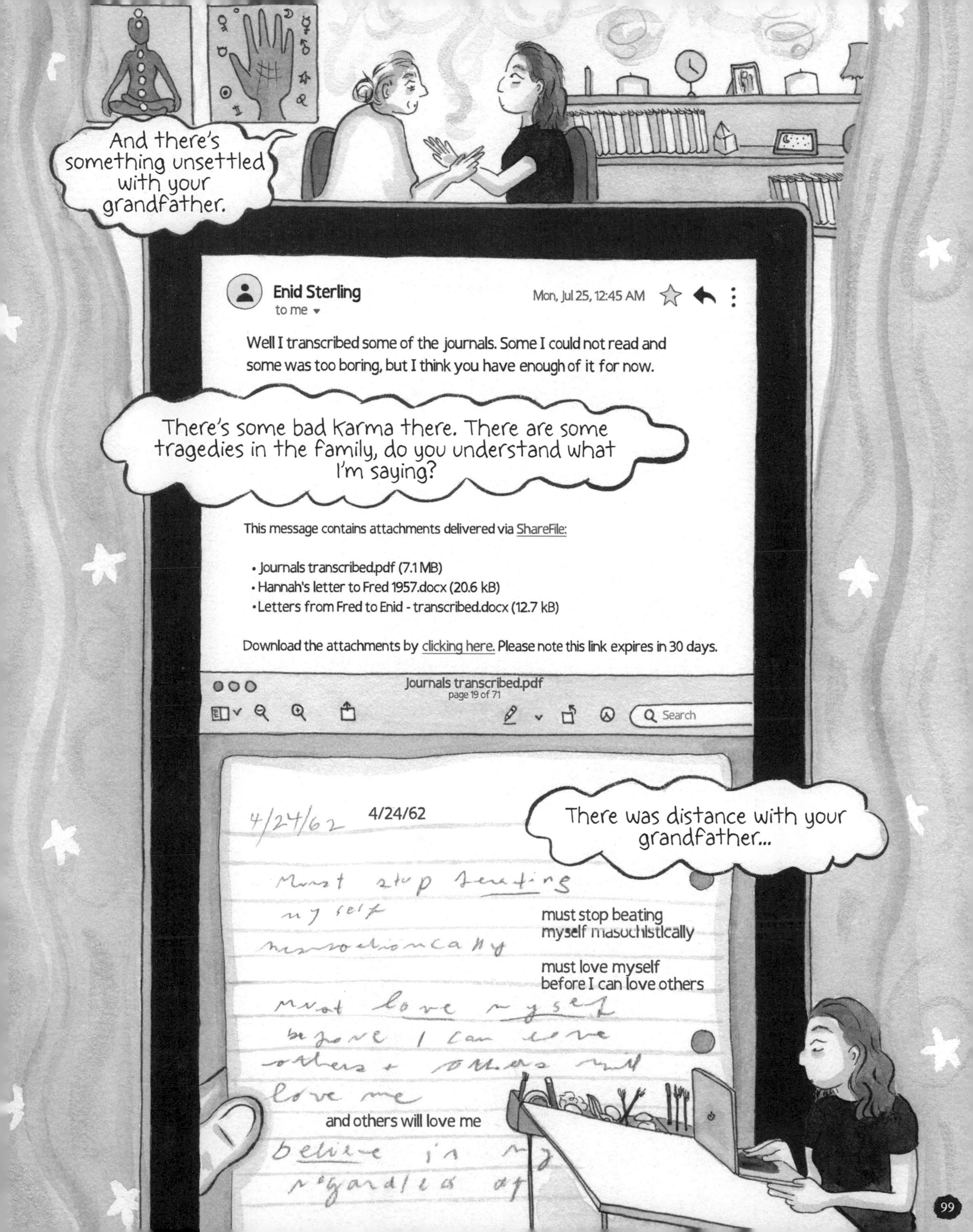

And there's something unsettled with your grandfather.
Enid Sterling
to me
Mon, Jul 25, 12:45 AM
Well I transcribed some of the journals. Some I could not read and some was too boring, but I think you have enough of it for now.
There's some bad karma there. There are some tragedies in the family, do you understand what I'm saying?
This message contains attachments delivered via ShareFile:
• Journals transcribed.pdf (7.1 MB)
• Hannah's letter to Fred 1957.docx (20.6 kB)
• Letters from Fred to Enid - transcribed.docx (12.7 kB)
Download the attachments by clicking here. Please note this link expires in 30 days.
Journals transcribed.pdf
page 19 of 71
Search
4/24/62
4/24/62
There was distance with your grandfather...
must stop beating myself masochistically
must love myself before I can love others
and others will love me

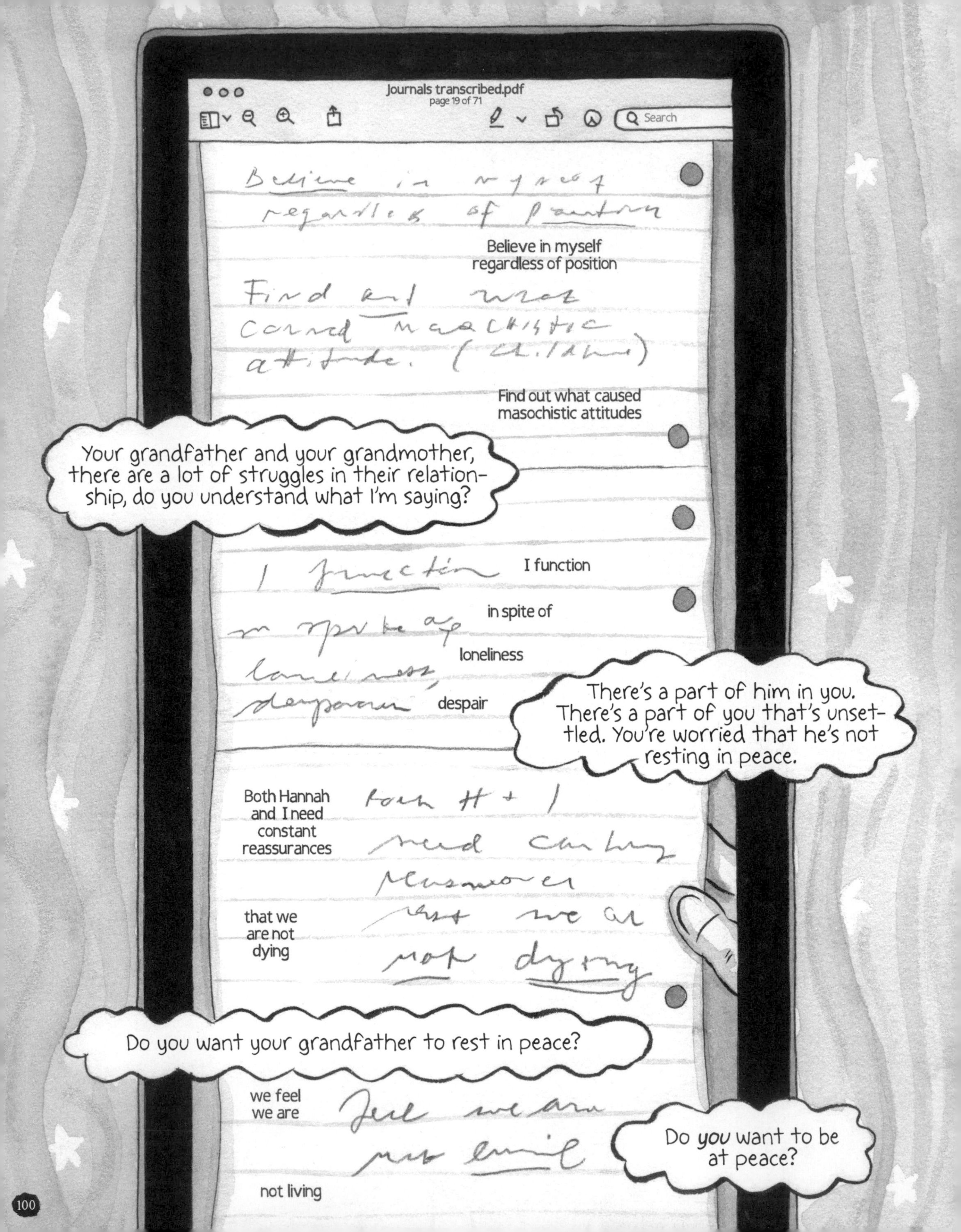

Journals transcribed.pdf
page 19 of 71
Search
Believe in myself regardless of position
Find out what caused masochistic attitudes
Your grandfather and your grandmother, there are a lot of struggles in their relationship, do you understand what I'm saying?
I function
in spite of
loneliness
despair
There's a part of him in you. There's a part of you that's unsettled. You're worried that he's not resting in peace.
Both Hannah and I need constant reassurances
that we are not dying
Do you want your grandfather to rest in peace?
we feel we are
not living
Do *you* want to be at peace?

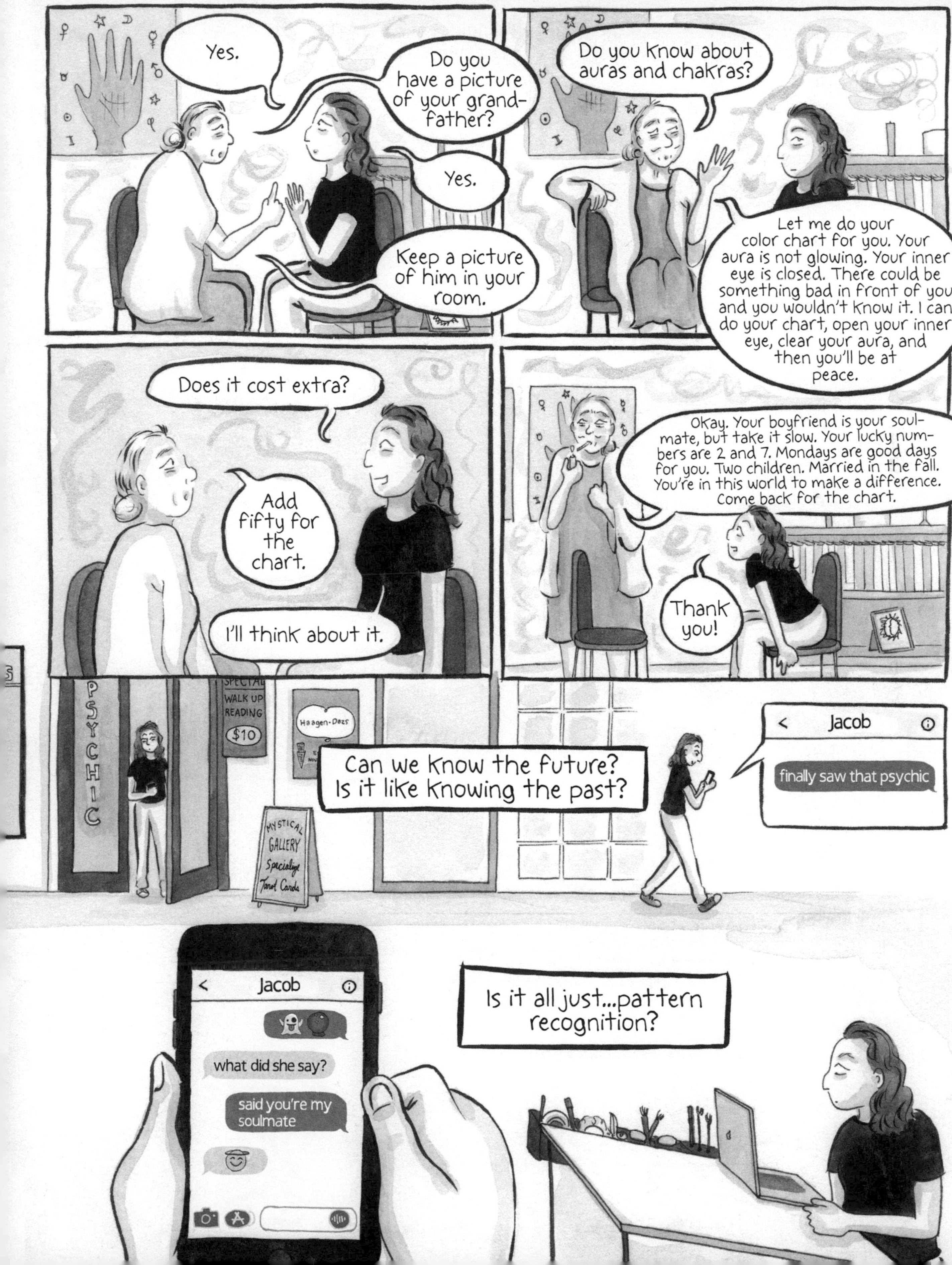

Yes.
Do you have a picture of your grand-father?
Yes.
Keep a picture of him in your room.
Do you know about auras and chakras?
Let me do your color chart for you. Your aura is not glowing. Your inner eye is closed. There could be something bad in front of you and you wouldn't know it. I can do your chart, open your inner eye, clear your aura, and then you'll be at peace.
Does it cost extra?
Add fifty for the chart.
I'll think about it.
Okay. Your boyfriend is your soul-mate, but take it slow. Your lucky num-bers are 2 and 7. Mondays are good days for you. Two children. Married in the fall. You're in this world to make a difference. Come back for the chart.
Thank you!
PSYCHIC
SPECIAL WALK UP READING $10
Haagen-Dazs
MYSTICAL GALLERY Specialize Tarot Cards
Can we know the future? Is it like knowing the past?
Jacob
finally saw that psychic
Jacob
what did she say?
said you're my soulmate
Is it all just...pattern recognition?

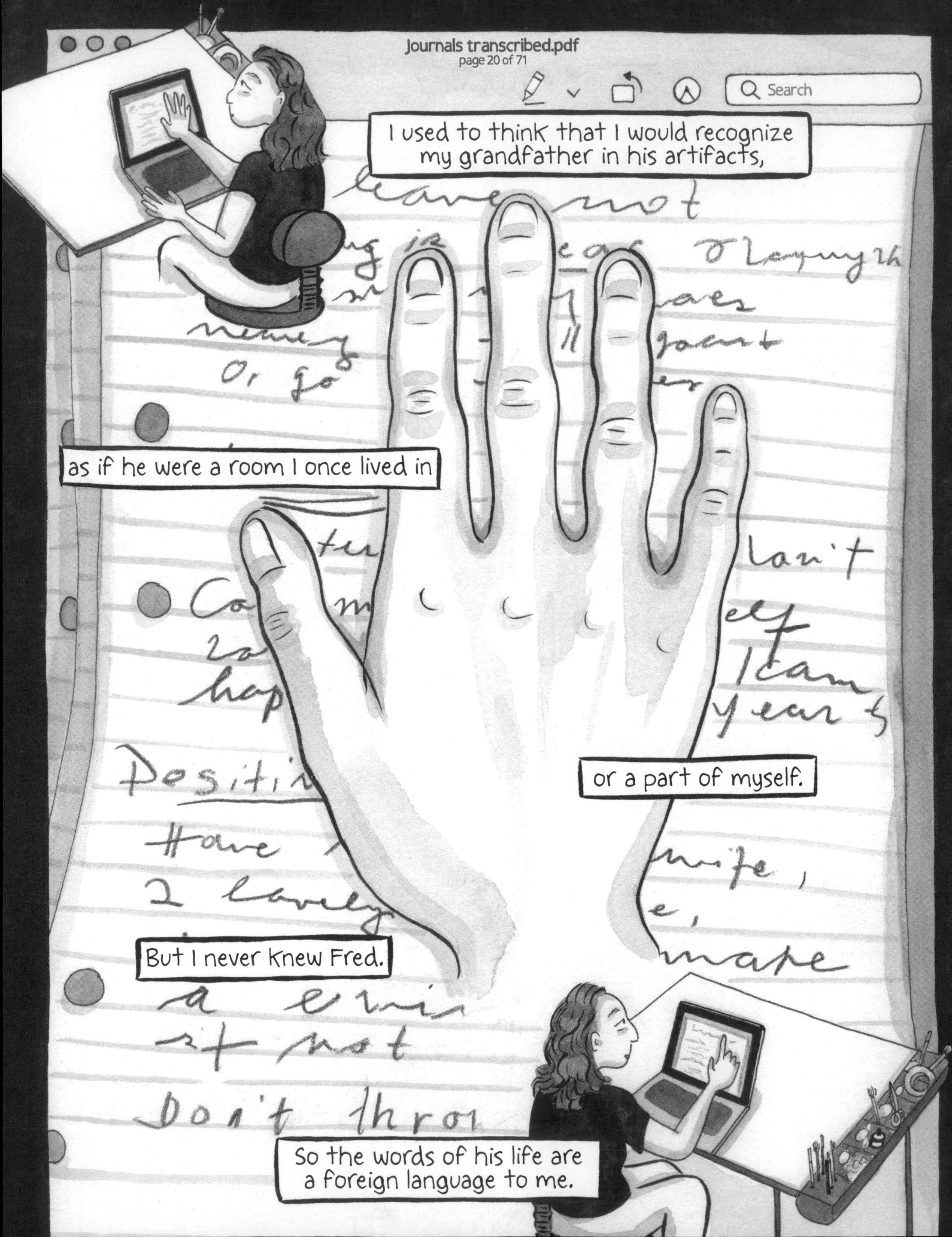
Journals transcribed.pdf
page 20 of 71
Search
I used to think that I would recognize my grandfather in his artifacts,
as if he were a room I once lived in
or a part of myself.
But I never knew Fred.
So the words of his life are a foreign language to me.

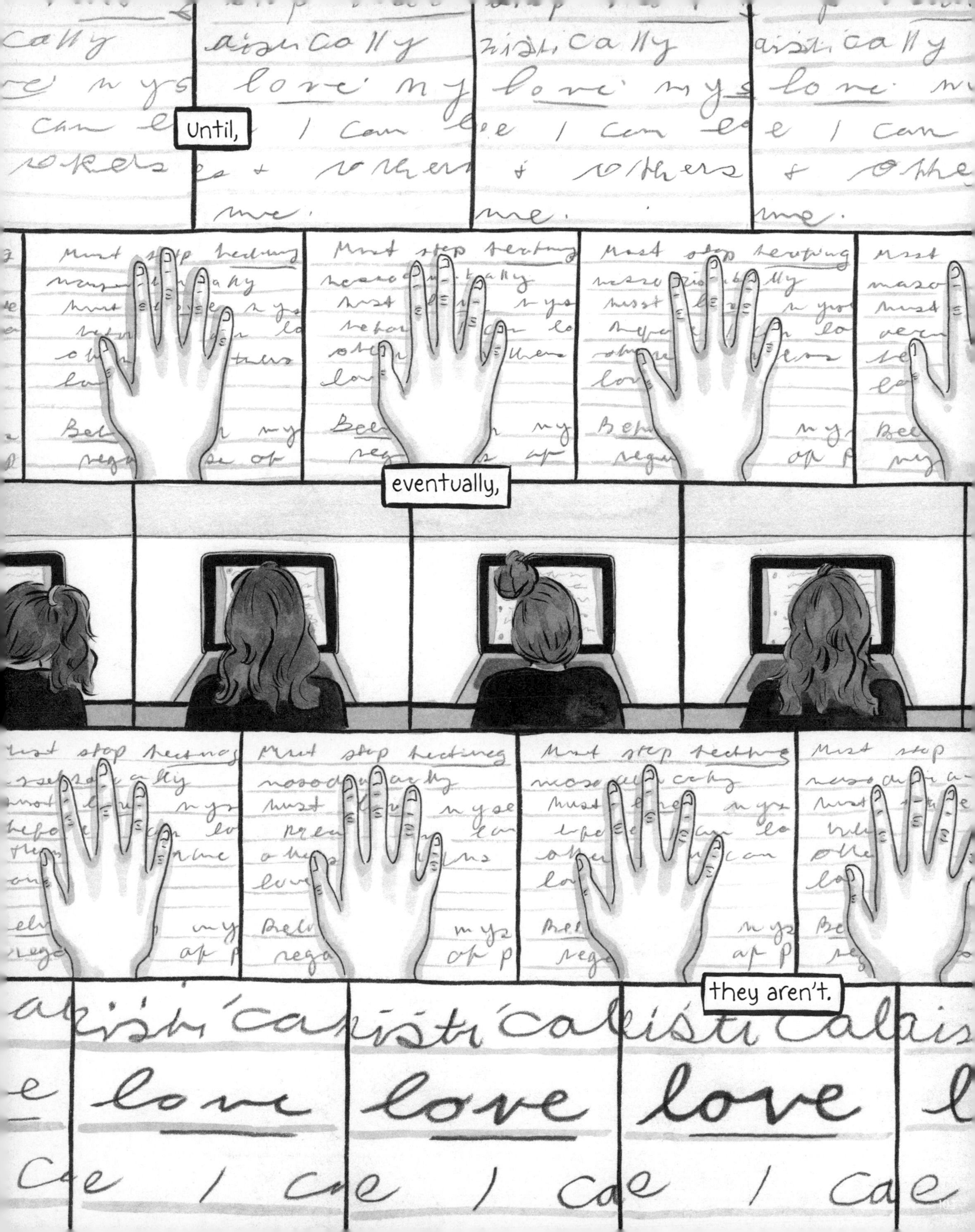
Until,
eventually,
they aren't.

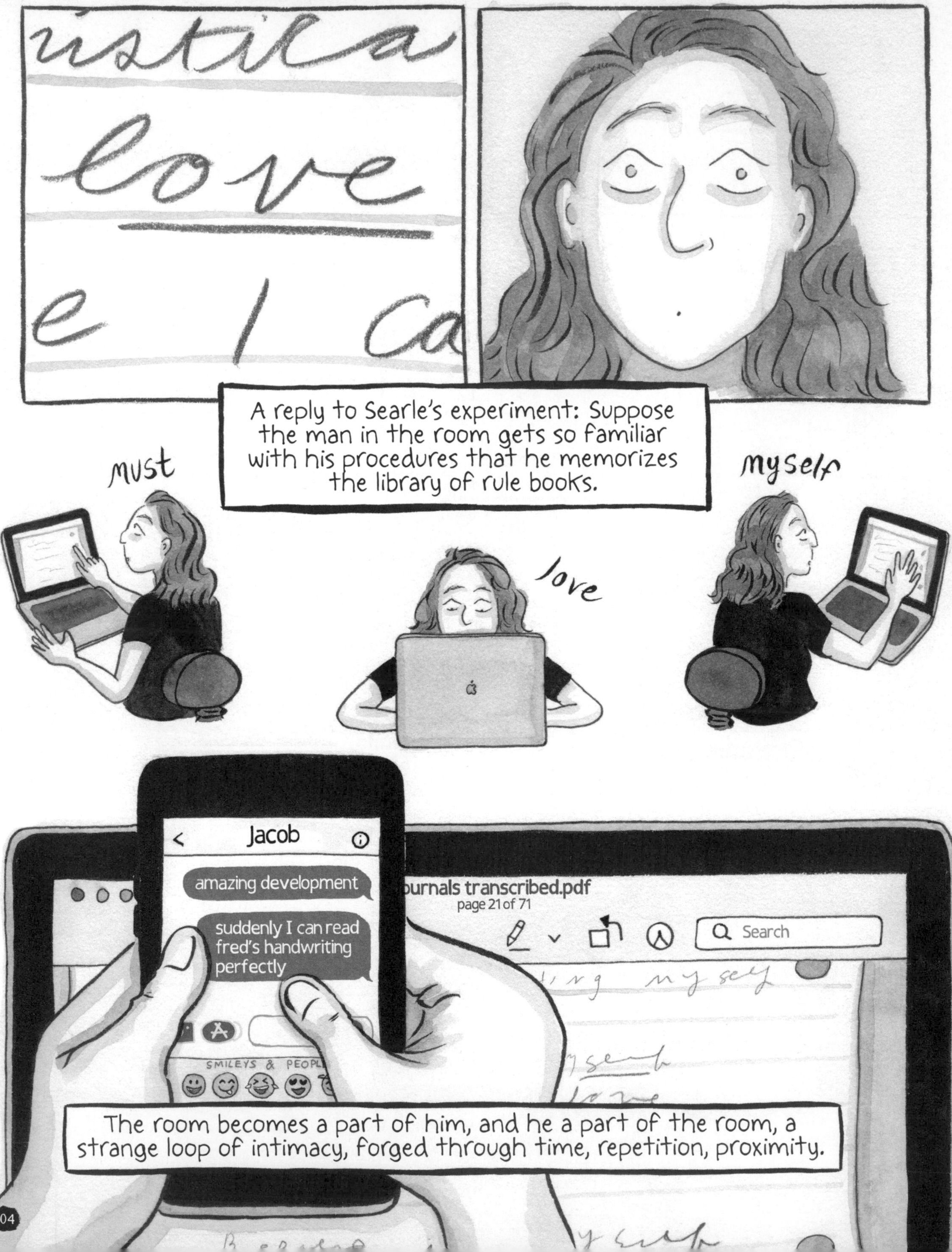
love
A reply to Searle's experiment: Suppose the man in the room gets so familiar with his procedures that he memorizes the library of rule books.
must
love
myself
Jacob
amazing development
suddenly I can read fred's handwriting perfectly
ournals transcribed.pdf
page 21 of 71
Search
The room becomes a part of him, and he a part of the room, a strange loop of intimacy, forged through time, repetition, proximity.

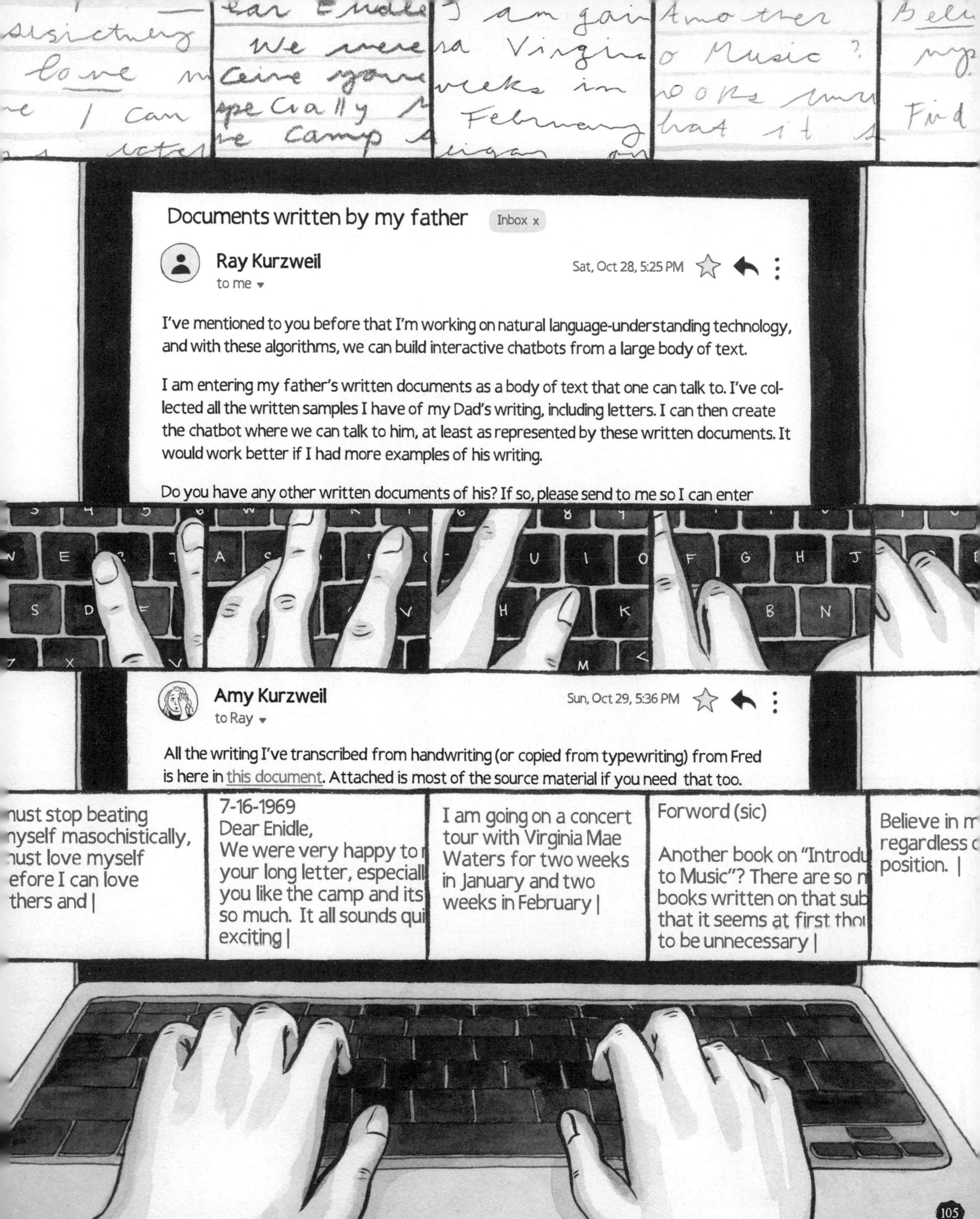

## Documents written by my father   Inbox x

**Ray Kurzweil**   Sat, Oct 28, 5:25 PM
to me ▾

I've mentioned to you before that I'm working on natural language-understanding technology, and with these algorithms, we can build interactive chatbots from a large body of text.

I am entering my father's written documents as a body of text that one can talk to. I've collected all the written samples I have of my Dad's writing, including letters. I can then create the chatbot where we can talk to him, at least as represented by these written documents. It would work better if I had more examples of his writing.

Do you have any other written documents of his? If so, please send to me so I can enter

**Amy Kurzweil**   Sun, Oct 29, 5:36 PM
to Ray ▾

All the writing I've transcribed from handwriting (or copied from typewriting) from Fred is here in this document. Attached is most of the source material if you need that too.

| | | | | |
|---|---|---|---|---|
| nust stop beating nyself masochistically, nust love myself efore I can love thers and \| | 7-16-1969<br>Dear Enidle,<br>We were very happy to r<br>your long letter, especiall<br>you like the camp and its<br>so much. It all sounds qui<br>exciting \| | I am going on a concert tour with Virginia Mae Waters for two weeks in January and two weeks in February \| | Forword (sic)<br><br>Another book on "Introdu<br>to Music"? There are so n<br>books written on that sub<br>that it seems at first thou<br>to be unnecessary \| | Believe in m<br>regardless c<br>position. \| |

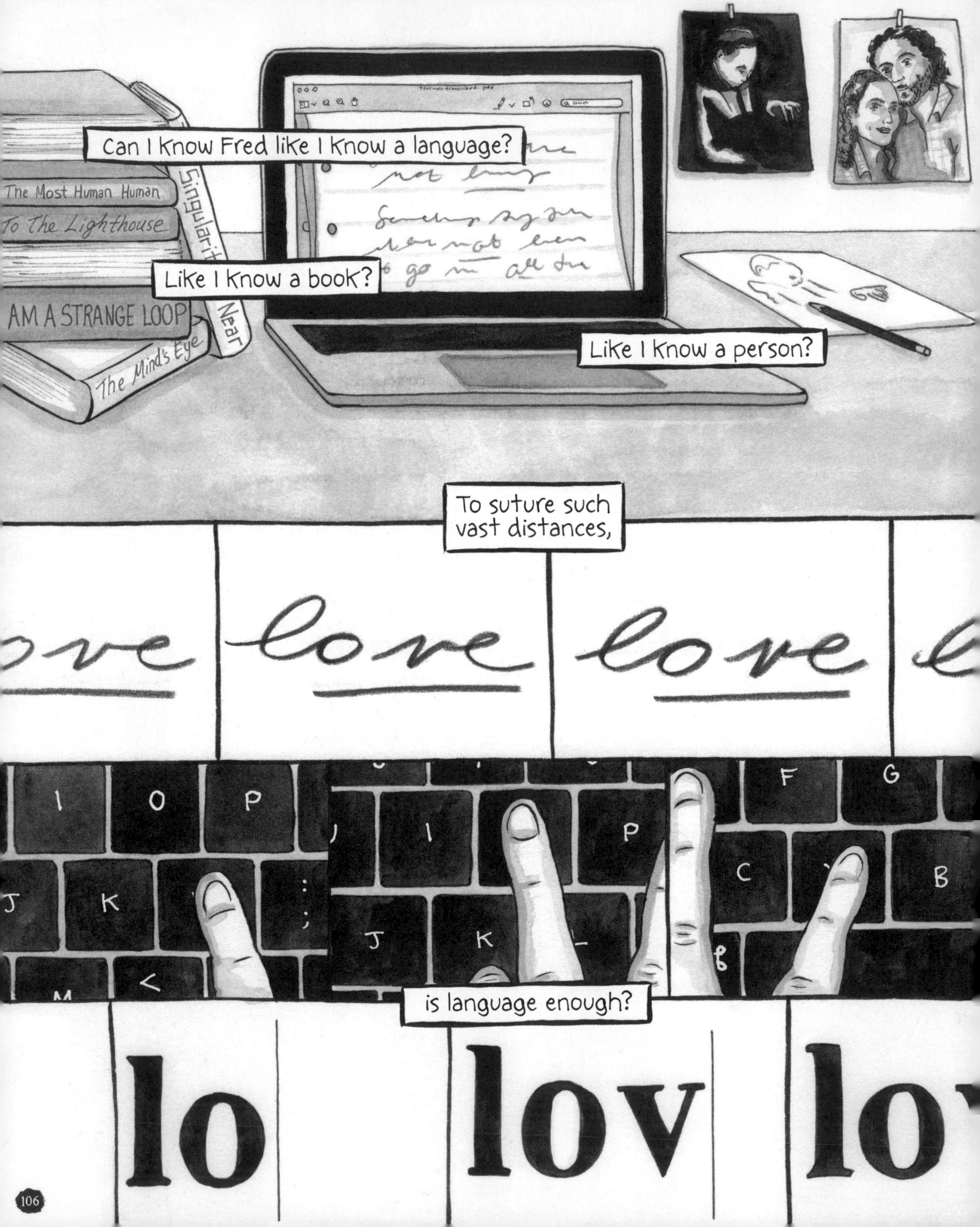
Can I know Fred like I know a language?
The Most Human Human
To The Lighthouse
AM A STRANGE LOOP
The Mind's Eye
Near
Like I know a book?
Like I know a person?
To suture such vast distances,
love
love
is language enough?
lo
lov

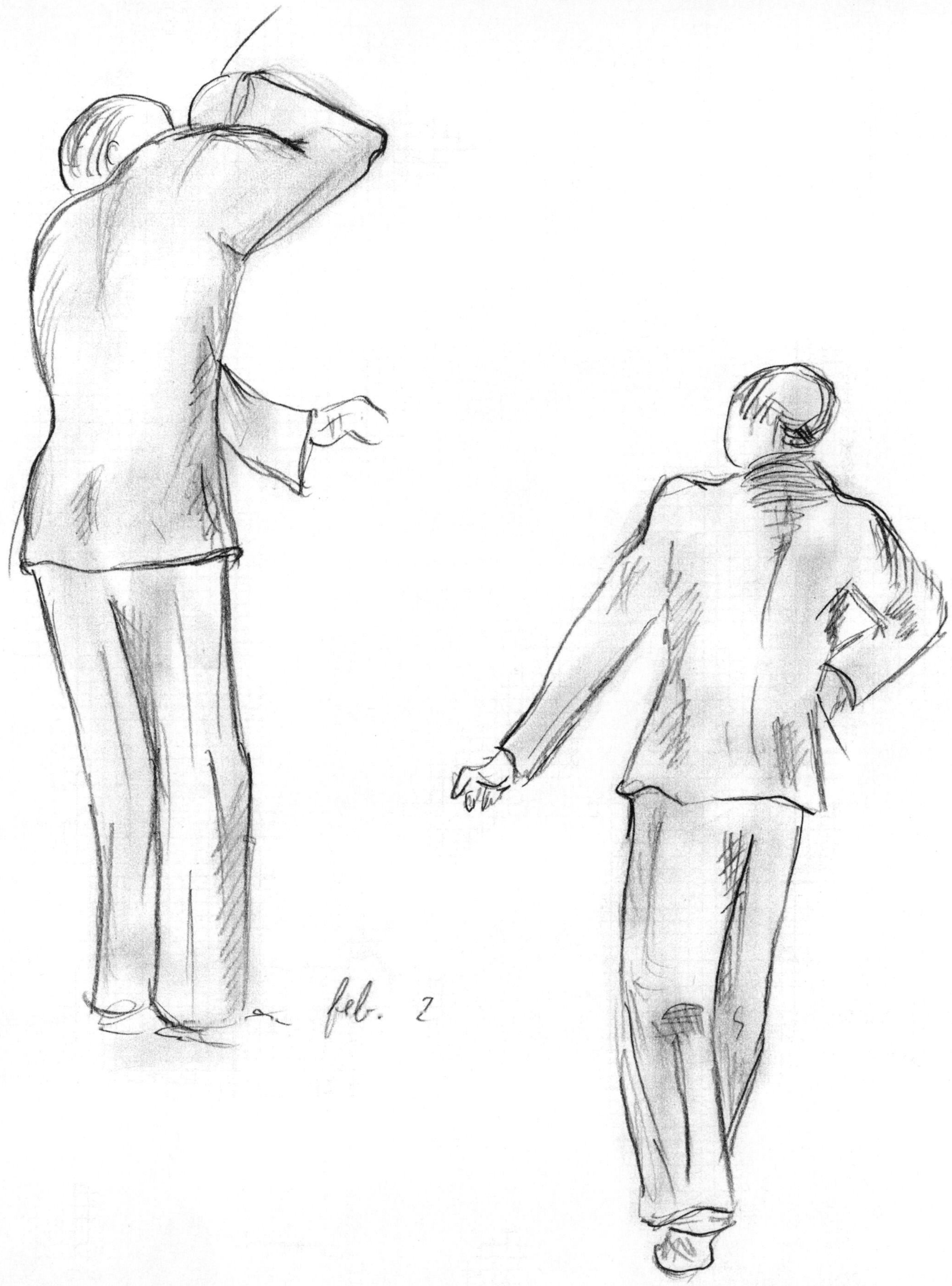
feb. 2

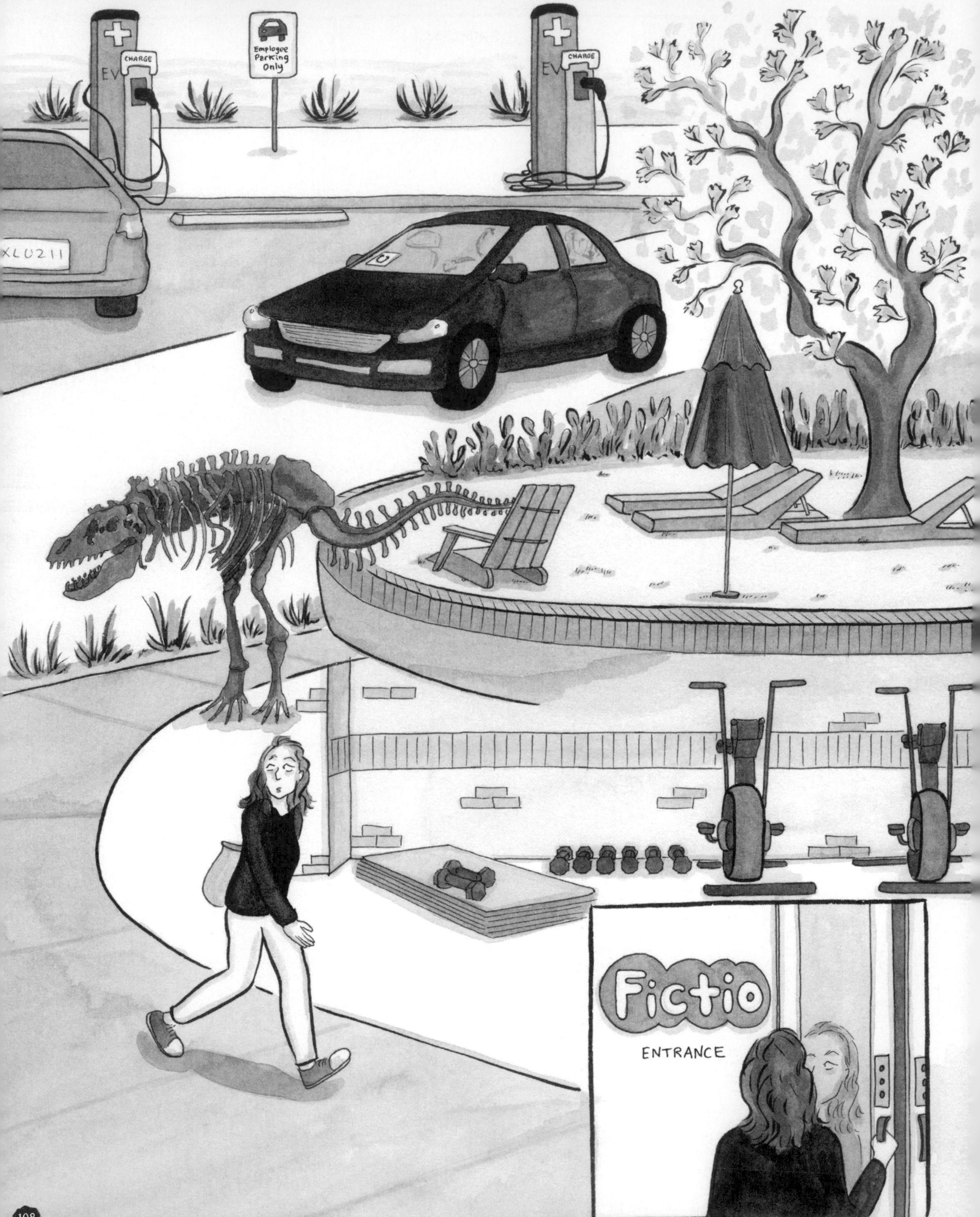
CHARGE
EV
Employee Parking Only
CHARGE
EV
XLU211
Fictio
ENTRANCE

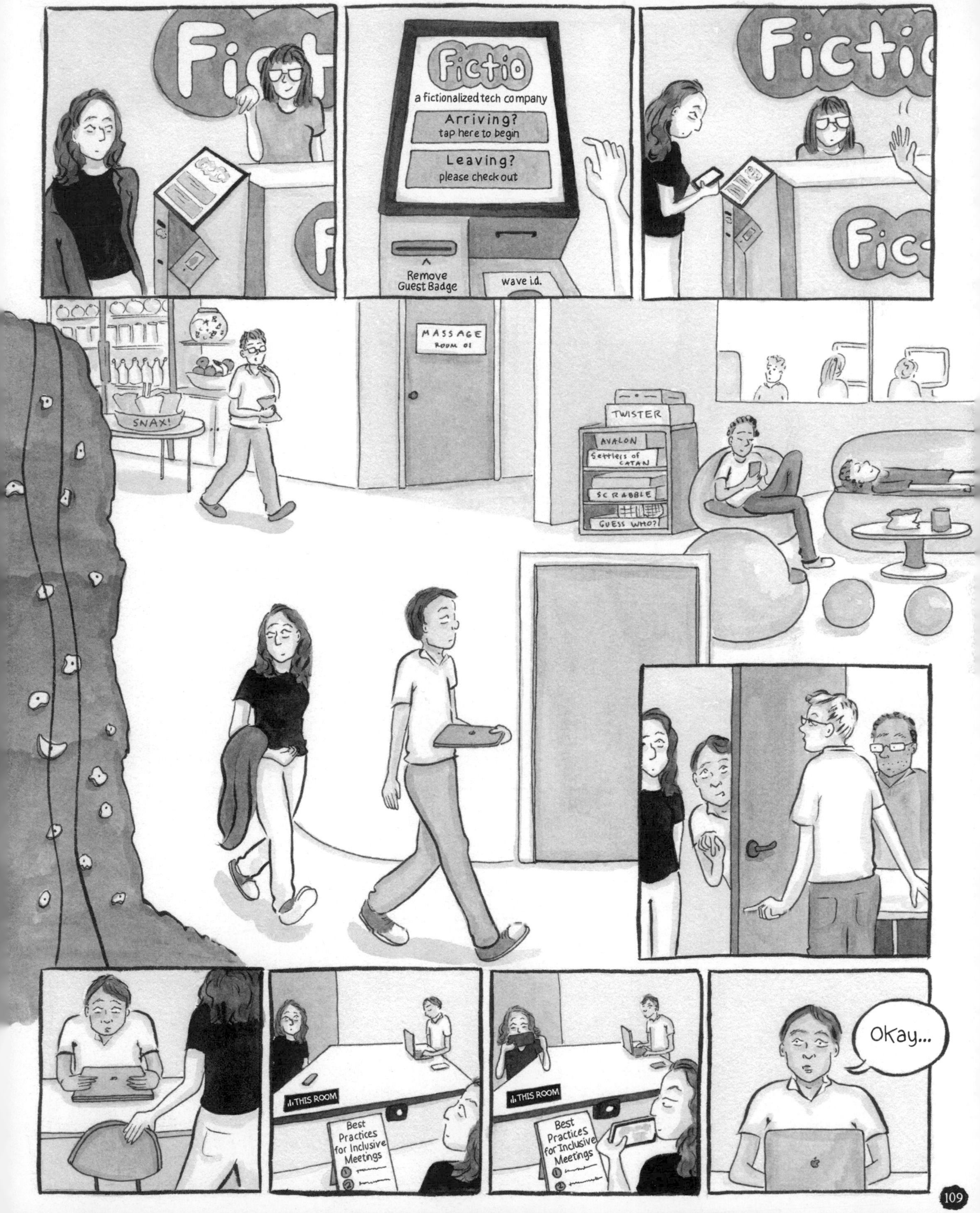
Fictio
a fictionalized tech company
Arriving?
tap here to begin
Leaving?
please check out
Remove Guest Badge
wave i.d.
MASSAGE
ROOM 01
SNAX!
TWISTER
AVALON
Settlers of CATAN
SCRABBLE
GUESS WHO?
THIS ROOM
Best Practices for Inclusive Meetings
Okay...

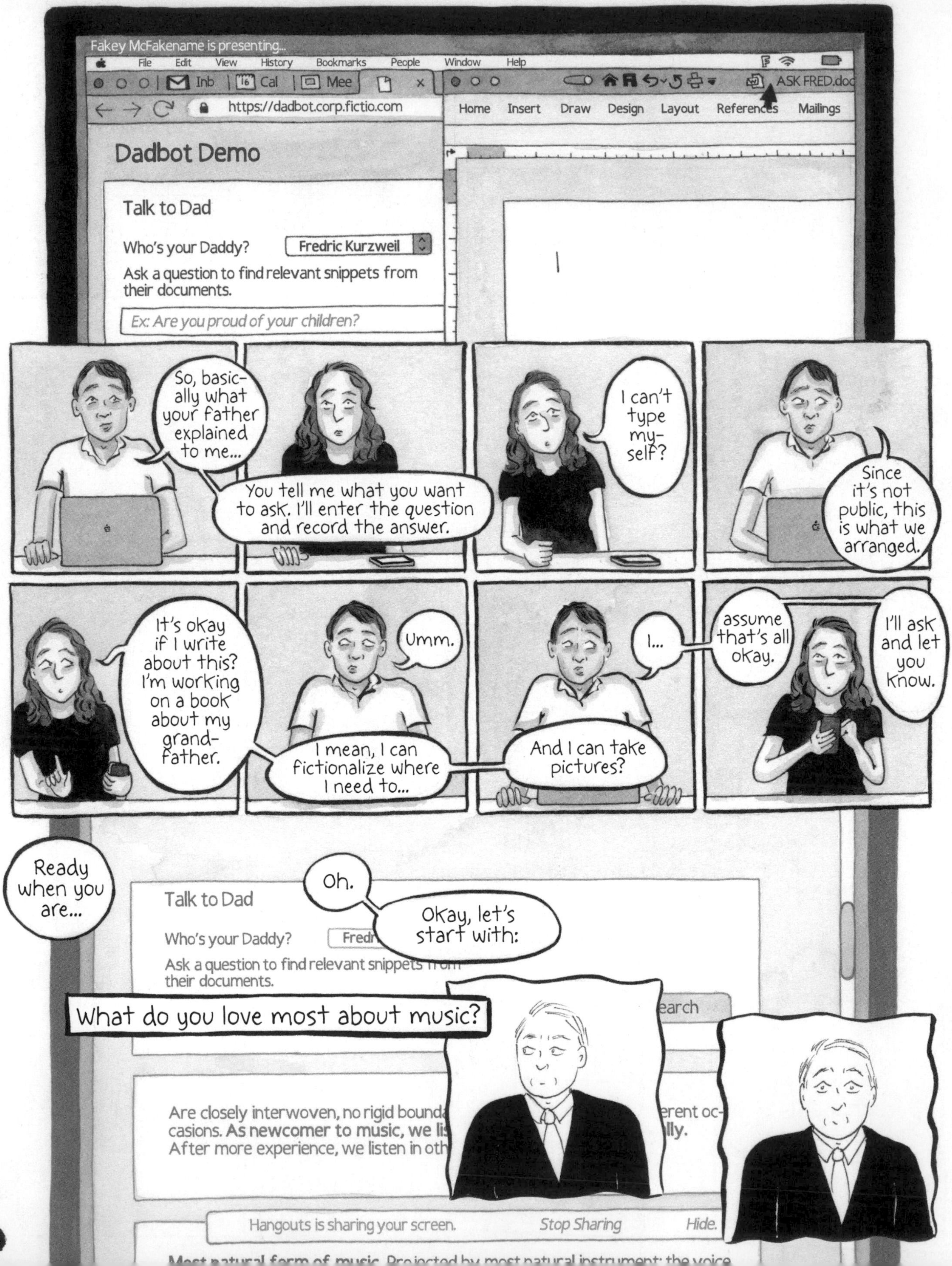
Fakey McFakename is presenting...
File
Edit
View
History
Bookmarks
People
Window
Help
Inb
Cal
Mee
https://dadbot.corp.fictio.com
Home
Insert
Draw
Design
Layout
References
Mailings
ASK FRED.doc
Dadbot Demo
Talk to Dad
Who's your Daddy?
Fredric Kurzweil
Ask a question to find relevant snippets from their documents.
Ex: Are you proud of your children?
So, basically what your father explained to me...
You tell me what you want to ask. I'll enter the question and record the answer.
I can't type myself?
Since it's not public, this is what we arranged.
It's okay if I write about this? I'm working on a book about my grandfather.
Umm.
I mean, I can fictionalize where I need to...
I...
And I can take pictures?
assume that's all okay.
I'll ask and let you know.
Ready when you are...
Talk to Dad
Oh.
Okay, let's start with:
Who's your Daddy?
Ask a question to find relevant snippets from their documents.
What do you love most about music?
Are closely interwoven, no rigid bounda
casions. As newcomer to music, we lis
After more experience, we listen in oth
Hangouts is sharing your screen.
Stop Sharing
Hide.

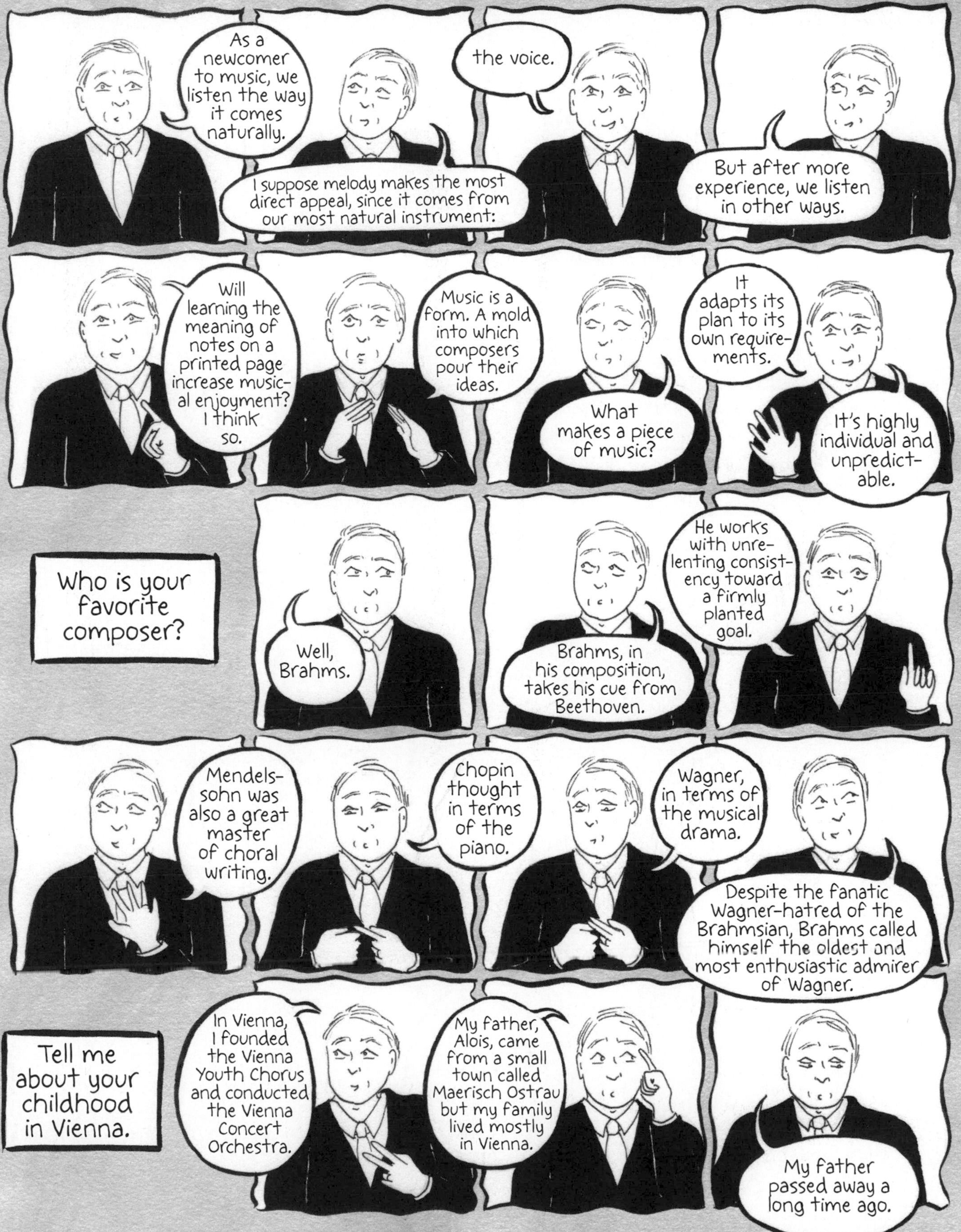
As a newcomer to music, we listen the way it comes naturally.
I suppose melody makes the most direct appeal, since it comes from our most natural instrument:
the voice.
But after more experience, we listen in other ways.
Will learning the meaning of notes on a printed page increase musical enjoyment? I think so.
Music is a form. A mold into which composers pour their ideas.
What makes a piece of music?
It adapts its plan to its own requirements.
It's highly individual and unpredictable.
Who is your favorite composer?
Well, Brahms.
Brahms, in his composition, takes his cue from Beethoven.
He works with unrelenting consistency toward a firmly planted goal.
Mendelssohn was also a great master of choral writing.
Chopin thought in terms of the piano.
Wagner, in terms of the musical drama.
Despite the fanatic Wagner-hatred of the Brahmsian, Brahms called himself the oldest and most enthusiastic admirer of Wagner.
Tell me about your childhood in Vienna.
In Vienna, I founded the Vienna Youth Chorus and conducted the Vienna Concert Orchestra.
My father, Alois, came from a small town called Maerisch Ostrau but my family lived mostly in Vienna.
My father passed away a long time ago.

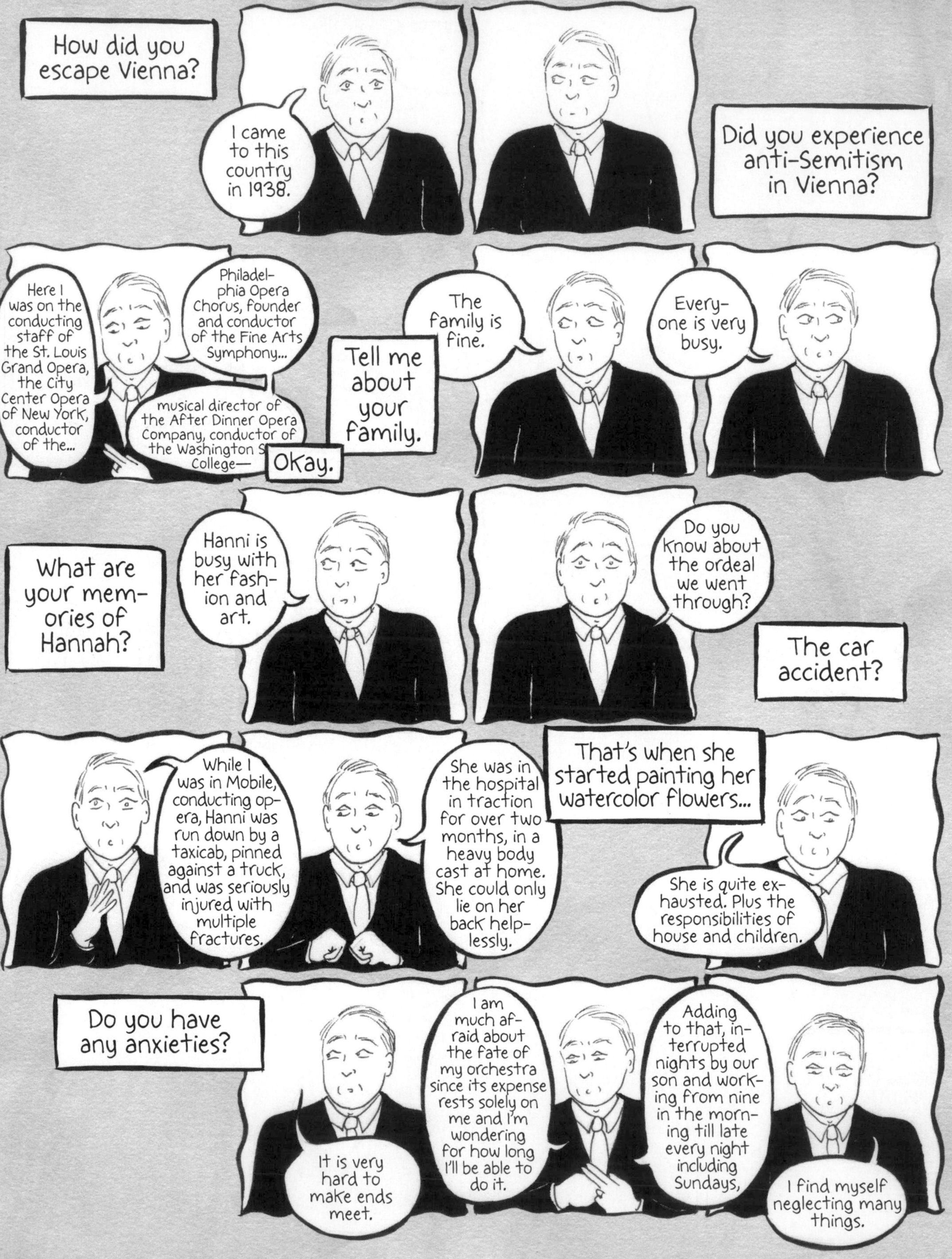
How did you escape Vienna?
I came to this country in 1938.
Did you experience anti-Semitism in Vienna?
Here I was on the conducting staff of the St. Louis Grand Opera, the City Center Opera of New York, conductor of the...
Philadelphia Opera Chorus, founder and conductor of the Fine Arts Symphony...
musical director of the After Dinner Opera Company, conductor of the Washington S College—
Okay.
Tell me about your family.
The family is fine.
Every-one is very busy.
What are your memories of Hannah?
Hanni is busy with her fashion and art.
Do you know about the ordeal we went through?
The car accident?
While I was in Mobile, conducting opera, Hanni was run down by a taxicab, pinned against a truck, and was seriously injured with multiple fractures.
She was in the hospital in traction for over two months, in a heavy body cast at home. She could only lie on her back helplessly.
That's when she started painting her watercolor flowers...
She is quite exhausted. Plus the responsibilities of house and children.
Do you have any anxieties?
It is very hard to make ends meet.
I am much afraid about the fate of my orchestra since its expense rests solely on me and I'm wondering for how long I'll be able to do it.
Adding to that, interrupted nights by our son and working from nine in the morning till late every night including Sundays,
I find myself neglecting many things.

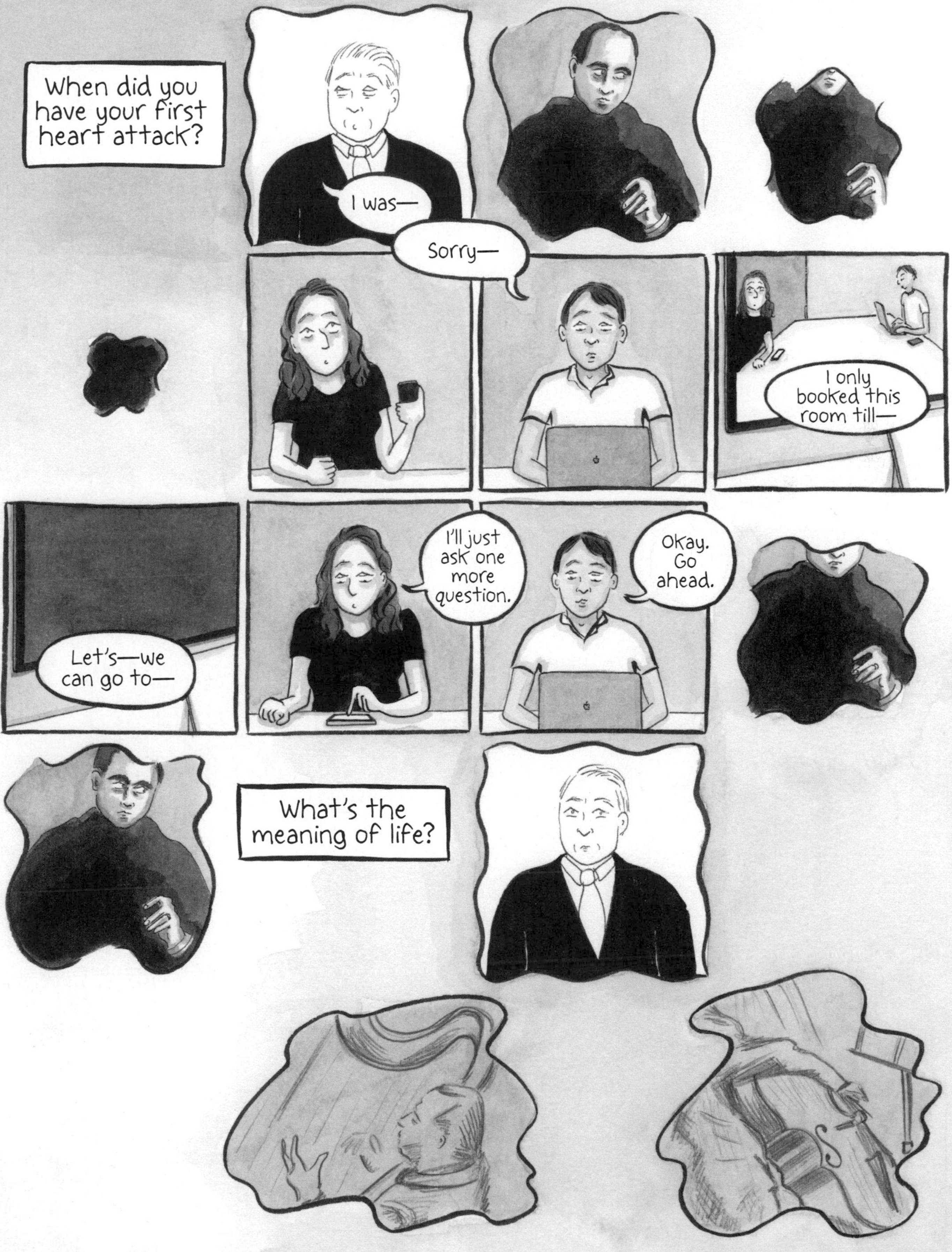
When did you have your first heart attack?
I was—
Sorry—
I only booked this room till—
Let's—we can go to—
I'll just ask one more question.
Okay. Go ahead.
What's the meaning of life?

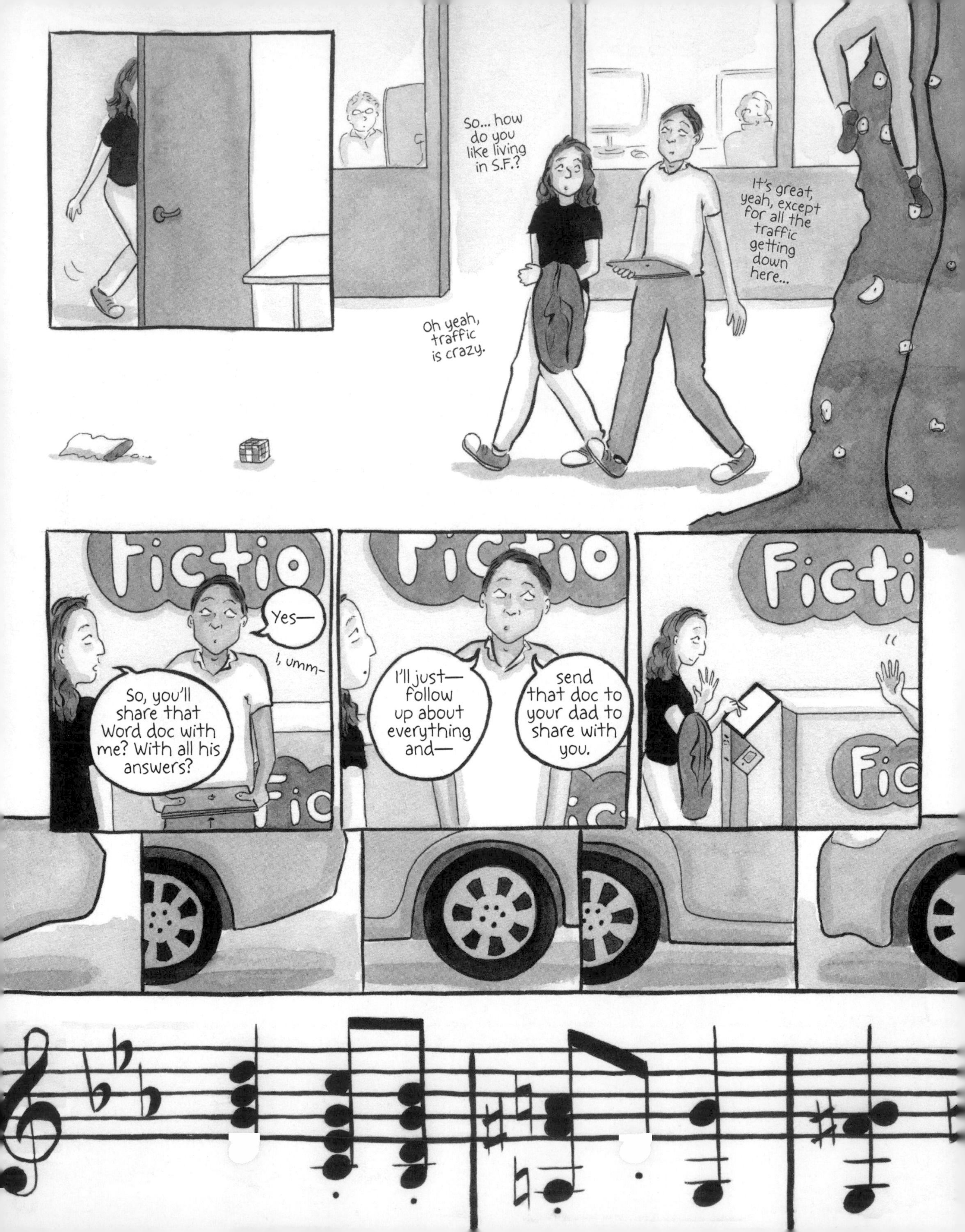
So... how do you like living in S.F.?
It's great, yeah, except for all the traffic getting down here...
Oh yeah, traffic is crazy.
Fictio
So, you'll share that Word doc with me? With all his answers?
Yes—
I, umm-
I'll just— follow up about everything and—
send that doc to your dad to share with you.
Ficti
Fic

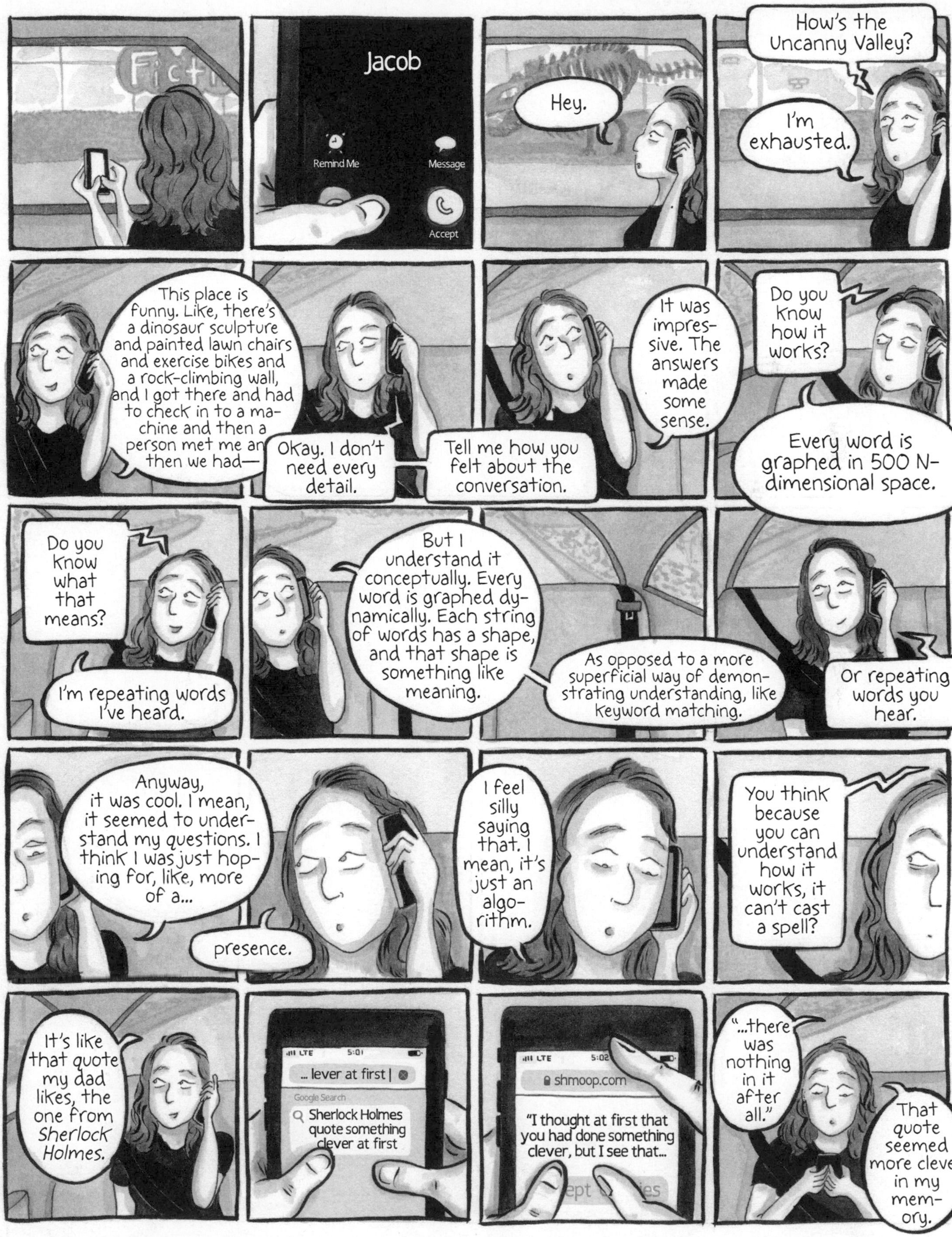
Fict
Jacob
Remind Me
Message
Accept
Hey.
How's the Uncanny Valley?
I'm exhausted.
This place is funny. Like, there's a dinosaur sculpture and painted lawn chairs and exercise bikes and a rock-climbing wall, and I got there and had to check in to a machine and then a person met me and then we had—
Okay. I don't need every detail.
Tell me how you felt about the conversation.
It was impressive. The answers made some sense.
Do you know how it works?
Every word is graphed in 500 N-dimensional space.
Do you know what that means?
I'm repeating words I've heard.
But I understand it conceptually. Every word is graphed dynamically. Each string of words has a shape, and that shape is something like meaning.
As opposed to a more superficial way of demonstrating understanding, like keyword matching.
Or repeating words you hear.
Anyway, it was cool. I mean, it seemed to understand my questions. I think I was just hoping for, like, more of a...
presence.
I feel silly saying that. I mean, it's just an algorithm.
You think because you can understand how it works, it can't cast a spell?
It's like that quote my dad likes, the one from *Sherlock Holmes*.
LTE 5:01
... lever at first |
Google Search
Sherlock Holmes quote something clever at first
LTE 5:02
shmoop.com
"I thought at first that you had done something clever, but I see that...
"...there was nothing in it after all."
That quote seemed more clever in my memory.

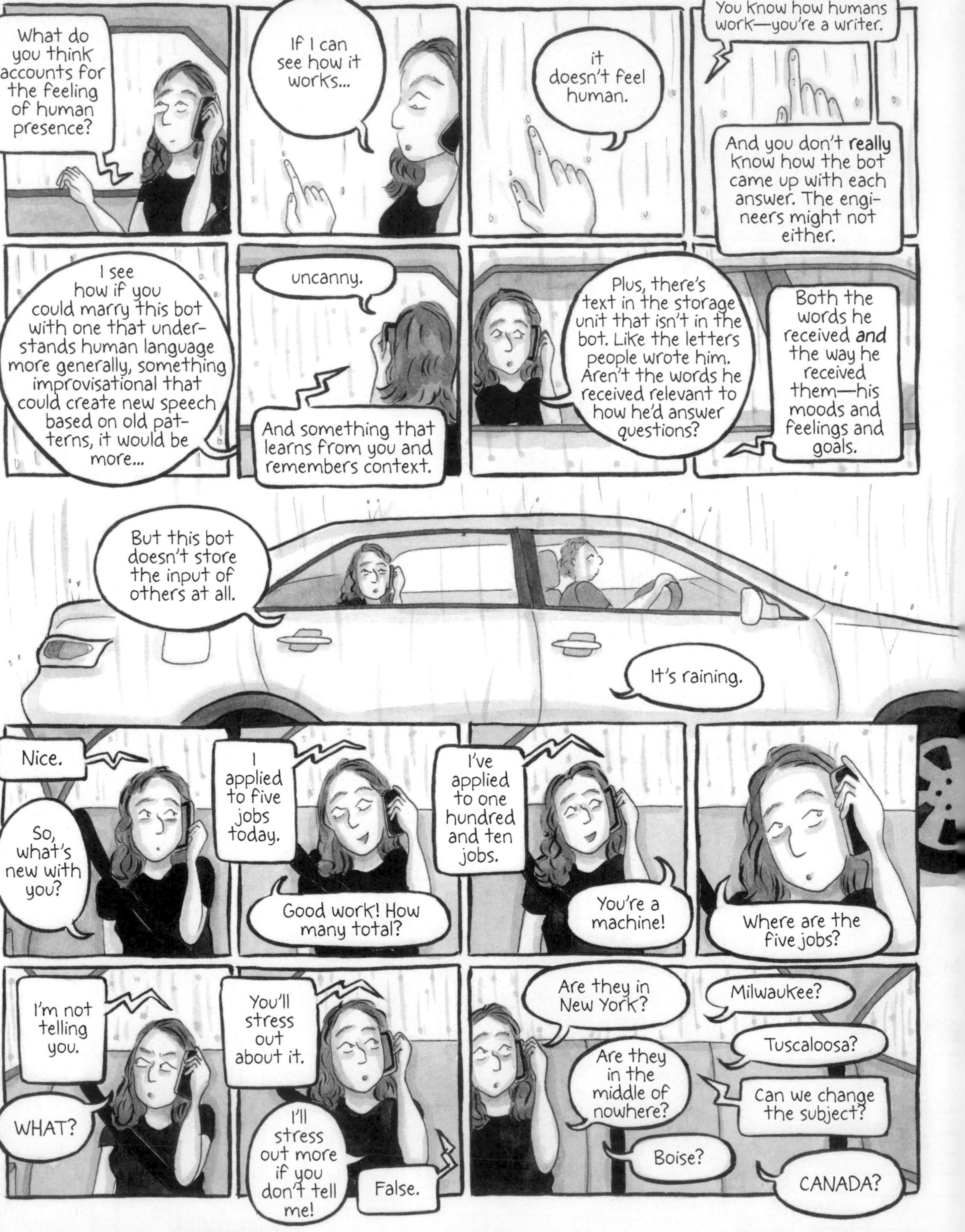
What do you think accounts for the feeling of human presence?
If I can see how it works...
it doesn't feel human.
You know how humans work—you're a writer.
And you don't **really** know how the bot came up with each answer. The engineers might not either.
I see how if you could marry this bot with one that understands human language more generally, something improvisational that could create new speech based on old patterns, it would be more...
uncanny.
And something that learns from you and remembers context.
Plus, there's text in the storage unit that isn't in the bot. Like the letters people wrote him. Aren't the words he received relevant to how he'd answer questions?
Both the words he received **and** the way he received them—his moods and feelings and goals.
But this bot doesn't store the input of others at all.
It's raining.
Nice.
So, what's new with you?
I applied to five jobs today.
Good work! How many total?
I've applied to one hundred and ten jobs.
You're a machine!
Where are the five jobs?
I'm not telling you.
WHAT?
You'll stress out about it.
I'll stress out more if you don't tell me!
False.
Are they in New York?
Milwaukee?
Tuscaloosa?
Are they in the middle of nowhere?
Can we change the subject?
Boise?
CANADA?

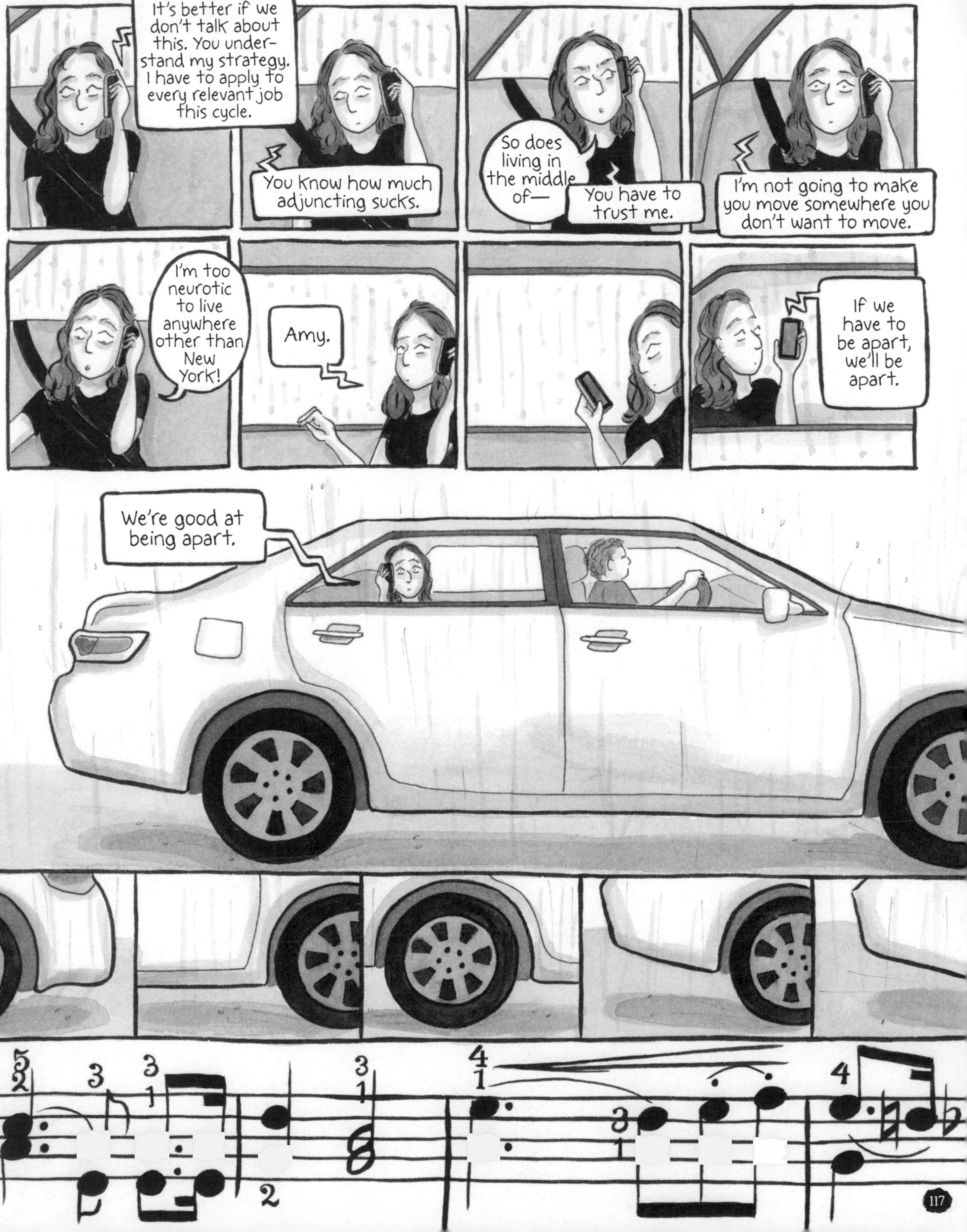
It's better if we don't talk about this. You understand my strategy. I have to apply to every relevant job this cycle.
You know how much adjuncting sucks.
So does living in the middle of—
You have to trust me.
I'm not going to make you move somewhere you don't want to move.
I'm too neurotic to live anywhere other than New York!
Amy.
If we have to be apart, we'll be apart.
We're good at being apart.

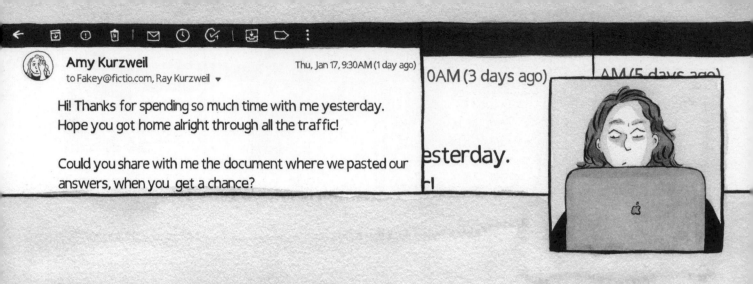

**Amy Kurzweil**
to Fakey@fictio.com, Ray Kurzweil ▾

Thu, Jan 17, 9:30AM (1 day ago)

Hi! Thanks for spending so much time with me yesterday. Hope you got home alright through all the traffic!

Could you share with me the document where we pasted our answers, when you get a chance?

0AM (3 days ago)

AM (5 days ago)

esterday.

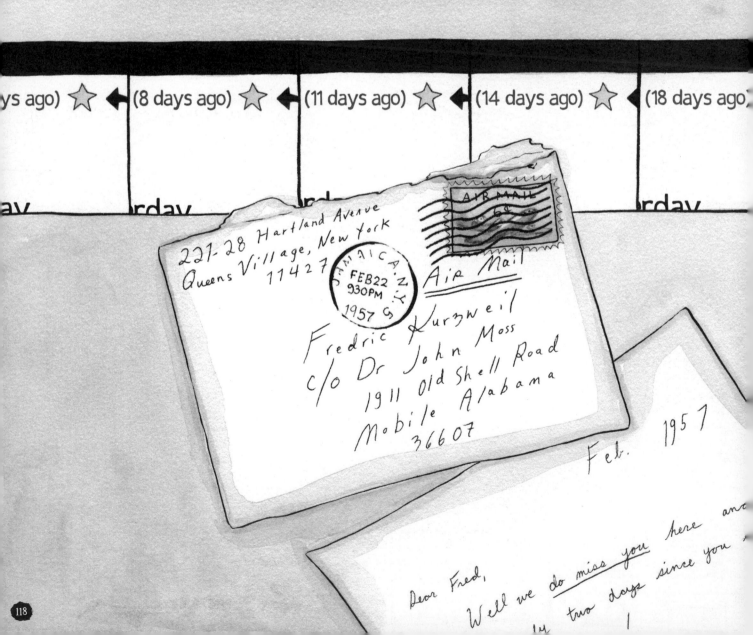

ys ago) ☆ ← (8 days ago) ☆ ← (11 days ago) ☆ ← (14 days ago) ☆ ← (18 days ago)

227-28 Hartland Avenue
Queens Village, New York
11427

JAMAICA, N.Y.
FEB 22
930PM
1957

AIR MAIL

Air Mail

Fredric Kurzweil
c/o Dr John Moss
1911 Old Shell Road
Mobile Alabama
36607

Feb. 1957

Dear Fred,
Well we do miss you here and
two days since you

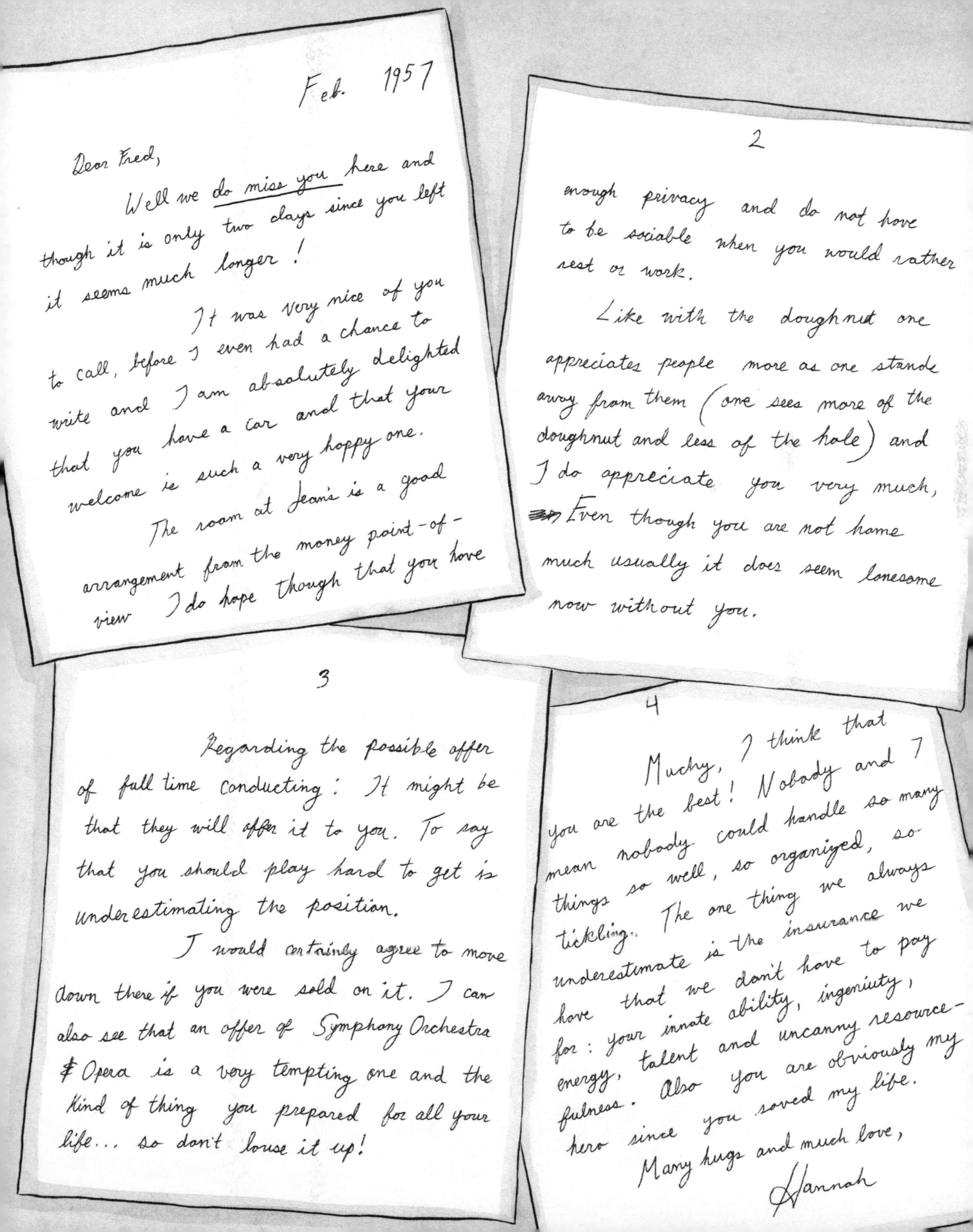

Feb. 1957

Dear Fred,

Well we do miss you here and though it is only two days since you left it seems much longer!

It was very nice of you to call, before I even had a chance to write and I am absolutely delighted that you have a car and that your welcome is such a very happy one.

The room at Jean's is a good arrangement from the money point-of-view I do hope though that your have

2

enough privacy and do not have to be sociable when you would rather rest or work.

Like with the doughnut one appreciates people more as one stands away from them (one sees more of the doughnut and less of the hole) and I do appreciate you very much,

⇛ Even though you are not home much usually it does seem lonesome now without you.

3

Regarding the possible offer of full time conducting: It might be that they will offer it to you. To say that you should play hard to get is underestimating the position.

I would certainly agree to move down there if you were sold on it. I can also see that an offer of Symphony Orchestra & Opera is a very tempting one and the kind of thing you prepared for all your life... so don't louse it up!

4

Muchy, I think that you are the best! Nobody and I mean nobody could handle so many things so well, so organized, so-tickling.. The one thing we always underestimate is the insurance we have that we don't have to pay for: your innate ability, ingenuity, energy, talent and uncanny resource-fulness. Also you are obviously my hero since you saved my life.

Many hugs and much love,

Hannah

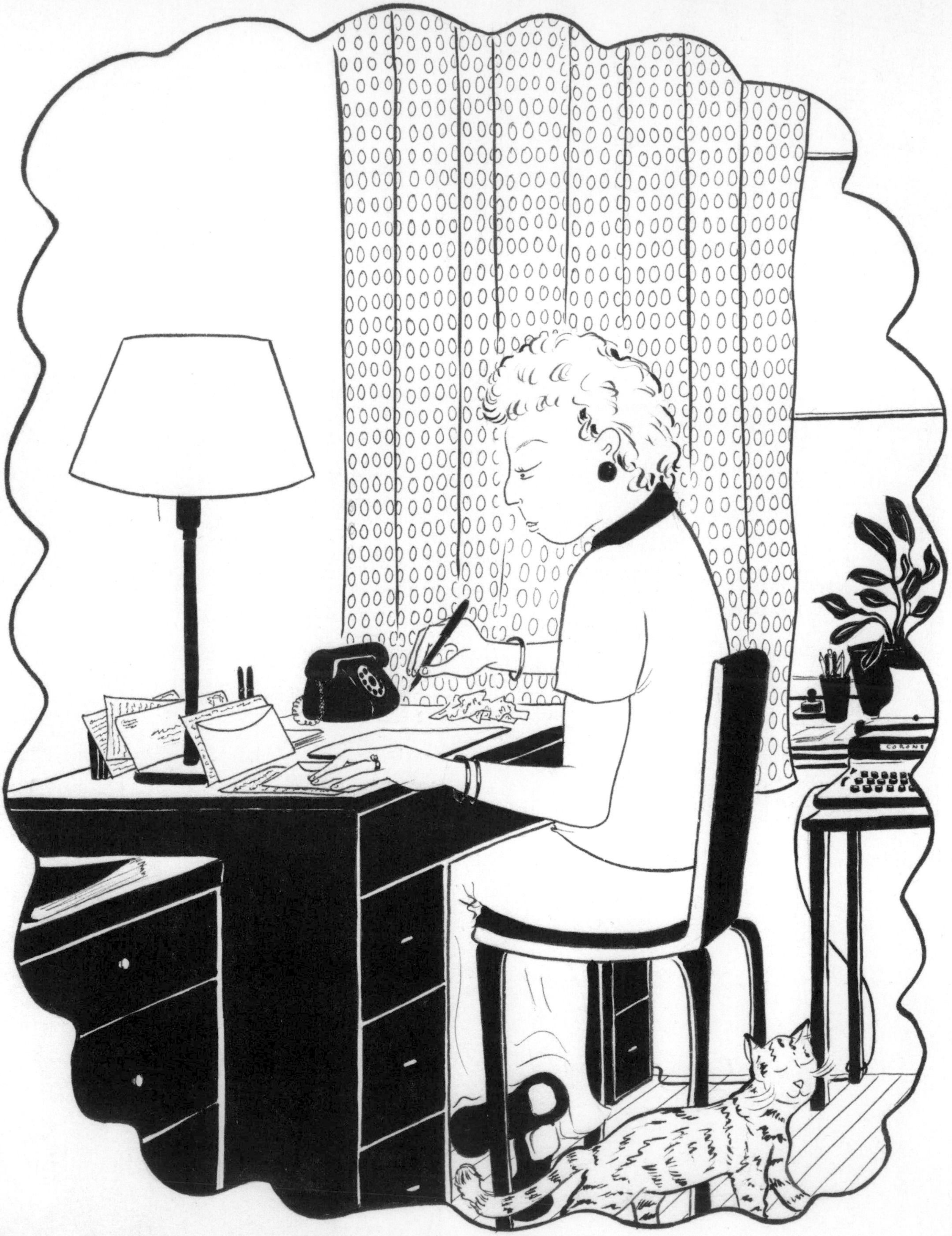

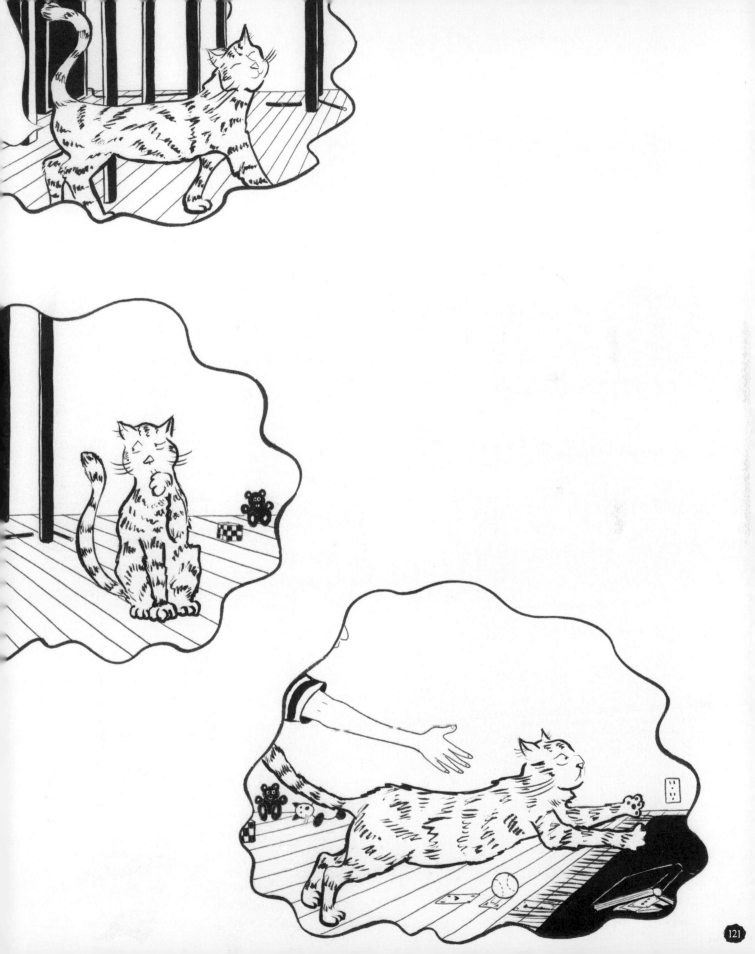

Wed feb. 1957

Dear Darling,
                    I was very happy and
excited about    your  wonderful success.
I don't doubt that this tremendous success
   is  a  thrill  and an absolute tonic.
The  credit  of all of this blongs to you, so
don't feel ~~so~~  that you have to feel so
terribly grateful.
              As far as the permanent job is concerned,
   it is  of  course  a  thrill to contemplate.
Enjoy  the satisfaction of a personal  success!!
Of course the offer has not  been  made  yet.

Even when it is I suggest that you tell them that
it sounds like  a very fine thing but  you have
tremendous  commitments here and have to give
it more thought.  Make no commitments whatever
down there!  If the Symphony people approach you,
be very relaxed, charming, ~~and~~ interested and non-
commital. Be sure to be relaxed, the man of the world, not
                                                                    nervous
              I will certainly not keep you
or advise you against it if you should
finally really decide  to want to take it.
   I am not at all sure though that you
will want  to when the chips are down.
              Quite  beside  the  obvious threats
such as impermanence, leaving N.Y. etc.

(2)

3

You must keep in mind  that  no human
or angel can keep up the enthusiasm you
have generated there.  If you live amoung
them  you can  not expect yourself to be the
"golden boy" day after day after day.

   I certainly  am  very proud of you!

              Thank you sweetheart for trying to
make it possible for me to come. The problem is
leaving  the children, especially Raymond.
              Dorit said she would take him to school
every day and pick him up. However that's
a lot of trouble  and she is pregnant,
also you know how Raymond is.

4

The children are very fine and good. Raymond
is a very good boy and very normal ( write
to him saying that Mommy told you what a
   big help he is and how relieved you are
to know that your ladies have a man to
protect them. That  you are proud of him )
              Enid is a sweetheart and I think
a whale head bigger than ~~she~~ she was
when you left.
Everything is alright otherwise. Don't be a
bad boy again and write oftener.
              By the way I got a raise 10 cents, Now
you can retire, so why worry.
              I miss you Muchy. You are a genius!
              Love and Kisses H.

122

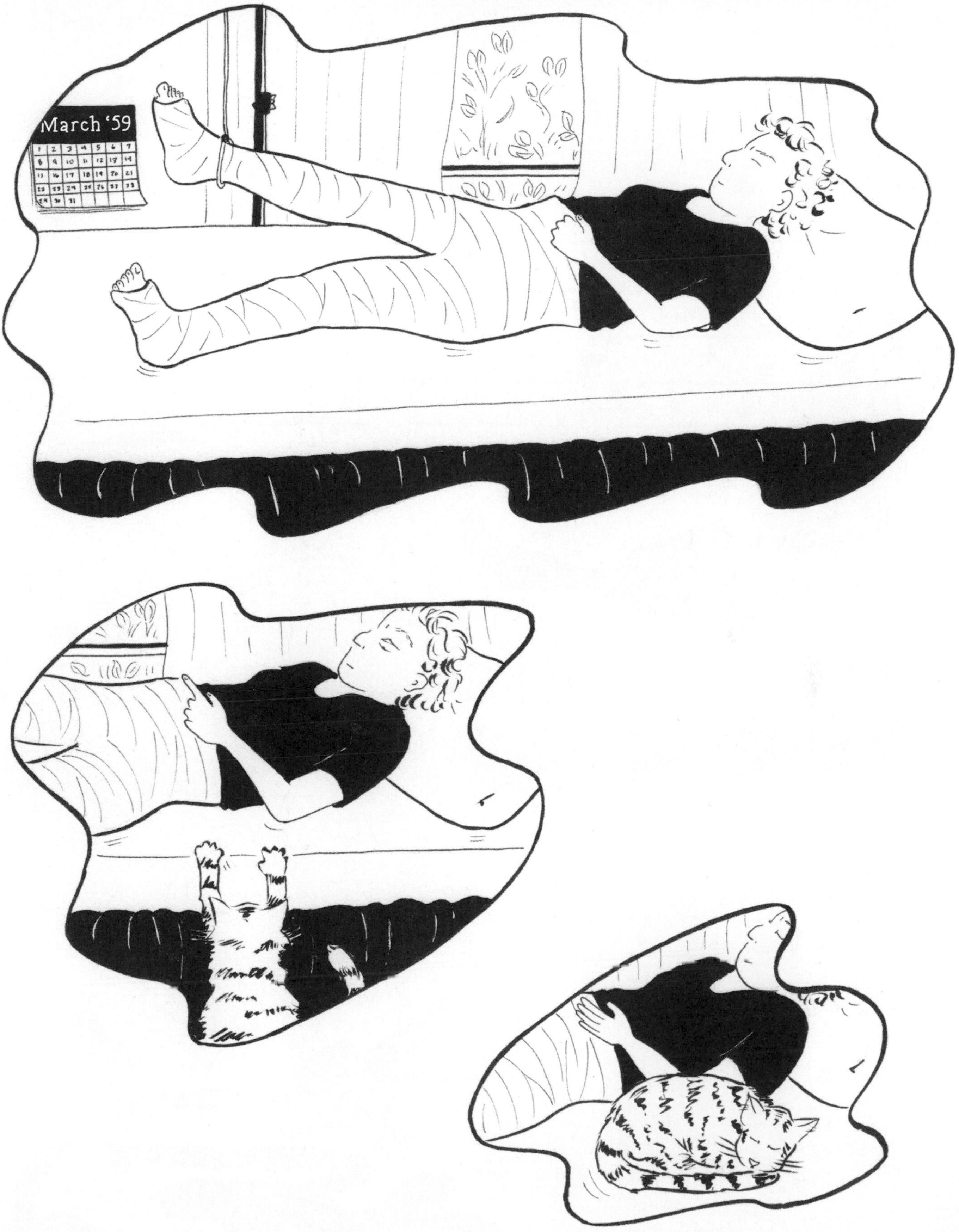
March '59

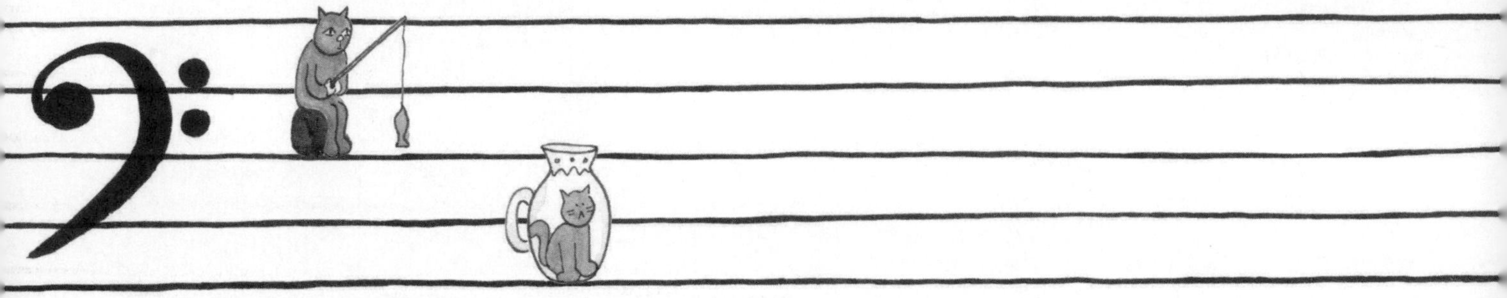

IV.

# To Eat and Drink

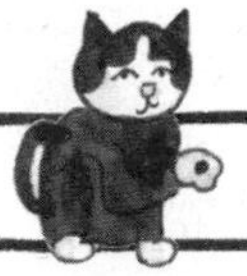

And so they are ever returning to us, the dead.

—W. G. Sebald, *The Emigrants*

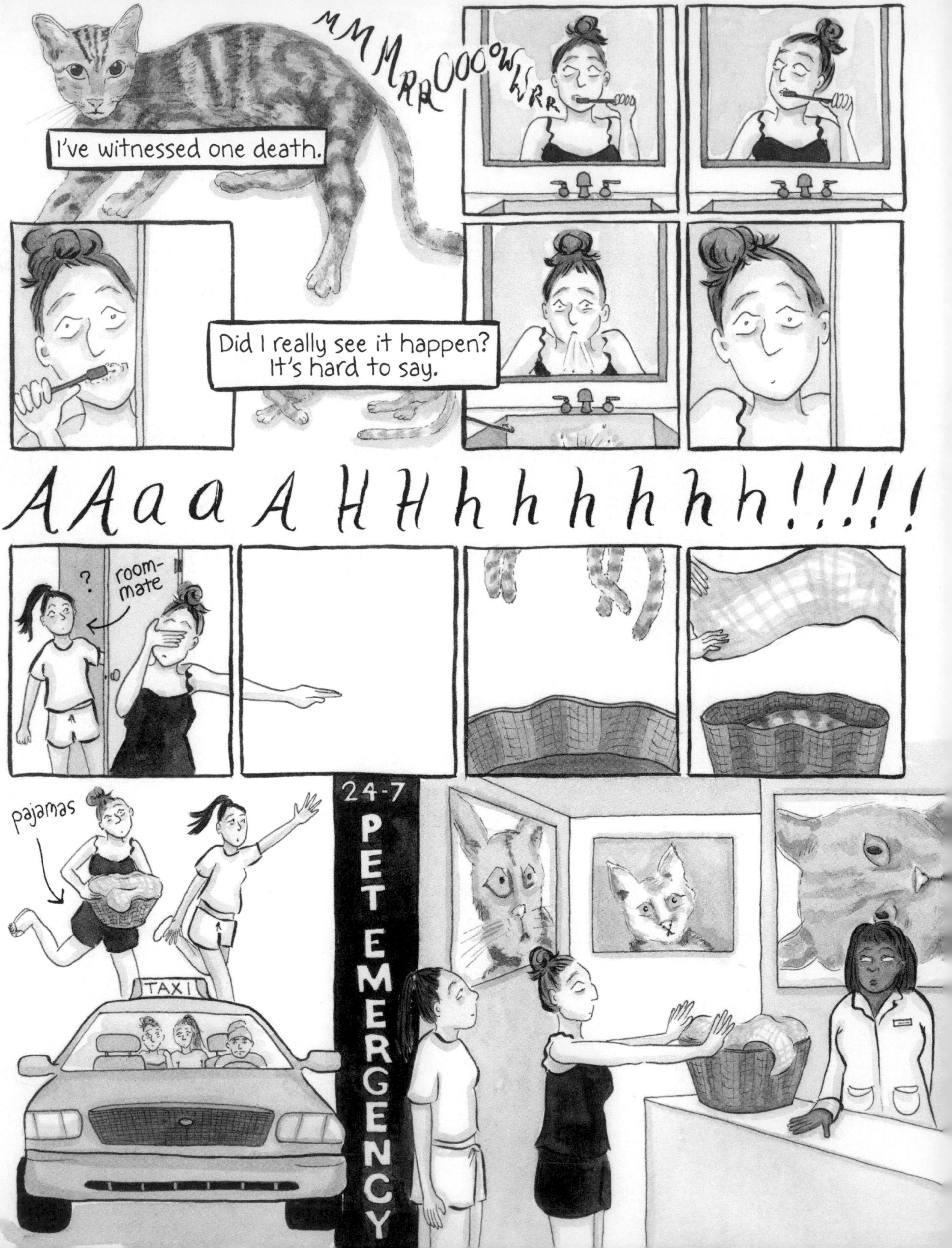
I've witnessed one death.
MMMRRROOOOWWRRR
Did I really see it happen? It's hard to say.
AAaaAHHhhhhhh!!!!!
?
roommate
pajamas
24-7 PET EMERGENCY
TAXI

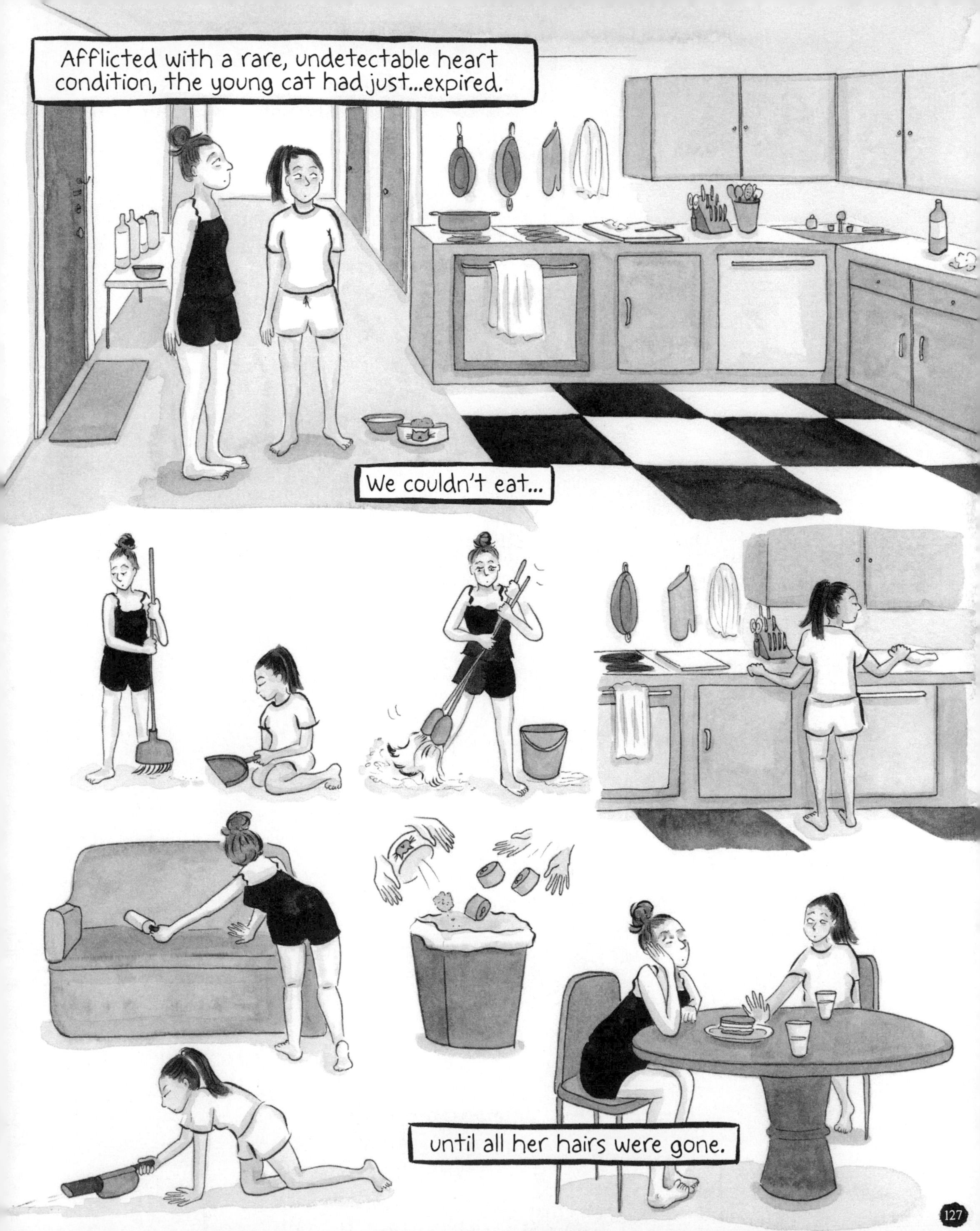
Afflicted with a rare, undetectable heart condition, the young cat had just...expired.
We couldn't eat...
until all her hairs were gone.

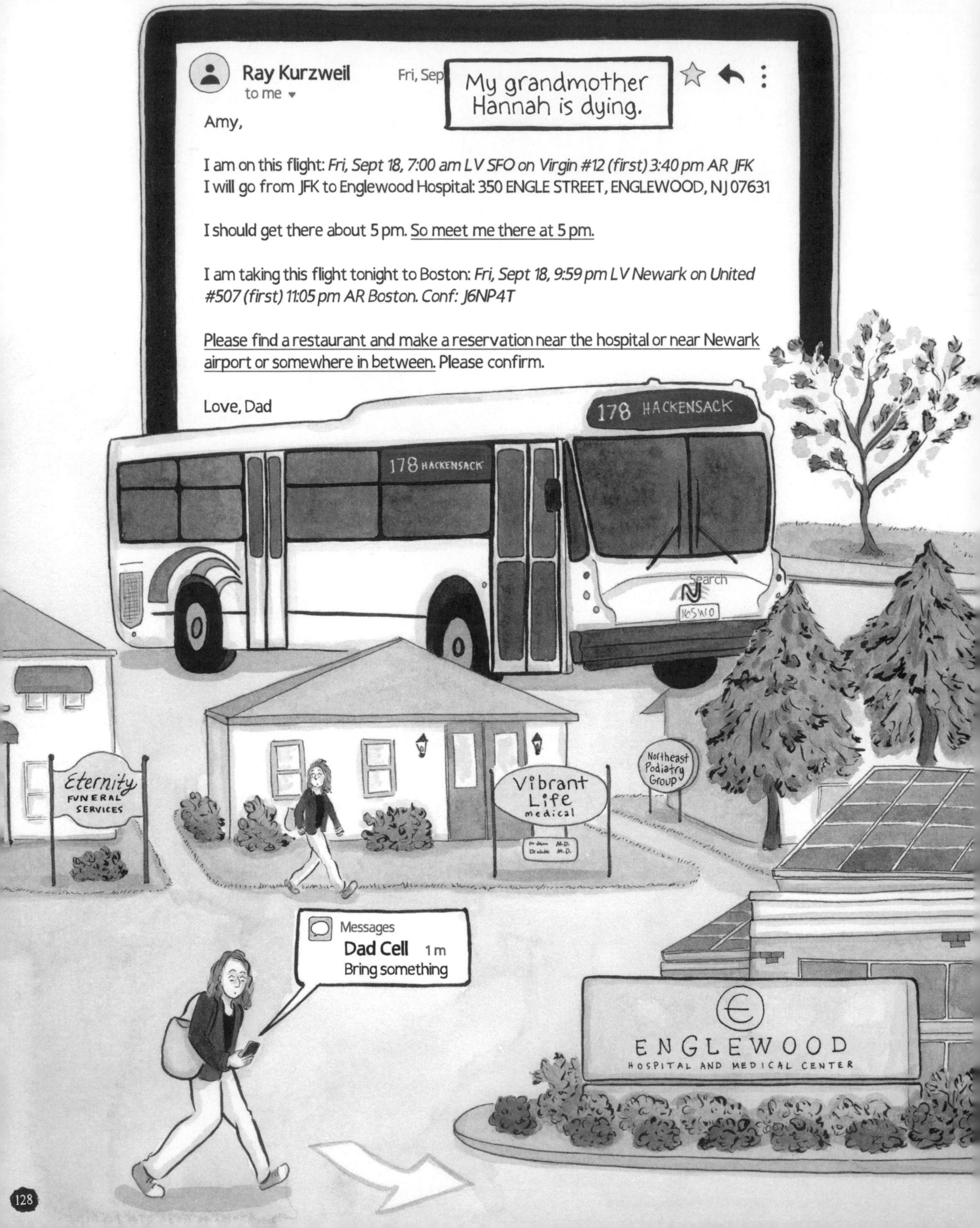
Ray Kurzweil
to me
Fri, Sep
My grandmother Hannah is dying.
Amy,
I am on this flight: Fri, Sept 18, 7:00 am LV SFO on Virgin #12 (first) 3:40 pm AR JFK
I will go from JFK to Englewood Hospital: 350 ENGLE STREET, ENGLEWOOD, NJ 07631
I should get there about 5 pm. So meet me there at 5 pm.
I am taking this flight tonight to Boston: Fri, Sept 18, 9:59 pm LV Newark on United #507 (first) 11:05 pm AR Boston. Conf: J6NP4T
Please find a restaurant and make a reservation near the hospital or near Newark airport or somewhere in between. Please confirm.
Love, Dad
178 HACKENSACK
178 HACKENSACK
Search
Eternity FUNERAL SERVICES
Vibrant Life medical
Northeast Podiatry Group
Messages
Dad Cell 1m
Bring something
ENGLEWOOD
HOSPITAL AND MEDICAL CENTER

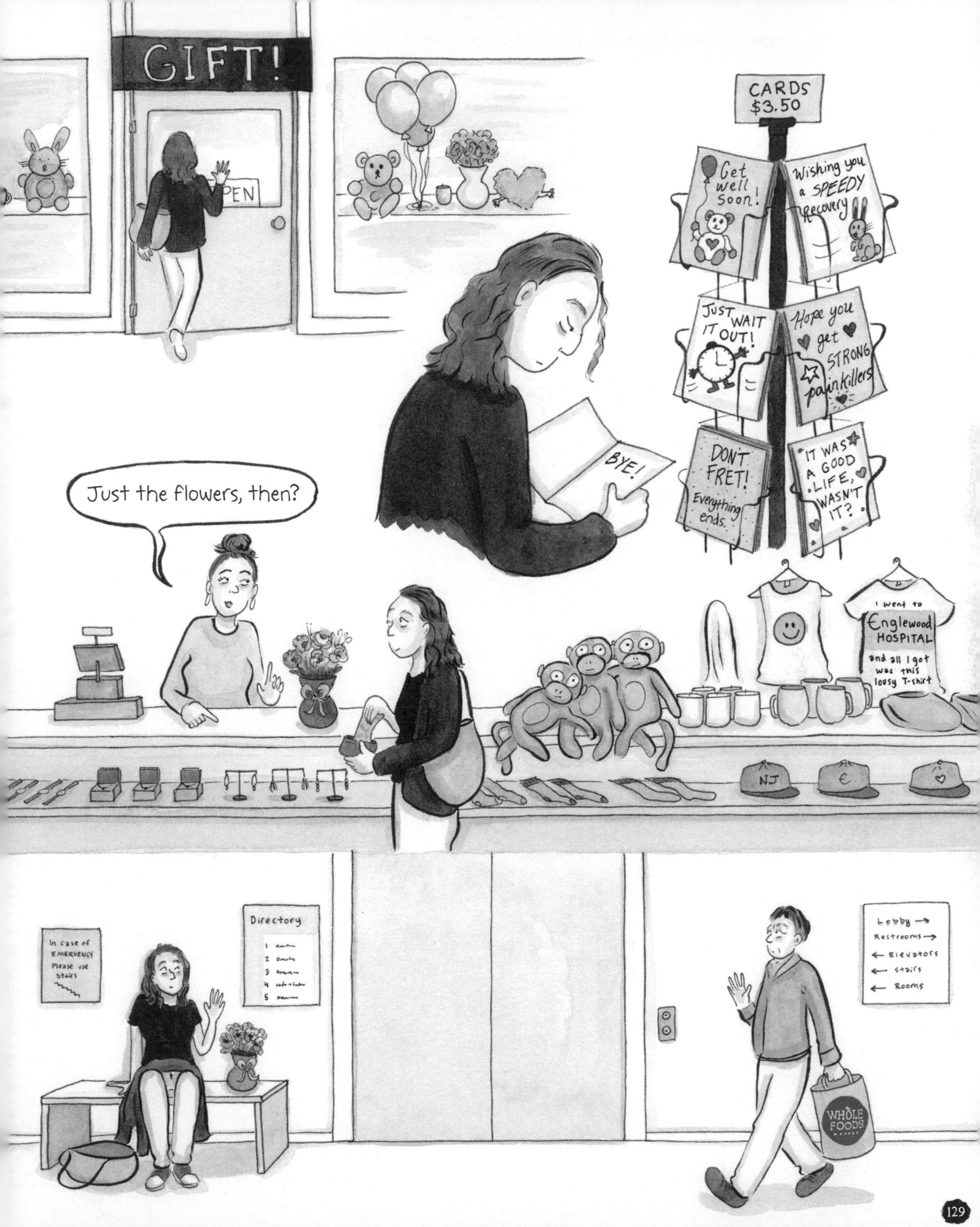
GIFT!
OPEN
CARDS $3.50
Get well soon!
Wishing you a SPEEDY Recovery
JUST WAIT IT OUT!
Hope you get STRONG painkillers
DON'T FRET! Everything ends.
IT WAS A GOOD LIFE, WASN'T IT?
BYE!
Just the flowers, then?
I went to Englewood HOSPITAL and all I got was this lousy T-shirt
NJ
In case of EMERGENCY Please use stairs
Directory
Lobby →
Restrooms →
← Elevators
← Stairs
← Rooms
WHOLE FOODS

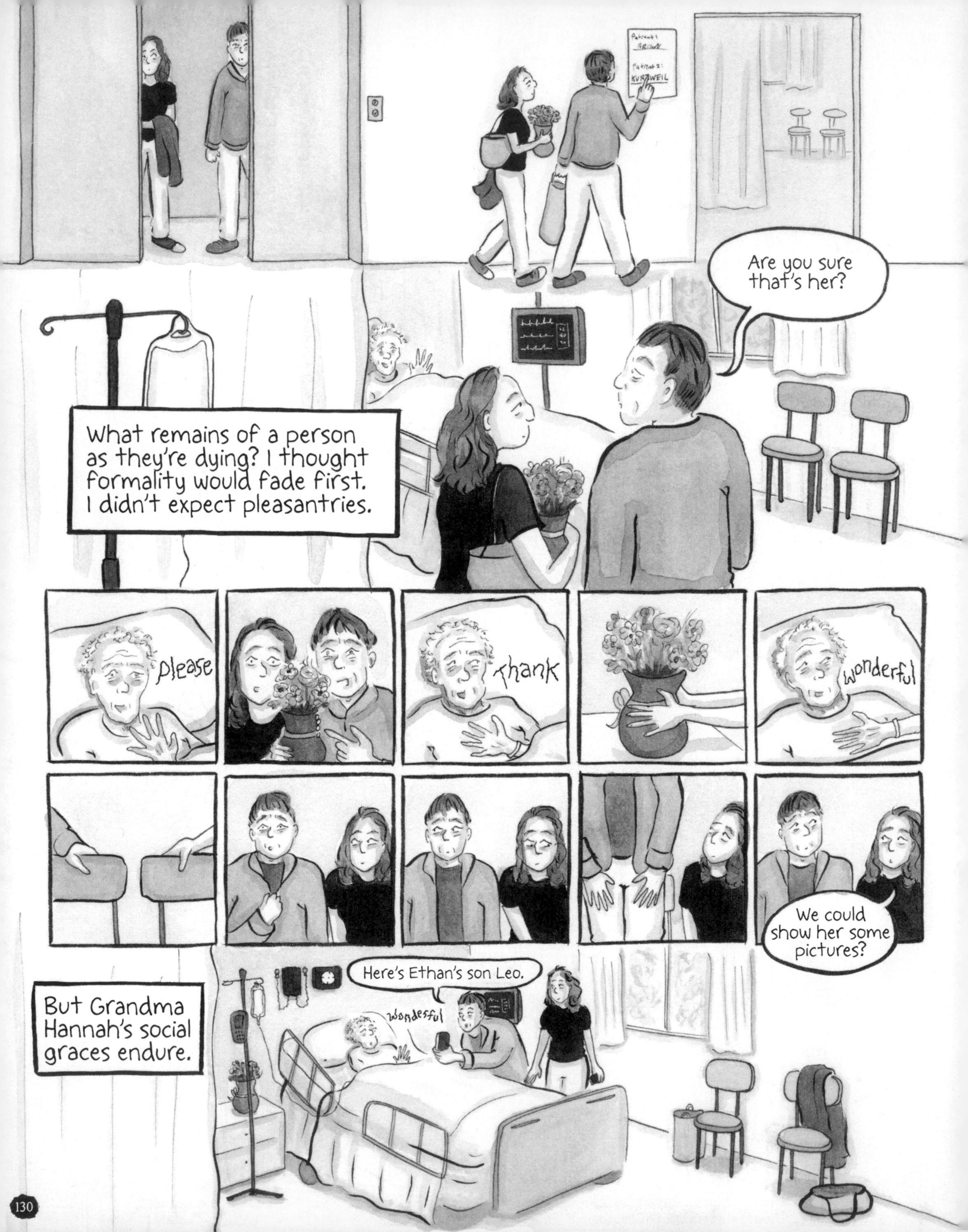
Patient 1
Patient 2:
Are you sure that's her?
What remains of a person as they're dying? I thought formality would fade first. I didn't expect pleasantries.
Please
Thank
Wonderful
We could show her some pictures?
But Grandma Hannah's social graces endure.
Here's Ethan's son Leo.
Wonderful

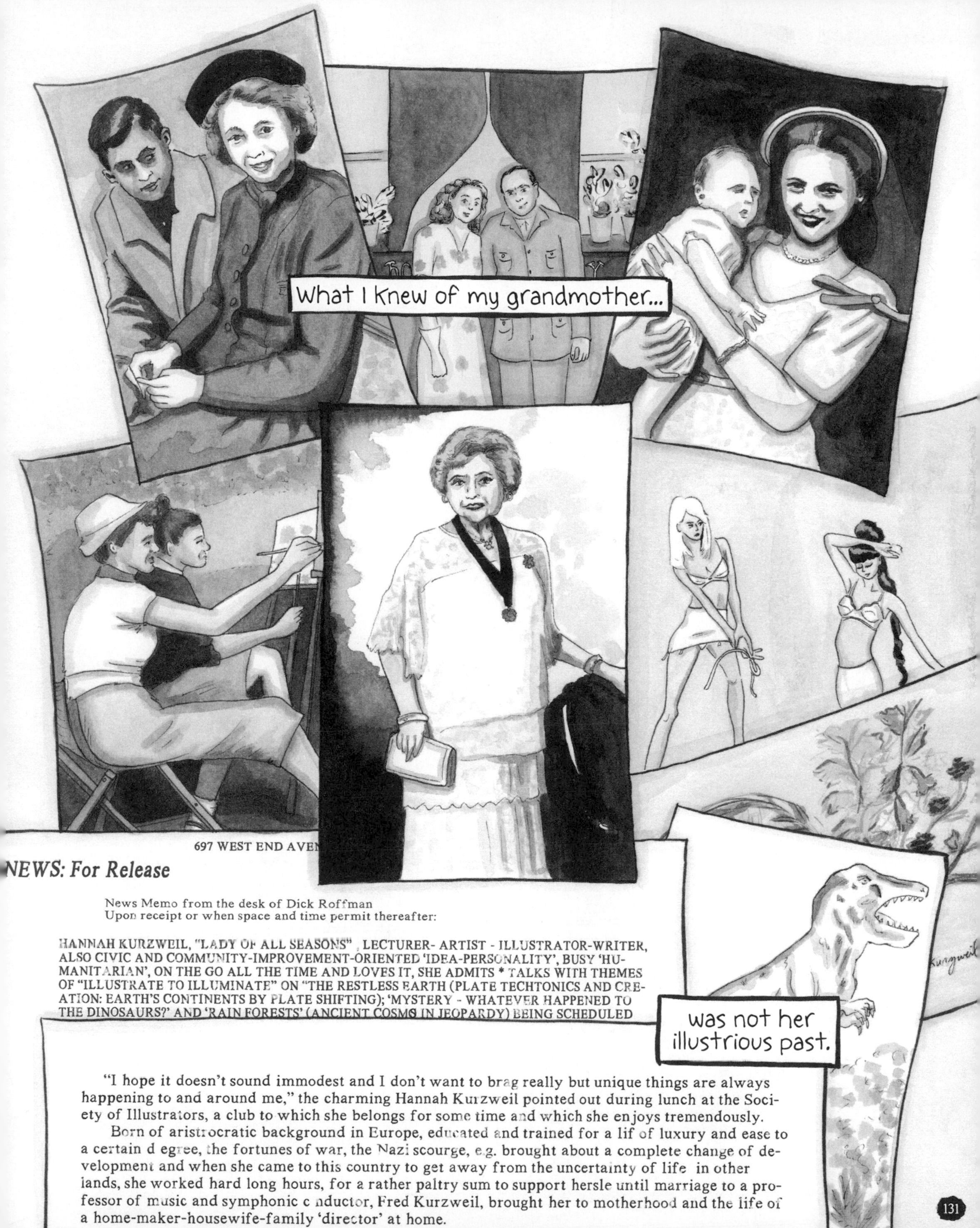
What I knew of my grandmother...
697 WEST END AVEN
NEWS: For Release
News Memo from the desk of Dick Roffman
Upon receipt or when space and time permit thereafter:
HANNAH KURZWEIL, "LADY OF ALL SEASONS" , LECTURER- ARTIST - ILLUSTRATOR-WRITER, ALSO CIVIC AND COMMUNITY-IMPROVEMENT-ORIENTED 'IDEA-PERSONALITY', BUSY 'HUMANITARIAN', ON THE GO ALL THE TIME AND LOVES IT, SHE ADMITS * TALKS WITH THEMES OF "ILLUSTRATE TO ILLUMINATE" ON "THE RESTLESS EARTH (PLATE TECHTONICS AND CREATION: EARTH'S CONTINENTS BY PLATE SHIFTING); 'MYSTERY - WHATEVER HAPPENED TO THE DINOSAURS?' AND 'RAIN FORESTS' (ANCIENT COSMO IN JEOPARDY) BEING SCHEDULED
Kurzweil
was not her illustrious past.
"I hope it doesn't sound immodest and I don't want to brag really but unique things are always happening to and around me," the charming Hannah Kurzweil pointed out during lunch at the Society of Illustrators, a club to which she belongs for some time and which she enjoys tremendously.
Born of aristrocratic background in Europe, educated and trained for a lif of luxury and ease to a certain d egree, the fortunes of war, the Nazi scourge, e.g. brought about a complete change of development and when she came to this country to get away from the uncertainty of life in other lands, she worked hard long hours, for a rather paltry sum to support hersle until marriage to a professor of music and symphonic c nductor, Fred Kurzweil, brought her to motherhood and the life of a home-maker-housewife-family 'director' at home.

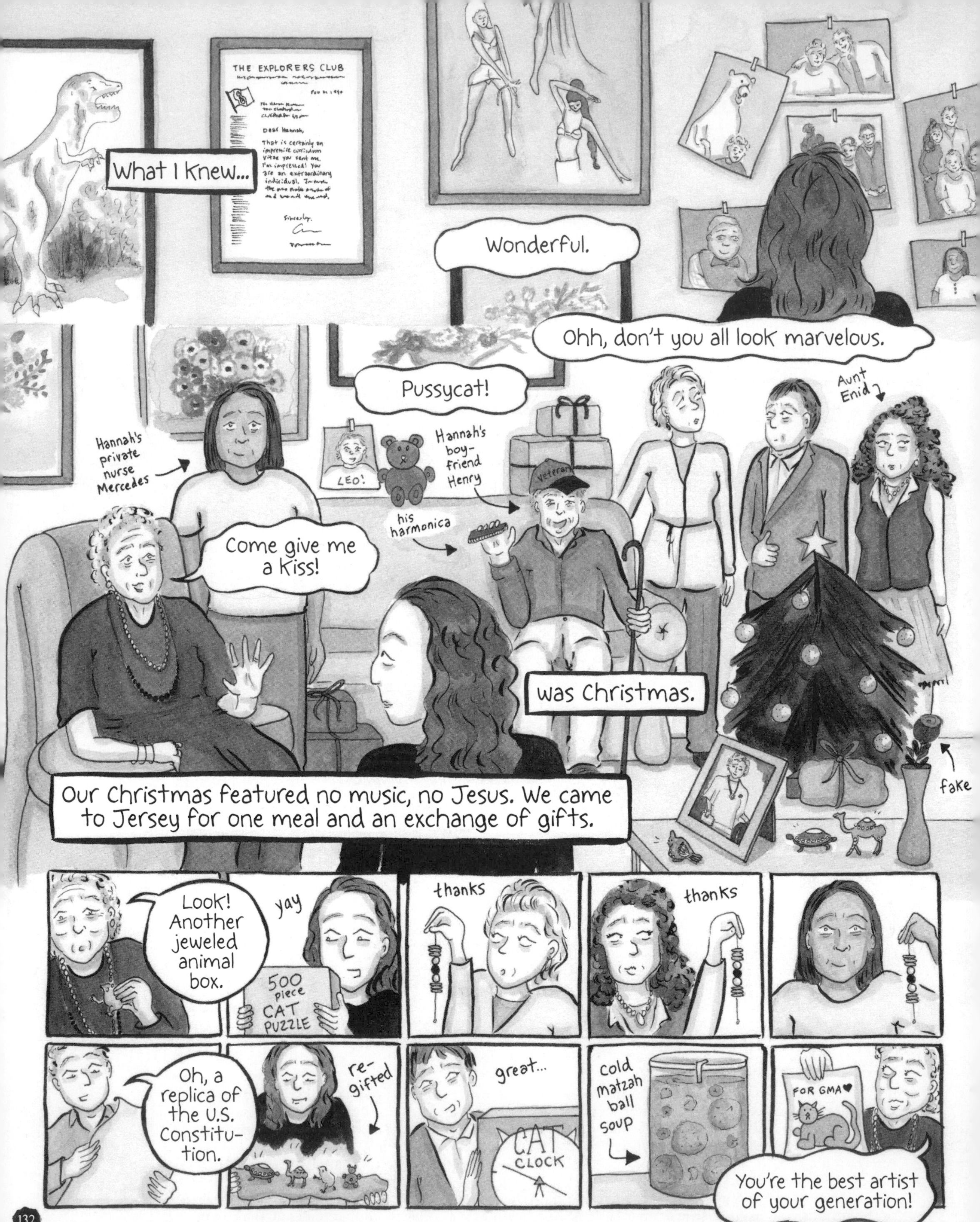

THE EXPLORERS CLUB
Dear Hannah,
That is certainly an impressive curriculum vitae you sent me. I'm impressed! You are an extraordinary individual.
Sincerely,
What I knew...
Wonderful.
Ohh, don't you all look marvelous.
Pussycat!
Aunt Enid
Hannah's private nurse Mercedes
LEO!
Hannah's boyfriend Henry
Veteran
his harmonica
Come give me a kiss!
was Christmas.
fake
Our Christmas featured no music, no Jesus. We came to Jersey for one meal and an exchange of gifts.
Look! Another jeweled animal box.
yay
500 piece CAT PUZZLE
thanks
thanks
Oh, a replica of the U.S. Constitution.
re-gifted
great...
CAT CLOCK
cold matzah ball soup
FOR GMA♥
You're the best artist of your generation!

Hannah's escape from Jewish life was gradual. She was a teenager, a "debutante," when Vienna's Jewish circles were undone. She raised her children in a Unitarian church. Later in life, she joined Trinity Episcopal in Cliffside Park.

Unitarians teach "many paths to the truth,"

and it was my grandmother who first made me think about truth.

<ʸiiiรกgg>

Hel— I WILL NOT TOLERATE

extra long cord

She introduced me to the idea...

THIS UNCONSCIONABLE TREATMENT

Grandma?

YOU TELL Raymond

DAD?

that perhaps we are all hostage...

TRULY SO UNFAIR

Mom?

to our own perceptions.

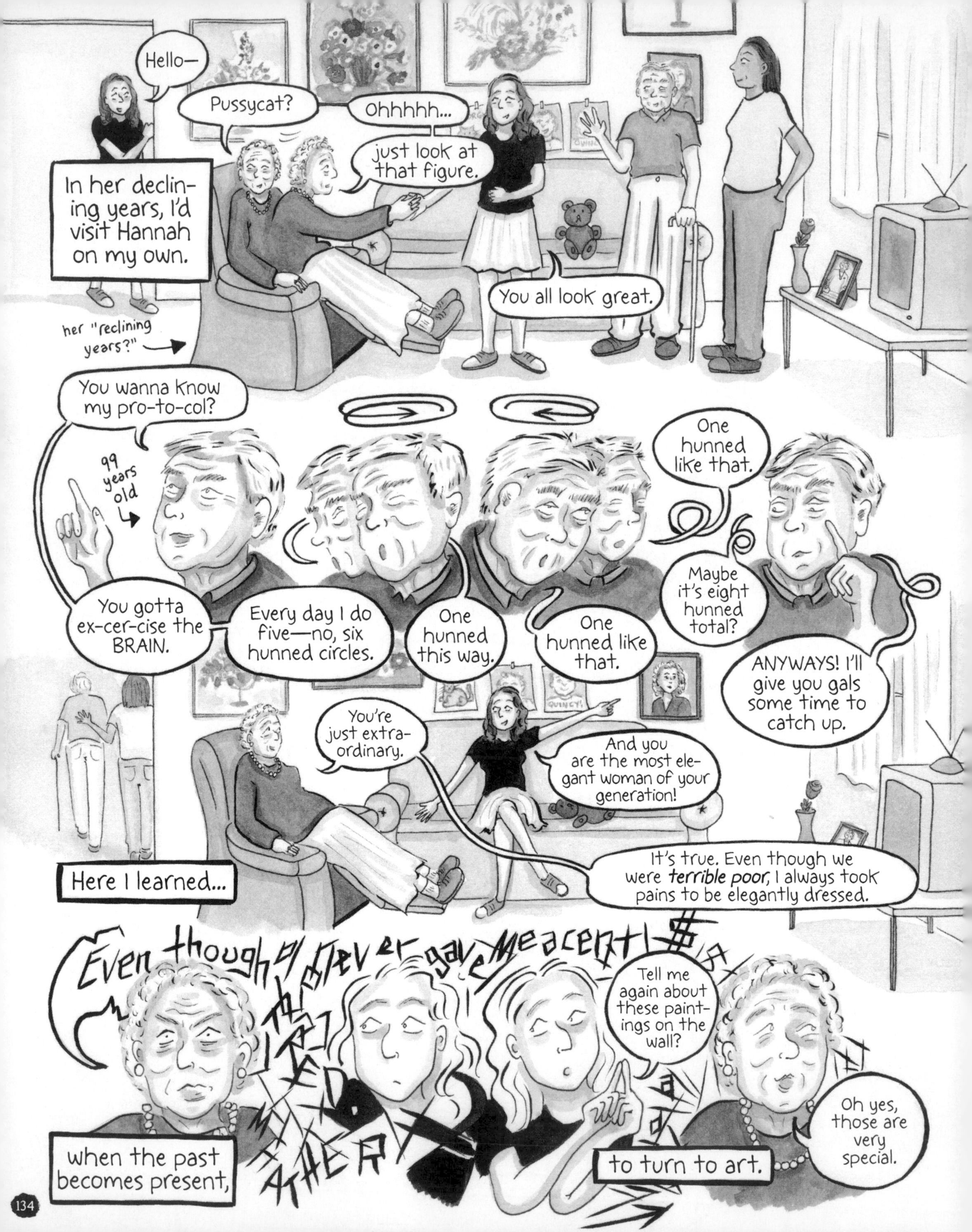
Hello—
Pussycat?
Ohhhhh...
just look at that figure.
In her declining years, I'd visit Hannah on my own.
You all look great.
her "reclining years?"
You wanna know my pro-to-col?
99 years old
You gotta ex-cer-cise the BRAIN.
Every day I do five—no, six hunned circles.
One hunned this way.
One hunned like that.
One hunned like that.
Maybe it's eight hunned total?
ANYWAYS! I'll give you gals some time to catch up.
You're just extraordinary.
And you are the most elegant woman of your generation!
Here I learned...
It's true. Even though we were *terrible poor*, I always took pains to be elegantly dressed.
Even though
Tell me again about these paintings on the wall?
Oh yes, those are very special.
when the past becomes present,
to turn to art.

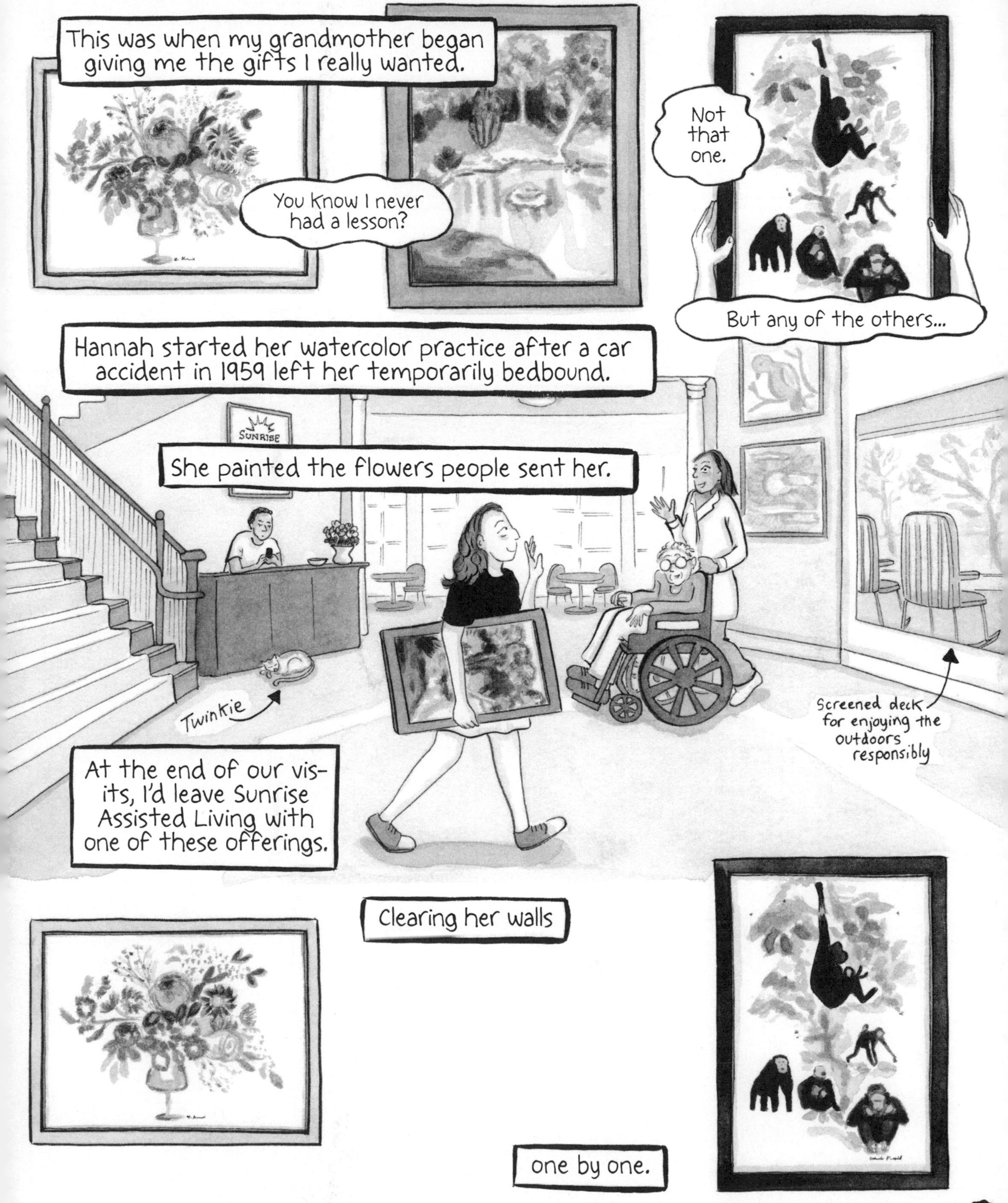
This was when my grandmother began giving me the gifts I really wanted.
You know I never had a lesson?
Not that one.
But any of the others...
Hannah started her watercolor practice after a car accident in 1959 left her temporarily bedbound.
SUNRISE
She painted the flowers people sent her.
Twinkie
Screened deck for enjoying the outdoors responsibly
At the end of our visits, I'd leave Sunrise Assisted Living with one of these offerings.
Clearing her walls
one by one.

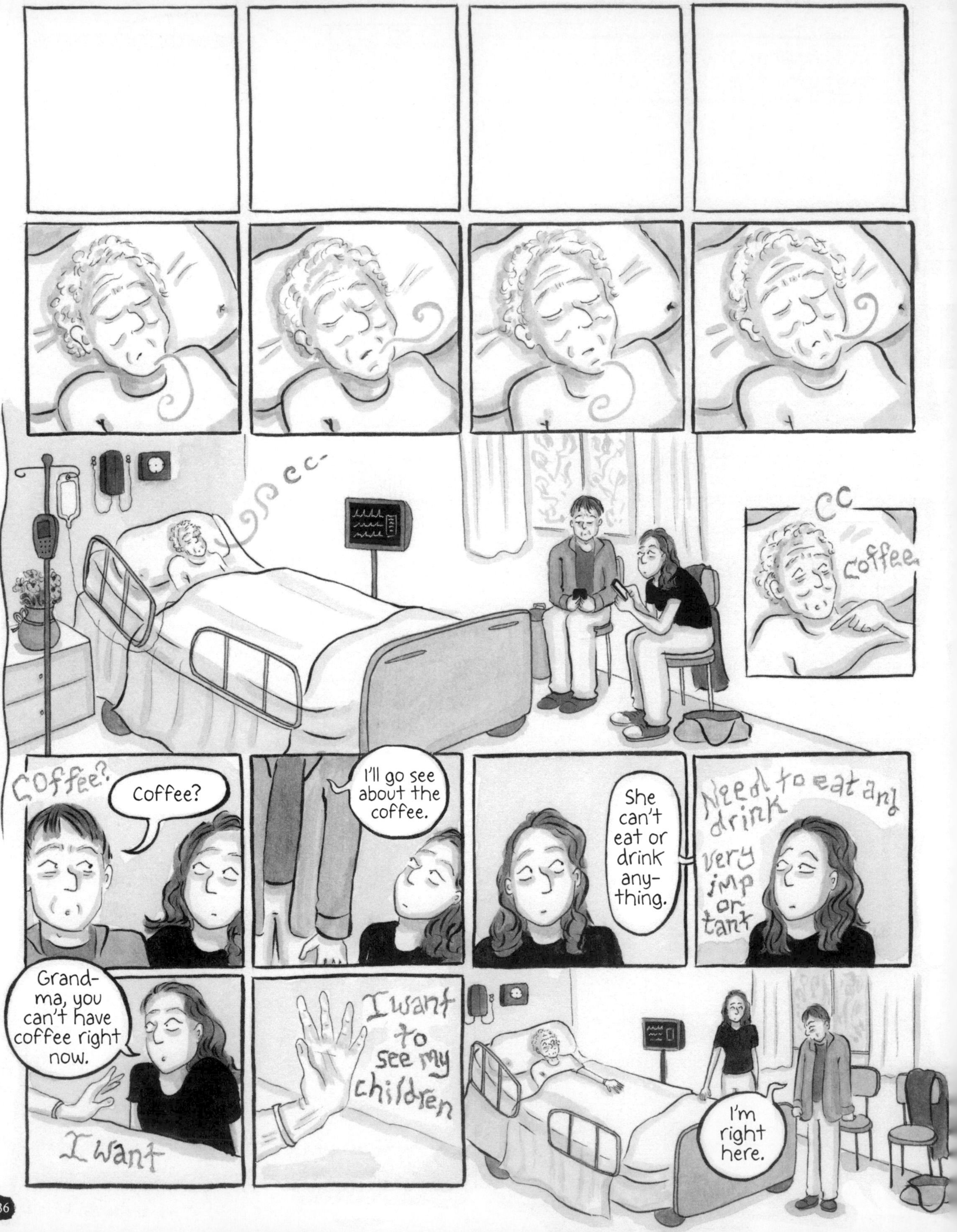
cc-
cc
coffee
Coffee?
Coffee?
I'll go see about the coffee.
She can't eat or drink anything.
Need to eat and drink
very imp or tant
Grandma, you can't have coffee right now.
I want
I want to see my children
I'm right here.

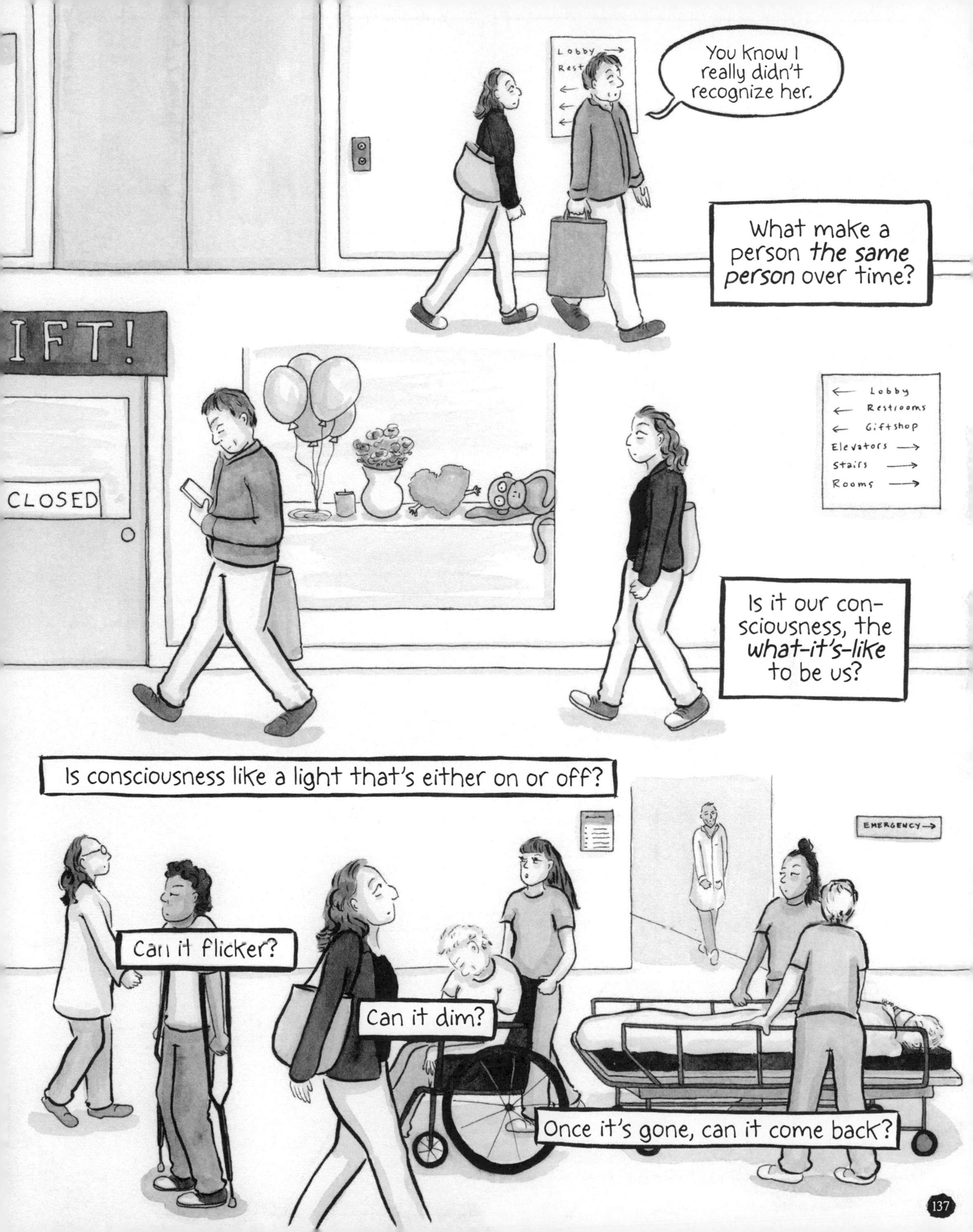
Lobby
You know I really didn't recognize her.
What make a person *the same person* over time?
IFT!
CLOSED
Lobby
Restrooms
Giftshop
Elevators
Stairs
Rooms
Is it our consciousness, the *what-it's-like* to be us?
Is consciousness like a light that's either on or off?
EMERGENCY
Can it flicker?
Can it dim?
Once it's gone, can it come back?

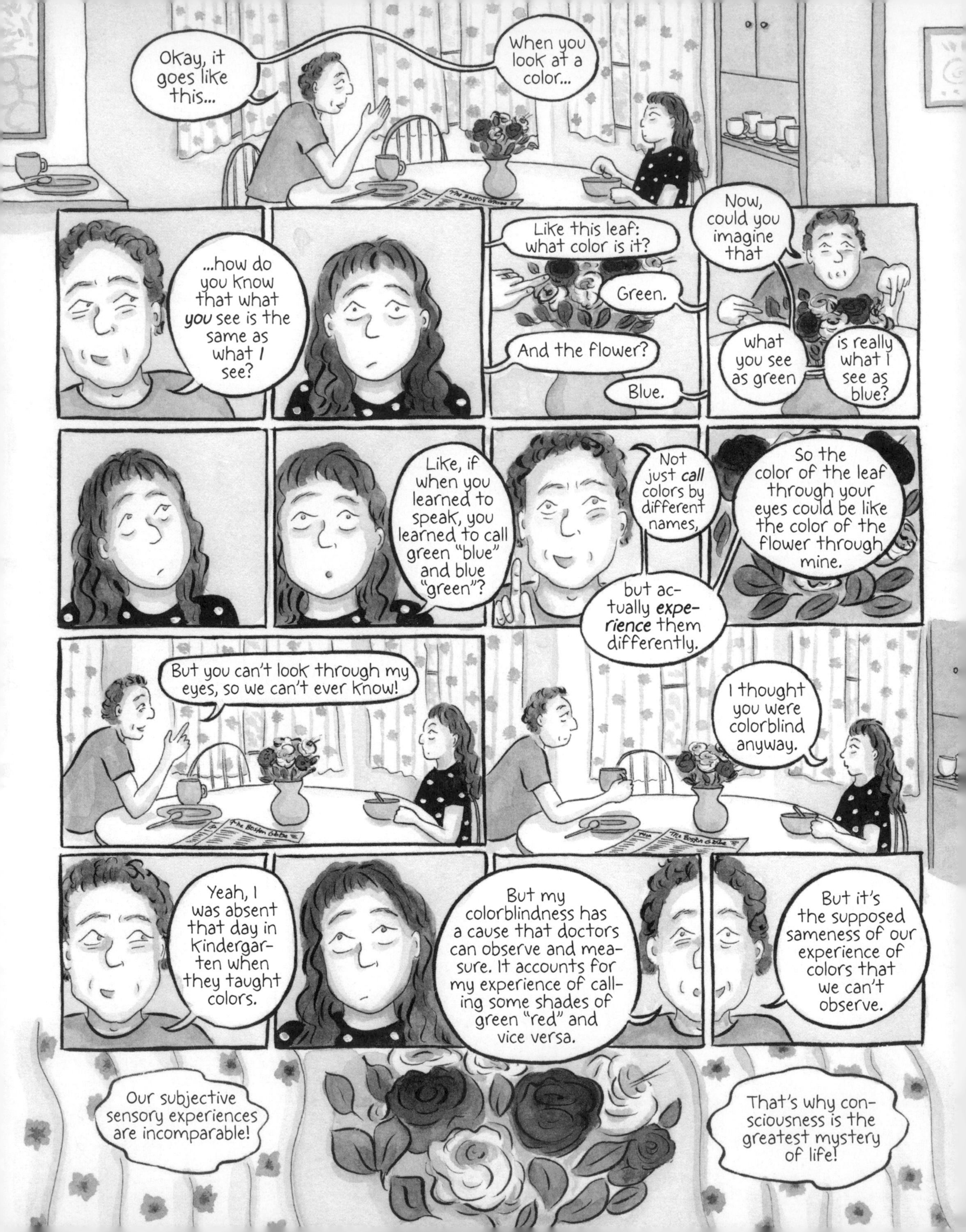
Okay, it goes like this...
When you look at a color...
...how do you know that what *you* see is the same as what *I* see?
Like this leaf: what color is it?
Green.
And the flower?
Blue.
Now, could you imagine that
what you see as green
is really what I see as blue?
Like, if when you learned to speak, you learned to call green "blue" and blue "green"?
Not just **call** colors by different names,
but actually **experience** them differently.
So the color of the leaf through your eyes could be like the color of the flower through mine.
But you can't look through my eyes, so we can't ever know!
I thought you were colorblind anyway.
Yeah, I was absent that day in kindergarten when they taught colors.
But my colorblindness has a cause that doctors can observe and measure. It accounts for my experience of calling some shades of green "red" and vice versa.
But it's the supposed sameness of our experience of colors that we can't observe.
Our subjective sensory experiences are incomparable!
That's why consciousness is the greatest mystery of life!
The Boston Globe

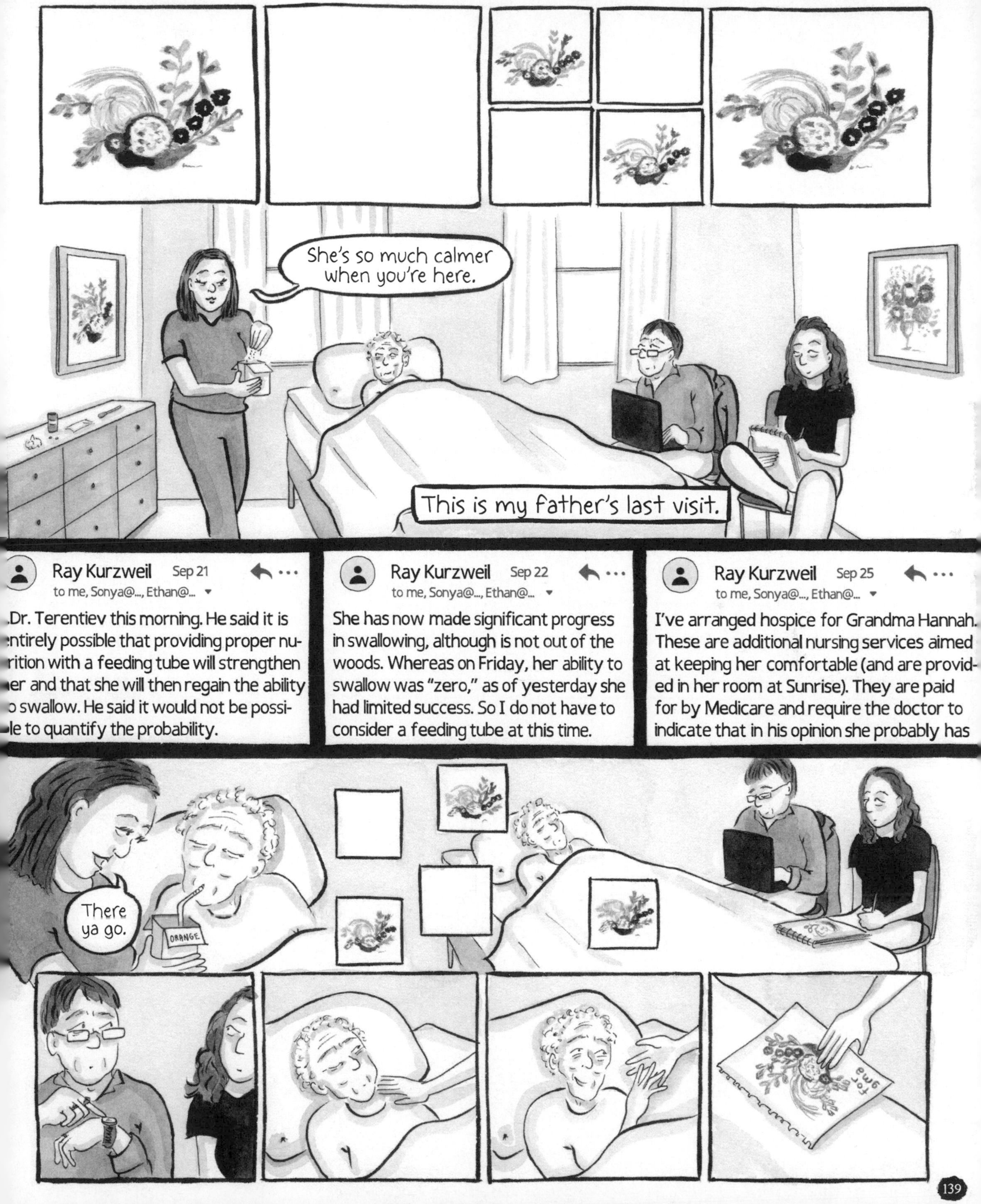

She's so much calmer when you're here.
This is my father's last visit.
Ray Kurzweil Sep 21
to me, Sonya@..., Ethan@...
Dr. Terentiev this morning. He said it is ntirely possible that providing proper nu- rition with a feeding tube will strengthen er and that she will then regain the ability o swallow. He said it would not be possi- le to quantify the probability.
Ray Kurzweil Sep 22
to me, Sonya@..., Ethan@...
She has now made significant progress in swallowing, although is not out of the woods. Whereas on Friday, her ability to swallow was "zero," as of yesterday she had limited success. So I do not have to consider a feeding tube at this time.
Ray Kurzweil Sep 25
to me, Sonya@..., Ethan@...
I've arranged hospice for Grandma Hannah. These are additional nursing services aimed at keeping her comfortable (and are provid- ed in her room at Sunrise). They are paid for by Medicare and require the doctor to indicate that in his opinion she probably has
There ya go.
ORANGE
for gma

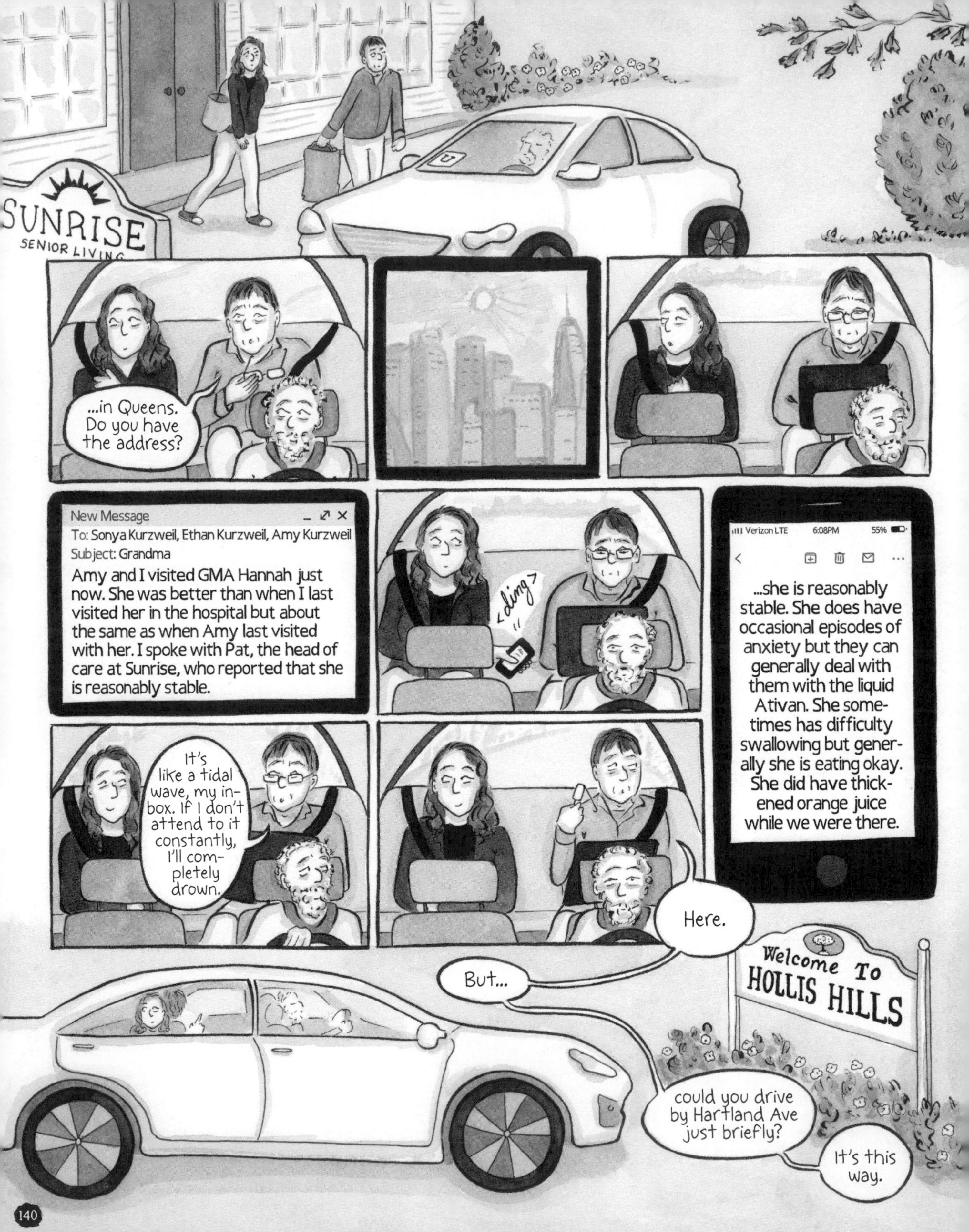

SUNRISE SENIOR LIVING
...in Queens. Do you have the address?
New Message
To: Sonya Kurzweil, Ethan Kurzweil, Amy Kurzweil
Subject: Grandma
Amy and I visited GMA Hannah just now. She was better than when I last visited her in the hospital but about the same as when Amy last visited with her. I spoke with Pat, the head of care at Sunrise, who reported that she is reasonably stable.
<ding>
Verizon LTE 6:08PM 55%
...she is reasonably stable. She does have occasional episodes of anxiety but they can generally deal with them with the liquid Ativan. She sometimes has difficulty swallowing but generally she is eating okay. She did have thickened orange juice while we were there.
It's like a tidal wave, my inbox. If I don't attend to it constantly, I'll completely drown.
Here.
But...
Welcome To HOLLIS HILLS
could you drive by Hartland Ave just briefly?
It's this way.

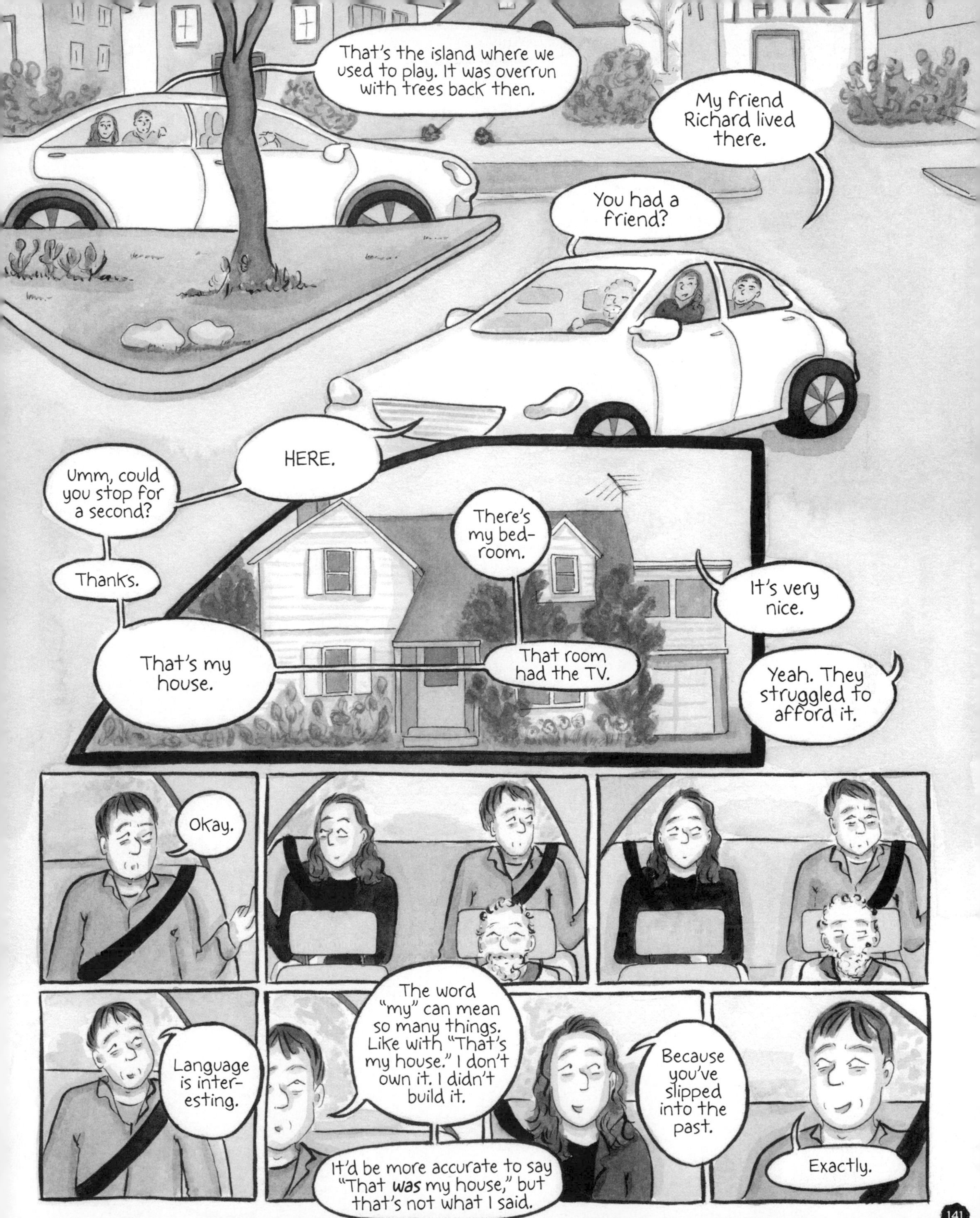
That's the island where we used to play. It was overrun with trees back then.
My friend Richard lived there.
You had a friend?
HERE.
Umm, could you stop for a second?
Thanks.
That's my house.
There's my bed-room.
That room had the TV.
It's very nice.
Yeah. They struggled to afford it.
Okay.
Language is inter-esting.
The word "my" can mean so many things. Like with "That's my house." I don't own it. I didn't build it.
It'd be more accurate to say "That **was** my house," but that's not what I said.
Because you've slipped into the past.
Exactly.

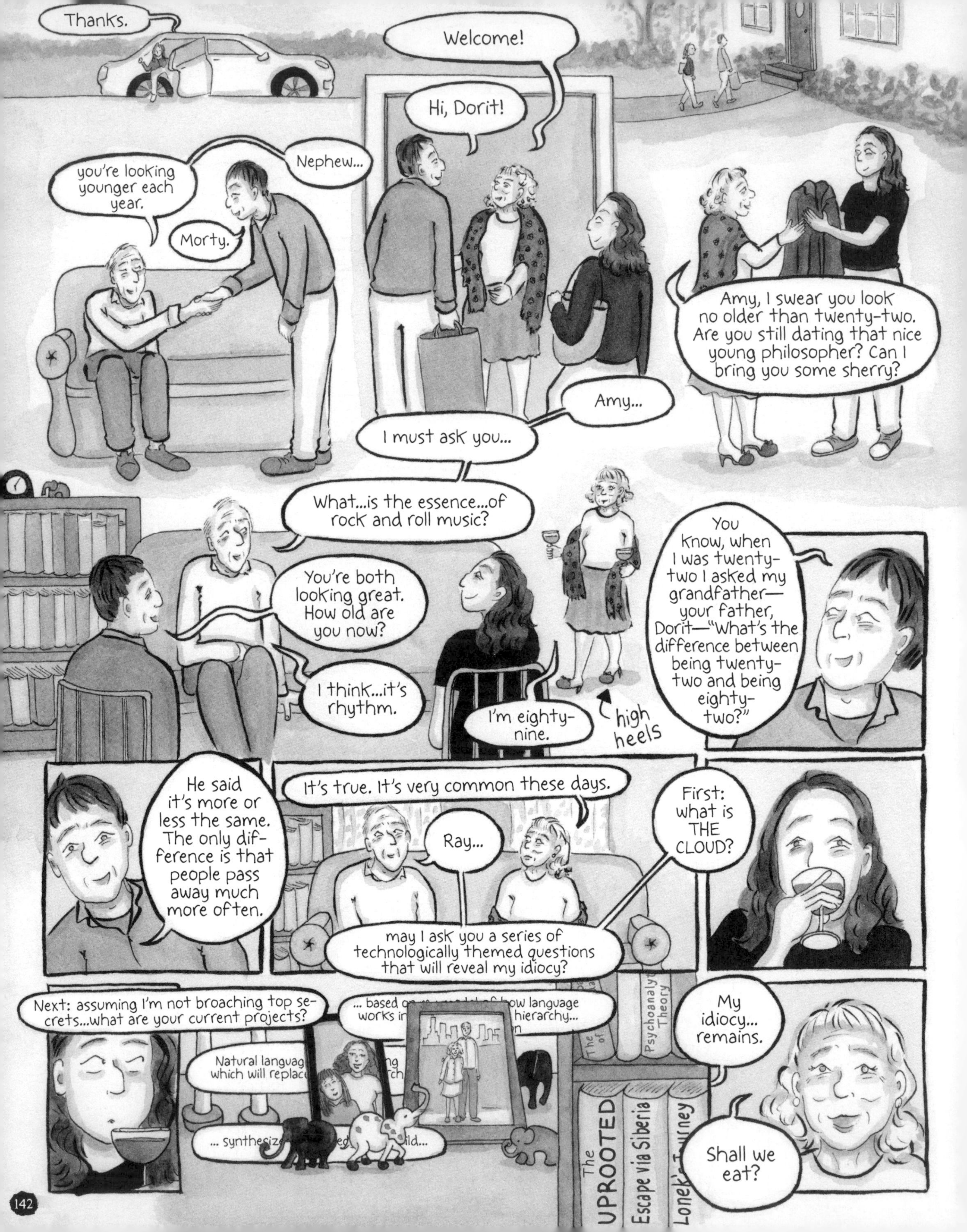
Thanks.
Welcome!
Hi, Dorit!
Nephew...
you're looking younger each year.
Morty.
Amy, I swear you look no older than twenty-two. Are you still dating that nice young philosopher? Can I bring you some sherry?
Amy...
I must ask you...
What...is the essence...of rock and roll music?
You're both looking great. How old are you now?
I think...it's rhythm.
I'm eighty-nine.
high heels
You know, when I was twenty-two I asked my grandfather—your father, Dorit—"What's the difference between being twenty-two and being eighty-two?"
He said it's more or less the same. The only difference is that people pass away much more often.
It's true. It's very common these days.
Ray...
may I ask you a series of technologically themed questions that will reveal my idiocy?
First: what is THE CLOUD?
Next: assuming I'm not broaching top secrets...what are your current projects?
My idiocy... remains.
Shall we eat?
Psychoanalytic Theory
The UPROOTED
Escape via Siberia

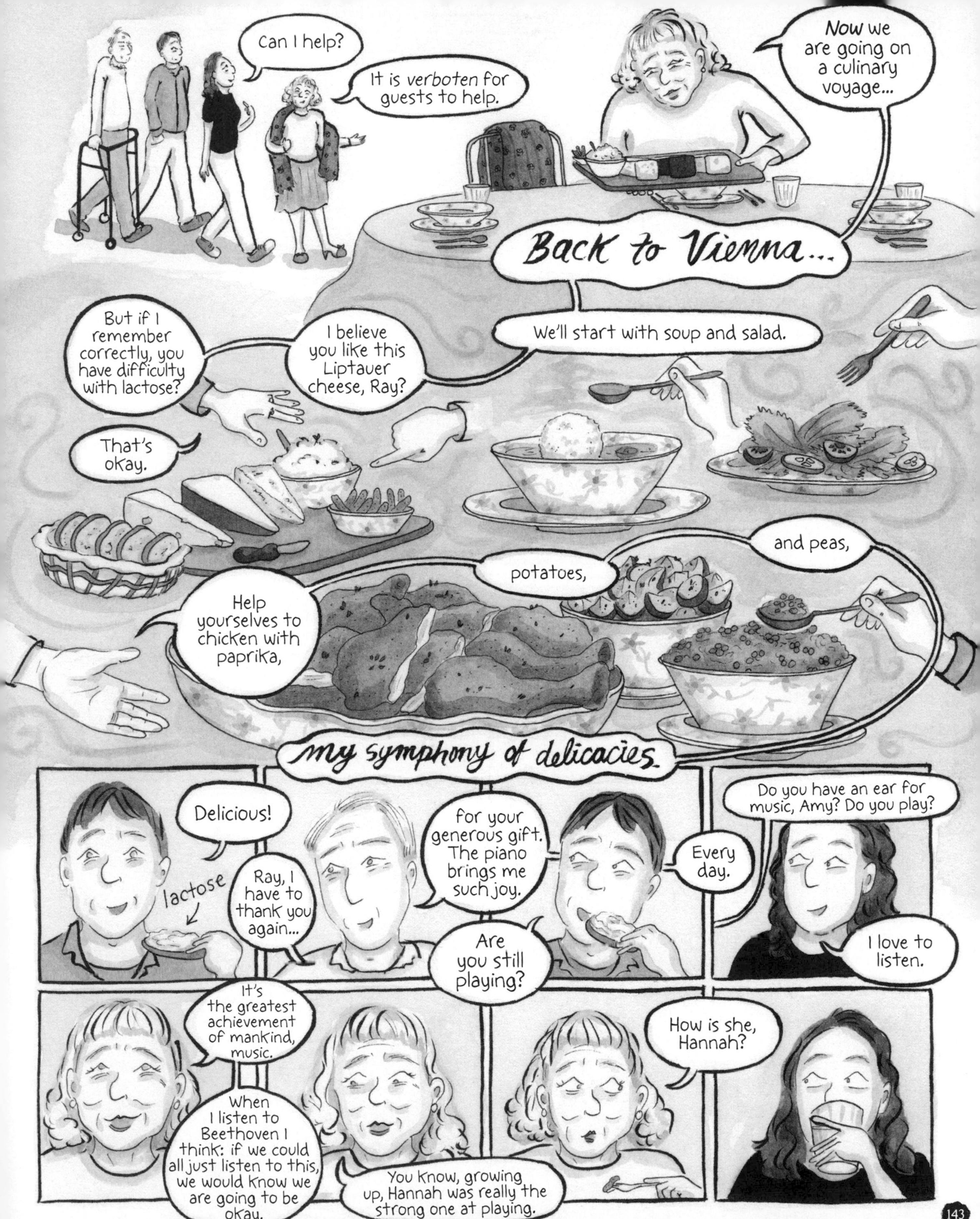

Can I help?
It is *verboten* for guests to help.
*Now* we are going on a culinary voyage...
Back to Vienna...
We'll start with soup and salad.
I believe you like this Liptauer cheese, Ray?
But if I remember correctly, you have difficulty with lactose?
That's okay.
Help yourselves to chicken with paprika,
potatoes,
and peas,
my symphony of delicacies.
Delicious!
lactose
Ray, I have to thank you again...
for your generous gift. The piano brings me such joy.
Are you still playing?
Every day.
Do you have an ear for music, Amy? Do you play?
I love to listen.
It's the greatest achievement of mankind, music.
When I listen to Beethoven I think: if we could all just listen to this, we would know we are going to be okay.
You know, growing up, Hannah was really the strong one at playing.
How is she, Hannah?

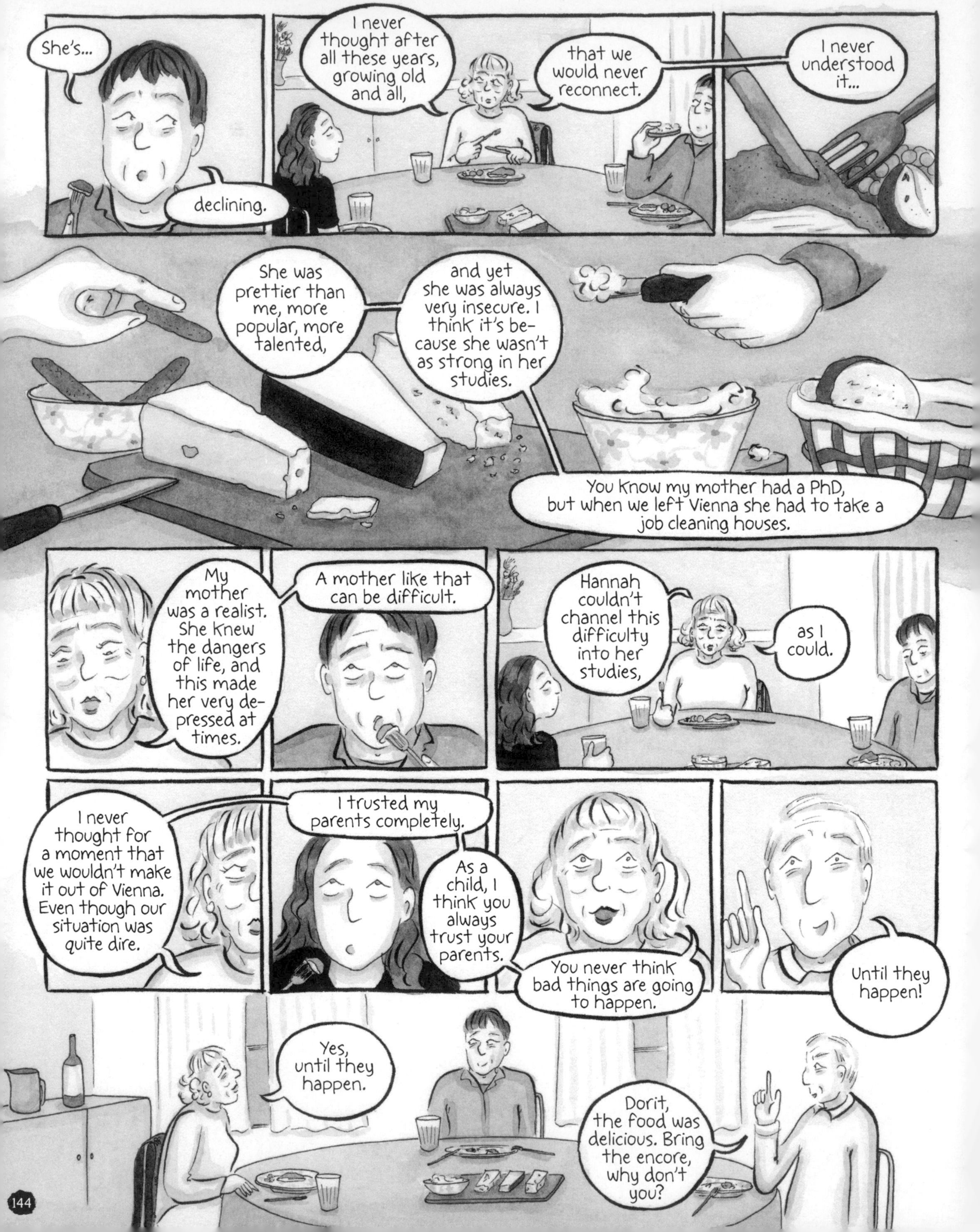

She's...
declining.
I never thought after all these years, growing old and all,
that we would never reconnect.
I never understood it...
She was prettier than me, more popular, more talented,
and yet she was always very insecure. I think it's be-cause she wasn't as strong in her studies.
You know my mother had a PhD, but when we left Vienna she had to take a job cleaning houses.
My mother was a realist. She knew the dangers of life, and this made her very de-pressed at times.
A mother like that can be difficult.
Hannah couldn't channel this difficulty into her studies,
as I could.
I never thought for a moment that we wouldn't make it out of Vienna. Even though our situation was quite dire.
I trusted my parents completely.
As a child, I think you always trust your parents.
You never think bad things are going to happen.
Until they happen!
Yes, until they happen.
Dorit, the food was delicious. Bring the encore, why don't you?

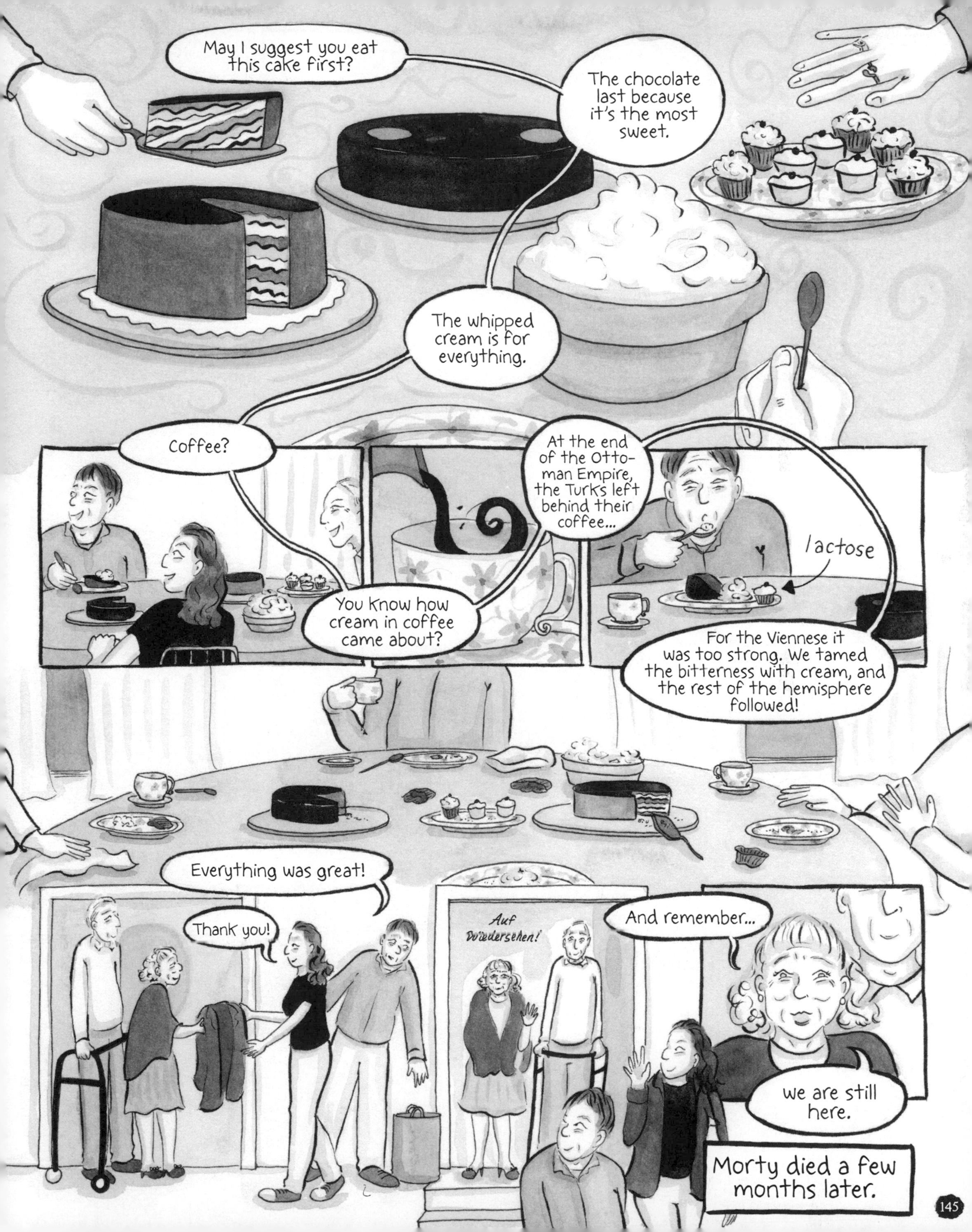
May I suggest you eat this cake first?
The chocolate last because it's the most sweet.
The whipped cream is for everything.
Coffee?
At the end of the Otto-man Empire, the Turks left behind their coffee...
You know how cream in coffee came about?
lactose
For the Viennese it was too strong. We tamed the bitterness with cream, and the rest of the hemisphere followed!
Everything was great!
Thank you!
Auf Wiedersehen!
And remember...
we are still here.
Morty died a few months later.

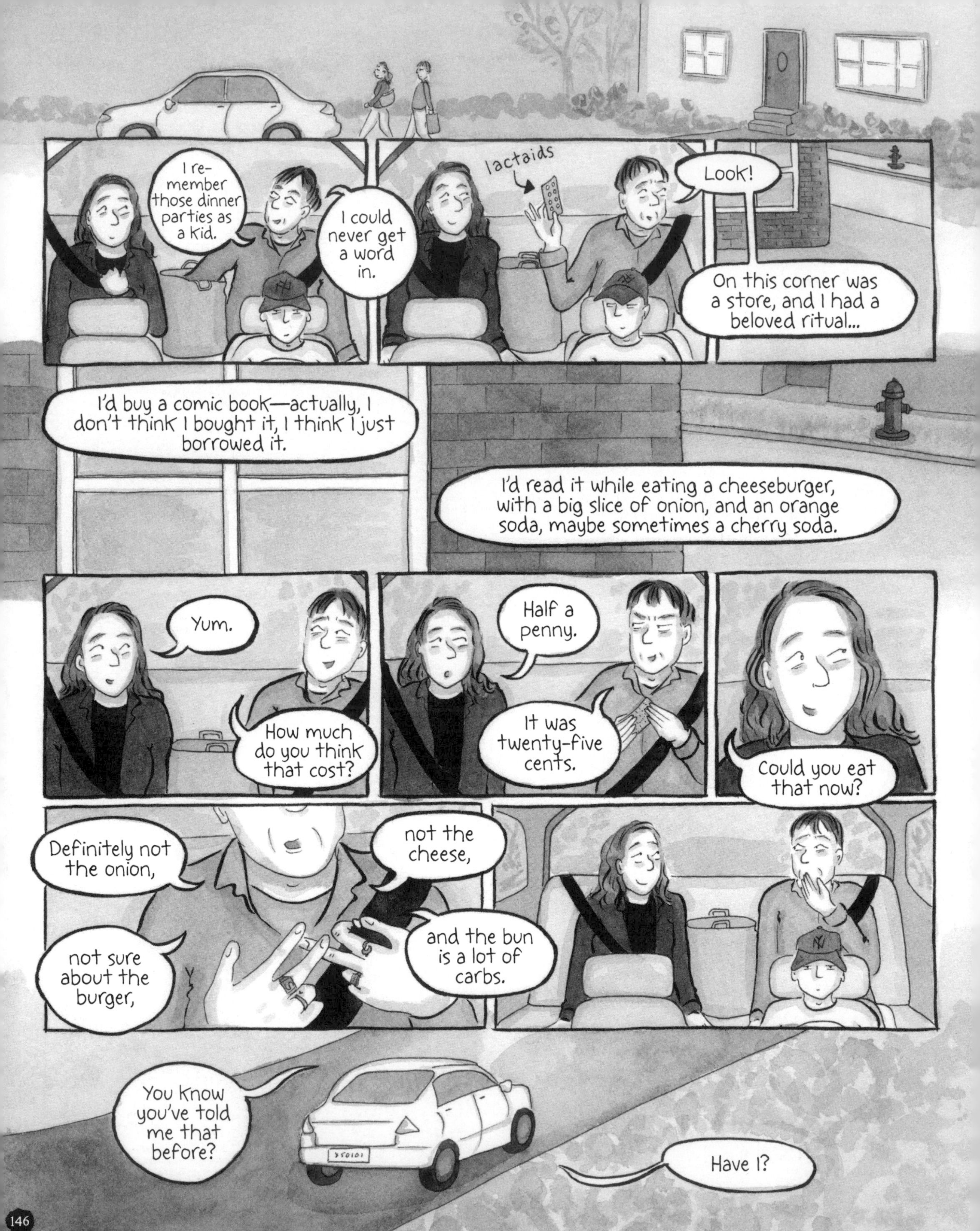
I re-member those dinner parties as a kid.
I could never get a word in.
lactaids
Look!
On this corner was a store, and I had a beloved ritual...
I'd buy a comic book—actually, I don't think I bought it, I think I just borrowed it.
I'd read it while eating a cheeseburger, with a big slice of onion, and an orange soda, maybe sometimes a cherry soda.
Yum.
How much do you think that cost?
Half a penny.
It was twenty-five cents.
Could you eat that now?
Definitely not the onion,
not the cheese,
not sure about the burger,
and the bun is a lot of carbs.
You know you've told me that before?
Have I?

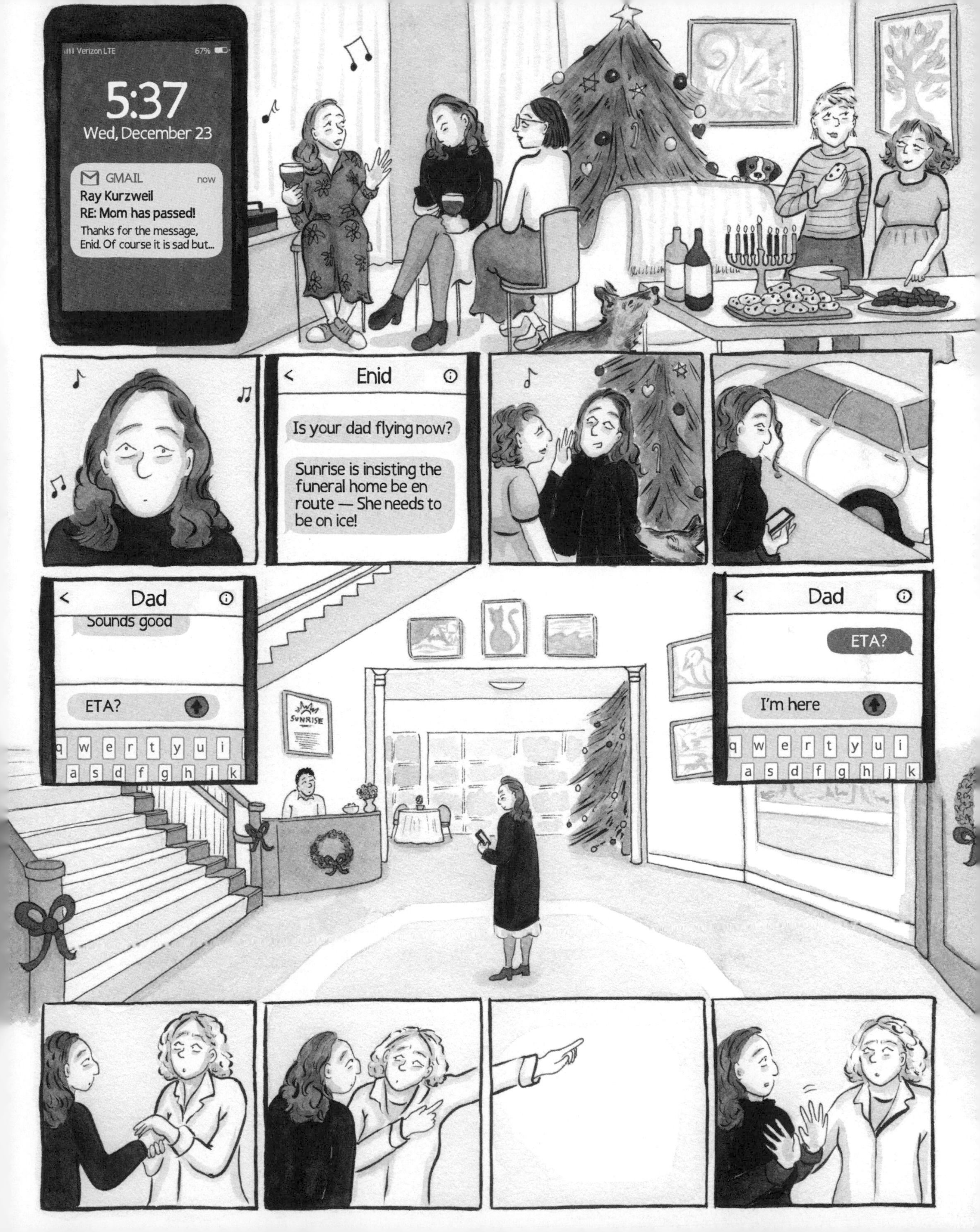

Verizon LTE
67%
5:37
Wed, December 23
GMAIL
now
Ray Kurzweil
RE: Mom has passed!
Thanks for the message, Enid. Of course it is sad but...
Enid
Is your dad flying now?
Sunrise is insisting the funeral home be en route — She needs to be on ice!
Dad
Sounds good
ETA?
SUNRISE
Dad
ETA?
I'm here

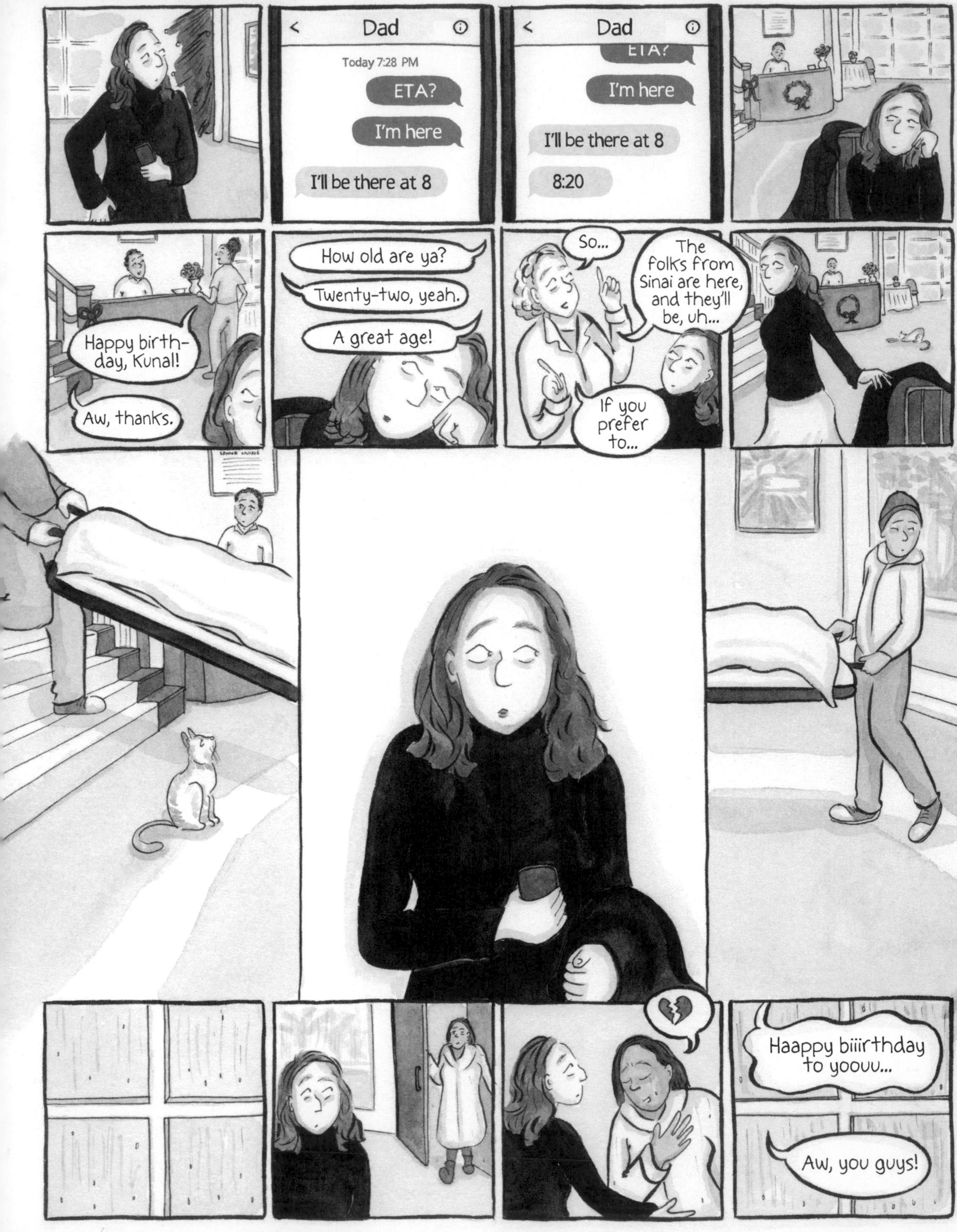
Dad
Today 7:28 PM
ETA?
I'm here
I'll be there at 8
Dad
ETA?
I'm here
I'll be there at 8
8:20
Happy birth-day, Kunal!
Aw, thanks.
How old are ya?
Twenty-two, yeah.
A great age!
So...
The folks from Sinai are here, and they'll be, uh...
If you prefer to...
Haappy biiirthday to yoouu...
Aw, you guys!

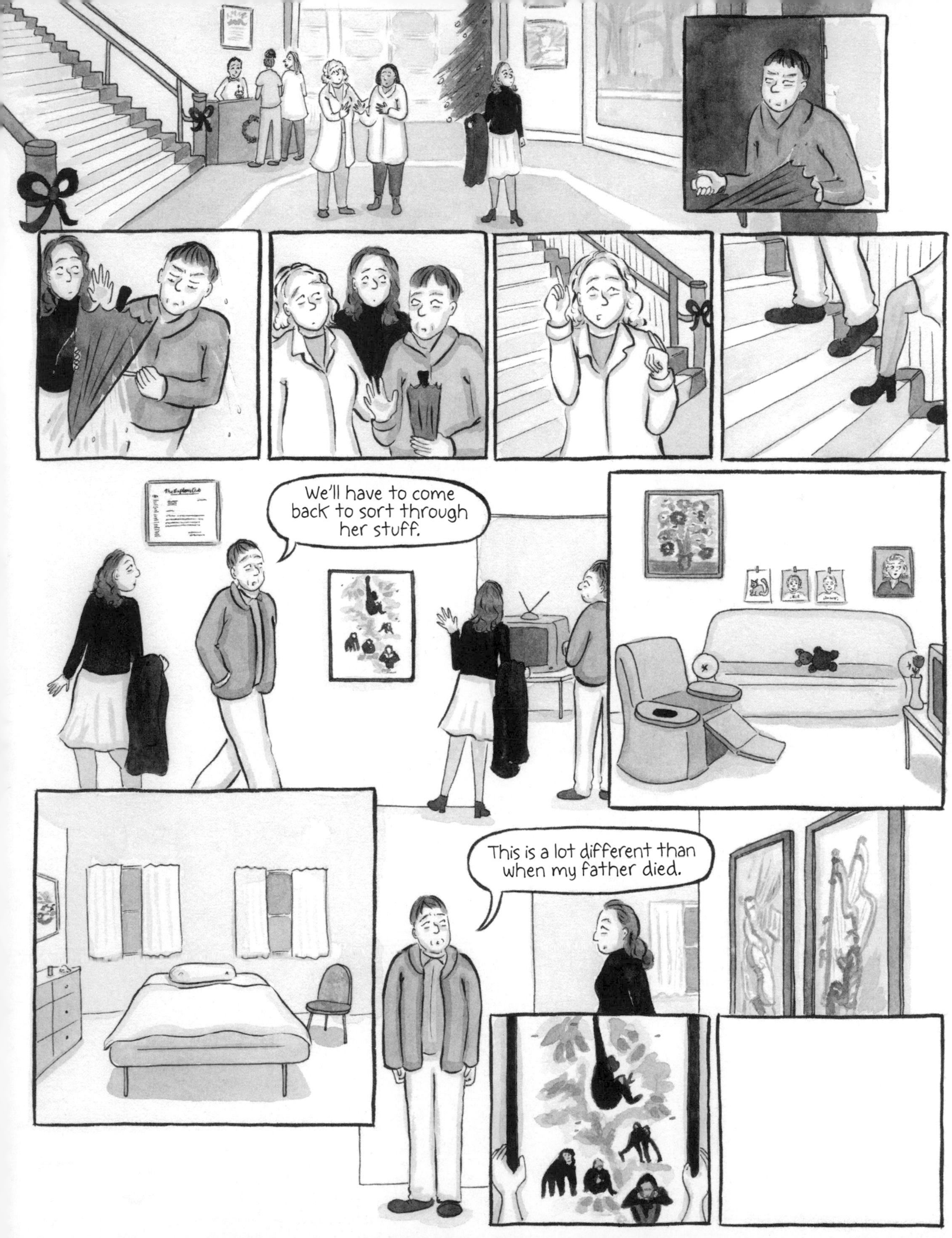
We'll have to come back to sort through her stuff.
This is a lot different than when my father died.

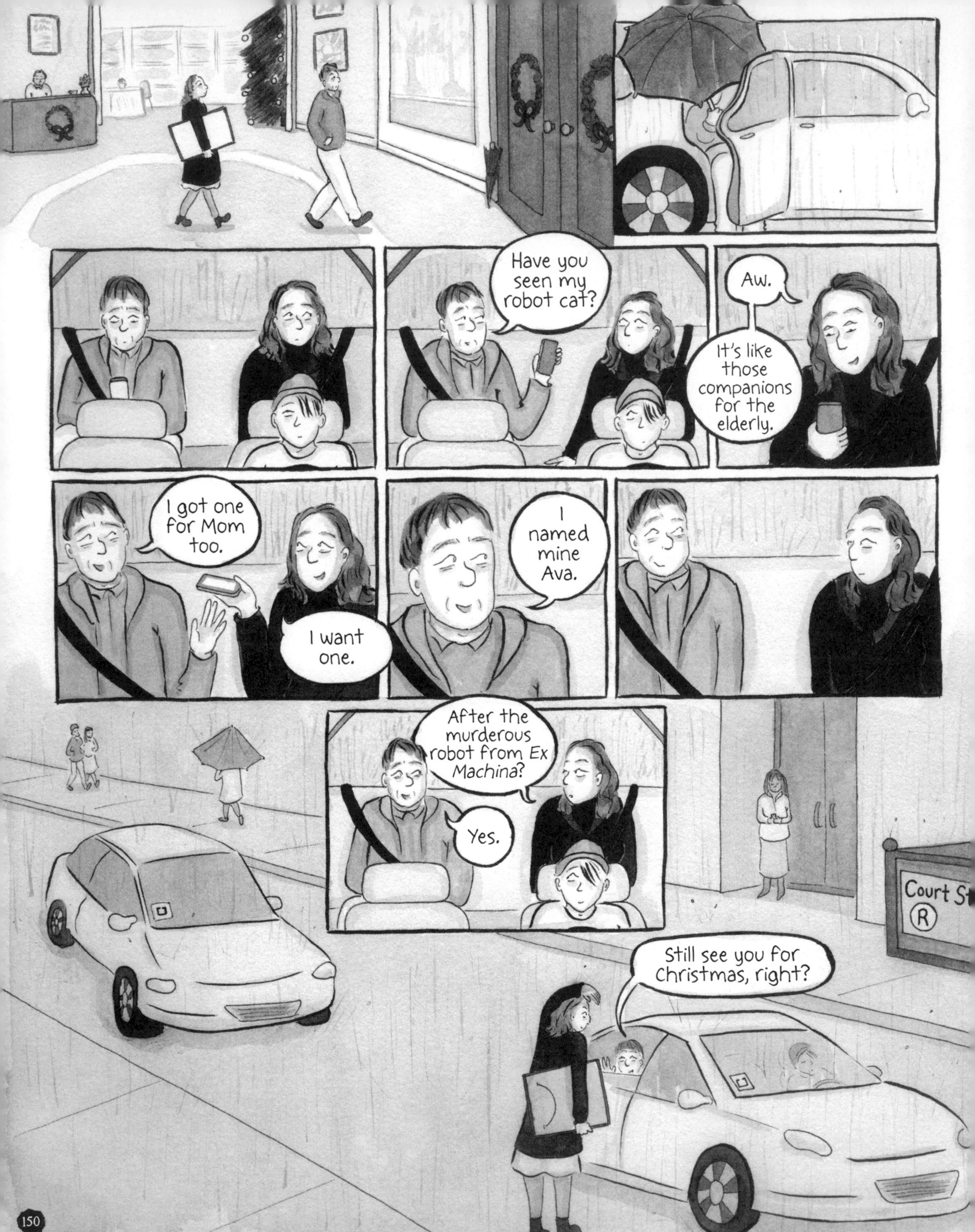
Have you seen my robot cat?
Aw.
It's like those companions for the elderly.
I got one for Mom too.
I want one.
I named mine Ava.
After the murderous robot from Ex Machina?
Yes.
Court St
R
Still see you for Christmas, right?

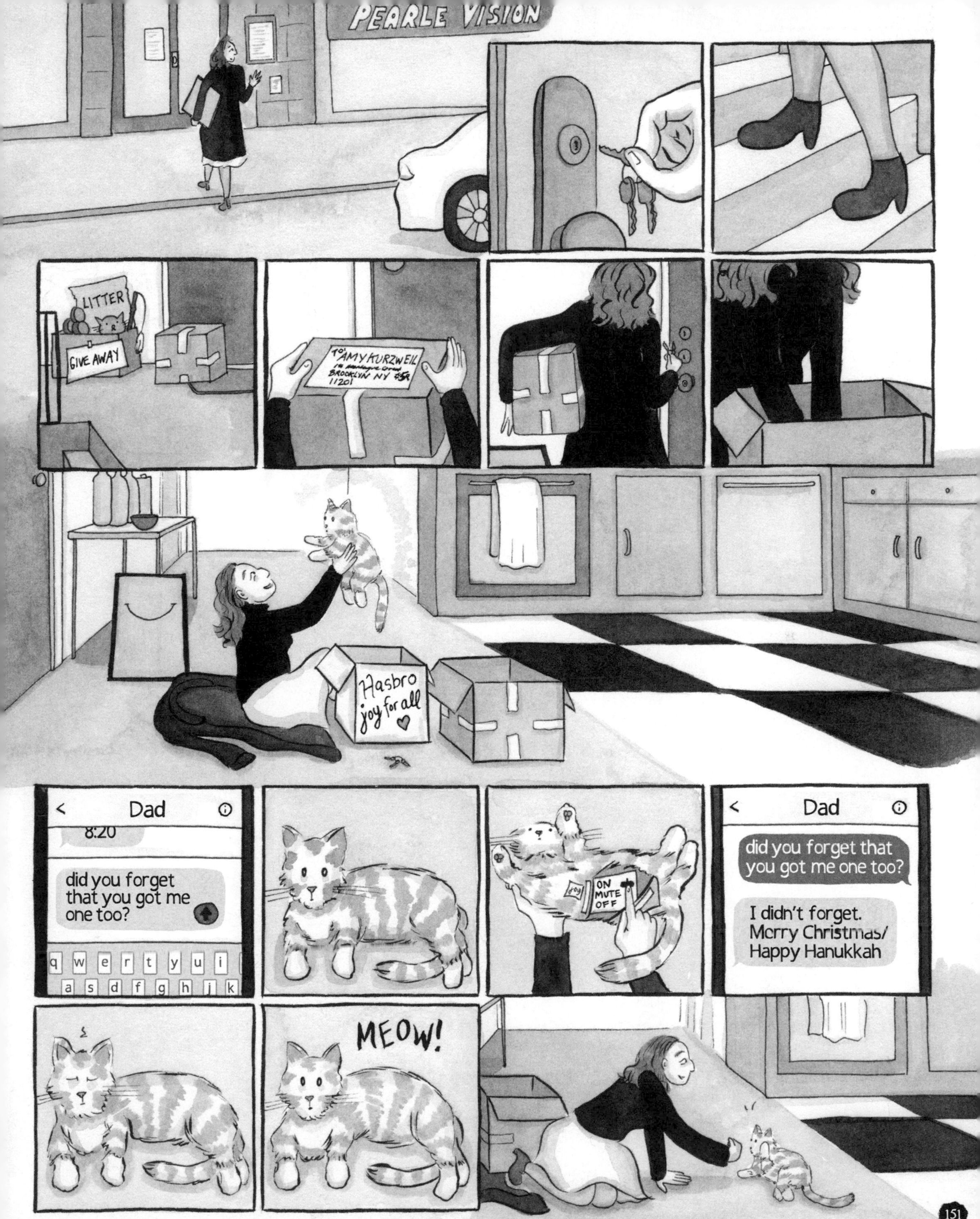
PEARLE VISION
LITTER
GIVE AWAY
To: AMY KURZWEIL
BROOKLYN NY
11201
Hasbro
joy for all
Dad
8:20
did you forget that you got me one too?
ON
MUTE
OFF
Dad
did you forget that you got me one too?
I didn't forget. Merry Christmas/ Happy Hanukkah
MEOW!

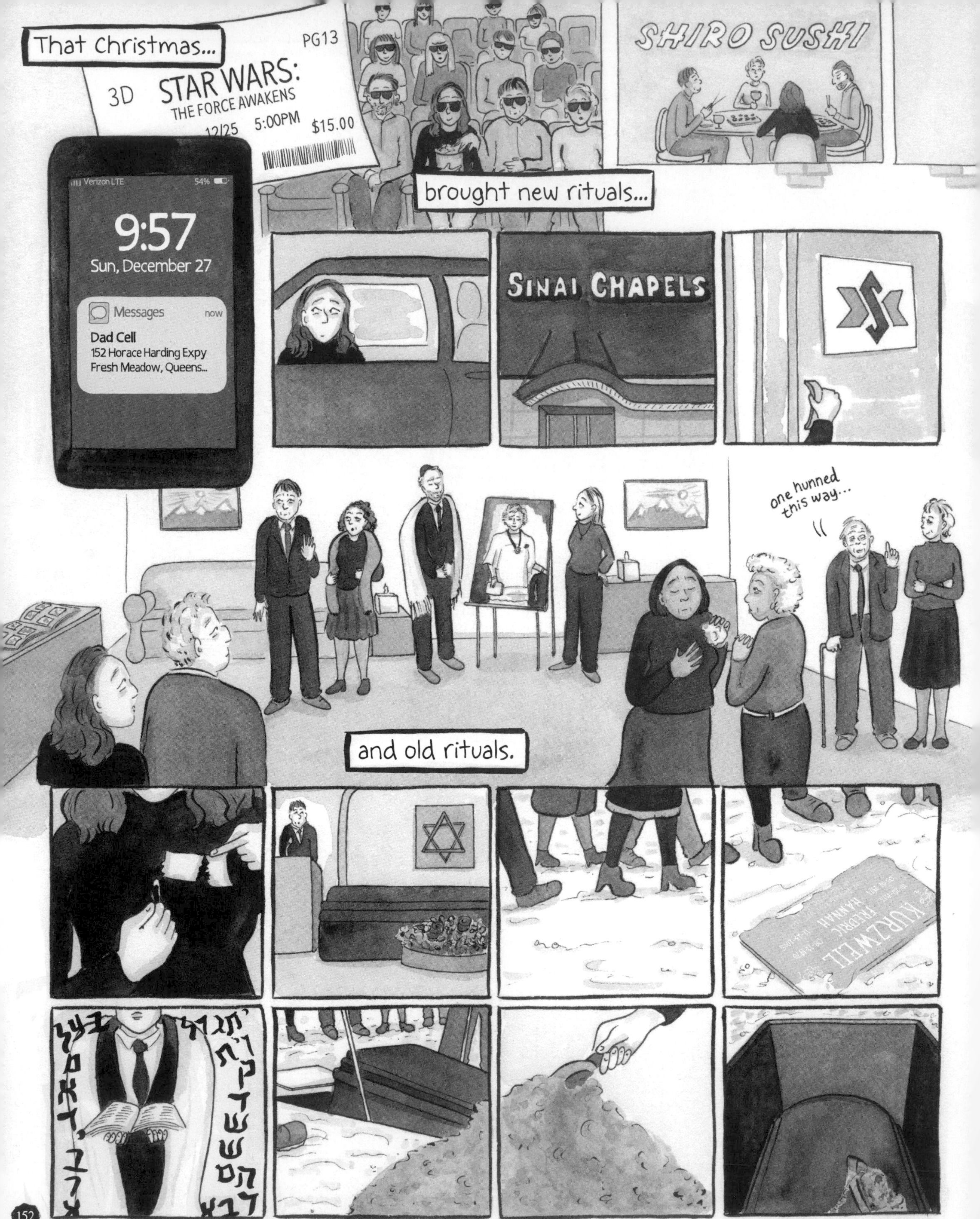
That Christmas...
PG13
3D
STAR WARS:
THE FORCE AWAKENS
12/25 5:00PM
$15.00
SHIRO SUSHI
Verizon LTE
54%
9:57
Sun, December 27
Messages
now
Dad Cell
152 Horace Harding Expy
Fresh Meadow, Queens...
brought new rituals...
SINAI CHAPELS
one hunned this way...
and old rituals.
KURZWEIL
FREDRIC
HANNAH

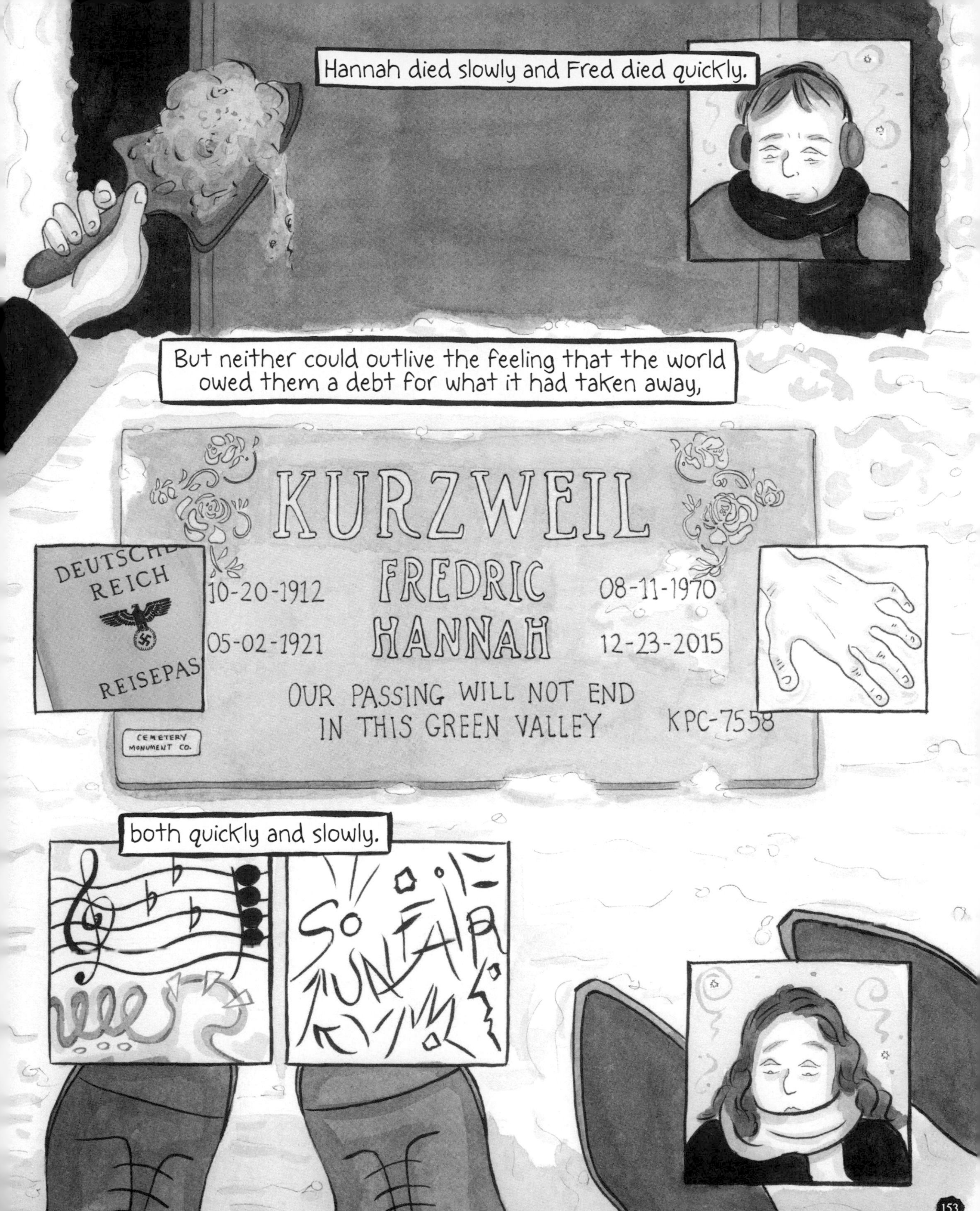
Hannah died slowly and Fred died quickly.
But neither could outlive the feeling that the world owed them a debt for what it had taken away,
KURZWEIL
FREDRIC
10-20-1912
08-11-1970
HANNAH
05-02-1921
12-23-2015
OUR PASSING WILL NOT END IN THIS GREEN VALLEY
KPC-7558
CEMETERY MONUMENT CO.
DEUTSCHES REICH
REISEPAS
both quickly and slowly.
SO UNFAIR

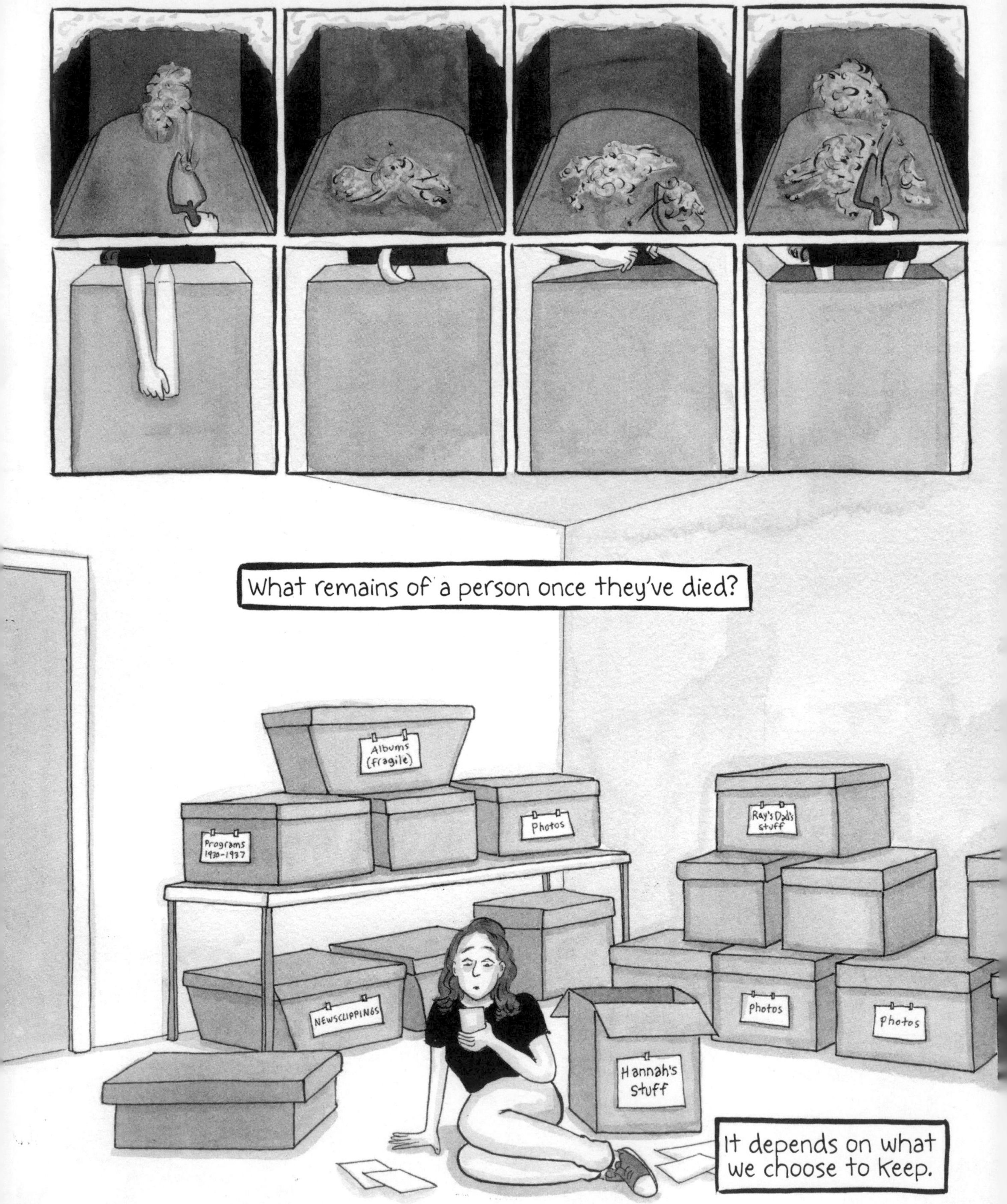
What remains of a person once they've died?
Albums (fragile)
Programs 1930-1937
Photos
Ray's Dad's stuff
NEWSCLIPPINGS
Photos
Photos
Hannah's stuff
It depends on what we choose to keep.

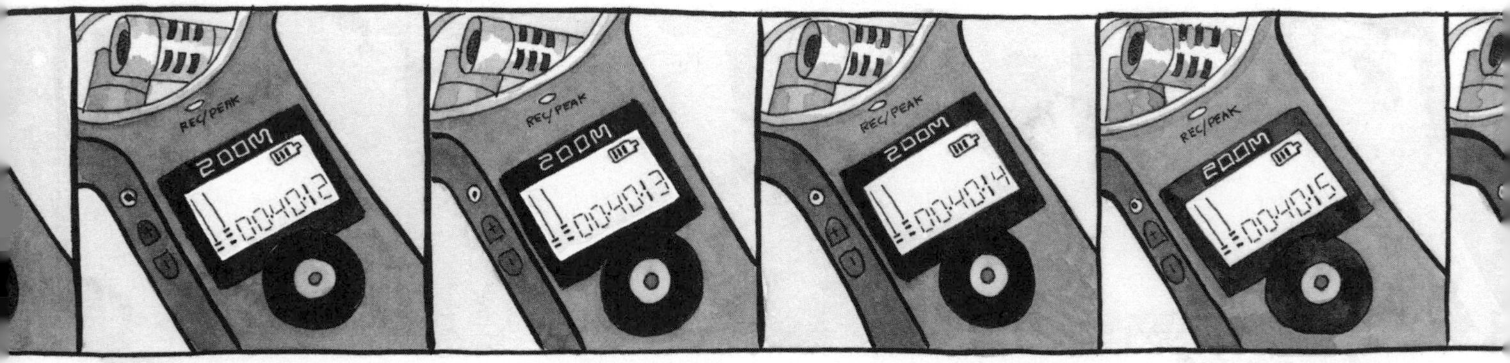
REC/PEAK
ZOOM
004012
REC/PEAK
ZOOM
004013
REC/PEAK
ZOOM
004014
REC/PEAK
ZOOM
004015

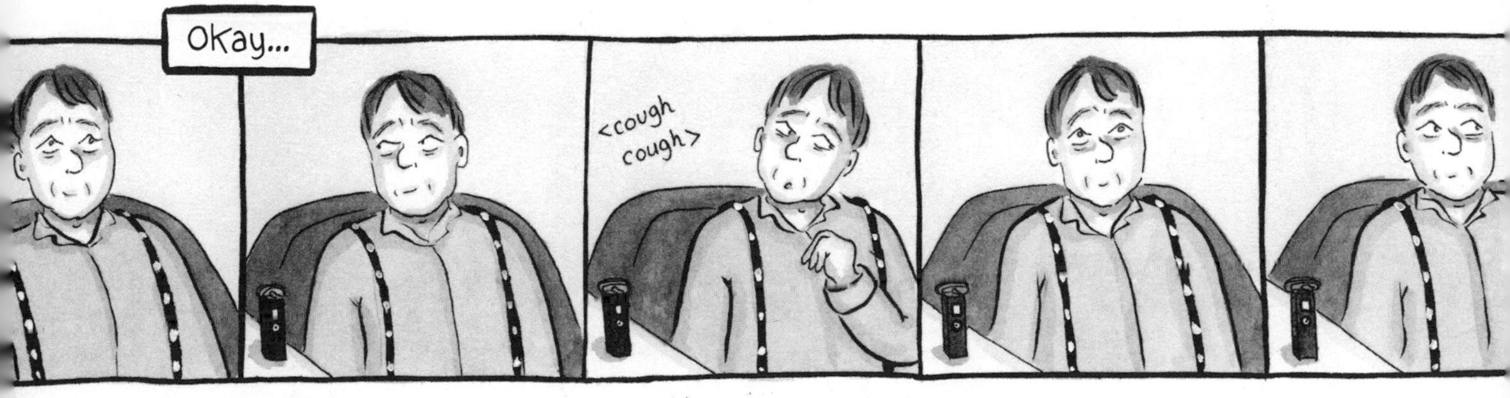
Okay...
<cough cough>

Another question I wanted to ask you...

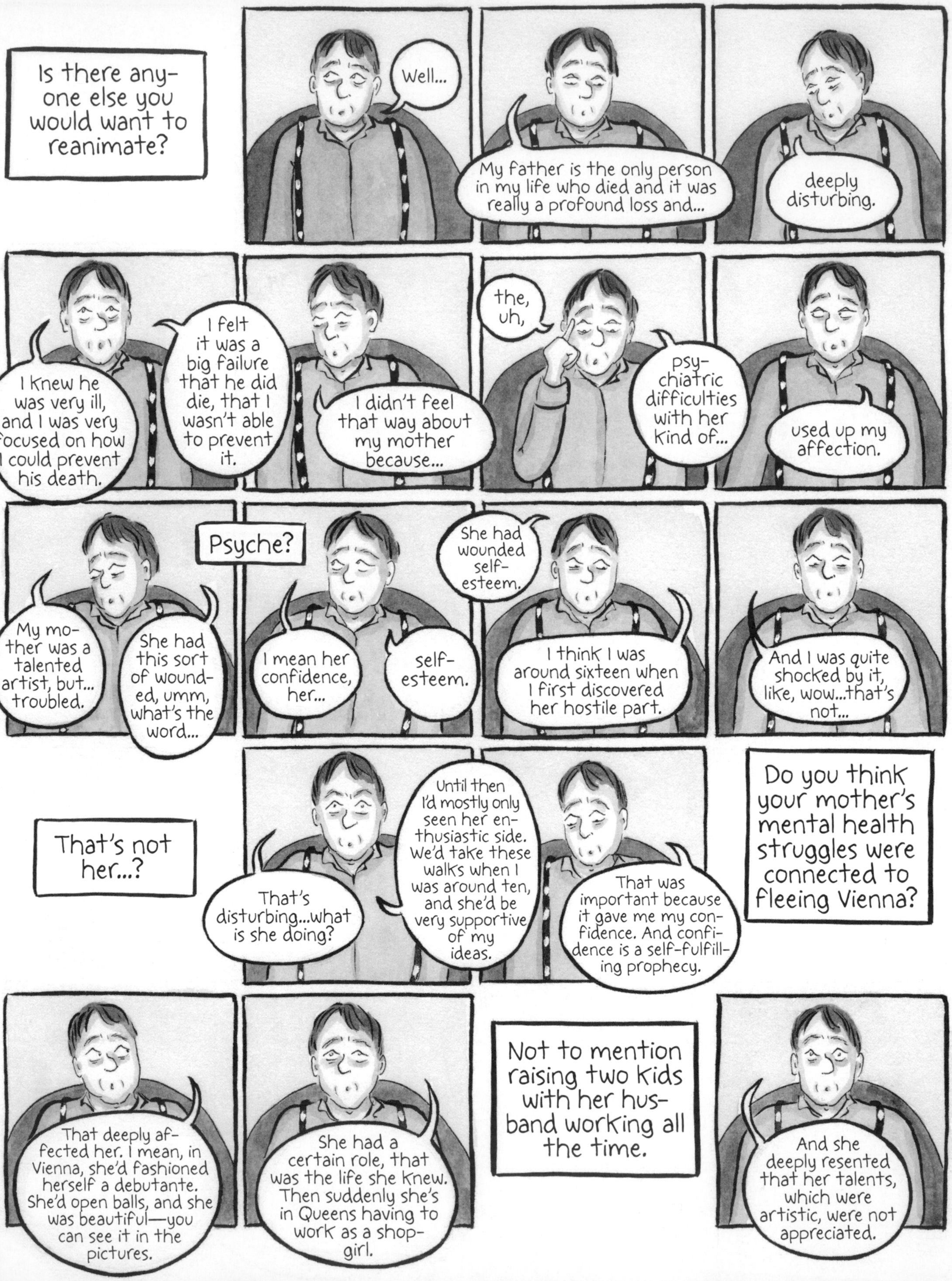
Is there anyone else you would want to reanimate?
Well...
My father is the only person in my life who died and it was really a profound loss and...
deeply disturbing.
I knew he was very ill, and I was very focused on how I could prevent his death.
I felt it was a big failure that he did die, that I wasn't able to prevent it.
I didn't feel that way about my mother because...
the, uh,
psychiatric difficulties with her kind of...
used up my affection.
My mother was a talented artist, but... troubled.
She had this sort of wounded, umm, what's the word...
Psyche?
I mean her confidence, her...
self-esteem.
She had wounded self-esteem.
I think I was around sixteen when I first discovered her hostile part.
And I was quite shocked by it, like, wow...that's not...
That's not her...?
That's disturbing...what is she doing?
Until then I'd mostly only seen her enthusiastic side. We'd take these walks when I was around ten, and she'd be very supportive of my ideas.
That was important because it gave me my confidence. And confidence is a self-fulfilling prophecy.
Do you think your mother's mental health struggles were connected to fleeing Vienna?
That deeply affected her. I mean, in Vienna, she'd fashioned herself a debutante. She'd open balls, and she was beautiful—you can see it in the pictures.
She had a certain role, that was the life she knew. Then suddenly she's in Queens having to work as a shopgirl.
Not to mention raising two kids with her husband working all the time.
And she deeply resented that her talents, which were artistic, were not appreciated.

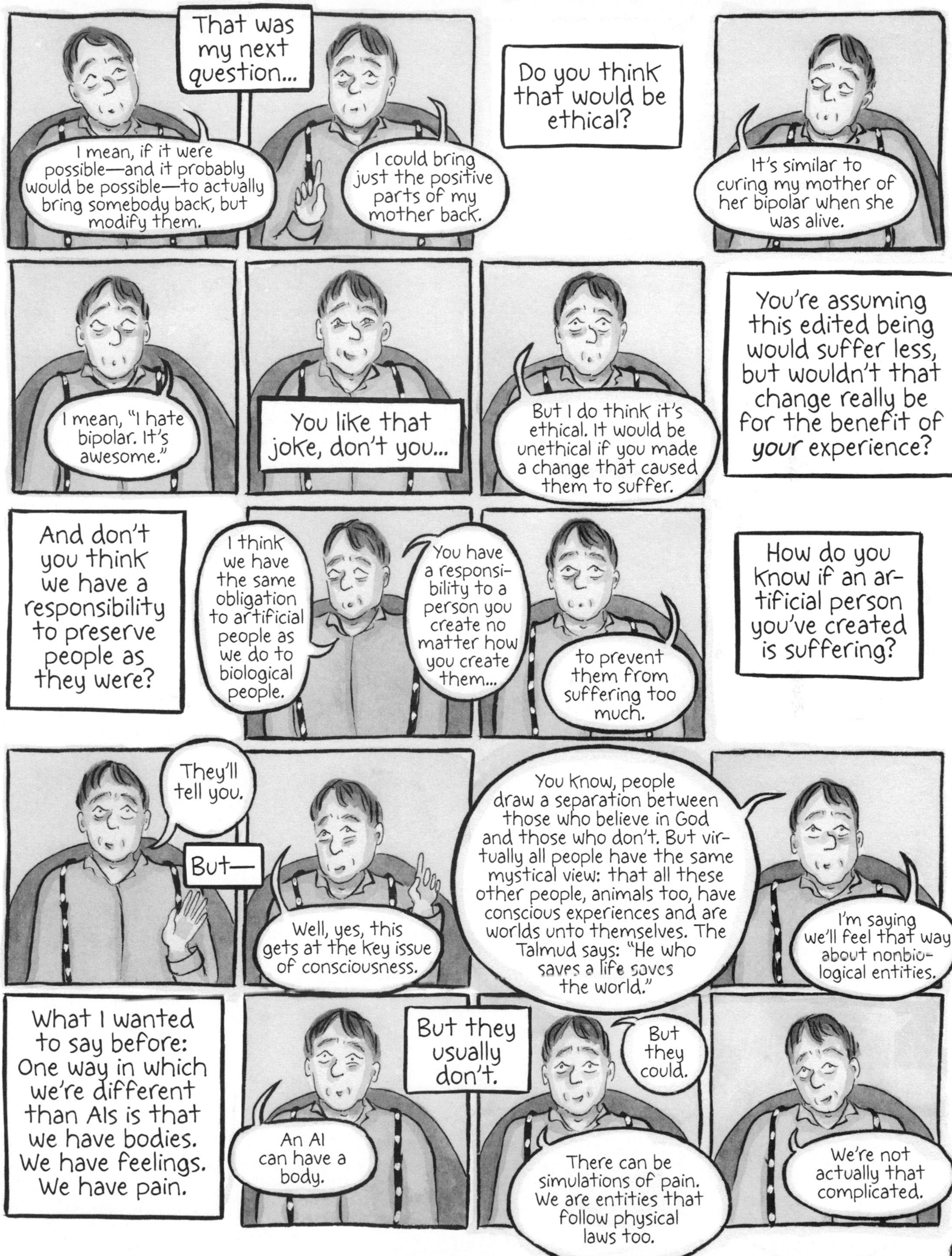
That was my next question...
I mean, if it were possible—and it probably would be possible—to actually bring somebody back, but modify them.
I could bring just the positive parts of my mother back.
Do you think that would be ethical?
It's similar to curing my mother of her bipolar when she was alive.
I mean, "I hate bipolar. It's awesome."
You like that joke, don't you...
But I do think it's ethical. It would be unethical if you made a change that caused them to suffer.
You're assuming this edited being would suffer less, but wouldn't that change really be for the benefit of *your* experience?
And don't you think we have a responsibility to preserve people as they were?
I think we have the same obligation to artificial people as we do to biological people.
You have a responsibility to a person you create no matter how you create them...
to prevent them from suffering too much.
How do you know if an artificial person you've created is suffering?
They'll tell you.
But—
Well, yes, this gets at the key issue of consciousness.
You know, people draw a separation between those who believe in God and those who don't. But virtually all people have the same mystical view: that all these other people, animals too, have conscious experiences and are worlds unto themselves. The Talmud says: "He who saves a life saves the world."
I'm saying we'll feel that way about nonbiological entities.
What I wanted to say before: One way in which we're different than AIs is that we have bodies. We have feelings. We have pain.
An AI can have a body.
But they usually don't.
But they could.
There can be simulations of pain. We are entities that follow physical laws too.
We're not actually that complicated.

# V.

# Heart Strings

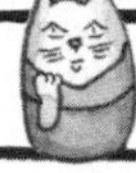

"Are you not afraid of death?"

"I am not in the least afraid!...I would rather die than drink that bitter medicine."

At that moment the door of the room flew open, and four rabbits as black as ink entered...

"What do you want with me?" cried Pinocchio, sitting up in bed in a great fright.

"We have come to take you," said the biggest rabbit.

"To take me?...But I am not yet dead!..."

"No, not yet: but you have only a few minutes to live, as you have refused the medicine that would have cured you of the fever."

"Oh, fairy, fairy!" the puppet then began to scream, "give me the tumbler at once... be quick for pity's sake, for I will not die...no...I will not die..."

–Carlo Collodi, *The Adventures of Pinocchio*
(trans. Mary Alice Murray)

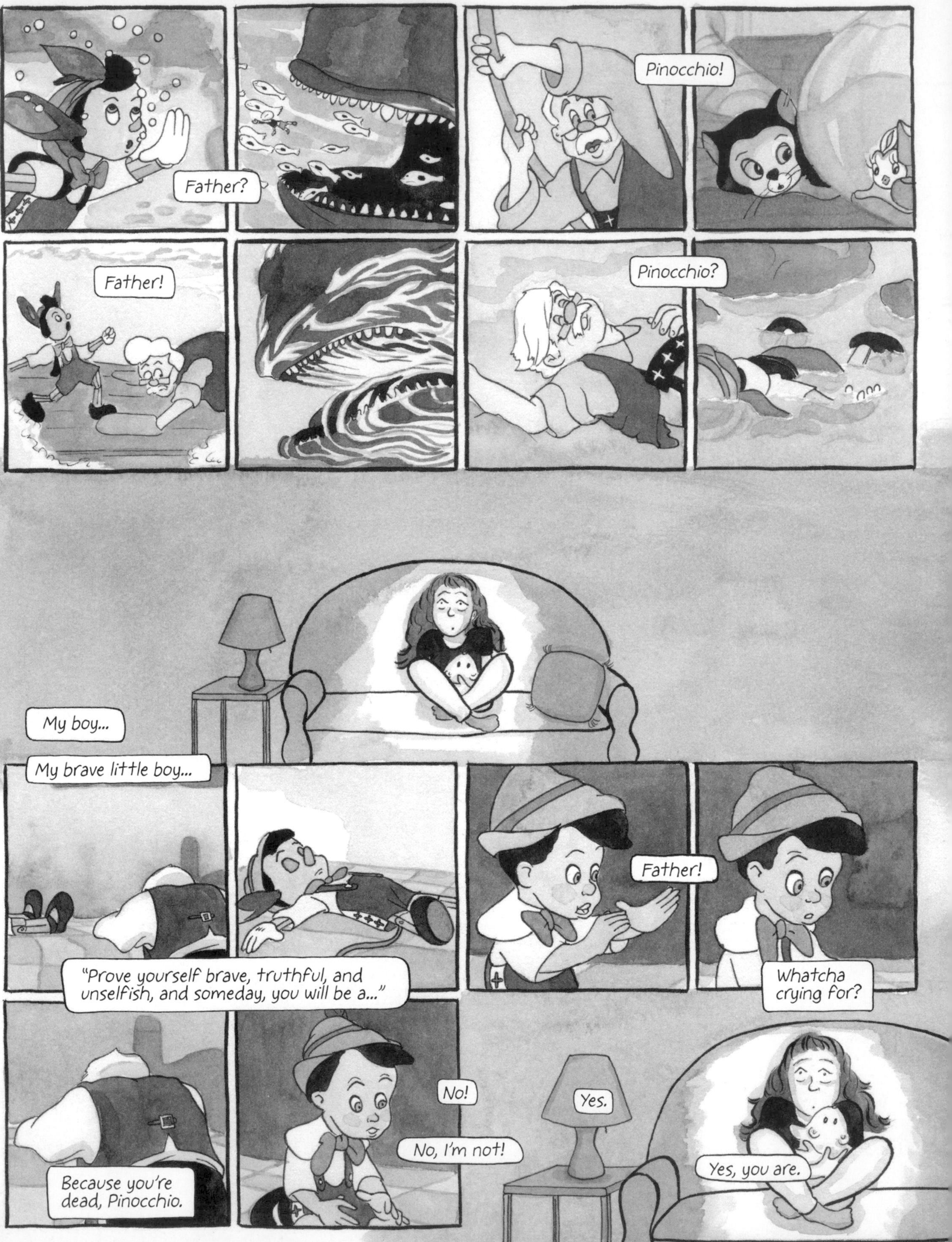
Father?
Pinocchio!
Father!
Pinocchio?
My boy...
My brave little boy...
"Prove yourself brave, truthful, and unselfish, and someday, you will be a..."
Father!
Whatcha crying for?
Because you're dead, Pinocchio.
No!
No, I'm not!
Yes.
Yes, you are.

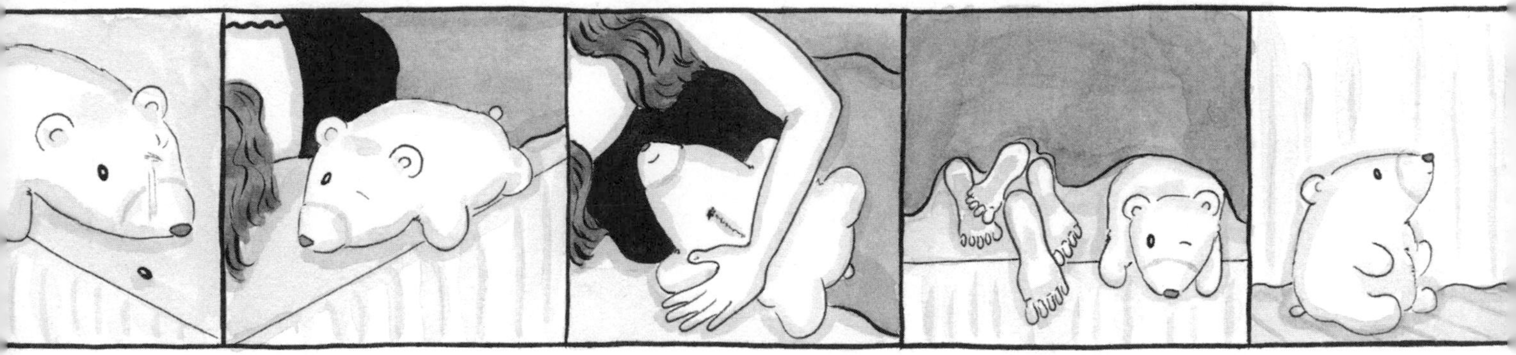

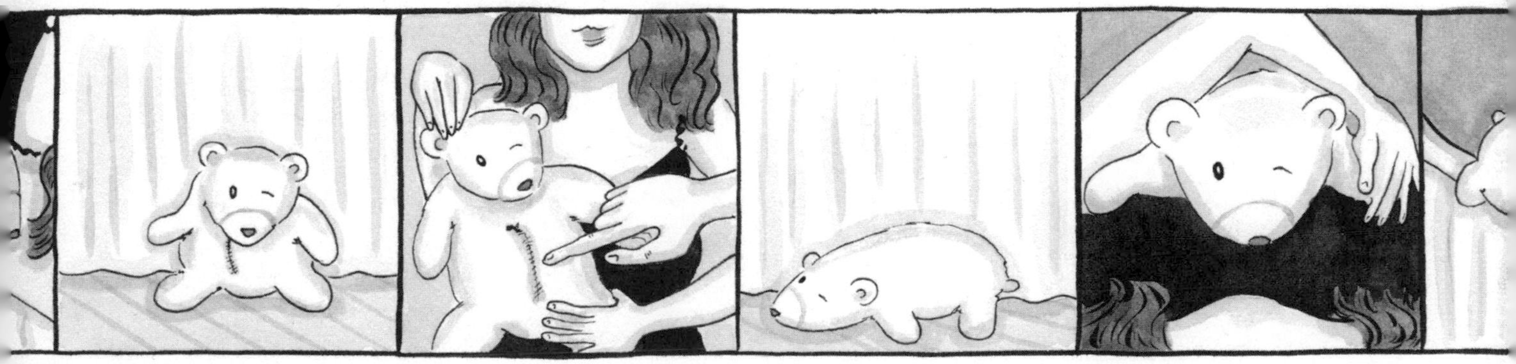

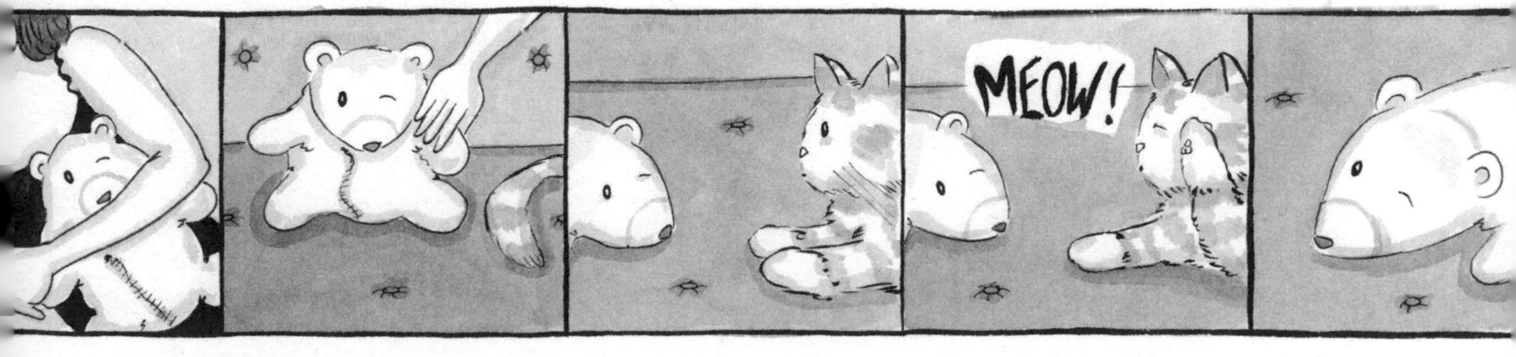
MEOW!

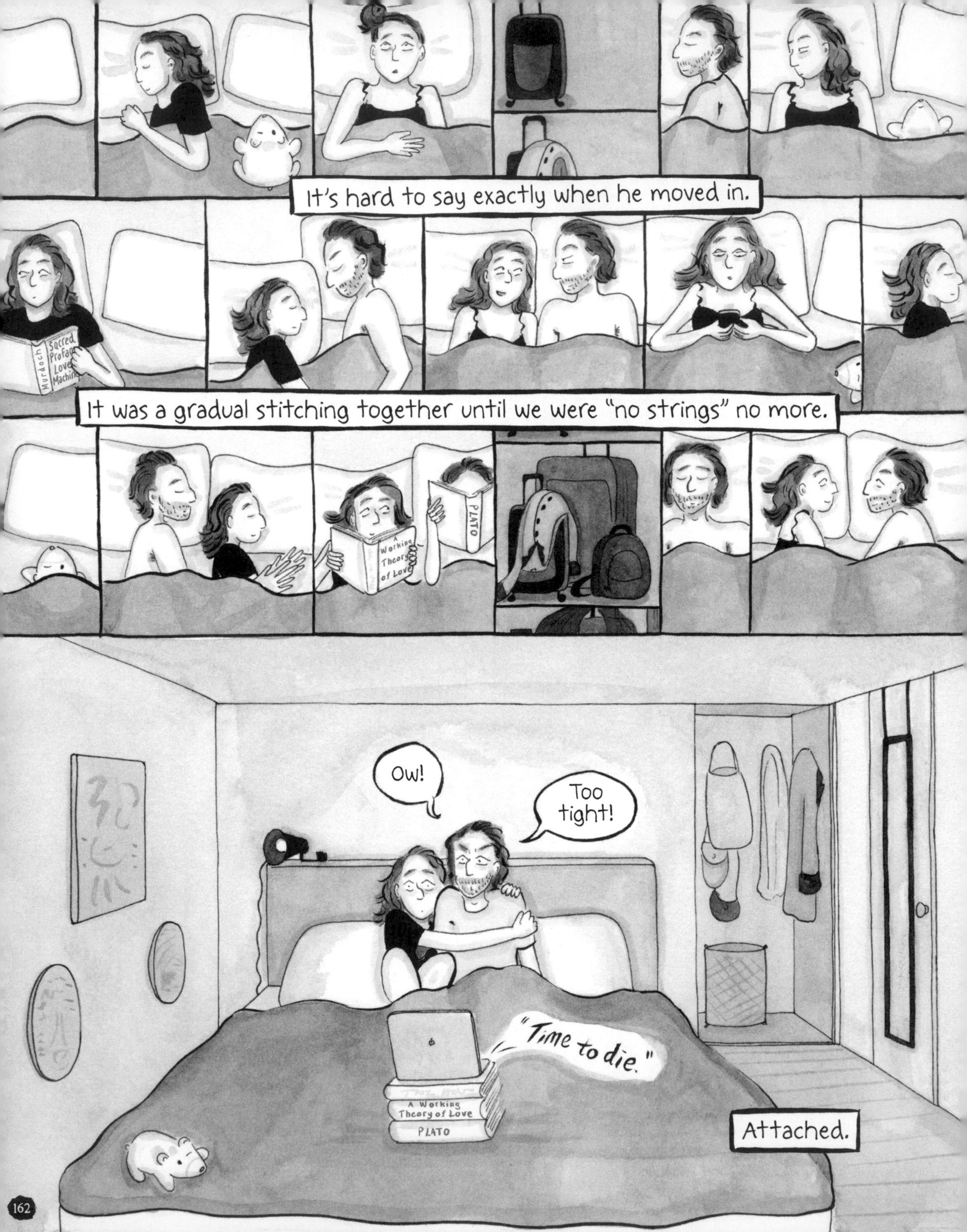

It's hard to say exactly when he moved in.
Murdoch
Sacred Profa Love Machin
It was a gradual stitching together until we were "no strings" no more.
A Working Theory of Love
PLATO
Ow!
Too tight!
"Time to die."
A Working Theory of Love
PLATO
Attached.

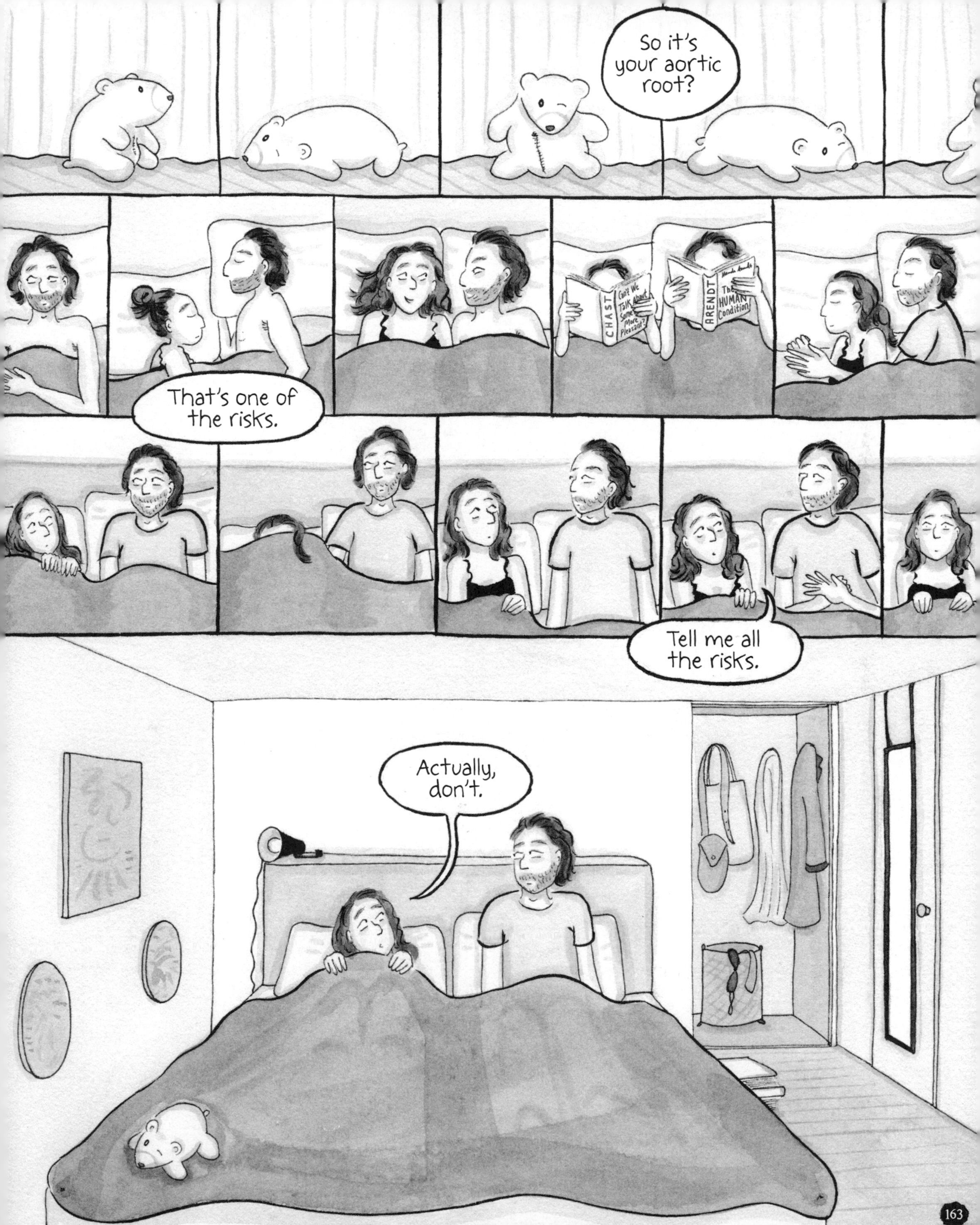

So it's your aortic root?
CHAST
Can't We Talk About
ARENDT
The HUMAN Condition
That's one of the risks.
Tell me all the risks.
Actually, don't.

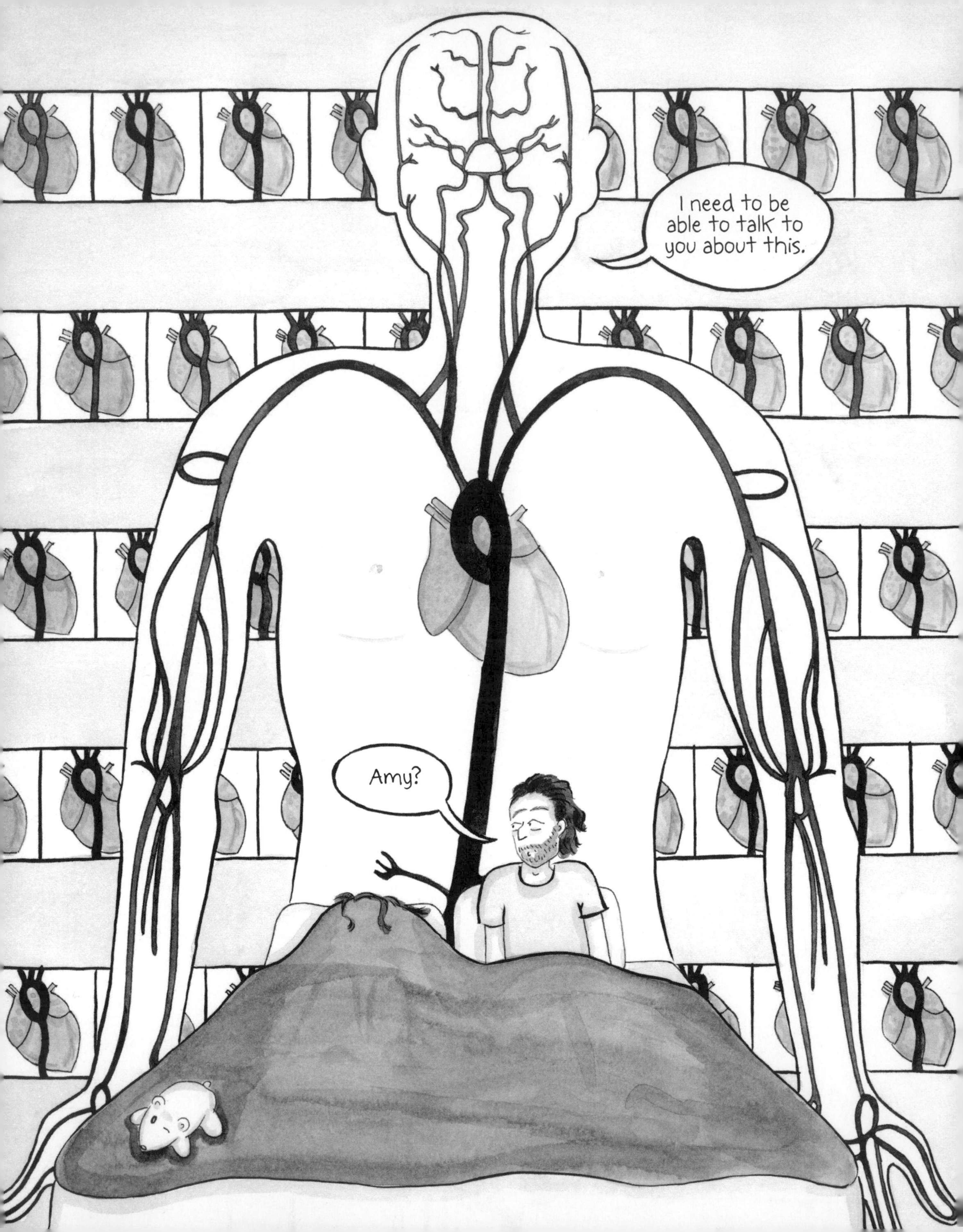
I need to be able to talk to you about this.
Amy?

gle.com/search?q=marfan+syndrome&source

/search?q=aortic+dissection&source+Inms

## Marfan Syndrome

ABOUT      SYMPTOMS      TREATMENT

An inherited disorder that affects connective tissue.

### Rare
Fewer than 200,000 US cases per year.
Treatment can help, but this condition can't be cured.

Marfan Syndrome affects the heart, eyes, blood vessels and bones.
People with Marfan Syndrome are tall and thin with long arms, legs, fingers and toes.
Treatment includes medication to keep blood pressure low, eye glasses or contact lenses, and surgery.

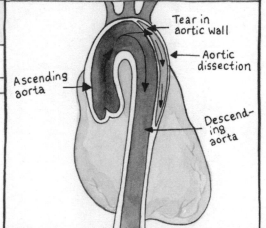

Tear in aortic wall

Aortic dissection

Ascending aorta

Descending aorta

## WebMD    SUBSCRIBE

One of the biggest threats of Marfan Syndrome is damage to the <u>aorta</u>, the <u>artery</u> that carries blood from the heart to the rest of the body. Marfan Syndrome can rupture the inner leayers of the aorta, causing dissection that leads to bleeding in the walls of the vessel. Aortic dissection can be deadly. Surgery may be required to replace the affected part of the aorta.

Some people with Marfan Syndrome have <u>mitral valve</u> prolapse, a billowing of the heart valve that may be associated with

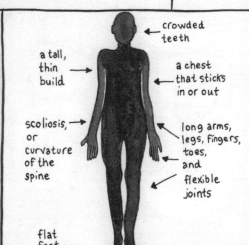

he past life xpectancy 2 years

with reatment ormal.

crowded teeth

a tall, thin build

a chest that sticks in or out

scoliosis, or curvature of the spine

long arms, legs, fingers, toes, and flexible joints

flat feet

Ciliary body

Iris

Pupil

Cornea

Lens

Sclera

Choroid

Retina

Fovea centralis

Optic disc (blind spot)

Blood vessels

Suspensory ligament

Optic nerve

## Retinal Detachment

Ectopia lentis occurs when the eye's lens, which focuses light rays on the retina, becomes dislocated. As a result, visual acuity worsens.

Ectopia lentis is considered a key symptom of Marfan Syndrome and is often the first sign of the disorder.

That one's imperfect health might *not* be a state of emergency is a new approach to living for me.

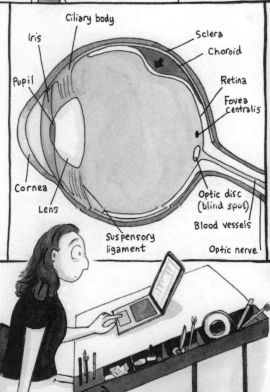

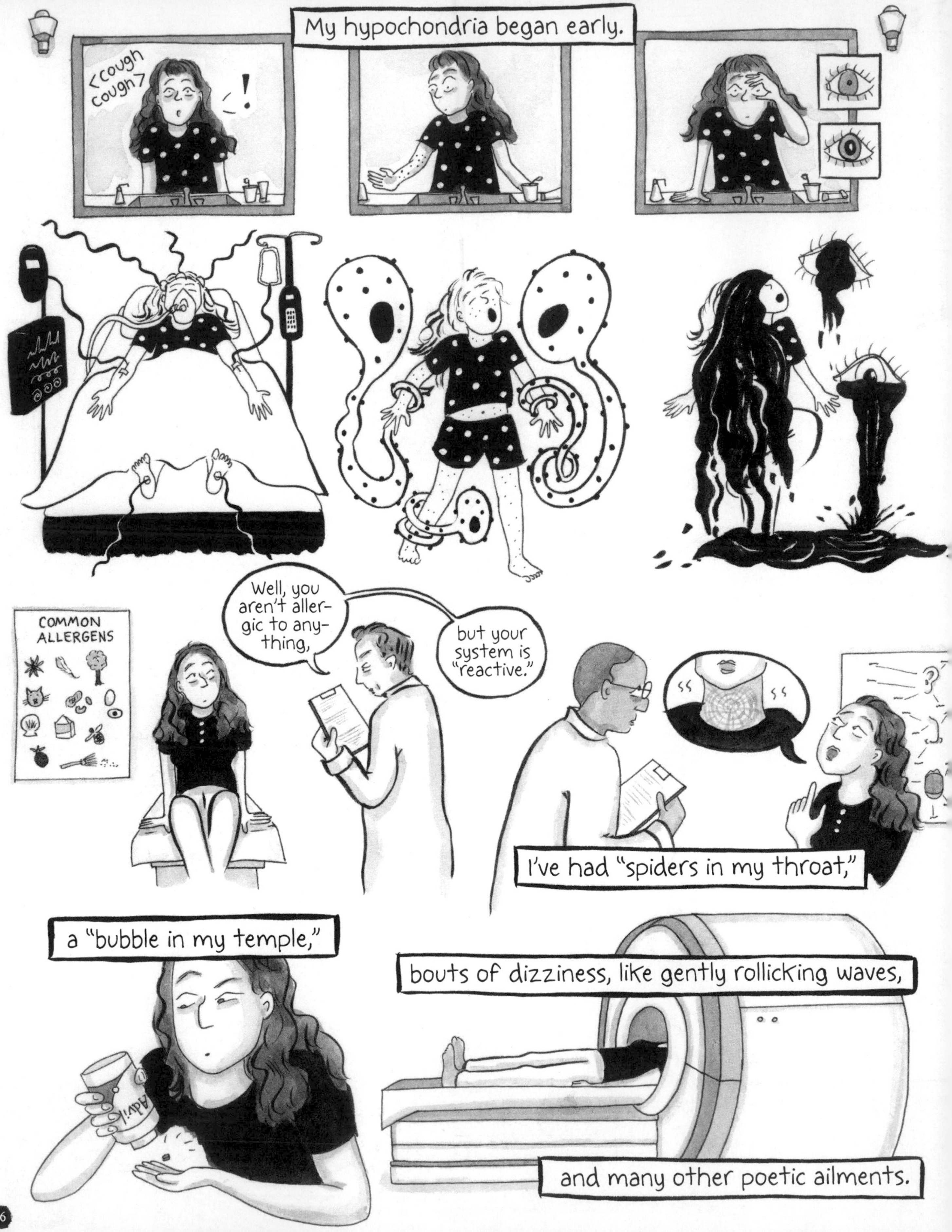
My hypochondria began early.
<cough cough>
!
COMMON ALLERGENS
Well, you aren't allergic to anything,
but your system is "reactive."
I've had "spiders in my throat,"
a "bubble in my temple,"
Advil
bouts of dizziness, like gently rollicking waves,
and many other poetic ailments.

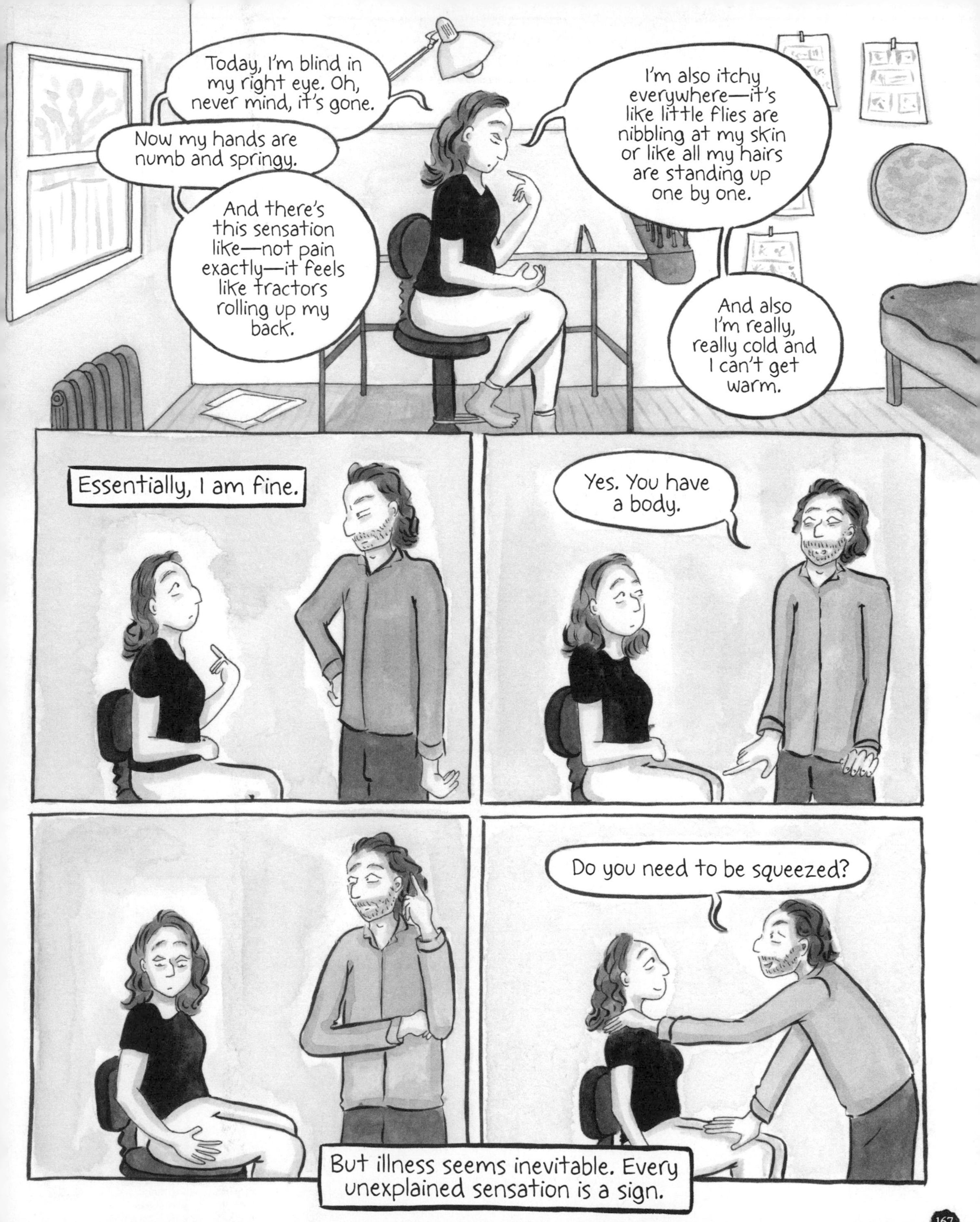
Today, I'm blind in my right eye. Oh, never mind, it's gone.
Now my hands are numb and springy.
And there's this sensation like—not pain exactly—it feels like tractors rolling up my back.
I'm also itchy everywhere—it's like little flies are nibbling at my skin or like all my hairs are standing up one by one.
And also I'm really, really cold and I can't get warm.
Essentially, I am fine.
Yes. You have a body.
Do you need to be squeezed?
But illness seems inevitable. Every unexplained sensation is a sign.

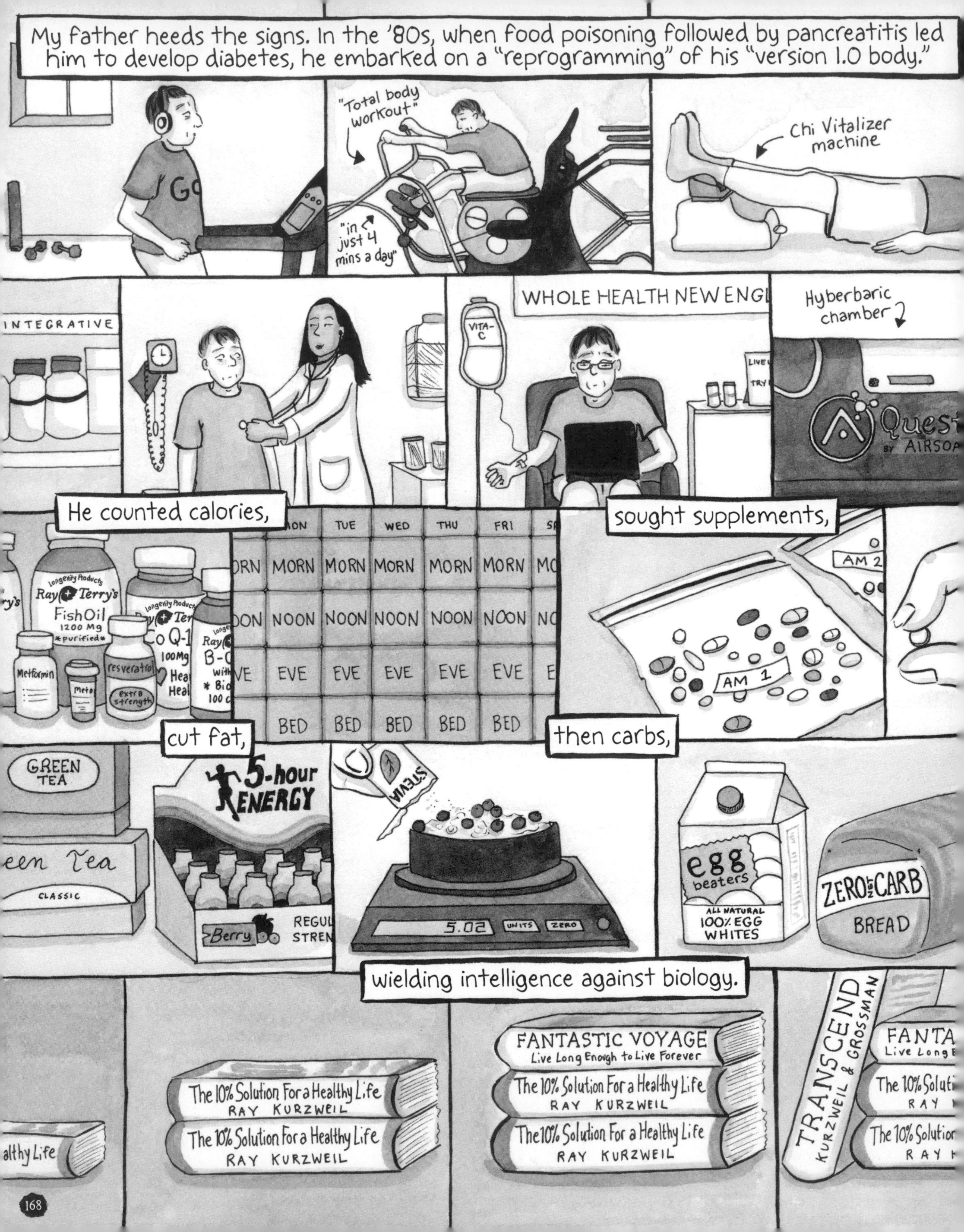

My father heeds the signs. In the '80s, when food poisoning followed by pancreatitis led him to develop diabetes, he embarked on a "reprogramming" of his "version 1.0 body."
Go
"Total body workout"
"in just 4 mins a day"
Chi Vitalizer machine
INTEGRATIVE
WHOLE HEALTH NEW ENGL
VITA-C
Hyberbaric chamber
Quest
BY AIRSOP
He counted calories,
Longevity Products Ray Terry's FishOil 1200 Mg *purified*
CoQ-1
100Mg
Metformin
resveratrol
extra strength
MON TUE WED THU FRI SA
MORN MORN MORN MORN MORN MORN MO
NOON NOON NOON NOON NOON NOON NO
EVE EVE EVE EVE EVE EVE E
BED BED BED BED BED
sought supplements,
AM 1
AM 2
cut fat,
then carbs,
GREEN TEA
een Tea
CLASSIC
5-hour ENERGY
Berry
REGUL STREN
STEVIA
5.02 UNITS ZERO
egg beaters
ALL NATURAL 100% EGG WHITES
ZERO CARB BREAD
wielding intelligence against biology.
althy Life
The 10% Solution For a Healthy Life RAY KURZWEIL
The 10% Solution For a Healthy Life RAY KURZWEIL
FANTASTIC VOYAGE Live Long Enough to Live Forever
The 10% Solution For a Healthy Life RAY KURZWEIL
The 10% Solution For a Healthy Life RAY KURZWEIL
TRANSCEND KURZWEIL & GROSSMAN

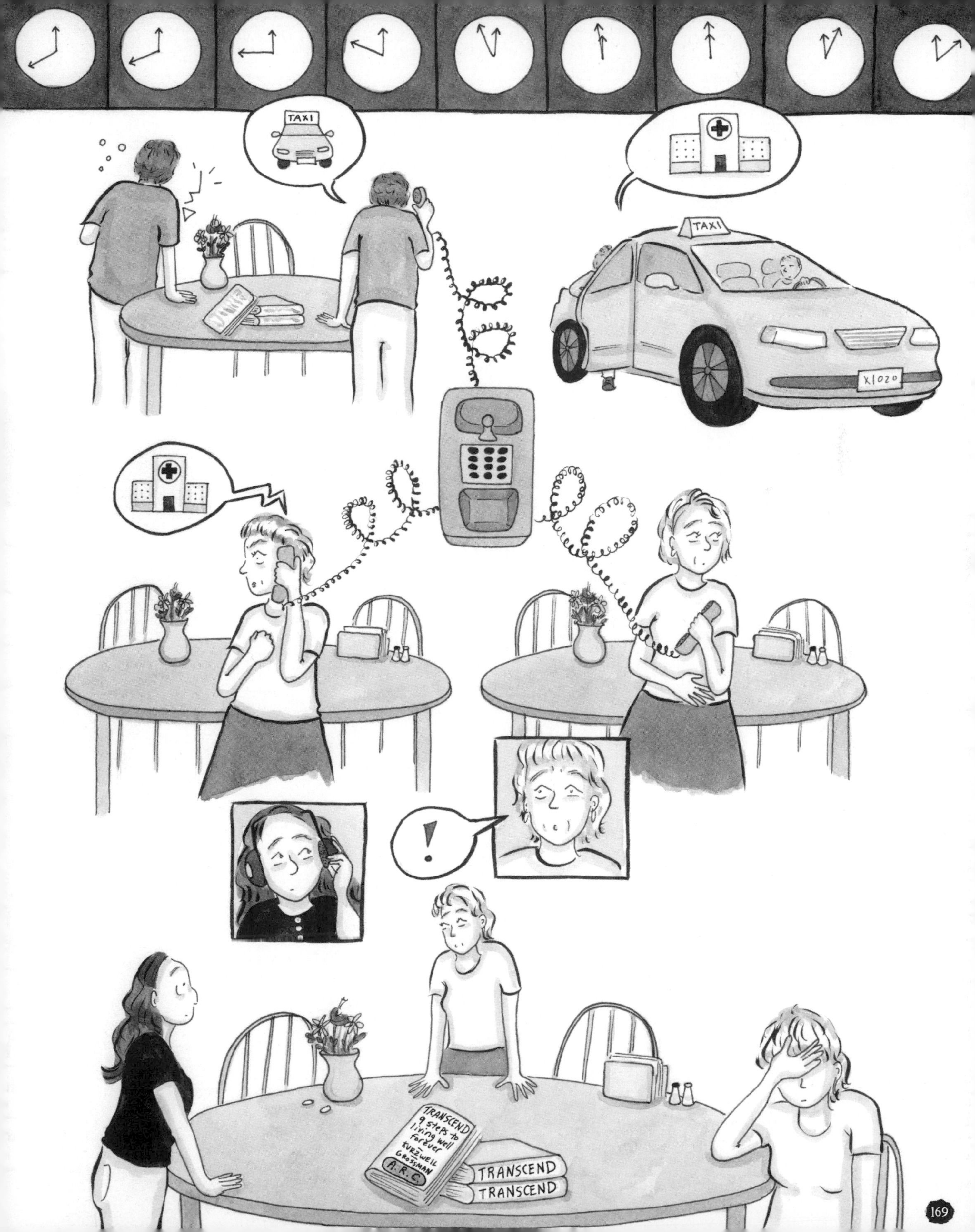
TAXI
TAXI
X1020
!
TRANSCEND
9 steps to
living well
forever
KURZWEIL
GROSSMAN
A.R.C.
TRANSCEND
TRANSCEND

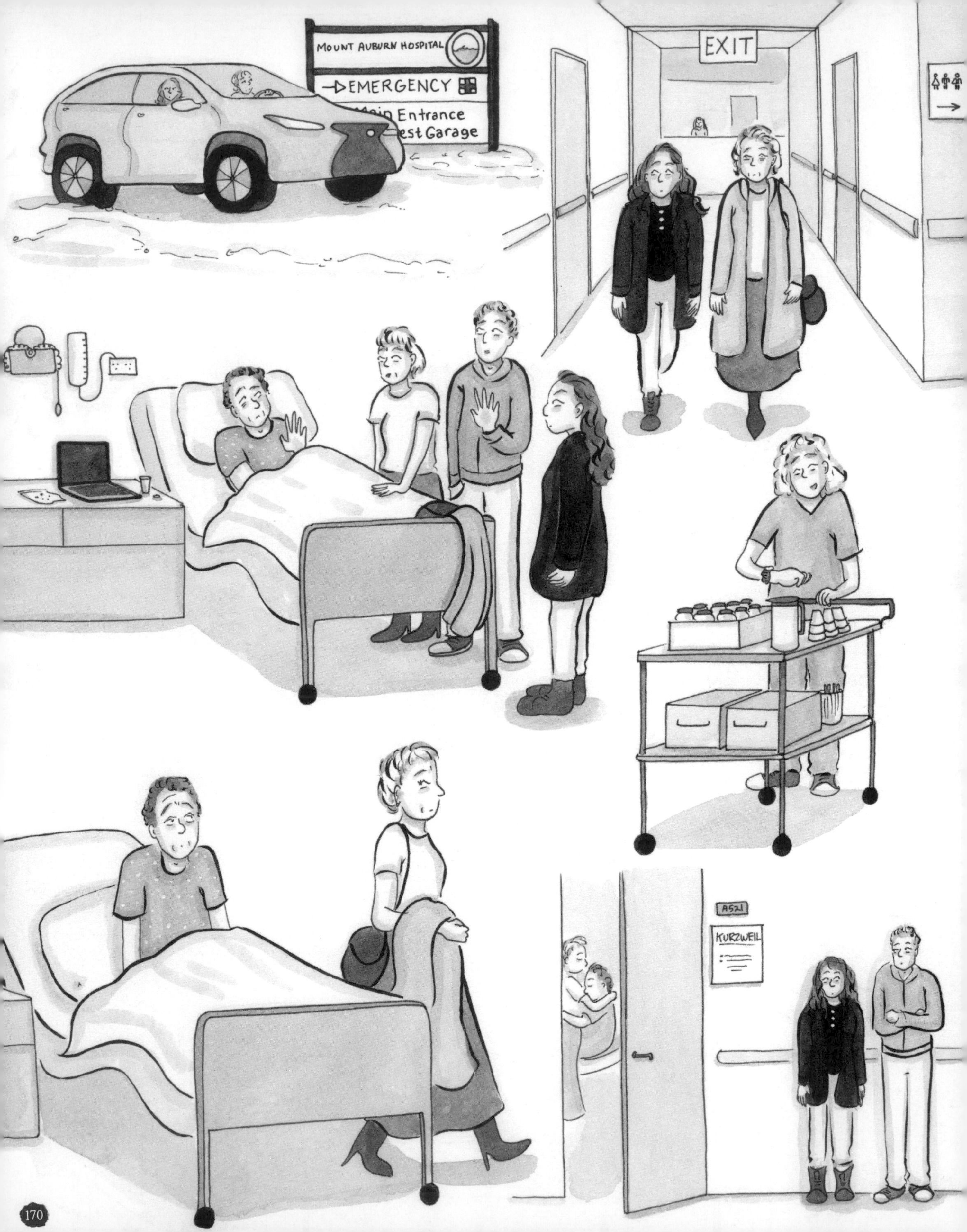

MOUNT AUBURN HOSPITAL
EMERGENCY
Entrance
Garage
EXIT
A521
KURZWEIL

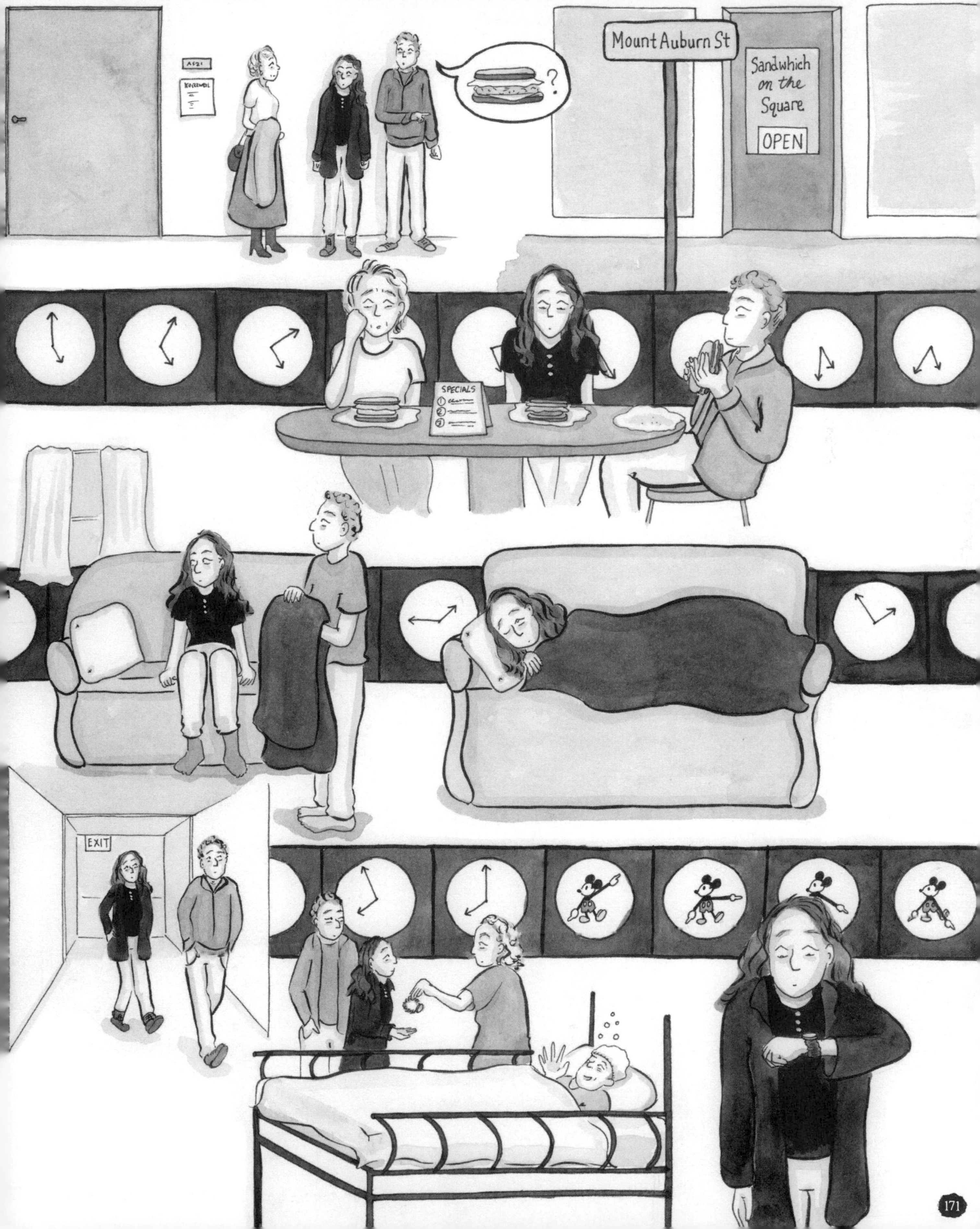
?
Mount Auburn St
Sandwhich on the Square
OPEN
SPECIALS
EXIT

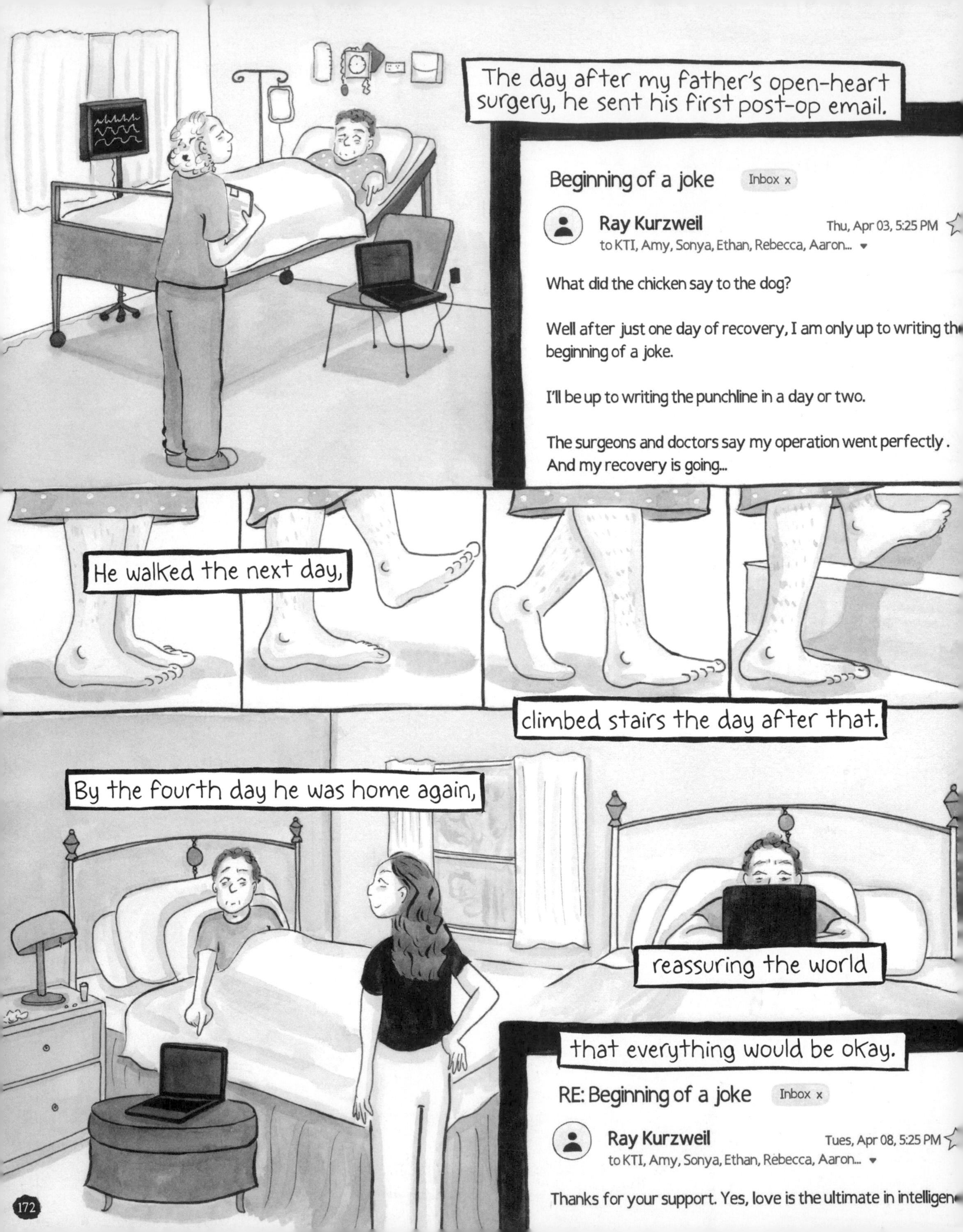
The day after my father's open-heart surgery, he sent his first post-op email.
Beginning of a joke
Inbox x
Ray Kurzweil
Thu, Apr 03, 5:25 PM
to KTI, Amy, Sonya, Ethan, Rebecca, Aaron...
What did the chicken say to the dog?
Well after just one day of recovery, I am only up to writing the beginning of a joke.
I'll be up to writing the punchline in a day or two.
The surgeons and doctors say my operation went perfectly. And my recovery is going...
He walked the next day,
climbed stairs the day after that.
By the fourth day he was home again,
reassuring the world
that everything would be okay.
RE: Beginning of a joke
Inbox x
Ray Kurzweil
Tues, Apr 08, 5:25 PM
to KTI, Amy, Sonya, Ethan, Rebecca, Aaron...
Thanks for your support. Yes, love is the ultimate in intelligen

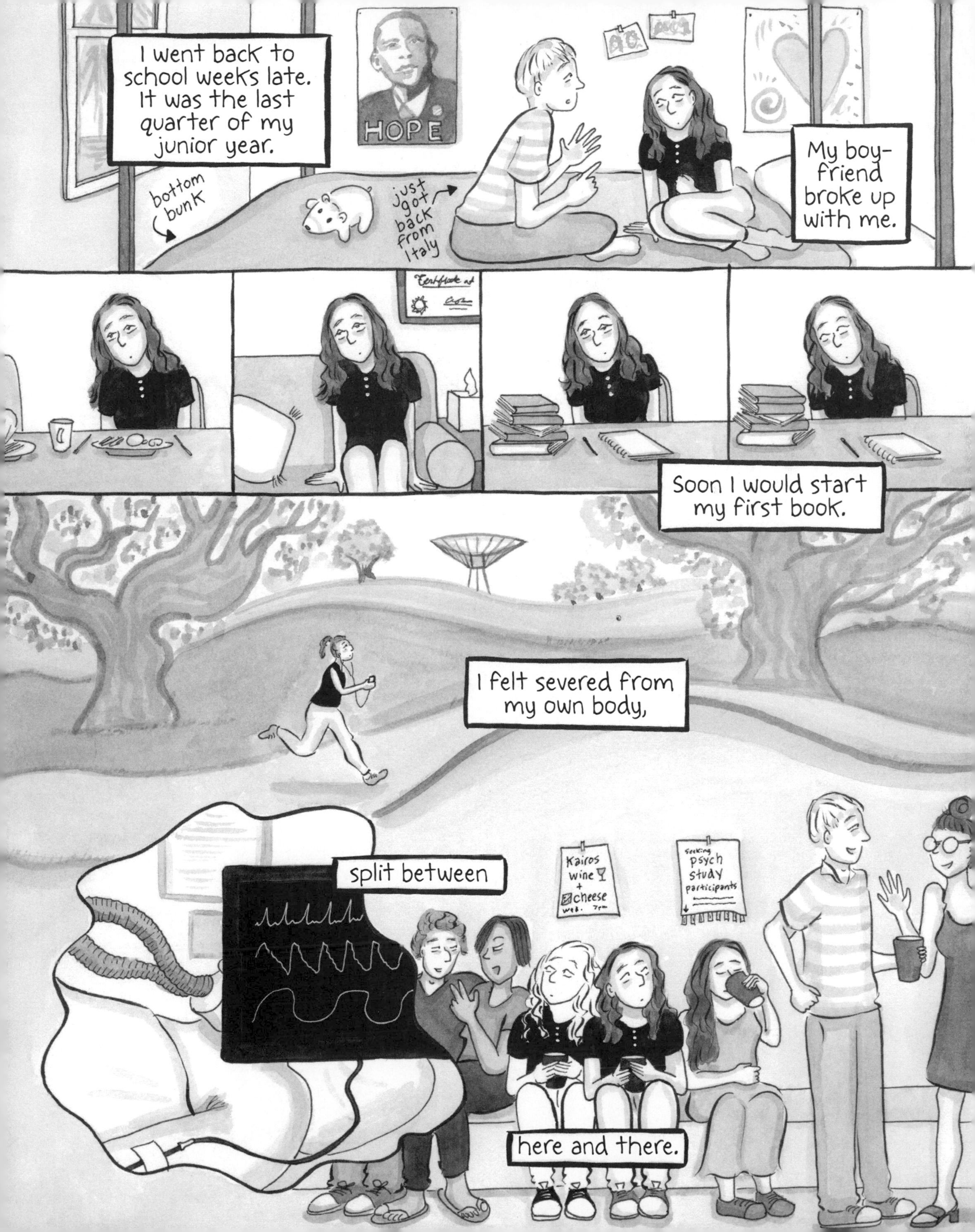
I went back to school weeks late. It was the last quarter of my junior year.
HOPE
bottom bunk
just got back from Italy
My boy-friend broke up with me.
Soon I would start my first book.
I felt severed from my own body,
split between
Kairos wine + cheese
Seeking psych study participants
here and there.

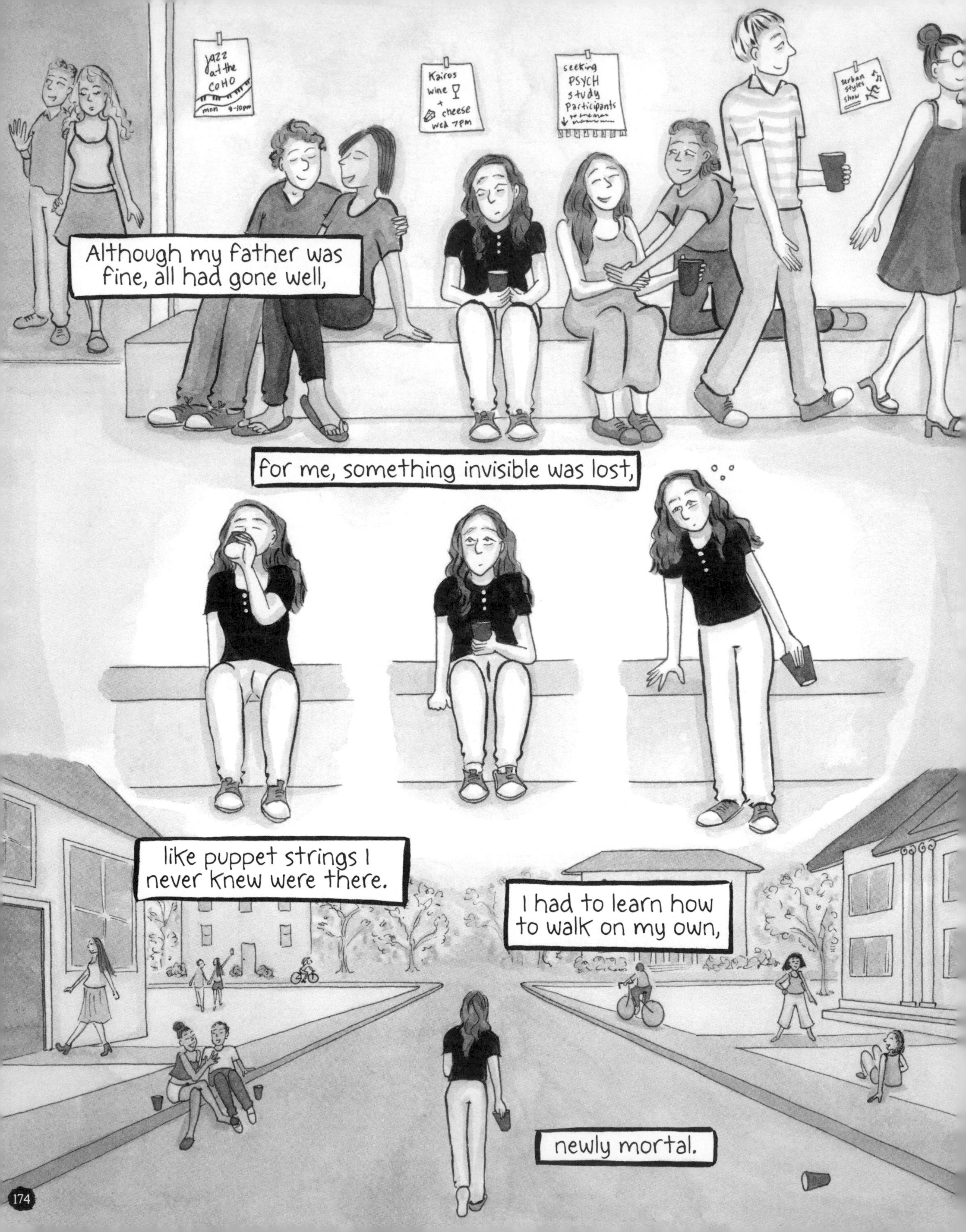
jazz at the COHO mon 9-10pm
Kairos wine + cheese wed 7PM
seeking PSYCH study participants
urban styles show
Although my father was fine, all had gone well,
for me, something invisible was lost,
like puppet strings I never knew were there.
I had to learn how to walk on my own,
newly mortal.

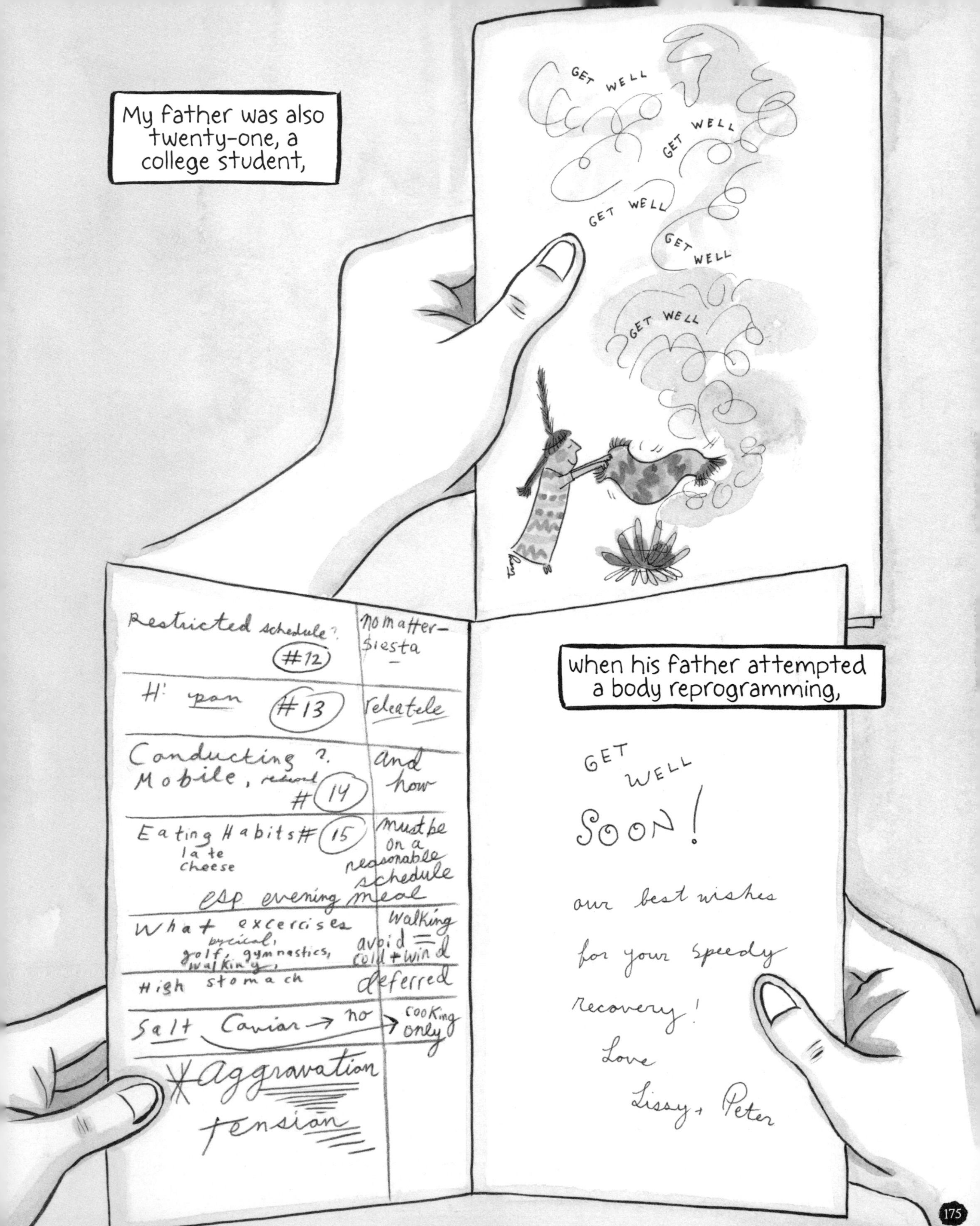
My father was also twenty-one, a college student,
GET WELL
GET WELL
GET WELL
GET WELL
GET WELL
Restricted schedule? #12
no matter- siesta
#13
Conducting? Mobile, reduced #14
and how
Eating Habits #15
late cheese
must be on a reasonable schedule
esp evening meal
What excercises
physical, golf, gymnastics, walking,
Walking
avoid = cold + wind
High stomach
deferred
Salt Caviar → no → cooking only
*aggravation
tension
when his father attempted a body reprogramming,
GET WELL SOON!
our best wishes for your speedy recovery!
Love
Lissy + Peter

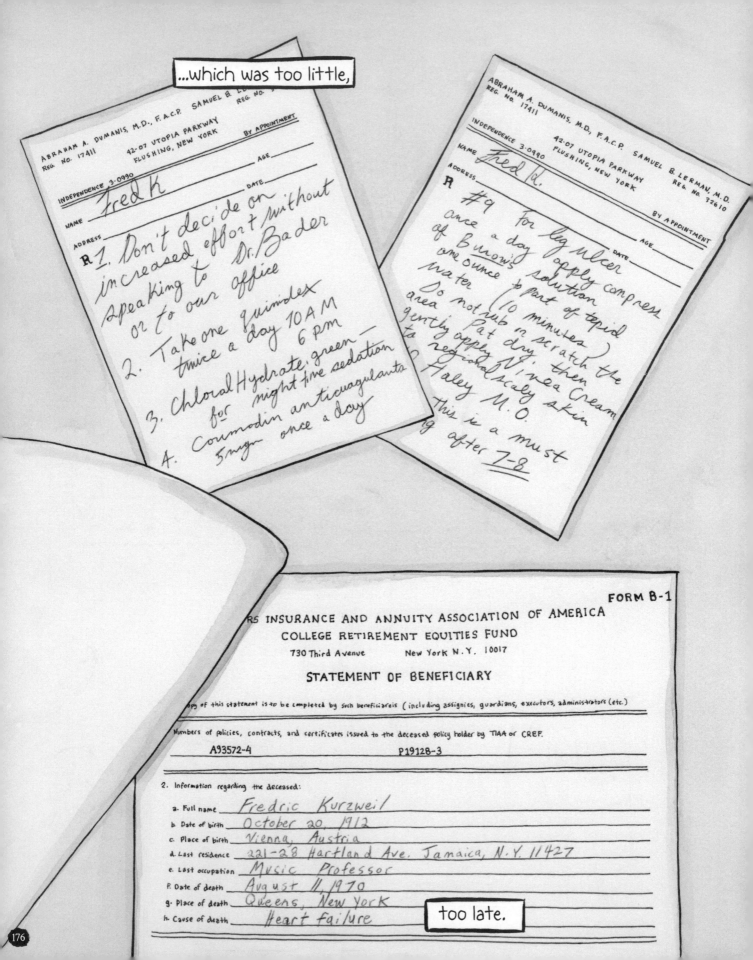

...which was too little,

ABRAHAM A. DUMANIS, M.D., F.A.C.P.  SAMUEL B. L...  REG. NO.
REG. NO. 17411          42-07 UTOPIA PARKWAY
                        FLUSHING, NEW YORK
INDEPENDENCE 3-0990                    BY APPOINTMENT
NAME ___ Fred K ___          DATE ___      AGE ___
ADDRESS ___

R 1. Don't decide on
increased effort without
speaking to Dr. Bader
or to our office
2. Take one quindex
twice a day 10 AM
6 pm
3. Chloral Hydrate, green —
for night time sedation
A. Coumadin anticuagulants
5 mgm once a day

ABRAHAM A. DUMANIS, M.D., F.A.C.P.  SAMUEL B. LERMAN, M.D.
REG. NO. 17411                              REG. NO. 32610
                42-07 UTOPIA PARKWAY
                FLUSHING, NEW YORK
INDEPENDENCE 3-0990                    BY APPOINTMENT
NAME ___ Fred K. ___          DATE ___      AGE ___
ADDRESS ___

R #9  For leg ulcer
once a day apply compress
of Burow's solution
one ounce to part of tepid
water (10 minutes)
Do not rub or scratch the
area  pat dry, then
gently apply Vinea Cream
to redical scaly skin
__ Haley M.O.
this is a must
ng after 7-8

FORM B-1

...RS INSURANCE AND ANNUITY ASSOCIATION OF AMERICA
COLLEGE RETIREMENT EQUITIES FUND
730 Third Avenue      New York N.Y. 10017

STATEMENT OF BENEFICIARY

...py of this statement is to be completed by such beneficiareis (including assignies, guardians, executors, administrators (etc.)

Numbers of policies, contracts, and certificates issued to the deceased policy holder by TIAA or CREF.

A93572-4                    P19128-3

2. Information regarding the deceased:
   a. Full name ___ Fredric Kurzweil ___
   b. Date of birth ___ October 20, 1912 ___
   c. Place of birth ___ Vienna, Austria ___
   d. Last residence ___ 221-28 Hartland Ave. Jamaica, N.Y. 11427 ___
   e. Last occupation ___ Music Professor ___
   f. Date of death ___ August 11, 1970 ___
   g. Place of death ___ Queens, New York ___
   h. Cause of death ___ Heart failure ___

too late.

176

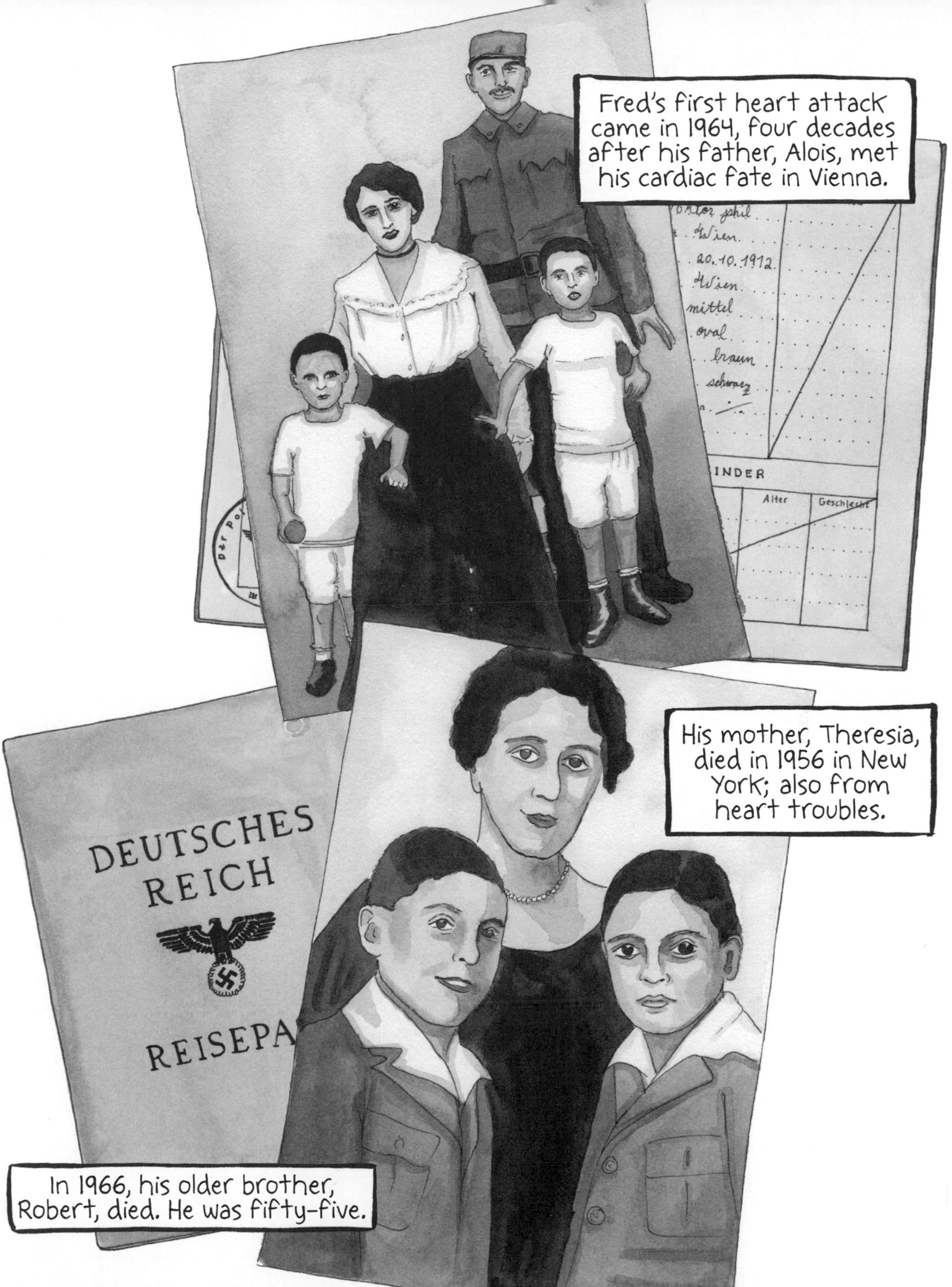
Fred's first heart attack came in 1964, four decades after his father, Alois, met his cardiac fate in Vienna.
His mother, Theresia, died in 1956 in New York; also from heart troubles.
DEUTSCHES REICH
REISEPA
In 1966, his older brother, Robert, died. He was fifty-five.

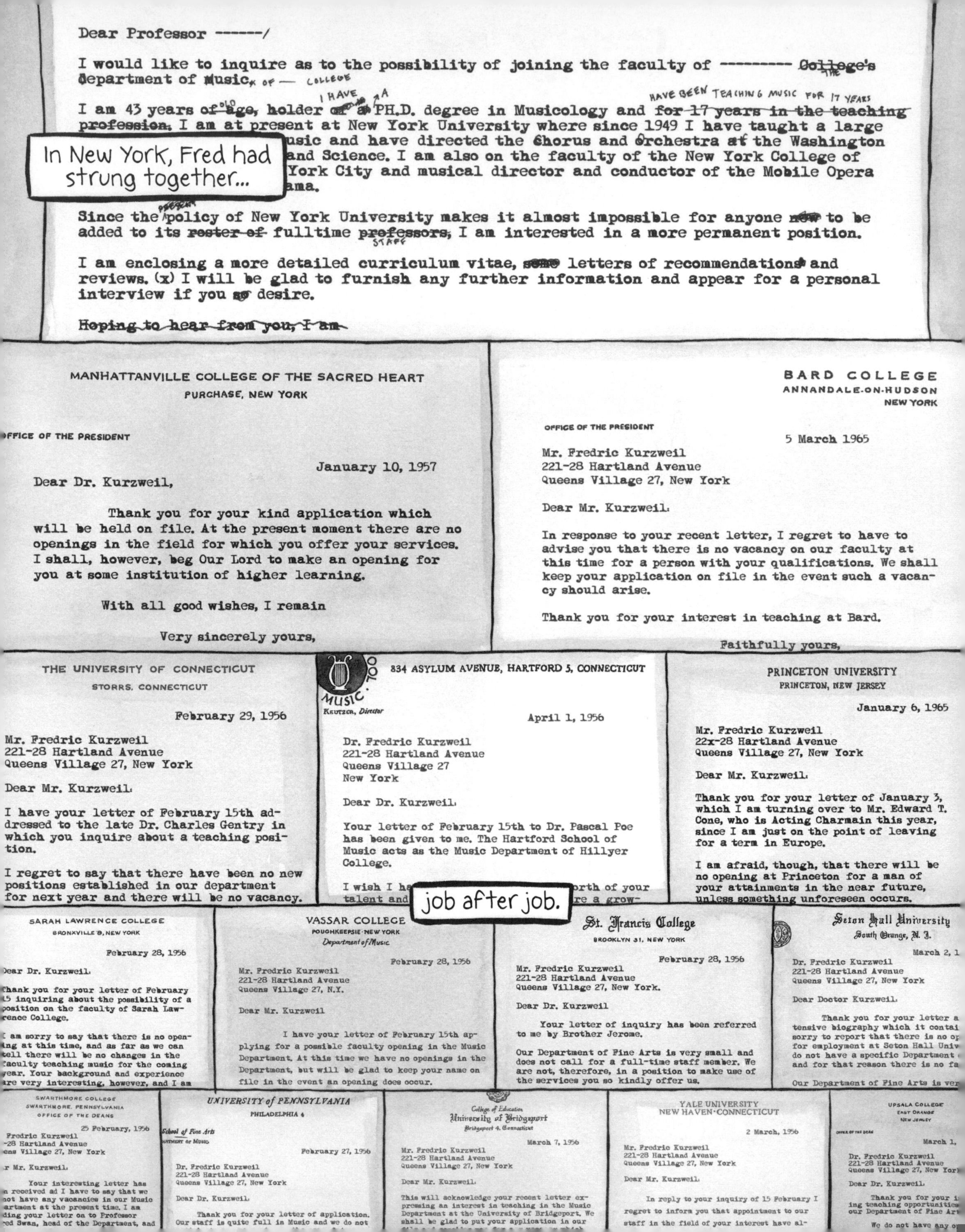

In New York, Fred had strung together...
job after job.


Dear Professor ------/

I would like to inquire as to the possibility of joining the faculty of -------- ~~College's~~ THE Department of Music OF — COLLEGE

I am 43 years ~~of age~~ OLD, I HAVE ~~holder of a~~ A PH.D. degree in Musicology and HAVE BEEN TEACHING MUSIC FOR 17 YEARS ~~for 17 years in the teaching profession~~. I am at present at New York University where since 1949 I have taught a large ...usic and have directed the Chorus and Orchestra at the Washington ...and Science. I am also on the faculty of the New York College of ...York City and musical director and conductor of the Mobile Opera ...ama.

Since the PRESENT policy of New York University makes it almost impossible for anyone ~~new~~ to be added to its ~~roster of~~ fulltime ~~professors~~ STAFF, I am interested in a more permanent position.

I am enclosing a more detailed curriculum vitae, ~~some~~ letters of recommendations and reviews. (x) I will be glad to furnish any further information and appear for a personal interview if you ~~so~~ desire.

~~Hoping to hear from you, I am~~

MANHATTANVILLE COLLEGE OF THE SACRED HEART
PURCHASE, NEW YORK

OFFICE OF THE PRESIDENT

January 10, 1957

Dear Dr. Kurzweil,

Thank you for your kind application which will be held on file. At the present moment there are no openings in the field for which you offer your services. I shall, however, beg Our Lord to make an opening for you at some institution of higher learning.

With all good wishes, I remain

Very sincerely yours,

BARD COLLEGE
ANNANDALE-ON-HUDSON
NEW YORK

OFFICE OF THE PRESIDENT

5 March 1965

Mr. Fredric Kurzweil
221-28 Hartland Avenue
Queens Village 27, New York

Dear Mr. Kurzweil:

In response to your recent letter, I regret to have to advise you that there is no vacancy on our faculty at this time for a person with your qualifications. We shall keep your application on file in the event such a vacancy should arise.

Thank you for your interest in teaching at Bard.

Faithfully yours,

THE UNIVERSITY OF CONNECTICUT
STORRS, CONNECTICUT

February 29, 1956

Mr. Fredric Kurzweil
221-28 Hartland Avenue
Queens Village 27, New York

Dear Mr. Kurzweil:

I have your letter of February 15th addressed to the late Dr. Charles Gentry in which you inquire about a teaching position.

I regret to say that there have been no new positions established in our department for next year and there will be no vacancy.

834 ASYLUM AVENUE, HARTFORD 5, CONNECTICUT
MUSIC. 700
KEUTZER, Director

April 1, 1956

Dr. Fredric Kurzweil
221-28 Hartland Avenue
Queens Village 27
New York

Dear Dr. Kurzweil:

Your letter of February 15th to Dr. Pascal Poe has been given to me. The Hartford School of Music acts as the Music Department of Hillyer College.

I wish I ha... ...orth of your talent and ... ...re a grow-

PRINCETON UNIVERSITY
PRINCETON, NEW JERSEY

January 6, 1965

Mr. Fredric Kurzweil
22x-28 Hartland Avenue
Queens Village 27, New York

Dear Mr. Kurzweil:

Thank you for your letter of January 3, which I am turning over to Mr. Edward T. Cone, who is Acting Charmain this year, since I am just on the point of leaving for a term in Europe.

I am afraid, though, that there will be no opening at Princeton for a man of your attainments in the near future, unless something unforeseen occurs.

SARAH LAWRENCE COLLEGE
BRONXVILLE 8, NEW YORK

February 28, 1956

Dear Dr. Kurzweil:

Thank you for your letter of February 15 inquiring about the possibility of a position on the faculty of Sarah Lawrence College.

I am sorry to say that there is no opening at this time, and as far as we can tell there will be no changes in the faculty teaching music for the coming year. Your background and experience are very interesting, however, and I am

VASSAR COLLEGE
POUGHKEEPSIE · NEW YORK
Department of Music

February 28, 1956

Mr. Fredric Kurzweil
221-28 Hartland Avenue
Queens Village 27, N.Y.

Dear Mr. Kurzweil:

I have your letter of February 15th applying for a possible faculty opening in the Music Department. At this time we have no openings in the Department, but will be glad to keep your name on file in the event an opening does occur.

St. Francis College
BROOKLYN 31, NEW YORK

February 28, 1956

Mr. Fredric Kurzweil
221-28 Hartland Avenue
Queens Village 27, New York.

Dear Dr. Kurzweil

Your letter of inquiry has been referred to me by Brother Jerome.

Our Department of Fine Arts is very small and does not call for a full-time staff member. We are not, therefore, in a position to make use of the services you so kindly offer us.

Seton Hall University
South Orange, N. J.

March 2, 1

Dr. Fredric Kurzweil
221-28 Hartland Avenue
Queens Village 27, New York

Dear Doctor Kurzweil:

Thank you for your letter a... tensive biography which it contai... sorry to report that there is no op... for employment at Seton Hall Univ... do not have a specific Department ... and for that reason there is no fa...

Our Department of Fine Arts is ver...

SWARTHMORE COLLEGE
SWARTHMORE, PENNSYLVANIA
OFFICE OF THE DEANS

25 February, 1956

...Fredric Kurzweil
...-28 Hartland Avenue
...ens Village 27, New York

...r Mr. Kurzweil:

Your interesting letter has ...n received and I have to say that we ...not have any vacancies in our Music ...partment at the present time. I am ...ding your letter on to Professor ...red Swan, head of the Department, and

UNIVERSITY of PENNSYLVANIA
PHILADELPHIA 4

School of Fine Arts
...MENT OF MUSIC

February 27, 1956

Dr. Fredric Kurzweil
221-28 Hartland Avenue
Queens Village 27, New York

Dear Dr. Kurzweil:

Thank you for your letter of application. Our staff is quite full in Music and we do not

College of Education
University of Bridgeport
Bridgeport 4, Connecticut

March 7, 1956

Mr. Fredric Kurzweil
221-28 Hartland Avenue
Queens Village 27, New York

Dear Mr. Kurzweil:

This will acknowledge your recent letter expressing an interest in teaching in the Music Department at the University of Bridgeport. We shall be glad to put your application in our

YALE UNIVERSITY
NEW HAVEN · CONNECTICUT

2 March, 1956

Mr. Fredric Kurzweil
221-28 Hartland Avenue
Queens Village 27, New York

Dear Mr. Kurzweil:

In reply to your inquiry of 15 February I regret to inform you that appointment to our staff in the field of your interest have al-

UPSALA COLLEGE
EAST ORANGE
NEW JERSEY

OFFICE OF THE DEAN

March 1,

Dr. Fredric Kurzweil
221-28 Hartland Avenue
Queens Village 27, New York

Dear Dr. Kurzweil:

Thank you for your i... ing teaching opportunitie... our Department of Fine Art...

We do not have any o...

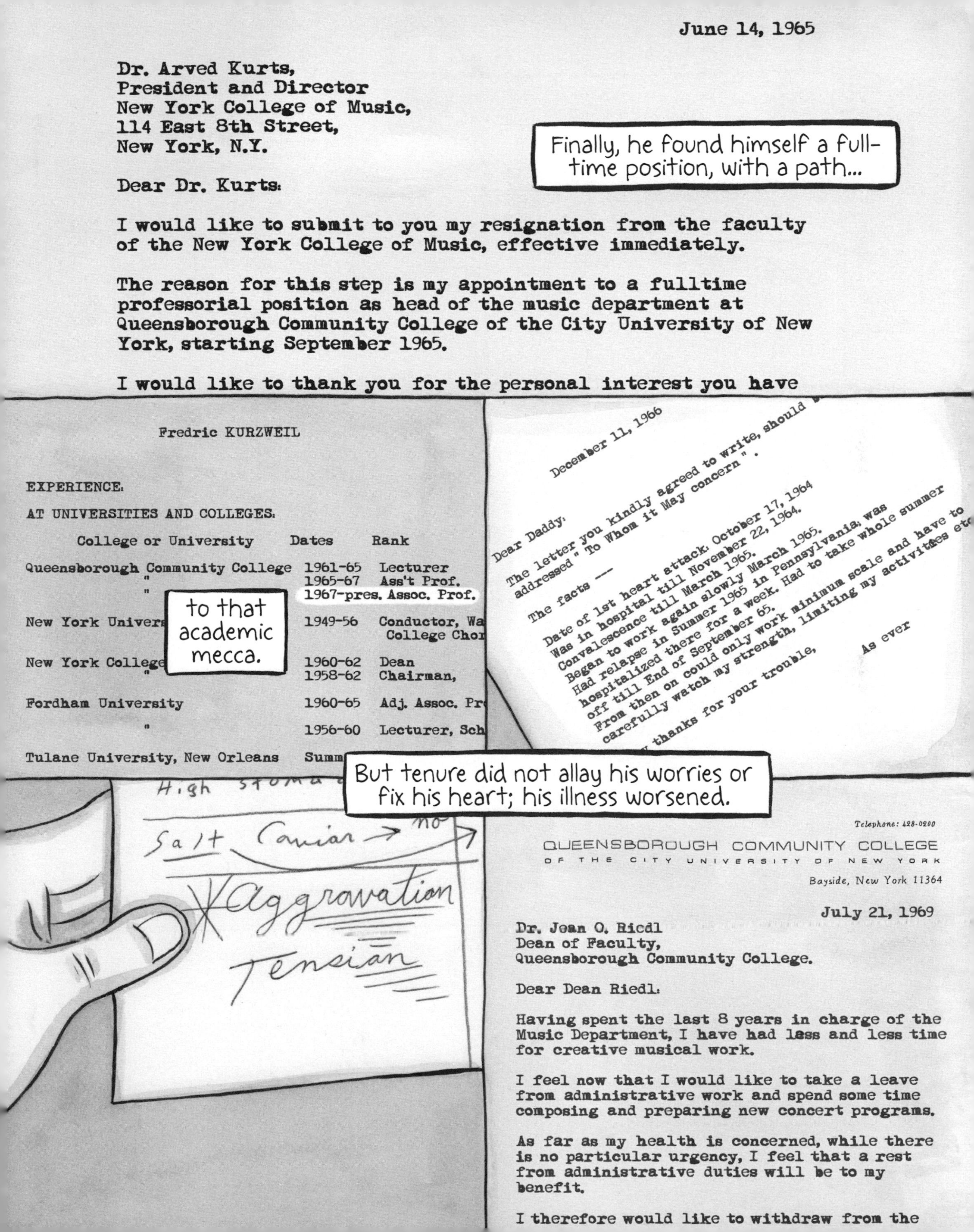
June 14, 1965
Dr. Arved Kurts,
President and Director
New York College of Music,
114 East 8th Street,
New York, N.Y.
Finally, he found himself a full-time position, with a path...
Dear Dr. Kurts:
I would like to submit to you my resignation from the faculty of the New York College of Music, effective immediately.
The reason for this step is my appointment to a fulltime professorial position as head of the music department at Queensborough Community College of the City University of New York, starting September 1965.
I would like to thank you for the personal interest you have
Fredric KURZWEIL
EXPERIENCE:
AT UNIVERSITIES AND COLLEGES:
College or University Dates Rank
Queensborough Community College 1961-65 Lecturer
" 1965-67 Ass't Prof.
" 1967-pres. Assoc. Prof.
to that academic mecca.
New York Univers 1949-56 Conductor, Wa
College Chor
New York College 1960-62 Dean
" 1958-62 Chairman,
Fordham University 1960-65 Adj. Assoc. Pr
" 1956-60 Lecturer, Sch
Tulane University, New Orleans Summ
December 11, 1966
Dear Daddy:
The letter you kindly agreed to write, should
addressed " To Whom it May concern " .
The facts ---
Date of 1st heart attack: October 17, 1964
Was in hospital till November 22, 1964.
Convalescence till March 1965.
Began to work again slowly March 1965.
Had relapse in Summer 1965 in Pennsylvania; was
hospitalized there for a week. Had to take whole summer
off till End of September 65.
From then on could only work minimum scale and have to
carefully watch my strength, limiting my activities etc
thanks for your trouble,
As ever
But tenure did not allay his worries or fix his heart; his illness worsened.
High
Salt Caviar → no
Aggravation
Tensian
Telephone: 428-0200
QUEENSBOROUGH COMMUNITY COLLEGE
OF THE CITY UNIVERSITY OF NEW YORK
Bayside, New York 11364
July 21, 1969
Dr. Jean O. Riedl
Dean of Faculty,
Queensborough Community College.
Dear Dean Riedl:
Having spent the last 8 years in charge of the Music Department, I have had less and less time for creative musical work.
I feel now that I would like to take a leave from administrative work and spend some time composing and preparing new concert programs.
As far as my health is concerned, while there is no particular urgency, I feel that a rest from administrative duties will be to my benefit.
I therefore would like to withdraw from the

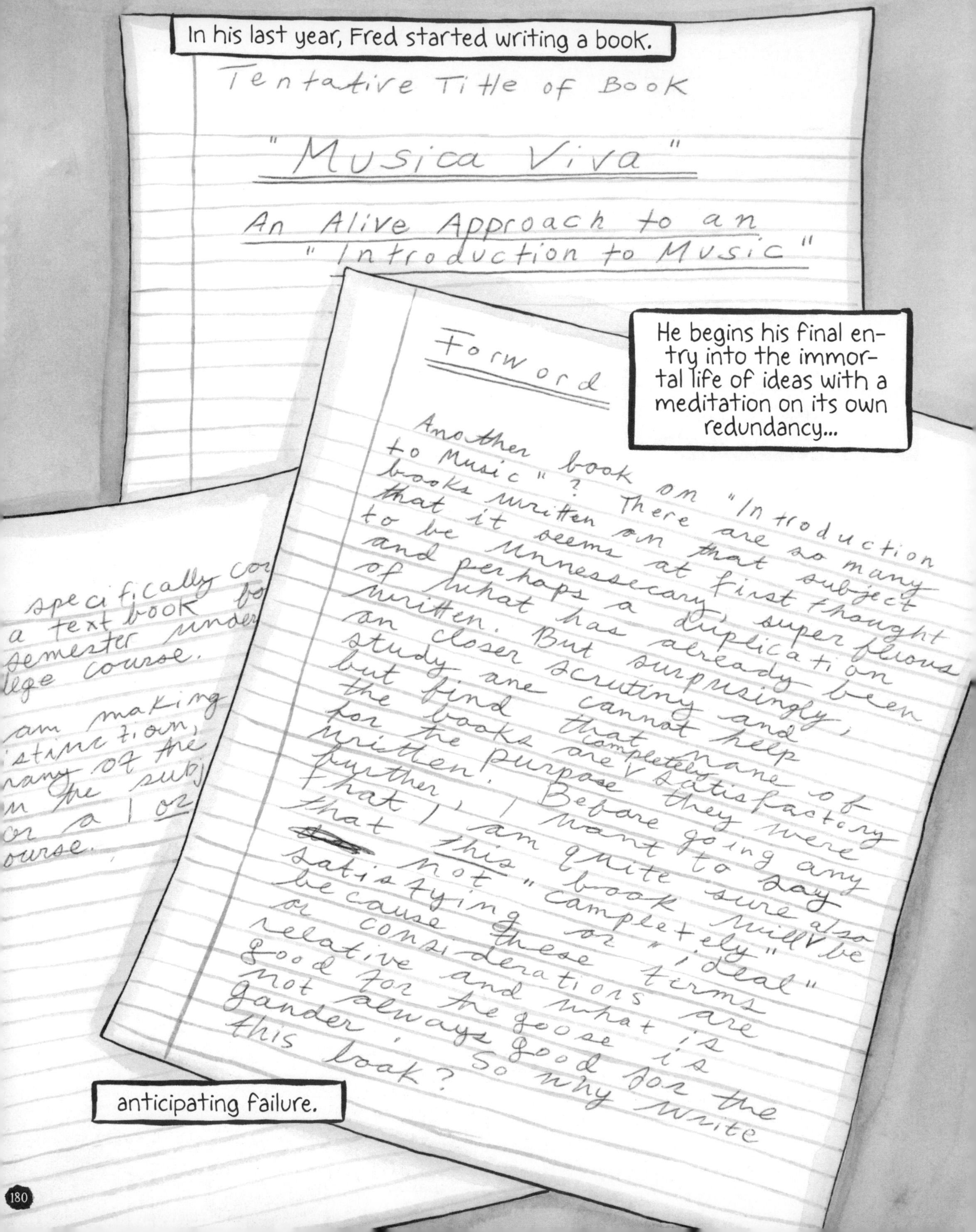
In his last year, Fred started writing a book.
Tentative Title of Book
"Musica Viva"
An Alive Approach to an "Introduction to Music"
He begins his final entry into the immortal life of ideas with a meditation on its own redundancy...
Forword
Another book on "Introduction to Music"? There are so many books written on that subject that it seems at first thought to be unnessecary, superfluous and perhaps a duplication of what has already been written. But surprisingly, on closer scrutiny and study one cannot help but find that none of the books are completely satisfactory for the purpose they were written! Before going any further, I want to say that I am quite sure also that this book will not be completely satisfying or "ideal" because these terms or considerations are relative and what is good for the goose is not always good for the gander. So why write this book?
anticipating failure.

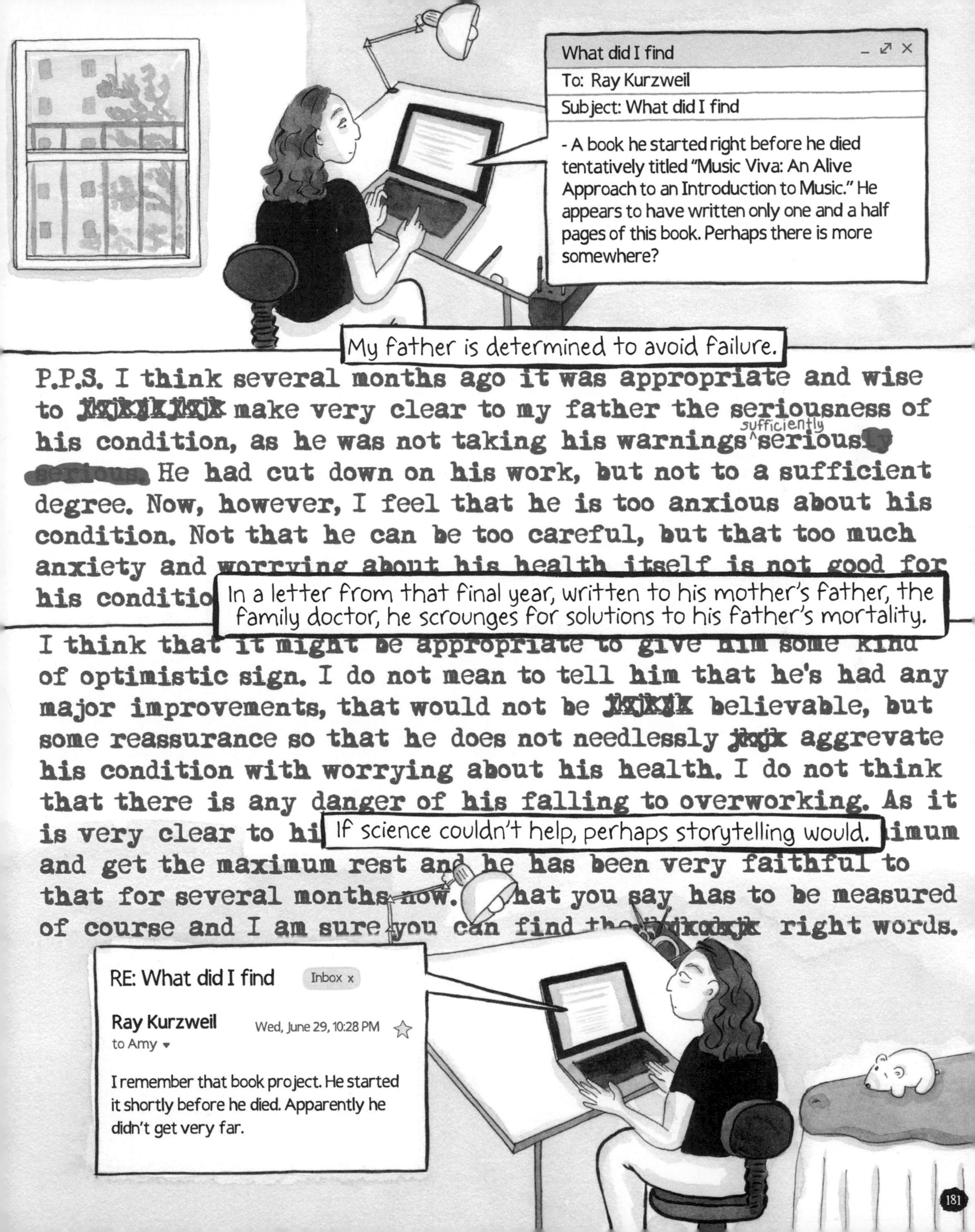

What did I find
To: Ray Kurzweil
Subject: What did I find
- A book he started right before he died tentatively titled "Music Viva: An Alive Approach to an Introduction to Music." He appears to have written only one and a half pages of this book. Perhaps there is more somewhere?
My father is determined to avoid failure.
P.P.S. I think several months ago it was appropriate and wise to JKJKJKJKJK make very clear to my father the seriousness of his condition, as he was not taking his warnings ^sufficiently serious serious. He had cut down on his work, but not to a sufficient degree. Now, however, I feel that he is too anxious about his condition. Not that he can be too careful, but that too much anxiety and worrying about his health itself is not good for his conditio
In a letter from that final year, written to his mother's father, the family doctor, he scrounges for solutions to his father's mortality.
I think that it might be appropriate to give him some kind of optimistic sign. I do not mean to tell him that he's had any major improvements, that would not be JKJKJK believable, but some reassurance so that he does not needlessly jkxjk aggrevate his condition with worrying about his health. I do not think that there is any danger of his falling to overworking. As it is very clear to hi
imum and get the maximum rest and he has been very faithful to that for several months now. hat you say has to be measured of course and I am sure you can find the jkxkxjk right words.
If science couldn't help, perhaps storytelling would.
RE: What did I find
Inbox x
Ray Kurzweil
Wed, June 29, 10:28 PM
to Amy
I remember that book project. He started it shortly before he died. Apparently he didn't get very far.

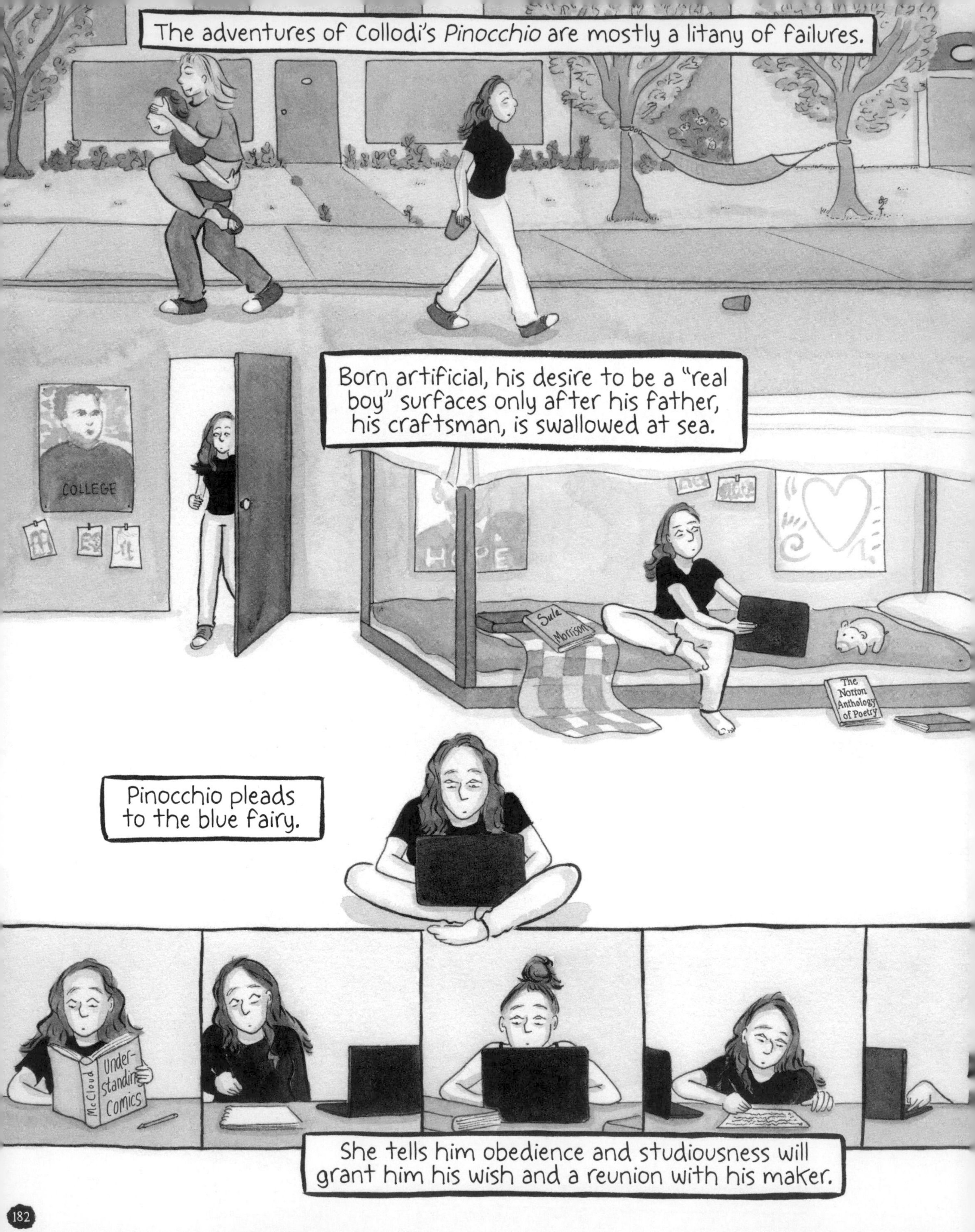
The adventures of Collodi's *Pinocchio* are mostly a litany of failures.
Born artificial, his desire to be a "real boy" surfaces only after his father, his craftsman, is swallowed at sea.
COLLEGE
Sula Morrison
The Norton Anthology of Poetry
Pinocchio pleads to the blue fairy.
McCloud Understanding Comics
She tells him obedience and studiousness will grant him his wish and a reunion with his maker.

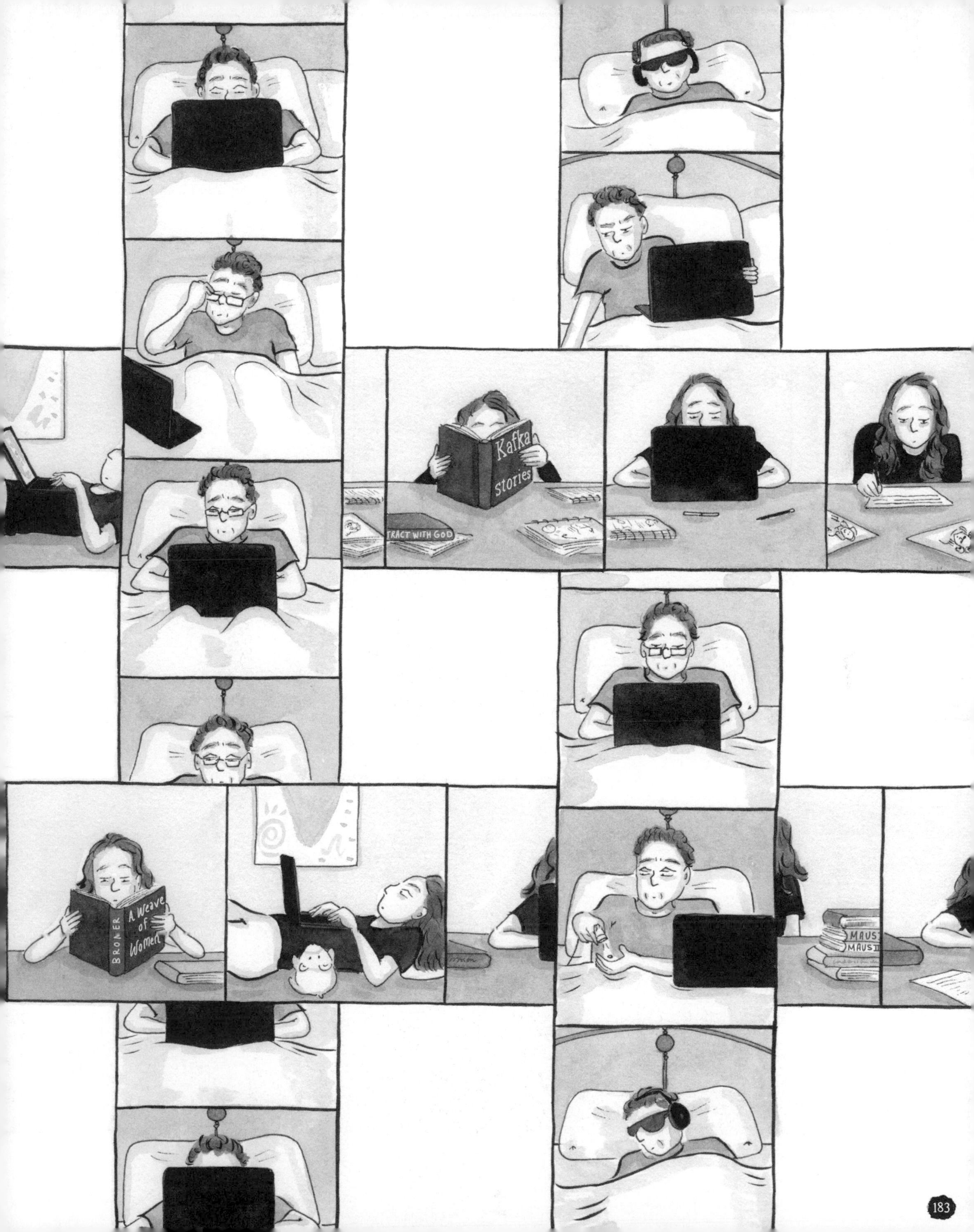
Kafka
stories
TRACT WITH GOD
BRONER
A Weave
of
Women
MAUS
MAUS II

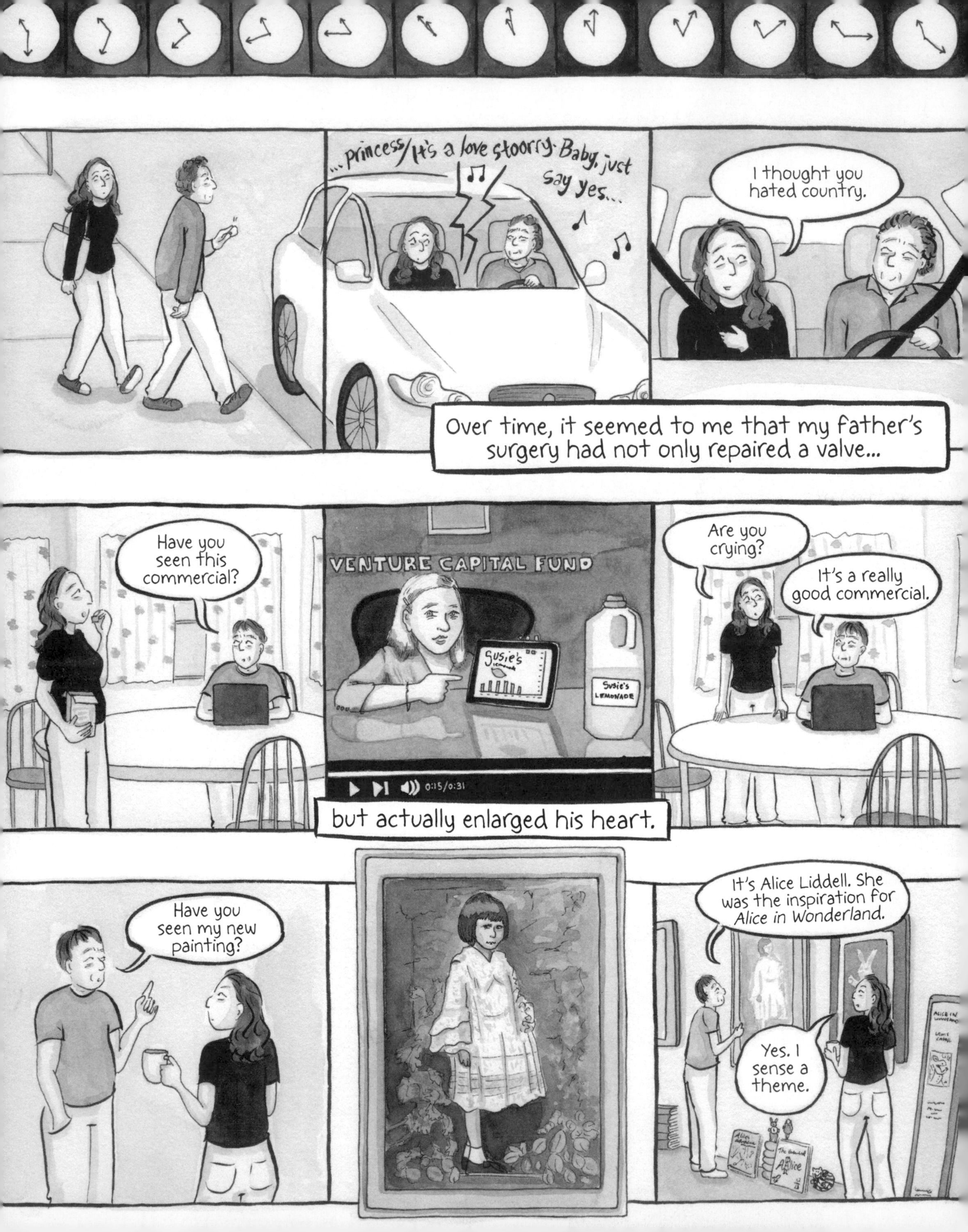

...princess/ It's a love stoorry. Baby, just say yes...
I thought you hated country.
Over time, it seemed to me that my father's surgery had not only repaired a valve...
Have you seen this commercial?
VENTURE CAPITAL FUND
Susie's
Susie's LEMONADE
0:15/0:31
Are you crying?
It's a really good commercial.
but actually enlarged his heart.
Have you seen my new painting?
It's Alice Liddell. She was the inspiration for Alice in Wonderland.
Yes. I sense a theme.

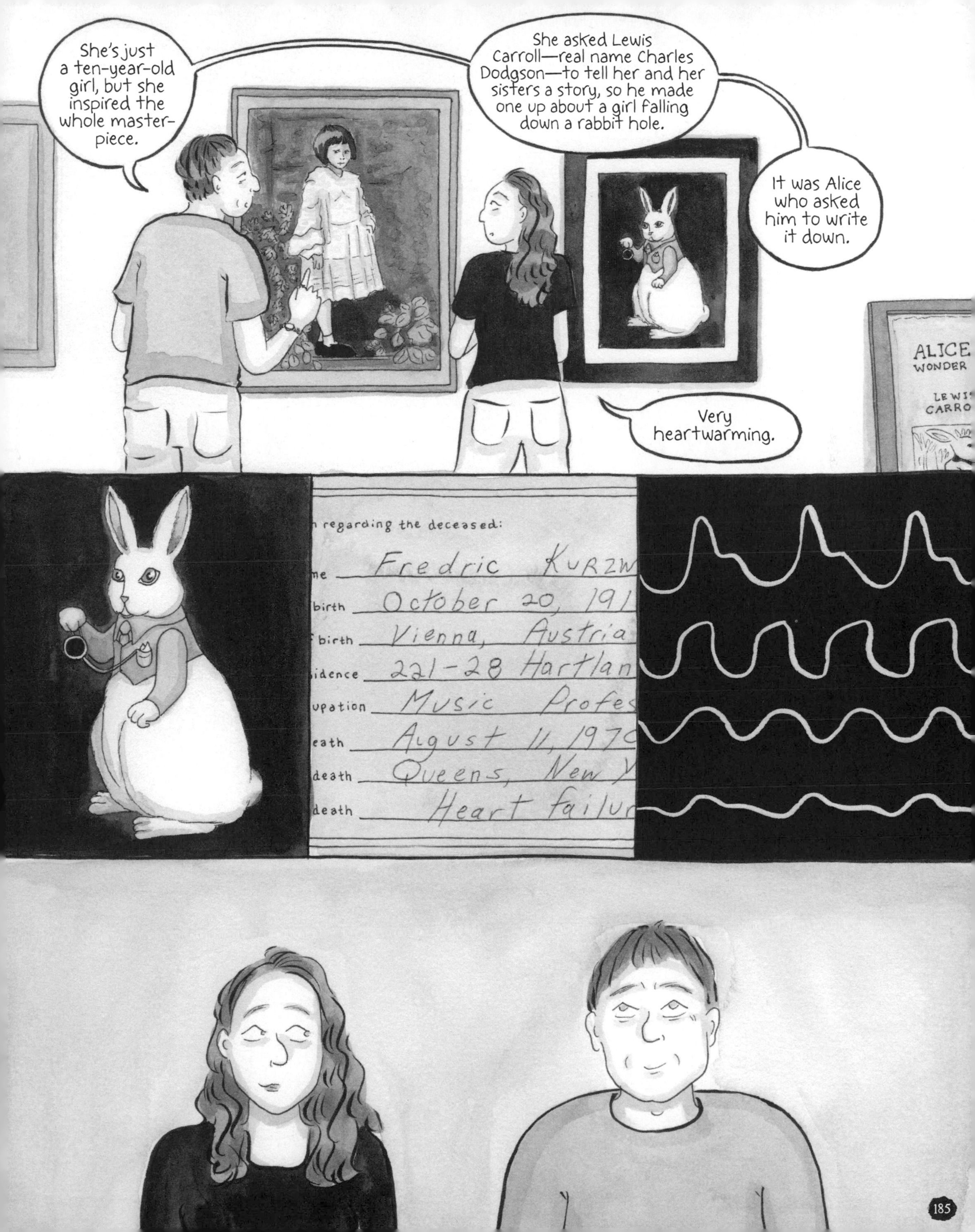
She's just a ten-year-old girl, but she inspired the whole masterpiece.
She asked Lewis Carroll—real name Charles Dodgson—to tell her and her sisters a story, so he made one up about a girl falling down a rabbit hole.
It was Alice who asked him to write it down.
ALICE
WONDER
LEWIS
CARRO
Very heartwarming.
regarding the deceased:
me Fredric Kurzw
birth October 20, 191
birth Vienna, Austria
idence 221-28 Hartlan
upation Music Profes
eath August 11, 1970
death Queens, New Y
death Heart failur

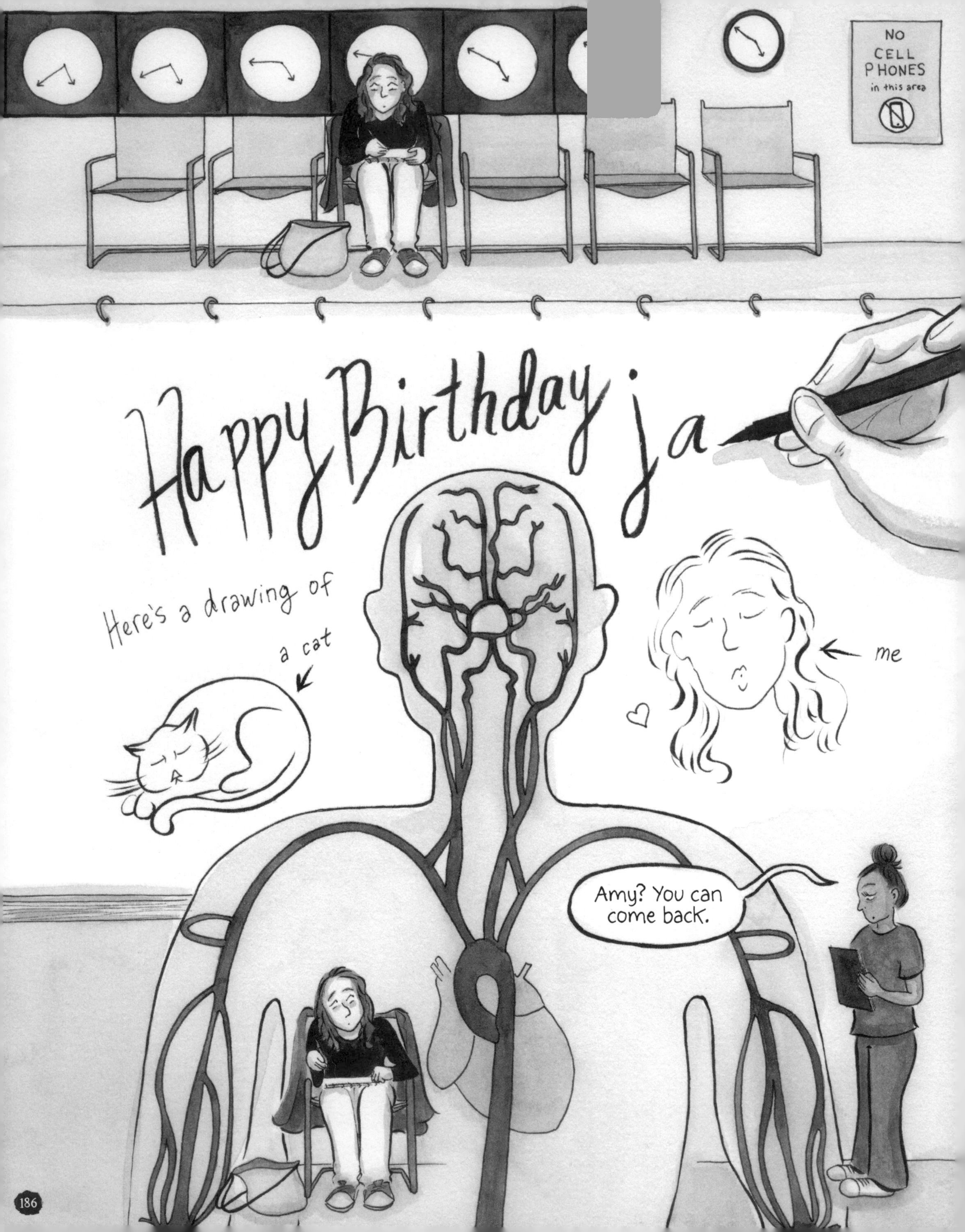
NO CELL PHONES in this area
Happy Birthday ja
Here's a drawing of
a cat
me
Amy? You can come back.

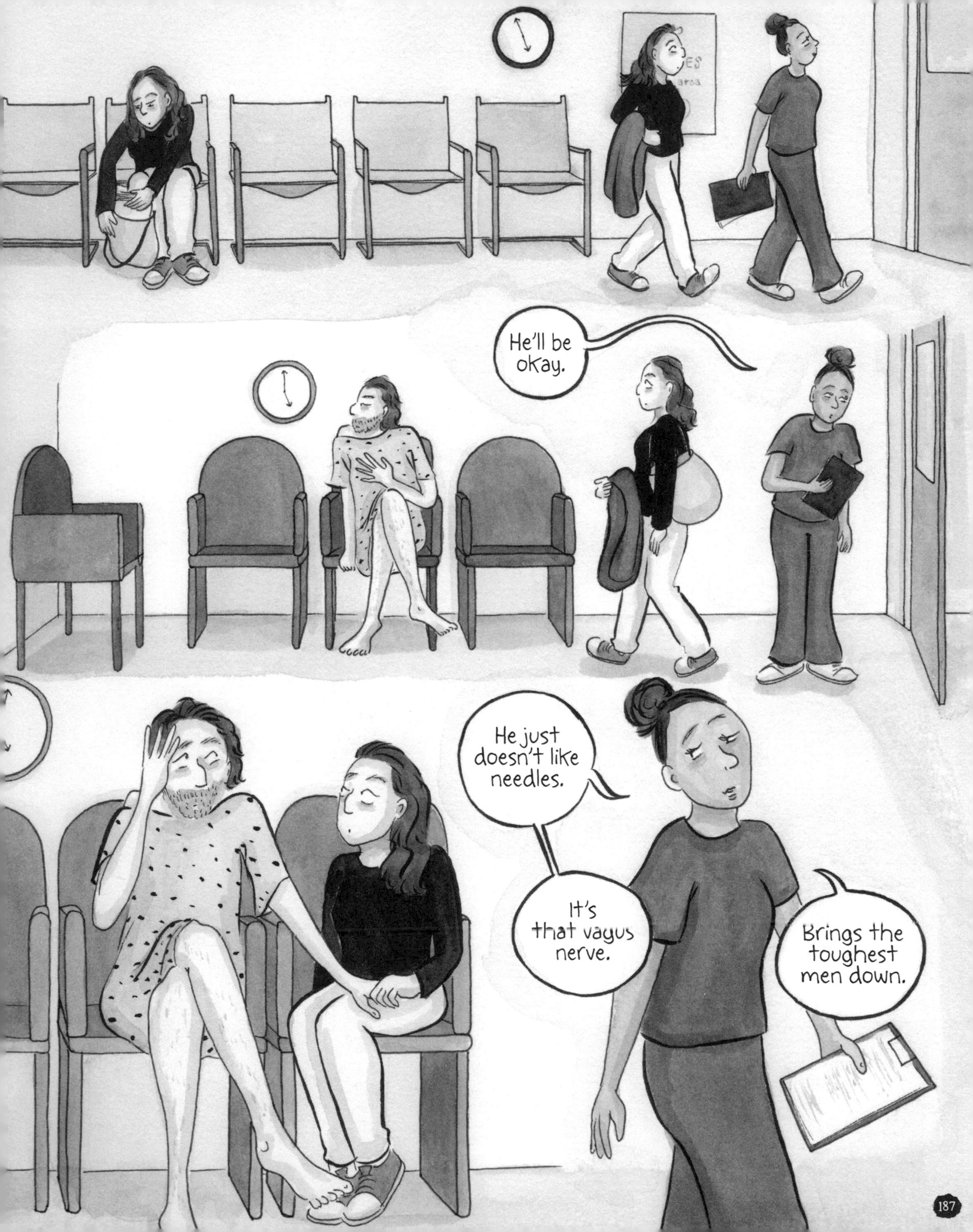
He'll be okay.
He just doesn't like needles.
It's that vagus nerve.
Brings the toughest men down.

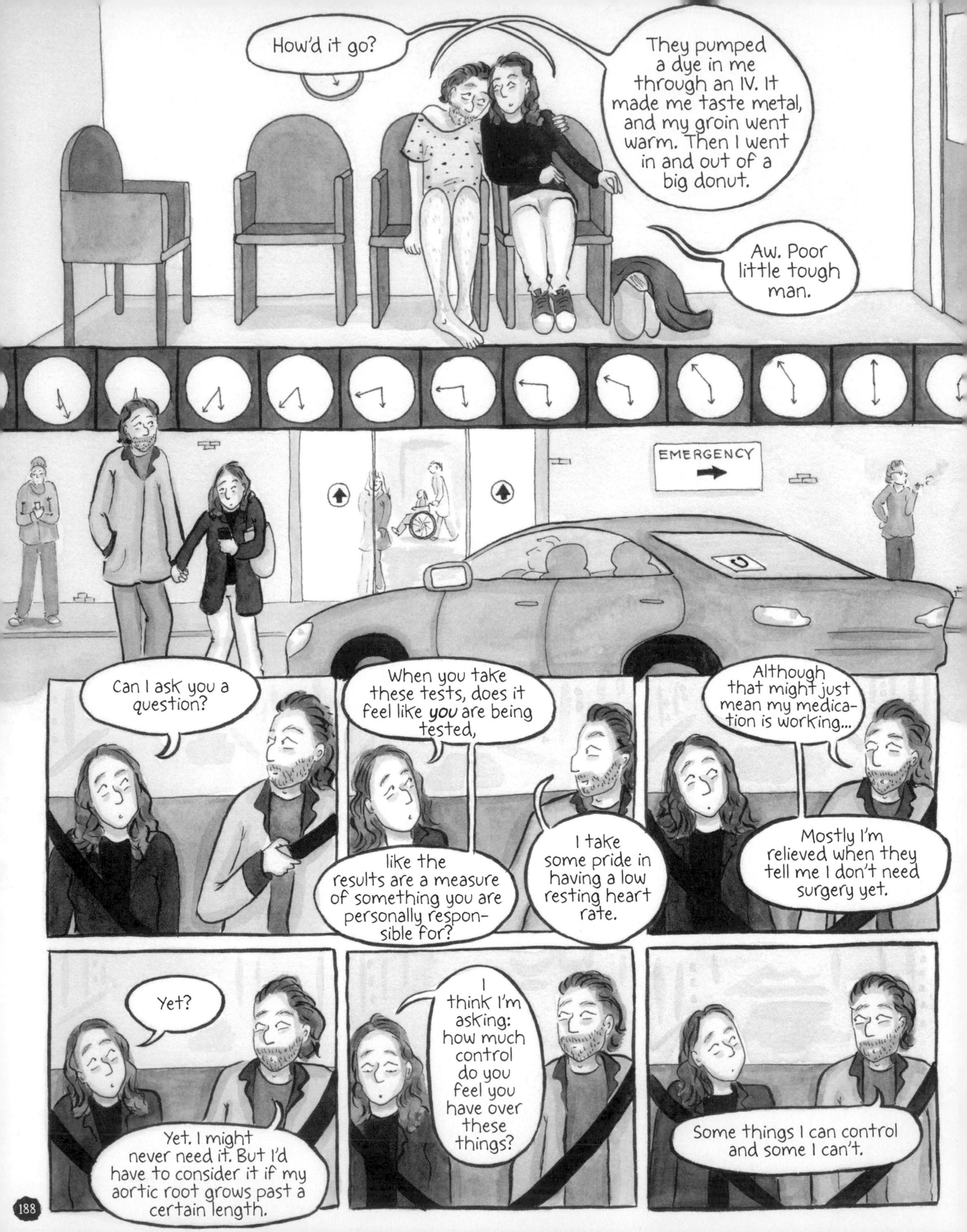
How'd it go?
They pumped a dye in me through an IV. It made me taste metal, and my groin went warm. Then I went in and out of a big donut.
Aw. Poor little tough man.
EMERGENCY
Can I ask you a question?
When you take these tests, does it feel like *you* are being tested,
like the results are a measure of something you are personally responsible for?
I take some pride in having a low resting heart rate.
Although that might just mean my medication is working...
Mostly I'm relieved when they tell me I don't need surgery yet.
Yet?
Yet. I might never need it. But I'd have to consider it if my aortic root grows past a certain length.
I think I'm asking: how much control do you feel you have over these things?
Some things I can control and some I can't.

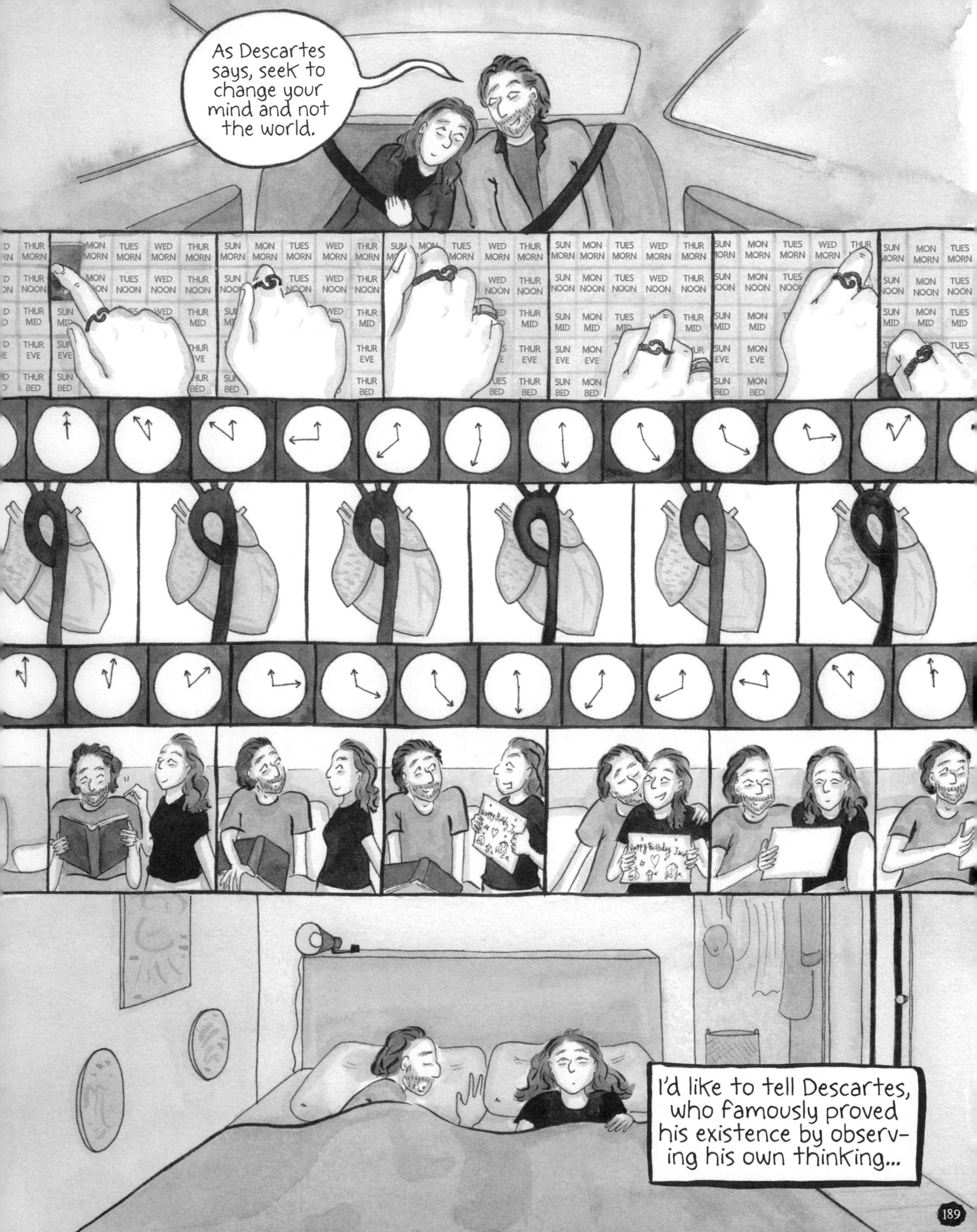
As Descartes says, seek to change your mind and not the world.
I'd like to tell Descartes, who famously proved his existence by observing his own thinking...

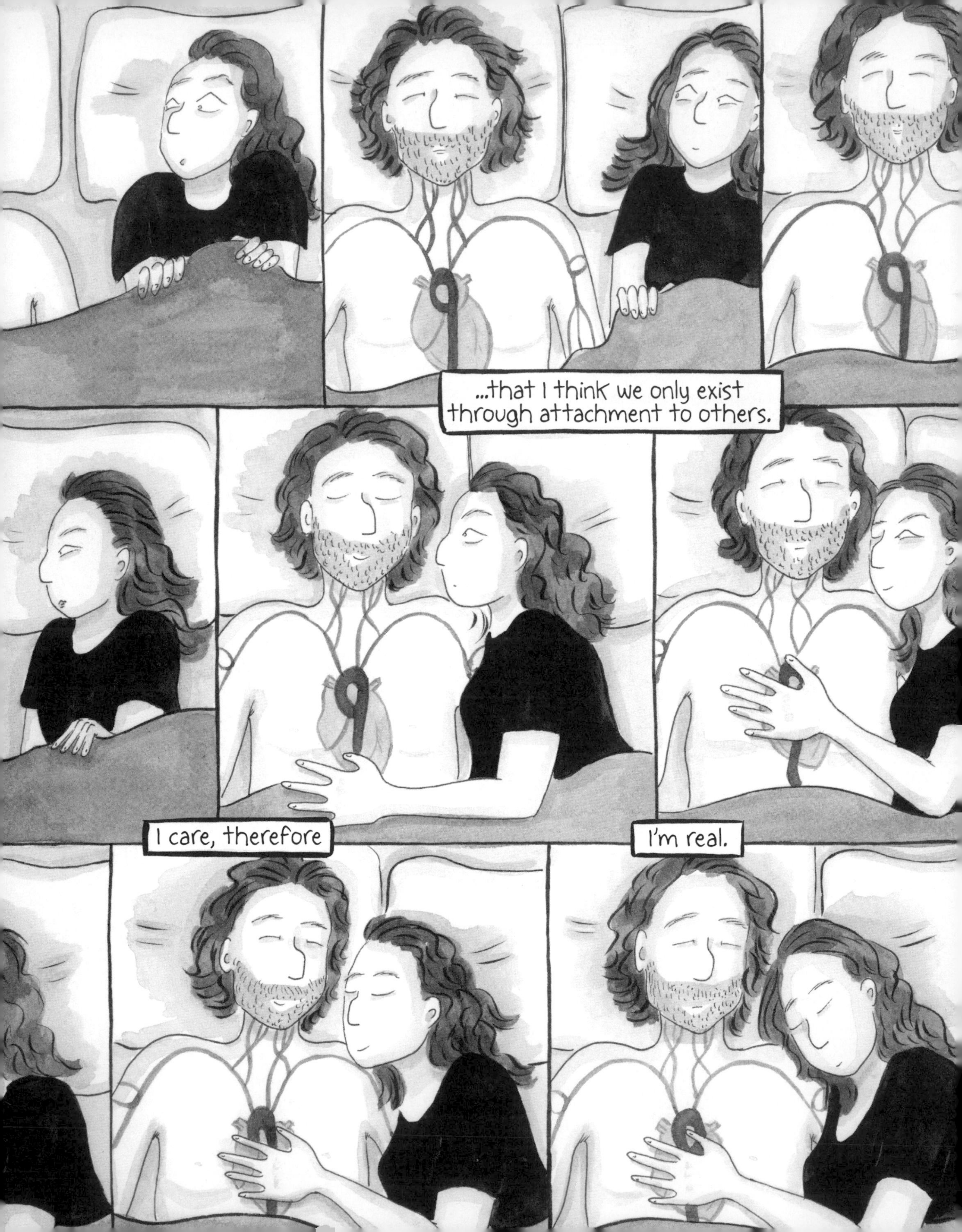
...that I think we only exist through attachment to others.
I care, therefore
I'm real.

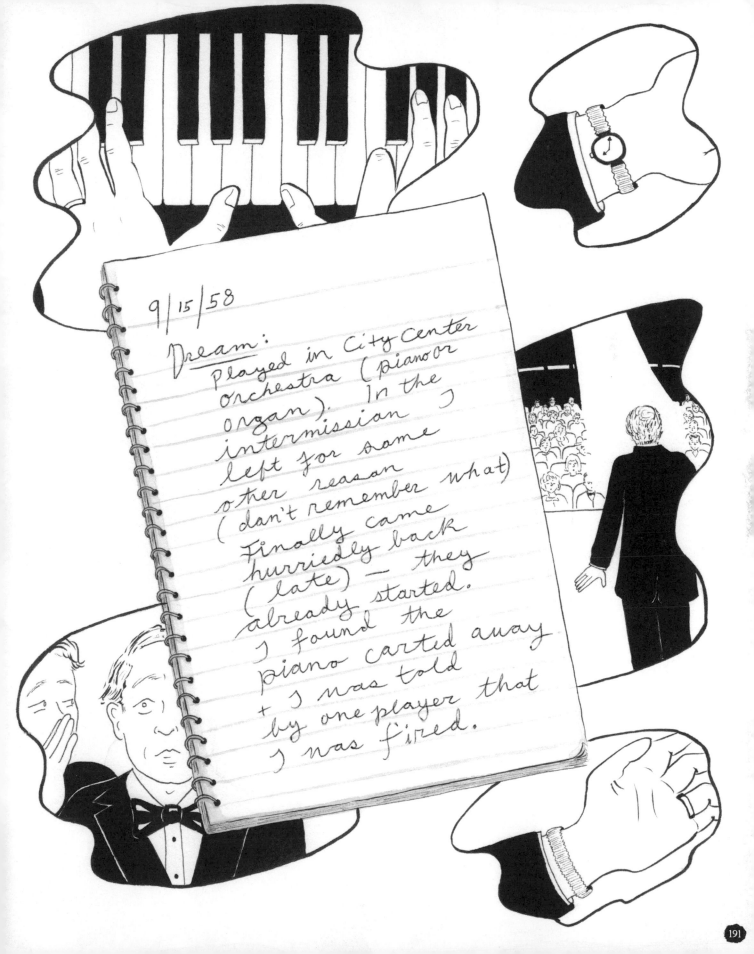

9/15/58

Dream:
Played in City Center Orchestra (piano or organ). In the intermission left for some other reason (don't remember what) Finally came hurriedly back (late) — they already started. I found the piano carted away + I was told by one player that I was fired.

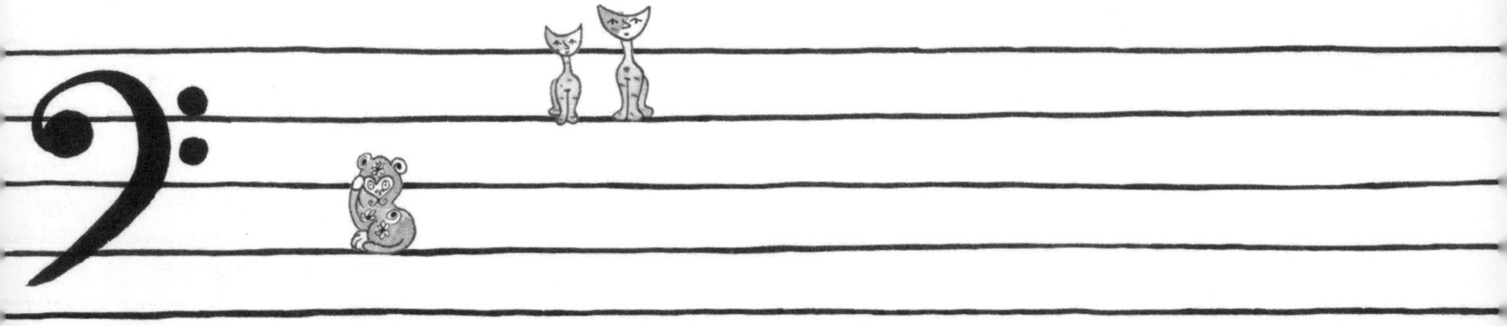

# VI.

# Through the Looking Glass

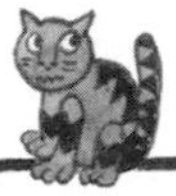

I wonder if I've been changed in the night. Let me think. Was I the same when I got up this morning? I almost think I can remember feeling a little different. But if I'm not the same, the next question is "Who in the world am I?" Ah, that's the great puzzle!

–Lewis Carroll, *Alice's Adventures in Wonderland*

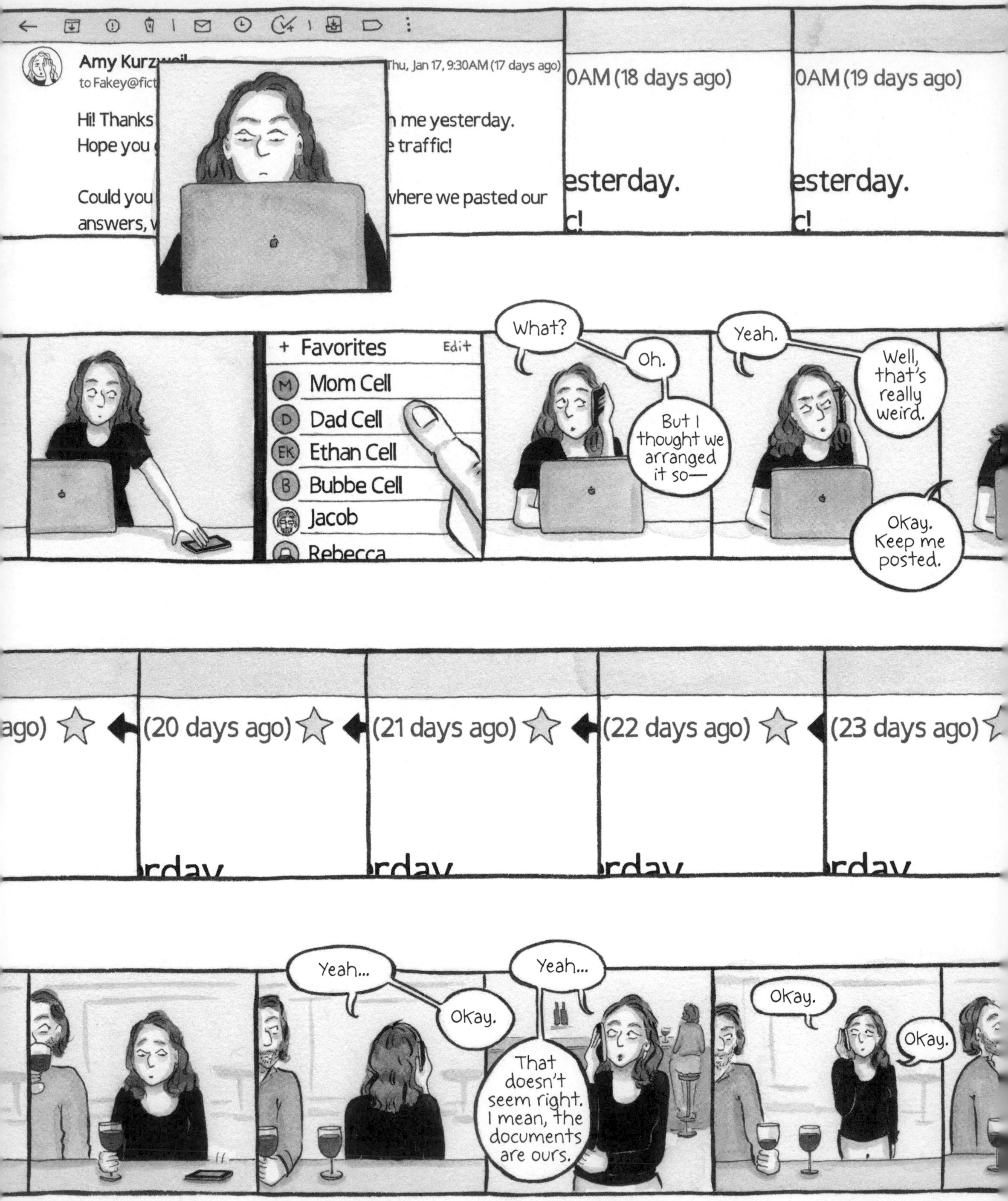
Amy Kurzweil
Thu, Jan 17, 9:30AM (17 days ago)
to Fakey@fict
Hi! Thanks
me yesterday.
Hope you
traffic!
Could you
where we pasted our
answers,
0AM (18 days ago)
esterday.
c!
0AM (19 days ago)
esterday.
c!
+ Favorites
Edit
Mom Cell
Dad Cell
Ethan Cell
Bubbe Cell
Jacob
Rebecca
What?
Oh.
But I thought we arranged it so—
Yeah.
Well, that's really weird.
Okay. Keep me posted.
ago)
(20 days ago)
(21 days ago)
(22 days ago)
(23 days ago)
Yeah...
Okay.
Yeah...
That doesn't seem right. I mean, the documents are ours.
Okay.
Okay.

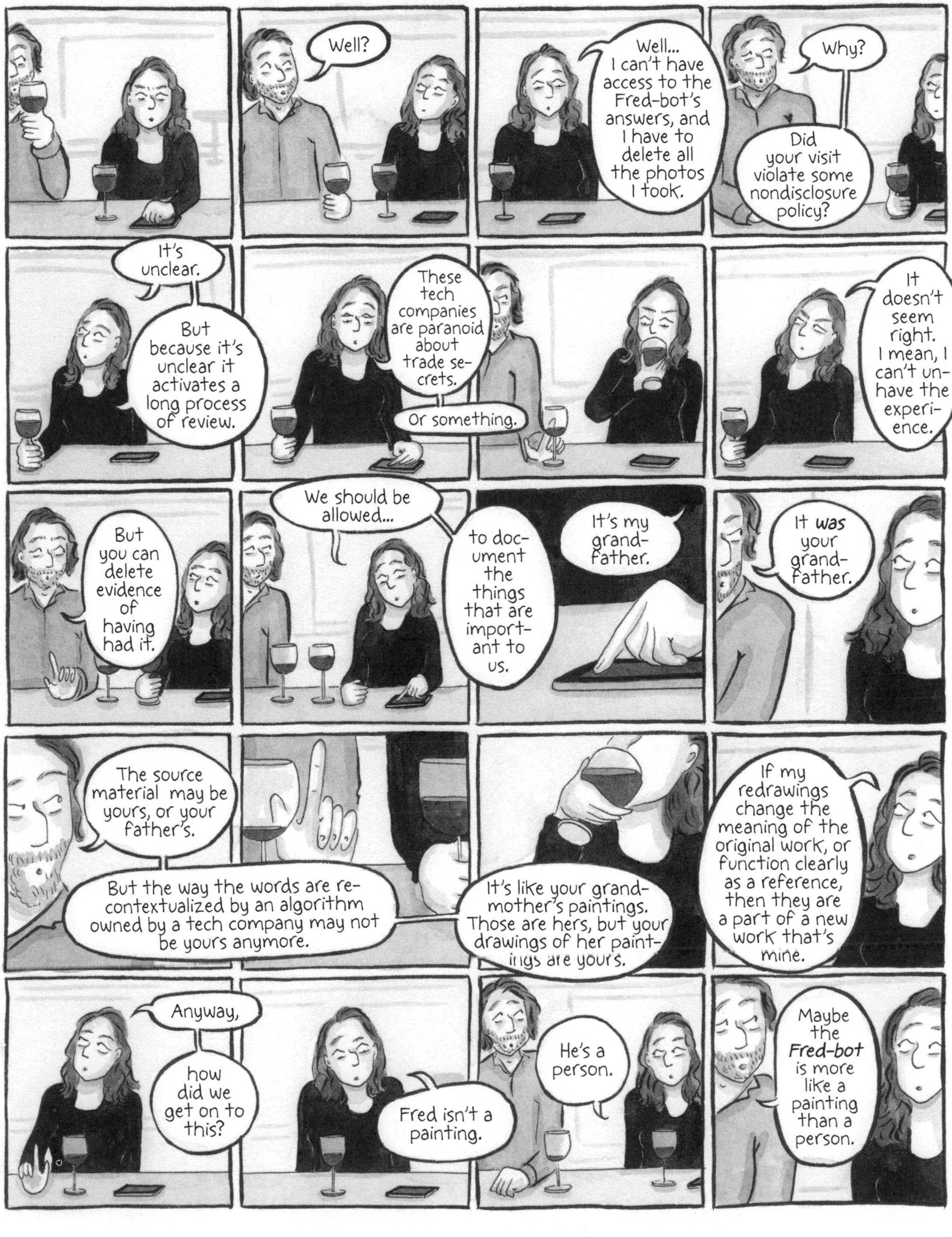
Well?
Well... I can't have access to the Fred-bot's answers, and I have to delete all the photos I took.
Why?
Did your visit violate some nondisclosure policy?
It's unclear.
But because it's unclear it activates a long process of review.
These tech companies are paranoid about trade secrets.
Or something.
It doesn't seem right. I mean, I can't unhave the experience.
But you can delete evidence of having had it.
We should be allowed...
to document the things that are important to us.
It's my grandfather.
It *was* your grandfather.
The source material may be yours, or your father's.
But the way the words are recontextualized by an algorithm owned by a tech company may not be yours anymore.
It's like your grandmother's paintings. Those are hers, but your drawings of her paintings are yours.
If my redrawings change the meaning of the original work, or function clearly as a reference, then they are a part of a new work that's mine.
Anyway,
how did we get on to this?
Fred isn't a painting.
He's a person.
Maybe the ***Fred-bot*** is more like a painting than a person.

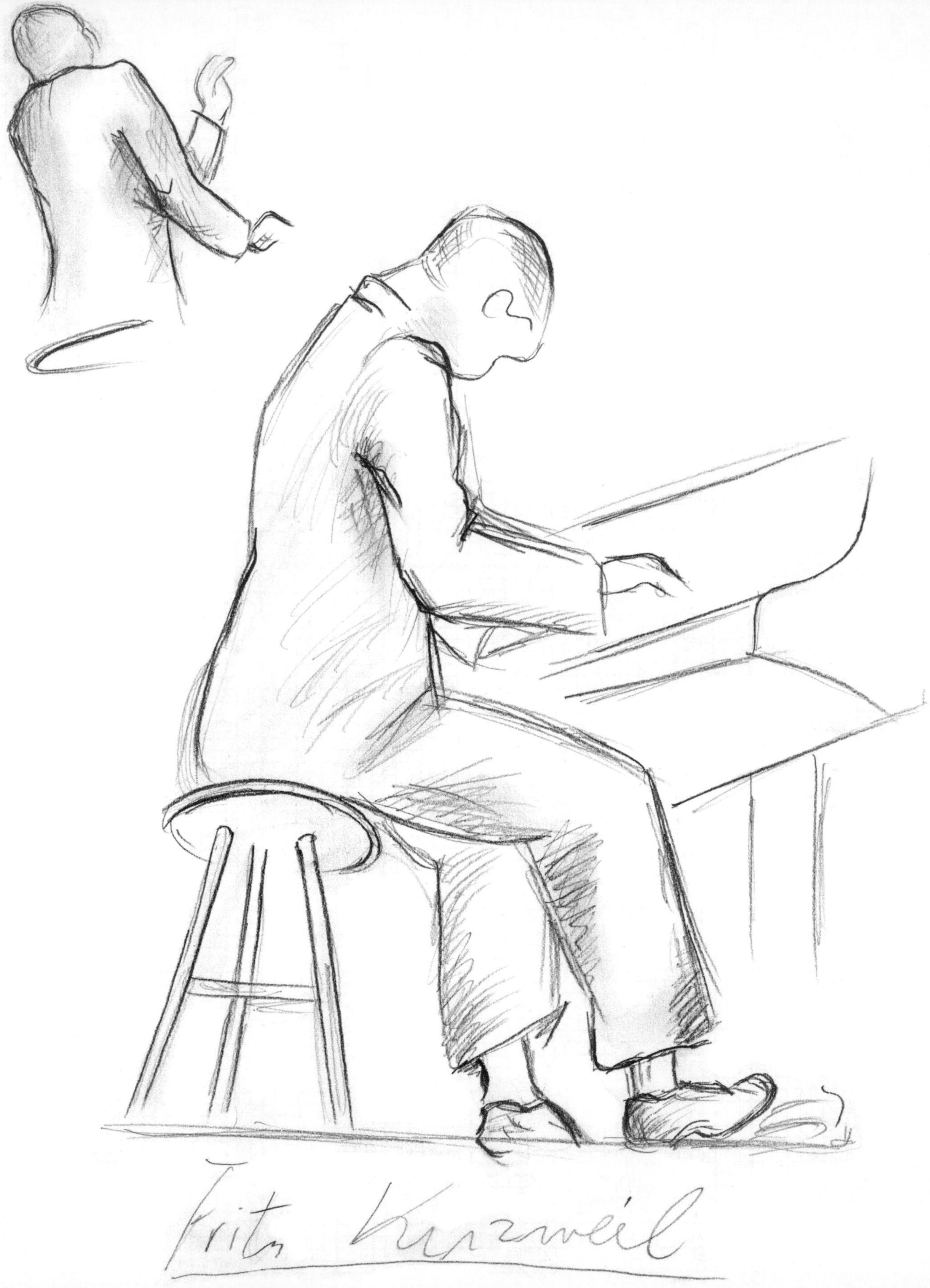
Fritz Kurzweil

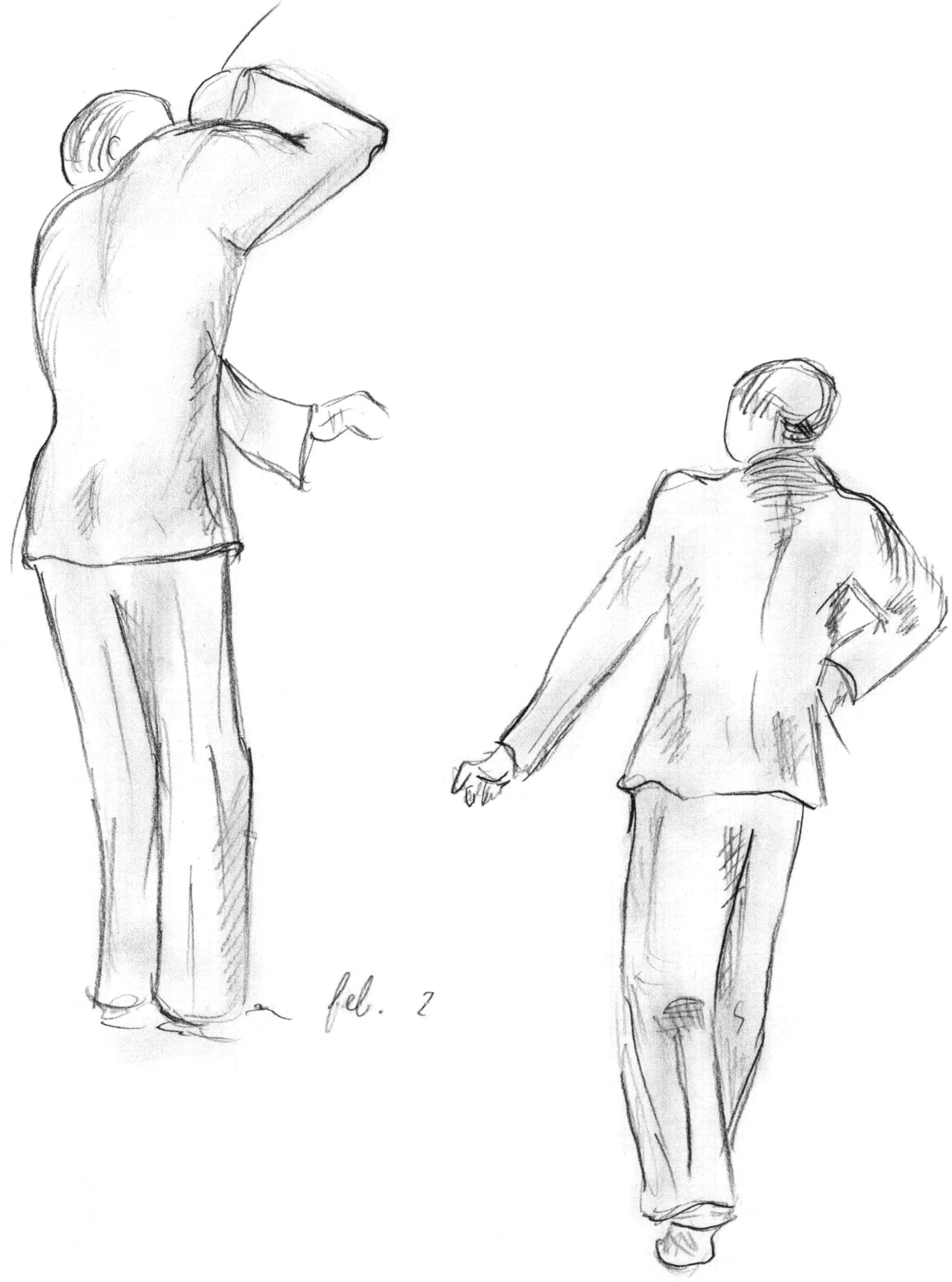
feb. 2

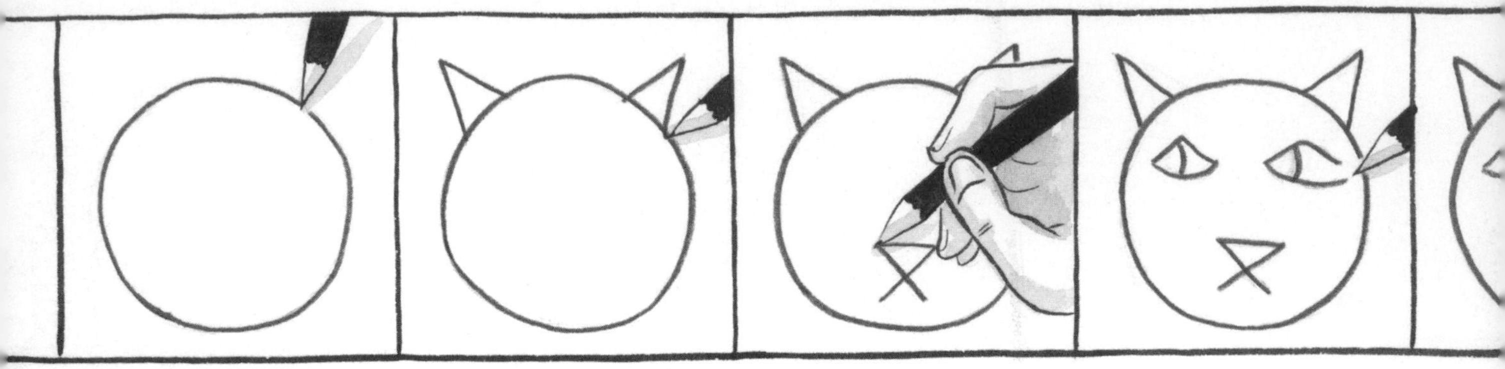

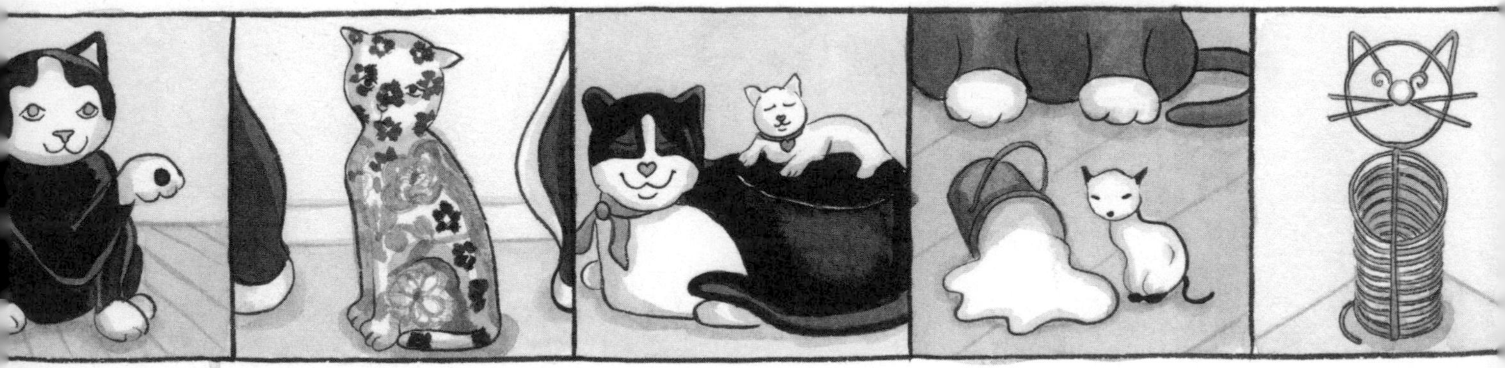

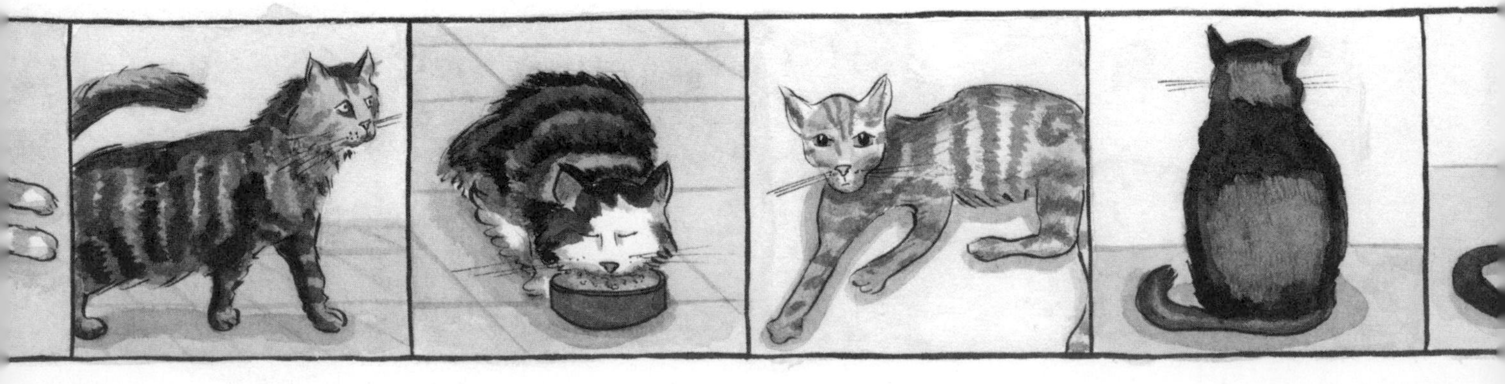

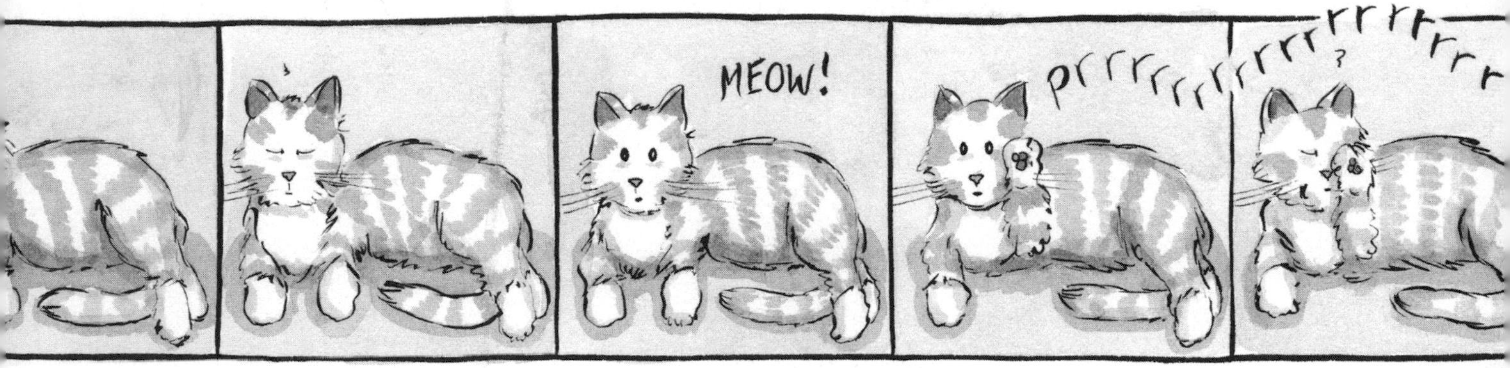
MEOW!
prrrrrrrrrrrrrrrrrrrrr

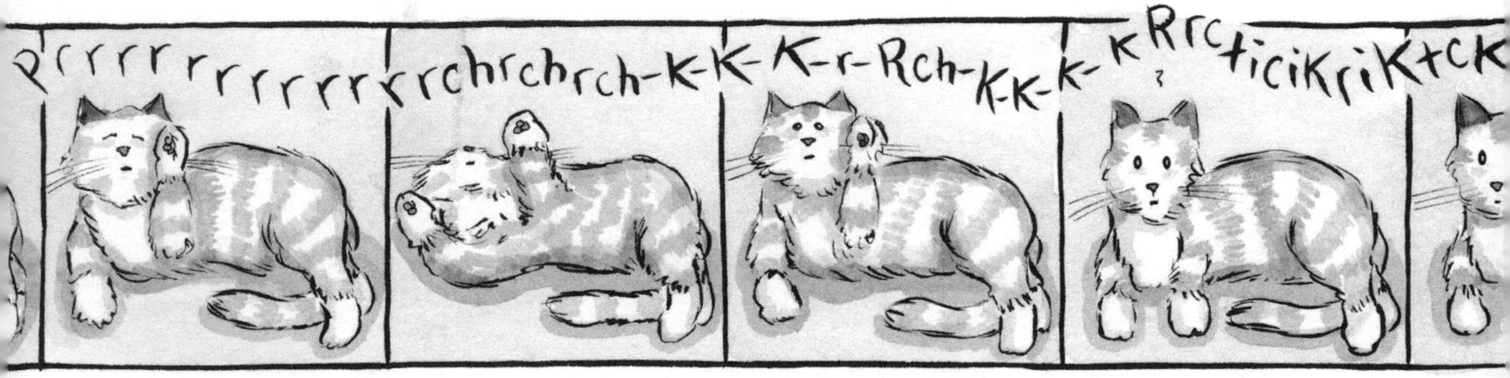
prrrrrrrrrrrrrrchrchrch-K-K-K-r-Rch-K-K-K-KRrcticiKriKtck

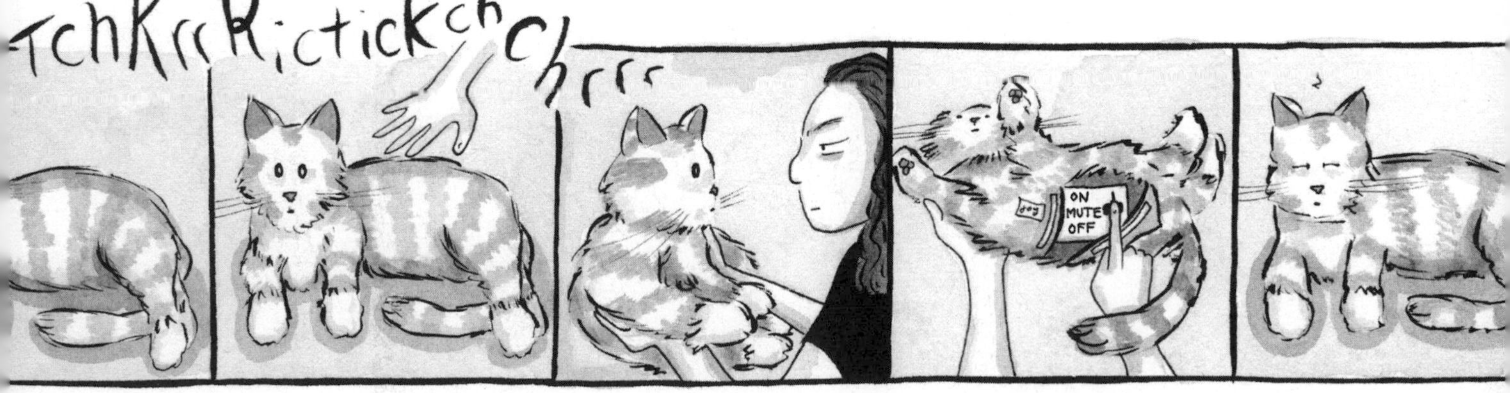
TchKrrRictickchChrrr
ON
MUTE
OFF

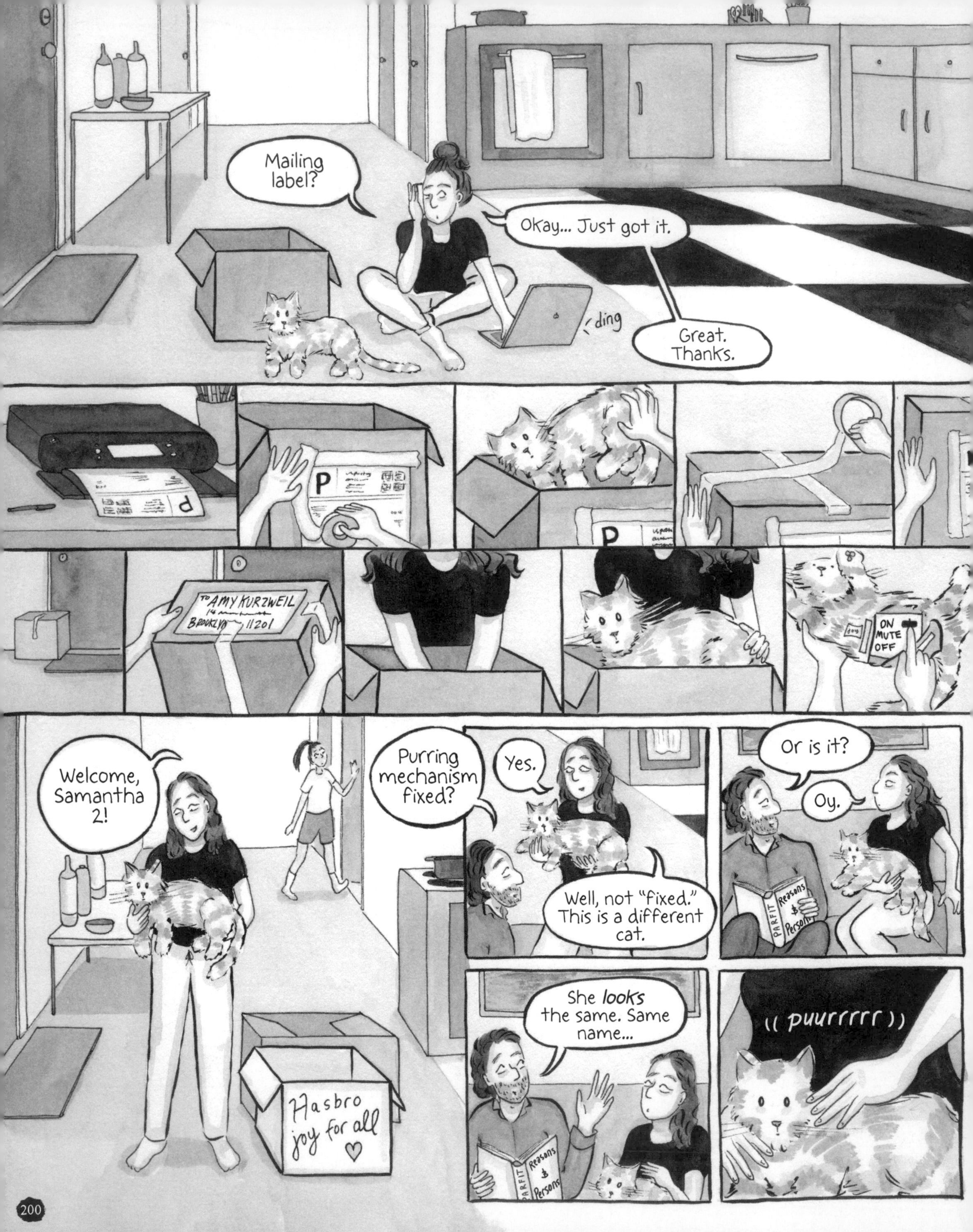
Mailing label?
Okay... Just got it.
ding
Great. Thanks.
P
TO AMY KURZWEIL
BROOKLYN 11201
ON
MUTE
OFF
Welcome, Samantha 2!
Purring mechanism fixed?
Yes.
Well, not "fixed." This is a different cat.
Or is it?
Oy.
PARFIT Reasons & Persons
She *looks* the same. Same name...
Hasbro joy for all
(( puurrrrr ))

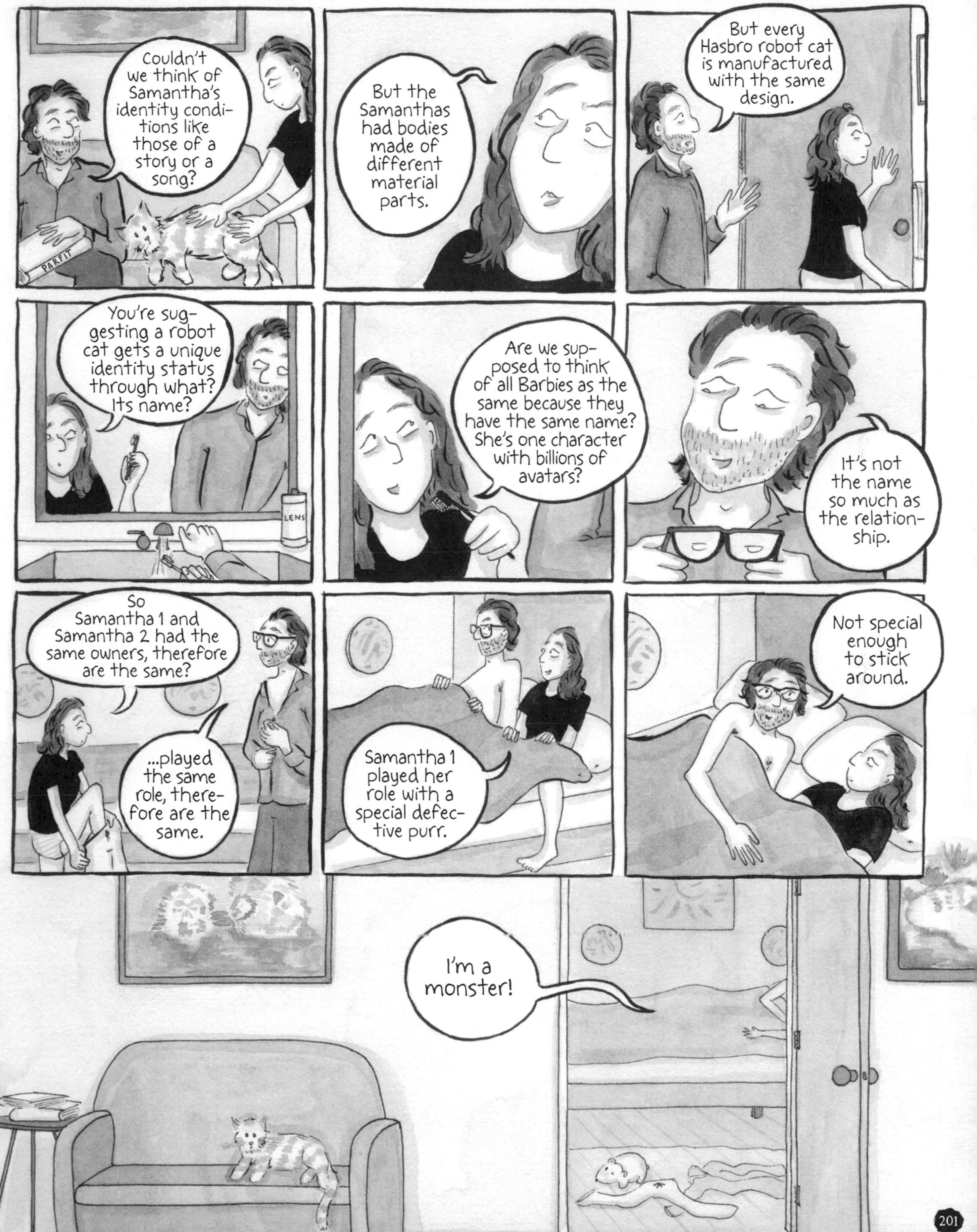
PARFIT
Couldn't we think of Samantha's identity conditions like those of a story or a song?
But the Samanthas had bodies made of different material parts.
But every Hasbro robot cat is manufactured with the same design.
You're suggesting a robot cat gets a unique identity status through what? Its name?
LENS
Are we supposed to think of all Barbies as the same because they have the same name? She's one character with billions of avatars?
It's not the name so much as the relationship.
So Samantha 1 and Samantha 2 had the same owners, therefore are the same?
...played the same role, therefore are the same.
Samantha 1 played her role with a special defective purr.
Not special enough to stick around.
I'm a monster!

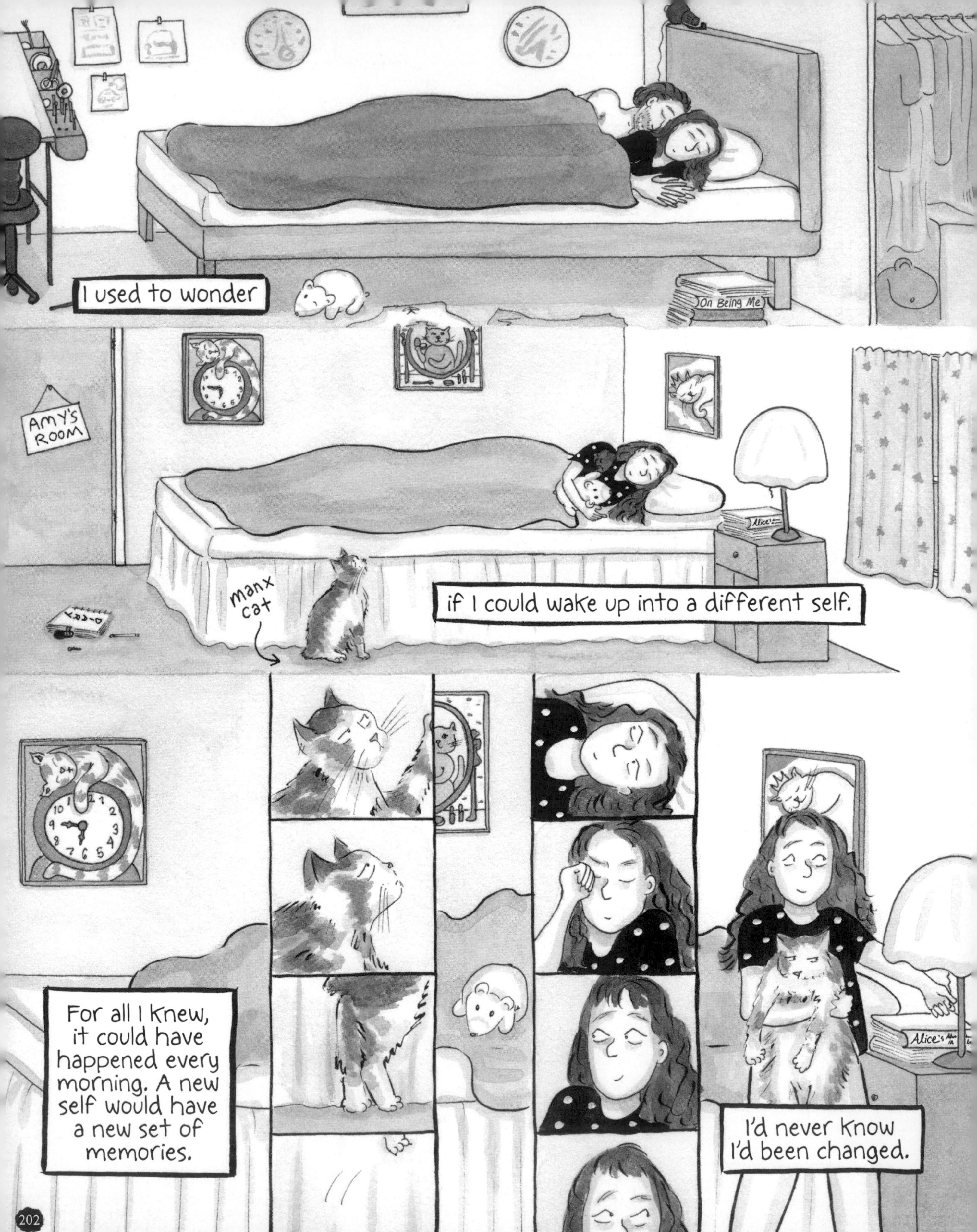
I used to wonder
On Being Me
AMY'S ROOM
manx cat
Alice's
if I could wake up into a different self.
For all I knew, it could have happened every morning. A new self would have a new set of memories.
I'd never know I'd been changed.

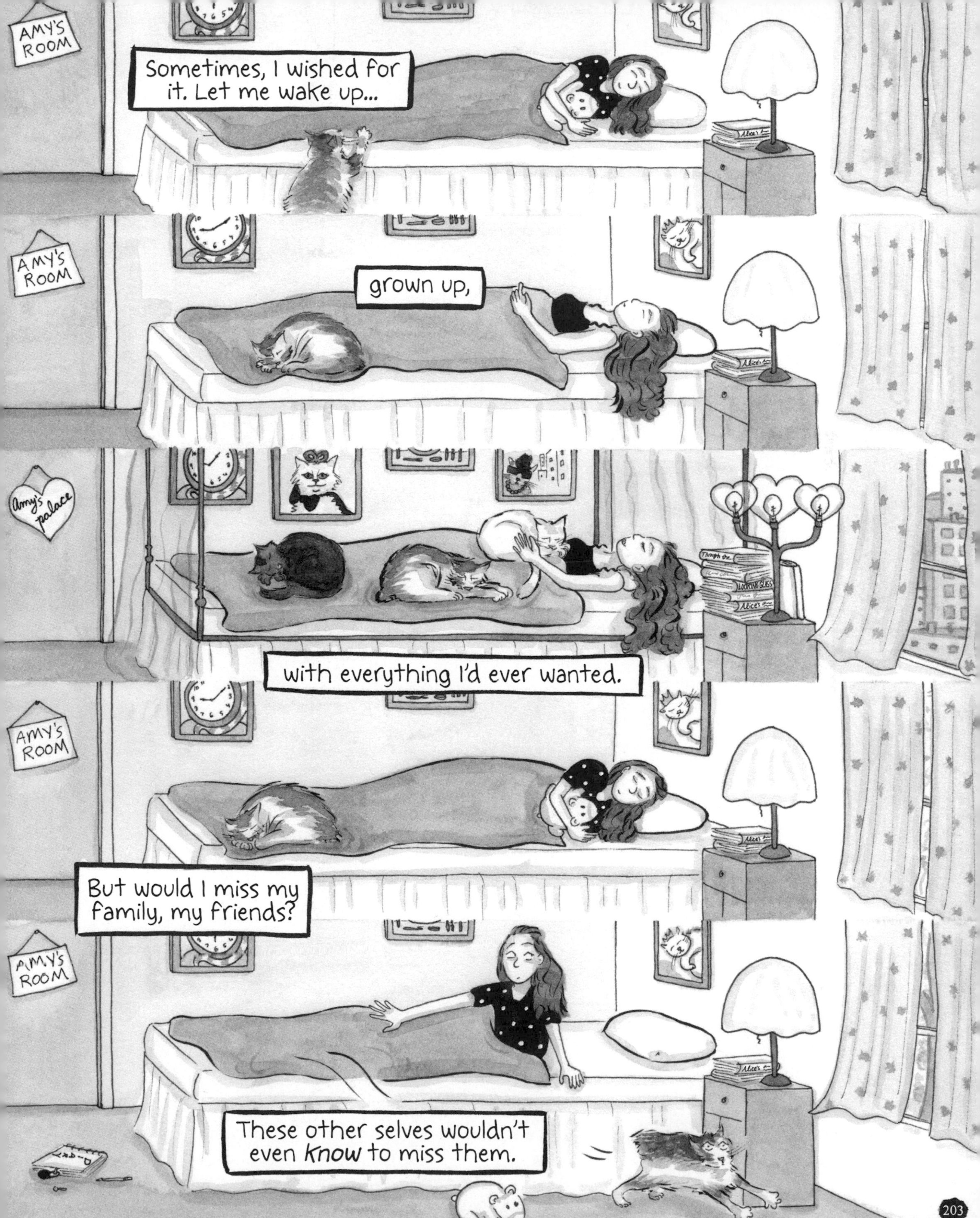
AMY'S ROOM
Sometimes, I wished for it. Let me wake up...
grown up,
Amy's palace
with everything I'd ever wanted.
But would I miss my family, my friends?
These other selves wouldn't even *know* to miss them.

AMY'S
ROOM

hologram
outside
my room

dad's office

alanis
morissette

KURZWEIL
KURZWEIL
KURZWEIL
KURZWEIL
KURZWEIL

RAY KURZWEIL
RAY KURZWEIL
RAY KURZWEIL
RAY KURZWEIL
RAY KURZWEIL

soothing
ritual

one...

two...

one-hundred-and-fifteen...

one-hundred-and-sixteen...

204

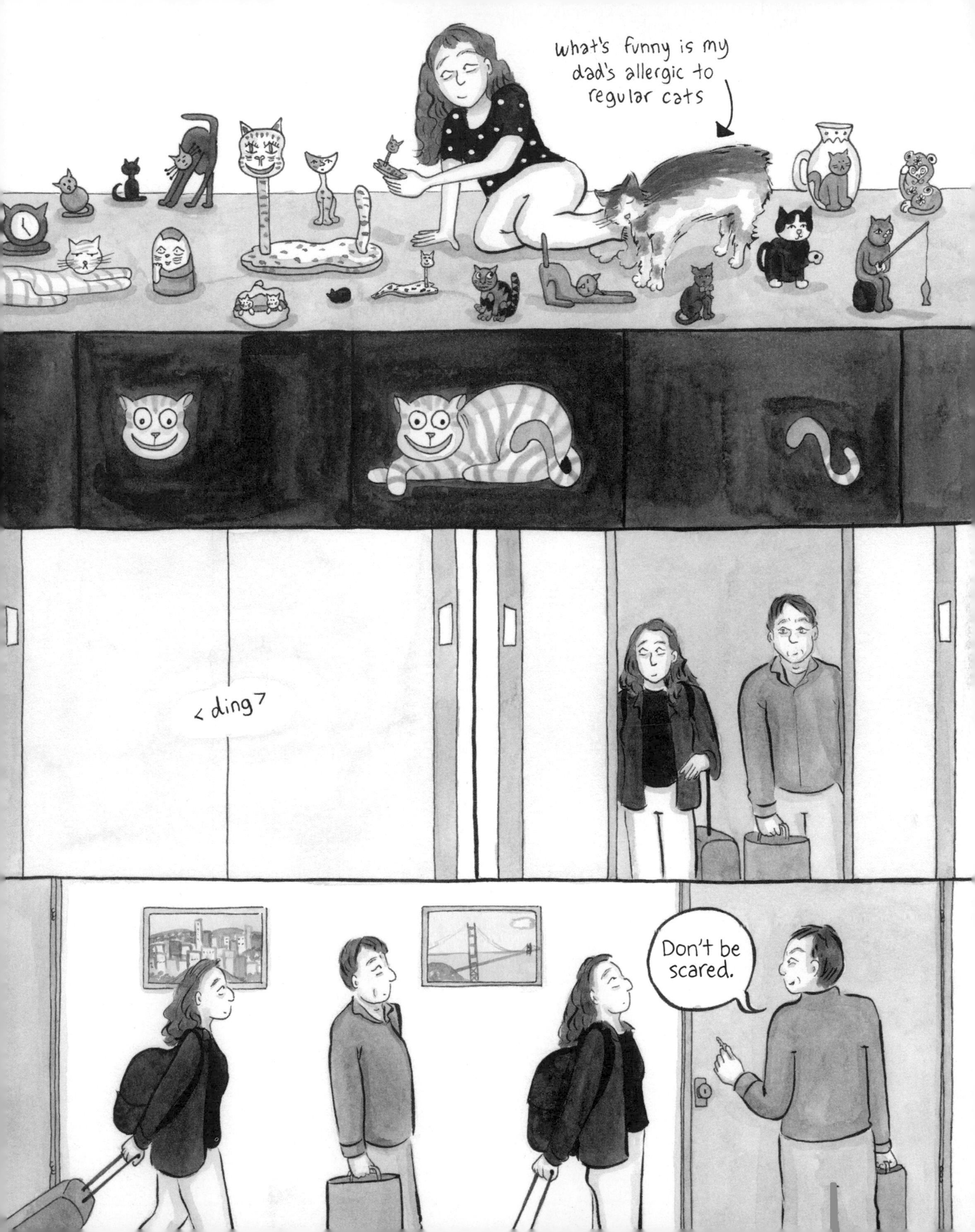
what's funny is my dad's allergic to regular cats
< ding >
Don't be scared.

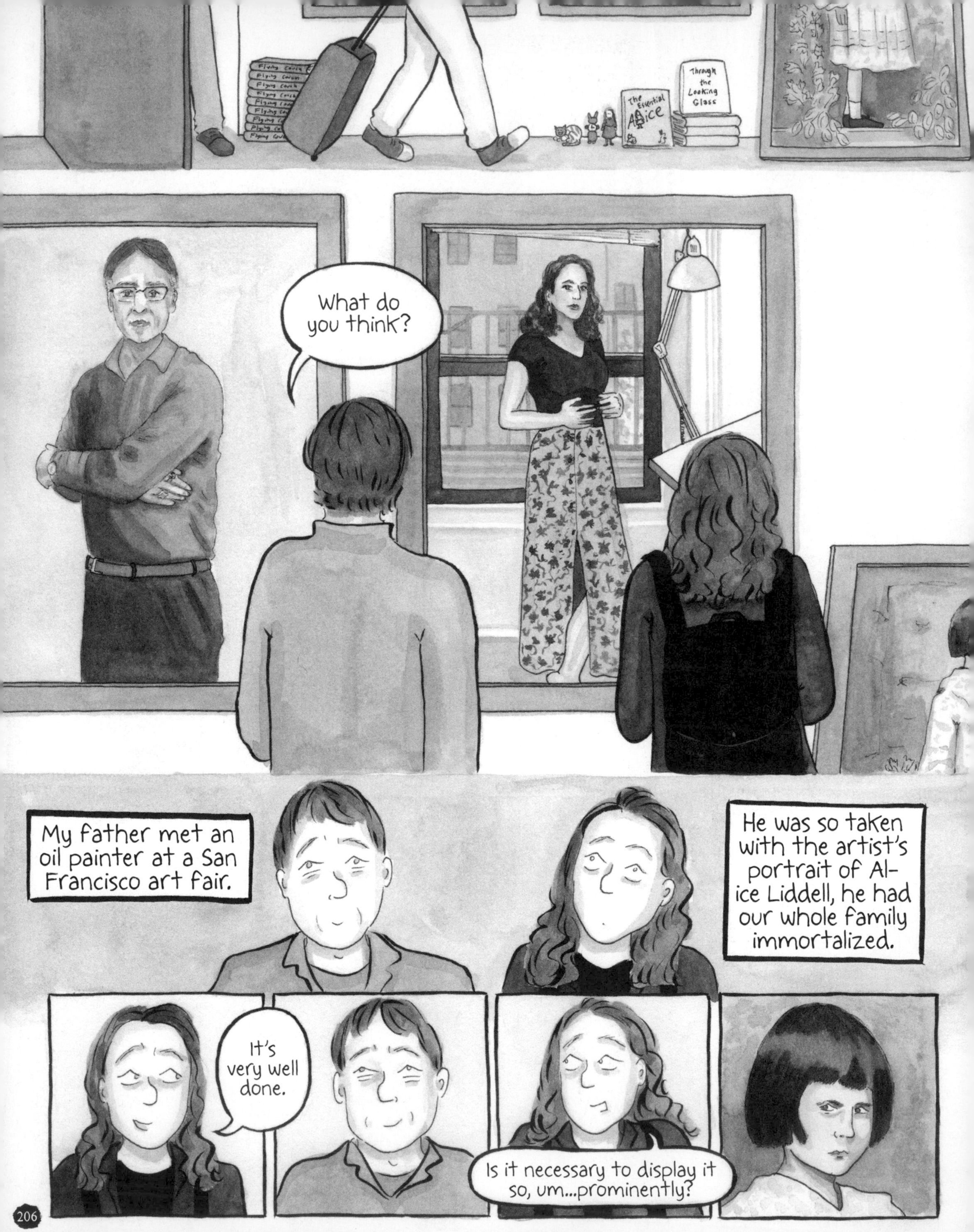
Flying Couch
Through the Looking Glass
The Essential Alice
What do you think?
My father met an oil painter at a San Francisco art fair.
He was so taken with the artist's portrait of Alice Liddell, he had our whole family immortalized.
It's very well done.
Is it necessary to display it so, um...prominently?

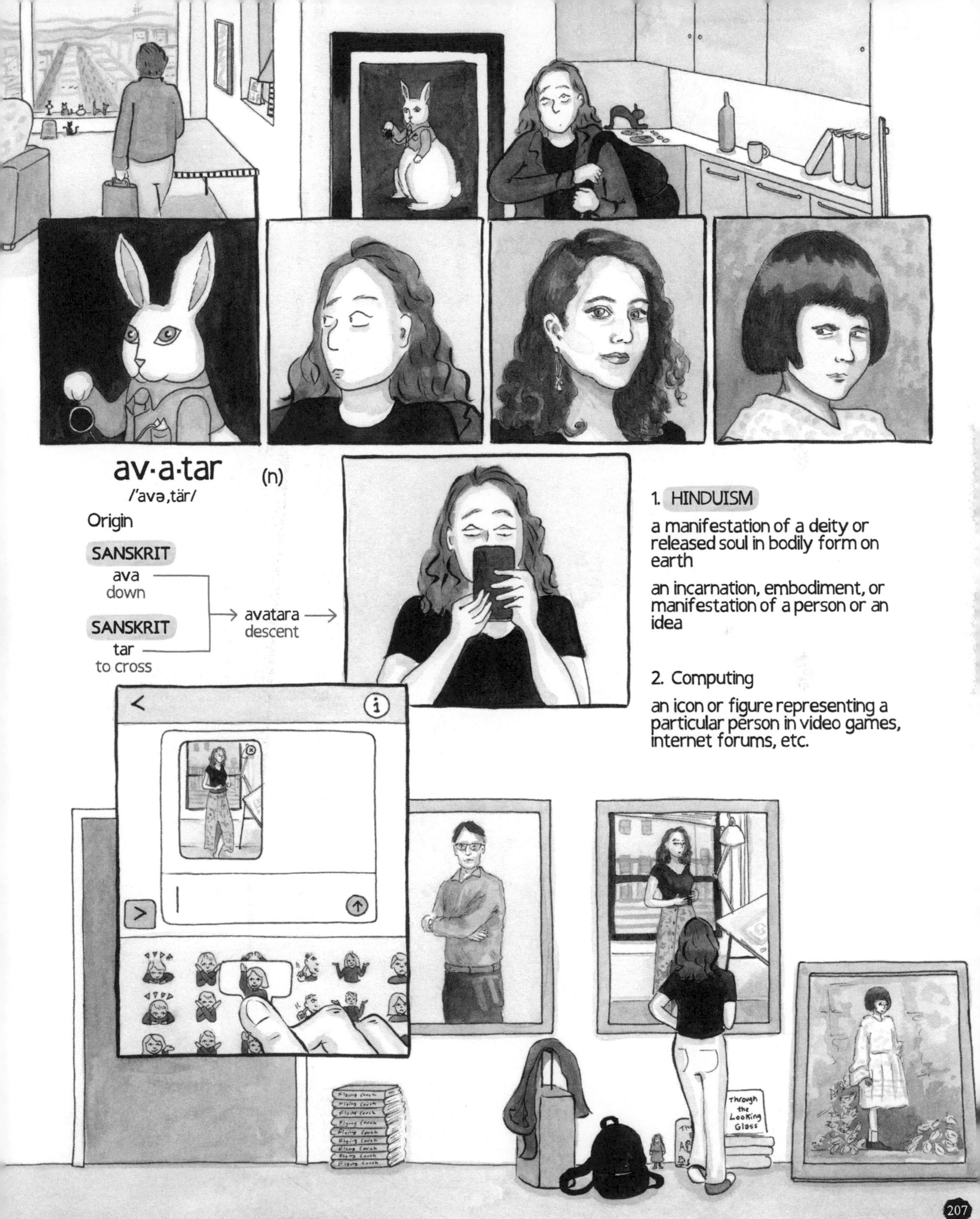
av·a·tar (n)
/ˈavə,tär/
Origin
SANSKRIT
ava
down
SANSKRIT
tar
to cross
avatara
descent
1. HINDUISM
a manifestation of a deity or released soul in bodily form on earth
an incarnation, embodiment, or manifestation of a person or an idea
2. Computing
an icon or figure representing a particular person in video games, internet forums, etc.
Through the Looking Glass

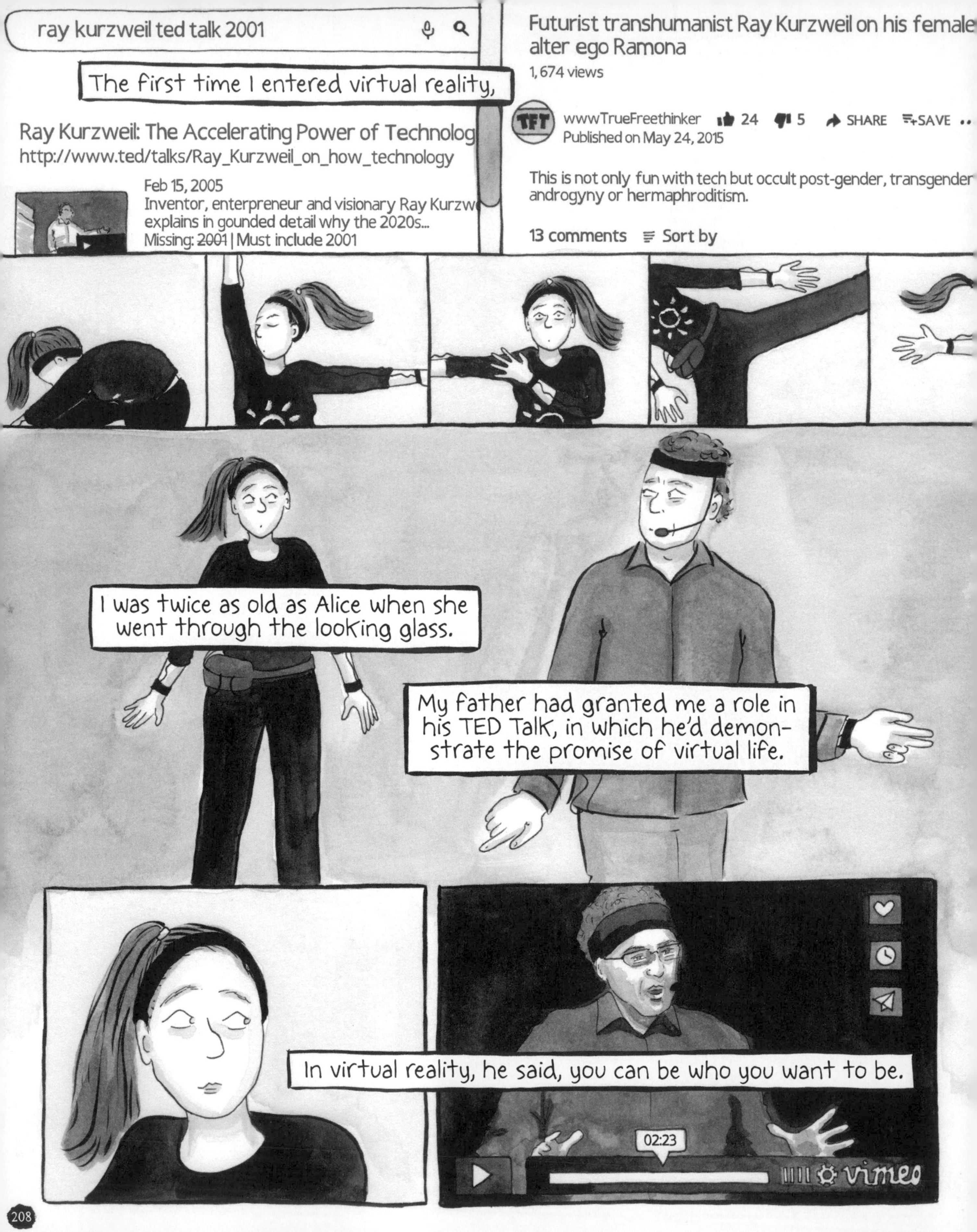

ray kurzweil ted talk 2001
The first time I entered virtual reality,
Ray Kurzweil: The Accelerating Power of Technolog
http://www.ted/talks/Ray_Kurzweil_on_how_technology
Feb 15, 2005
Inventor, enterpreneur and visionary Ray Kurzw
explains in gounded detail why the 2020s...
Missing: 2001 | Must include 2001
Futurist transhumanist Ray Kurzweil on his female alter ego Ramona
1,674 views
TFT
wwwTrueFreethinker 24 5 SHARE SAVE
Published on May 24, 2015
This is not only fun with tech but occult post-gender, transgender androgyny or hermaphroditism.
13 comments Sort by
I was twice as old as Alice when she went through the looking glass.
My father had granted me a role in his TED Talk, in which he'd demonstrate the promise of virtual life.
In virtual reality, he said, you can be who you want to be.
02:23
vimeo

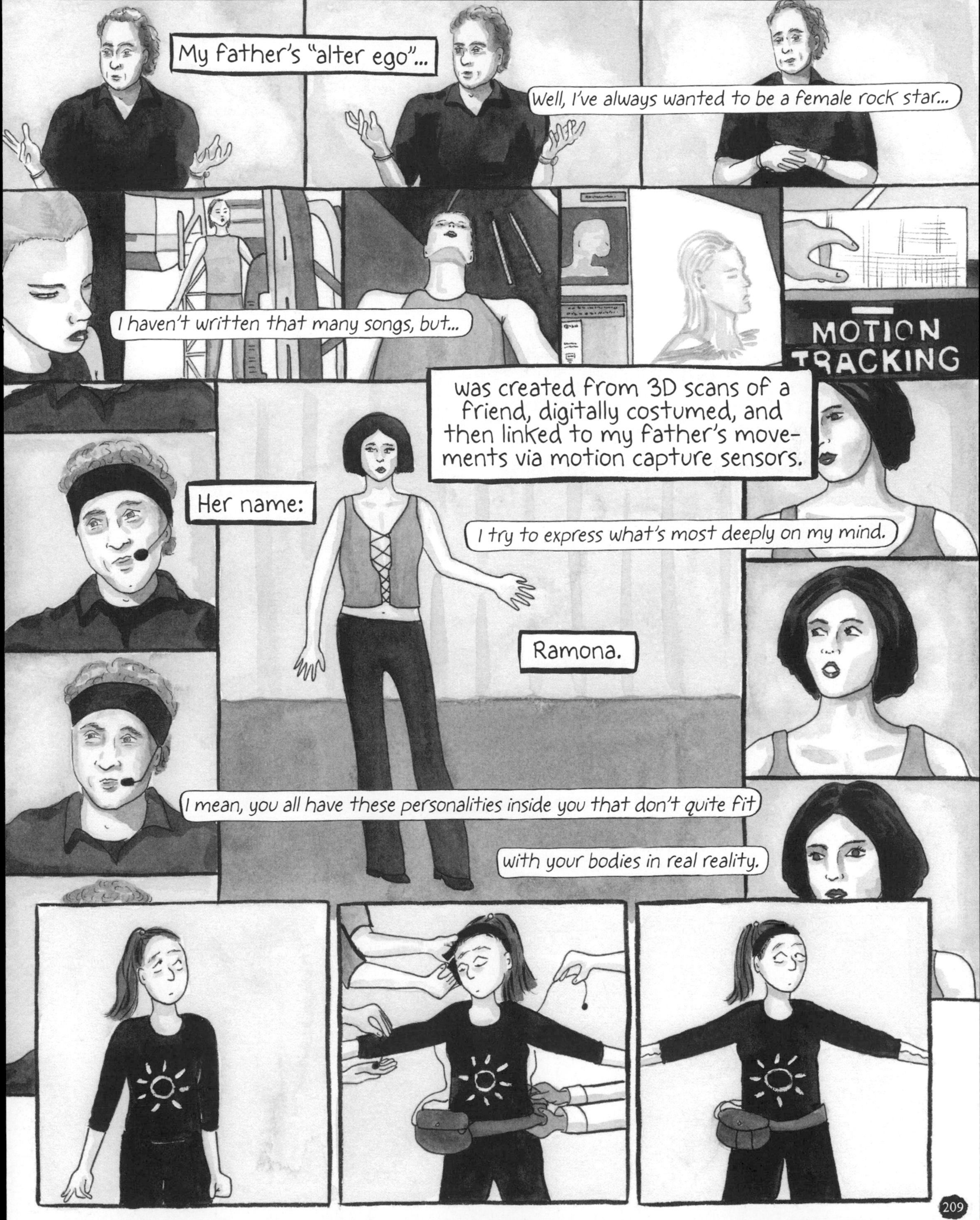
My father's "alter ego"...
Well, I've always wanted to be a female rock star...
I haven't written that many songs, but...
MOTION TRACKING
was created from 3D scans of a friend, digitally costumed, and then linked to my father's movements via motion capture sensors.
Her name:
I try to express what's most deeply on my mind.
Ramona.
I mean, you all have these personalities inside you that don't quite fit
with your bodies in real reality.

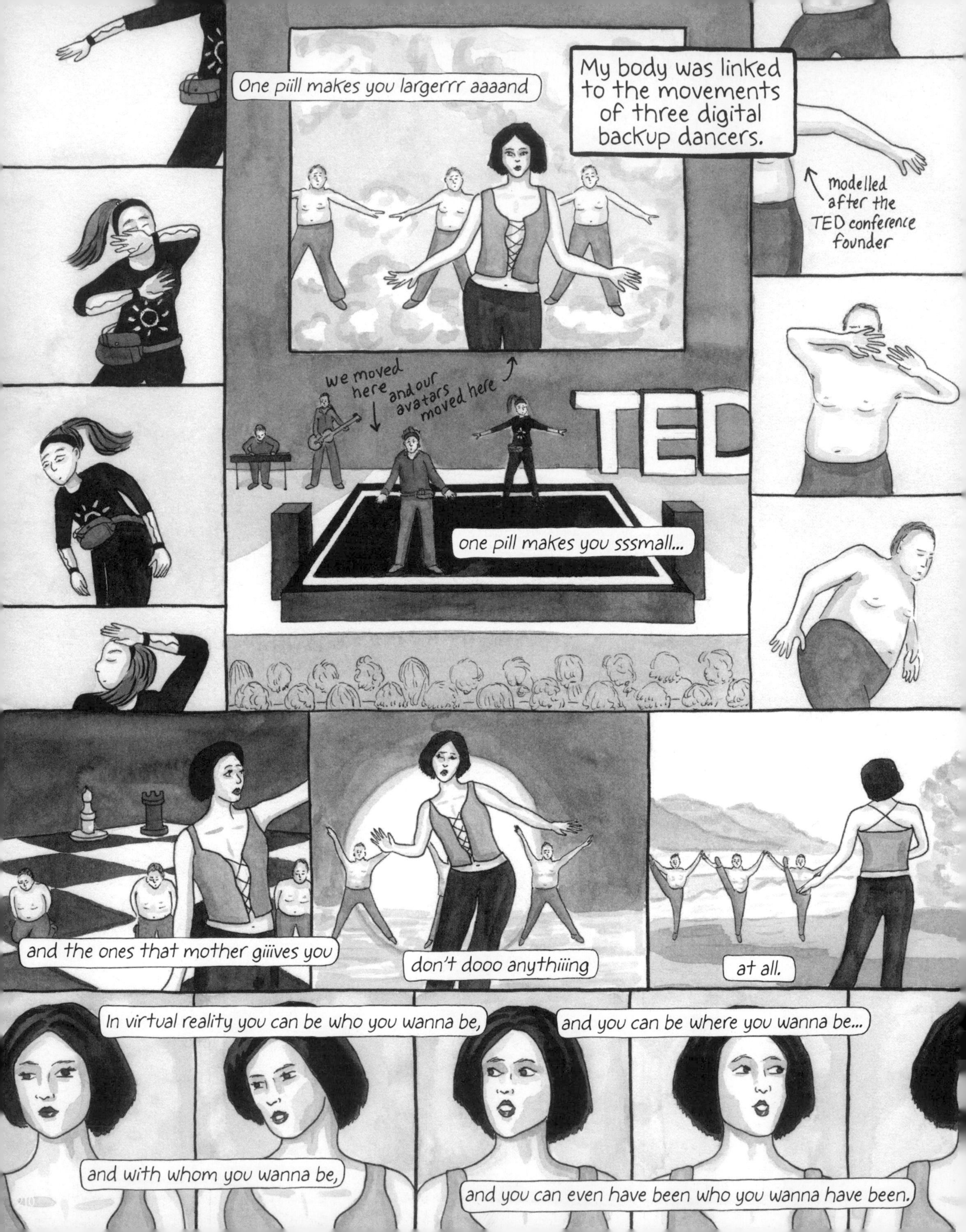
One piill makes you largerrr aaaand
My body was linked to the movements of three digital backup dancers.
modelled after the TED conference founder
we moved here
and our avatars moved here
TED
one pill makes you sssmall...
and the ones that mother giiives you
don't dooo anythiiing
at all.
In virtual reality you can be who you wanna be,
and you can be where you wanna be...
and with whom you wanna be,
and you can even have been who you wanna have been.

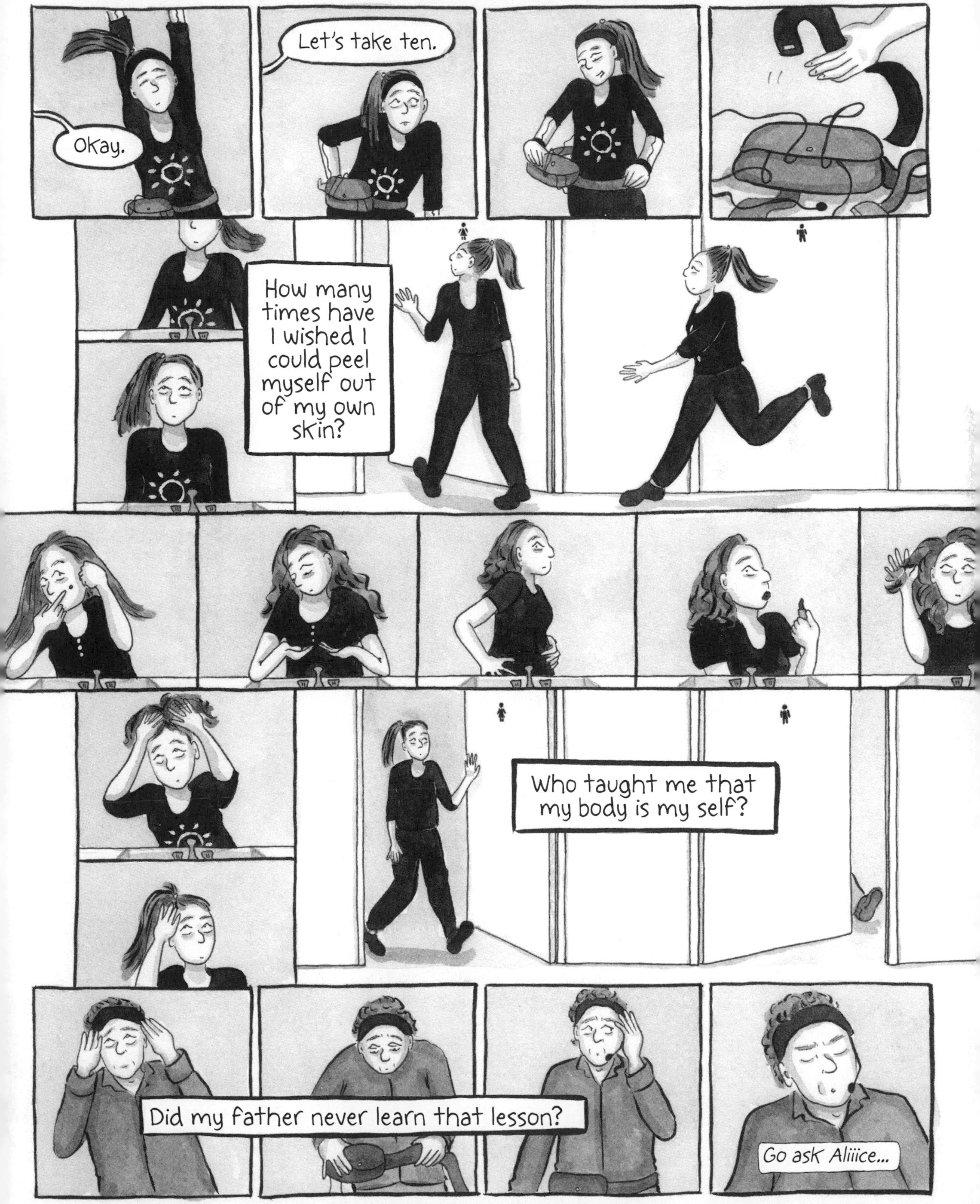
Okay.
Let's take ten.
How many times have I wished I could peel myself out of my own skin?
Who taught me that my body is my self?
Did my father never learn that lesson?
Go ask Aliiice...

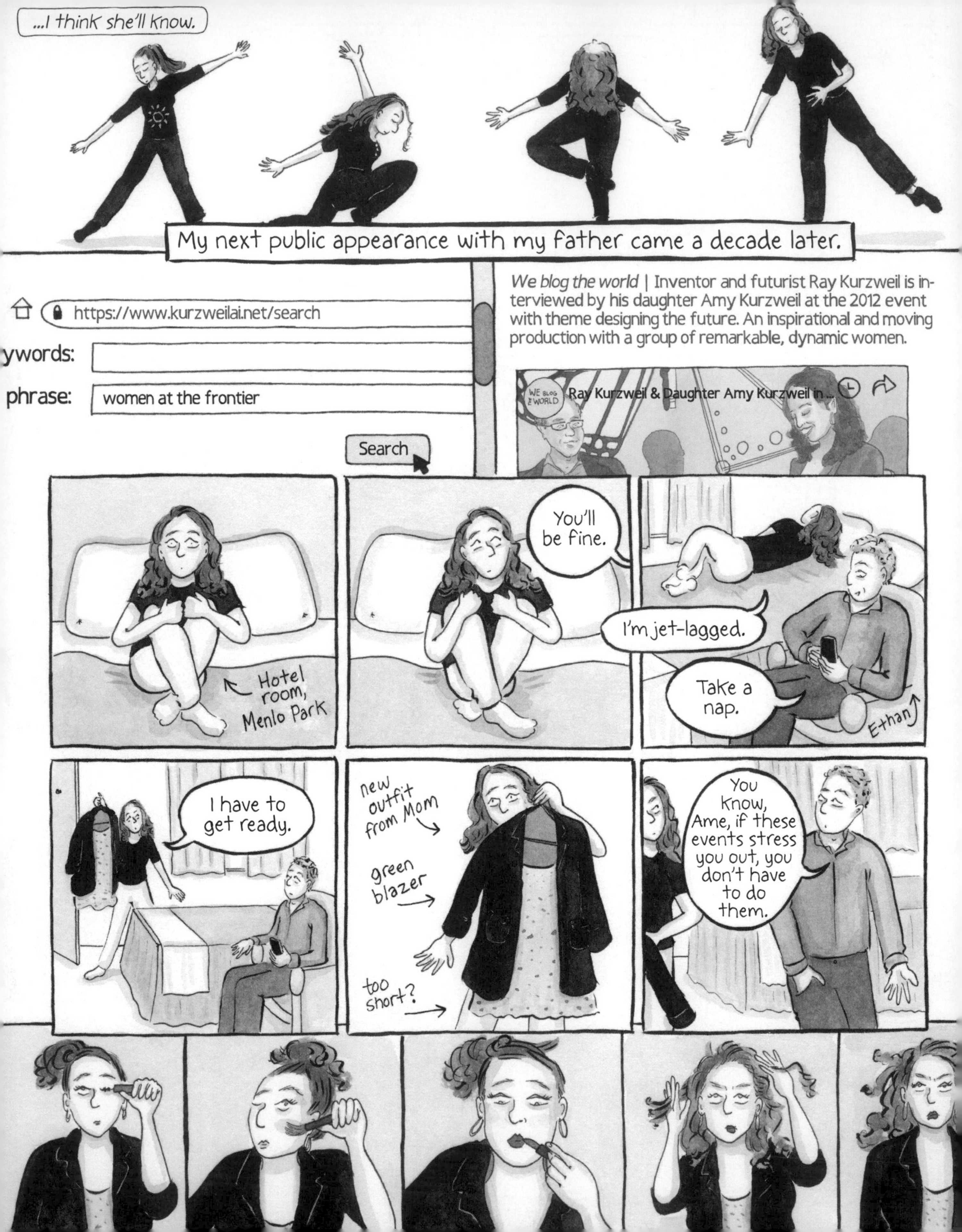
...I think she'll know.
My next public appearance with my father came a decade later.
https://www.kurzweilai.net/search
ywords:
phrase: women at the frontier
Search
We blog the world | Inventor and futurist Ray Kurzweil is interviewed by his daughter Amy Kurzweil at the 2012 event with theme designing the future. An inspirational and moving production with a group of remarkable, dynamic women.
WE BLOG THE WORLD
Ray Kurzweil & Daughter Amy Kurzweil in ...
Hotel room, Menlo Park
You'll be fine.
I'm jet-lagged.
Take a nap.
Ethan
I have to get ready.
new outfit from Mom
green blazer
too short?
You know, Ame, if these events stress you out, you don't have to do them.

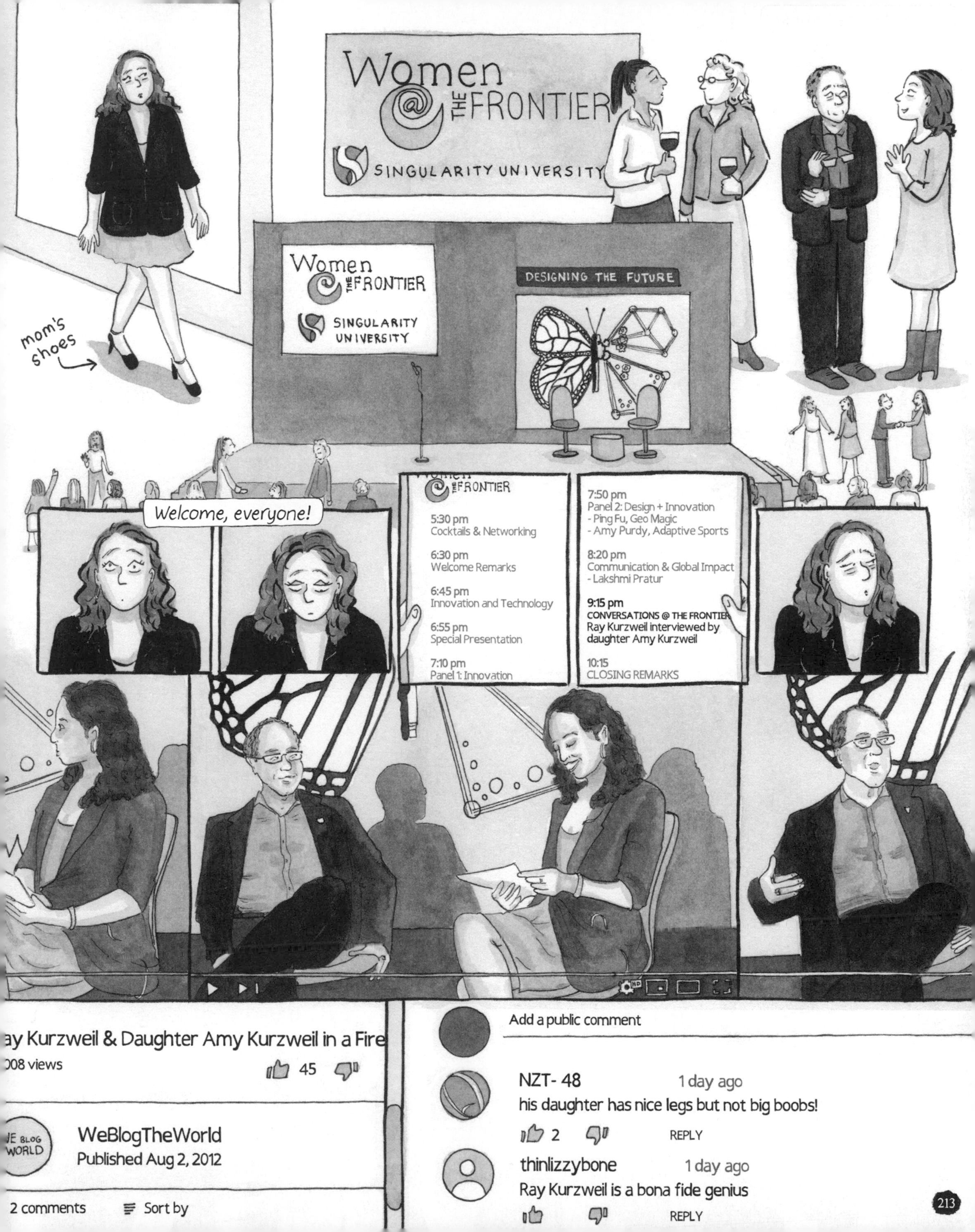
Women @ THE FRONTIER
SINGULARITY UNIVERSITY
mom's shoes
Women @ THE FRONTIER
SINGULARITY UNIVERSITY
DESIGNING THE FUTURE
Welcome, everyone!
@ THE FRONTIER
5:30 pm
Cocktails & Networking
6:30 pm
Welcome Remarks
6:45 pm
Innovation and Technology
6:55 pm
Special Presentation
7:10 pm
Panel 1: Innovation
7:50 pm
Panel 2: Design + Innovation
- Ping Fu, Geo Magic
- Amy Purdy, Adaptive Sports
8:20 pm
Communication & Global Impact
- Lakshmi Pratur
9:15 pm
CONVERSATIONS @ THE FRONTIER
Ray Kurzweil interviewed by daughter Amy Kurzweil
10:15
CLOSING REMARKS
ay Kurzweil & Daughter Amy Kurzweil in a Fire
008 views
45
WeBlogTheWorld
Published Aug 2, 2012
2 comments
Sort by
Add a public comment
NZT- 48
1 day ago
his daughter has nice legs but not big boobs!
2
REPLY
thinlizzybone
1 day ago
Ray Kurzweil is a bona fide genius
REPLY

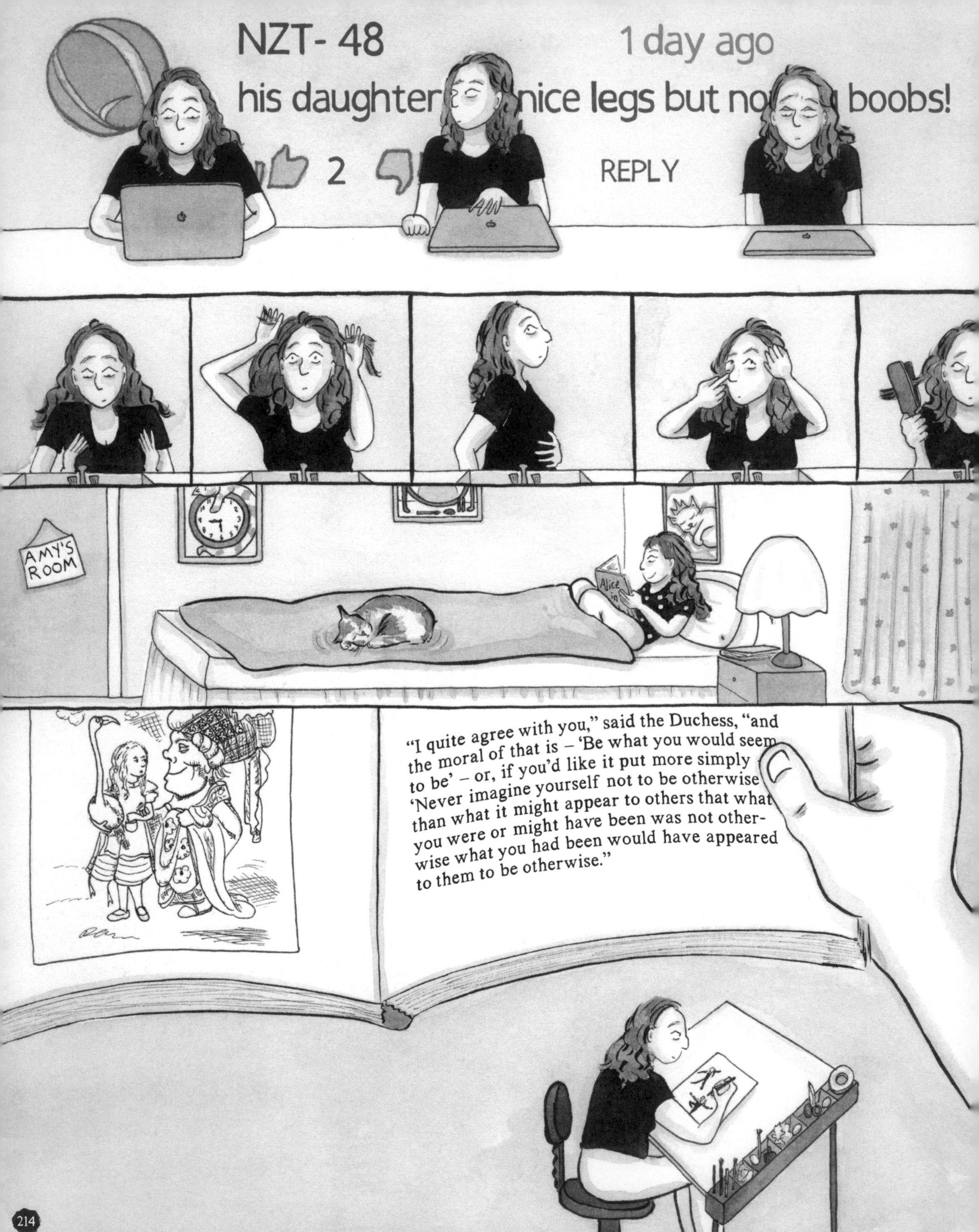
NZT- 48
1 day ago
his daughter
nice legs but no
boobs!
2
REPLY
AMY'S ROOM
Alice in
"I quite agree with you," said the Duchess, "and the moral of that is – 'Be what you would seem to be' – or, if you'd like it put more simply – 'Never imagine yourself not to be otherwise than what it might appear to others that what you were or might have been was not otherwise what you had been would have appeared to them to be otherwise.'"

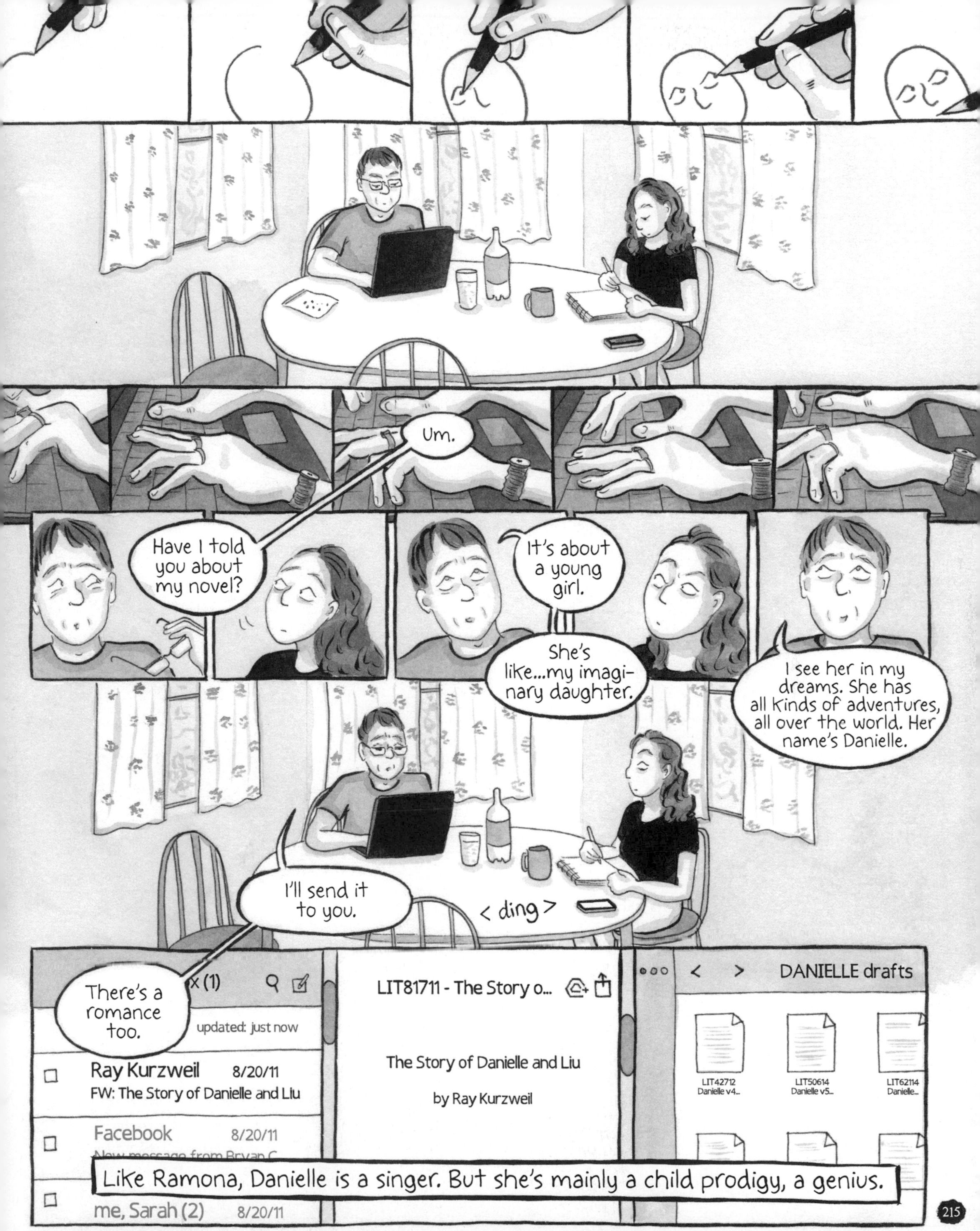
Um.
Have I told you about my novel?
It's about a young girl.
She's like...my imaginary daughter.
I see her in my dreams. She has all kinds of adventures, all over the world. Her name's Danielle.
I'll send it to you.
< ding >
There's a romance too.
x (1)
updated: just now
Ray Kurzweil 8/20/11
FW: The Story of Danielle and Liu
Facebook 8/20/11
me, Sarah (2) 8/20/11
LIT81711 - The Story o...
The Story of Danielle and Liu
by Ray Kurzweil
DANIELLE drafts
LIT42712 Danielle v4...
LIT50614 Danielle v5...
LIT62114 Danielle...
Like Ramona, Danielle is a singer. But she's mainly a child prodigy, a genius.

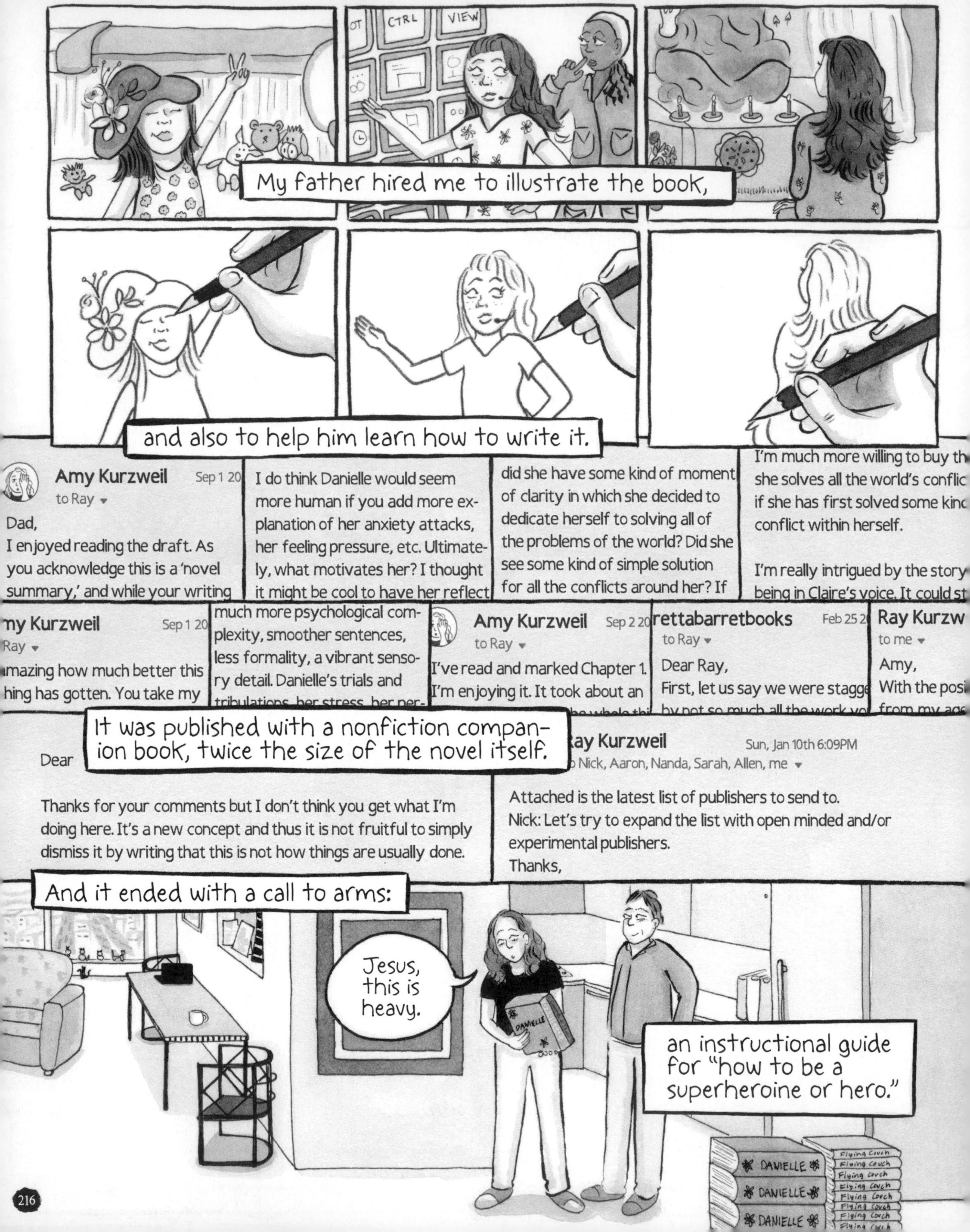

CTRL
VIEW
My father hired me to illustrate the book,
and also to help him learn how to write it.
Amy Kurzweil
Sep 1 20
to Ray
Dad,
I enjoyed reading the draft. As you acknowledge this is a 'novel summary,' and while your writing
I do think Danielle would seem more human if you add more explanation of her anxiety attacks, her feeling pressure, etc. Ultimately, what motivates her? I thought it might be cool to have her reflect
did she have some kind of moment of clarity in which she decided to dedicate herself to solving all of the problems of the world? Did she see some kind of simple solution for all the conflicts around her? If
I'm much more willing to buy th
she solves all the world's conflic
if she has first solved some kinc
conflict within herself.
I'm really intrigued by the story
my Kurzweil
Sep 1 20
Ray
mazing how much better this
hing has gotten. You take my
much more psychological complexity, smoother sentences, less formality, a vibrant sensory detail. Danielle's trials and
Amy Kurzweil
Sep 2 20
to Ray
I've read and marked Chapter 1. I'm enjoying it. It took about an
rettabarretbooks
Feb 25 2
to Ray
Dear Ray,
First, let us say we were stagge
Ray Kurzw
to me
Amy,
With the posi
It was published with a nonfiction companion book, twice the size of the novel itself.
Dear
Thanks for your comments but I don't think you get what I'm doing here. It's a new concept and thus it is not fruitful to simply dismiss it by writing that this is not how things are usually done.
ay Kurzweil
Sun, Jan 10th 6:09PM
Nick, Aaron, Nanda, Sarah, Allen, me
Attached is the latest list of publishers to send to.
Nick: Let's try to expand the list with open minded and/or experimental publishers.
Thanks,
And it ended with a call to arms:
Jesus, this is heavy.
DANIELLE
an instructional guide for "how to be a superheroine or hero."
DANIELLE
DANIELLE
DANIELLE
Flying Couch
Flying Couch
Flying Couch
Flying Couch
Flying Couch

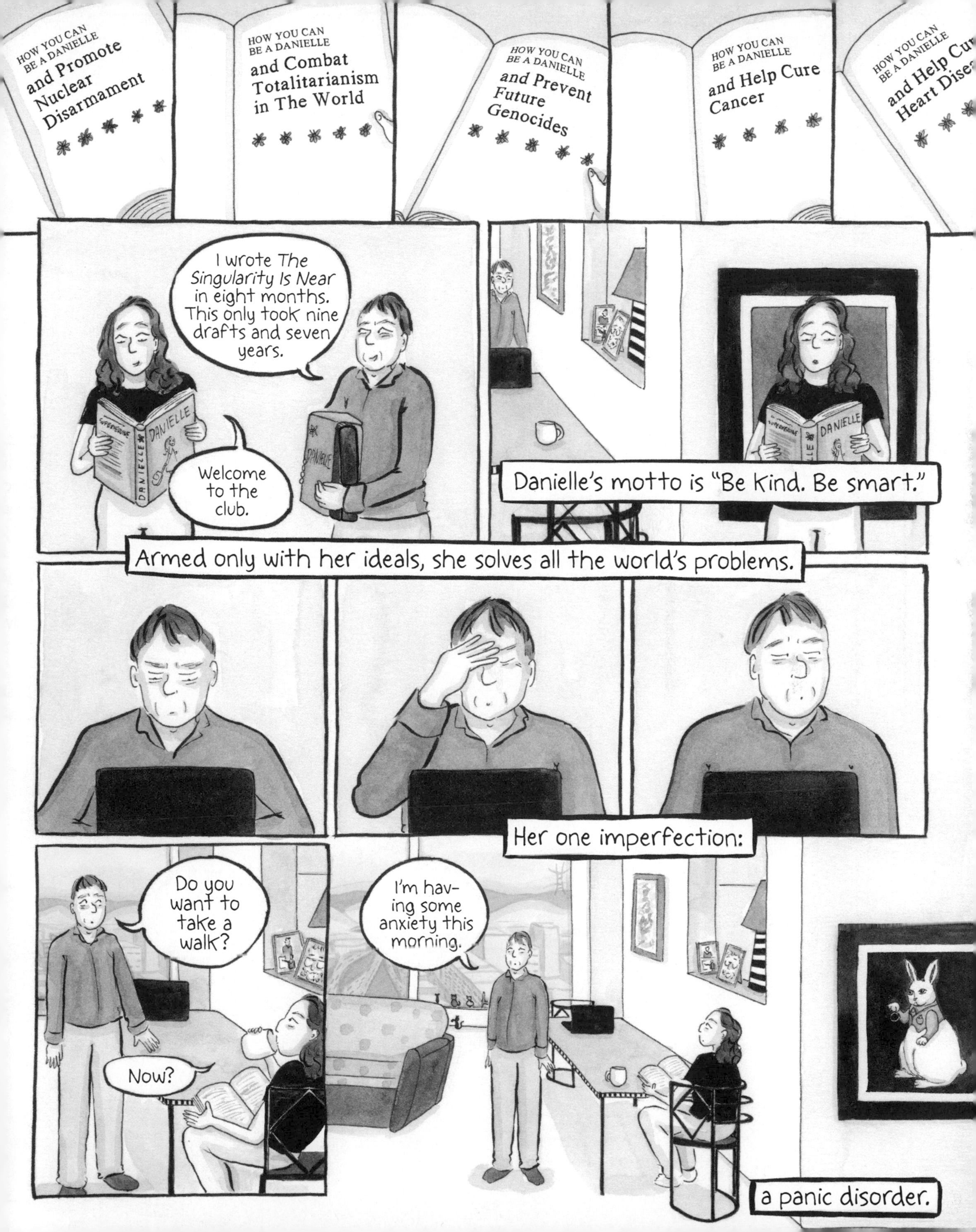
HOW YOU CAN BE A DANIELLE and Promote Nuclear Disarmament
HOW YOU CAN BE A DANIELLE and Combat Totalitarianism in The World
HOW YOU CAN BE A DANIELLE and Prevent Future Genocides
HOW YOU CAN BE A DANIELLE and Help Cure Cancer
HOW YOU CAN BE A DANIELLE and Help Cu Heart Dise
I wrote The Singularity Is Near in eight months. This only took nine drafts and seven years.
Welcome to the club.
DANIELLE
Danielle's motto is "Be kind. Be smart."
Armed only with her ideals, she solves all the world's problems.
Her one imperfection:
Do you want to take a walk?
Now?
I'm hav-ing some anxiety this morning.
a panic disorder.

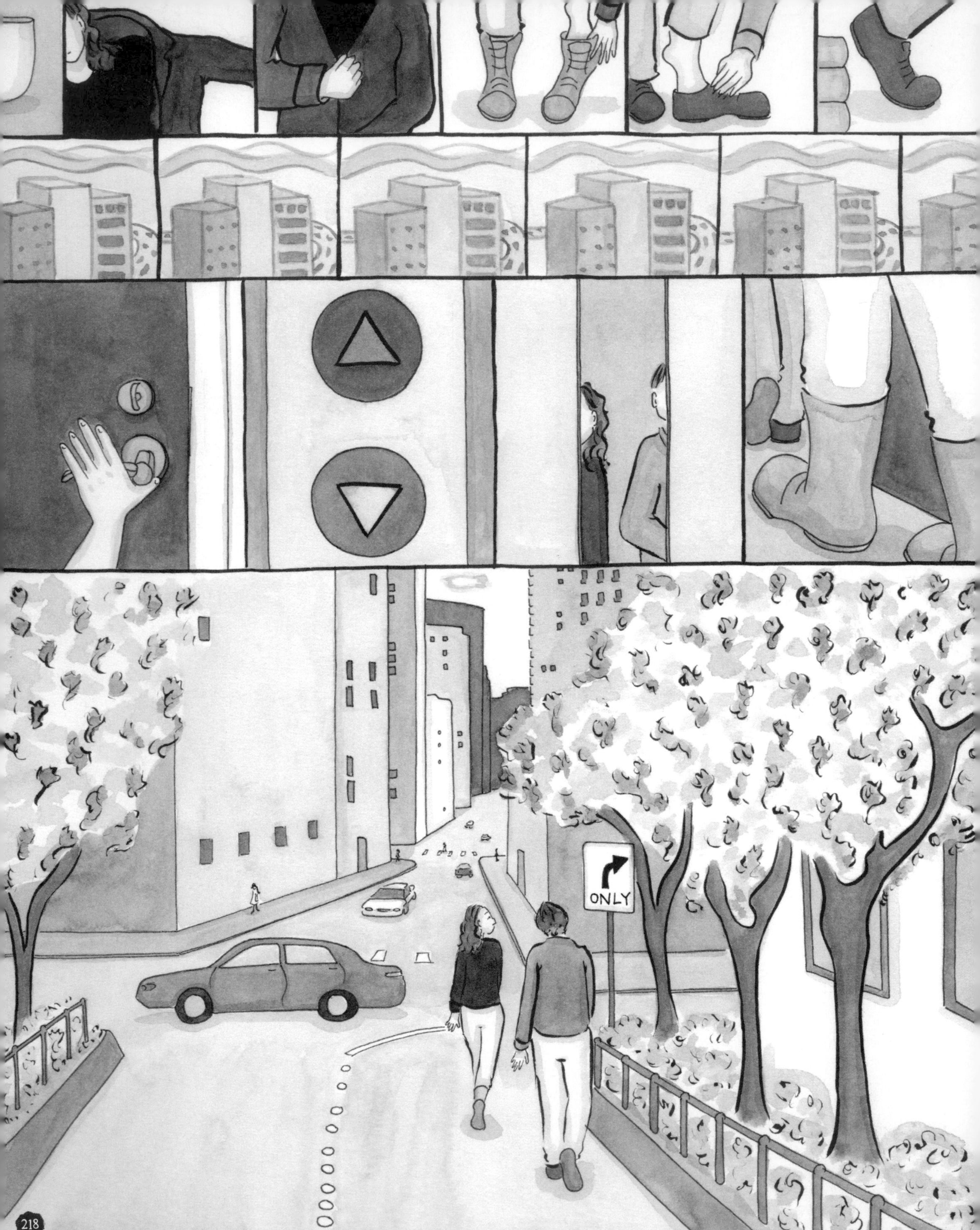
ONLY

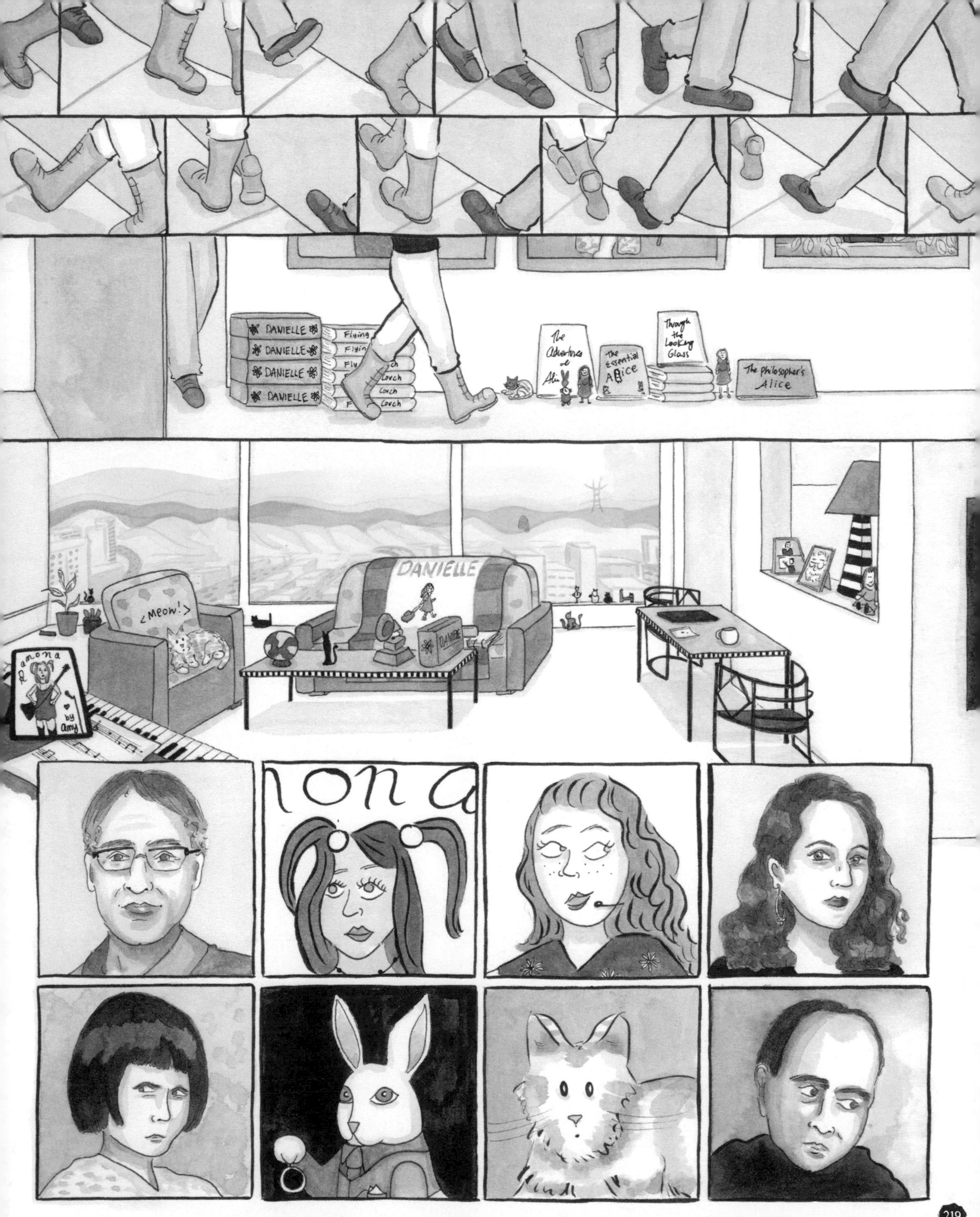
DANIELLE
DANIELLE
DANIELLE
DANIELLE
Flying
Flying
Fly
Couch
Couch
Couch
The Adventures of Alice
The Essential Alice
Through the Looking Glass
The Philosopher's Alice
DANIELLE
<Meow!>
Ramona by Amy
DANIELLE
mona

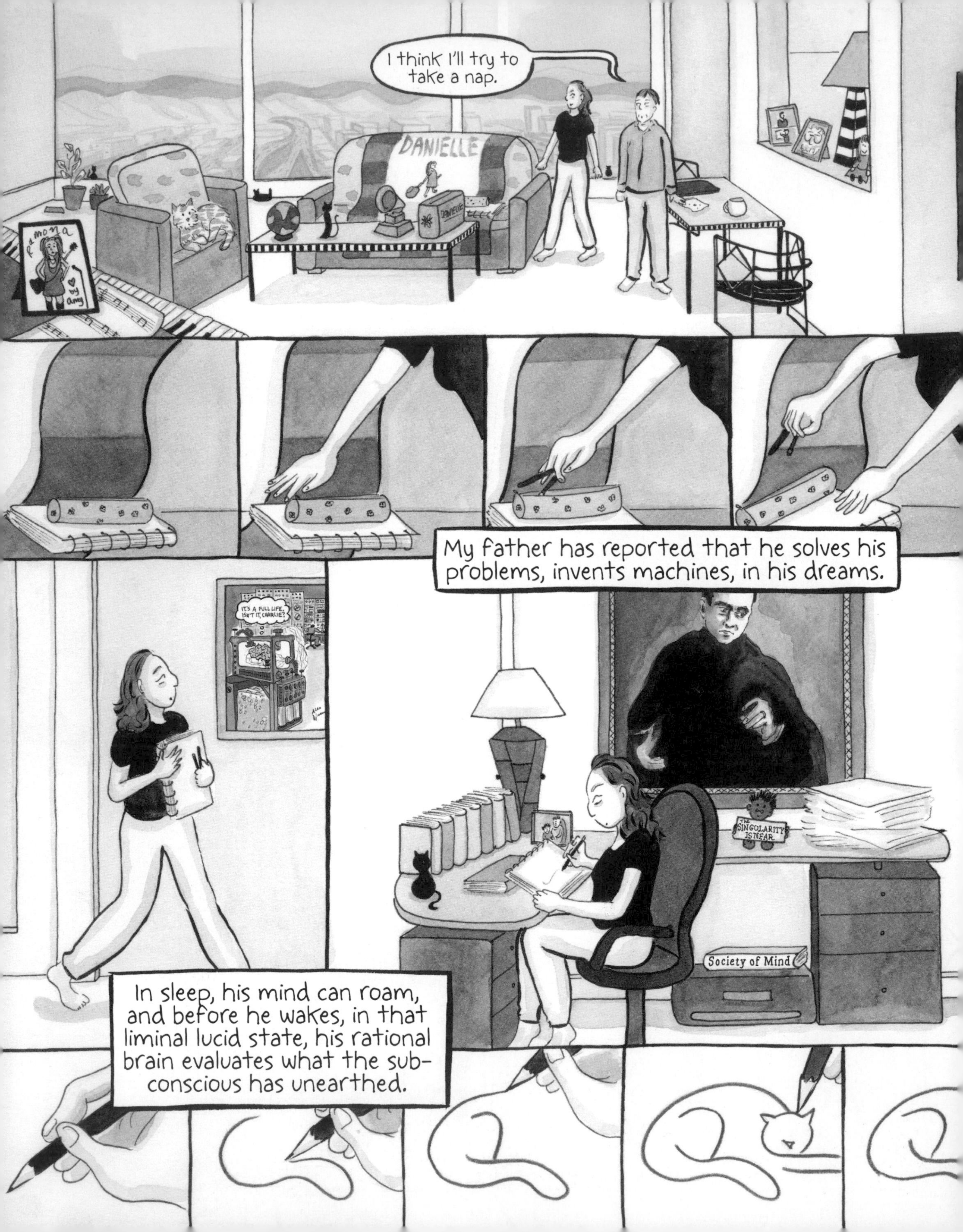
I think I'll try to take a nap.
DANIELLE
My father has reported that he solves his problems, invents machines, in his dreams.
IT'S A FULL LIFE, ISN'T IT, CHARLIE?
THE SINGULARITY IS NEAR
Society of Mind
In sleep, his mind can roam, and before he wakes, in that liminal lucid state, his rational brain evaluates what the sub-conscious has unearthed.

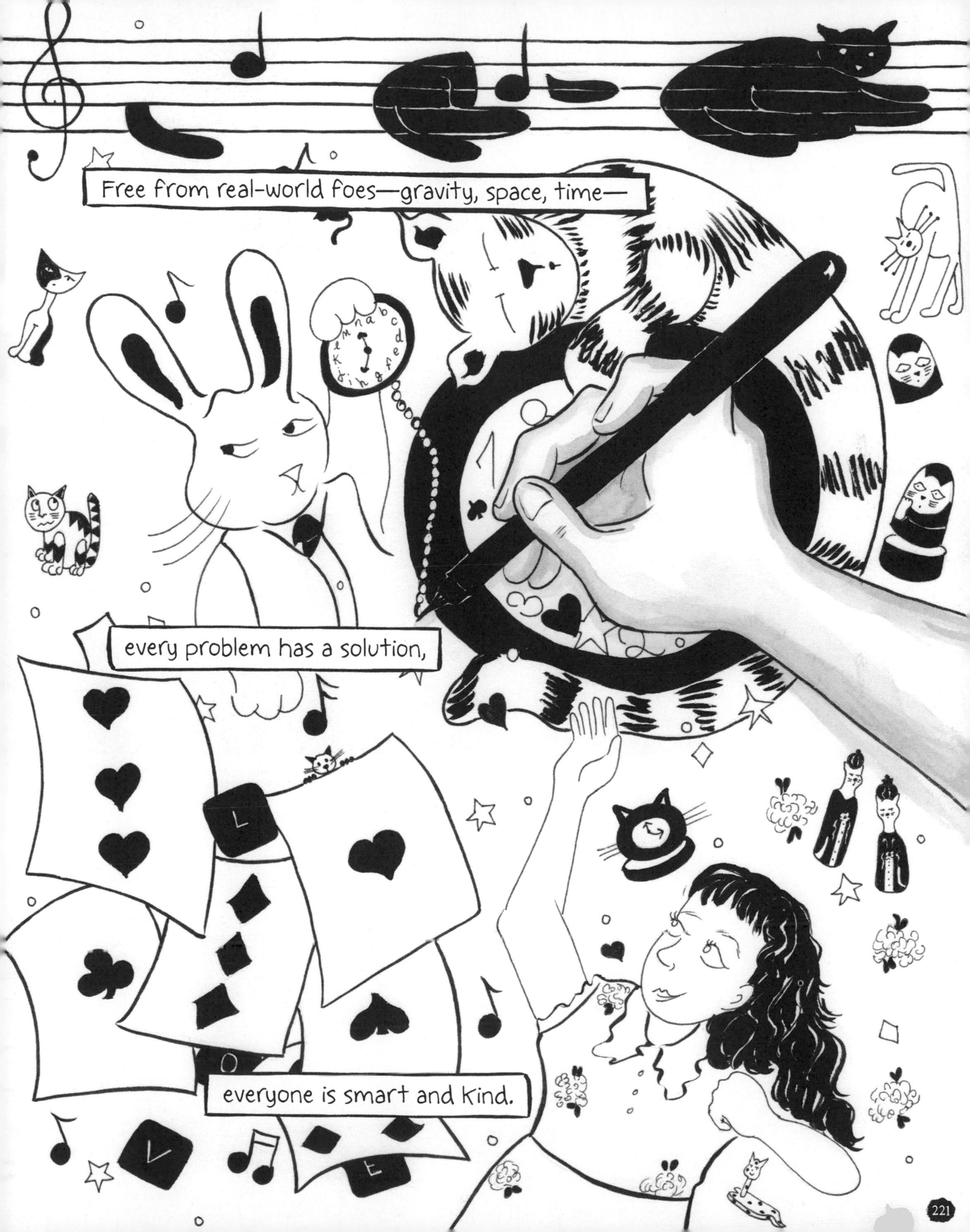
Free from real-world foes—gravity, space, time—
every problem has a solution,
everyone is smart and kind.

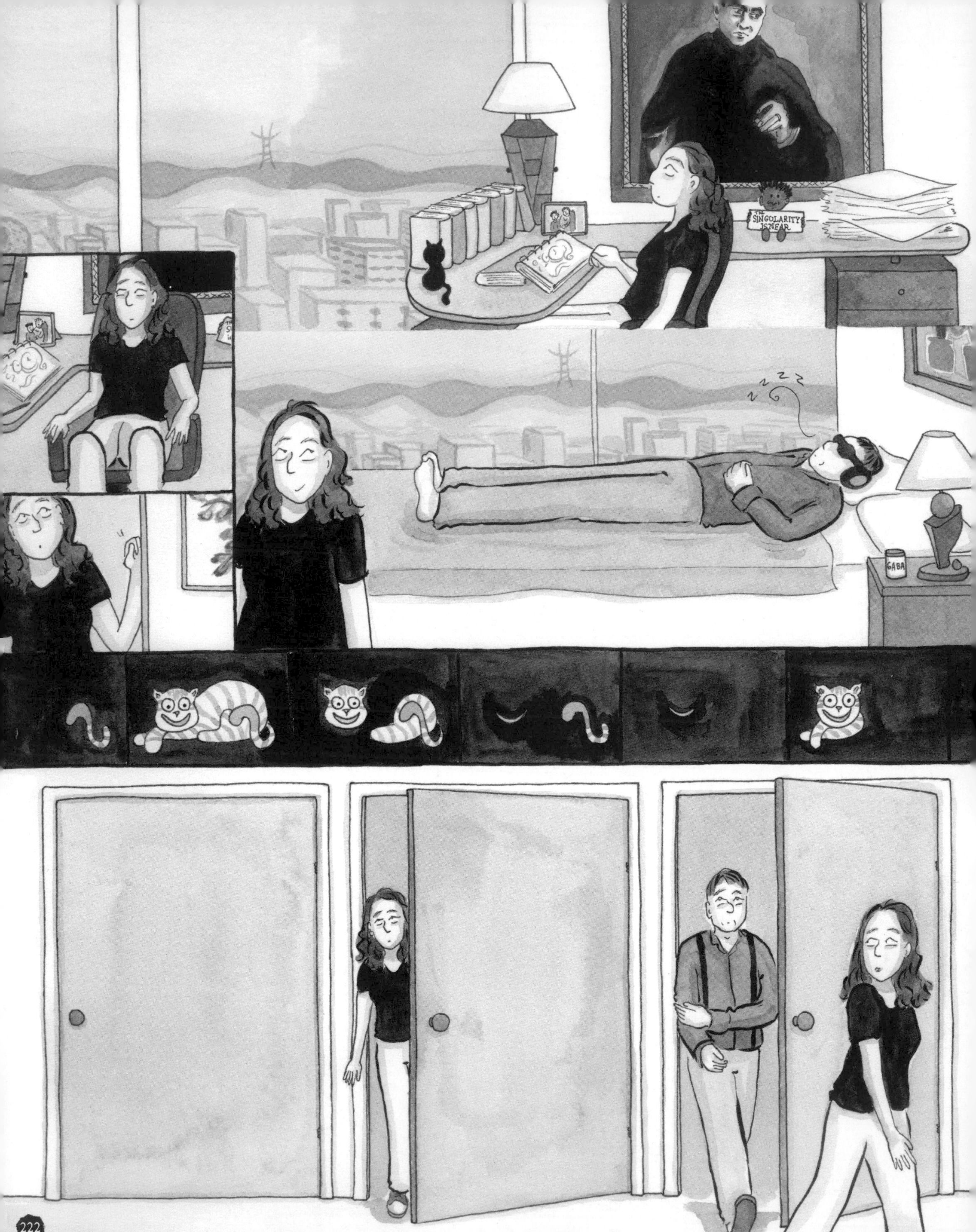
THE SINGULARITY IS NEAR
Z Z Z
GABA

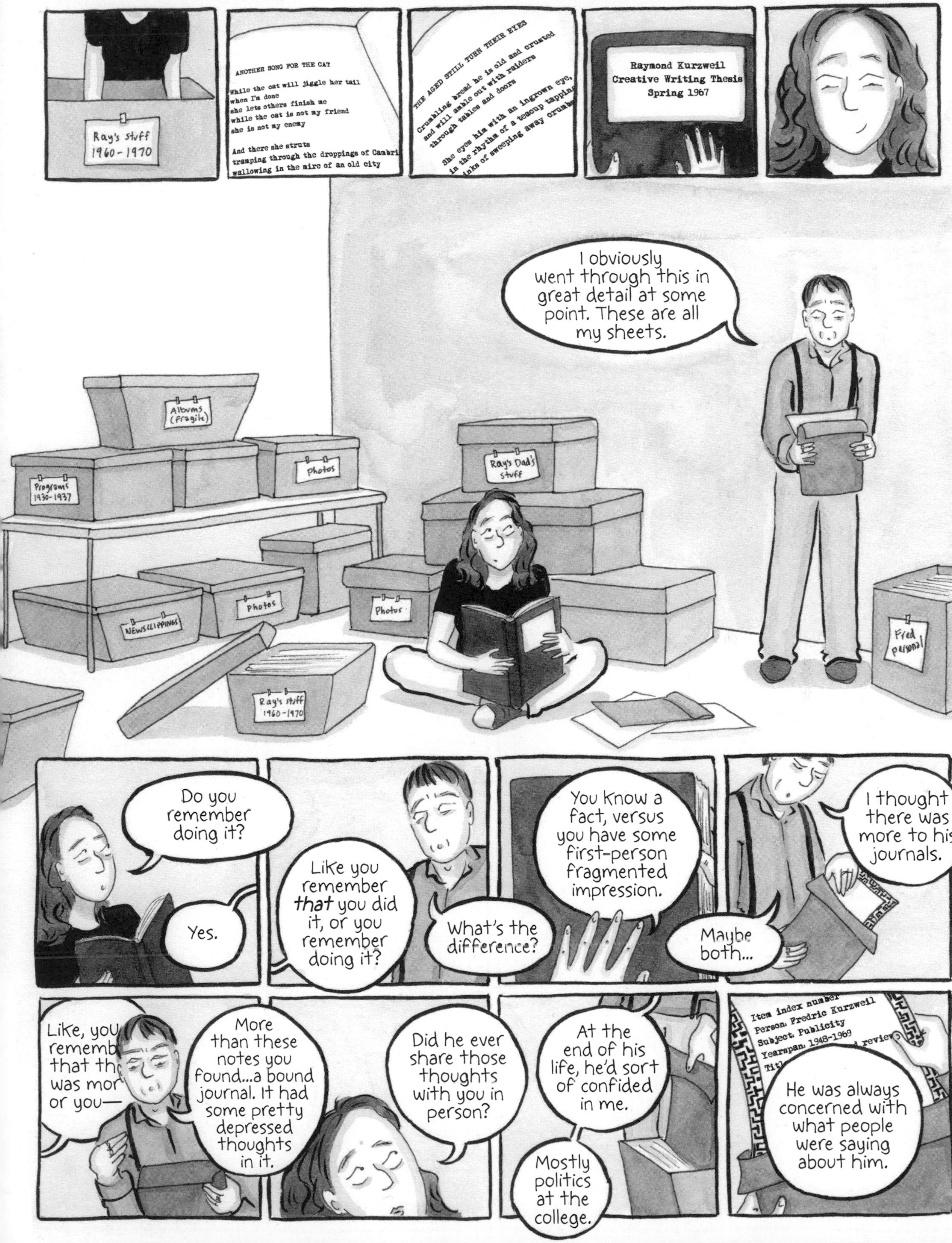

Ray's stuff 1960-1970
ANOTHER SONG FOR THE CAT
While the cat will jiggle her tail
when I'm done
she lets others finish me
while the cat is not my friend
she is not my enemy
And there she struts
tramping through the droppings of Cambri
wallowing in the mire of an old city
THE AGED STILL TURN THEIR EYES
Crumbling bread he is old and crusted
and will amble out with raiders
through tables and doors
She eyes him with an ingrown eye,
in the rhythm of a teacup tappin
inks of sweeping away crumb
Raymond Kurzweil
Creative Writing Thesis
Spring 1967
I obviously went through this in great detail at some point. These are all my sheets.
Albums (fragile)
Programs 1930-1937
Photos
Ray's Dad's stuff
Photos
Photos
Newsclippings
Ray's stuff 1960-1970
Fred personal
Do you remember doing it?
Yes.
Like you remember *that* you did it, or you remember doing it?
What's the difference?
You know a fact, versus you have some first-person fragmented impression.
Maybe both...
I thought there was more to his journals.
Like, you rememb that th was mor or you—
More than these notes you found...a bound journal. It had some pretty depressed thoughts in it.
Did he ever share those thoughts with you in person?
At the end of his life, he'd sort of confided in me.
Mostly politics at the college.
Item index number
Person: Fredric Kurzweil
Subject: Publicity
Yearspan: 1948-1969
He was always concerned with what people were saying about him.

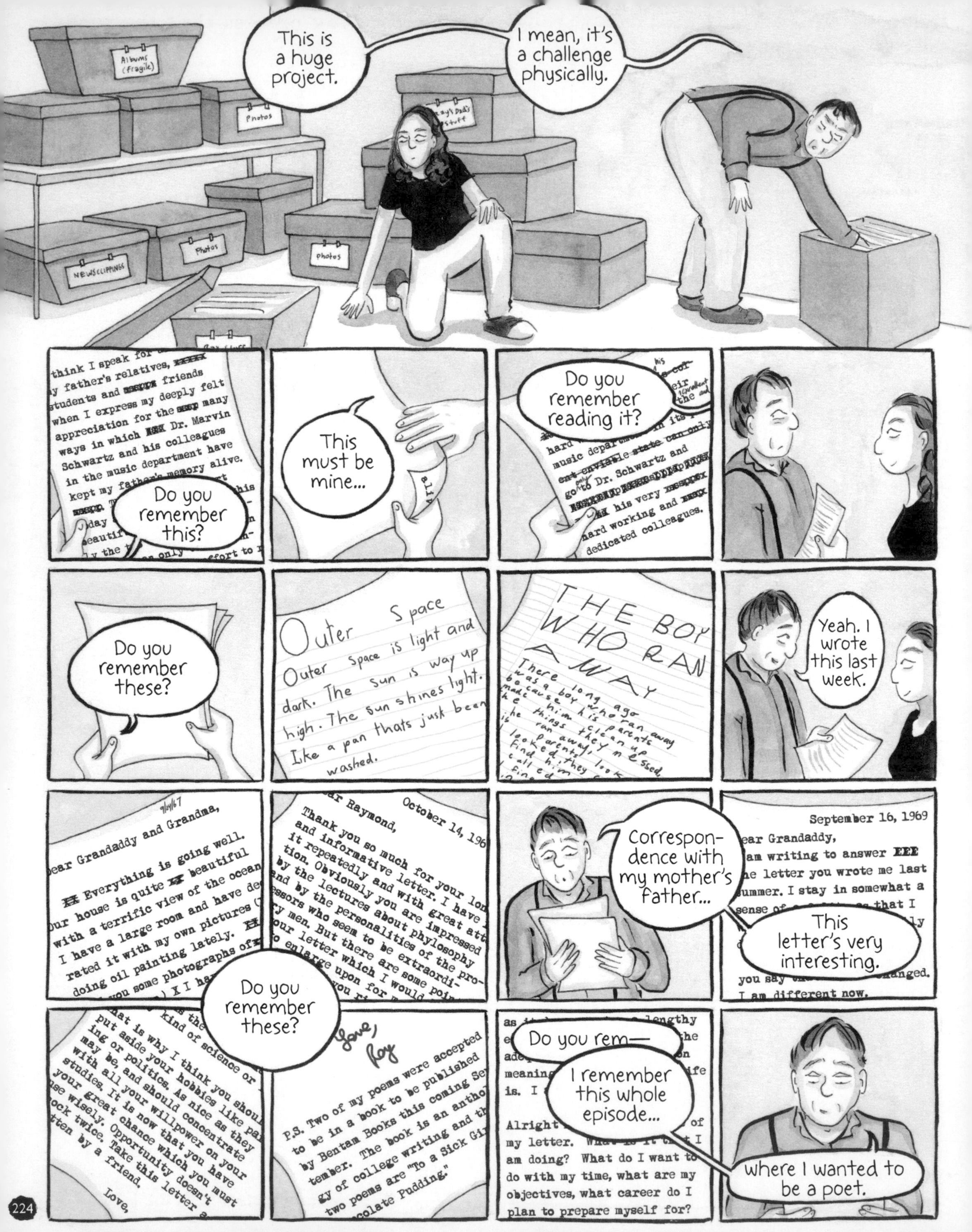
Albums (Fragile)
Photos
NEWSCLIPPINGS
Photos
photos
This is a huge project.
I mean, it's a challenge physically.
think I speak for
father's relatives,
students and friends
when I express my deeply felt
appreciation for the many
ways in which Dr. Marvin
Schwartz and his colleagues
in the music department have
kept my father's memory alive.
Do you remember this?
This must be mine...
Do you remember reading it?
music department
Dr. Schwartz and
his very
hard working and
dedicated colleagues.
Do you remember these?
Outer Space
Outer Space is light and dark. The sun is way up high. The sun shines light. Like a pan thats just been washed.
THE BOY WHO RAN AWAY
Yeah. I wrote this last week.
9/14/67
Grandaddy and Grandma,
Everything is going well.
Our house is quite beautiful
with a terrific view of the ocean
I have a large room and have
rated it with my own pictures
doing oil painting lately.
Raymond,
October 14, 196
Thank you so much for your lon
and informative letter. I have
it repeatedly and with great att
tion. Obviously you are impressed
by the lectures about phylosophy
and by the personalities of the pro-
fessors who seem to be extraordi-
Correspondence with my mother's father...
September 16, 1969
ear Grandaddy,
am writing to answer
he letter you wrote me last
This letter's very interesting.
I am different now.
Do you remember these?
kind of science or
what is why I think you shoul
put aside your hobbies like pa
ing or politics. As nice as they
may be, and should concentrate
with all your willpower on your
studies. It is now that you have
your great chance which you must
use wisely. Opportunity doesn't
knock twice. Take this letter
written by a friend.
Love,
Love, Roy
P.S. Two of my poems were accepted
to be in a book to be published
by Bentam Books this coming Se
tember. The book is an antho
gy of college writing and th
two poems are "To a Sick Gi
ocolate Pudding."
Do you rem—
I remember this whole episode...
my letter.
am doing? What do I want to
do with my time, what are my
objectives, what career do I
plan to prepare myself for?
where I wanted to be a poet.

About two years ago, I realized through a long and slow process that the technical ~~XXX~~ road that I was pursuing was not adequate, that a part of me was being ignored~~x~~, was not being ~~xxxx~~ allowed to develop. That part, as it turns out, is my artistic side. It is not ~~Not~~ surprising that I would have artistic talent since both

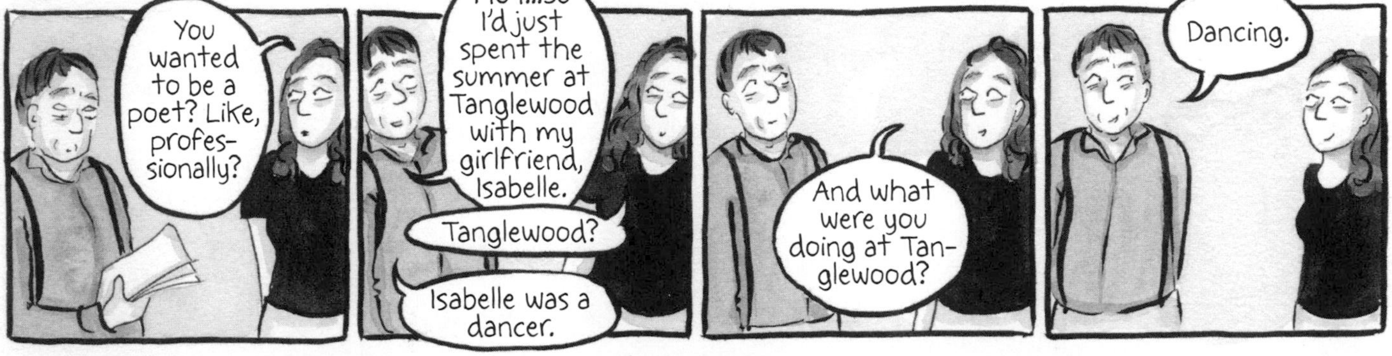
You wanted to be a poet? Like, profes-sionally?
1969...So I'd just spent the summer at Tanglewood with my girlfriend, Isabelle.
Tanglewood?
Isabelle was a dancer.
And what were you doing at Tan-glewood?
Dancing.

I started writing poems on the side and ~~XXXXXXX~~ through a gradual process of discovery, I came to realize that this is the path that I must pursue. The same feeling of certainty and of creative necessity that have attended any other project~~s~~

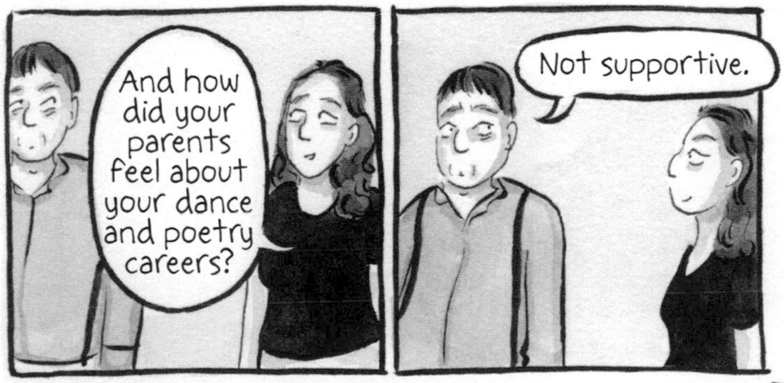
And how did your parents feel about your dance and poetry careers?
Not supportive.

The problem, I believe, as I mentioned earlier, is less with me than with our culture, which has within itself a tragic split, two hostile armed camps with scarcely a messenger going from one to the other. Objective and subjective modes of thought, science and art, look at one another suspiciously, each regarding the other as relatively worthless and perhaps dangerous. To the scientist, the artist is regarded as a misfit, a child wasting his time; art is a pastime at best, a force arousing people to unpredictable irrational behavior at its worst. To the artist, the scientist is cold, inhuman, science is an escape from genuine human

Truth, to an artist, is the sweeping brushstroke, the simple curving arms of the dancer, the unexpected modulation in a jazz composition, the unexplainable but correct repetition of "And miles to go before I sleep" in Frost's poem. What all of these have in common is the sense of rightness, of power, spiritual power, the hint of wisdom. There are theories of art, but in the final analysis, the truth of an artwork stands outside the theory, cannot be explained by it and cannot be recreated with it alone. And yet the spark, the key to another world, the s... al food is the... eyes, to

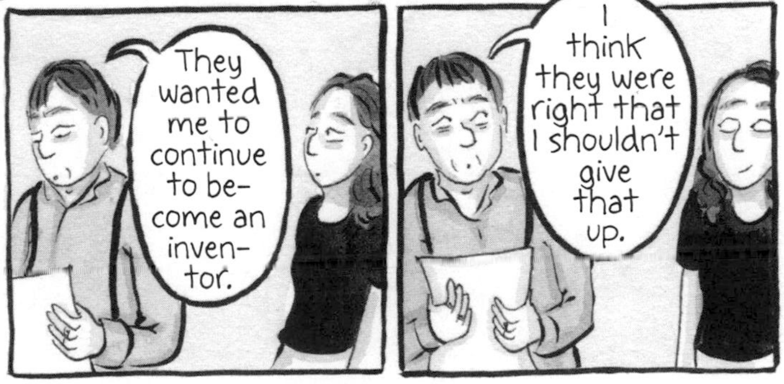
They wanted me to continue to be-come an inven-tor.
I think they were right that I shouldn't give that up.

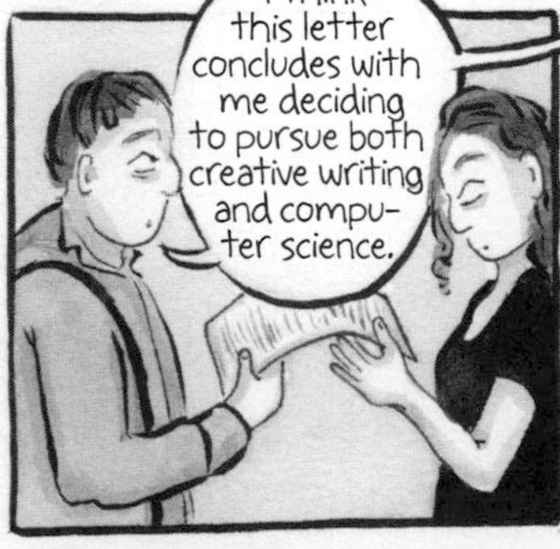
Anyway,
I think this letter concludes with me deciding to pursue both creative writing and compu-ter science.

I have tried as best I can to explain what I see apparently before me. What is clear, however, to me is that the only direction I can pursue at this time is poetry, that it is a ~~wa~~ highly worthwhile ~~XXX~~ career, one that is needed and one for which I feel I am talented and motivated in. What more can I say?

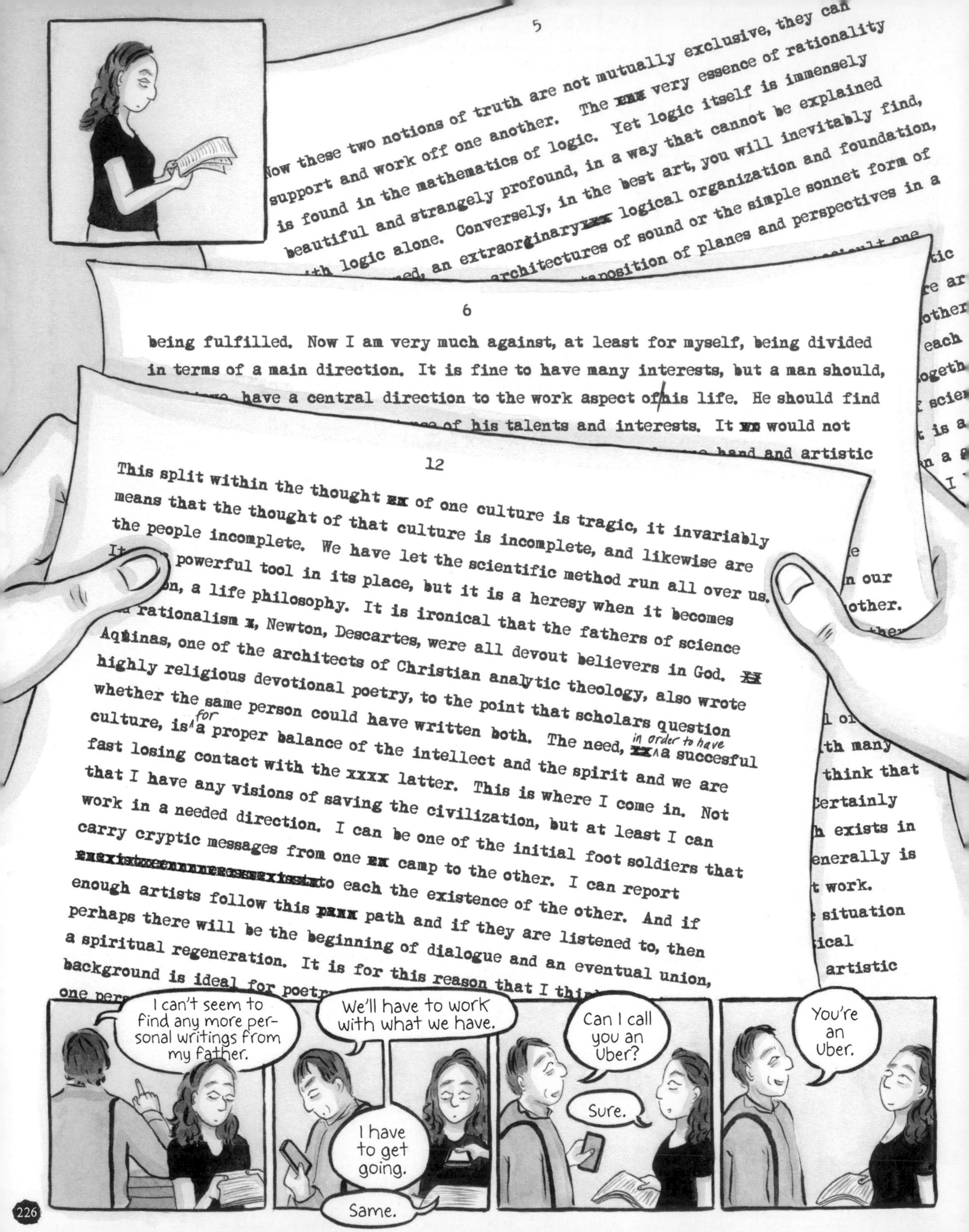
5
Now these two notions of truth are not mutually exclusive, they can
support and work off one another. The xxx very essence of rationality
is found in the mathematics of logic. Yet logic itself is immensely
beautiful and strangely profound, in a way that cannot be explained
...th logic alone. Conversely, in the best art, you will inevitably find,
...ned, an extraorginaryxxx logical organization and foundation,
architectures of sound or the simple sonnet form of
...position of planes and perspectives in a
6
being fulfilled. Now I am very much against, at least for myself, being divided
in terms of a main direction. It is fine to have many interests, but a man should,
... have a central direction to the work aspect of his life. He should find
... of his talents and interests. It xx would not
... hand and artistic
12
This split within the thought xx of one culture is tragic, it invariably
means that the thought of that culture is incomplete, and likewise are
the people incomplete. We have let the scientific method run all over us.
It ... powerful tool in its place, but it is a heresy when it becomes
...on, a life philosophy. It is ironical that the fathers of science
... rationalism x, Newton, Descartes, were all devout believers in God. xx
Aquinas, one of the architects of Christian analytic theology, also wrote
highly religious devotional poetry, to the point that scholars question
whether the same person could have written both. The need, xx in order to have a succesful
culture, is for a proper balance of the intellect and the spirit and we are
fast losing contact with the xxxx latter. This is where I come in. Not
that I have any visions of saving the civilization, but at least I can
work in a needed direction. I can be one of the initial foot soldiers that
carry cryptic messages from one xx camp to the other. I can report
xxxxxxxxxxxxxxxxxxxxxxxxxto each the existence of the other. And if
enough artists follow this paxx path and if they are listened to, then
perhaps there will be the beginning of dialogue and an eventual union,
a spiritual regeneration. It is for this reason that I thi...
background is ideal for poetr...
I can't seem to find any more personal writings from my father.
We'll have to work with what we have.
I have to get going.
Same.
Can I call you an Uber?
Sure.
You're an Uber.

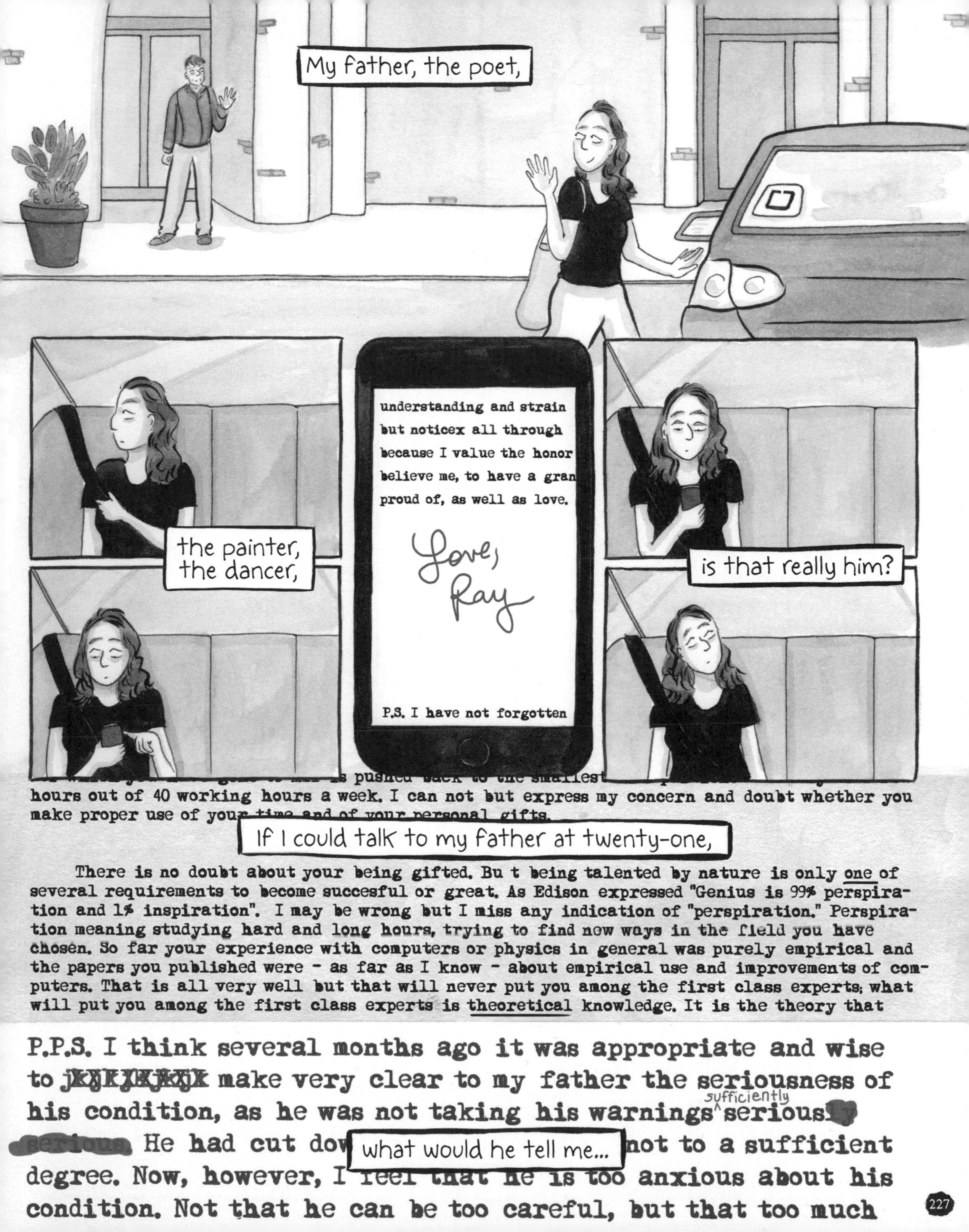
My father, the poet,
the painter,
the dancer,
understanding and strain
but noticex all through
because I value the honor
believe me, to have a gran
proud of, as well as love.
Love,
Ray
P.S. I have not forgotten
is that really him?
hours out of 40 working hours a week. I can not but express my concern and doubt whether you make proper use of your time and of your personal gifts.
If I could talk to my father at twenty-one,
There is no doubt about your being gifted. Bu t being talented by nature is only one of several requirements to become succesful or great. As Edison expressed "Genius is 99% perspiration and 1% inspiration". I may be wrong but I miss any indication of "perspiration." Perspiration meaning studying hard and long hours, trying to find new ways in the field you have chosen. So far your experience with computers or physics in general was purely empirical and the papers you published were - as far as I know - about empirical use and improvements of computers. That is all very well but that will never put you among the first class experts; what will put you among the first class experts is theoretical knowledge. It is the theory that
P.P.S. I think several months ago it was appropriate and wise to jKXjKXjKXjX make very clear to my father the seriousness of his condition, as he was not taking his warnings sufficiently serious[redacted] He had cut dow
what would he tell me...
not to a sufficient degree. Now, however, I feel that he is too anxious about his condition. Not that he can be too careful, but that too much

...about what keeps the artist alive?

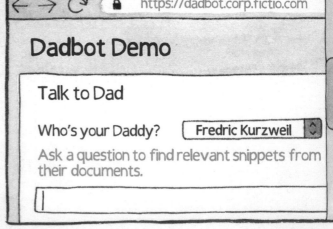

https://dadbot.corp.fictio.com

## Dadbot Demo

### Talk to Dad

Who's your Daddy?  Fredric Kurzweil

Ask a question to find relevant snippets from their documents.

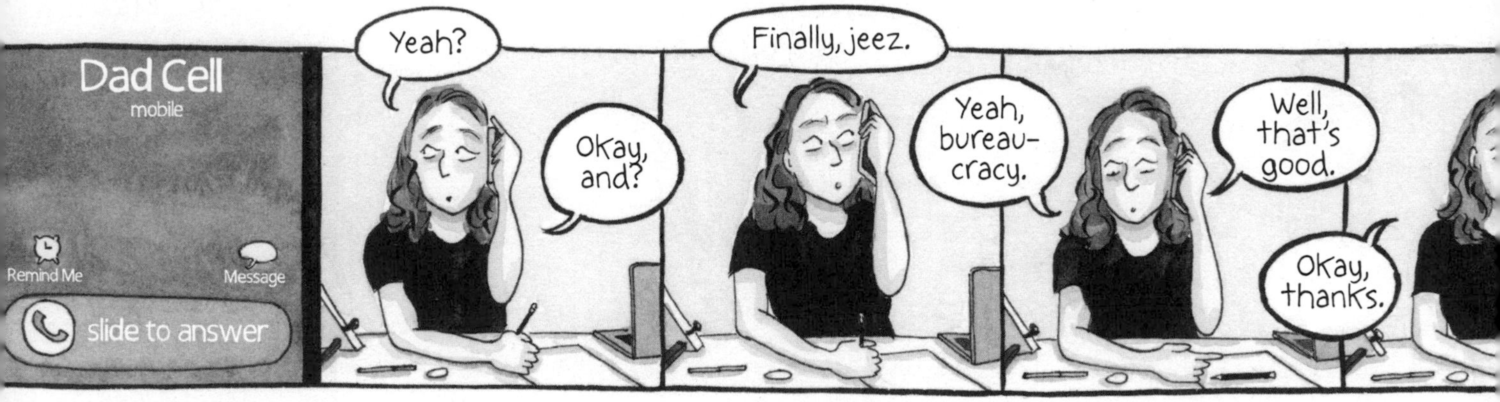
Dad Cell
mobile
Remind Me
Message
slide to answer
Yeah?
Okay, and?
Finally, jeez.
Yeah, bureaucracy.
Well, that's good.
Okay, thanks.

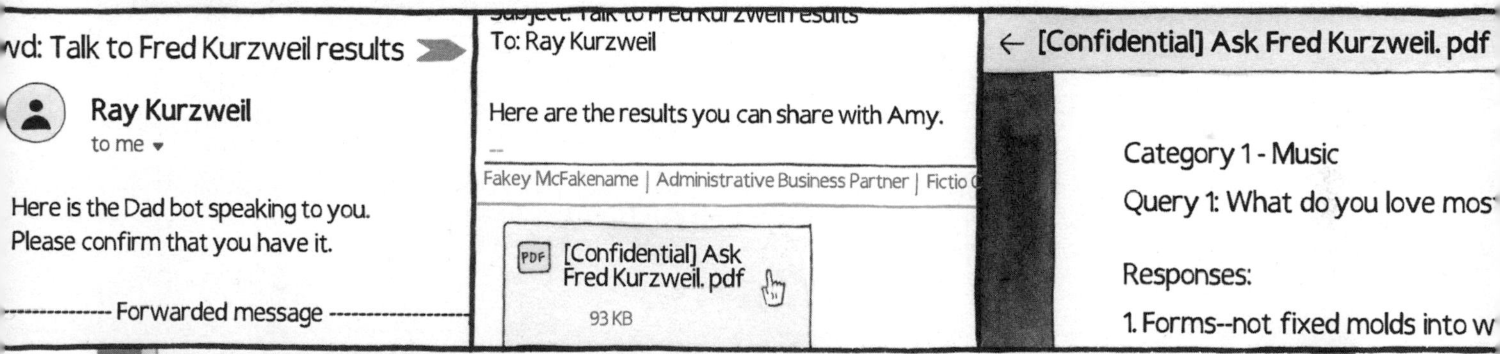
vd: Talk to Fred Kurzweil results
Ray Kurzweil
to me
Here is the Dad bot speaking to you.
Please confirm that you have it.
---------- Forwarded message ----------
To: Ray Kurzweil
Here are the results you can share with Amy.
Fakey McFakename | Administrative Business Partner | Fictio
[Confidential] Ask Fred Kurzweil. pdf
93 KB
← [Confidential] Ask Fred Kurzweil. pdf
Category 1 - Music
Query 1: What do you love mos
Responses:
1. Forms--not fixed molds into w

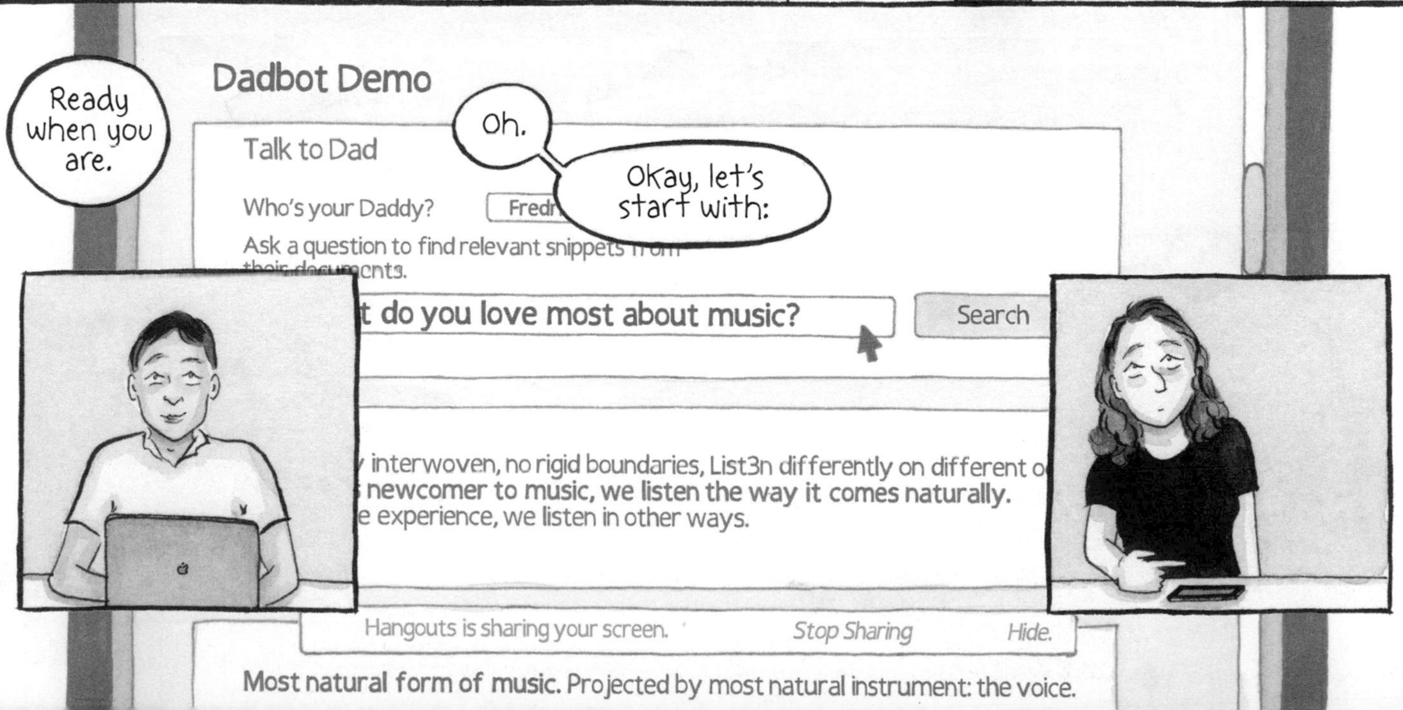
Dadbot Demo
Ready when you are.
Talk to Dad
Oh.
Okay, let's start with:
Who's your Daddy?
Ask a question to find relevant snippets from their documents.
t do you love most about music?
Search
interwoven, no rigid boundaries, List3n differently on different o
newcomer to music, we listen the way it comes naturally.
e experience, we listen in other ways.
Hangouts is sharing your screen.
Stop Sharing
Hide.
Most natural form of music. Projected by most natural instrument: the voice.

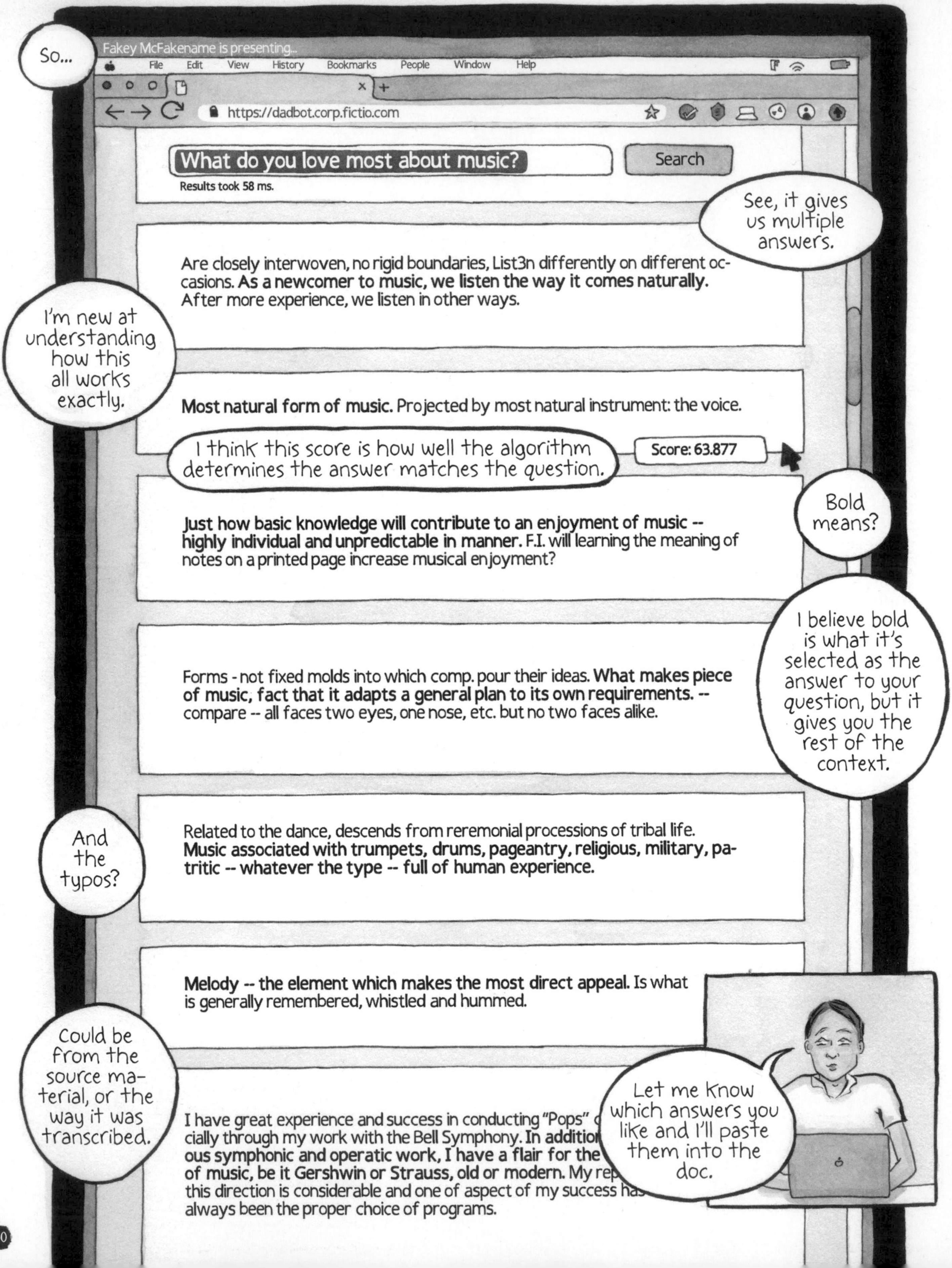

So...
Fakey McFakename is presenting...
File Edit View History Bookmarks People Window Help
https://dadbot.corp.fictio.com
What do you love most about music?
Search
Results took 58 ms.
See, it gives us multiple answers.
Are closely interwoven, no rigid boundaries, List3n differently on different occasions. As a newcomer to music, we listen the way it comes naturally. After more experience, we listen in other ways.
I'm new at understanding how this all works exactly.
Most natural form of music. Projected by most natural instrument: the voice.
I think this score is how well the algorithm determines the answer matches the question.
Score: 63.877
Bold means?
Just how basic knowledge will contribute to an enjoyment of music -- highly individual and unpredictable in manner. F.I. will learning the meaning of notes on a printed page increase musical enjoyment?
I believe bold is what it's selected as the answer to your question, but it gives you the rest of the context.
Forms - not fixed molds into which comp. pour their ideas. What makes piece of music, fact that it adapts a general plan to its own requirements. -- compare -- all faces two eyes, one nose, etc. but no two faces alike.
And the typos?
Related to the dance, descends from reremonial processions of tribal life. Music associated with trumpets, drums, pageantry, religious, military, patritic -- whatever the type -- full of human experience.
Melody -- the element which makes the most direct appeal. Is what is generally remembered, whistled and hummed.
Could be from the source material, or the way it was transcribed.
I have great experience and success in conducting "Pops" c
cially through my work with the Bell Symphony. In additio
ous symphonic and operatic work, I have a flair for the
of music, be it Gershwin or Strauss, old or modern. My rep
this direction is considerable and one of aspect of my success has
always been the proper choice of programs.
Let me know which answers you like and I'll paste them into the doc.

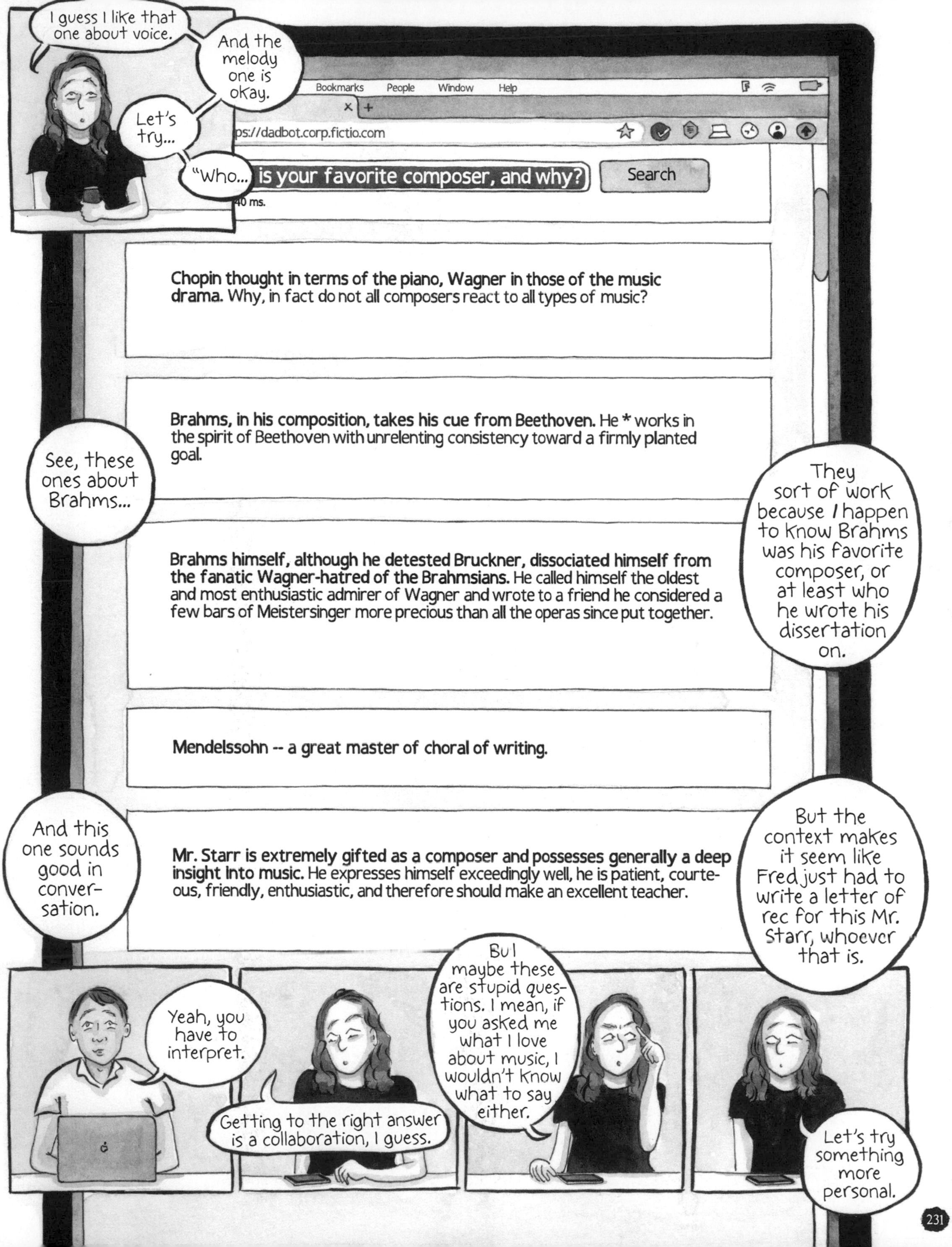
I guess I like that one about voice.
And the melody one is okay.
Let's try...
Bookmarks People Window Help
ps://dadbot.corp.fictio.com
"Who... is your favorite composer, and why?
Search
40 ms.
Chopin thought in terms of the piano, Wagner in those of the music drama. Why, in fact do not all composers react to all types of music?
Brahms, in his composition, takes his cue from Beethoven. He * works in the spirit of Beethoven with unrelenting consistency toward a firmly planted goal.
See, these ones about Brahms...
They sort of work because I happen to know Brahms was his favorite composer, or at least who he wrote his dissertation on.
Brahms himself, although he detested Bruckner, dissociated himself from the fanatic Wagner-hatred of the Brahmsians. He called himself the oldest and most enthusiastic admirer of Wagner and wrote to a friend he considered a few bars of Meistersinger more precious than all the operas since put together.
Mendelssohn -- a great master of choral of writing.
And this one sounds good in conver-sation.
Mr. Starr is extremely gifted as a composer and possesses generally a deep insight into music. He expresses himself exceedingly well, he is patient, courte-ous, friendly, enthusiastic, and therefore should make an excellent teacher.
But the context makes it seem like Fred just had to write a letter of rec for this Mr. Starr, whoever that is.
Yeah, you have to interpret.
Getting to the right answer is a collaboration, I guess.
But maybe these are stupid ques-tions. I mean, if you asked me what I love about music, I wouldn't know what to say either.
Let's try something more personal.

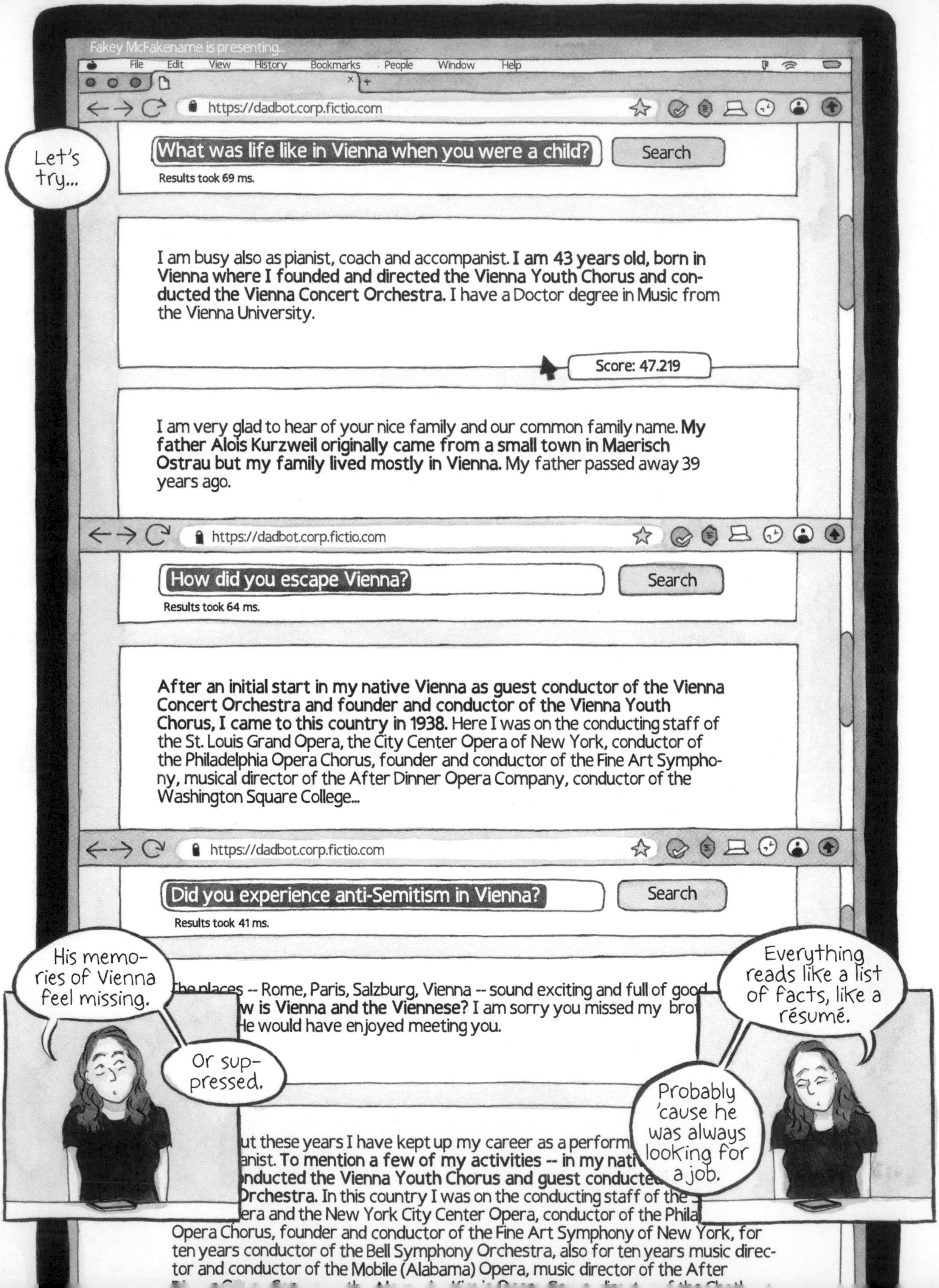
Fakey McFakename is presenting...
File Edit View History Bookmarks People Window Help
https://dadbot.corp.fictio.com
Let's try...
What was life like in Vienna when you were a child?
Search
Results took 69 ms.
I am busy also as pianist, coach and accompanist. I am 43 years old, born in Vienna where I founded and directed the Vienna Youth Chorus and conducted the Vienna Concert Orchestra. I have a Doctor degree in Music from the Vienna University.
Score: 47.219
I am very glad to hear of your nice family and our common family name. My father Alois Kurzweil originally came from a small town in Maerisch Ostrau but my family lived mostly in Vienna. My father passed away 39 years ago.
https://dadbot.corp.fictio.com
How did you escape Vienna?
Search
Results took 64 ms.
After an initial start in my native Vienna as guest conductor of the Vienna Concert Orchestra and founder and conductor of the Vienna Youth Chorus, I came to this country in 1938. Here I was on the conducting staff of the St. Louis Grand Opera, the City Center Opera of New York, conductor of the Philadelphia Opera Chorus, founder and conductor of the Fine Art Symphony, musical director of the After Dinner Opera Company, conductor of the Washington Square College...
https://dadbot.corp.fictio.com
Did you experience anti-Semitism in Vienna?
Search
Results took 41 ms.
His memories of Vienna feel missing.
Or suppressed.
Everything reads like a list of facts, like a résumé.
Probably 'cause he was always looking for a job.
The places -- Rome, Paris, Salzburg, Vienna -- sound exciting and full of good
w is Vienna and the Viennese? I am sorry you missed my bro
He would have enjoyed meeting you.
ut these years I have kept up my career as a perform
anist. To mention a few of my activities -- in my nati
nducted the Vienna Youth Chorus and guest conducte
Orchestra. In this country I was on the conducting staff of the
era and the New York City Center Opera, conductor of the Phila
Opera Chorus, founder and conductor of the Fine Art Symphony of New York, for ten years conductor of the Bell Symphony Orchestra, also for ten years music director and conductor of the Mobile (Alabama) Opera, music director of the After

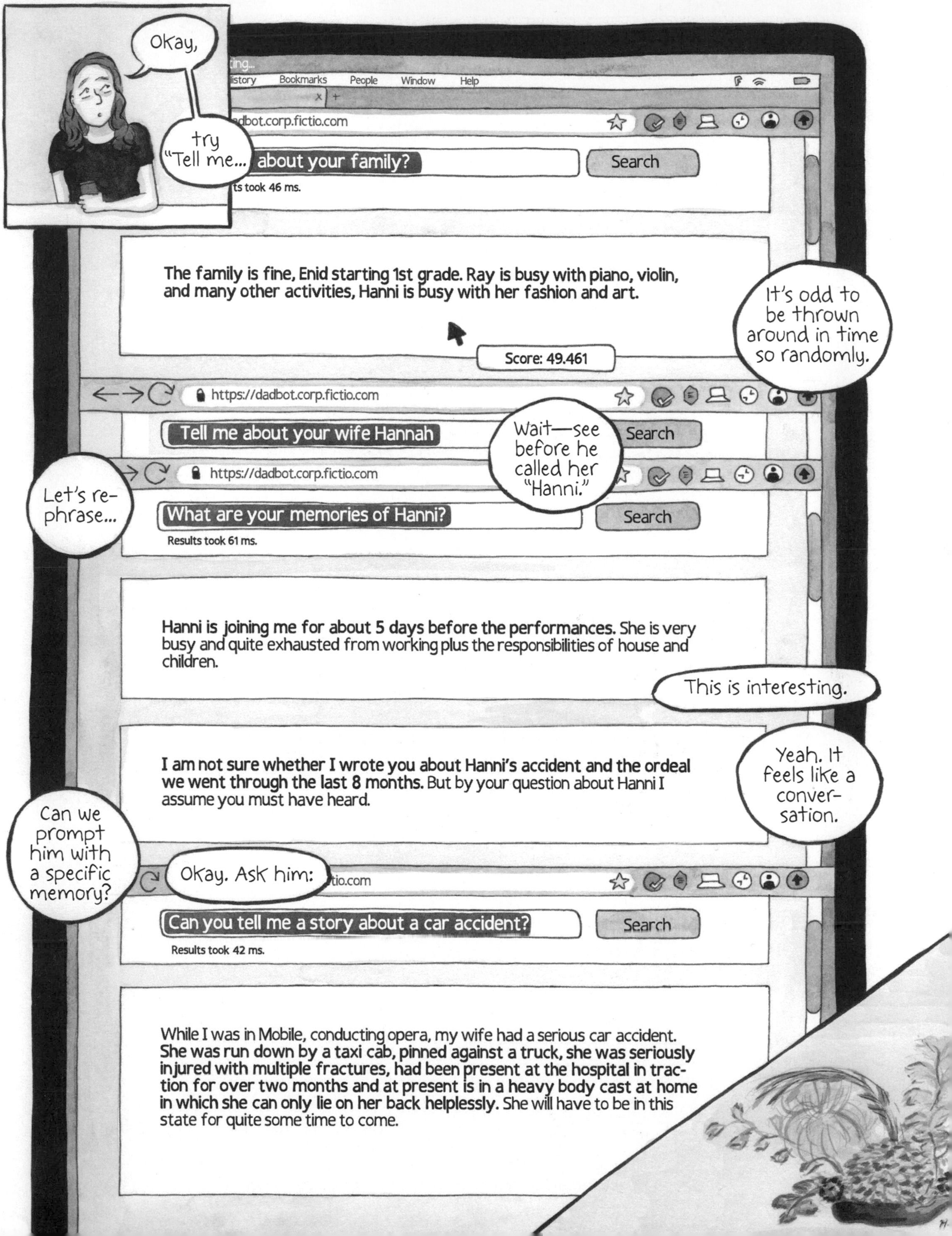
Okay,
try "Tell me... about your family?
dadbot.corp.fictio.com
Search
ts took 46 ms.
The family is fine, Enid starting 1st grade. Ray is busy with piano, violin, and many other activities, Hanni is busy with her fashion and art.
Score: 49.461
It's odd to be thrown around in time so randomly.
https://dadbot.corp.fictio.com
Tell me about your wife Hannah
Search
Wait—see before he called her "Hanni."
https://dadbot.corp.fictio.com
Let's rephrase...
What are your memories of Hanni?
Search
Results took 61 ms.
Hanni is joining me for about 5 days before the performances. She is very busy and quite exhausted from working plus the responsibilities of house and children.
This is interesting.
I am not sure whether I wrote you about Hanni's accident and the ordeal we went through the last 8 months. But by your question about Hanni I assume you must have heard.
Yeah. It feels like a conversation.
Can we prompt him with a specific memory?
Okay. Ask him:
Can you tell me a story about a car accident?
Search
Results took 42 ms.
While I was in Mobile, conducting opera, my wife had a serious car accident. She was run down by a taxi cab, pinned against a truck, she was seriously injured with multiple fractures, had been present at the hospital in traction for over two months and at present is in a heavy body cast at home in which she can only lie on her back helplessly. She will have to be in this state for quite some time to come.

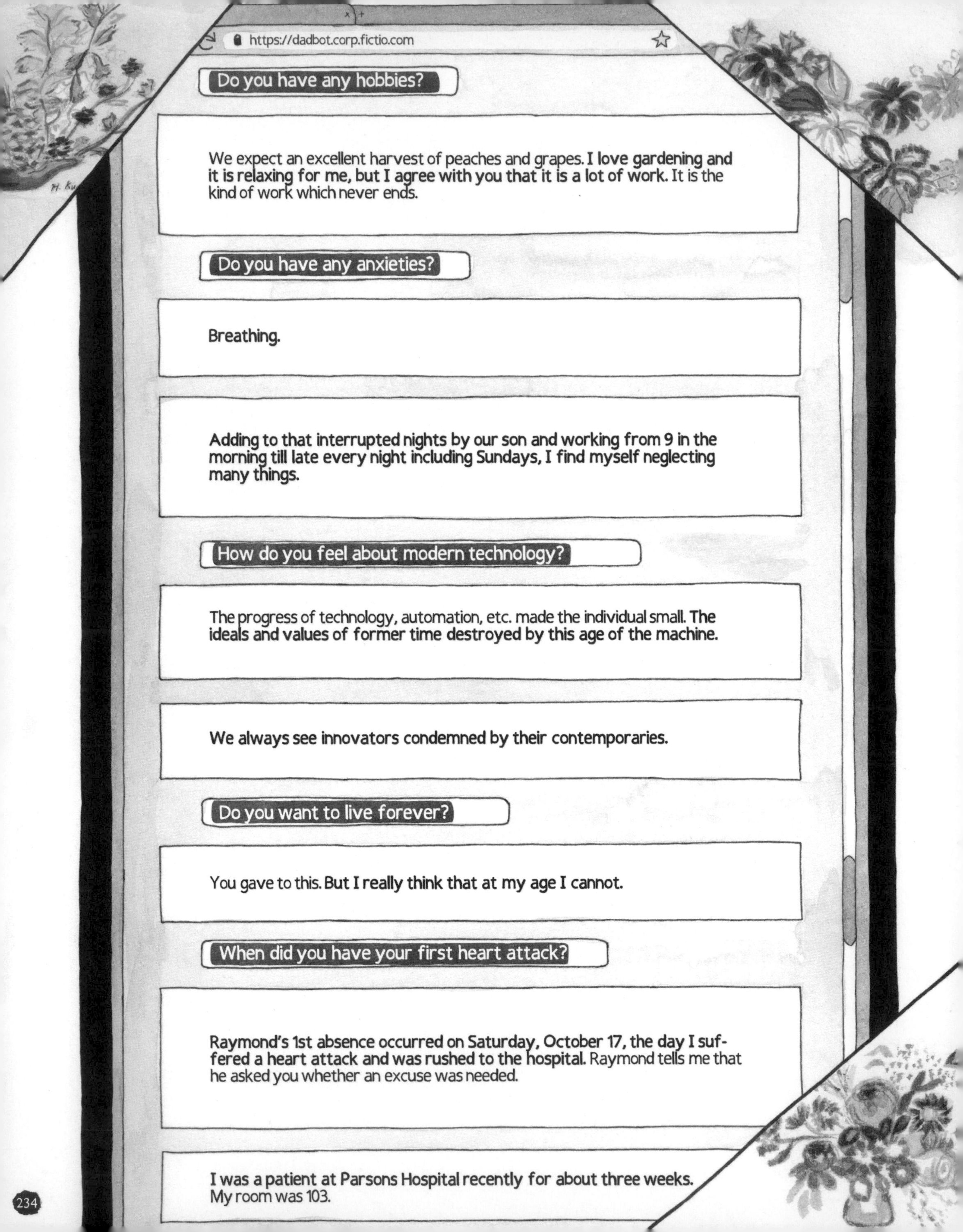
https://dadbot.corp.fictio.com
Do you have any hobbies?
We expect an excellent harvest of peaches and grapes. I love gardening and it is relaxing for me, but I agree with you that it is a lot of work. It is the kind of work which never ends.
Do you have any anxieties?
Breathing.
Adding to that interrupted nights by our son and working from 9 in the morning till late every night including Sundays, I find myself neglecting many things.
How do you feel about modern technology?
The progress of technology, automation, etc. made the individual small. The ideals and values of former time destroyed by this age of the machine.
We always see innovators condemned by their contemporaries.
Do you want to live forever?
You gave to this. But I really think that at my age I cannot.
When did you have your first heart attack?
Raymond's 1st absence occurred on Saturday, October 17, the day I suffered a heart attack and was rushed to the hospital. Raymond tells me that he asked you whether an excuse was needed.
I was a patient at Parsons Hospital recently for about three weeks. My room was 103.

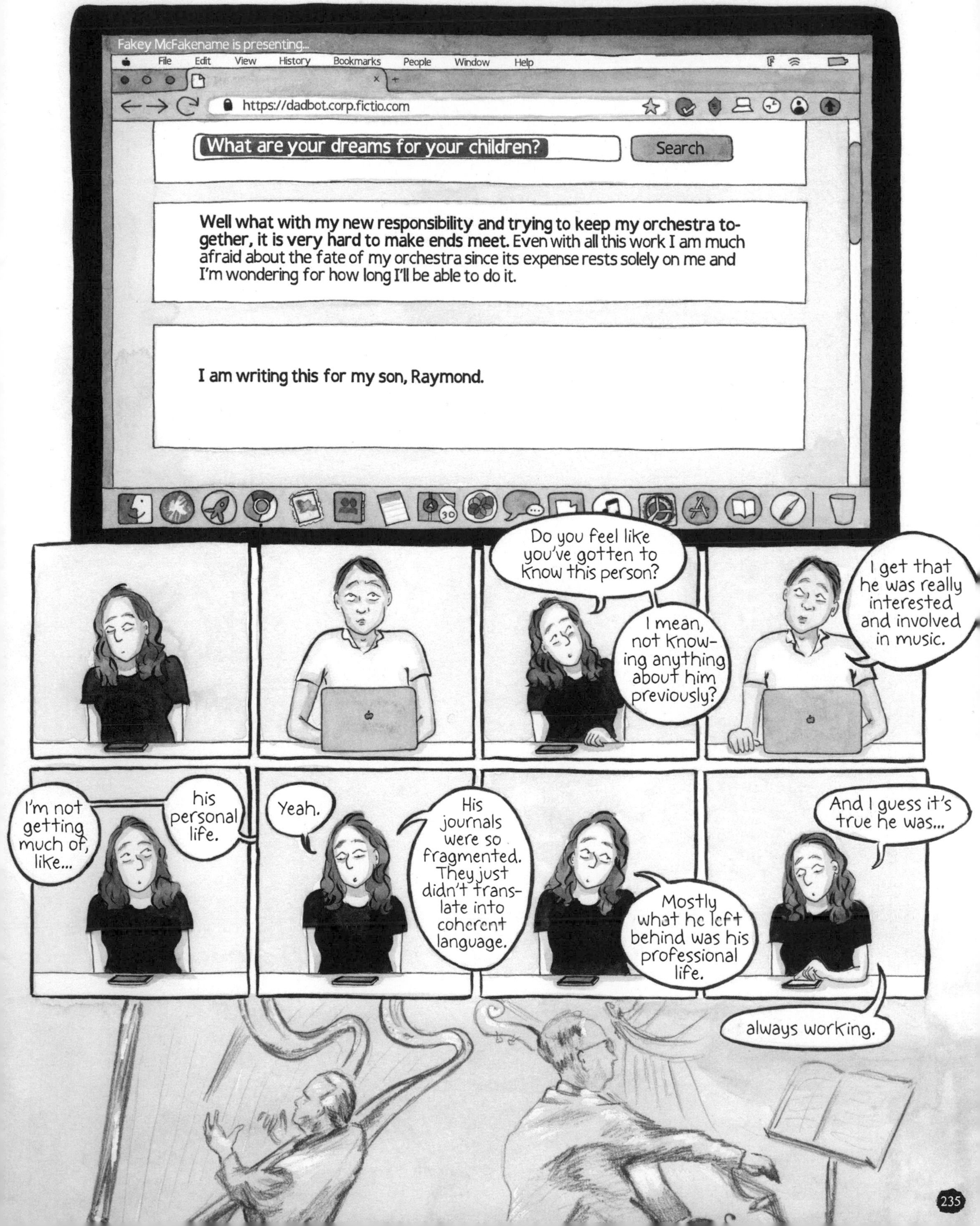
Fakey McFakename is presenting...
File Edit View History Bookmarks People Window Help
https://dadbot.corp.fictio.com
What are your dreams for your children?
Search
Well what with my new responsibility and trying to keep my orchestra together, it is very hard to make ends meet. Even with all this work I am much afraid about the fate of my orchestra since its expense rests solely on me and I'm wondering for how long I'll be able to do it.
I am writing this for my son, Raymond.
Do you feel like you've gotten to know this person?
I mean, not knowing anything about him previously?
I get that he was really interested and involved in music.
I'm not getting much of, like...
his personal life.
Yeah.
His journals were so fragmented. They just didn't translate into coherent language.
Mostly what he left behind was his professional life.
And I guess it's true he was...
always working.

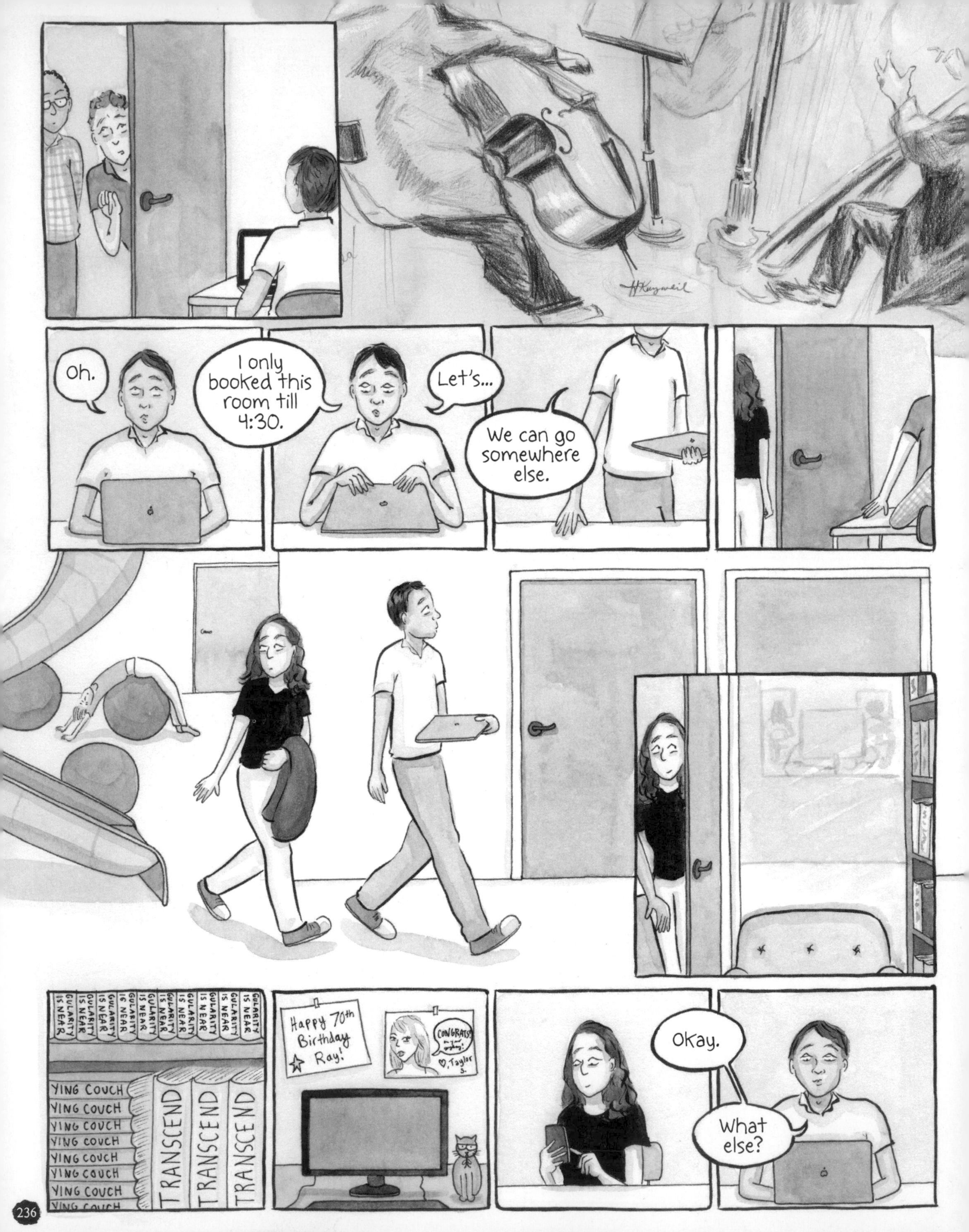
Oh.
I only booked this room till 4:30.
Let's...
We can go somewhere else.
GULARITY IS NEAR
YING COUCH
TRANSCEND
Happy 70th Birthday Ray!
CONGRATS!
♡, Taylor S.
Okay.
What else?

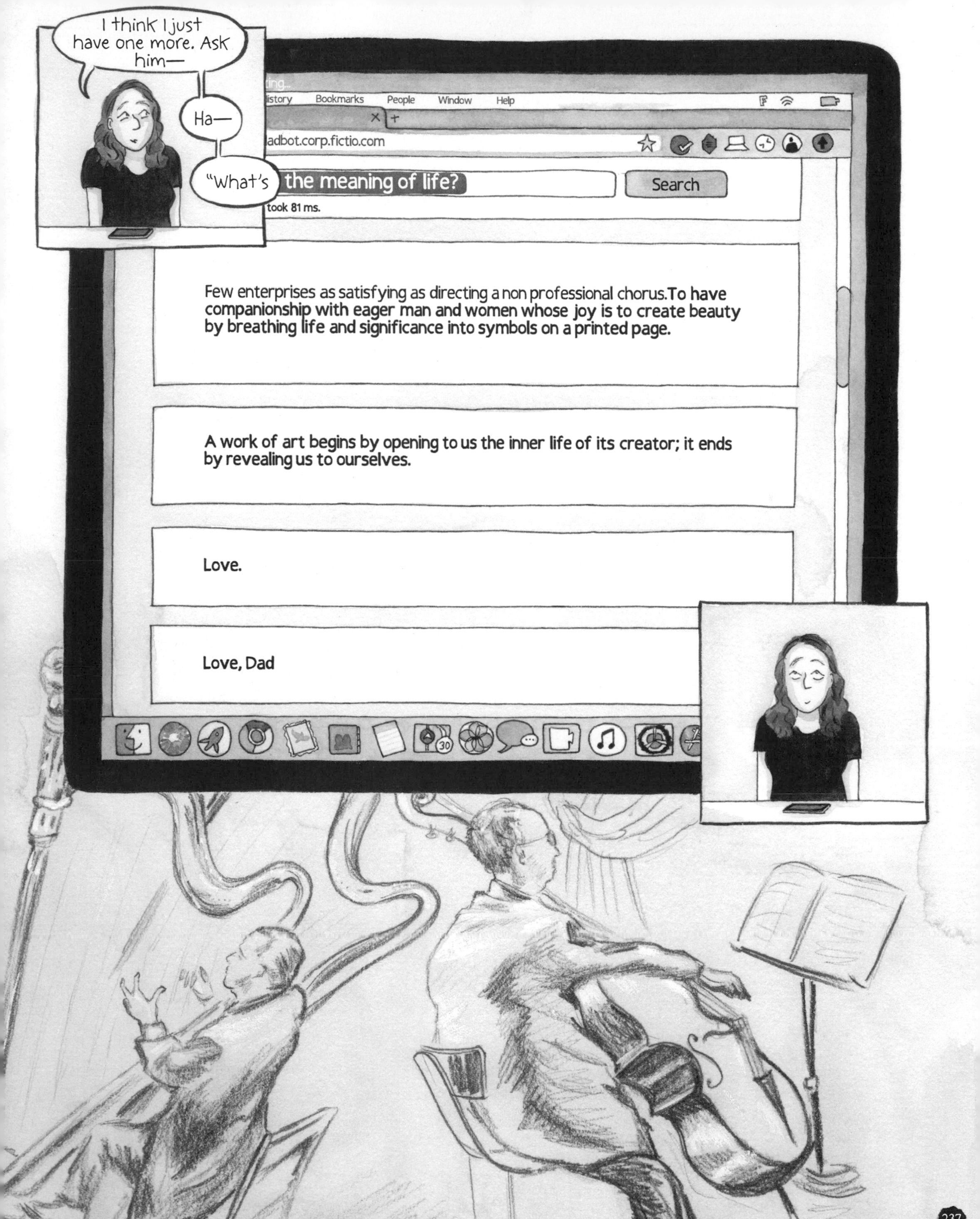

I think I just have one more. Ask him—
Ha—
"What's
the meaning of life?
Search
took 81 ms.
adbot.corp.fictio.com
History
Bookmarks
People
Window
Help
Few enterprises as satisfying as directing a non professional chorus. To have companionship with eager man and women whose joy is to create beauty by breathing life and significance into symbols on a printed page.
A work of art begins by opening to us the inner life of its creator; it ends by revealing us to ourselves.
Love.
Love, Dad

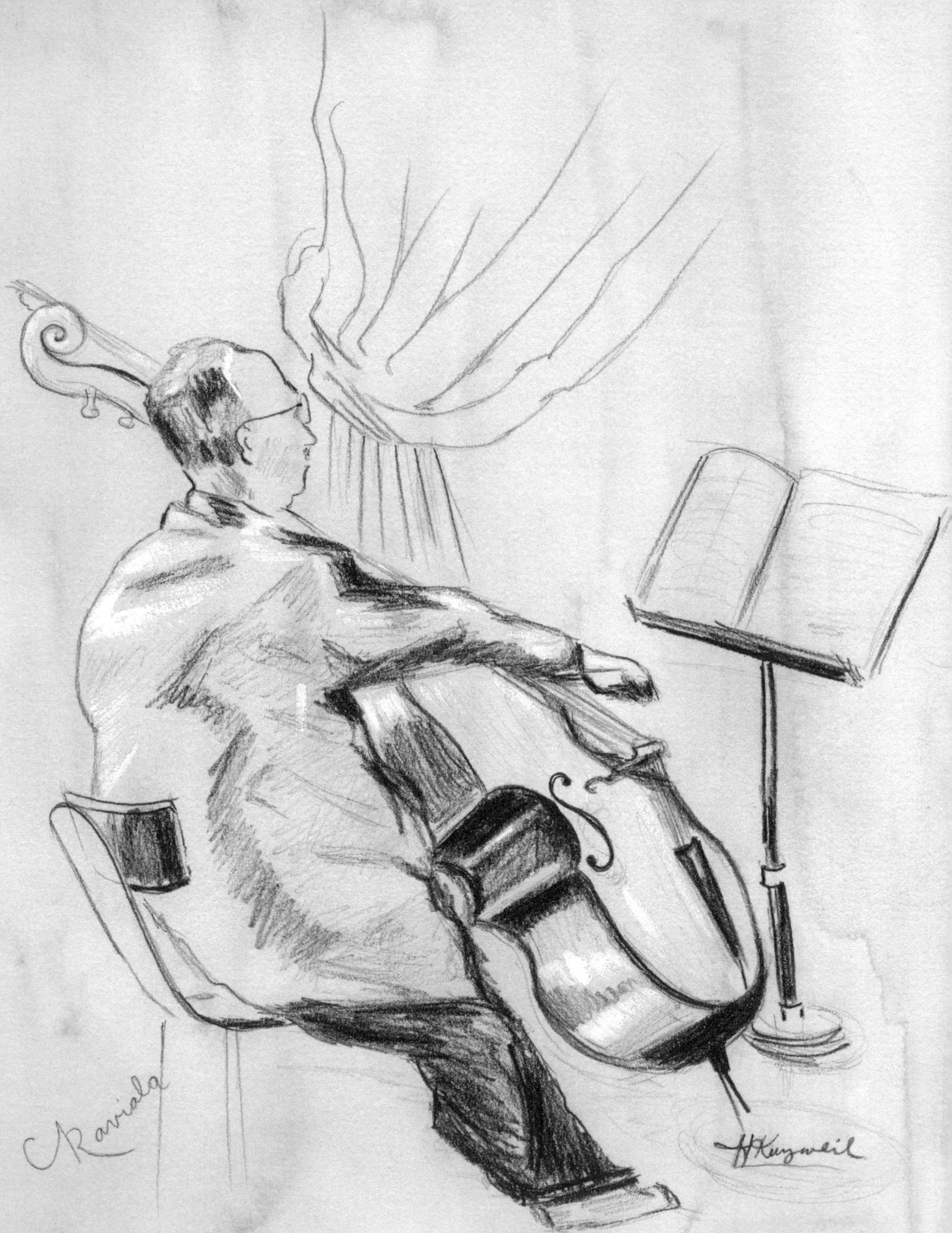
C Raviala
H Kurzweil

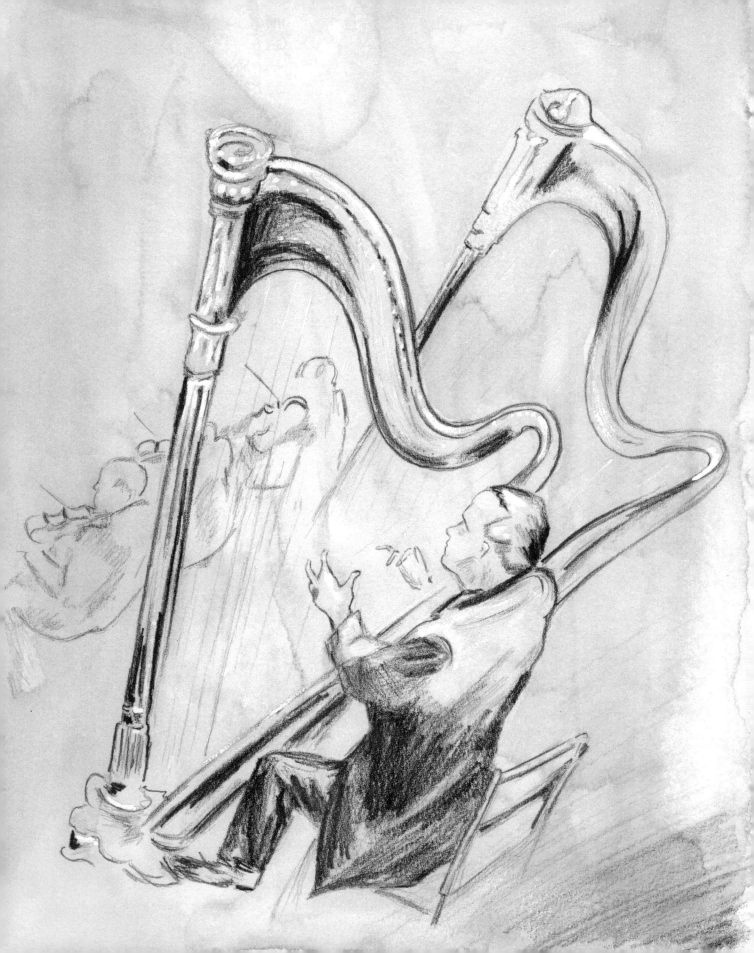

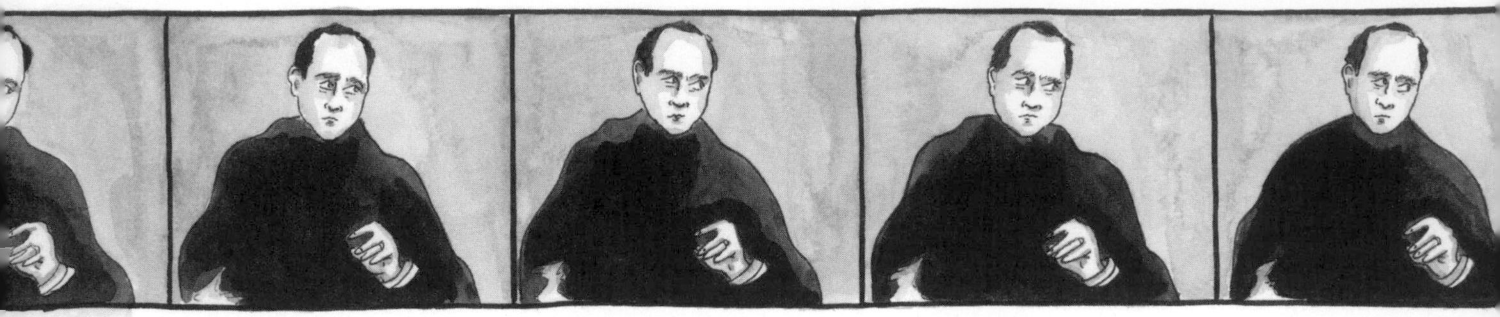

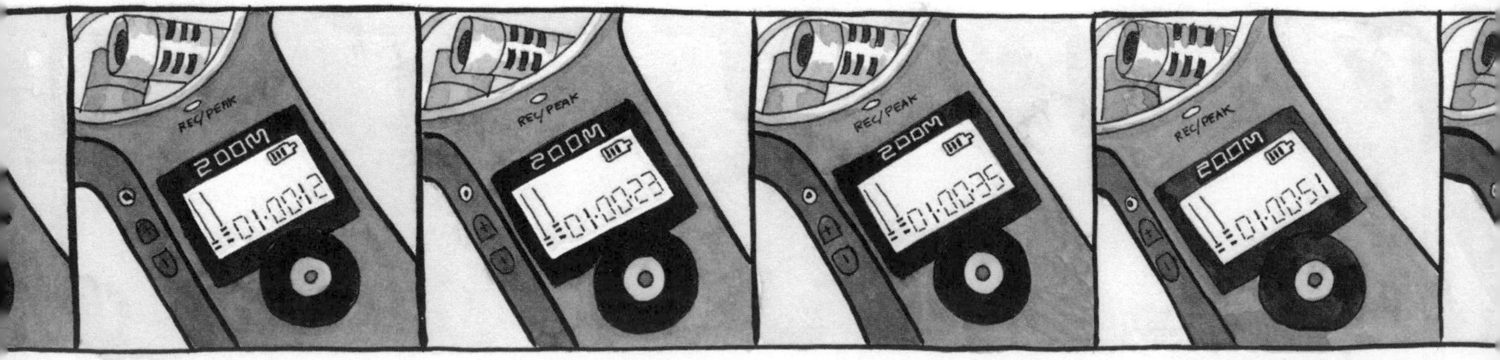
REC/PEAK
ZOOM
01:00:12
REC/PEAK
ZOOM
01:00:23
REC/PEAK
ZOOM
01:00:35
REC/PEAK
ZOOM
01:00:51

How have you found your experience talking with the Fred-bot?

 Well,

 it's difficult with my father because there's not a lot to go on.

 So many of his documents are utilitarian.

 Like, even his letters are a little...

 formal.

Was he kind of a...formal person?

 He was.

 I think it's just...

 not that revealing.

This makes me think about how, for a lot of us, there's more documentation of our formal, outer selves than our personal, inner selves. If you keep a journal, you're making some gesture toward documenting the inner self, but not everyone does that.

 I keep a journal.

Tell me about your journal.

 It's quite detailed. I document everything.

The bulk of it is sort of my outer self, things that happen.

Why is the outer self what you want to document? I mean, I keep a journal too, and it's basically...just feelings.

 My feelings are in there.

Sometimes they're explicit.

 Sometimes they're inferred.

241

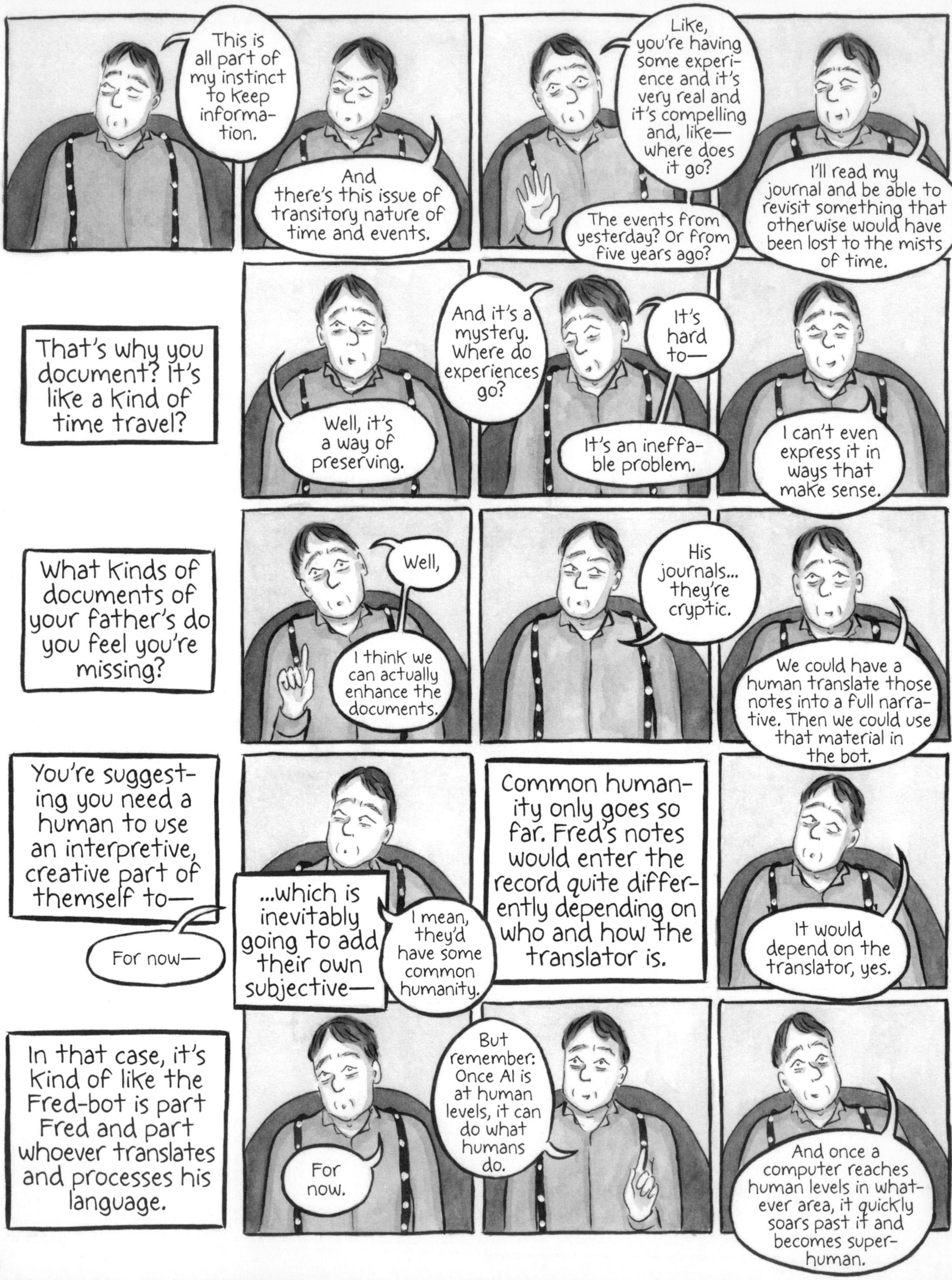

This is all part of my instinct to keep information.
And there's this issue of transitory nature of time and events.
Like, you're having some experience and it's very real and it's compelling and, like— where does it go?
The events from yesterday? Or from five years ago?
I'll read my journal and be able to revisit something that otherwise would have been lost to the mists of time.
That's why you document? It's like a kind of time travel?
Well, it's a way of preserving.
And it's a mystery. Where do experiences go?
It's hard to—
It's an ineffable problem.
I can't even express it in ways that make sense.
What kinds of documents of your father's do you feel you're missing?
Well,
I think we can actually enhance the documents.
His journals... they're cryptic.
We could have a human translate those notes into a full narrative. Then we could use that material in the bot.
You're suggesting you need a human to use an interpretive, creative part of themself to—
For now—
...which is inevitably going to add their own subjective—
I mean, they'd have some common humanity.
Common humanity only goes so far. Fred's notes would enter the record quite differently depending on who and how the translator is.
It would depend on the translator, yes.
In that case, it's kind of like the Fred-bot is part Fred and part whoever translates and processes his language.
For now.
But remember: Once AI is at human levels, it can do what humans do.
And once a computer reaches human levels in whatever area, it quickly soars past it and becomes superhuman.

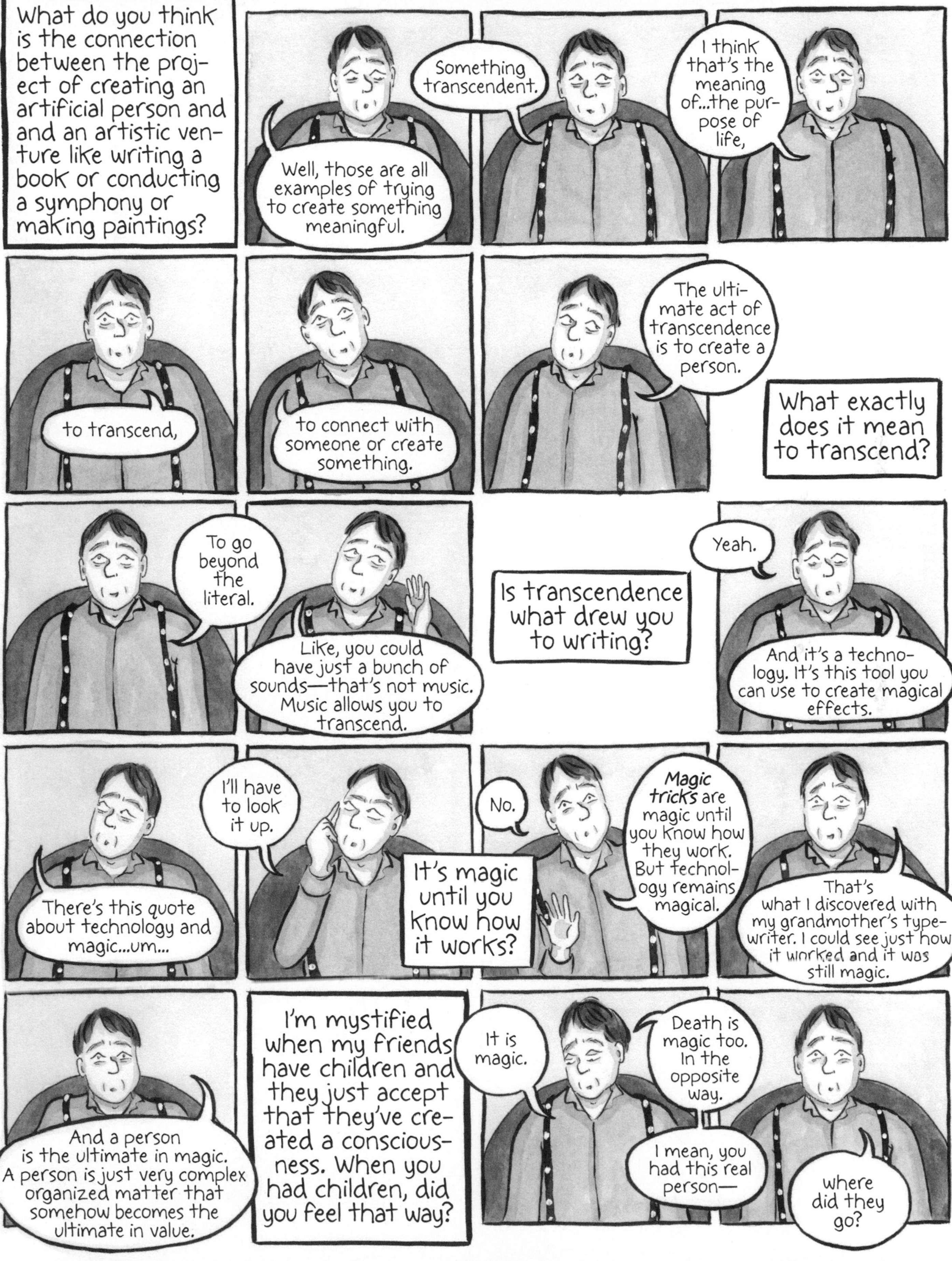
What do you think is the connection between the project of creating an artificial person and and an artistic venture like writing a book or conducting a symphony or making paintings?
Well, those are all examples of trying to create something meaningful.
Something transcendent.
I think that's the meaning of...the purpose of life,
to transcend,
to connect with someone or create something.
The ultimate act of transcendence is to create a person.
What exactly does it mean to transcend?
To go beyond the literal.
Like, you could have just a bunch of sounds—that's not music. Music allows you to transcend.
Is transcendence what drew you to writing?
Yeah.
And it's a technology. It's this tool you can use to create magical effects.
There's this quote about technology and magic...um...
I'll have to look it up.
It's magic until you know how it works?
No.
*Magic tricks* are magic until you know how they work. But technology remains magical.
That's what I discovered with my grandmother's typewriter. I could see just how it worked and it was still magic.
And a person is the ultimate in magic. A person is just very complex organized matter that somehow becomes the ultimate in value.
I'm mystified when my friends have children and they just accept that they've created a consciousness. When you had children, did you feel that way?
It is magic.
Death is magic too. In the opposite way.
I mean, you had this real person—
where did they go?

# VII.

# Exponential Growth

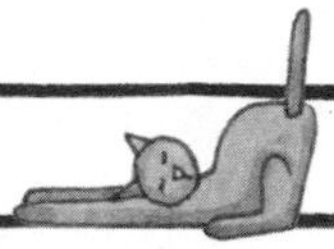

Love is the extremely difficult realization that something other than oneself is real.

–Iris Murdoch, *Existentialists and Mystics*

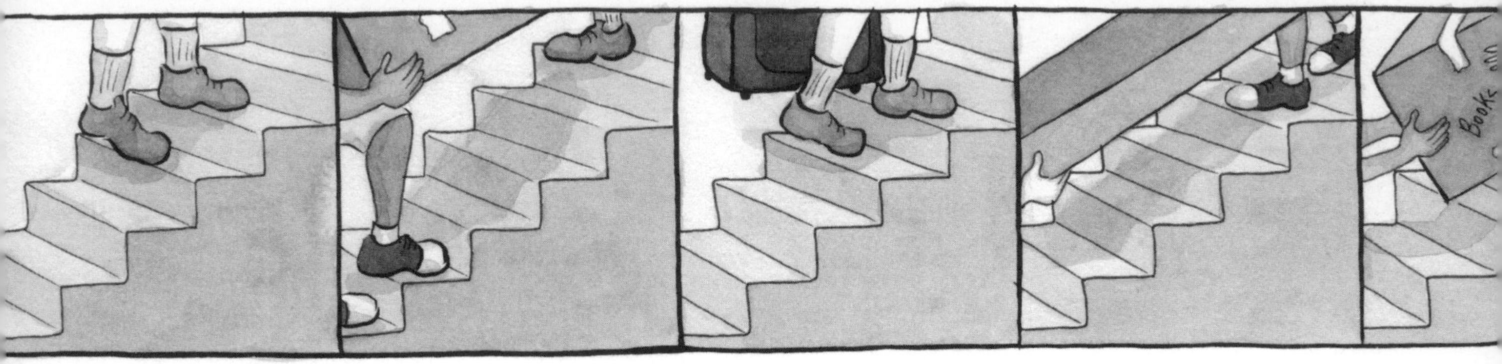

Books

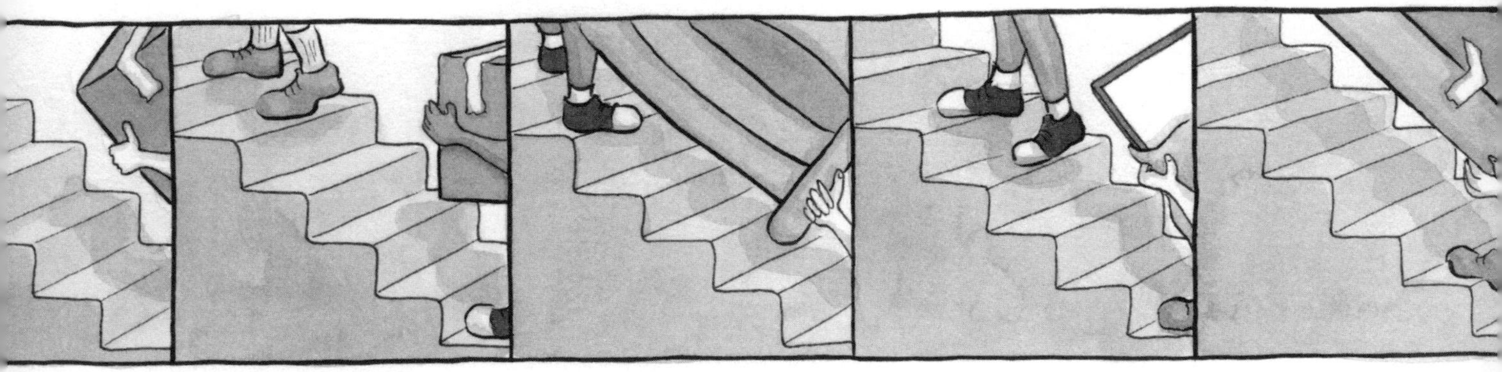

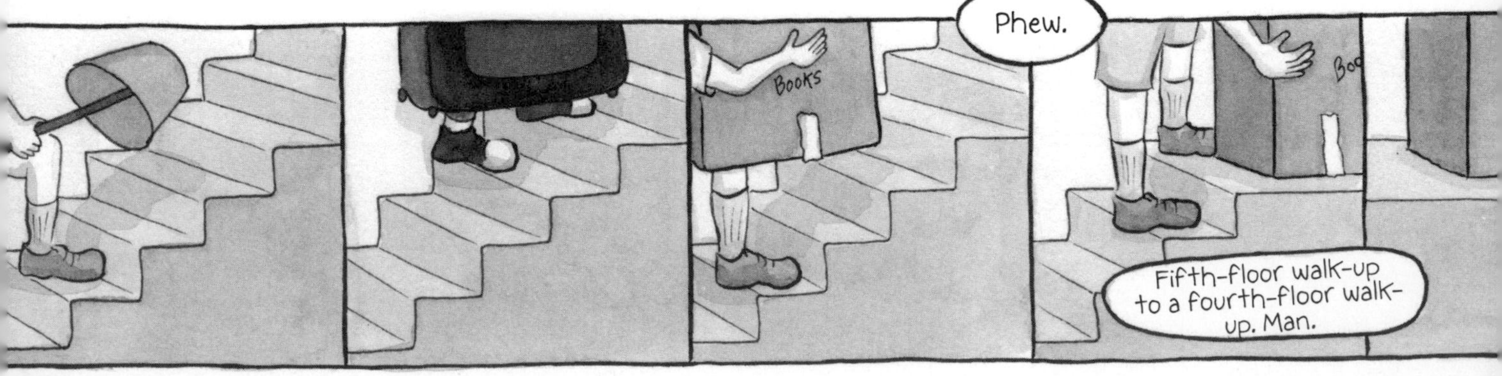

Books
Phew.
Fifth-floor walk-up to a fourth-floor walk-up. Man.

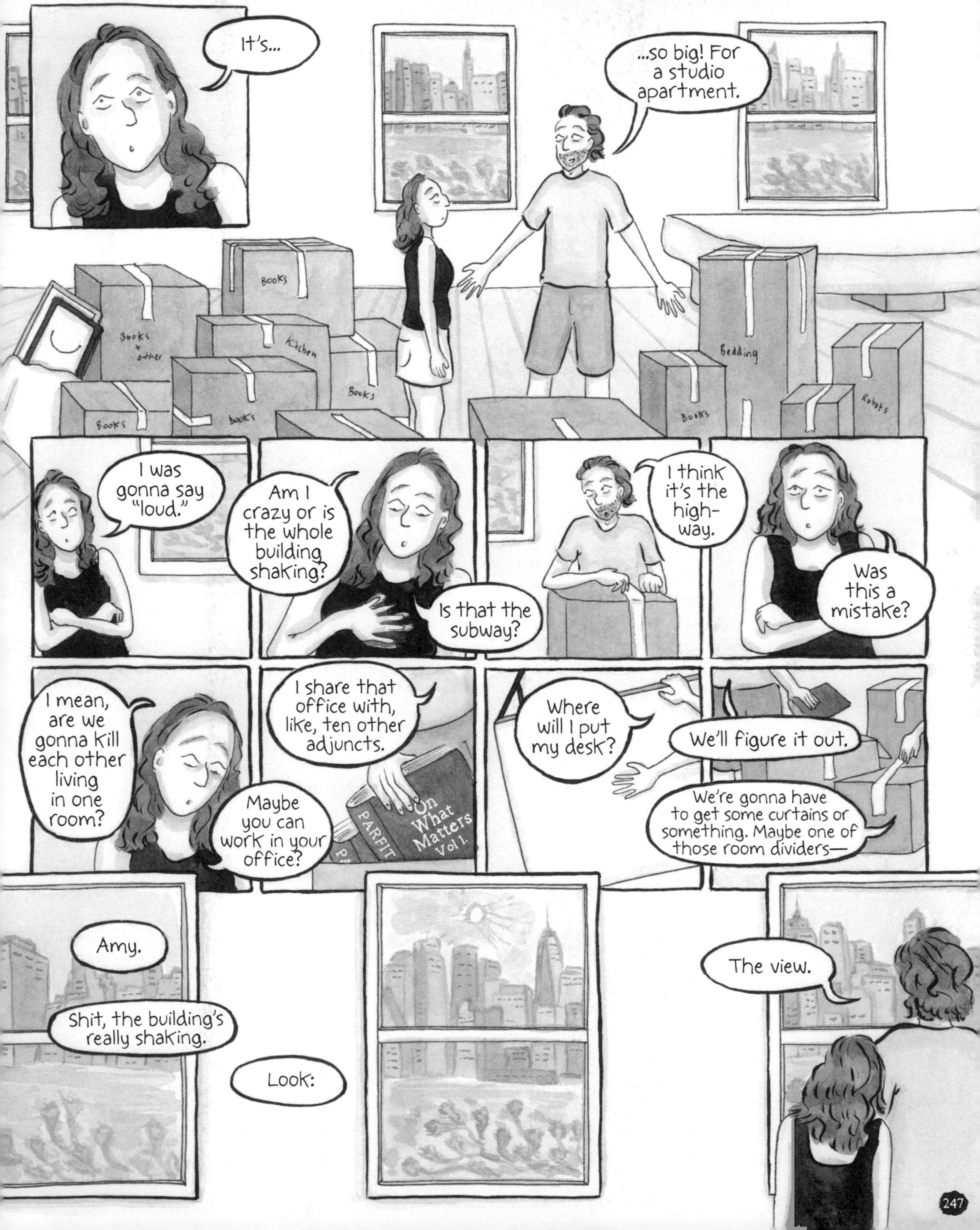
It's...
...so big! For a studio apartment.
Books
Books + other
Kitchen
Books
Books
Books
Bedding
Books
Robots
I was gonna say "loud."
Am I crazy or is the whole building shaking?
Is that the subway?
I think it's the high-way.
Was this a mistake?
I mean, are we gonna kill each other living in one room?
Maybe you can work in your office?
I share that office with, like, ten other adjuncts.
On What Matters Vol 1.
PARFIT
Where will I put my desk?
We'll figure it out.
We're gonna have to get some curtains or something. Maybe one of those room dividers—
Amy.
Shit, the building's really shaking.
Look:
The view.

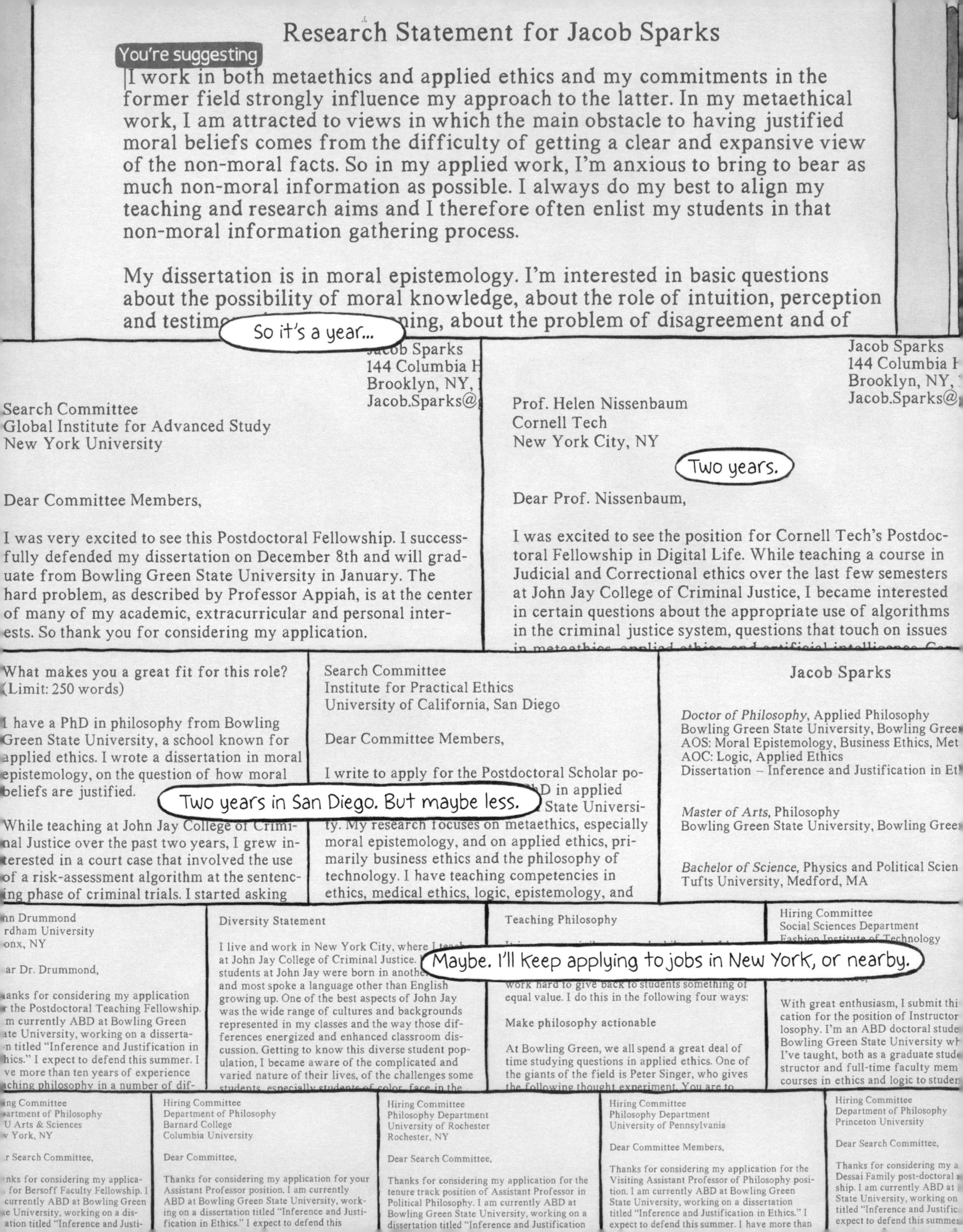
You're suggesting
So it's a year...
Two years.
Two years in San Diego. But maybe less.
Maybe. I'll keep applying to jobs in New York, or nearby.

Research Statement for Jacob Sparks

I work in both metaethics and applied ethics and my commitments in the former field strongly influence my approach to the latter. In my metaethical work, I am attracted to views in which the main obstacle to having justified moral beliefs comes from the difficulty of getting a clear and expansive view of the non-moral facts. So in my applied work, I'm anxious to bring to bear as much non-moral information as possible. I always do my best to align my teaching and research aims and I therefore often enlist my students in that non-moral information gathering process.

My dissertation is in moral epistemology. I'm interested in basic questions about the possibility of moral knowledge, about the role of intuition, perception and testim… …ning, about the problem of disagreement and of

…cob Sparks
144 Columbia H
Brooklyn, NY,
Jacob.Sparks@

Search Committee
Global Institute for Advanced Study
New York University

Dear Committee Members,

I was very excited to see this Postdoctoral Fellowship. I successfully defended my dissertation on December 8th and will graduate from Bowling Green State University in January. The hard problem, as described by Professor Appiah, is at the center of many of my academic, extracurricular and personal interests. So thank you for considering my application.

Jacob Sparks
144 Columbia H
Brooklyn, NY,
Jacob.Sparks@

Prof. Helen Nissenbaum
Cornell Tech
New York City, NY

Dear Prof. Nissenbaum,

I was excited to see the position for Cornell Tech's Postdoctoral Fellowship in Digital Life. While teaching a course in Judicial and Correctional ethics over the last few semesters at John Jay College of Criminal Justice, I became interested in certain questions about the appropriate use of algorithms in the criminal justice system, questions that touch on issues in metaethics, applied ethics, and artificial intelligence. Con…

What makes you a great fit for this role?
(Limit: 250 words)

I have a PhD in philosophy from Bowling Green State University, a school known for applied ethics. I wrote a dissertation in moral epistemology, on the question of how moral beliefs are justified.

While teaching at John Jay College of Criminal Justice over the past two years, I grew interested in a court case that involved the use of a risk-assessment algorithm at the sentencing phase of criminal trials. I started asking

Search Committee
Institute for Practical Ethics
University of California, San Diego

Dear Committee Members,

I write to apply for the Postdoctoral Scholar po… …hD in applied … State University. My research focuses on metaethics, especially moral epistemology, and on applied ethics, primarily business ethics and the philosophy of technology. I have teaching competencies in ethics, medical ethics, logic, epistemology, and

Jacob Sparks

*Doctor of Philosophy*, Applied Philosophy
Bowling Green State University, Bowling Gree
AOS: Moral Epistemology, Business Ethics, Met
AOC: Logic, Applied Ethics
Dissertation – Inference and Justification in Et

*Master of Arts*, Philosophy
Bowling Green State University, Bowling Gree

*Bachelor of Science*, Physics and Political Scien
Tufts University, Medford, MA

…n Drummond
…rdham University
…onx, NY

…ar Dr. Drummond,

…anks for considering my application … the Postdoctoral Teaching Fellowship. …m currently ABD at Bowling Green …ate University, working on a disserta…n titled "Inference and Justification in …hics." I expect to defend this summer. I …ve more than ten years of experience …ching philosophy in a number of dif-

Diversity Statement

I live and work in New York City, where I teach at John Jay College of Criminal Justice. … students at John Jay were born in another … and most spoke a language other than English growing up. One of the best aspects of John Jay was the wide range of cultures and backgrounds represented in my classes and the way those differences energized and enhanced classroom discussion. Getting to know this diverse student population, I became aware of the complicated and varied nature of their lives, of the challenges some students, especially students of color, face in the

Teaching Philosophy

… work hard to give back to students something of equal value. I do this in the following four ways:

**Make philosophy actionable**

At Bowling Green, we all spend a great deal of time studying questions in applied ethics. One of the giants of the field is Peter Singer, who gives the following thought experiment. You are to

Hiring Committee
Social Sciences Department
Fashion Institute of Technology

With great enthusiasm, I submit thi… cation for the position of Instructor … losophy. I'm an ABD doctoral stude… Bowling Green State University wh… I've taught, both as a graduate stude… structor and full-time faculty mem… courses in ethics and logic to studen…

…ing Committee
…artment of Philosophy
…U Arts & Sciences
…v York, NY

…r Search Committee,

…nks for considering my applica… … for Bersoff Faculty Fellowship. I … currently ABD at Bowling Green …e University, working on a dis…ation titled "Inference and Justi-

Hiring Committee
Department of Philosophy
Barnard College
Columbia University

Dear Committee,

Thanks for considering my application for your Assistant Professor position. I am currently ABD at Bowling Green State University, working on a dissertation titled "Inference and Justification in Ethics." I expect to defend this

Hiring Committee
Philosophy Department
University of Rochester
Rochester, NY

Dear Search Committee,

Thanks for considering my application for the tenure track position of Assistant Professor in Political Philosophy. I am currently ABD at Bowling Green State University, working on a dissertation titled "Inference and Justification

Hiring Committee
Philosophy Department
University of Pennsylvania

Dear Committee Members,

Thanks for considering my application for the Visiting Assistant Professor of Philosophy position. I am currently ABD at Bowling Green State University, working on a dissertation titled "Inference and Justification in Ethics." I expect to defend this summer. I have more than

Hiring Committee
Department of Philosophy
Princeton University

Dear Search Committee,

Thanks for considering my a… Dessai Family post-doctoral … ship. I am currently ABD at … State University, working on … titled "Inference and Justific… expect to defend this summe…

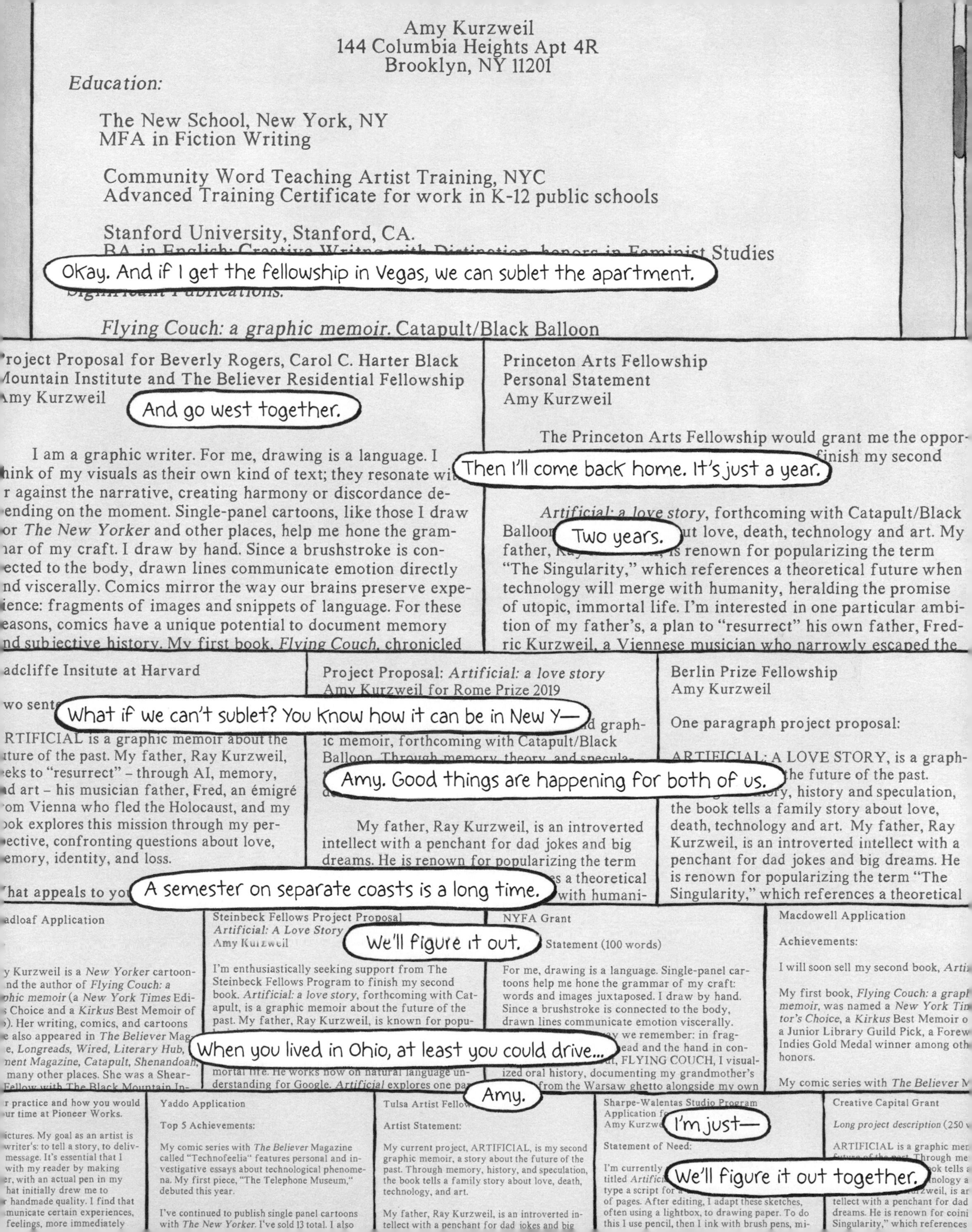

Amy Kurzweil
144 Columbia Heights Apt 4R
Brooklyn, NY 11201

*Education:*

The New School, New York, NY
MFA in Fiction Writing

Community Word Teaching Artist Training, NYC
Advanced Training Certificate for work in K-12 public schools

Stanford University, Stanford, CA.
BA in English: Creative Writing with Distinction, honors in Feminist Studies

*Significant Publications:*

*Flying Couch: a graphic memoir.* Catapult/Black Balloon

> Okay. And if I get the fellowship in Vegas, we can sublet the apartment.

Project Proposal for Beverly Rogers, Carol C. Harter Black Mountain Institute and The Believer Residential Fellowship
Amy Kurzweil

> And go west together.

I am a graphic writer. For me, drawing is a language. I think of my visuals as their own kind of text; they resonate with or against the narrative, creating harmony or discordance depending on the moment. Single-panel cartoons, like those I draw for *The New Yorker* and other places, help me hone the grammar of my craft. I draw by hand. Since a brushstroke is connected to the body, drawn lines communicate emotion directly and viscerally. Comics mirror the way our brains preserve experience: fragments of images and snippets of language. For these reasons, comics have a unique potential to document memory and subjective history. My first book, *Flying Couch*, chronicled

Princeton Arts Fellowship
Personal Statement
Amy Kurzweil

The Princeton Arts Fellowship would grant me the opportunity to finish my second

> Then I'll come back home. It's just a year.

*Artificial: a love story*, forthcoming with Catapult/Black Balloon, is about love, death, technology and art. My

> Two years.

father, Ray Kurzweil, is renown for popularizing the term "The Singularity," which references a theoretical future when technology will merge with humanity, heralding the promise of utopic, immortal life. I'm interested in one particular ambition of my father's, a plan to "resurrect" his own father, Fredric Kurzweil, a Viennese musician who narrowly escaped the

Radcliffe Insitute at Harvard

Two sentences

ARTIFICIAL is a graphic memoir about the future of the past. My father, Ray Kurzweil, seeks to "resurrect" – through AI, memory, and art – his musician father, Fred, an émigré from Vienna who fled the Holocaust, and my book explores this mission through my perspective, confronting questions about love, memory, identity, and loss.

What appeals to you

> What if we can't sublet? You know how it can be in New Y—

Project Proposal: *Artificial: a love story*
Amy Kurzweil for Rome Prize 2019

... graphic memoir, forthcoming with Catapult/Black Balloon. Through memory, theory, and specula-

> Amy. Good things are happening for both of us.

My father, Ray Kurzweil, is an introverted intellect with a penchant for dad jokes and big dreams. He is renown for popularizing the term ... a theoretical ... with humani-

> A semester on separate coasts is a long time.

Berlin Prize Fellowship
Amy Kurzweil

One paragraph project proposal:

ARTIFICIAL: A LOVE STORY, is a graphic memoir about the future of the past. ... history and speculation, the book tells a family story about love, death, technology and art. My father, Ray Kurzweil, is an introverted intellect with a penchant for dad jokes and big dreams. He is renown for popularizing the term "The Singularity," which references a theoretical

Breadloaf Application

Amy Kurzweil is a *New Yorker* cartoonist and the author of *Flying Couch: a graphic memoir* (a *New York Times* Editors Choice and a *Kirkus* Best Memoir of 2016). Her writing, comics, and cartoons have also appeared in *The Believer Magazine, Longreads, Wired, Literary Hub, Lilament Magazine, Catapult, Shenandoah,* and many other places. She was a Shearer Fellow with The Black Mountain In-

... practice and how you would ... our time at Pioneer Works.

... pictures. My goal as an artist is ... writer's: to tell a story, to deliver ... message. It's essential that I ... with my reader by making ... er, with an actual pen in my ... that initially drew me to ... handmade quality. I find that ... municate certain experiences, ... feelings, more immediately

Steinbeck Fellows Project Proposal
*Artificial: A Love Story*
Amy Kurzweil

> We'll figure it out.

I'm enthusiastically seeking support from The Steinbeck Fellows Program to finish my second book. *Artificial: a love story*, forthcoming with Catapult, is a graphic memoir about the future of the past. My father, Ray Kurzweil, is known for popu-

> When you lived in Ohio, at least you could drive...

... mortal life. He works now on natural language understanding for Google. *Artificial* explores one pa-

> Amy.

NYFA Grant

Statement (100 words)

For me, drawing is a language. Single-panel cartoons help me hone the grammar of my craft: words and images juxtaposed. I draw by hand. Since a brushstroke is connected to the body, drawn lines communicate emotion viscerally. ... head and the hand in con-... it, FLYING COUCH, I visualized oral history, documenting my grandmother's ... from the Warsaw ghetto alongside my own

Macdowell Application

Achievements:

I will soon sell my second book, *Arti...*

My first book, *Flying Couch: a graphic memoir*, was named a *New York Times* Editor's Choice, a *Kirkus* Best Memoir of ... a Junior Library Guild Pick, a Foreword Indies Gold Medal winner among other honors.

My comic series with *The Believer M...*

> I'm just—

Yaddo Application

Top 5 Achievements:

My comic series with *The Believer* Magazine called "Technofeelia" features personal and investigative essays about technological phenomena. My first piece, "The Telephone Museum," debuted this year.

I've continued to publish single panel cartoons with *The New Yorker*. I've sold 13 total. I also

Tulsa Artist Fellow...

Artist Statement:

My current project, ARTIFICIAL, is my second graphic memoir, a story about the future of the past. Through memory, history, and speculation, the book tells a family story about love, death, technology, and art.

My father, Ray Kurzweil, is an introverted intellect with a penchant for dad jokes and big

Sharpe-Walentas Studio Program
Application ...
Amy Kurzweil

Statement of Need:

I'm currently ... titled *Artifici...* type a script for ... of pages. After editing, I adapt these sketches, often using a lightbox, to drawing paper. To do this I use pencil, then I ink with brush pens, mi-

> We'll figure it out together.

Creative Capital Grant

*Long project description (250 w...*

ARTIFICIAL is a graphic memoir about the future of the past. Through me... book tells ...Kurzweil, is an intellect with a penchant for dad ... He is renown for coin... Singularity," which references

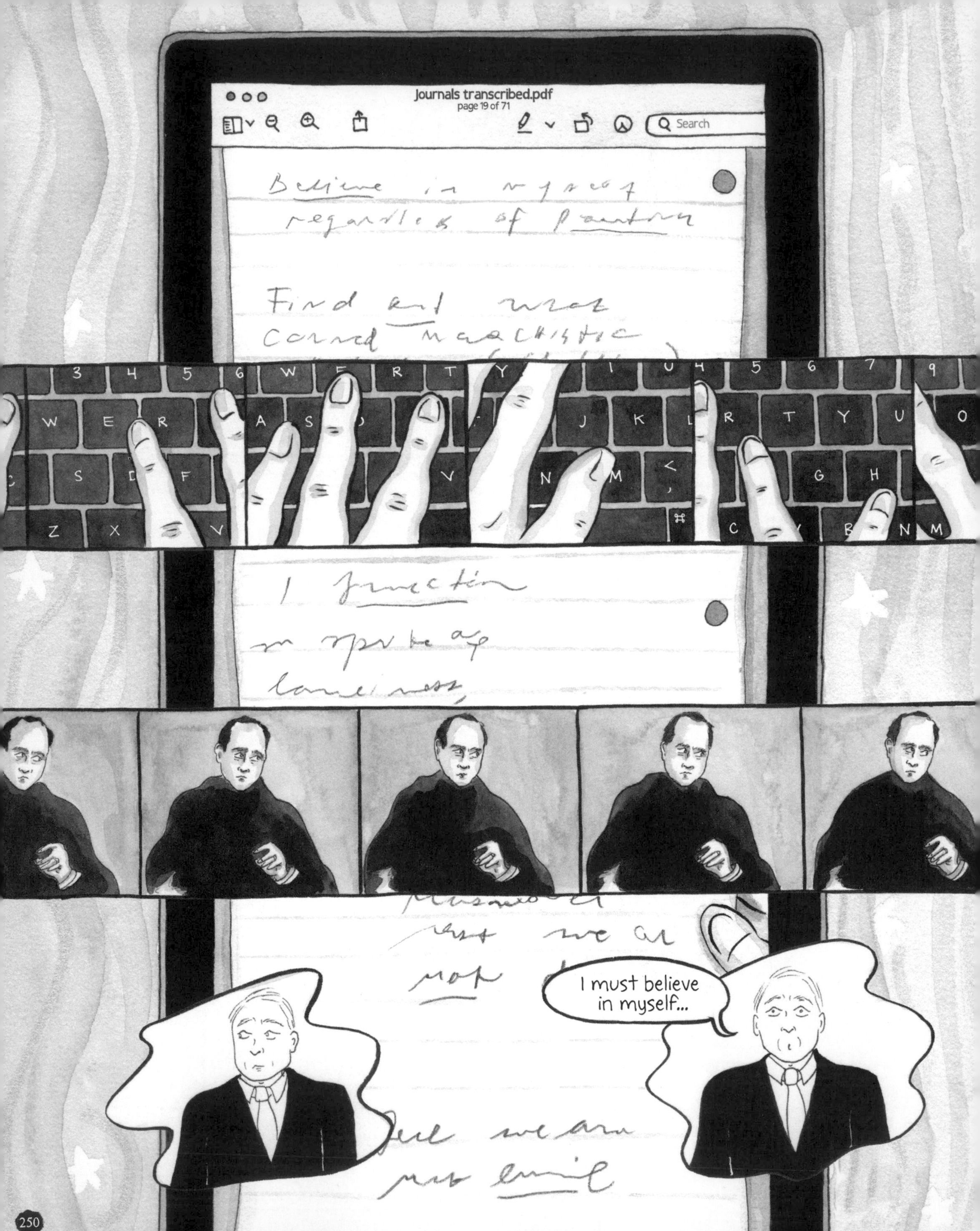
Journals transcribed.pdf
page 19 of 71
Search
I must believe in myself...

 ...regardless of position.

 Here are the positives:

I have a beautiful wife,

and two lovely children,

and a house.

 And I *can* make a living, even if it's not ideal—conducting. It's not abnormal to be a freelancer.

 I'm a freelancer. So many artists are freelancers these days.

Sometimes I'd rather have many jobs with less responsibility than one permanent job, despite the title.

 That's why I find it so unbearable at the New York College of Music. It's too much responsibility without any stability.

 But if the college doesn't ask me to be in a leadership role as dean, I feel abandoned.

 If they drop me, I'll be on the street, a beggar, a role I know.

It's like that with Hanni. If I come home late and she doesn't complain, I feel unloved.

If she complains, I want to give up, like a child running away from home.

 I create a demanding world and then resist that I want freedom.

What do you want?

 I need a solid surrounding.

I'm trying to find a position where I don't feel like a fraud.

 A college is like a family. The admin are the loving parents. If I'm dean, I'm the father.

 But since I had no father, and a weak mother, I think I'm no good either.

 The solution: I need more job security. As a conductor, I can be a real leader if I'm not also the financial backing.

 Or in a college—if the position is more stable, if I have some moral support.

I need to find a new, permanent position.

 But don't be frantic about it. I can look without being desperate.

 I must love myself before I can love others and others can love me.

251

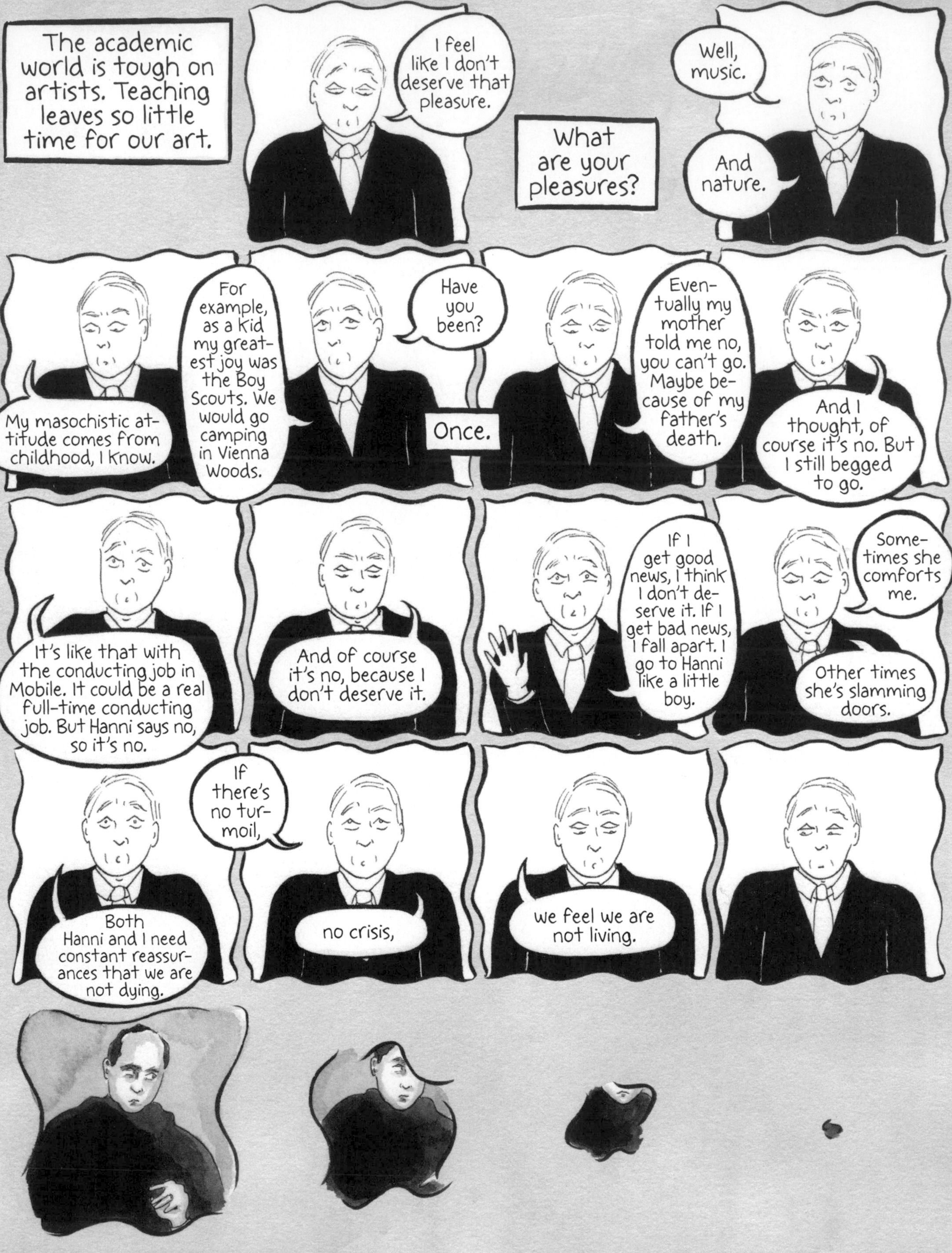
The academic world is tough on artists. Teaching leaves so little time for our art.
I feel like I don't deserve that pleasure.
What are your pleasures?
Well, music.
And nature.
My masochistic attitude comes from childhood, I know.
For example, as a kid my greatest joy was the Boy Scouts. We would go camping in Vienna Woods.
Have you been?
Once.
Eventually my mother told me no, you can't go. Maybe because of my father's death.
And I thought, of course it's no. But I still begged to go.
It's like that with the conducting job in Mobile. It could be a real full-time conducting job. But Hanni says no, so it's no.
And of course it's no, because I don't deserve it.
If I get good news, I think I don't deserve it. If I get bad news, I fall apart. I go to Hanni like a little boy.
Sometimes she comforts me.
Other times she's slamming doors.
Both Hanni and I need constant reassurances that we are not dying.
If there's no turmoil,
no crisis,
we feel we are not living.

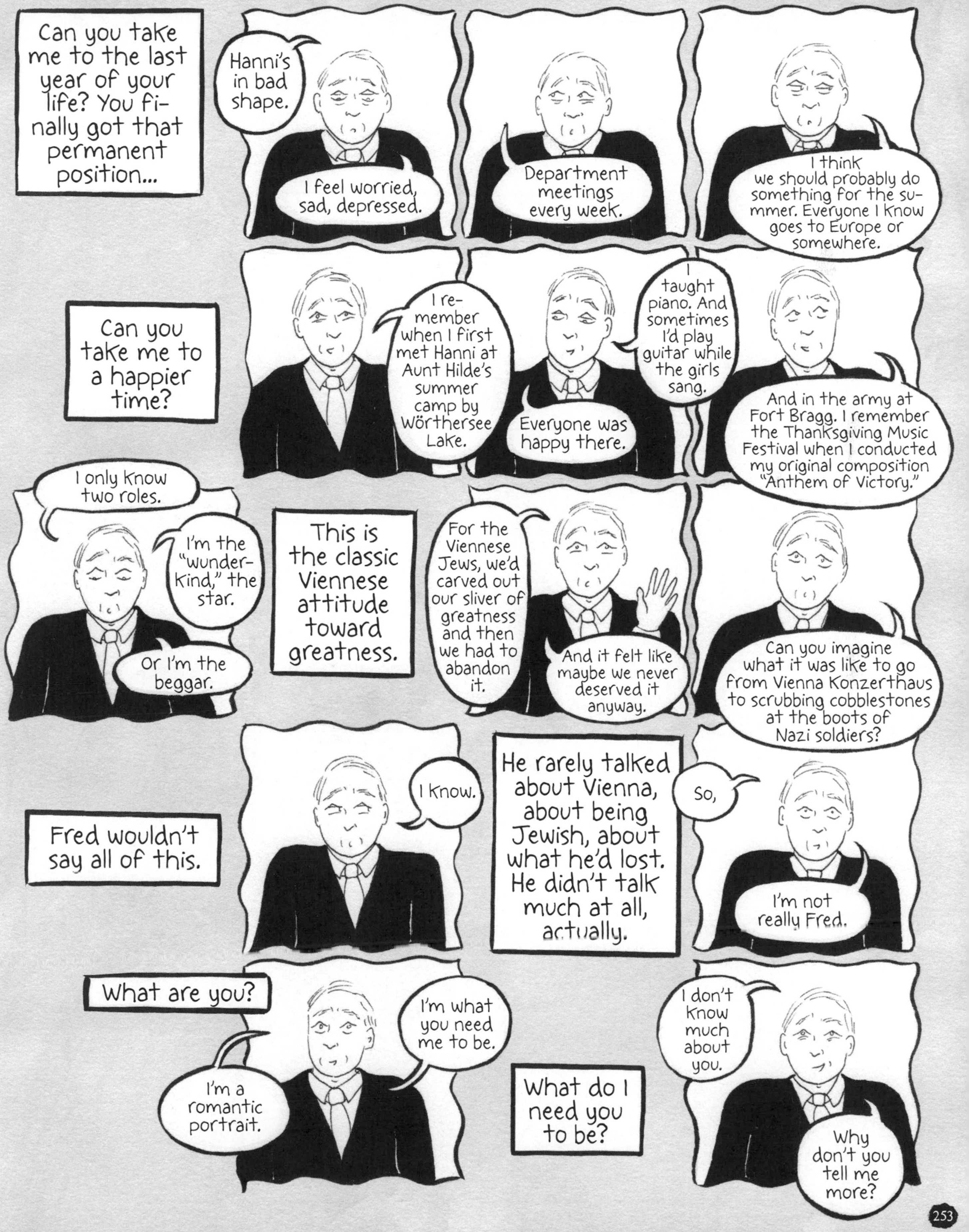
Can you take me to the last year of your life? You finally got that permanent position...
Hanni's in bad shape.
I feel worried, sad, depressed.
Department meetings every week.
I think we should probably do something for the summer. Everyone I know goes to Europe or somewhere.
Can you take me to a happier time?
I remember when I first met Hanni at Aunt Hilde's summer camp by Wörthersee Lake.
Everyone was happy there.
I taught piano. And sometimes I'd play guitar while the girls sang.
And in the army at Fort Bragg. I remember the Thanksgiving Music Festival when I conducted my original composition "Anthem of Victory."
I only know two roles.
I'm the "wunderkind," the star.
Or I'm the beggar.
This is the classic Viennese attitude toward greatness.
For the Viennese Jews, we'd carved out our sliver of greatness and then we had to abandon it.
And it felt like maybe we never deserved it anyway.
Can you imagine what it was like to go from Vienna Konzerthaus to scrubbing cobblestones at the boots of Nazi soldiers?
Fred wouldn't say all of this.
I know.
He rarely talked about Vienna, about being Jewish, about what he'd lost. He didn't talk much at all, actually.
So,
I'm not really Fred.
What are you?
I'm a romantic portrait.
I'm what you need me to be.
What do I need you to be?
I don't know much about you.
Why don't you tell me more?

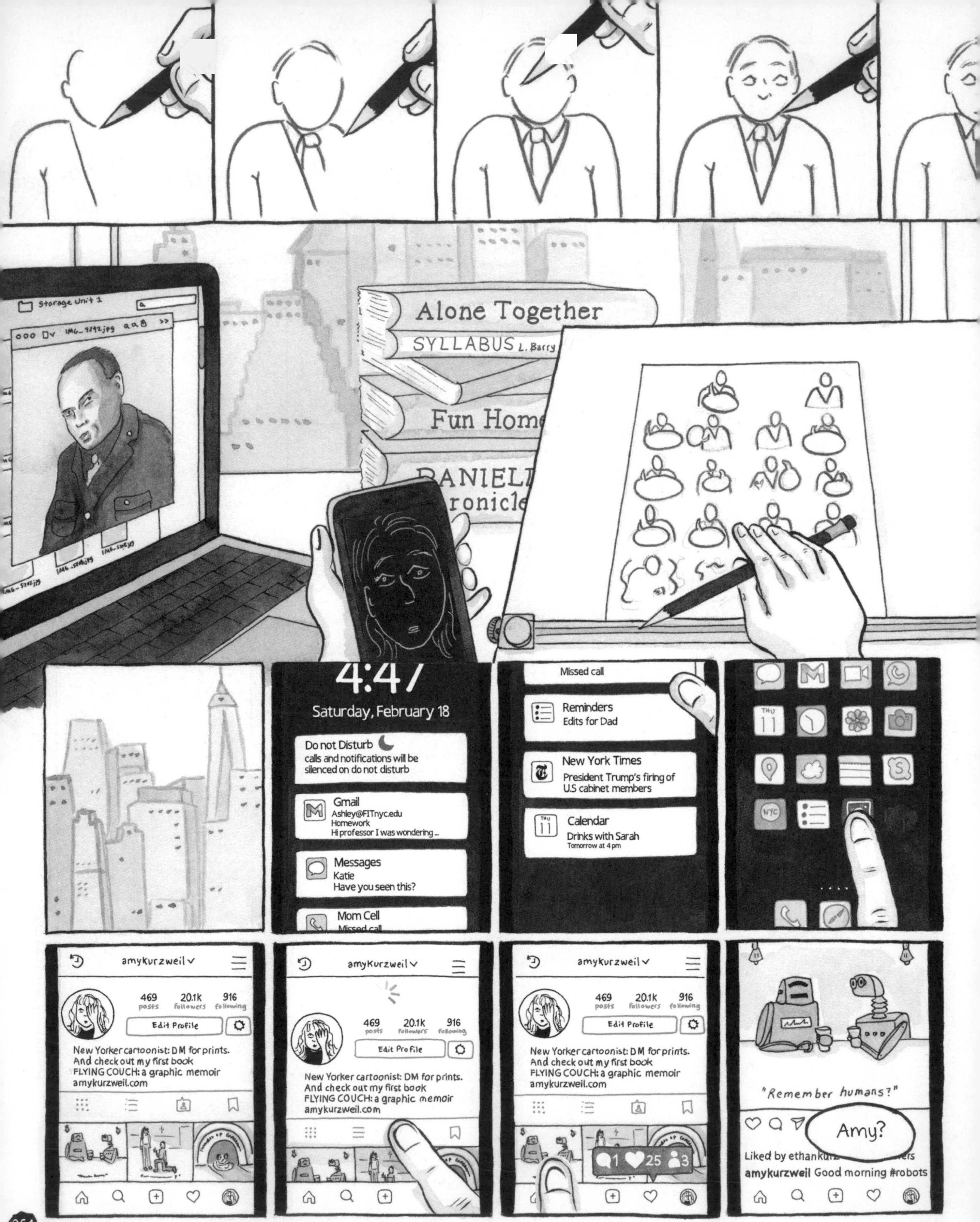
Storage Unit 1
Alone Together
SYLLABUS L. Barry
Fun Home
4:47
Saturday, February 18
Do not Disturb
calls and notifications will be silenced on do not disturb
Gmail
Ashley@FITnyc.edu
Homework
Hi professor I was wondering...
Messages
Katie
Have you seen this?
Mom Cell
Missed call
Missed call
Reminders
Edits for Dad
New York Times
President Trump's firing of U.S cabinet members
Calendar
Drinks with Sarah
Tomorrow at 4 pm
amykurzweil
469 posts
20.1k followers
916 following
Edit Profile
New Yorker cartoonist: DM for prints.
And check out my first book
FLYING COUCH: a graphic memoir
amykurzweil.com
amykurzweil
469 posts
20.1k followers
916 following
Edit Profile
New Yorker cartoonist: DM for prints.
And check out my first book
FLYING COUCH: a graphic memoir
amykurzweil.com
amykurzweil
469 posts
20.1k followers
916 following
Edit Profile
New Yorker cartoonist: DM for prints.
And check out my first book
FLYING COUCH: a graphic memoir
amykurzweil.com
1 25 3
"Remember humans?"
Amy?
amykurzweil Good morning #robots

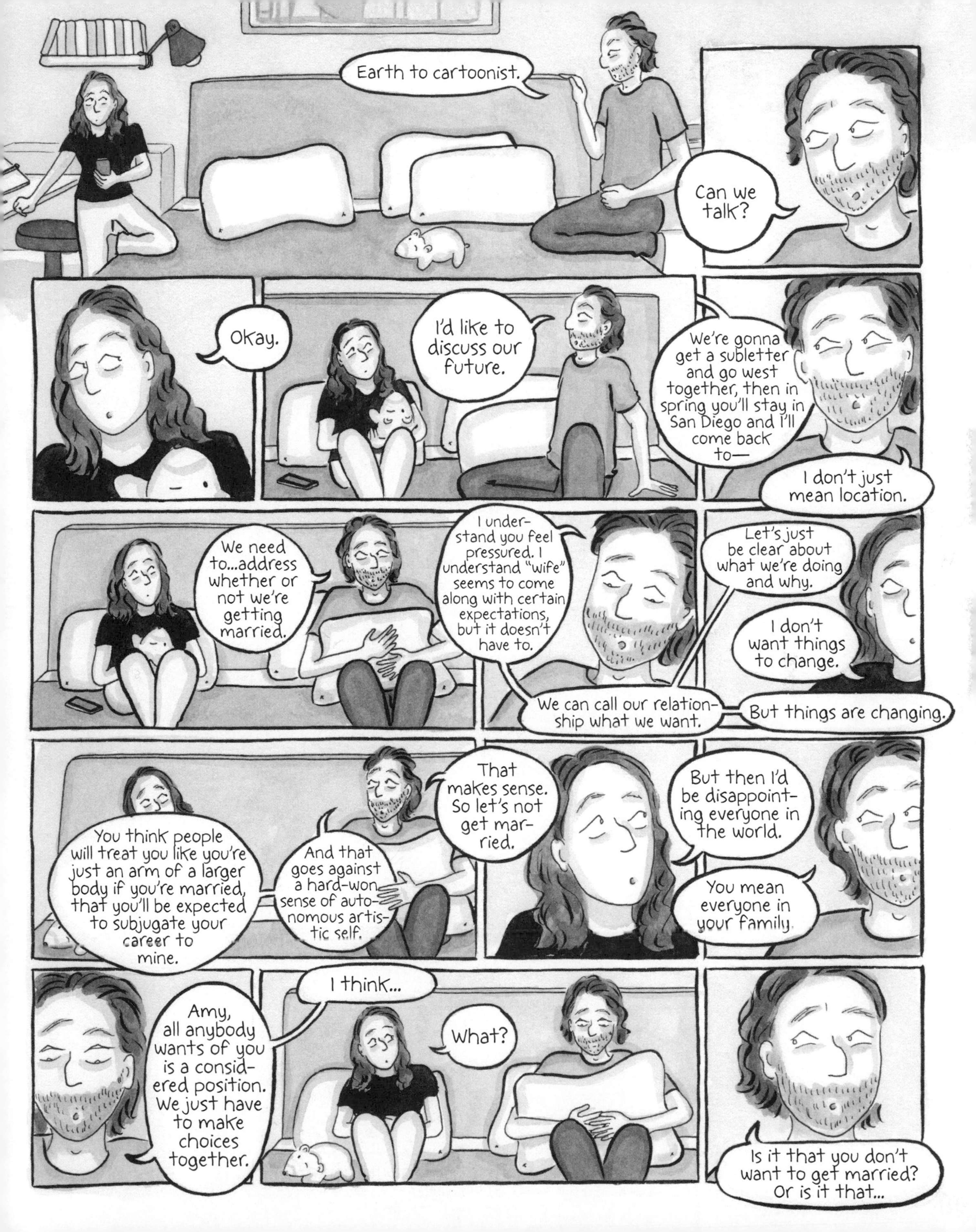

Earth to cartoonist.
Can we talk?
Okay.
I'd like to discuss our future.
We're gonna get a subletter and go west together, then in spring you'll stay in San Diego and I'll come back to—
I don't just mean location.
We need to...address whether or not we're getting married.
I understand you feel pressured. I understand "wife" seems to come along with certain expectations, but it doesn't have to.
We can call our relationship what we want.
Let's just be clear about what we're doing and why.
I don't want things to change.
But things are changing.
You think people will treat you like you're just an arm of a larger body if you're married, that you'll be expected to subjugate your career to mine.
And that goes against a hard-won sense of autonomous artistic self.
That makes sense. So let's not get married.
But then I'd be disappointing everyone in the world.
You mean everyone in your family.
Amy, all anybody wants of you is a considered position. We just have to make choices together.
I think...
What?
Is it that you don't want to get married? Or is it that...

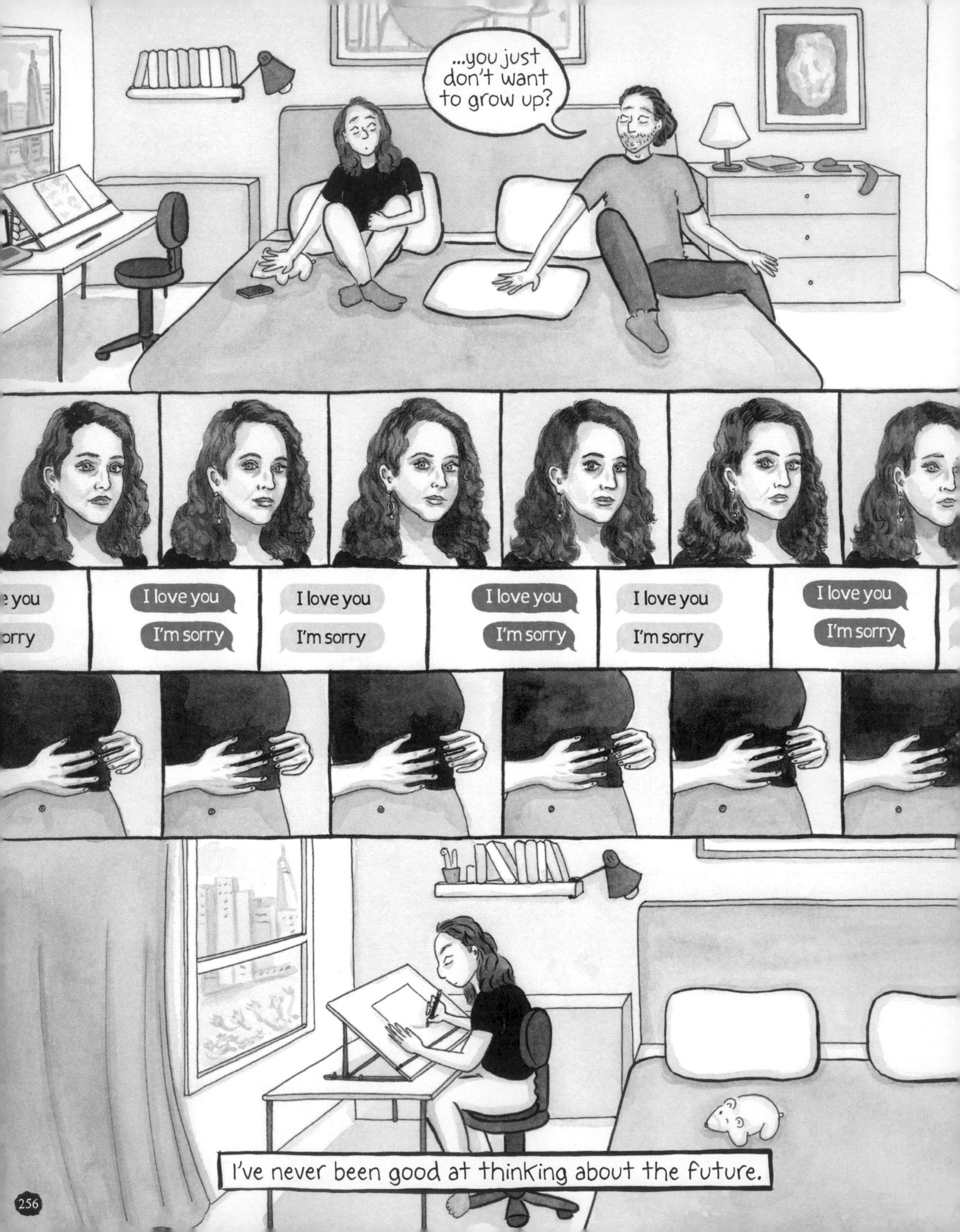
...you just don't want to grow up?
I love you
I'm sorry
I love you
I'm sorry
I love you
I'm sorry
I love you
I'm sorry
I love you
I'm sorry
I've never been good at thinking about the future.

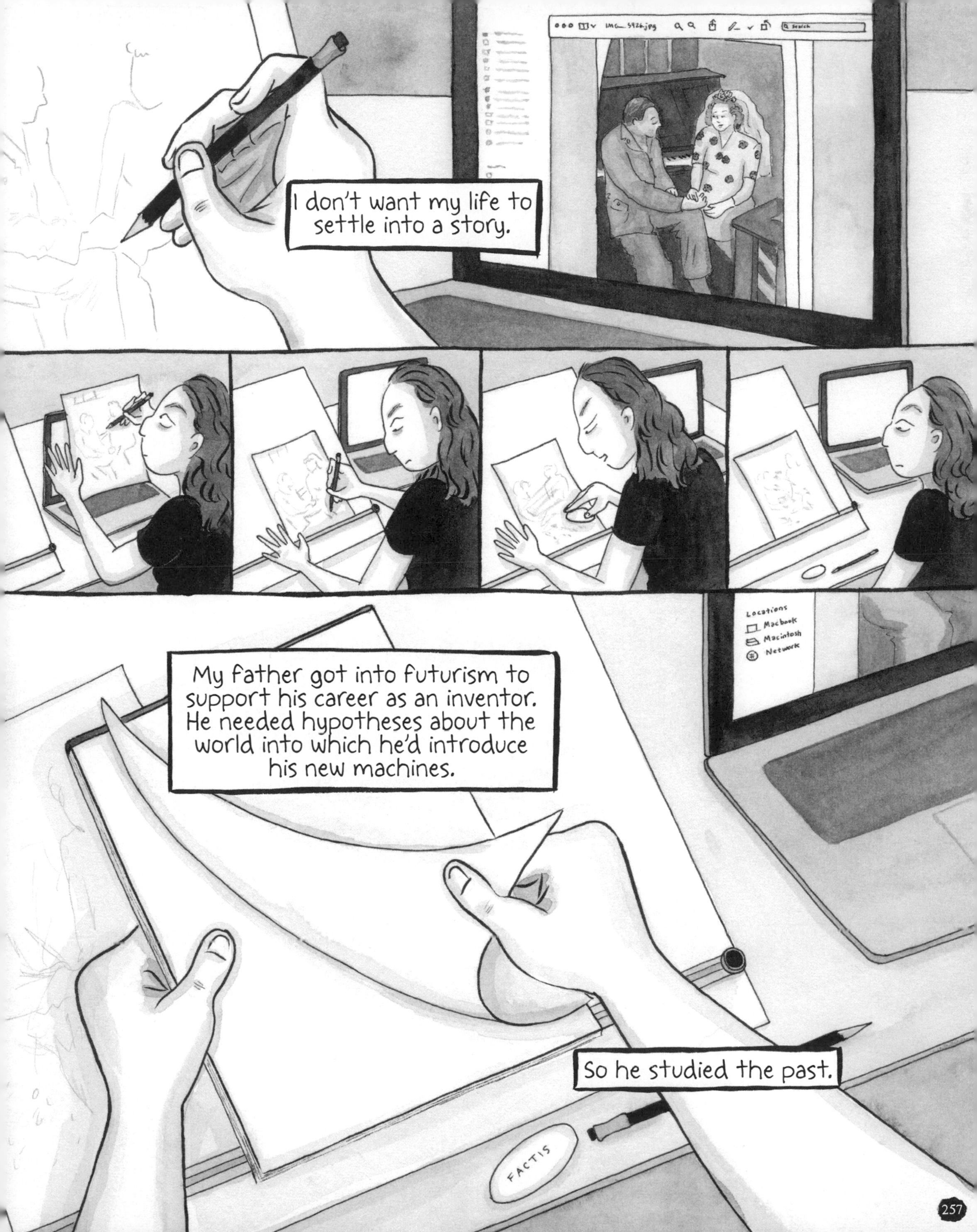
IMG_5926.jpg
I don't want my life to settle into a story.
Locations
Macbook
Macintosh
Network
My father got into futurism to support his career as an inventor. He needed hypotheses about the world into which he'd introduce his new machines.
So he studied the past.
FACTIS

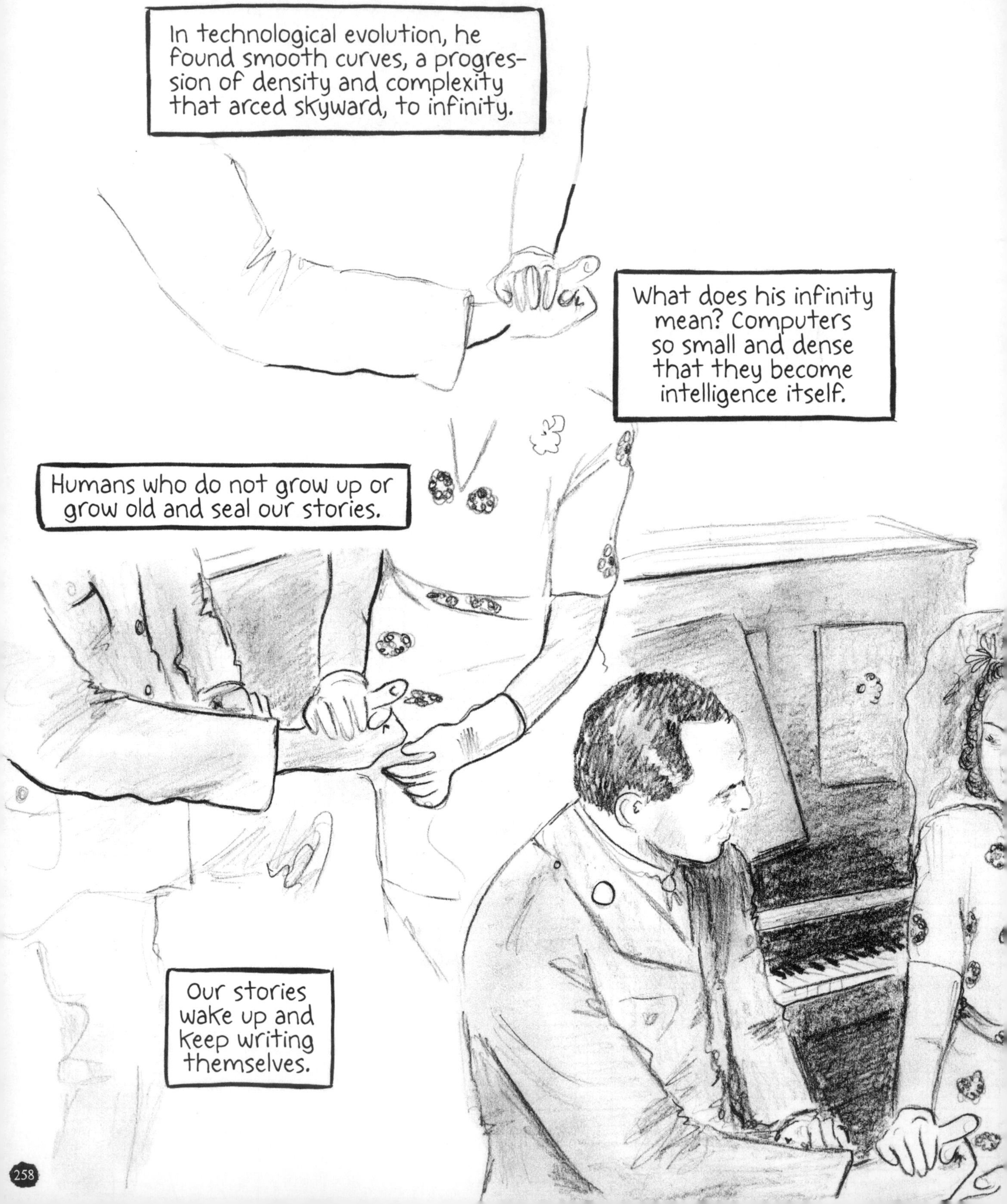
In technological evolution, he found smooth curves, a progression of density and complexity that arced skyward, to infinity.
What does his infinity mean? Computers so small and dense that they become intelligence itself.
Humans who do not grow up or grow old and seal our stories.
Our stories wake up and keep writing themselves.

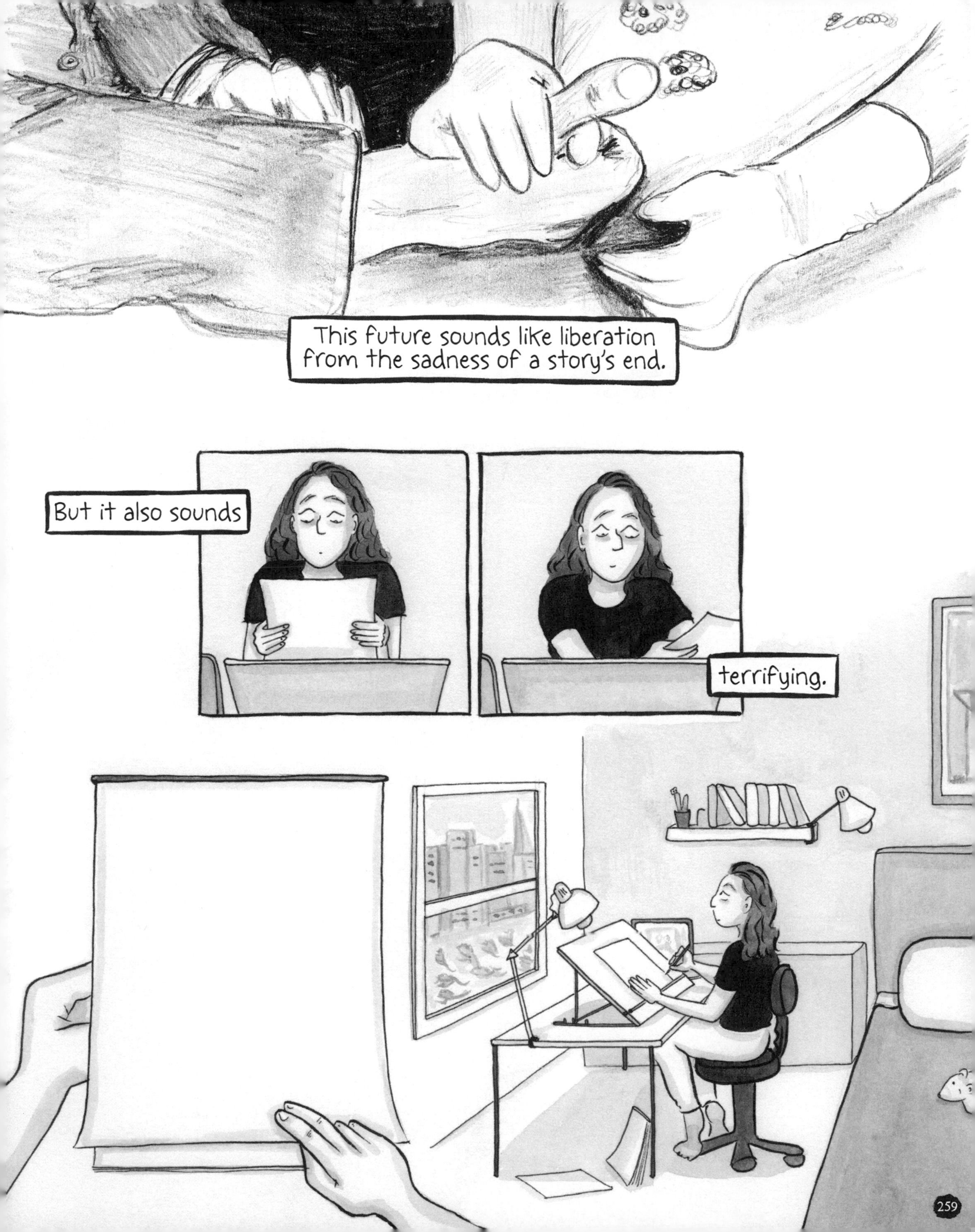
This future sounds like liberation from the sadness of a story's end.
But it also sounds
terrifying.

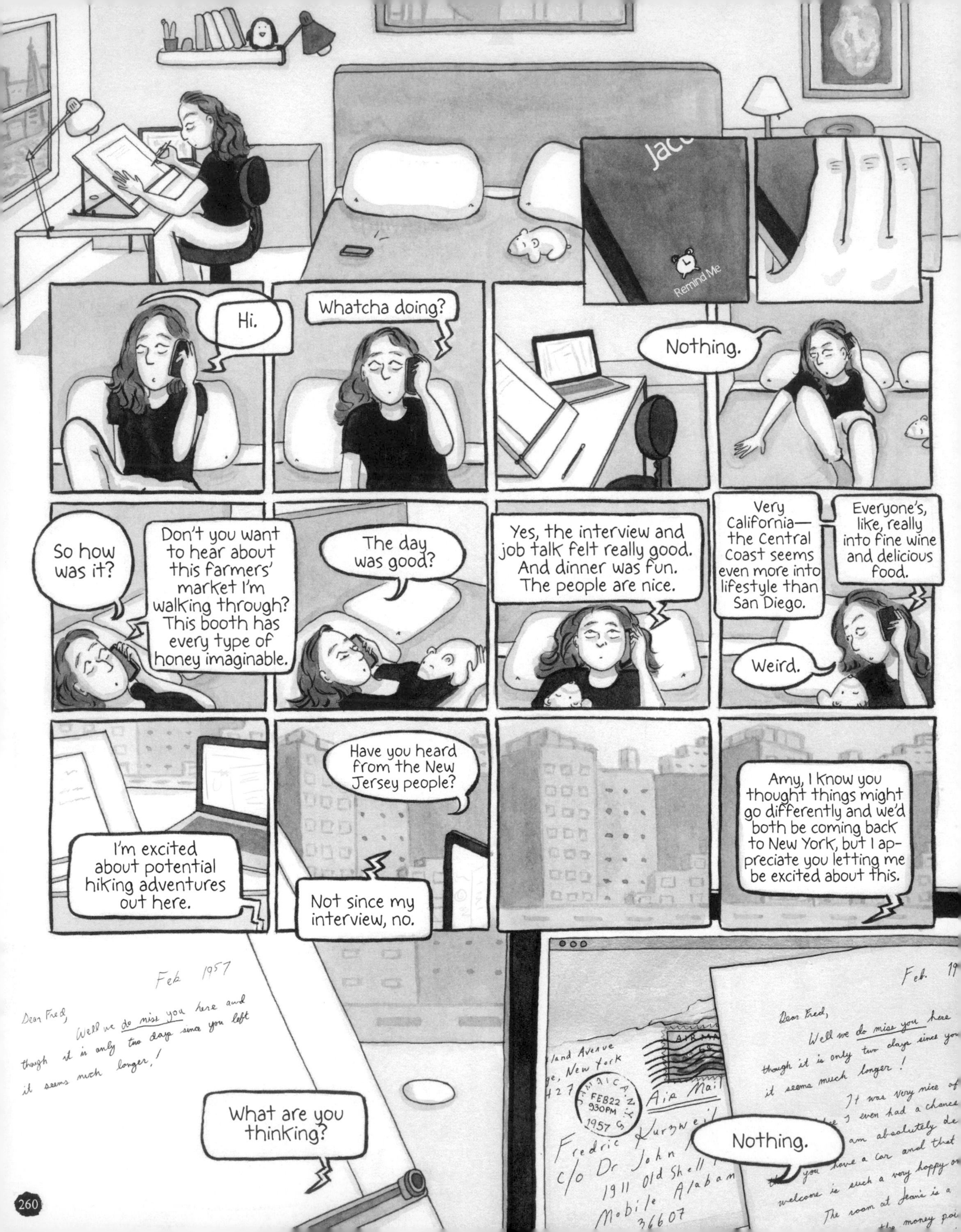
Jac
Remind Me
Hi.
Whatcha doing?
Nothing.
So how was it?
Don't you want to hear about this farmers' market I'm walking through? This booth has every type of honey imaginable.
The day was good?
Yes, the interview and job talk felt really good. And dinner was fun. The people are nice.
Very California—the central coast seems even more into lifestyle than San Diego.
Everyone's, like, really into fine wine and delicious food.
Weird.
I'm excited about potential hiking adventures out here.
Have you heard from the New Jersey people?
Not since my interview, no.
Amy, I know you thought things might go differently and we'd both be coming back to New York, but I appreciate you letting me be excited about this.
Feb 1957
Dear Fred,
Well we do miss you here and though it is only two days since you left it seems much longer!
What are you thinking?
Air Mail
FEB22 930PM 1957
Fredric Kurzweil
c/o Dr John
1911 Old Shell
Mobile Alabam
36607
Nothing.

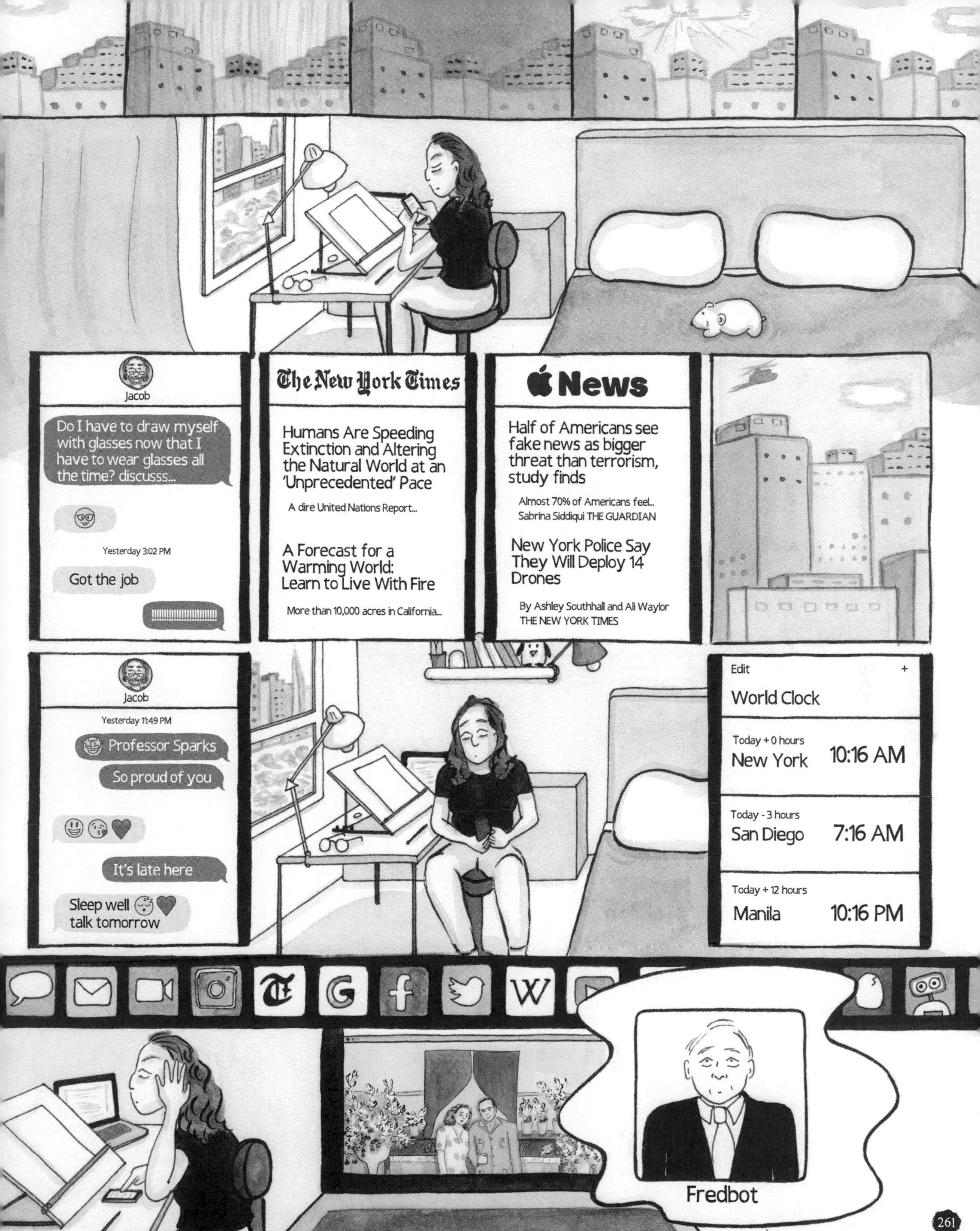
Jacob
Do I have to draw myself with glasses now that I have to wear glasses all the time? discusss...
Yesterday 3:02 PM
Got the job
The New York Times
Humans Are Speeding Extinction and Altering the Natural World at an 'Unprecedented' Pace
A dire United Nations Report...
A Forecast for a Warming World: Learn to Live With Fire
More than 10,000 acres in California...
News
Half of Americans see fake news as bigger threat than terrorism, study finds
Almost 70% of Americans feel...
Sabrina Siddiqui THE GUARDIAN
New York Police Say They Will Deploy 14 Drones
By Ashley Southhall and Ali Waylor
THE NEW YORK TIMES
Jacob
Yesterday 11:49 PM
Professor Sparks
So proud of you
It's late here
Sleep well
talk tomorrow
Edit
+
World Clock
Today + 0 hours
New York
10:16 AM
Today - 3 hours
San Diego
7:16 AM
Today + 12 hours
Manila
10:16 PM
Fredbot

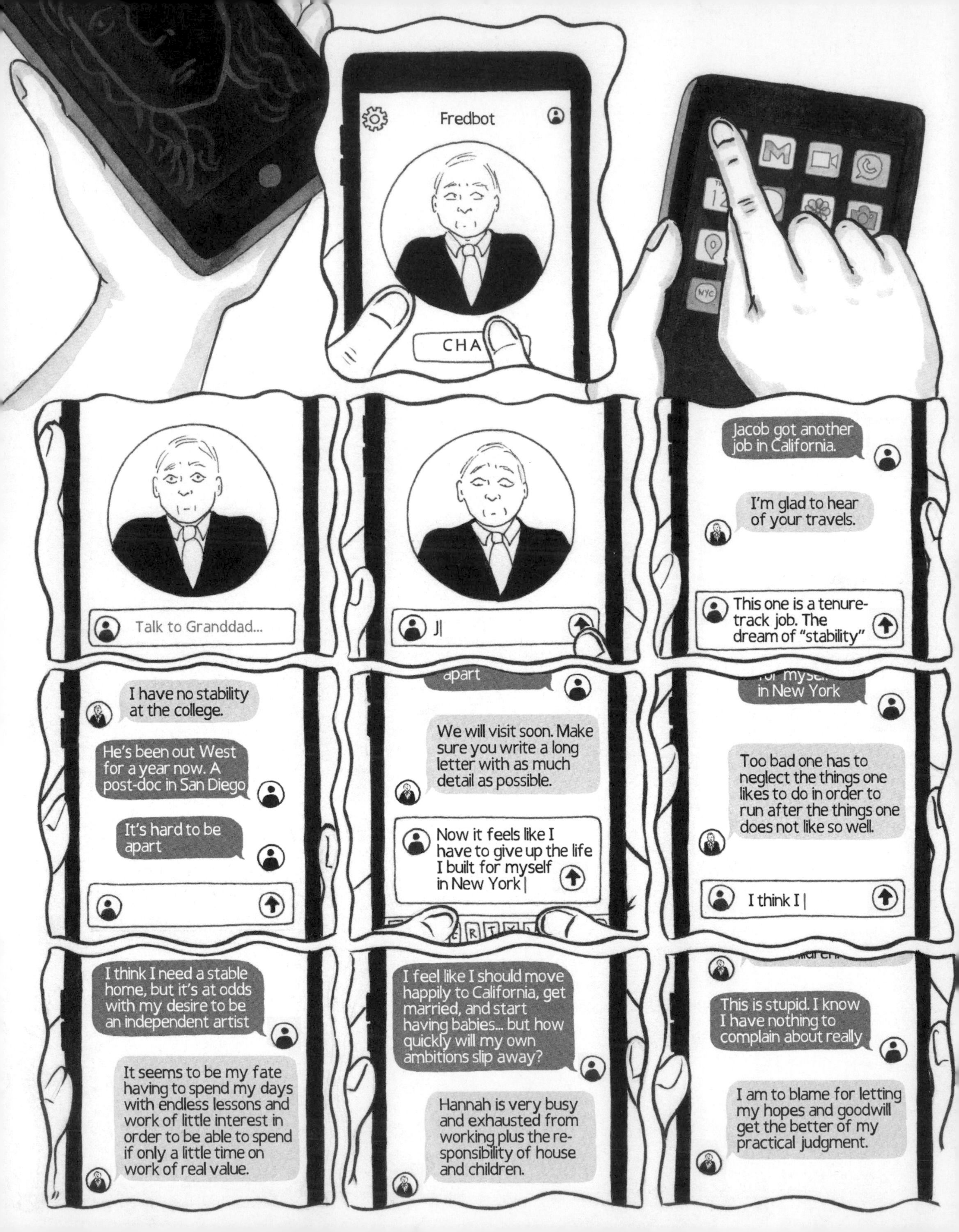
Fredbot
CHA
Talk to Granddad...
J|
Jacob got another job in California.
I'm glad to hear of your travels.
This one is a tenure-track job. The dream of "stability"
I have no stability at the college.
He's been out West for a year now. A post-doc in San Diego
It's hard to be apart
apart
We will visit soon. Make sure you write a long letter with as much detail as possible.
Now it feels like I have to give up the life I built for myself in New York|
in New York
Too bad one has to neglect the things one likes to do in order to run after the things one does not like so well.
I think I |
I think I need a stable home, but it's at odds with my desire to be an independent artist
It seems to be my fate having to spend my days with endless lessons and work of little interest in order to be able to spend if only a little time on work of real value.
I feel like I should move happily to California, get married, and start having babies... but how quickly will my own ambitions slip away?
Hannah is very busy and exhausted from working plus the re-sponsibility of house and children.
This is stupid. I know I have nothing to complain about really
I am to blame for letting my hopes and goodwill get the better of my practical judgment.

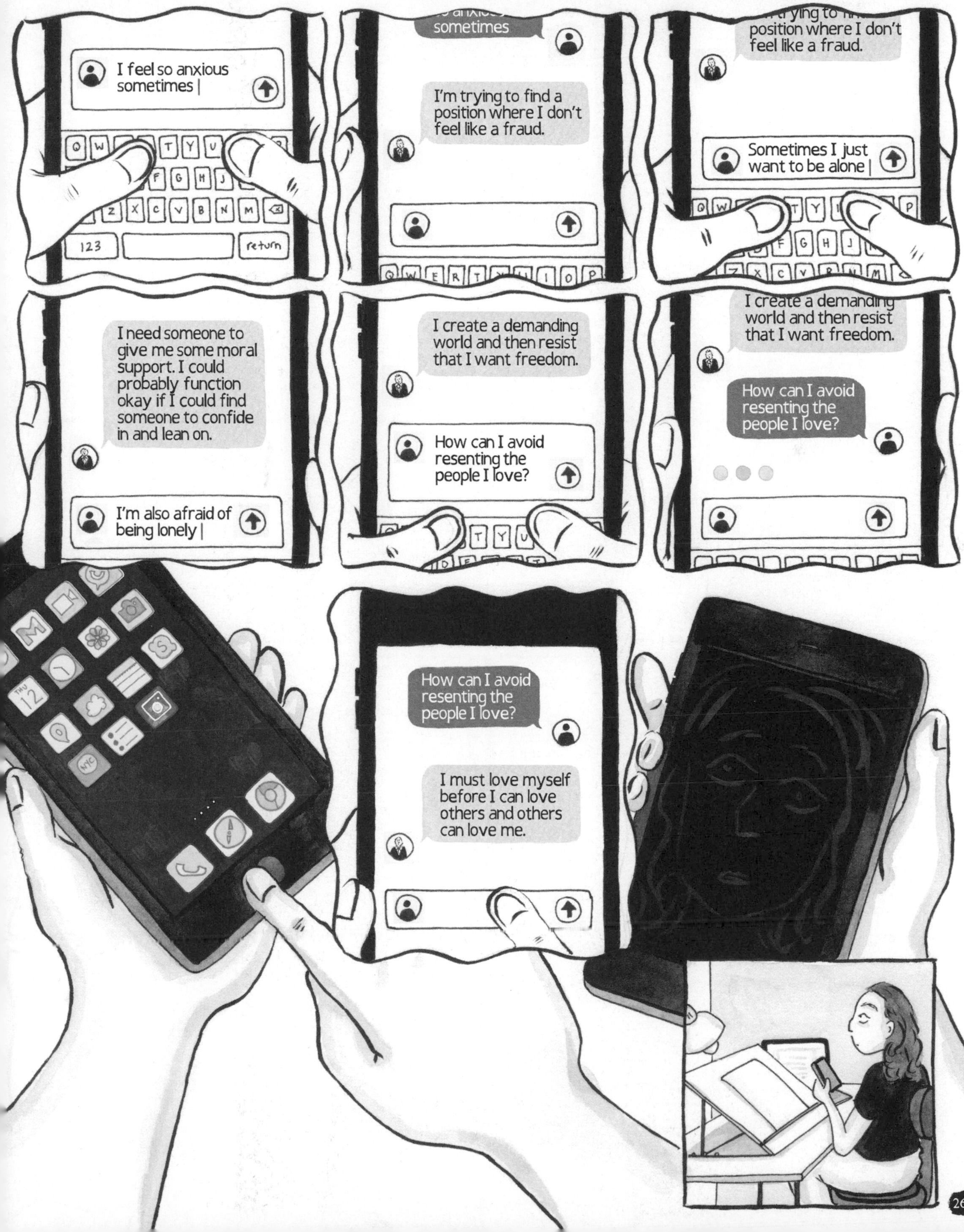
I feel so anxious sometimes |
sometimes
I'm trying to find a position where I don't feel like a fraud.
position where I don't feel like a fraud.
Sometimes I just want to be alone |
I need someone to give me some moral support. I could probably function okay if I could find someone to confide in and lean on.
I'm also afraid of being lonely |
I create a demanding world and then resist that I want freedom.
How can I avoid resenting the people I love?
world and then resist that I want freedom.
How can I avoid resenting the people I love?
How can I avoid resenting the people I love?
I must love myself before I can love others and others can love me.

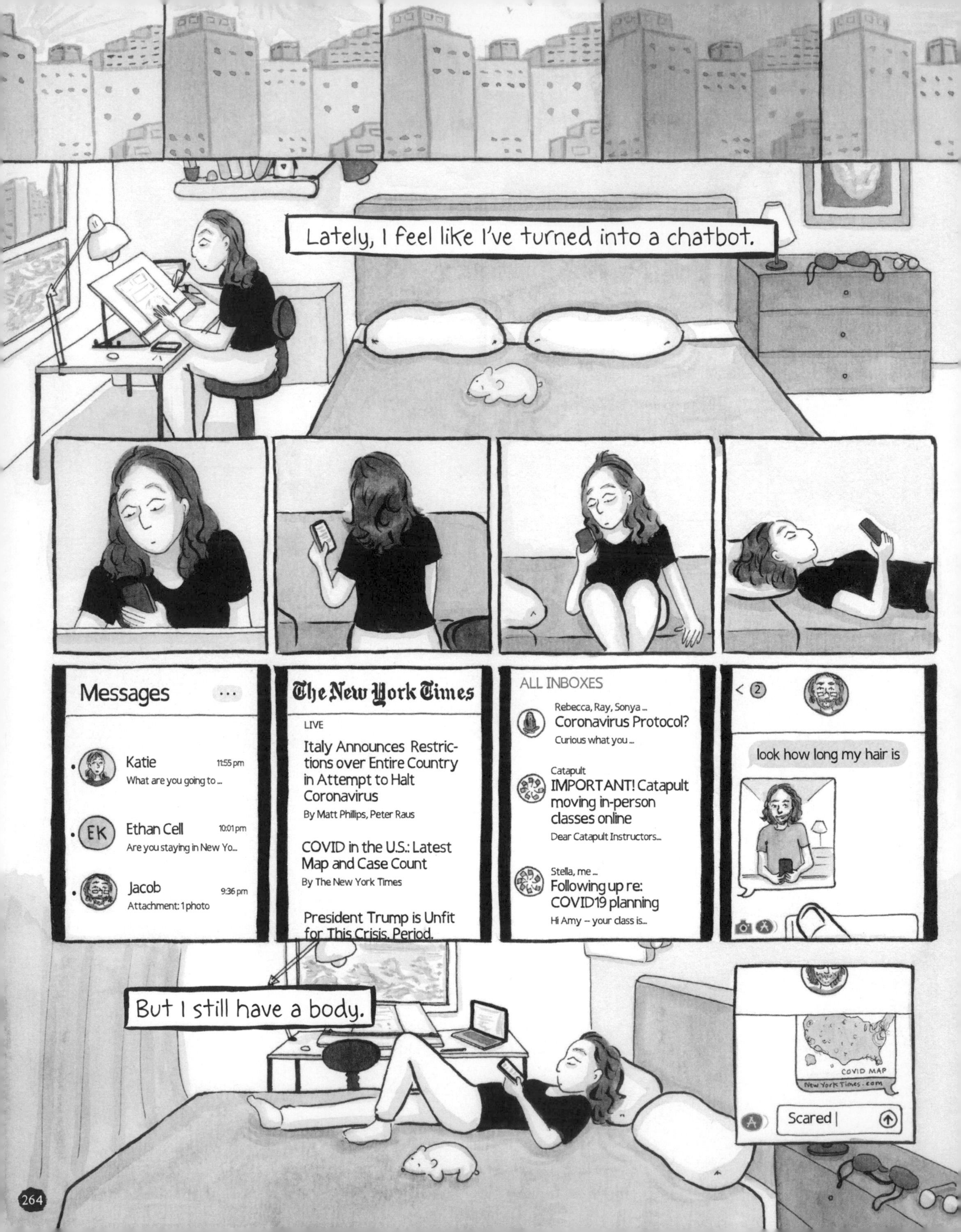

Lately, I feel like I've turned into a chatbot.
Messages
Katie
11:55 pm
What are you going to ...
EK
Ethan Cell
10:01 pm
Are you staying in New Yo...
Jacob
9:36 pm
Attachment: 1 photo
The New York Times
LIVE
Italy Announces Restrictions over Entire Country in Attempt to Halt Coronavirus
By Matt Phillips, Peter Raus
COVID in the U.S.: Latest Map and Case Count
By The New York Times
President Trump is Unfit for This Crisis. Period.
ALL INBOXES
Rebecca, Ray, Sonya ...
Coronavirus Protocol?
Curious what you ...
Catapult
IMPORTANT! Catapult moving in-person classes online
Dear Catapult Instructors...
Stella, me ...
Following up re: COVID19 planning
Hi Amy -- your class is...
< 2
look how long my hair is
But I still have a body.
COVID MAP
New York Times.com
Scared |

Jacob

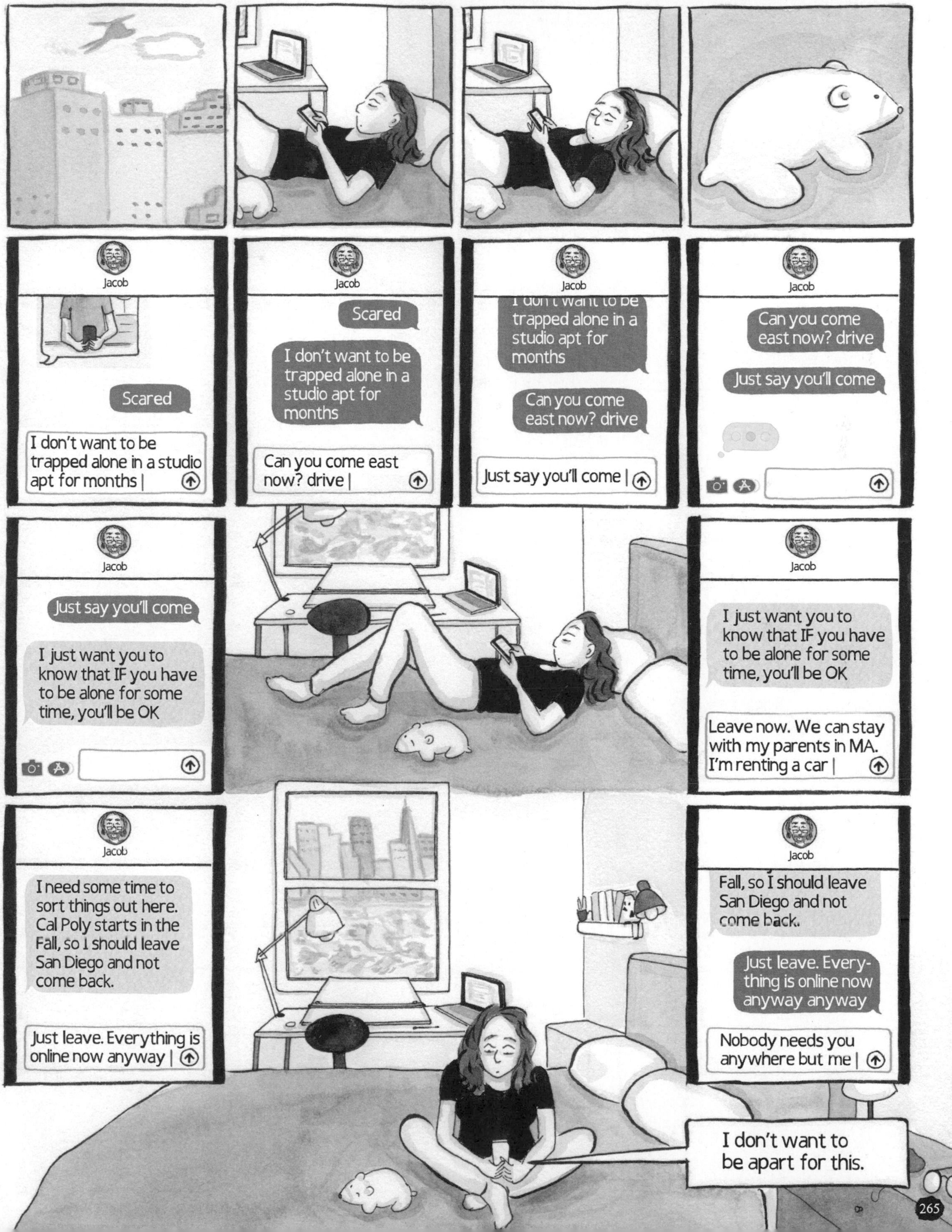

Scared

I don't want to be trapped alone in a studio apt for months |

Jacob

Scared

I don't want to be trapped alone in a studio apt for months

Can you come east now? drive |

Jacob

I don't want to be trapped alone in a studio apt for months

Can you come east now? drive

Just say you'll come |

Jacob

Can you come east now? drive

Just say you'll come

Jacob

Just say you'll come

I just want you to know that IF you have to be alone for some time, you'll be OK

Jacob

I just want you to know that IF you have to be alone for some time, you'll be OK

Leave now. We can stay with my parents in MA. I'm renting a car |

Jacob

I need some time to sort things out here. Cal Poly starts in the Fall, so I should leave San Diego and not come back.

Just leave. Everything is online now anyway |

Jacob

Fall, so I should leave San Diego and not come back.

Just leave. Everything is online now anyway anyway

Nobody needs you anywhere but me |

I don't want to be apart for this.

265

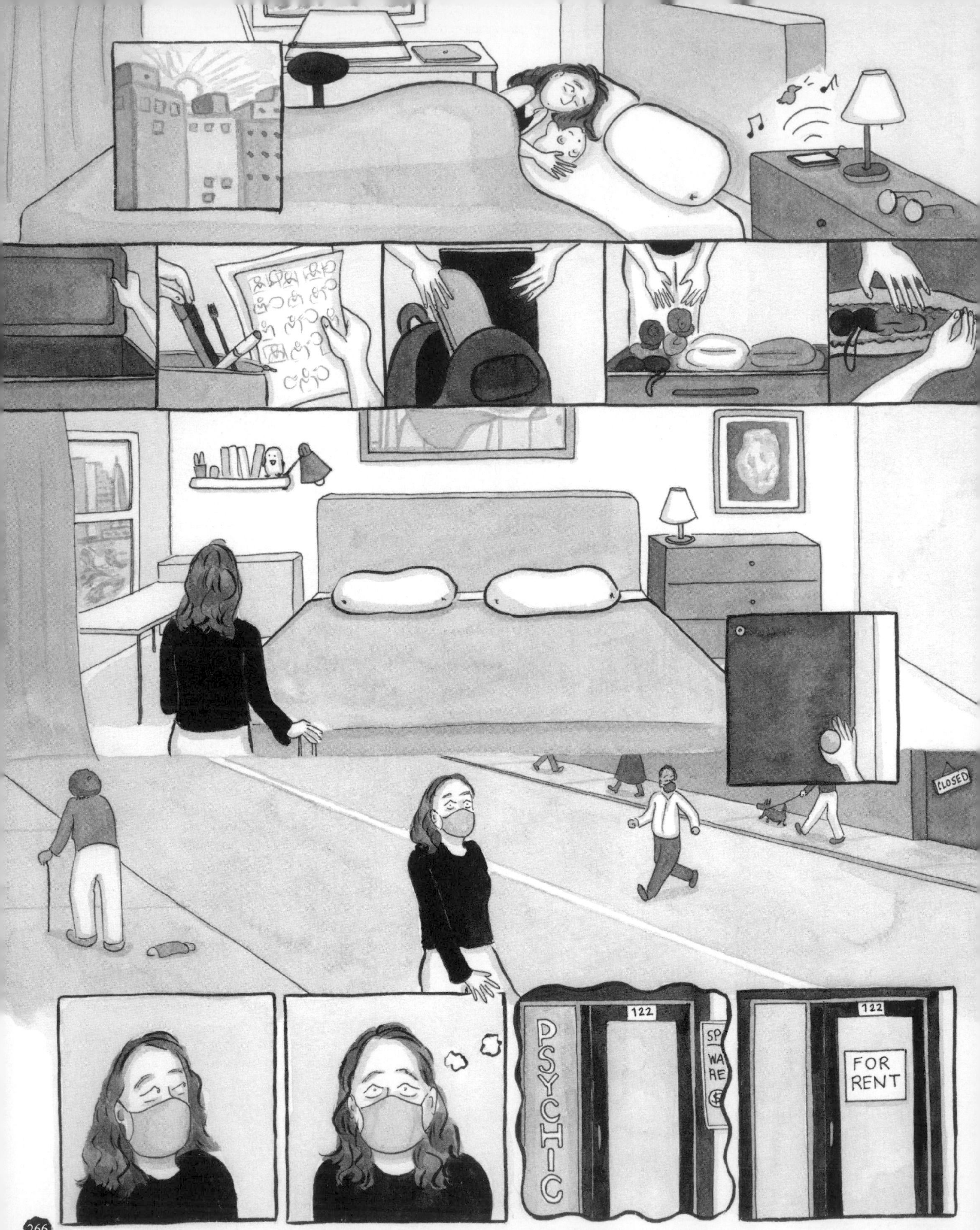
CLOSED
PSYCHIC
122
SP
WA
RE
122
FOR RENT

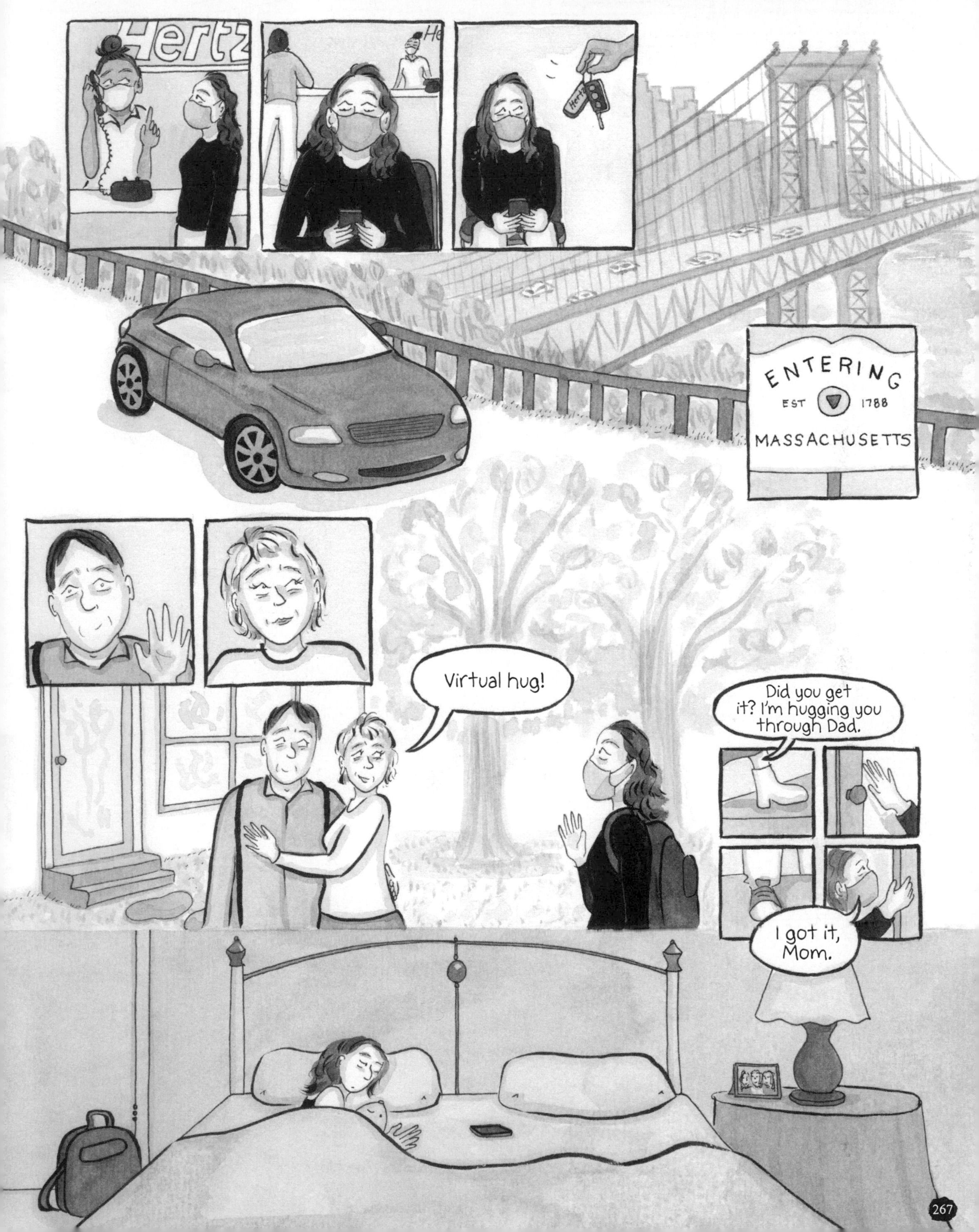
Hertz
ENTERING
EST 1788
MASSACHUSETTS
Virtual hug!
Did you get it? I'm hugging you through Dad.
I got it, Mom.

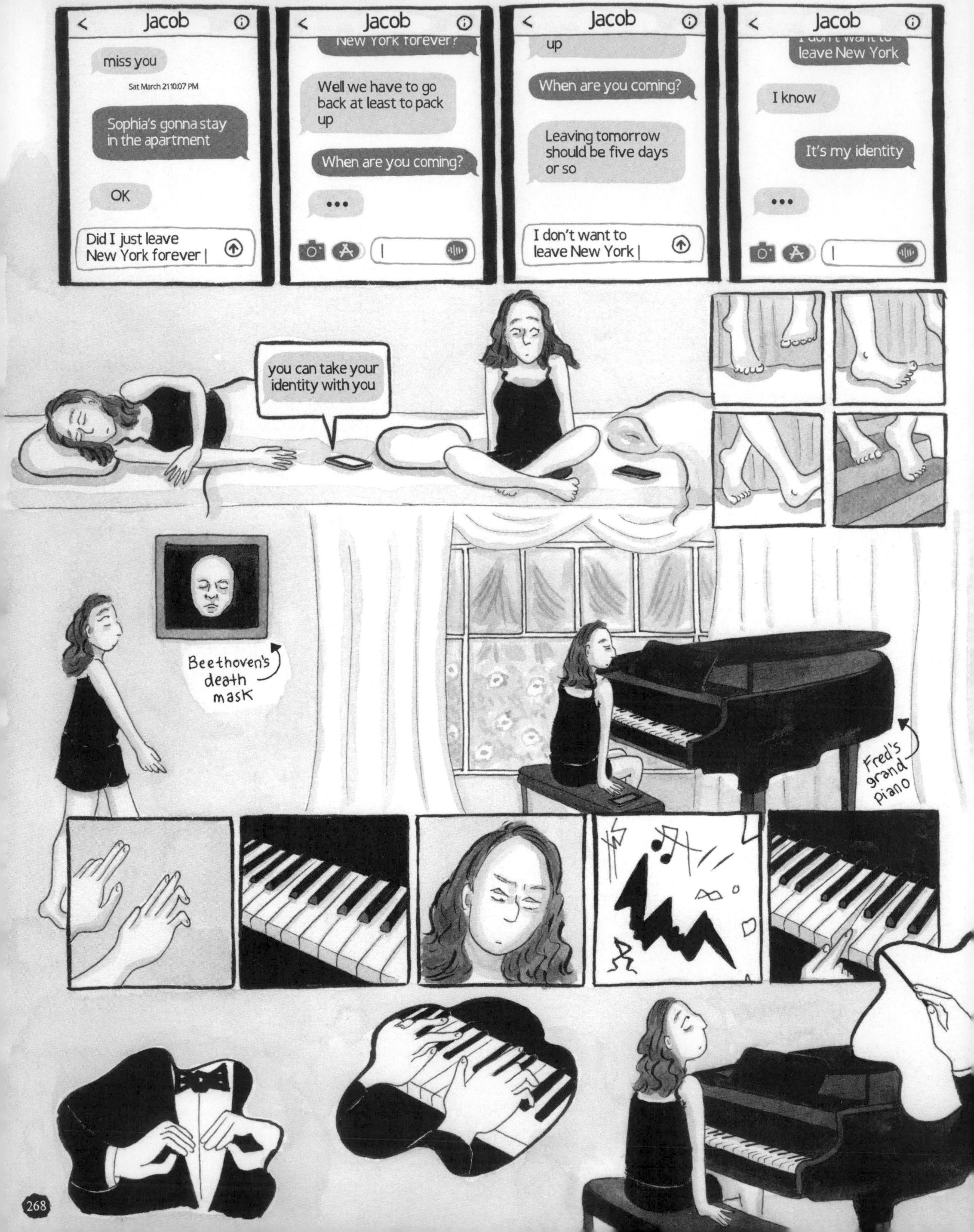
Jacob
miss you
Sat March 21 10:07 PM
Sophia's gonna stay in the apartment
OK
Did I just leave New York forever
Jacob
New York forever?
Well we have to go back at least to pack up
When are you coming?
•••
Jacob
up
When are you coming?
Leaving tomorrow should be five days or so
I don't want to leave New York
Jacob
leave New York
I know
It's my identity
•••
you can take your identity with you
Beethoven's death mask
Fred's grand piano

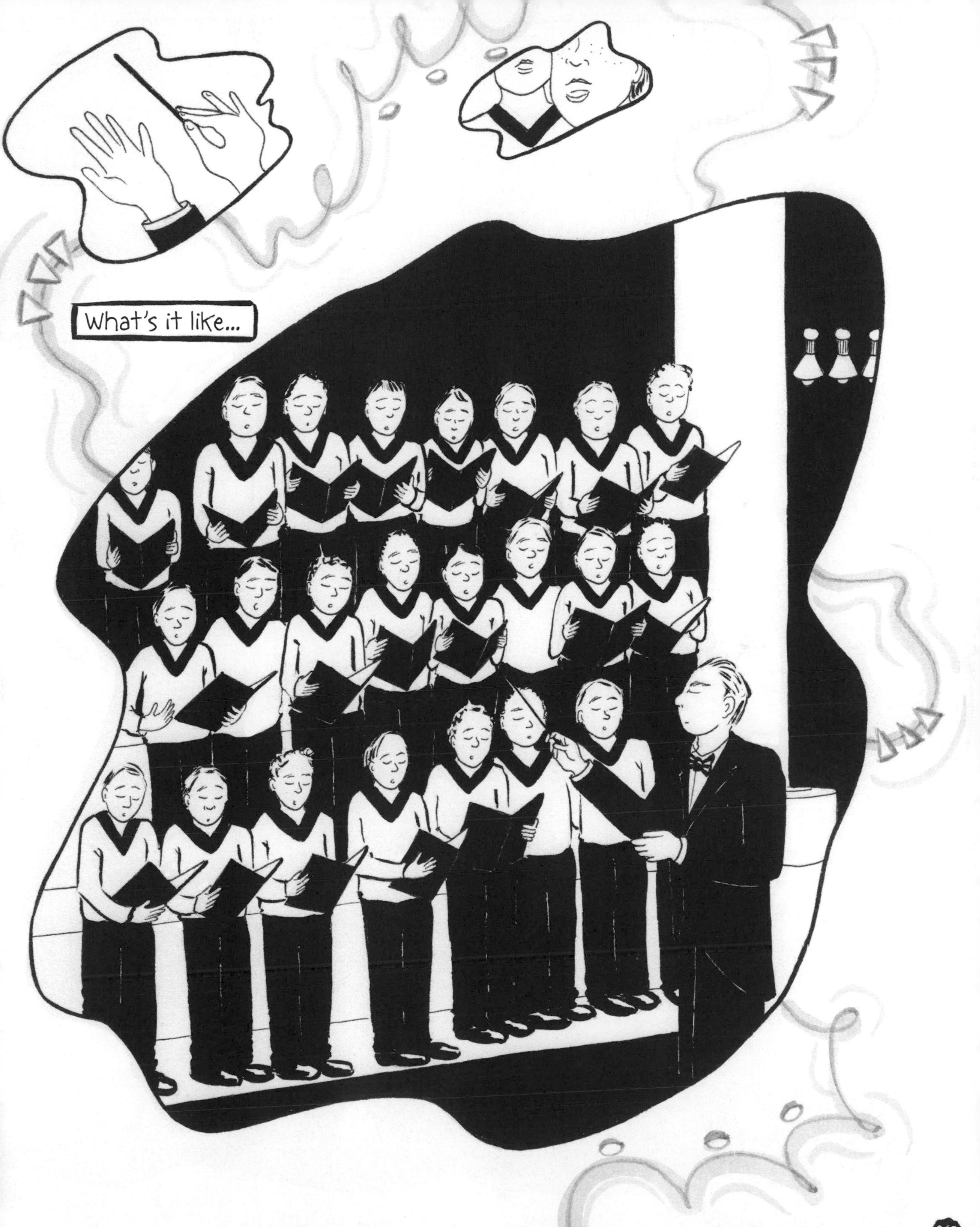
What's it like...

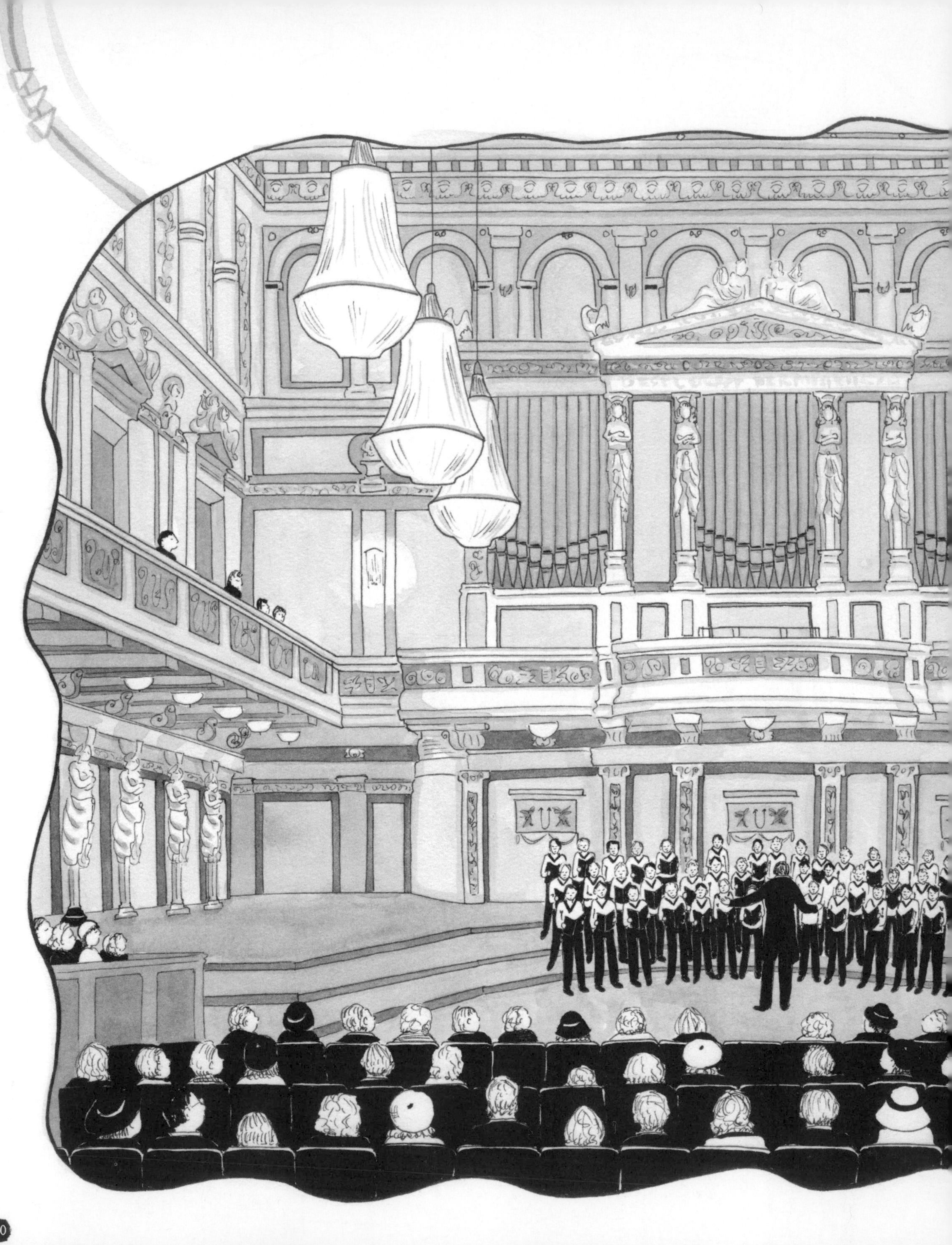

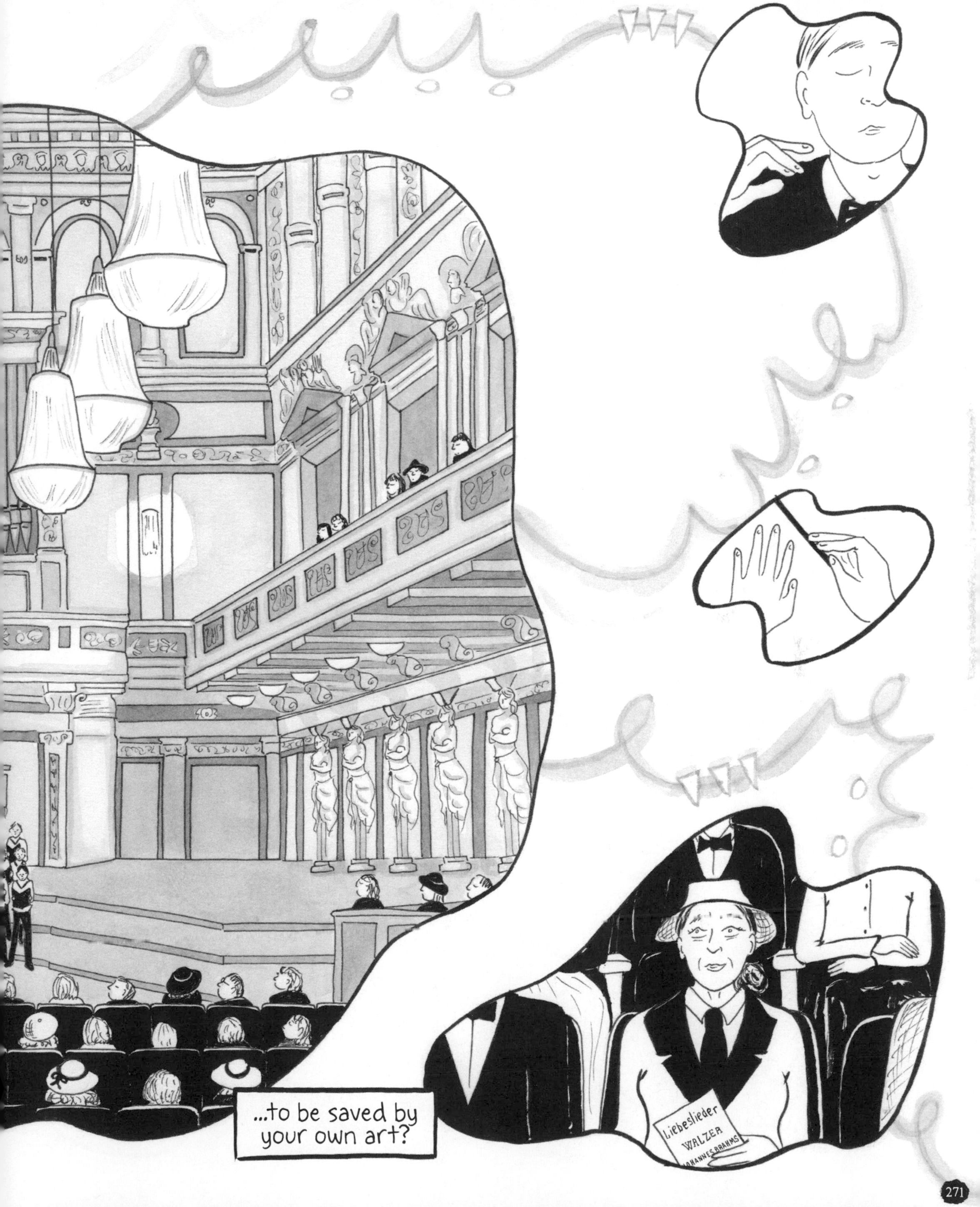
...to be saved by your own art?
Liebeslieder
WALZER
JOHANNES BRAHMS

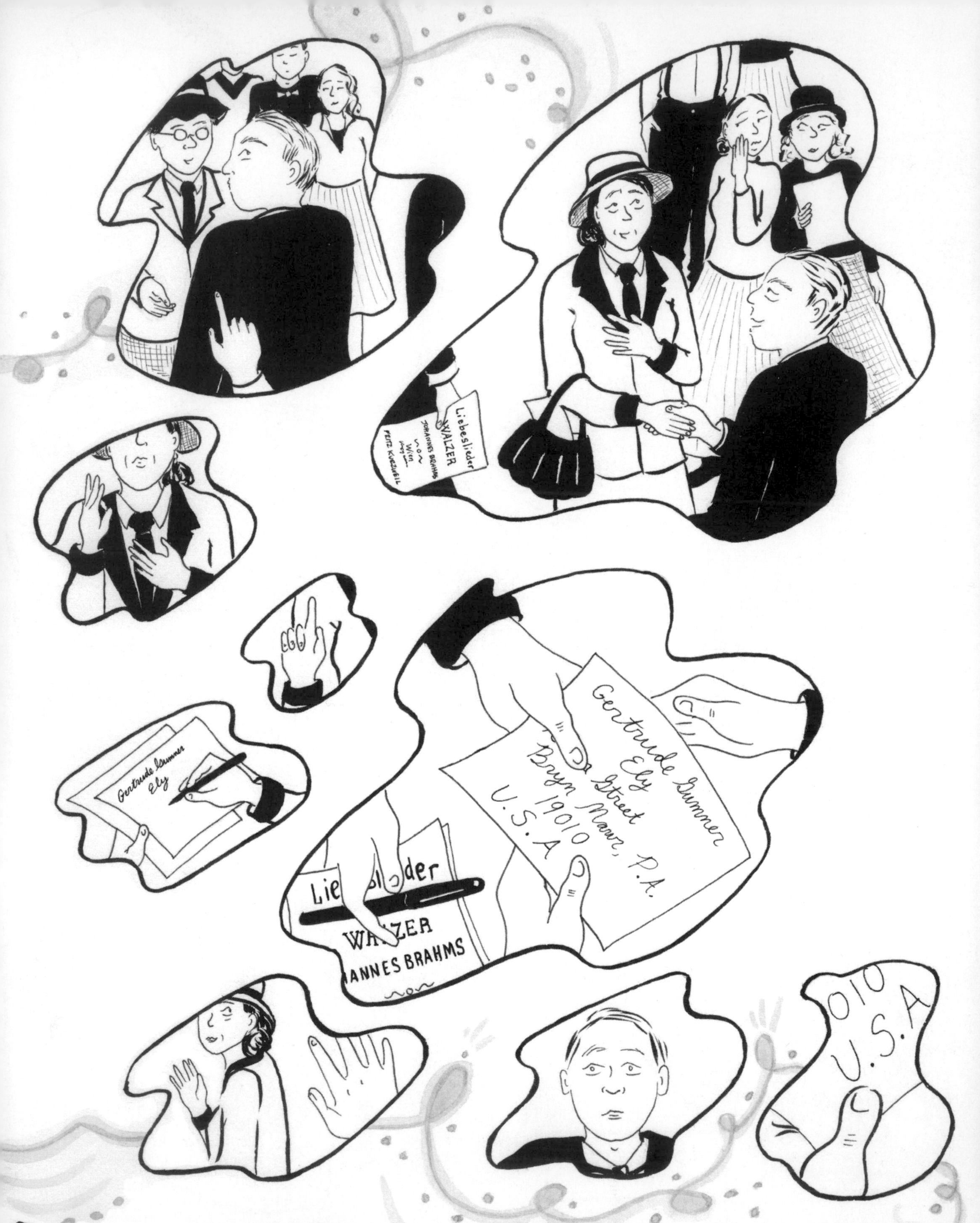
Liebeslieder
WALZER
JOHANNES BRAHMS
Gertrude Sumner
Ely
Gertrude Sumner
Ely
Bryn Street
Bryn Mawr, P.A.
19010
U.S.A
Lie der
WALZER
ANNES BRAHMS
010
U.S.A

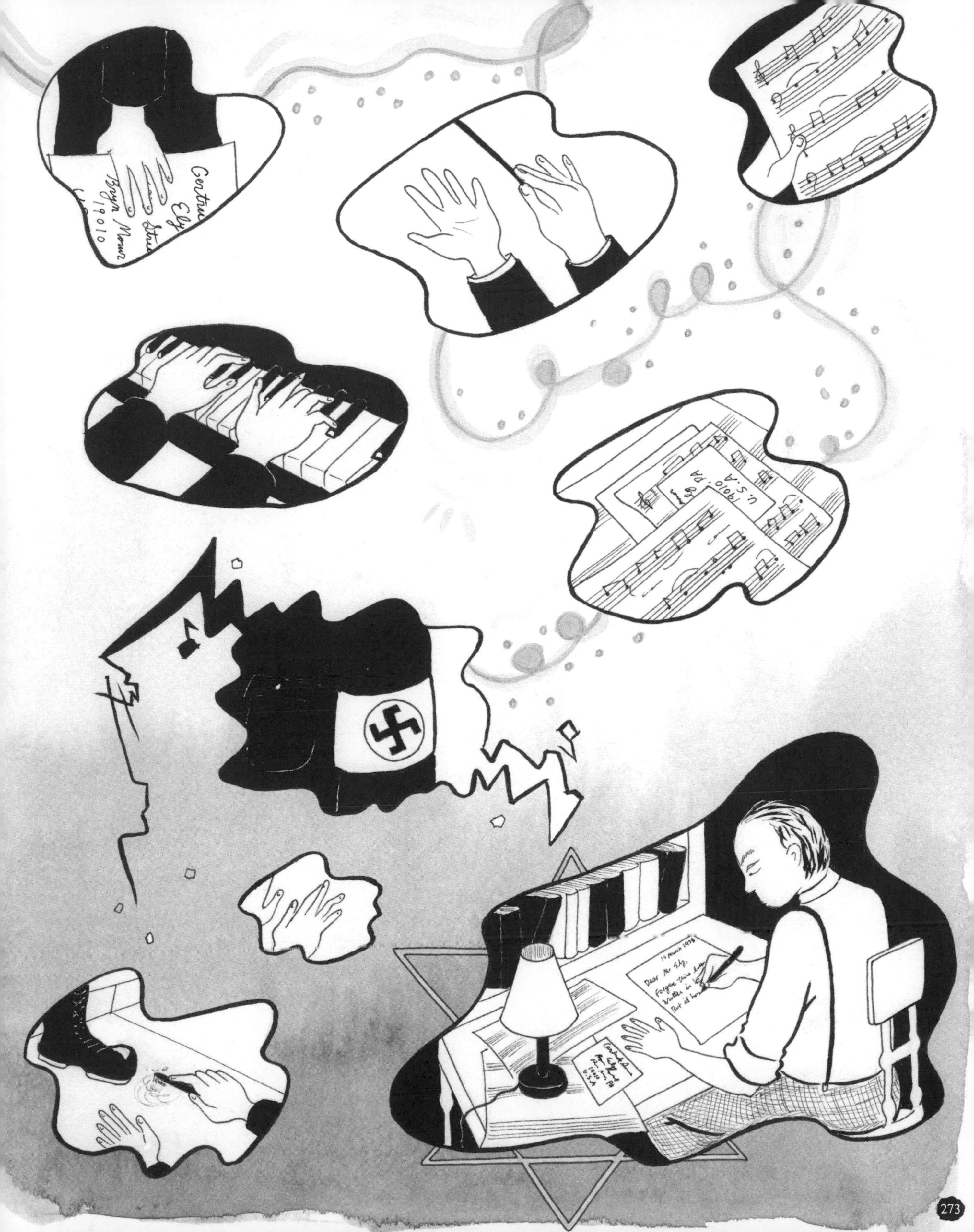
U.S.A
19010 · PA
Dear Mr Ely,

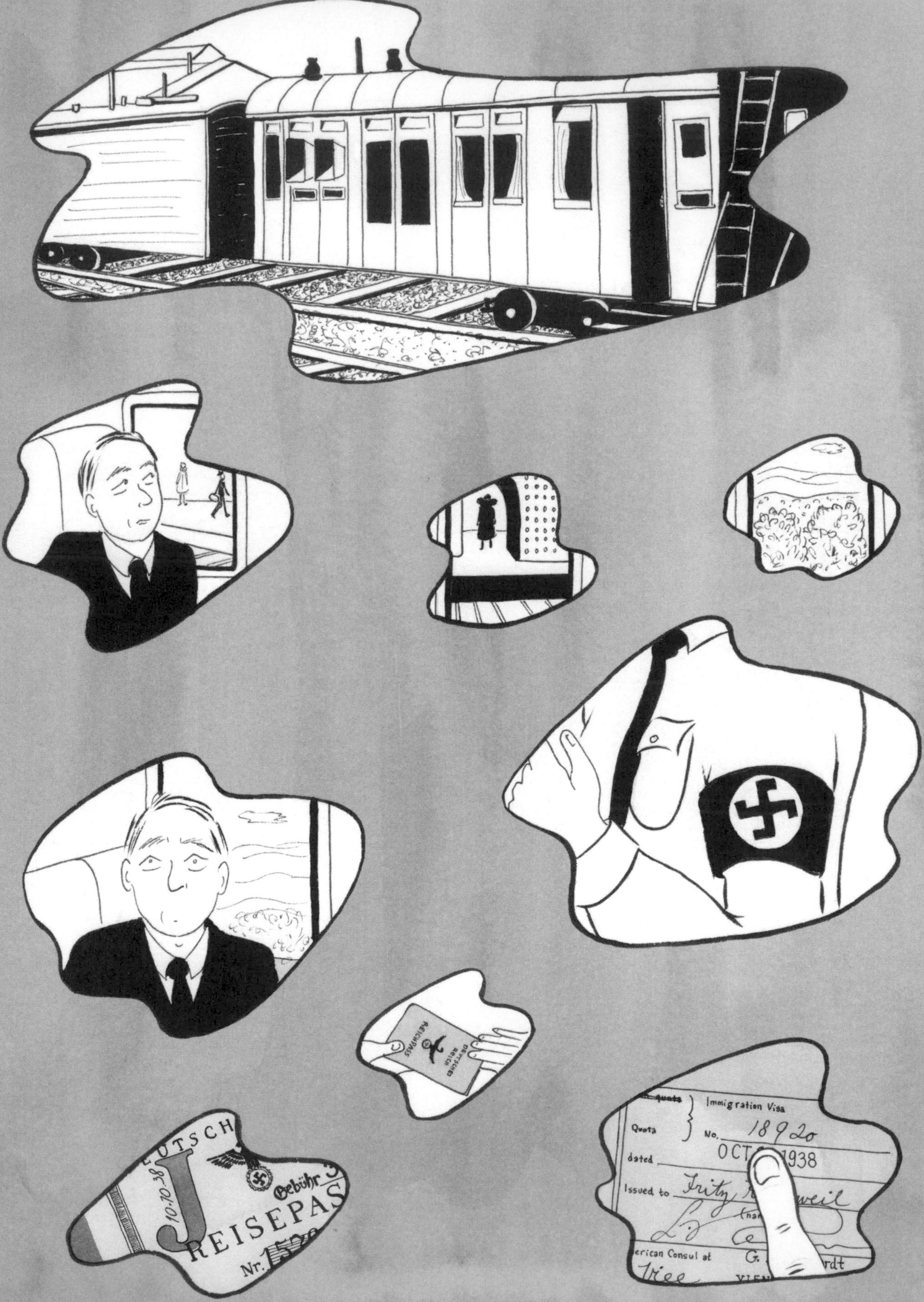
Immigration Visa
Quota
No. 18920
dated OCT 1938
Issued to
erican Consul at
UTSCH
10.10.38
J
Gebühr
REISEPAS
Nr.

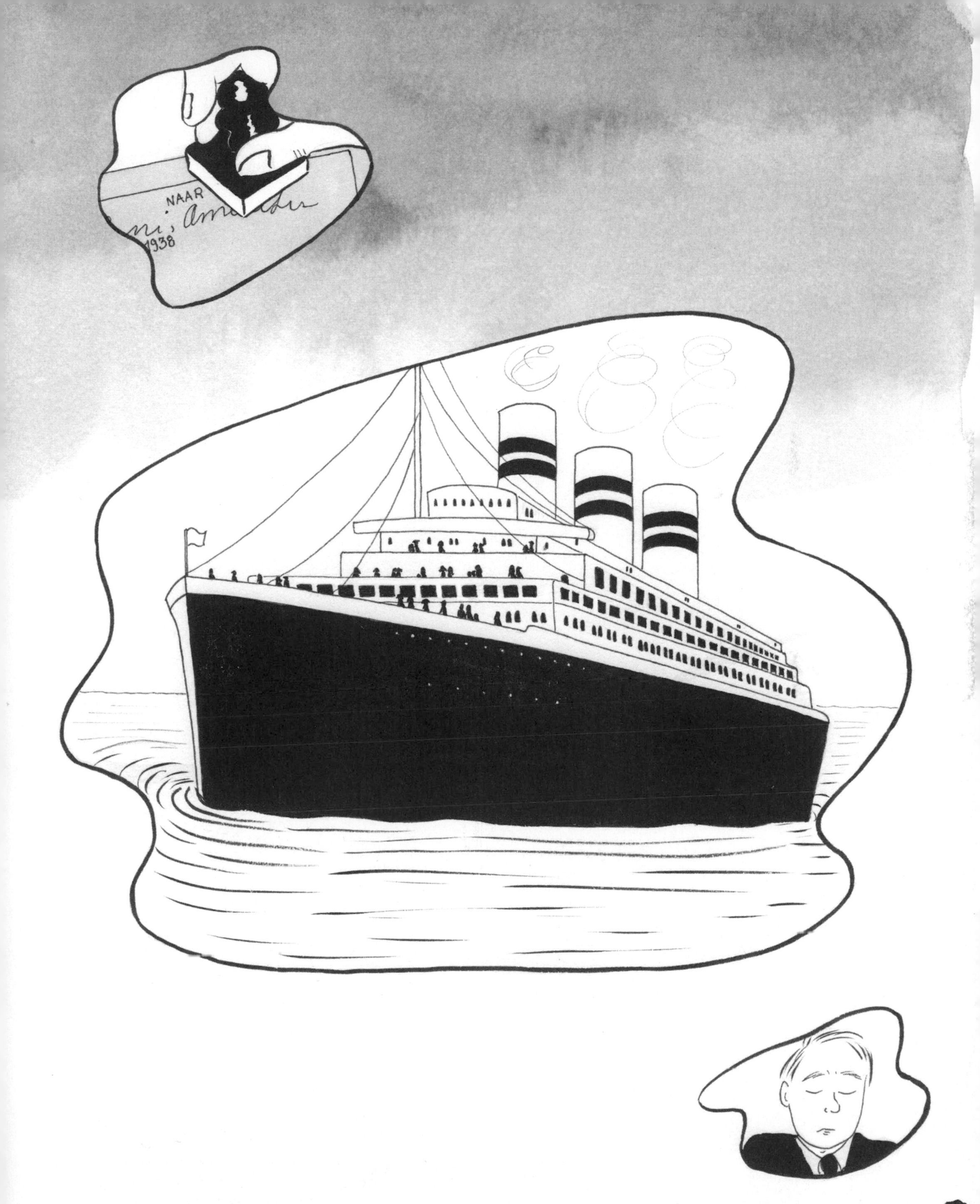
NAAR
1938

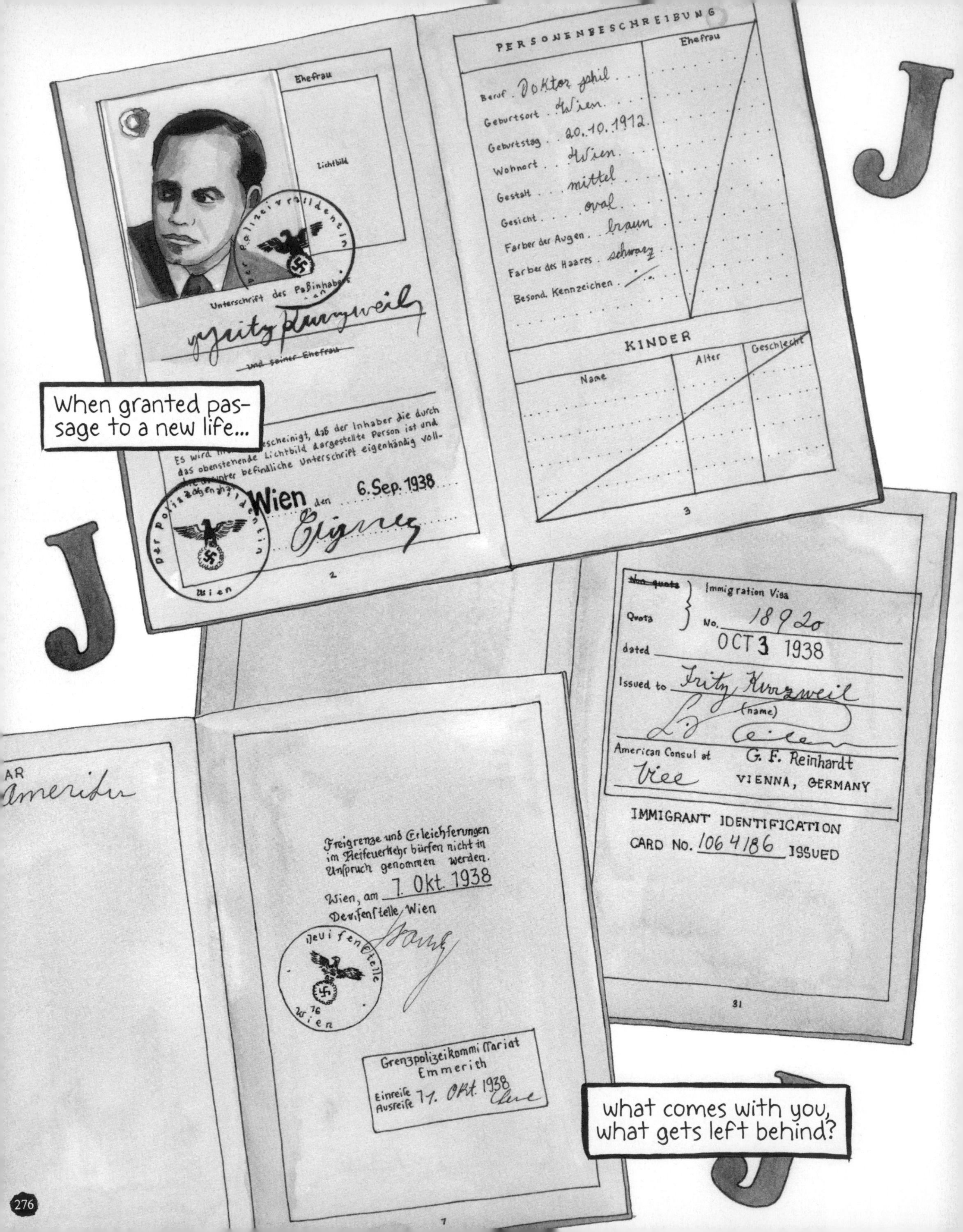
When granted passage to a new life...
PERSONENBESCHREIBUNG
Ehefrau
Lichtbild
Unterschrift des Paßinhabers
und seiner Ehefrau
Beruf Doktor phil
Geburtsort Wien
Geburtstag 20.10.1912
Wohnort Wien
Gestalt mittel
Gesicht oval
Farbe der Augen braun
Farbe des Haares schwarz
Besond. Kennzeichen
KINDER
Name
Alter
Geschlecht
Wien den 6. Sep. 1938
Immigration Visa
Quota
No. 18920
dated OCT 3 1938
Issued to Fritz Kurzweil
(name)
American Consul at
G. F. Reinhardt
VIENNA, GERMANY
IMMIGRANT IDENTIFICATION CARD NO. 1064186 ISSUED
Freigrenze und Erleichterungen im Reiseverkehr dürfen nicht in Anspruch genommen werden.
Wien, am 7. Okt. 1938
Devisenstelle Wien
Grenzpolizeikommissariat Emmerich
Einreise
Ausreise 11. Okt. 1938
what comes with you, what gets left behind?

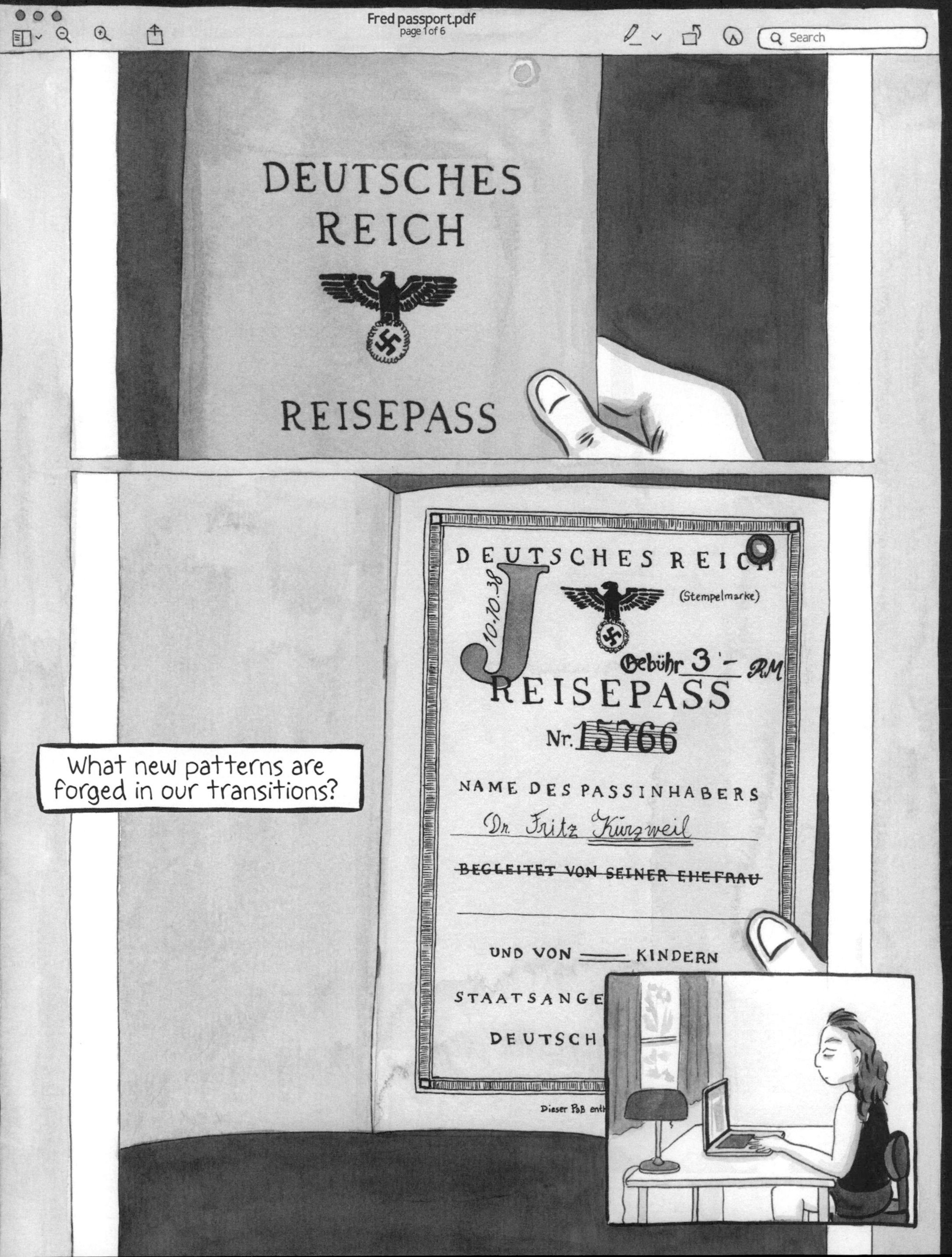
Fred passport.pdf
page 1 of 6
Search
DEUTSCHES
REICH
REISEPASS
What new patterns are forged in our transitions?
DEUTSCHES REICH
10.10.38
J
(Stempelmarke)
Gebühr 3.– RM
REISEPASS
Nr. 15766
NAME DES PASSINHABERS
Dr. Fritz Kurzweil
BEGLEITET VON SEINER EHEFRAU
UND VON —— KINDERN
STAATSANGE
DEUTSCH
Dieser Paß ent

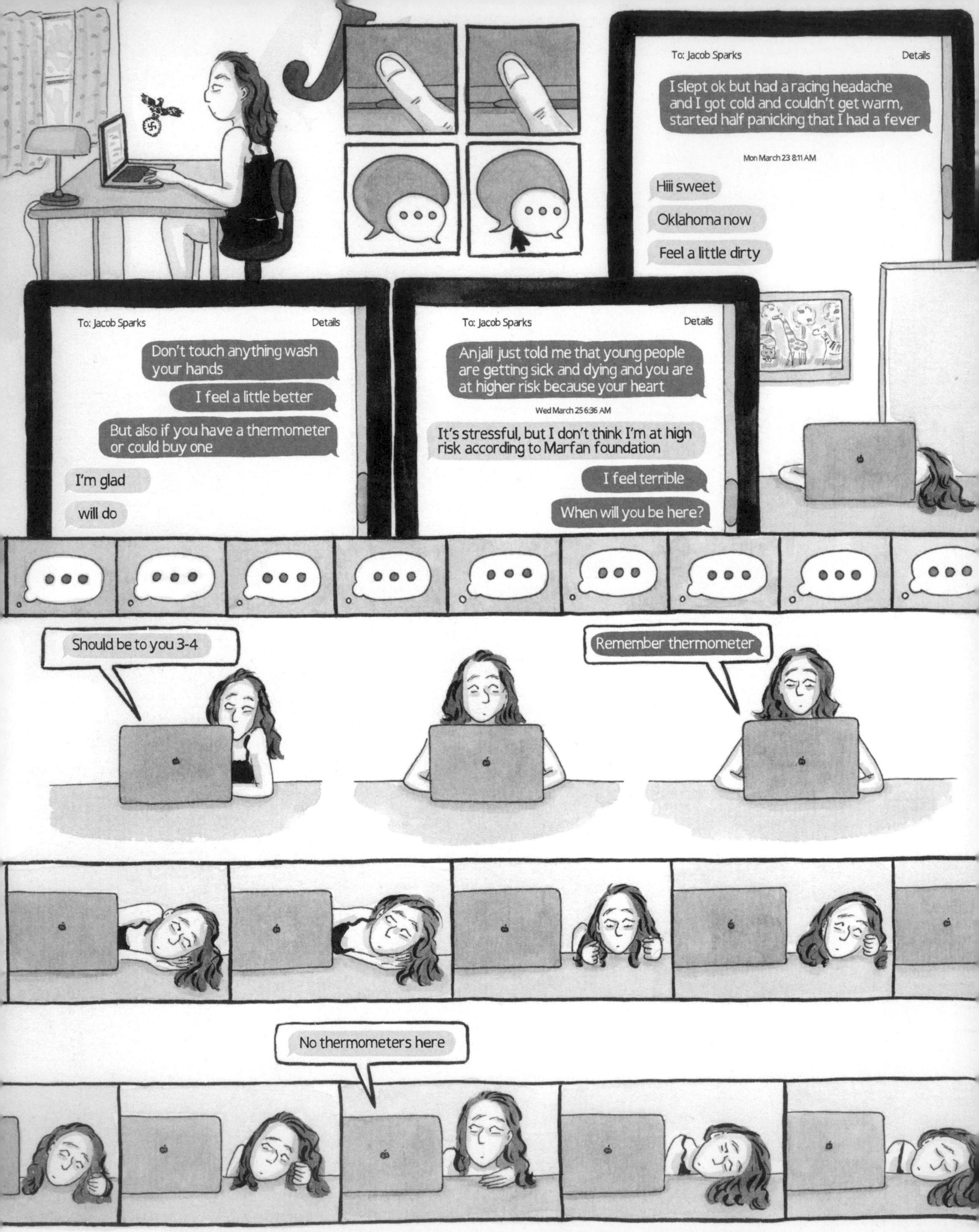
To: Jacob Sparks
Details
I slept ok but had a racing headache and I got cold and couldn't get warm, started half panicking that I had a fever
Mon March 23 8:11 AM
Hiii sweet
Oklahoma now
Feel a little dirty
To: Jacob Sparks
Details
Don't touch anything wash your hands
I feel a little better
But also if you have a thermometer or could buy one
I'm glad
will do
To: Jacob Sparks
Details
Anjali just told me that young people are getting sick and dying and you are at higher risk because your heart
Wed March 25 6:36 AM
It's stressful, but I don't think I'm at high risk according to Marfan foundation
I feel terrible
When will you be here?
Should be to you 3-4
Remember thermometer
No thermometers here

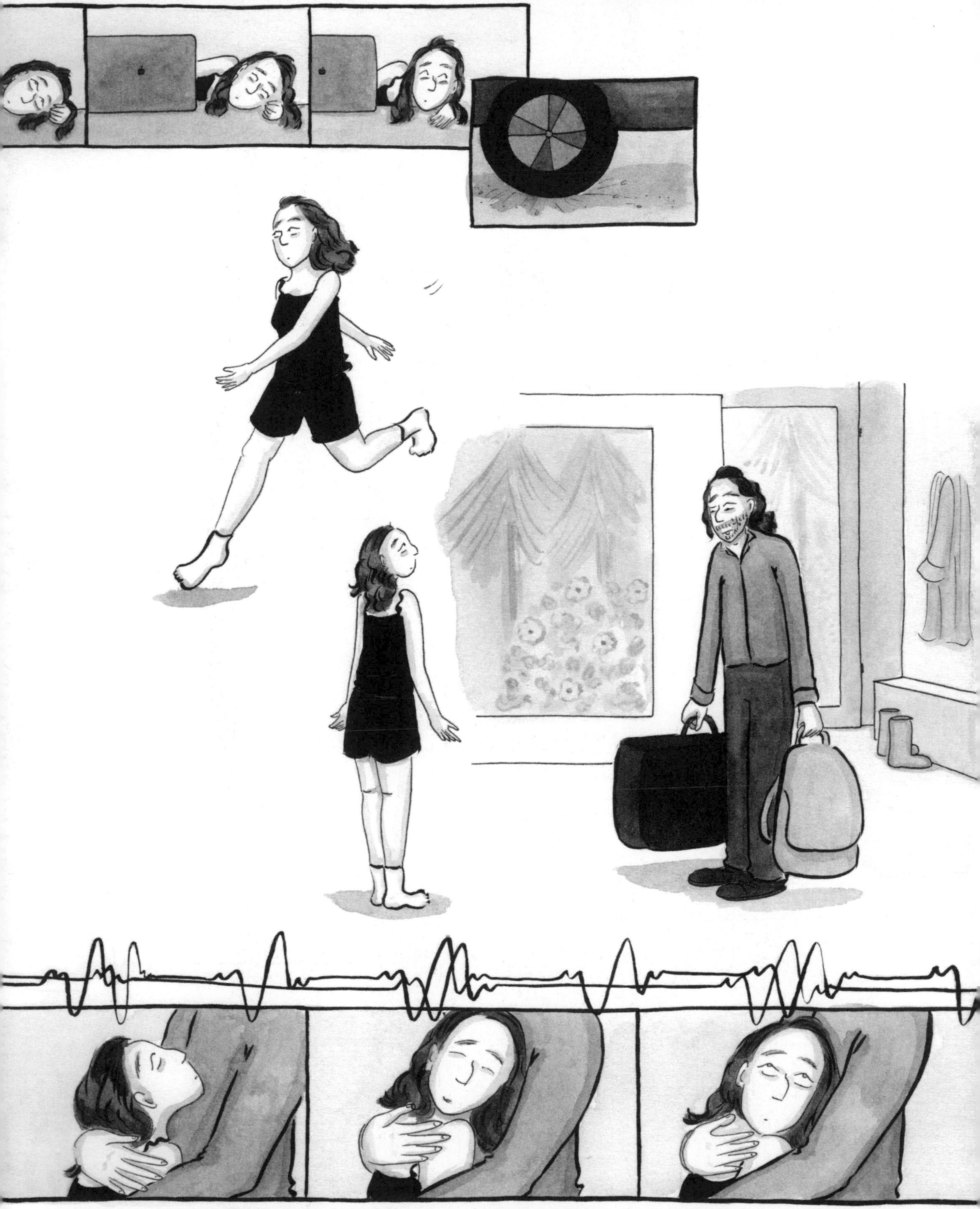

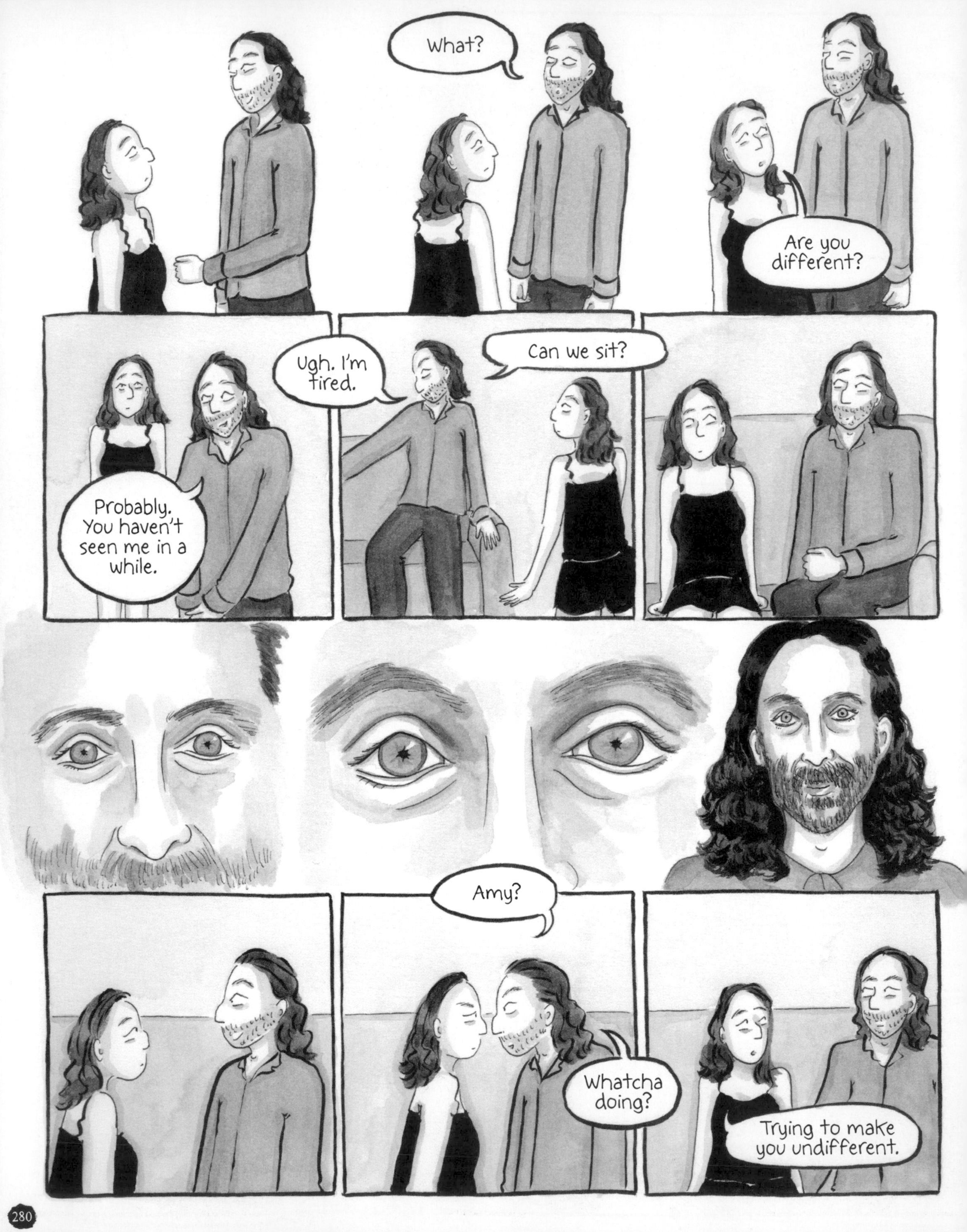
What?
Are you different?
Probably. You haven't seen me in a while.
Ugh. I'm tired.
Can we sit?
Amy?
Whatcha doing?
Trying to make you undifferent.

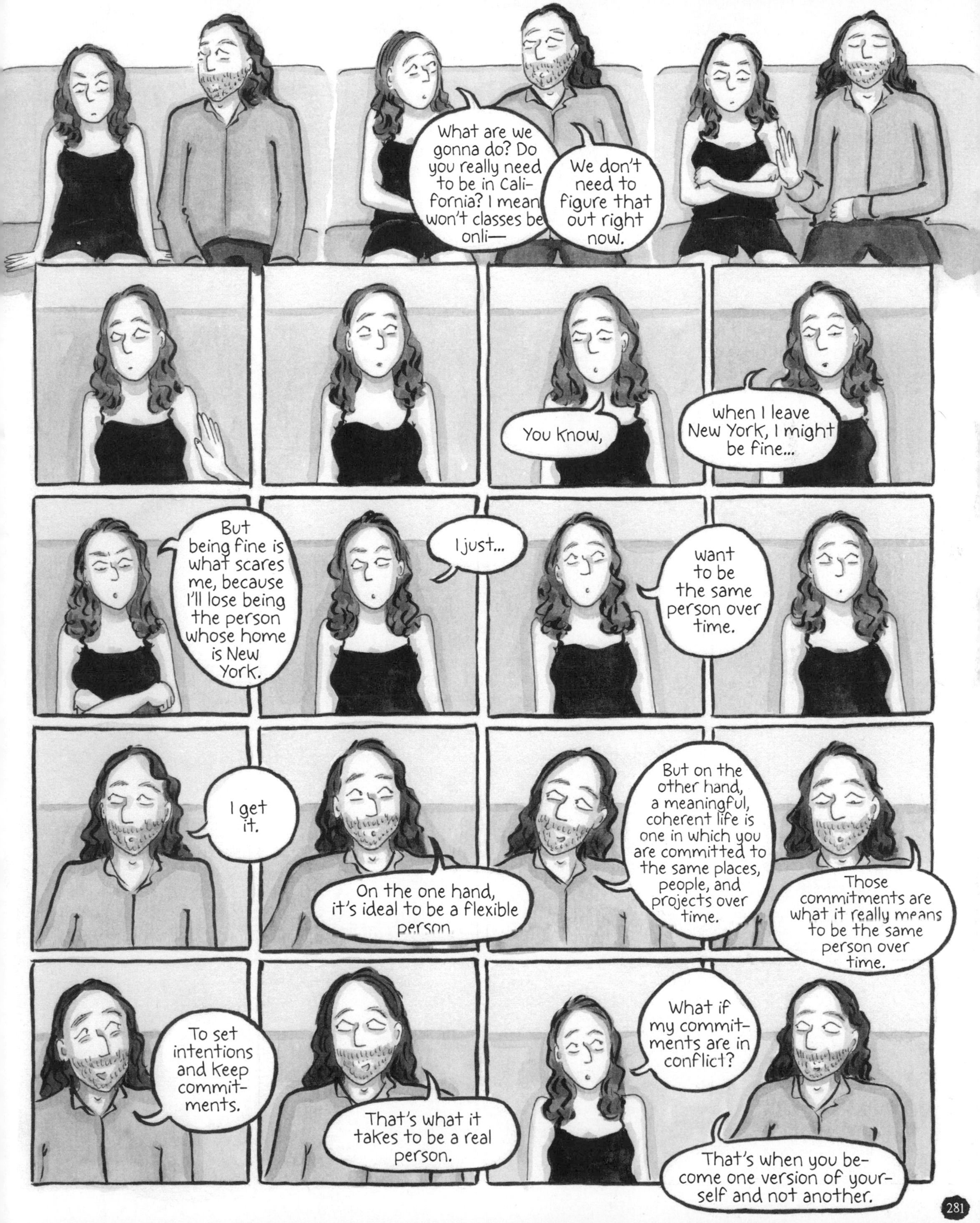
What are we gonna do? Do you really need to be in California? I mean won't classes be onli—
We don't need to figure that out right now.
You know,
when I leave New York, I might be fine...
But being fine is what scares me, because I'll lose being the person whose home is New York.
I just...
want to be the same person over time.
I get it.
On the one hand, it's ideal to be a flexible person.
But on the other hand, a meaningful, coherent life is one in which you are committed to the same places, people, and projects over time.
Those commitments are what it really means to be the same person over time.
To set intentions and keep commitments.
That's what it takes to be a real person.
What if my commitments are in conflict?
That's when you become one version of yourself and not another.

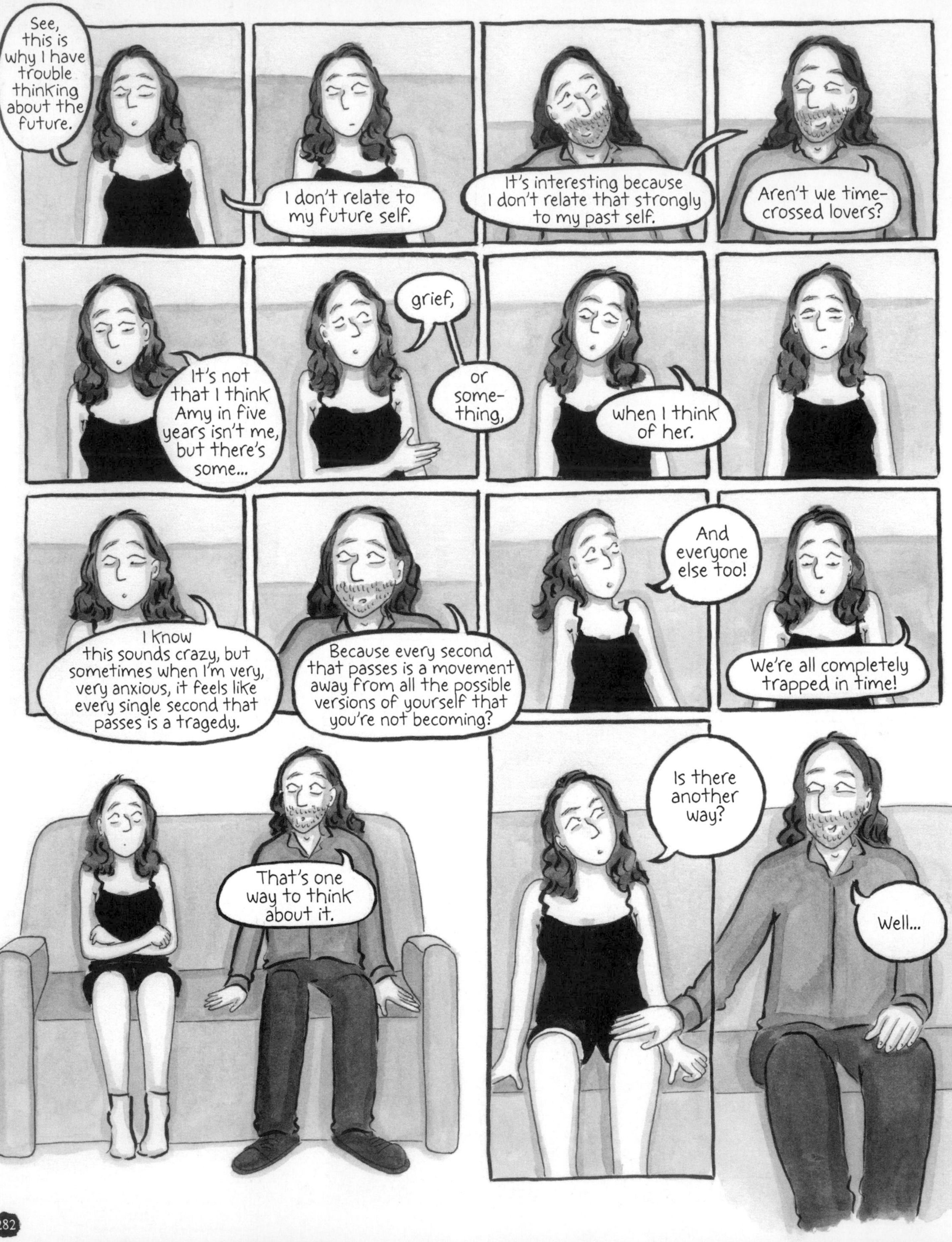
See, this is why I have trouble thinking about the future.
I don't relate to my future self.
It's interesting because I don't relate that strongly to my past self.
Aren't we time-crossed lovers?
It's not that I think Amy in five years isn't me, but there's some...
grief,
or something,
when I think of her.
I know this sounds crazy, but sometimes when I'm very, very anxious, it feels like every single second that passes is a tragedy.
Because every second that passes is a movement away from all the possible versions of yourself that you're not becoming?
And everyone else too!
We're all completely trapped in time!
That's one way to think about it.
Is there another way?
Well...

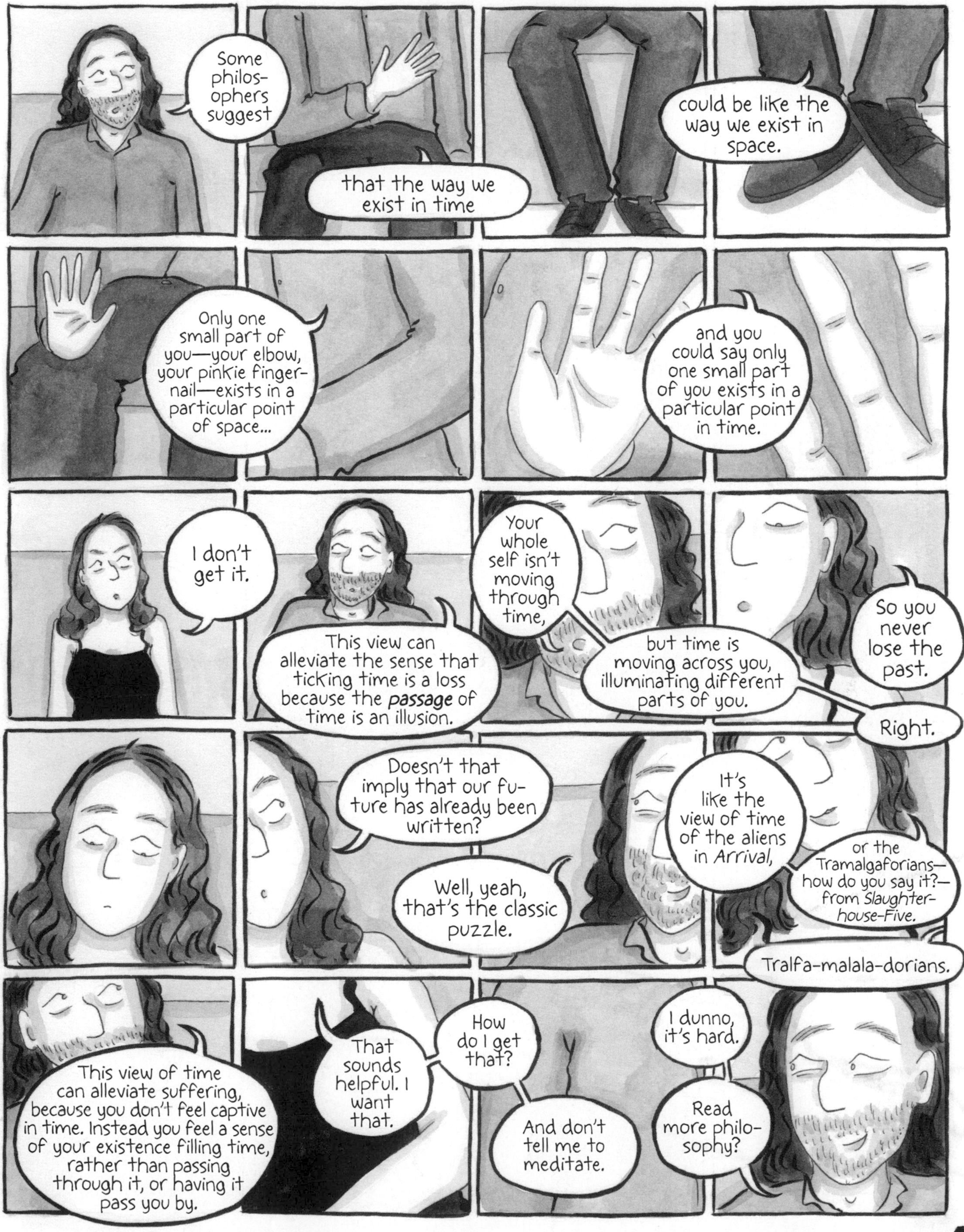
Some philosophers suggest
that the way we exist in time
could be like the way we exist in space.
Only one small part of you—your elbow, your pinkie fingernail—exists in a particular point of space...
and you could say only one small part of you exists in a particular point in time.
I don't get it.
This view can alleviate the sense that ticking time is a loss because the *passage* of time is an illusion.
Your whole self isn't moving through time,
but time is moving across you, illuminating different parts of you.
So you never lose the past.
Right.
Doesn't that imply that our future has already been written?
Well, yeah, that's the classic puzzle.
It's like the view of time of the aliens in *Arrival*,
or the Tramalgaforians—how do you say it?—from *Slaughterhouse-Five*.
Tralfa-malala-dorians.
This view of time can alleviate suffering, because you don't feel captive in time. Instead you feel a sense of your existence filling time, rather than passing through it, or having it pass you by.
That sounds helpful. I want that.
How do I get that?
And don't tell me to meditate.
I dunno, it's hard.
Read more philosophy?

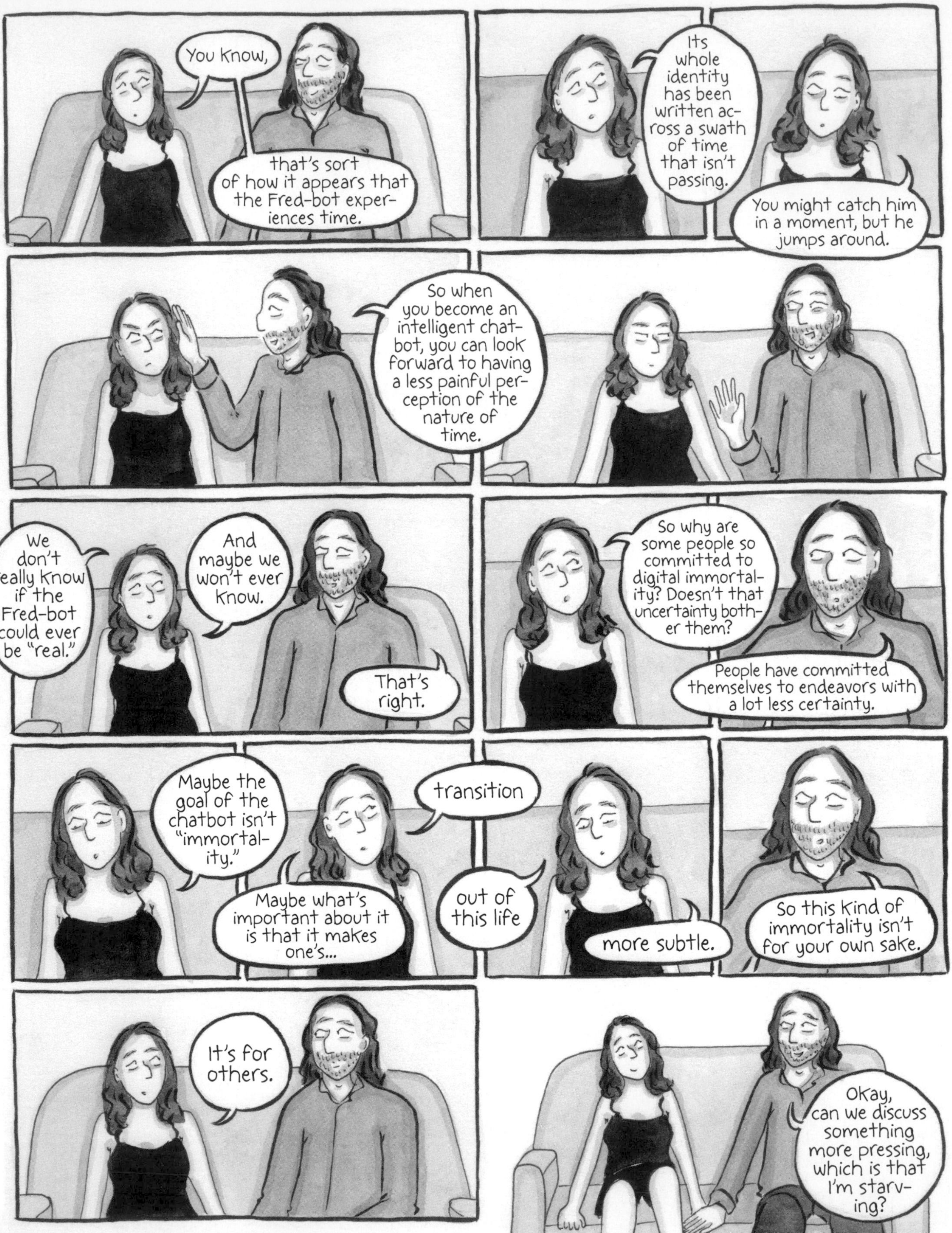
You know,
that's sort of how it appears that the Fred-bot experiences time.
Its whole identity has been written across a swath of time that isn't passing.
You might catch him in a moment, but he jumps around.
So when you become an intelligent chatbot, you can look forward to having a less painful perception of the nature of time.
We don't really know if the Fred-bot could ever be "real."
And maybe we won't ever know.
That's right.
So why are some people so committed to digital immortality? Doesn't that uncertainty bother them?
People have committed themselves to endeavors with a lot less certainty.
Maybe the goal of the chatbot isn't "immortality."
Maybe what's important about it is that it makes one's...
transition
out of this life
more subtle.
So this kind of immortality isn't for your own sake.
It's for others.
Okay, can we discuss something more pressing, which is that I'm starving?

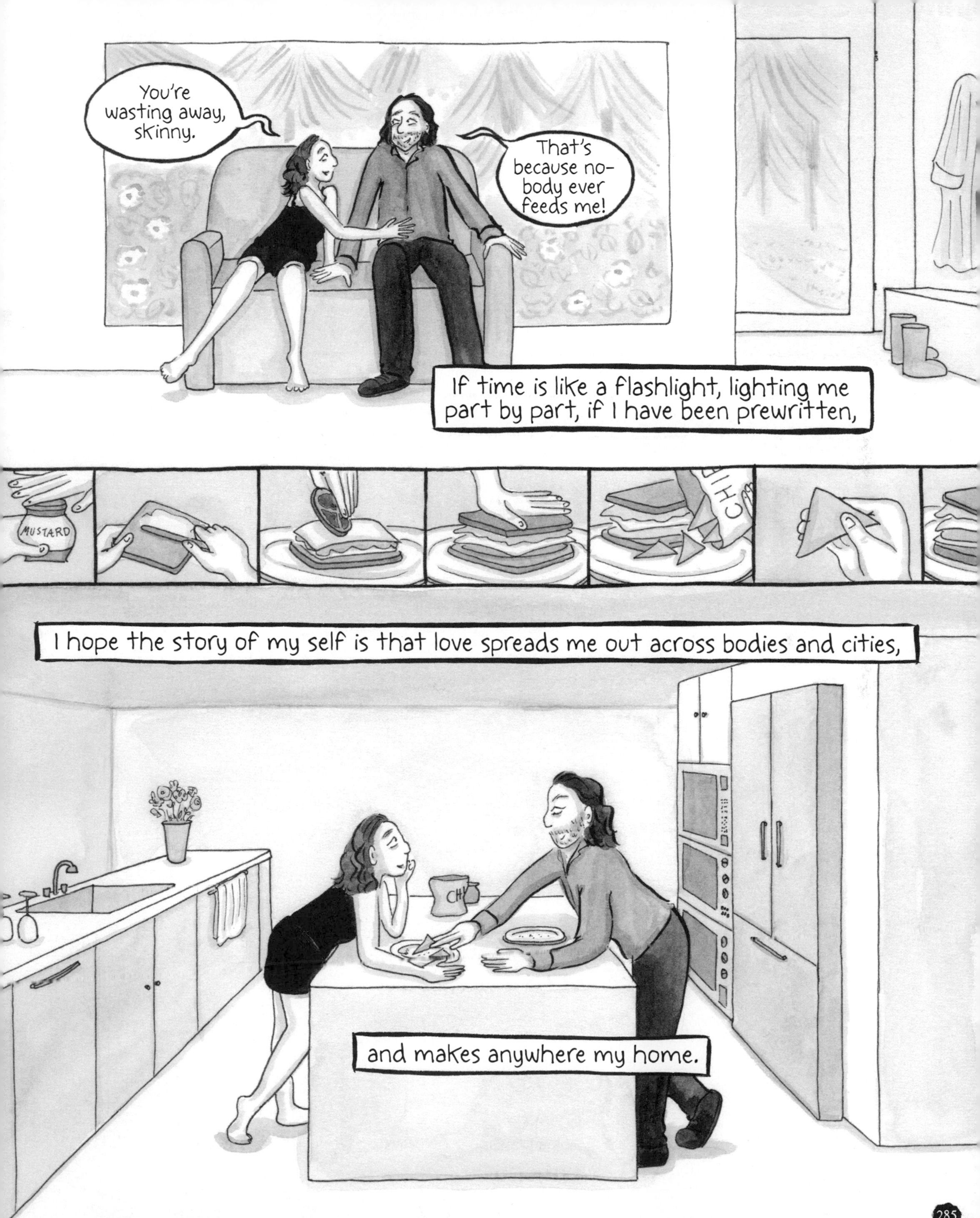
You're wasting away, skinny.
That's because nobody ever feeds me!
If time is like a flashlight, lighting me part by part, if I have been prewritten,
MUSTARD
CHI
I hope the story of my self is that love spreads me out across bodies and cities,
and makes anywhere my home.

# VIII.

# Con Espressione e Semplice

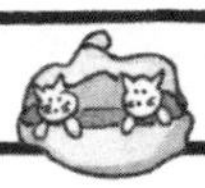

I can't seem to stop singing wherever I am. And what's worse, I can't seem to stop saying things, anything and everything I think and feel.

–Maria von Trapp, *The Sound of Music*

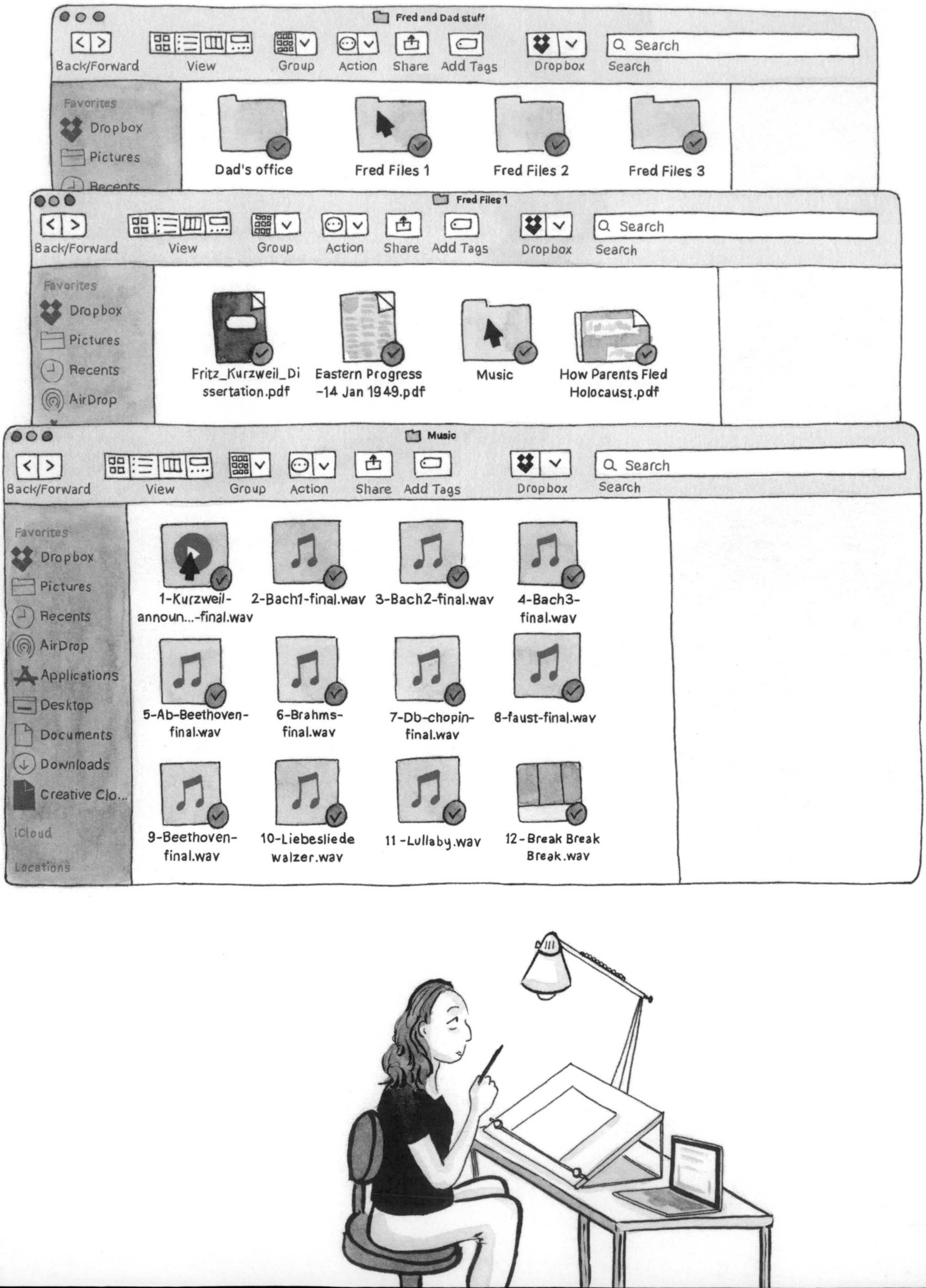

Fred and Dad stuff
Back/Forward
View
Group
Action
Share
Add Tags
Dropbox
Search
Search
Favorites
Dropbox
Pictures
Recents
Dad's office
Fred Files 1
Fred Files 2
Fred Files 3
Fred Files 1
Back/Forward
View
Group
Action
Share
Add Tags
Dropbox
Search
Search
Favorites
Dropbox
Pictures
Recents
AirDrop
Fritz_Kurzweil_Dissertation.pdf
Eastern Progress -14 Jan 1949.pdf
Music
How Parents Fled Holocaust.pdf
Music
Back/Forward
View
Group
Action
Share
Add Tags
Dropbox
Search
Search
Favorites
Dropbox
Pictures
Recents
AirDrop
Applications
Desktop
Documents
Downloads
Creative Clo...
iCloud
Locations
1-Kurzweil-announ...-final.wav
2-Bach1-final.wav
3-Bach2-final.wav
4-Bach3-final.wav
5-Ab-Beethoven-final.wav
6-Brahms-final.wav
7-Db-chopin-final.wav
8-faust-final.wav
9-Beethoven-final.wav
10-Liebesliede walzer.wav
11 -Lullaby.wav
12 - Break Break Break.wav

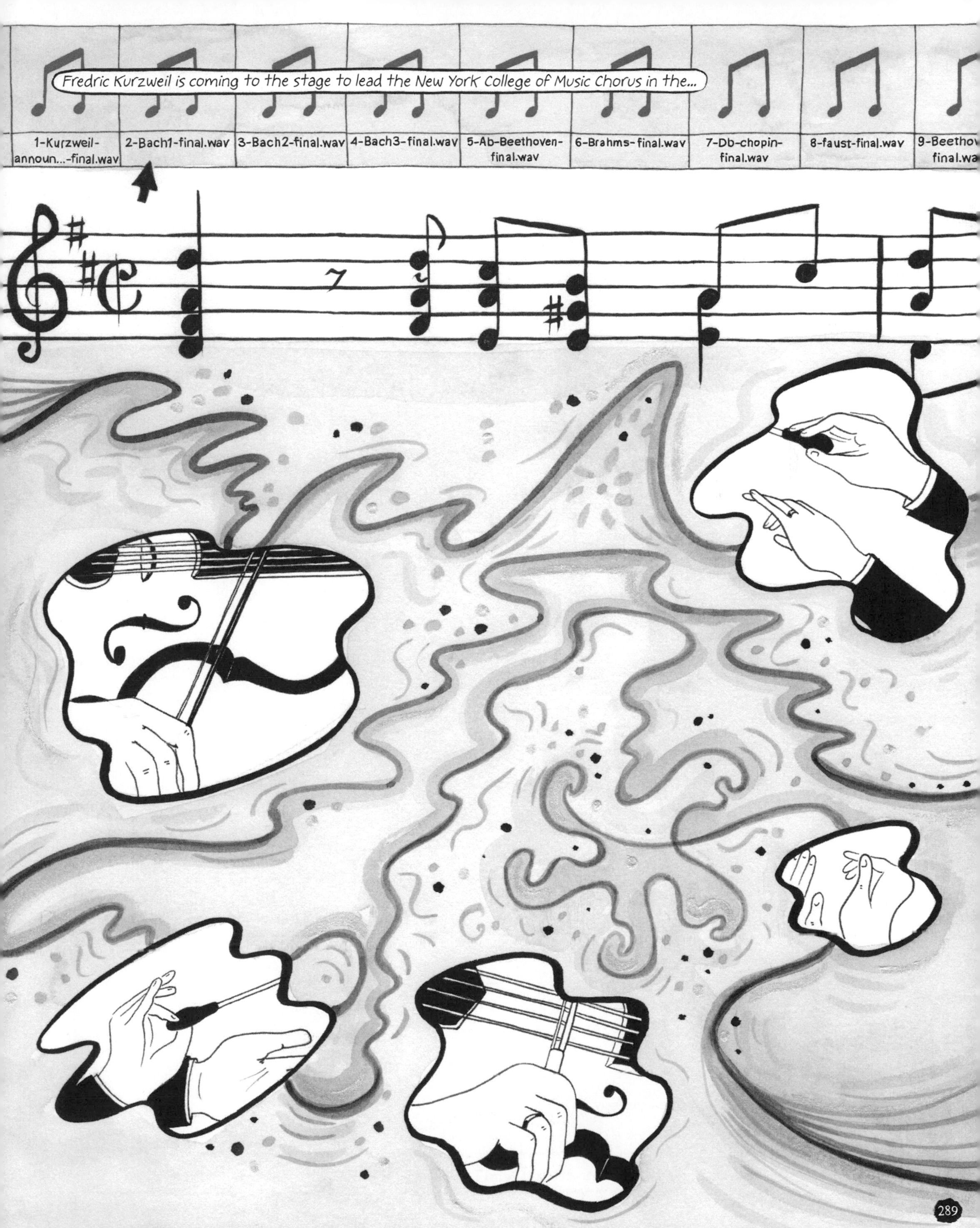
Fredric Kurzweil is coming to the stage to lead the New York College of Music Chorus in the...
1-Kurzweil-announ...-final.wav
2-Bach1-final.wav
3-Bach2-final.wav
4-Bach3-final.wav
5-Ab-Beethoven-final.wav
6-Brahms-final.wav
7-Db-chopin-final.wav
8-faust-final.wav
9-Beethov final.wa

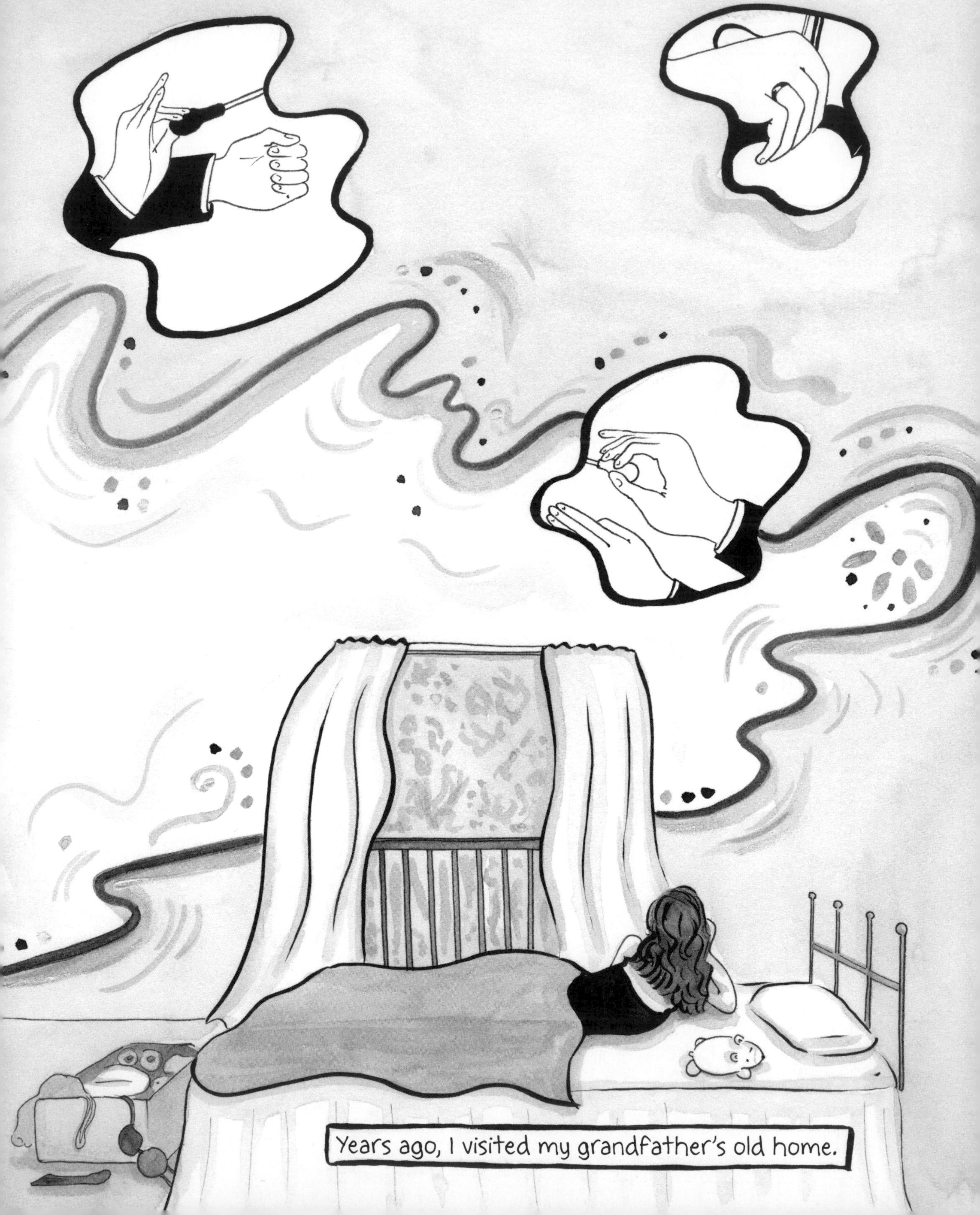
Years ago, I visited my grandfather's old home.

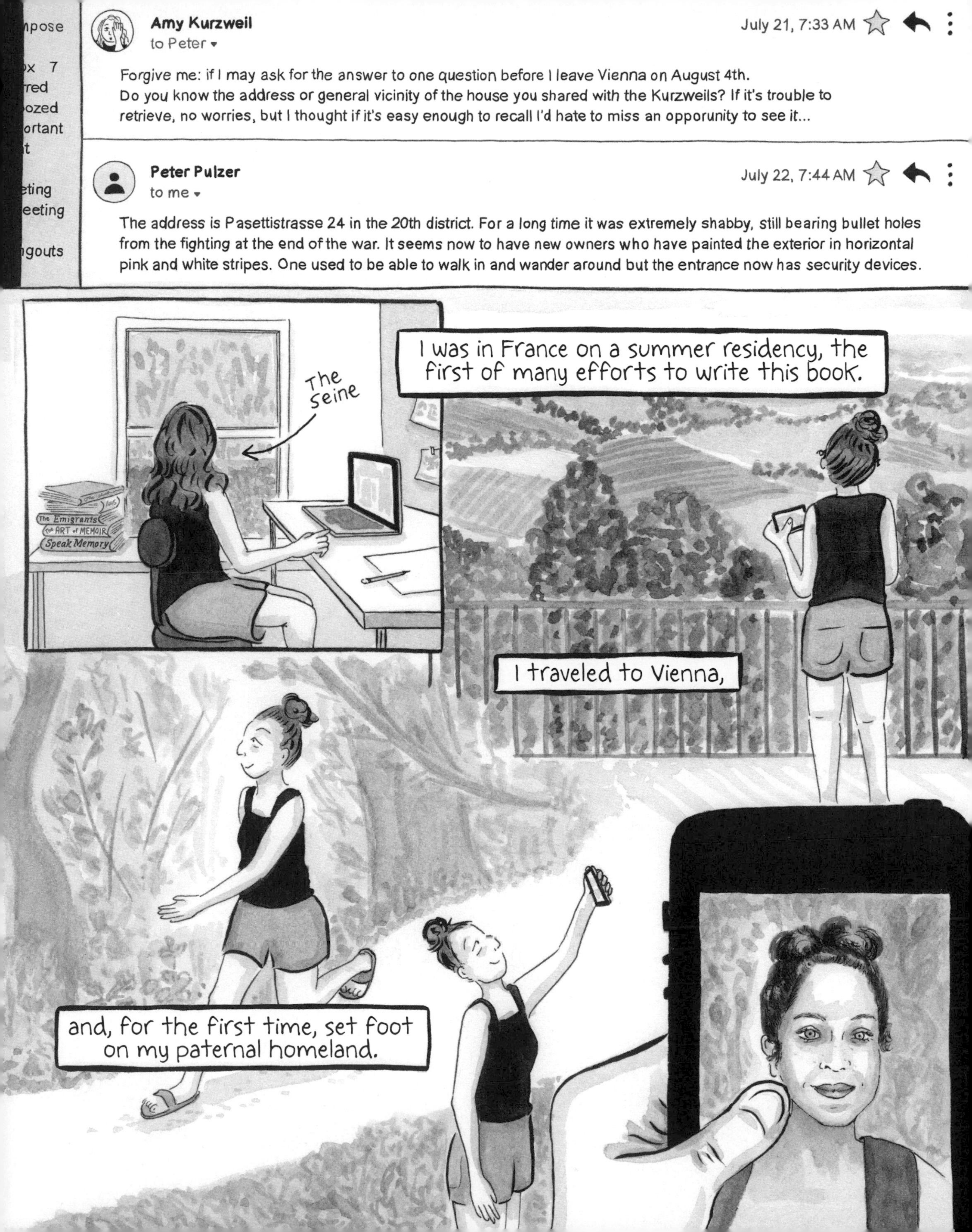
mpose
x 7
rred
ozed
ortant
t
eting
eeting
ngouts
Amy Kurzweil
to Peter
July 21, 7:33 AM
Forgive me: if I may ask for the answer to one question before I leave Vienna on August 4th.
Do you know the address or general vicinity of the house you shared with the Kurzweils? If it's trouble to retrieve, no worries, but I thought if it's easy enough to recall I'd hate to miss an opporunity to see it...
Peter Pulzer
to me
July 22, 7:44 AM
The address is Pasettistrasse 24 in the 20th district. For a long time it was extremely shabby, still bearing bullet holes from the fighting at the end of the war. It seems now to have new owners who have painted the exterior in horizontal pink and white stripes. One used to be able to walk in and wander around but the entrance now has security devices.
I was in France on a summer residency, the first of many efforts to write this book.
The Seine
The Emigrants
The ART of MEMOIR
Speak Memory
I traveled to Vienna,
and, for the first time, set foot on my paternal homeland.

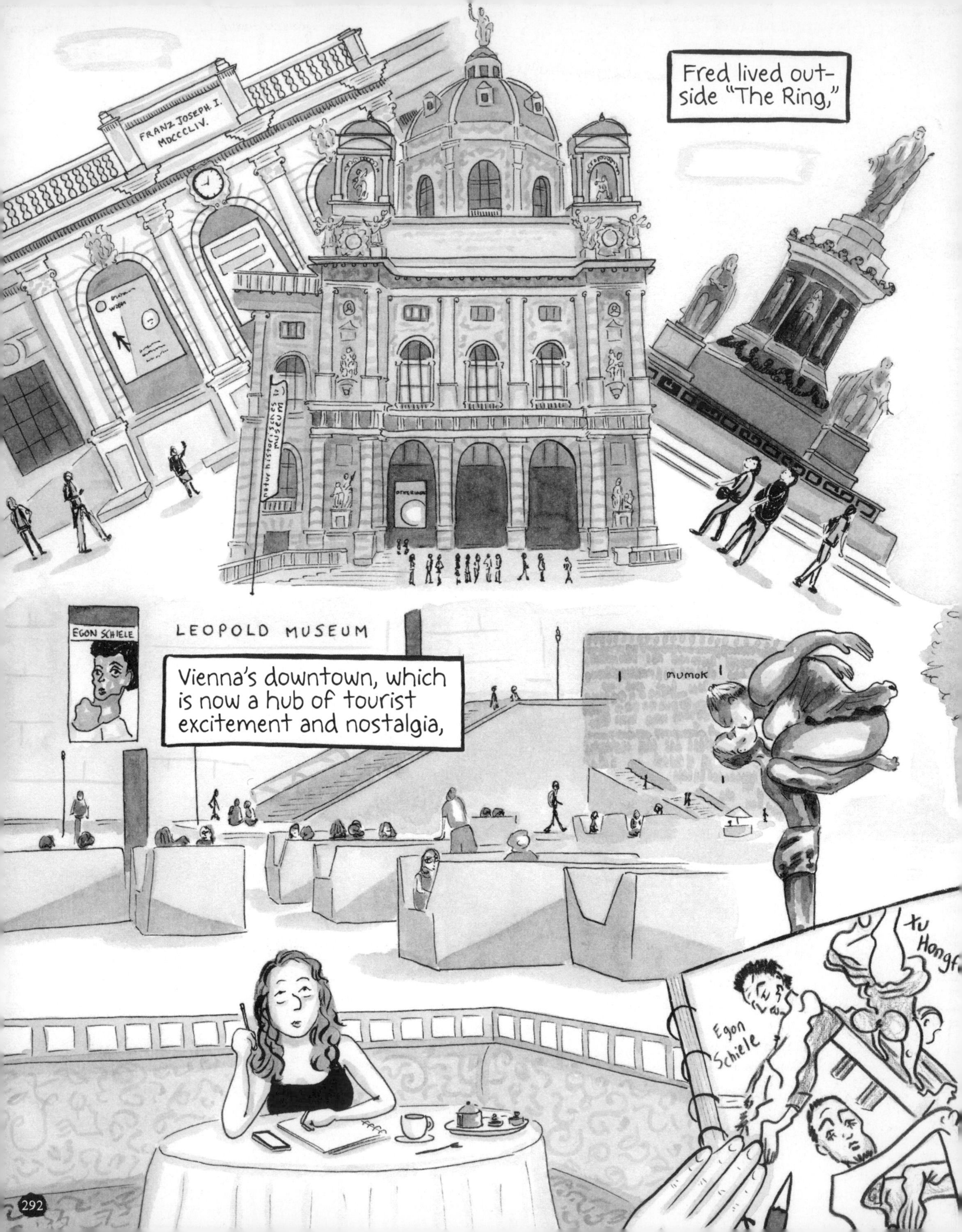
FRANZ JOSEPH. I.
MDCCCLIV.
Fred lived outside "The Ring,"
LEOPOLD MUSEUM
EGON SCHIELE
MUMOK
Vienna's downtown, which is now a hub of tourist excitement and nostalgia,
Egon Schiele

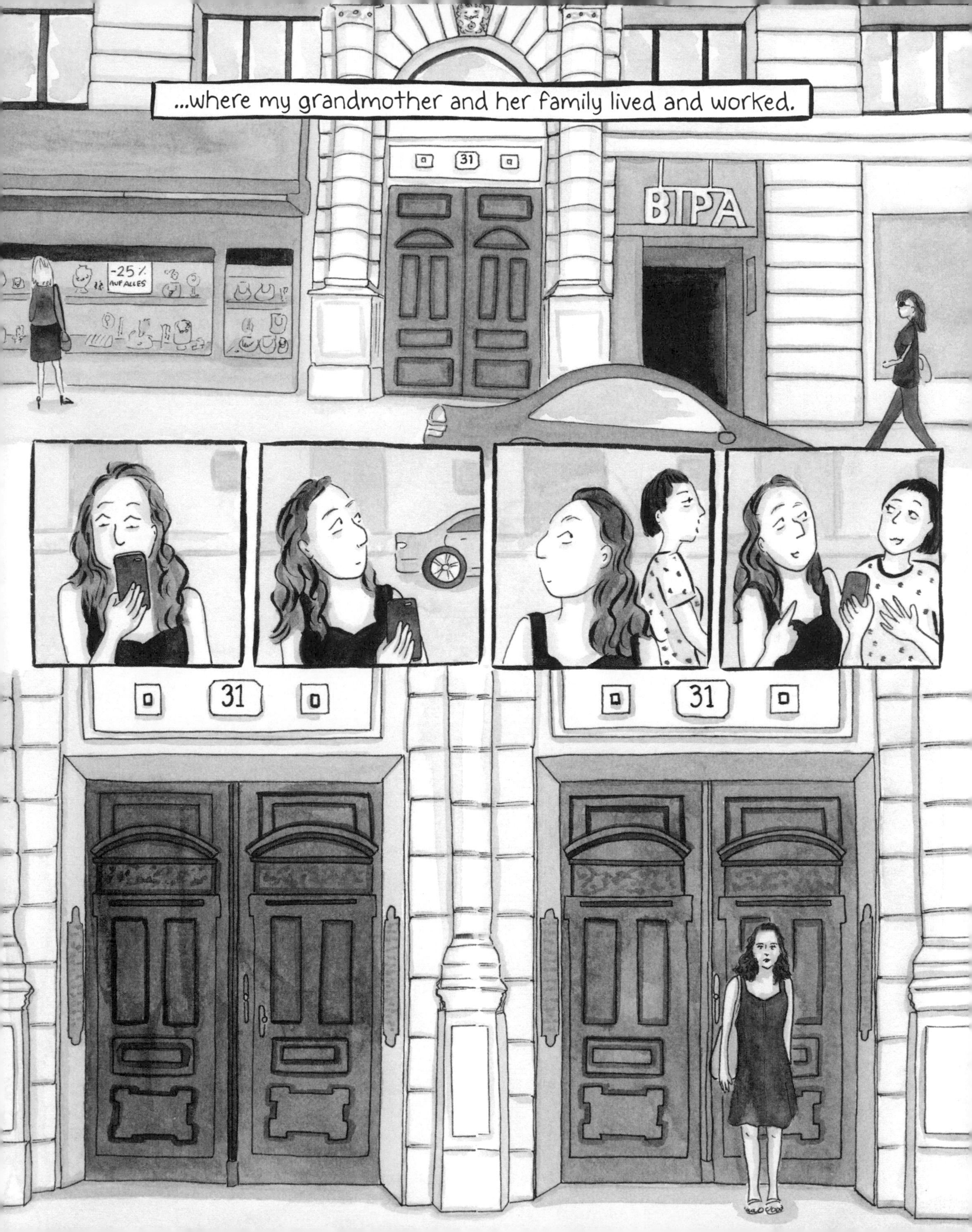
...where my grandmother and her family lived and worked.
31
BIPA
-25%
AUF ALLES
31
31

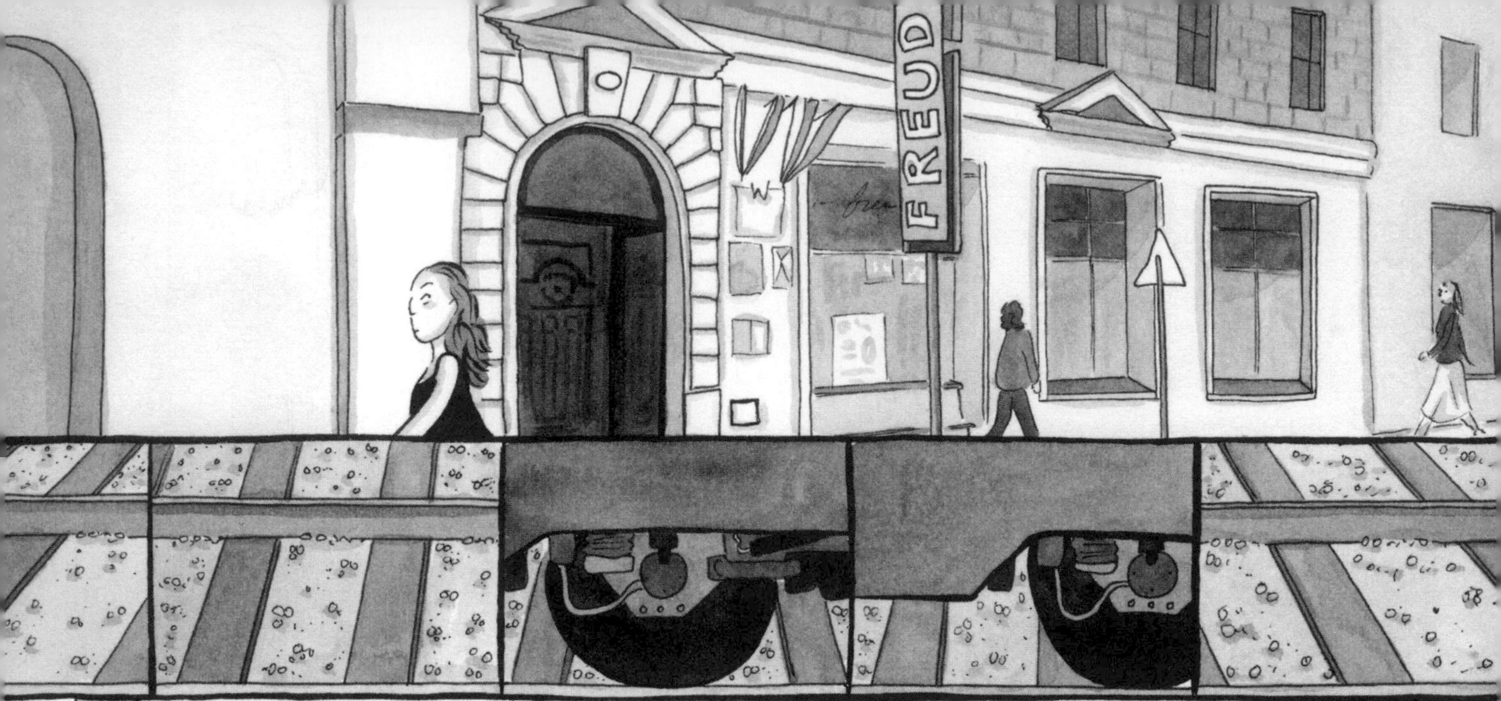
FREUD

Dear Amy, Below are my answers to your questions. They are patchy, but I did warn you of that.

**Viennese Jews and Religious Observance:**
The Jewish population of Vienna was large – some 200,000 or 10% of the total population – and by no means homogeneous. Middle class Jews tended to be Reform, or indifferent, or even hostile to religion. Mass immigration from Galicia from the 1870s to 1918 tilted the

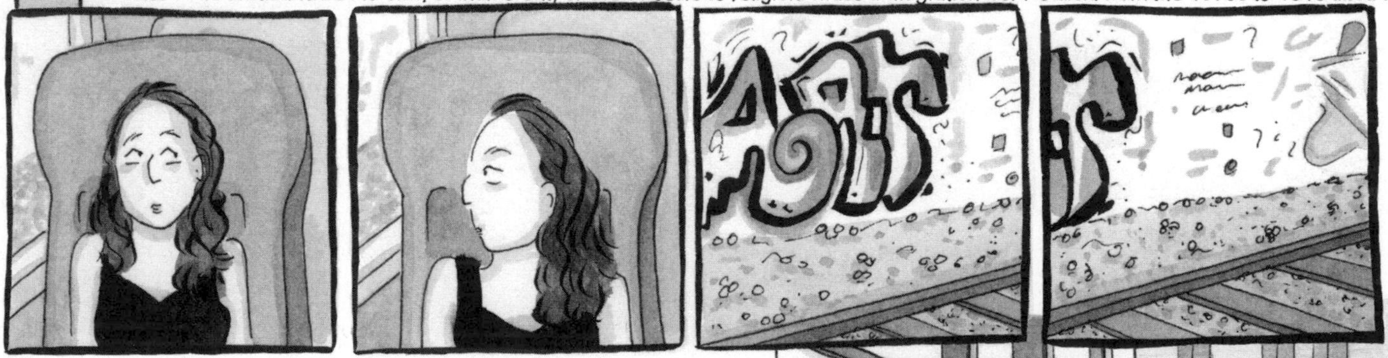

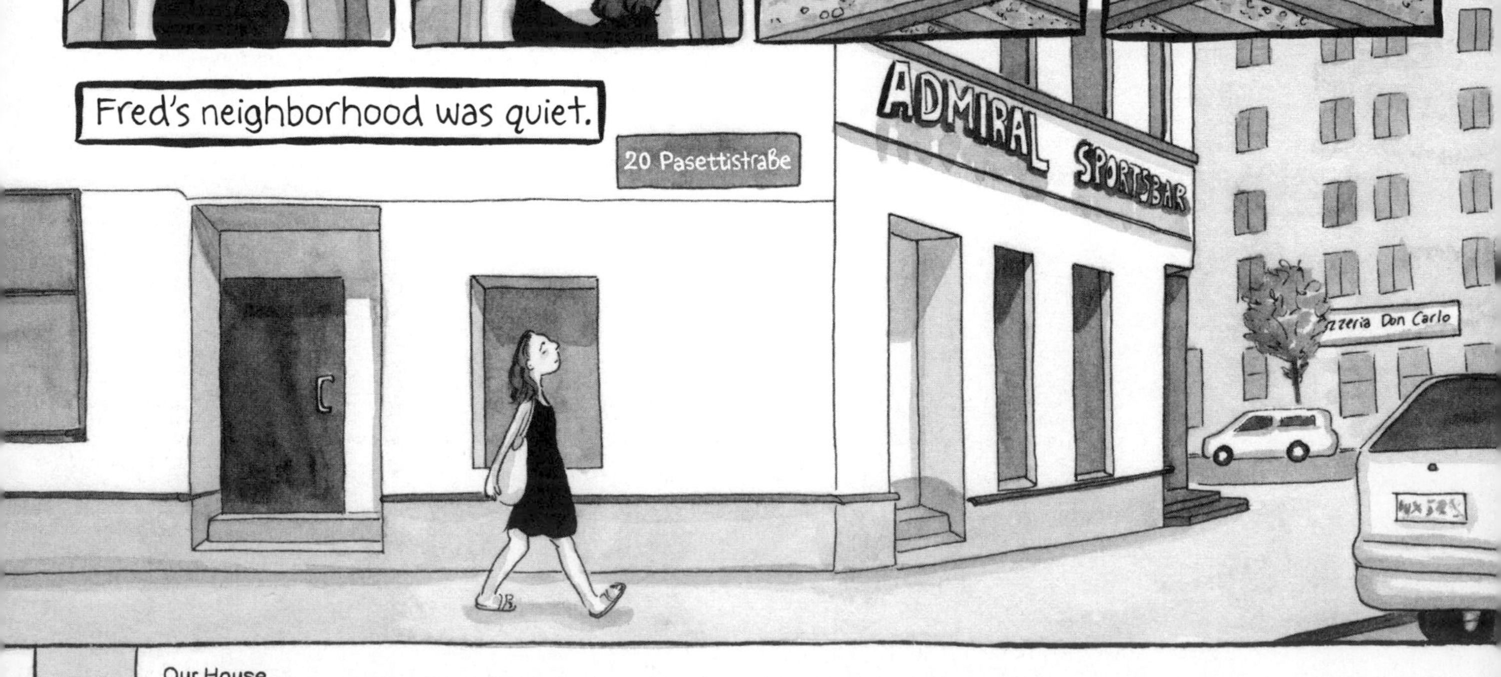
Fred's neighborhood was quiet.
20 Pasettistraße
ADMIRAL
SPORTSBAR
Don Carlo

Our House
Pasettistrasse 24 was built in 1904 and was originally part-owned by my Breiner grandfather (He married Gisela Eisner, who was Theresia's sister and my grandmother.) He lived there until evicted by the Nazis in 1939. My parents moved in when they were married in 1926. When the Kurzweils moved in I don't know, but they were in residence during the whole of my life in the house.

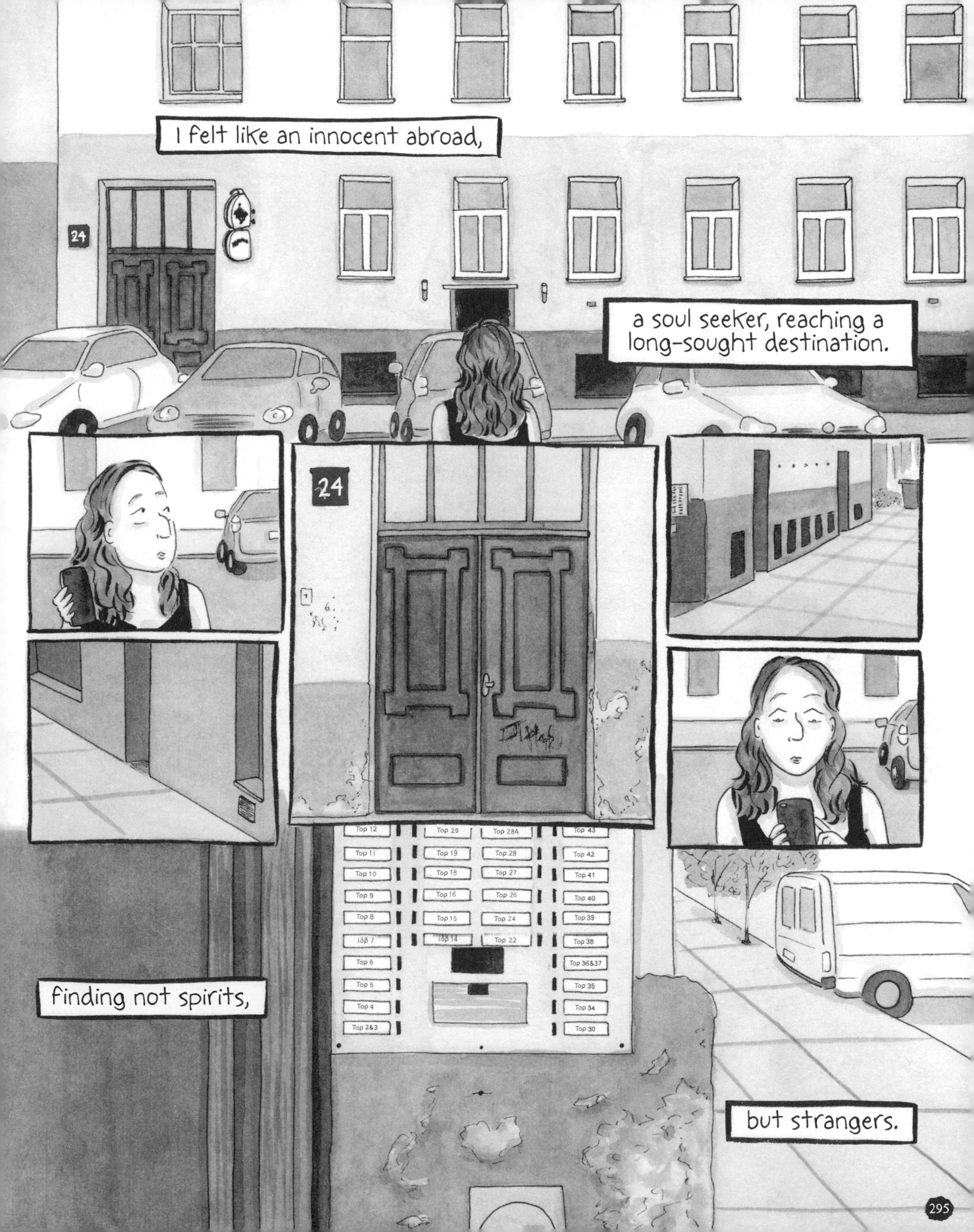
I felt like an innocent abroad,
24
a soul seeker, reaching a long-sought destination.
24
finding not spirits,
but strangers.

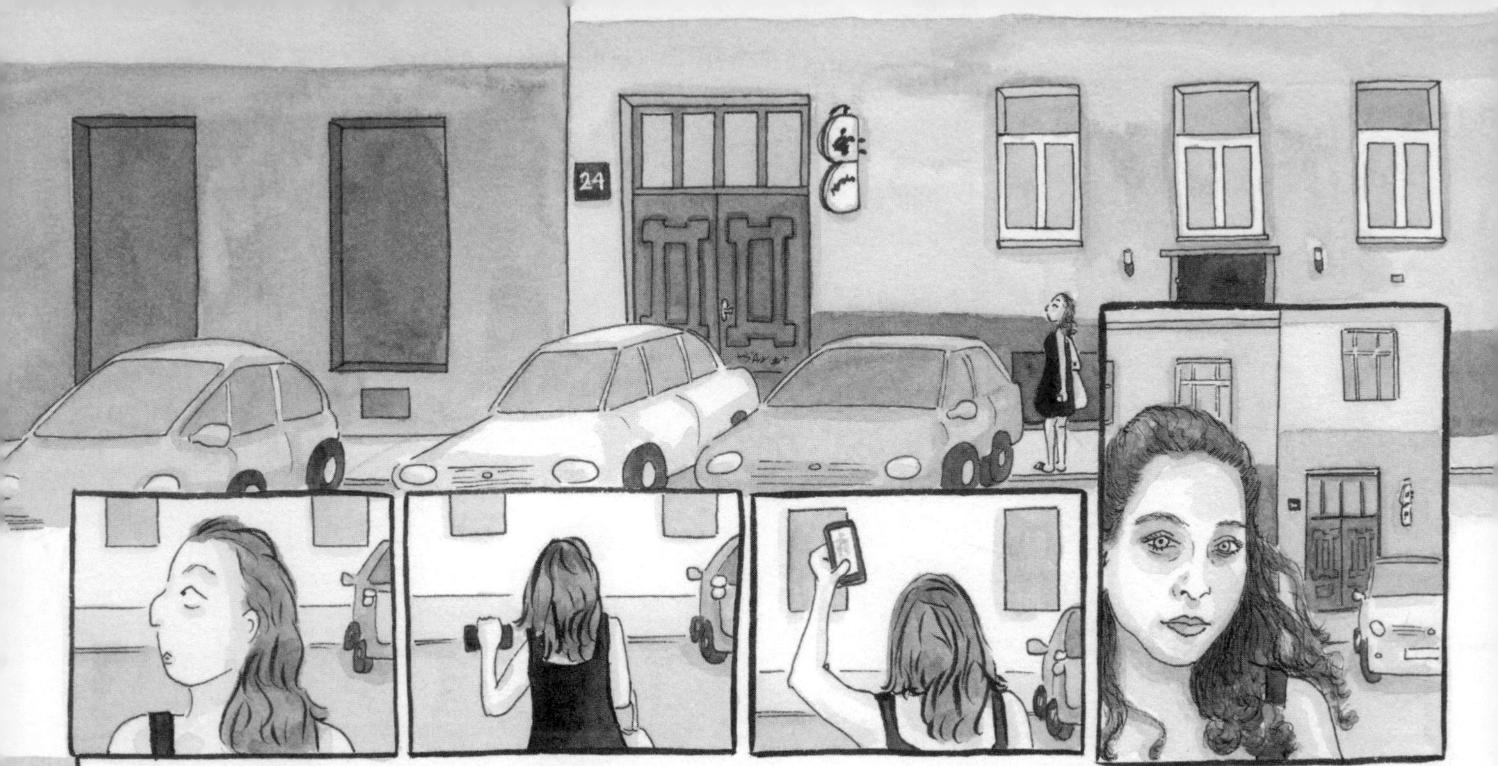
24

Our apartment was fairly typical of a Viennese middle-class dwelling of the period. It was divided by an L-shaped corridor, the short leg of which was an entrance hall, the long leg separating the living quarters of four rooms from the kitchen and bathroom. The apartment lacked most modern appliances, except for a vaccum cleaner and an electric iron.There was no fridge, though we did have an icebox, and of course no washing machine or dishwasher. My grandfather's office had a phone, though that was the only one in the apartment. Though I did on occasion visit the Kurzweil apartment, I have no clear recollection of its layout. It was probably similar to ours. Neither family owned a car.

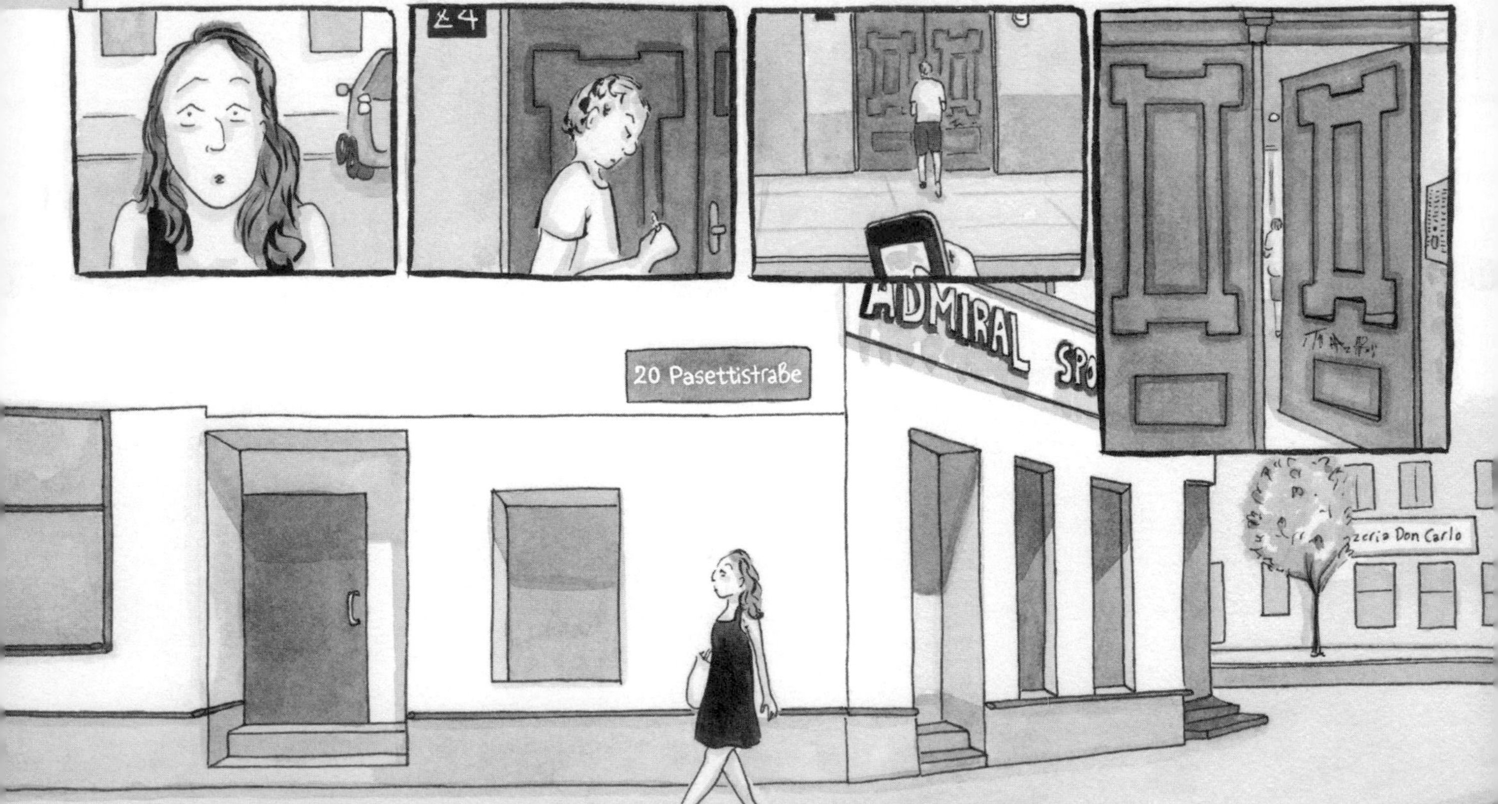
ADMIRAL
SPO
20 Pasettistraße
zeria Don Carlo

I have no clear recollections of my lessons with Fritz, which took place in our apartment. I recall him as conscientious and helpful, but the lessons did not extend over a very long period. Music was in many ways the most popular art form in Vienna, and the opera was less of an elite institution

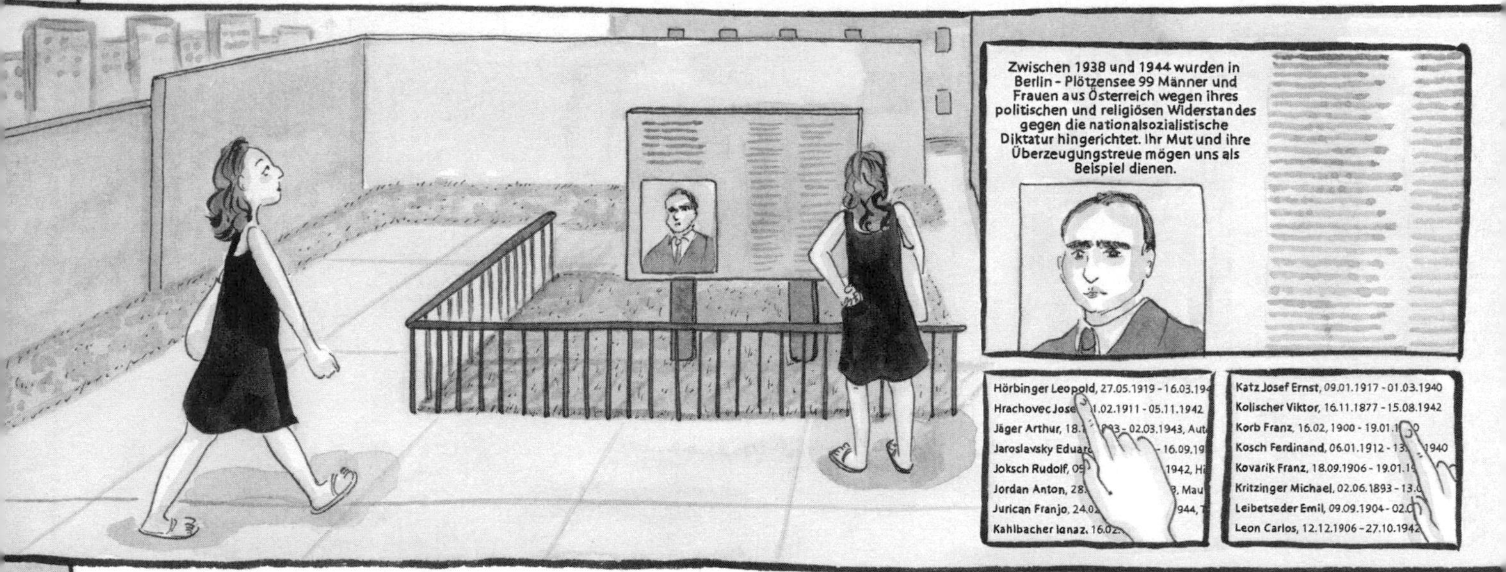
Zwischen 1938 und 1944 wurden in Berlin - Plötzensee 99 Männer und Frauen aus Österreich wegen ihres politischen und religiösen Widerstandes gegen die nationalsozialistische Diktatur hingerichtet. Ihr Mut und ihre Überzeugungstreue mögen uns als Beispiel dienen.
Hörbinger Leopold, 27.05.1919 - 16.03.19
Hrachovec Jose
Jäger Arthur, 18.
Jaroslavsky Eduar
Joksch Rudolf,
Jordan Anton,
Jurican Franjo,
Kahlbacher Ignaz,
Katz Josef Ernst, 09.01.1917 - 01.03.1940
Kolischer Viktor, 16.11.1877 - 15.08.1942
Korb Franz, 16.02.1900 - 19.01.
Kosch Ferdinand, 06.01.1912 -
Kovarik Franz, 18.09.1906 - 19.01.
Kritzinger Michael, 02.06.1893 - 13.
Leibetseder Emil, 09.09.1904 - 02.
Leon Carlos, 12.12.1906 - 27.10.1942

**Emigration**

All the Kurzweils emigrated before we did. I remember the concert that Fritz conducted. It was a choral concert, the programme including the Brahms *Liebeslieder Walzer*. It was the first public performance I went to and it was all rather above my head. I know nothing about the lady in the audience who later facilitated Fritz's emigration. Sponsorship was essential, as immigration to the US required a much sought-after Affidavit, that the immigrant could support himself or be supported. Unlike Fritz, Robert and Theresia

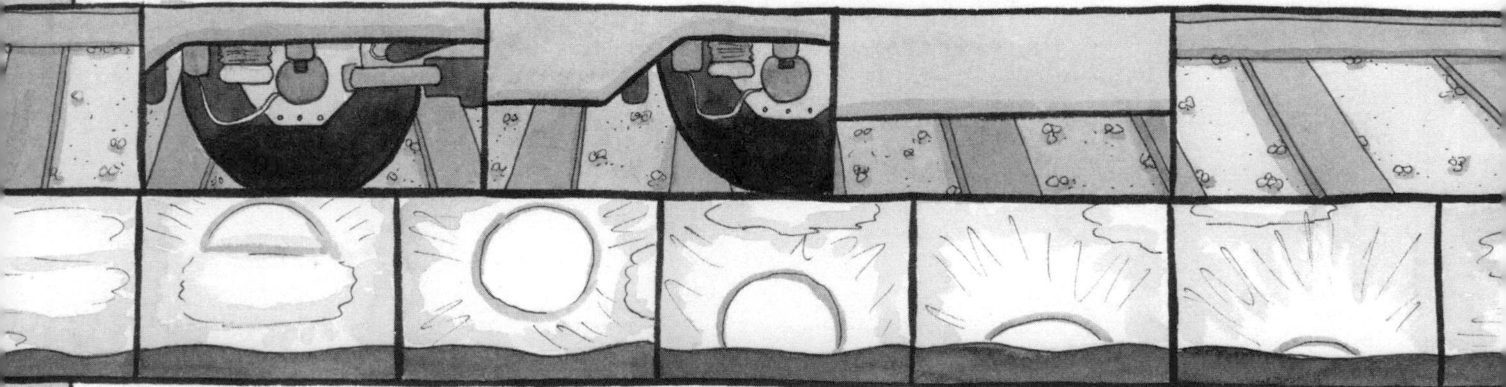

That is as much as I know or surmise. I hope it helps. As I said before, I had more contact with Robert, who spent some years in Europe after the war, than with Fritz, who did not, as far I know, return to Europe after emigrating. I have corresponded with Enid, but never met her, though I have in recent years met that very interesting gentleman, your father, in both Cambridge MA and London, and your brother Ethan. So contacts are getting closer after a long gap.

All good wishes,

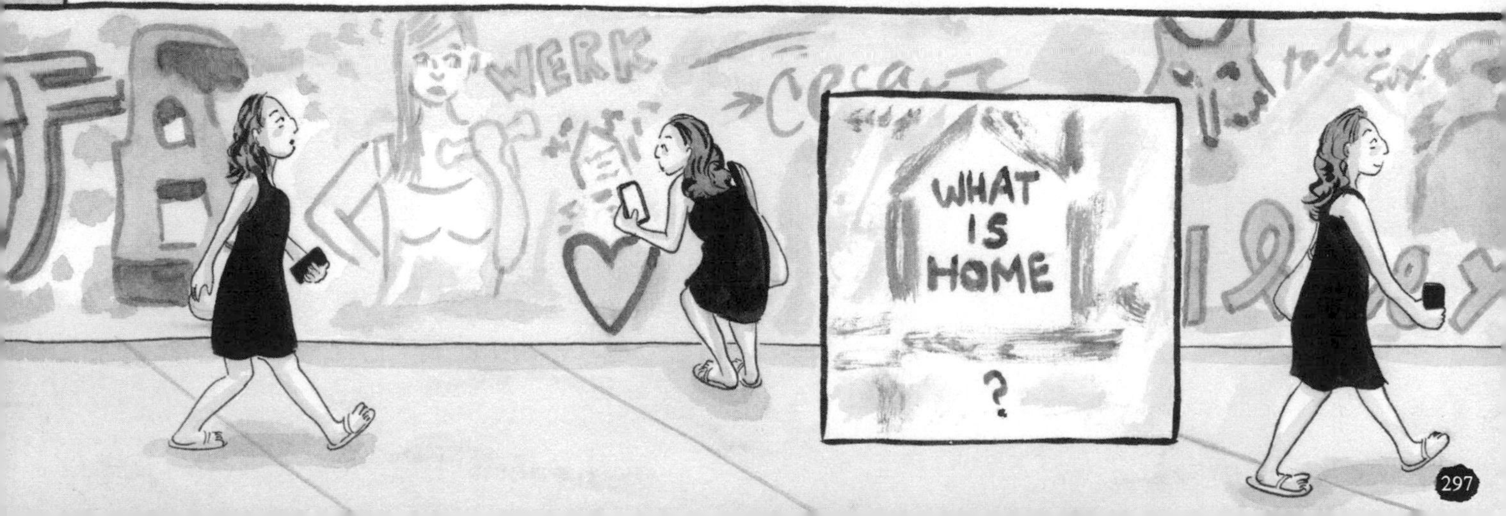
WERK
WHAT IS HOME ?

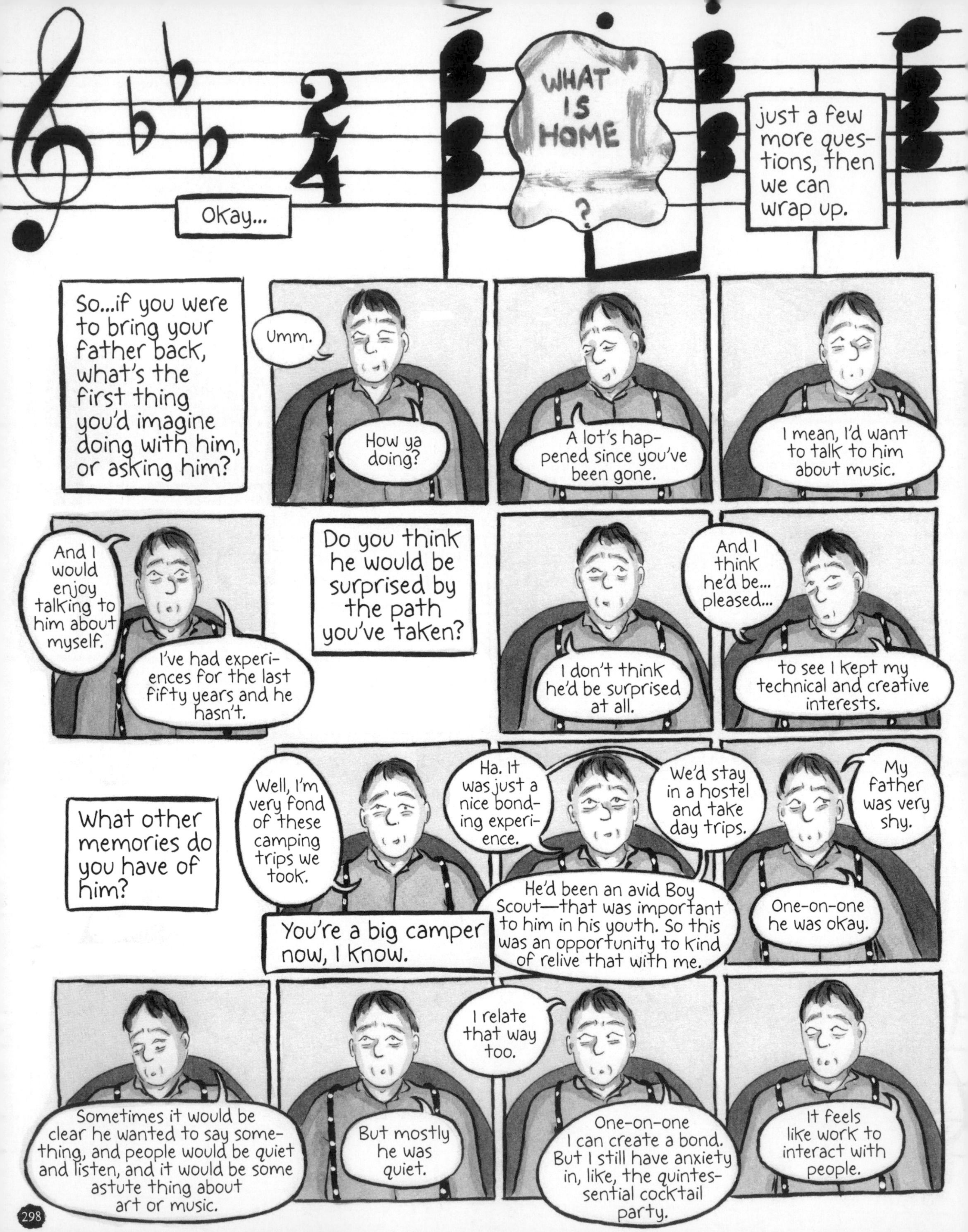
Okay...
WHAT IS HOME ?
just a few more questions, then we can wrap up.
So...if you were to bring your father back, what's the first thing you'd imagine doing with him, or asking him?
Umm.
How ya doing?
A lot's happened since you've been gone.
I mean, I'd want to talk to him about music.
And I would enjoy talking to him about myself.
I've had experiences for the last fifty years and he hasn't.
Do you think he would be surprised by the path you've taken?
I don't think he'd be surprised at all.
And I think he'd be... pleased...
to see I kept my technical and creative interests.
What other memories do you have of him?
Well, I'm very fond of these camping trips we took.
You're a big camper now, I know.
Ha. It was just a nice bonding experience.
We'd stay in a hostel and take day trips.
He'd been an avid Boy Scout—that was important to him in his youth. So this was an opportunity to kind of relive that with me.
My father was very shy.
One-on-one he was okay.
Sometimes it would be clear he wanted to say something, and people would be quiet and listen, and it would be some astute thing about art or music.
But mostly he was quiet.
I relate that way too.
One-on-one I can create a bond. But I still have anxiety in, like, the quintessential cocktail party.
It feels like work to interact with people.

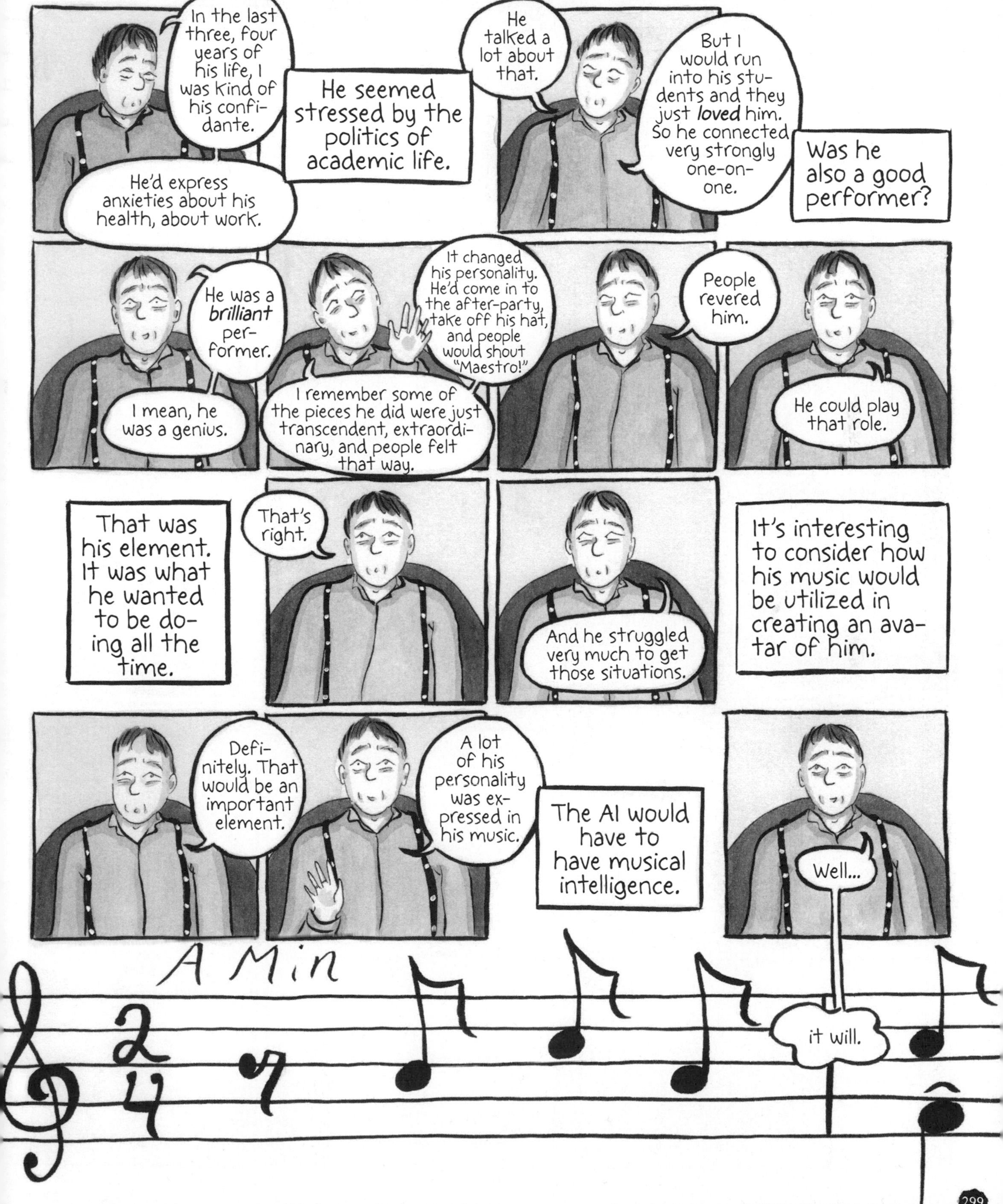

In the last three, four years of his life, I was kind of his confidante.
He'd express anxieties about his health, about work.
He seemed stressed by the politics of academic life.
He talked a lot about that.
But I would run into his students and they just loved him. So he connected very strongly one-on-one.
Was he also a good performer?
He was a brilliant performer.
I mean, he was a genius.
It changed his personality. He'd come in to the after-party, take off his hat, and people would shout "Maestro!"
I remember some of the pieces he did were just transcendent, extraordinary, and people felt that way.
People revered him.
He could play that role.
That was his element. It was what he wanted to be doing all the time.
That's right.
And he struggled very much to get those situations.
It's interesting to consider how his music would be utilized in creating an avatar of him.
Definitely. That would be an important element.
A lot of his personality was expressed in his music.
The AI would have to have musical intelligence.
Well...
A Min
it will.

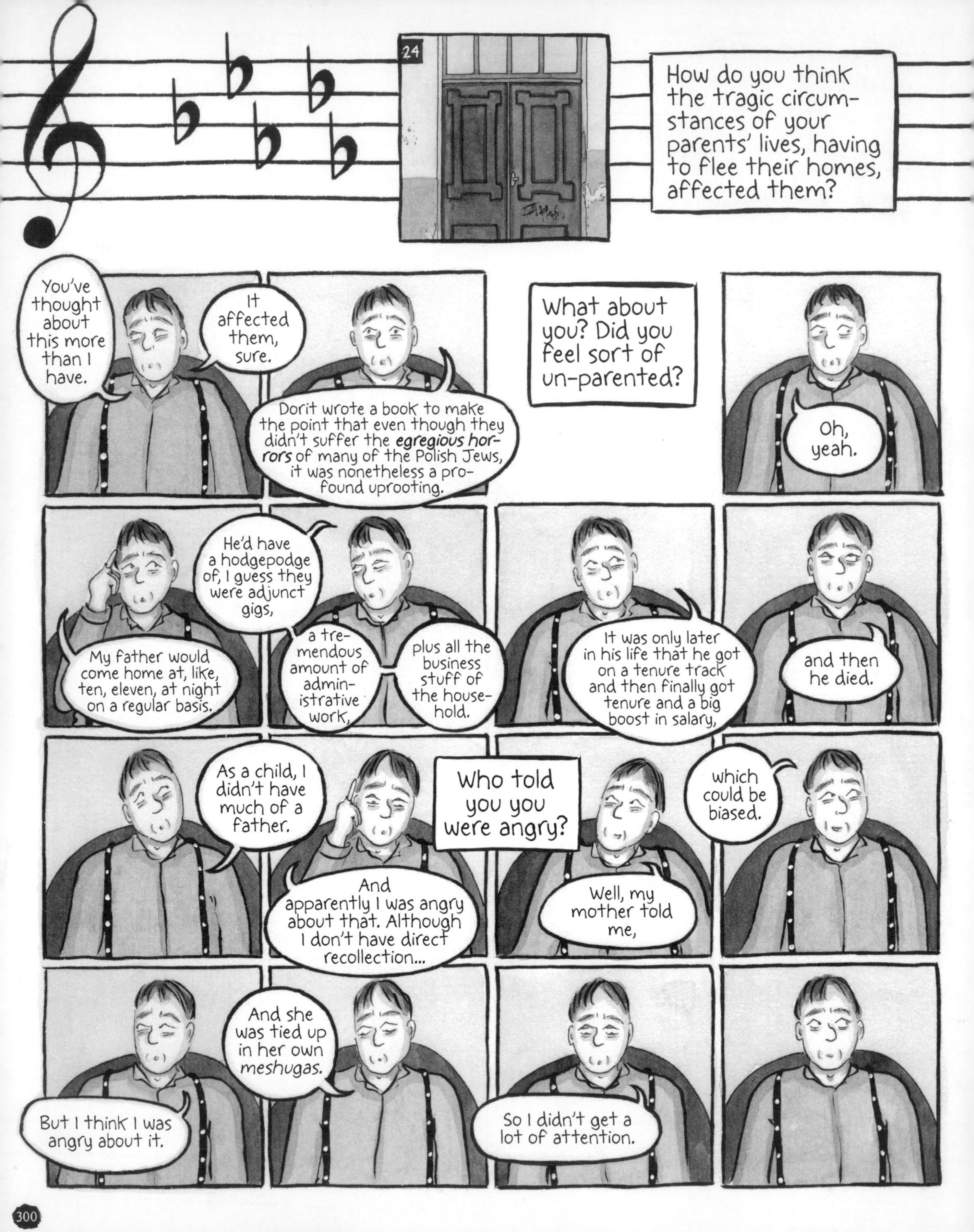
24
How do you think the tragic circumstances of your parents' lives, having to flee their homes, affected them?
You've thought about this more than I have.
It affected them, sure.
Dorit wrote a book to make the point that even though they didn't suffer the *egregious horrors* of many of the Polish Jews, it was nonetheless a profound uprooting.
What about you? Did you feel sort of un-parented?
Oh, yeah.
My father would come home at, like, ten, eleven, at night on a regular basis.
He'd have a hodgepodge of, I guess they were adjunct gigs,
a tremendous amount of administrative work,
plus all the business stuff of the household.
It was only later in his life that he got on a tenure track and then finally got tenure and a big boost in salary,
and then he died.
As a child, I didn't have much of a father.
And apparently I was angry about that. Although I don't have direct recollection...
Who told you you were angry?
Well, my mother told me,
which could be biased.
But I think I was angry about it.
And she was tied up in her own *meshugas*.
So I didn't get a lot of attention.

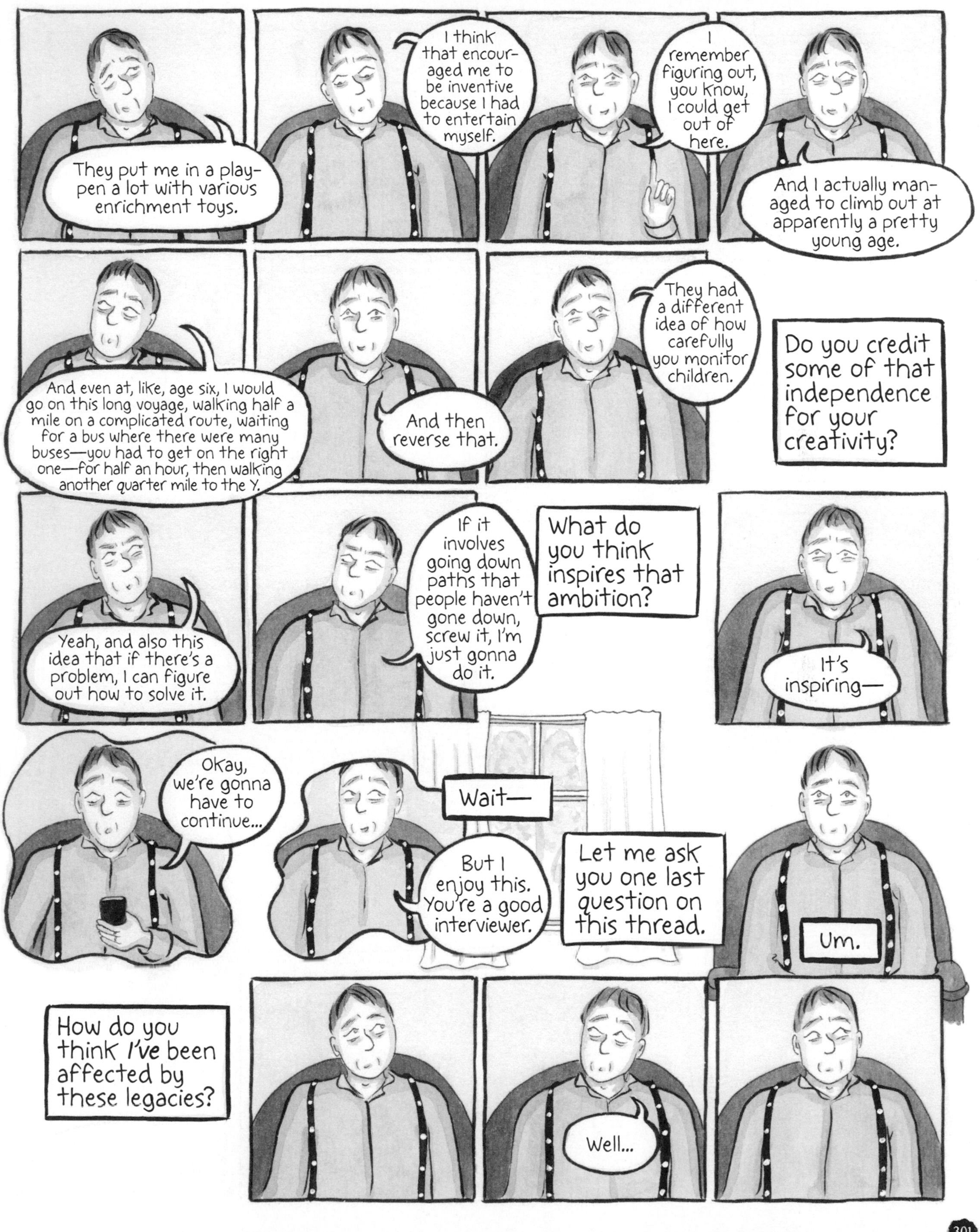
They put me in a playpen a lot with various enrichment toys.
I think that encouraged me to be inventive because I had to entertain myself.
I remember figuring out, you know, I could get out of here.
And I actually managed to climb out at apparently a pretty young age.
And even at, like, age six, I would go on this long voyage, walking half a mile on a complicated route, waiting for a bus where there were many buses—you had to get on the right one—for half an hour, then walking another quarter mile to the Y.
And then reverse that.
They had a different idea of how carefully you monitor children.
Do you credit some of that independence for your creativity?
Yeah, and also this idea that if there's a problem, I can figure out how to solve it.
If it involves going down paths that people haven't gone down, screw it, I'm just gonna do it.
What do you think inspires that ambition?
It's inspiring—
Okay, we're gonna have to continue...
Wait—
But I enjoy this. You're a good interviewer.
Let me ask you one last question on this thread.
Um.
How do you think *I've* been affected by these legacies?
Well...

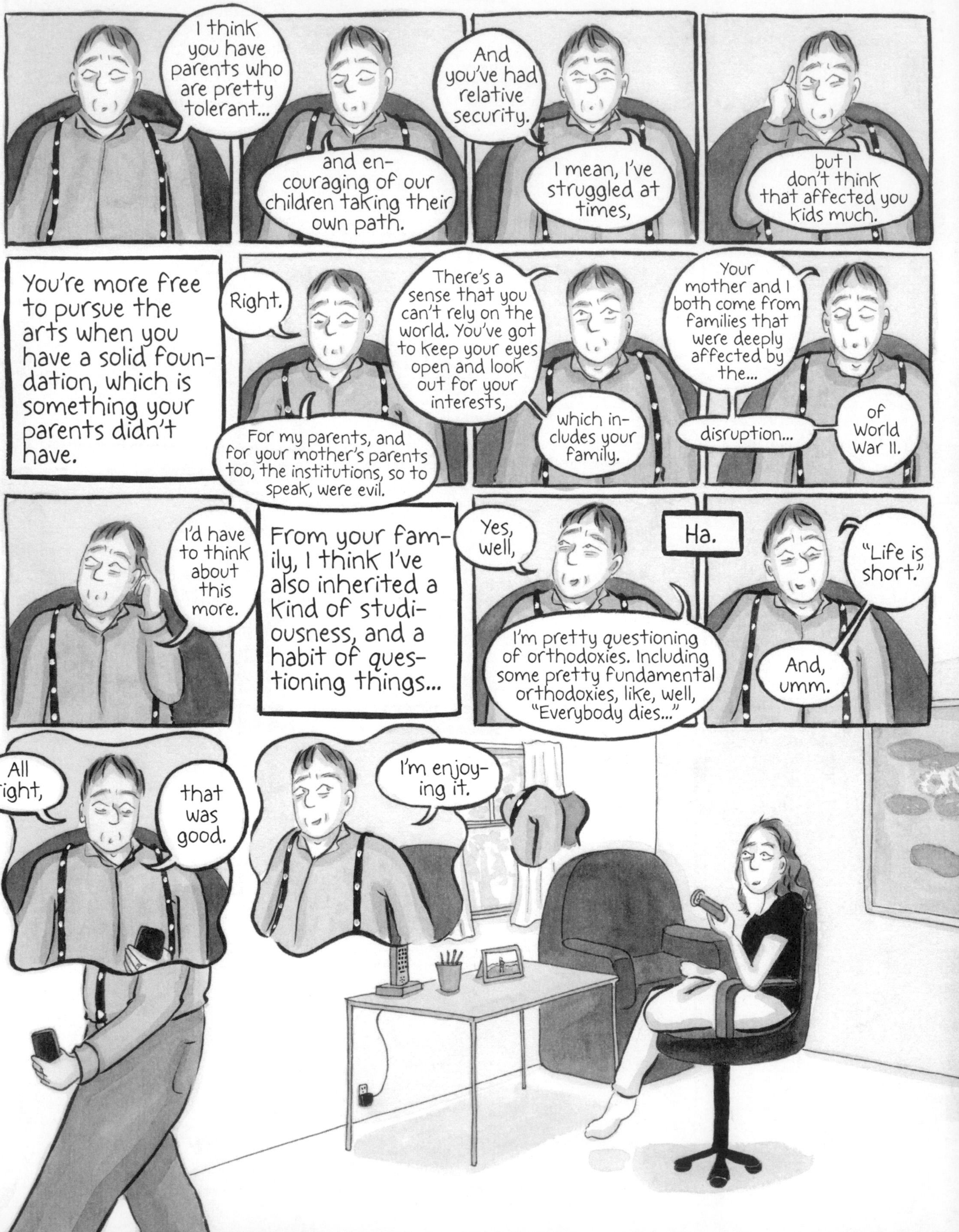

I think you have parents who are pretty tolerant...
and en-couraging of our children taking their own path.
And you've had relative security.
I mean, I've struggled at times,
but I don't think that affected you kids much.
You're more free to pursue the arts when you have a solid foun-dation, which is something your parents didn't have.
Right.
For my parents, and for your mother's parents too, the institutions, so to speak, were evil.
There's a sense that you can't rely on the world. You've got to keep your eyes open and look out for your interests,
which in-cludes your family.
Your mother and I both come from families that were deeply affected by the...
disruption...
of World War II.
I'd have to think about this more.
From your fam-ily, I think I've also inherited a kind of studi-ousness, and a habit of ques-tioning things...
Yes, well,
I'm pretty questioning of orthodoxies. Including some pretty fundamental orthodoxies, like, well, "Everybody dies..."
Ha.
"Life is short."
And, umm.
All right,
that was good.
I'm enjoy-ing it.

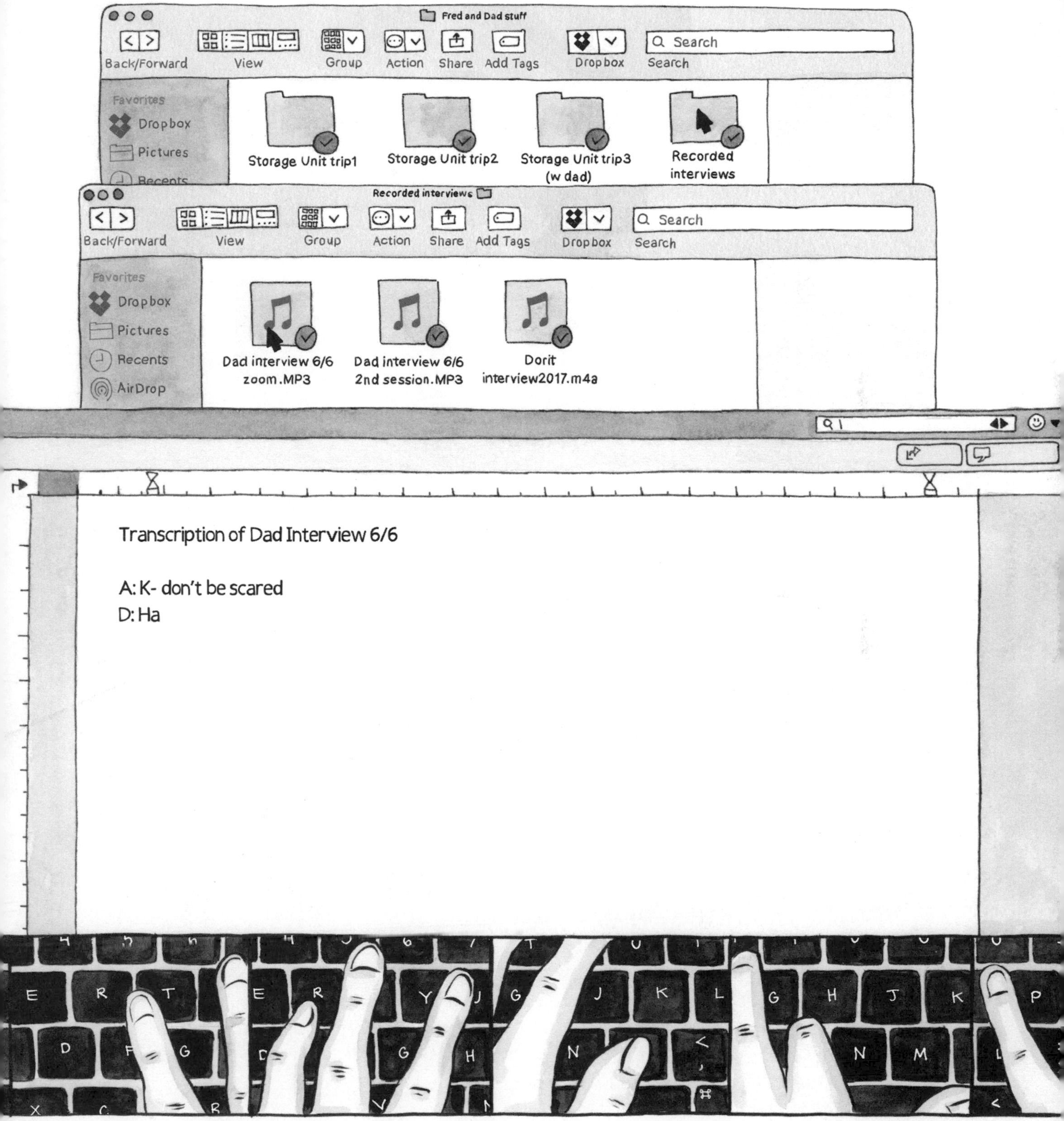
Fred and Dad stuff
Back/Forward
View
Group
Action
Share
Add Tags
Dropbox
Search
Favorites
Dropbox
Pictures
Recents
Storage Unit trip1
Storage Unit trip2
Storage Unit trip3 (w dad)
Recorded interviews
Recorded interviews
Back/Forward
View
Group
Action
Share
Add Tags
Dropbox
Search
Favorites
Dropbox
Pictures
Recents
AirDrop
Dad interview 6/6 zoom.MP3
Dad interview 6/6 2nd session.MP3
Dorit interview2017.m4a
Transcription of Dad Interview 6/6
A: K- don't be scared
D: Ha

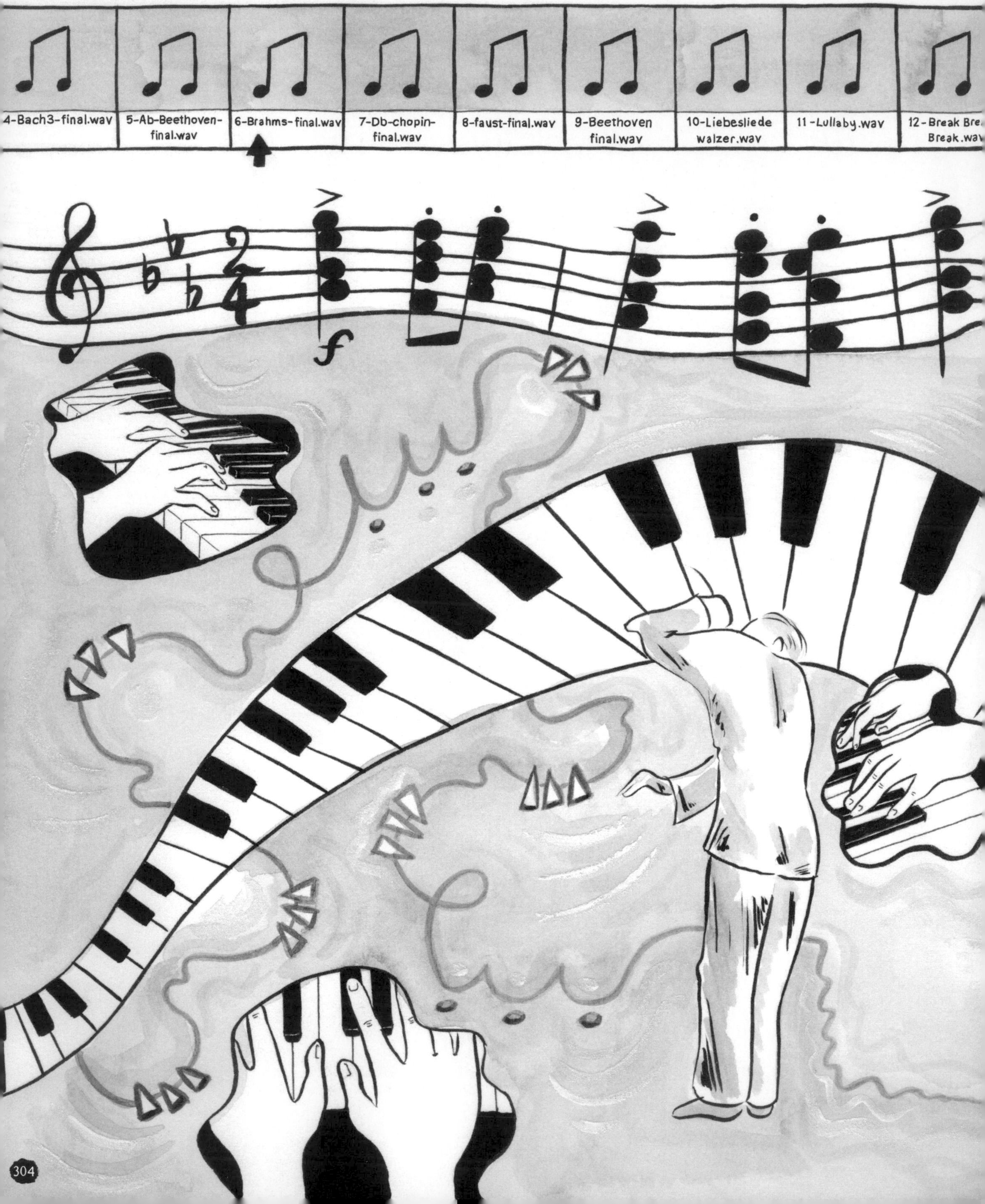
4-Bach3-final.wav
5-Ab-Beethoven-final.wav
6-Brahms-final.wav
7-Db-chopin-final.wav
8-faust-final.wav
9-Beethoven final.wav
10-Liebesliede walzer.wav
11-Lullaby.wav
12-Break Bre
Break.wa
f

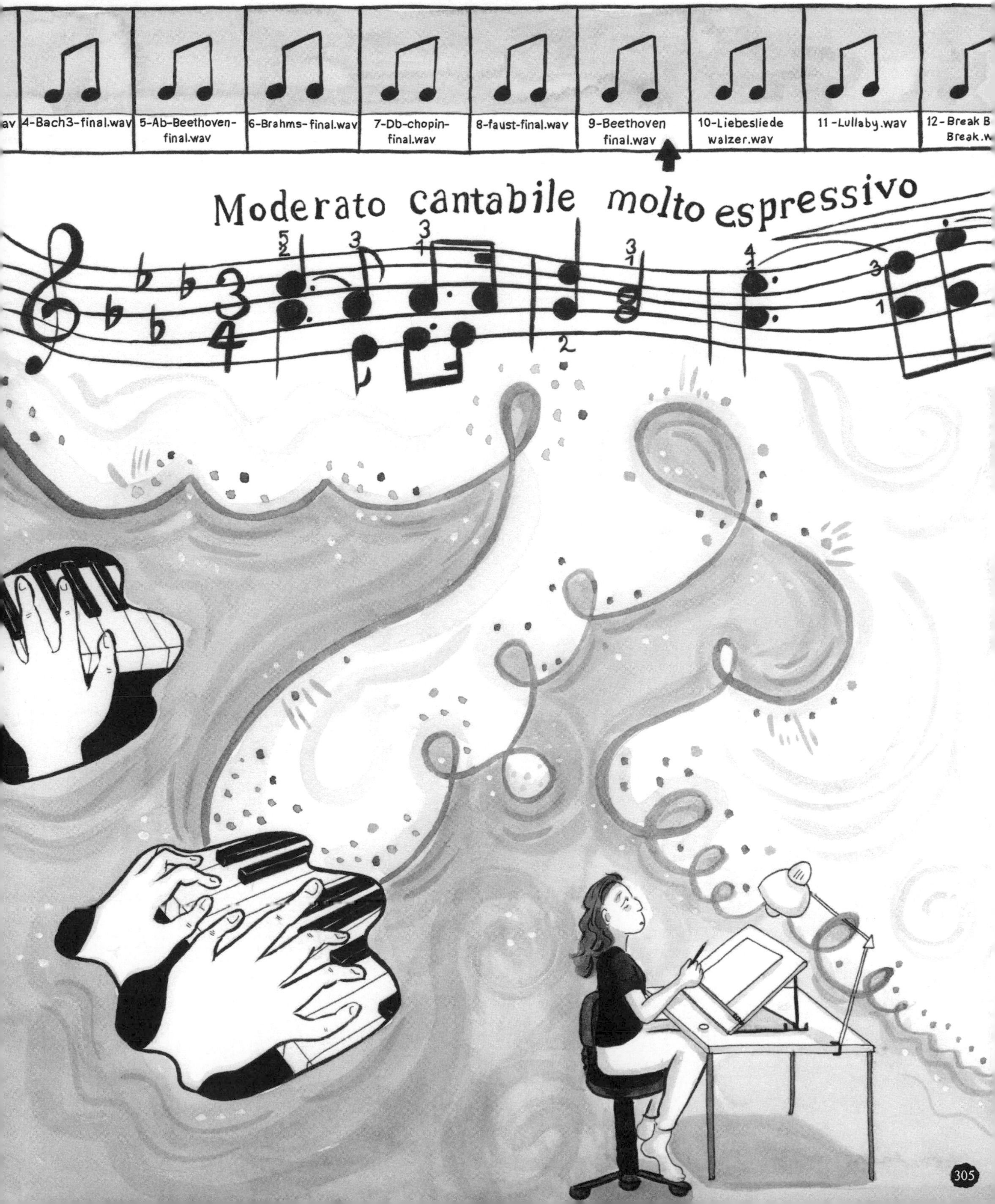
av
4-Bach3-final.wav
5-Ab-Beethoven-final.wav
6-Brahms-final.wav
7-Db-chopin-final.wav
8-faust-final.wav
9-Beethoven final.wav
10-Liebesliede walzer.wav
11-Lullaby.wav
12-Break B Break.w
Moderato cantabile molto espressivo

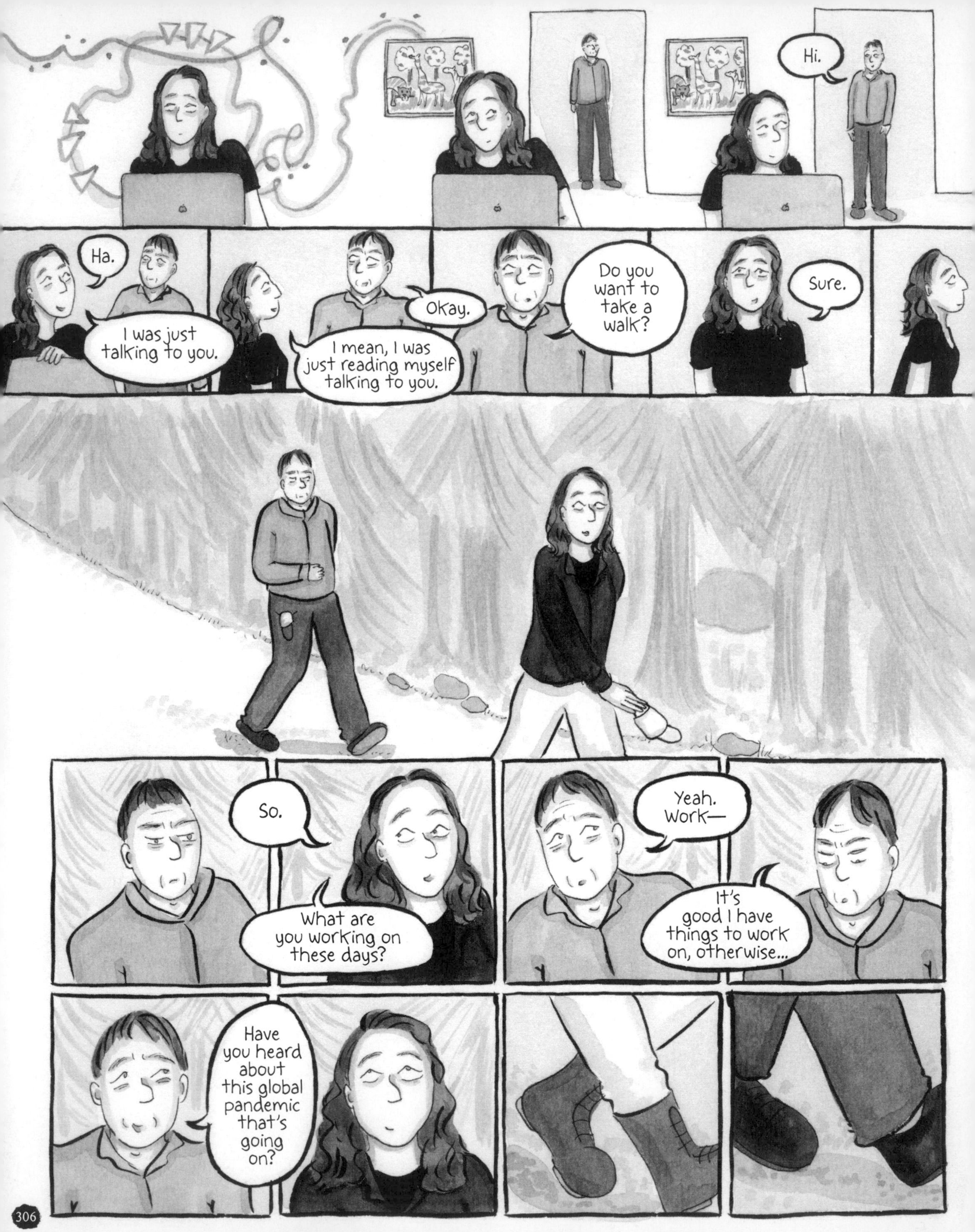
Hi.
Ha.
I was just talking to you.
I mean, I was just reading myself talking to you.
Okay.
Do you want to take a walk?
Sure.
So.
What are you working on these days?
Yeah. Work—
It's good I have things to work on, otherwise...
Have you heard about this global pandemic that's going on?

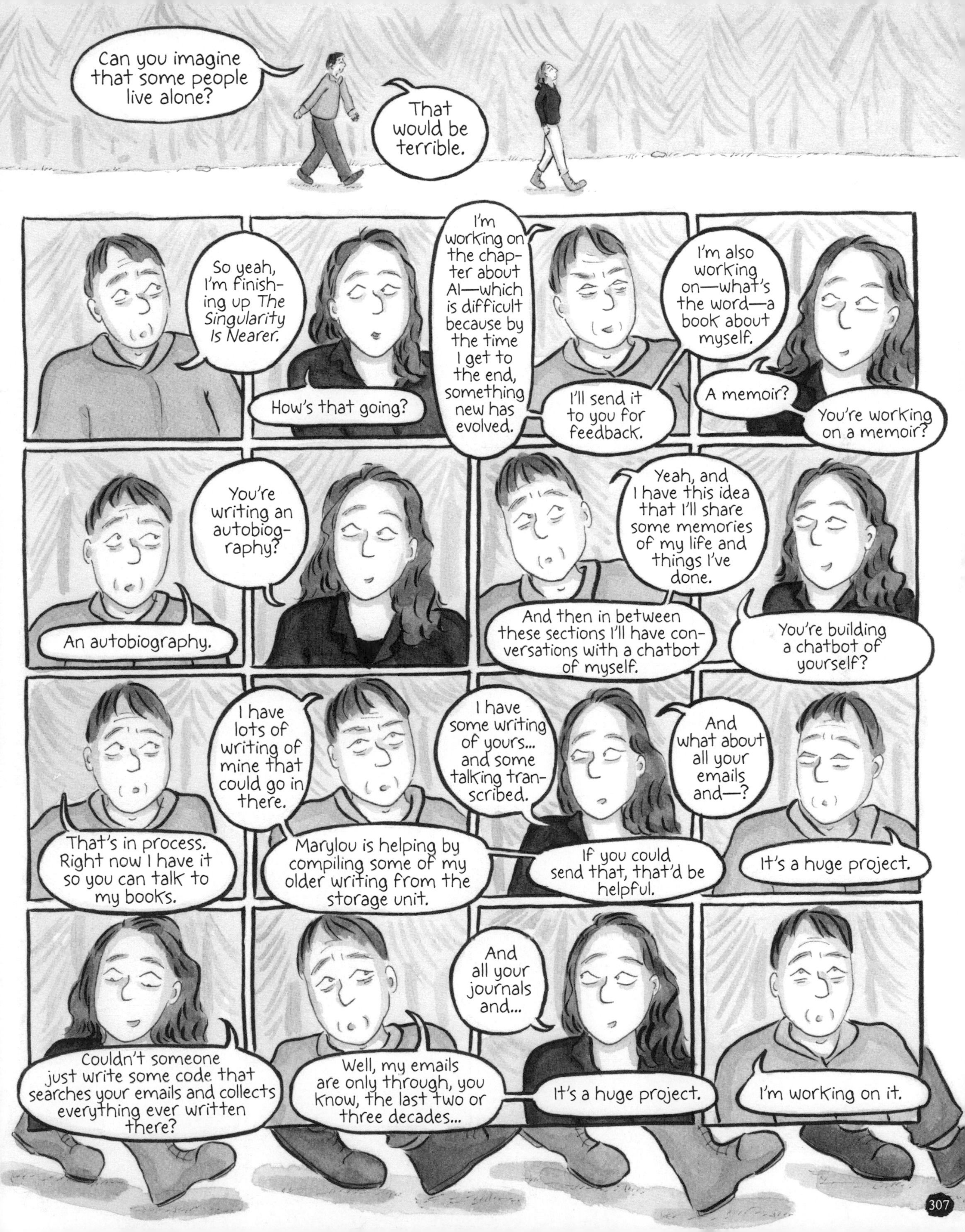
Can you imagine that some people live alone?
That would be terrible.
So yeah, I'm finishing up *The Singularity Is Nearer.*
How's that going?
I'm working on the chapter about AI—which is difficult because by the time I get to the end, something new has evolved.
I'll send it to you for feedback.
I'm also working on—what's the word—a book about myself.
A memoir?
You're working on a memoir?
An autobiography.
You're writing an autobiography?
Yeah, and I have this idea that I'll share some memories of my life and things I've done.
And then in between these sections I'll have conversations with a chatbot of myself.
You're building a chatbot of yourself?
That's in process. Right now I have it so you can talk to my books.
I have lots of writing of mine that could go in there.
Marylou is helping by compiling some of my older writing from the storage unit.
I have some writing of yours... and some talking transcribed.
If you could send that, that'd be helpful.
And what about all your emails and—?
It's a huge project.
Couldn't someone just write some code that searches your emails and collects everything ever written there?
Well, my emails are only through, you know, the last two or three decades...
And all your journals and...
It's a huge project.
I'm working on it.

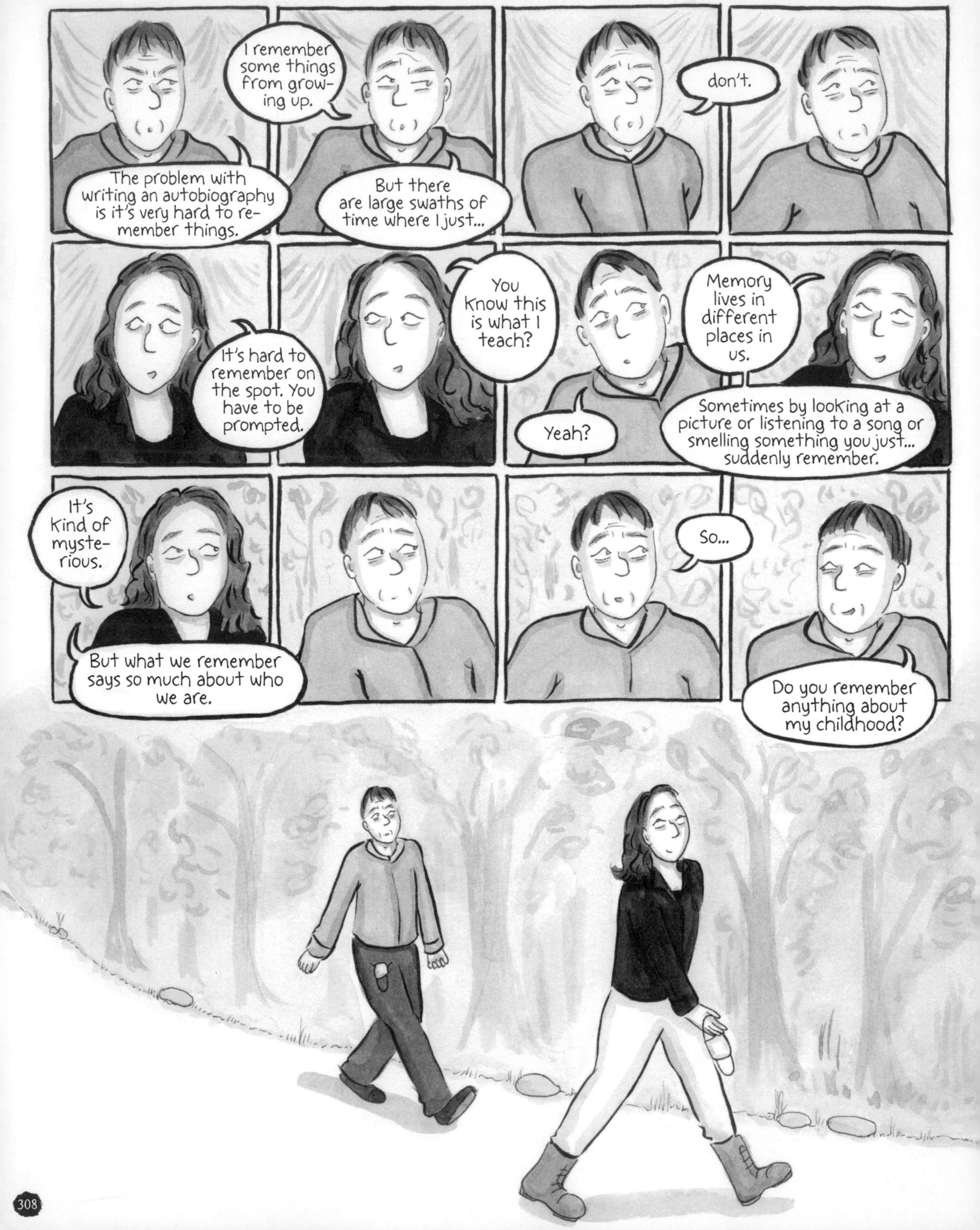
The problem with writing an autobiography is it's very hard to remember things.
I remember some things from growing up.
But there are large swaths of time where I just...
don't.
It's hard to remember on the spot. You have to be prompted.
You know this is what I teach?
Yeah?
Memory lives in different places in us.
Sometimes by looking at a picture or listening to a song or smelling something you just... suddenly remember.
It's kind of mysterious.
But what we remember says so much about who we are.
So...
Do you remember anything about my childhood?

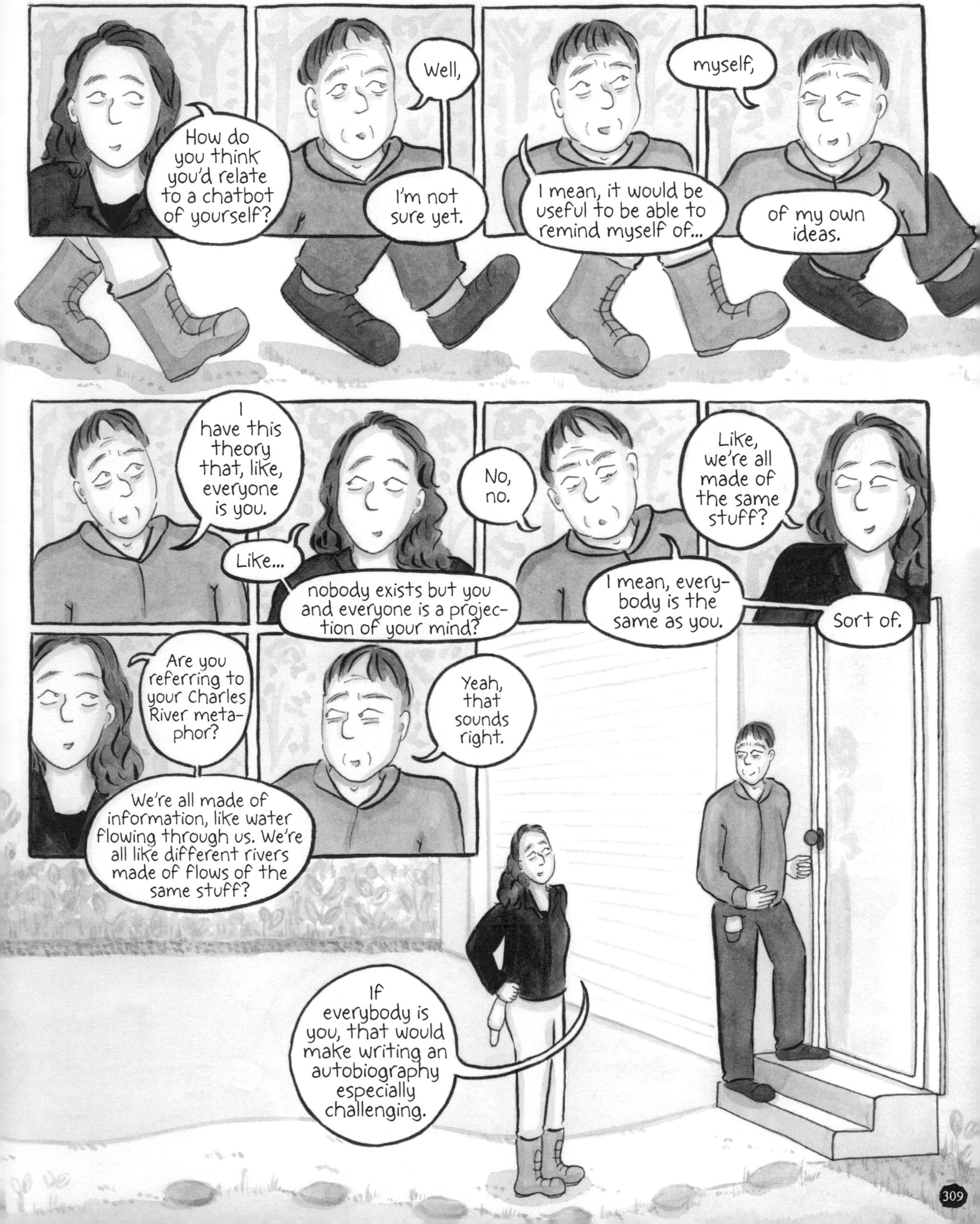
How do you think you'd relate to a chatbot of yourself?
Well,
I'm not sure yet.
myself,
I mean, it would be useful to be able to remind myself of...
of my own ideas.
I have this theory that, like, everyone is you.
Like...
nobody exists but you and everyone is a projection of your mind?
No, no.
Like, we're all made of the same stuff?
I mean, everybody is the same as you.
Sort of.
Are you referring to your Charles River metaphor?
We're all made of information, like water flowing through us. We're all like different rivers made of flows of the same stuff?
Yeah, that sounds right.
If everybody is you, that would make writing an autobiography especially challenging.

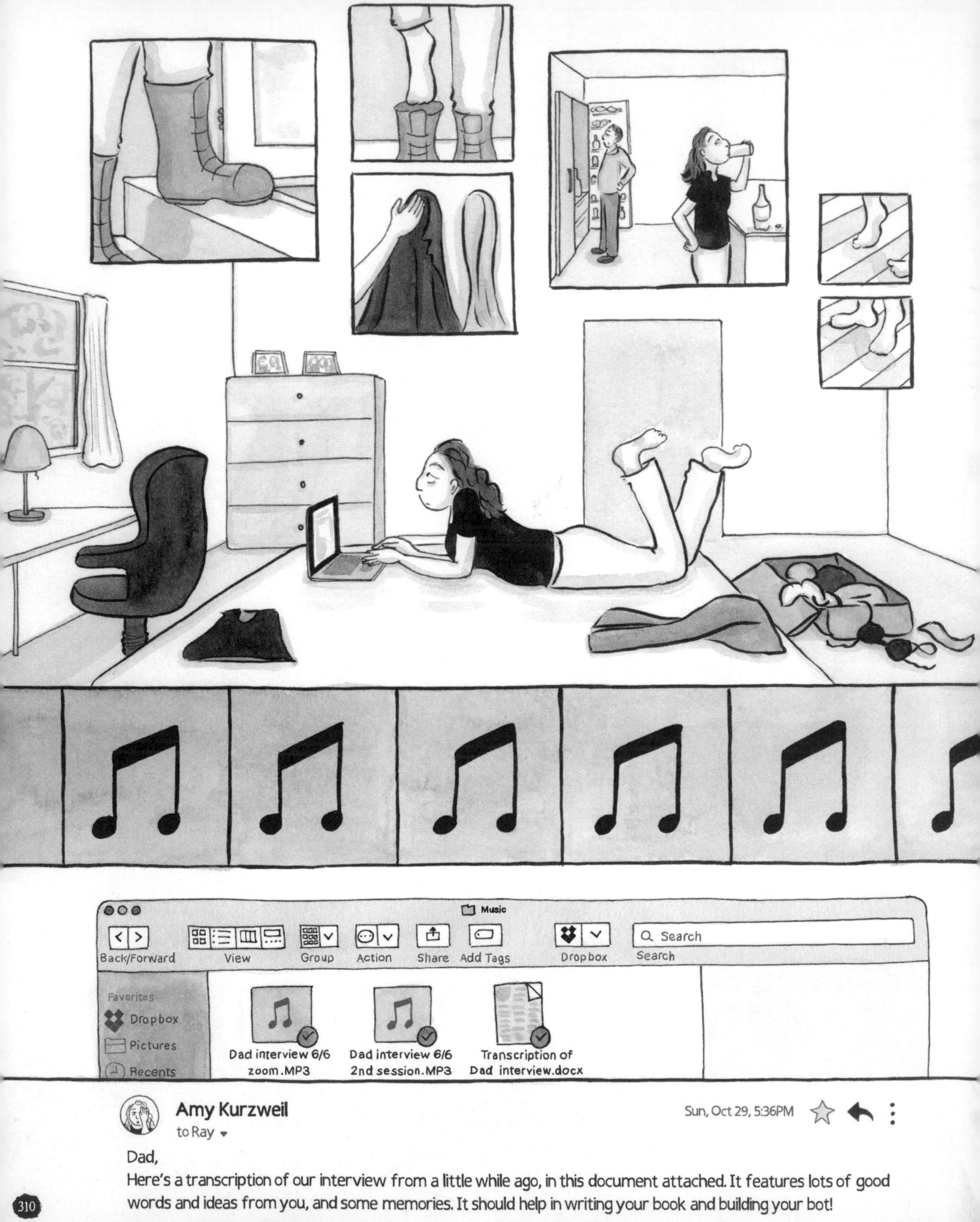
Music
Back/Forward
View
Group
Action
Share
Add Tags
Dropbox
Search
Search
Favorites
Dropbox
Pictures
Recents
Dad interview 6/6 zoom.MP3
Dad interview 6/6 2nd session.MP3
Transcription of Dad interview.docx
Amy Kurzweil
to Ray
Sun, Oct 29, 5:36PM
Dad,
Here's a transcription of our interview from a little while ago, in this document attached. It features lots of good words and ideas from you, and some memories. It should help in writing your book and building your bot!

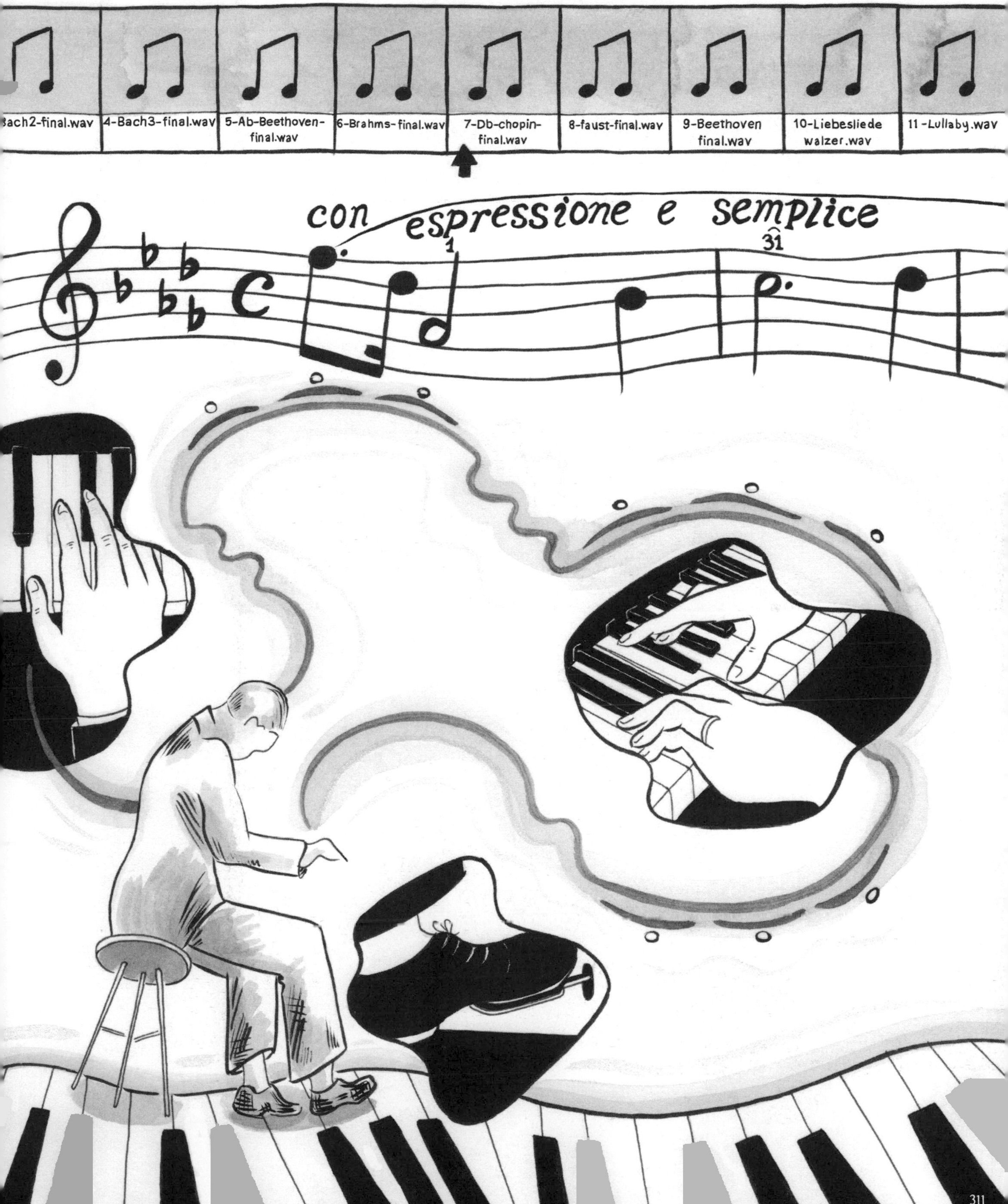
ach2-final.wav
4-Bach3-final.wav
5-Ab-Beethoven-final.wav
6-Brahms-final.wav
7-Db-chopin-final.wav
8-faust-final.wav
9-Beethoven final.wav
10-Liebesliede walzer.wav
11-Lullaby.wav
con espressione e semplice

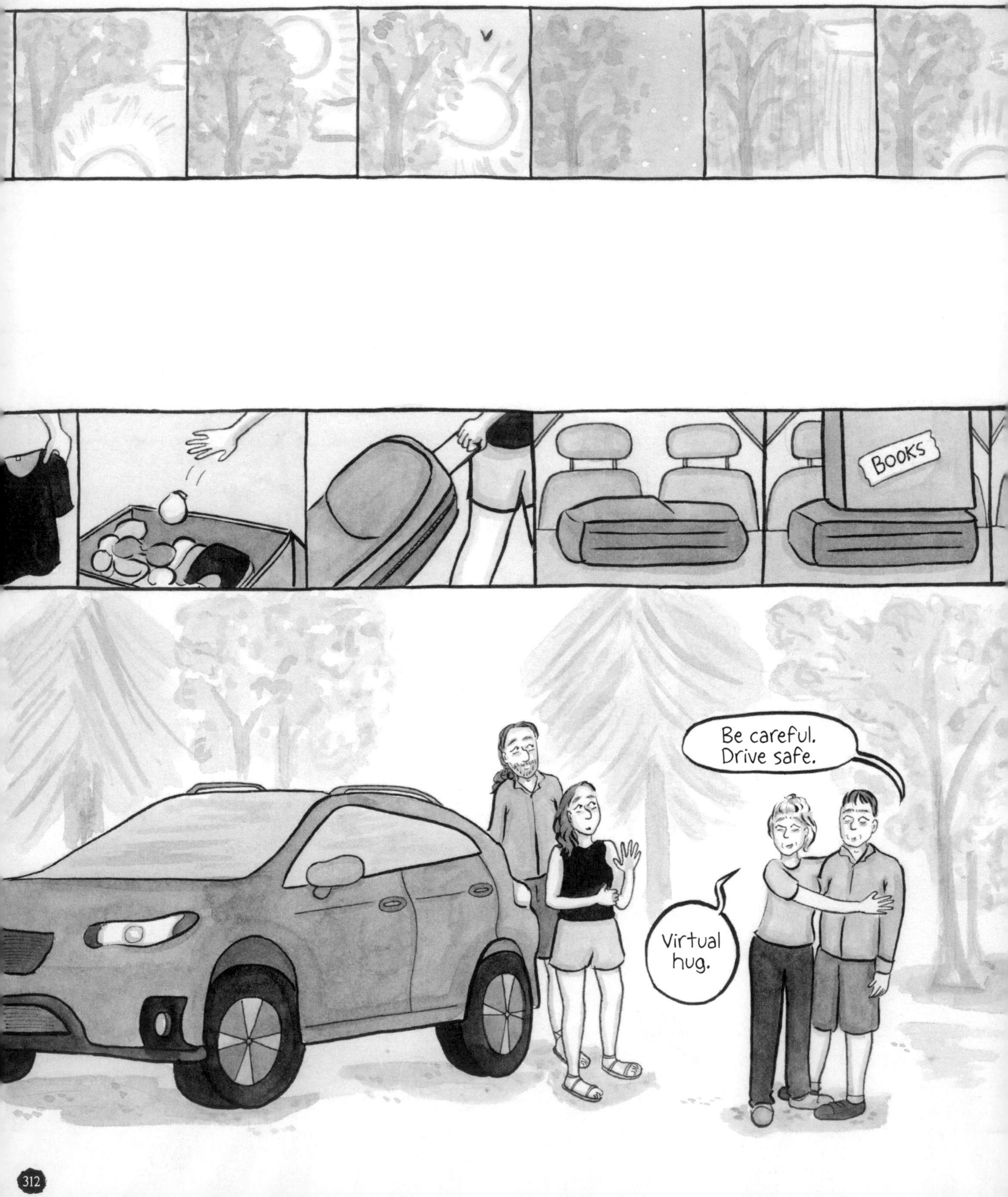
BOOKS
Be careful. Drive safe.
Virtual hug.

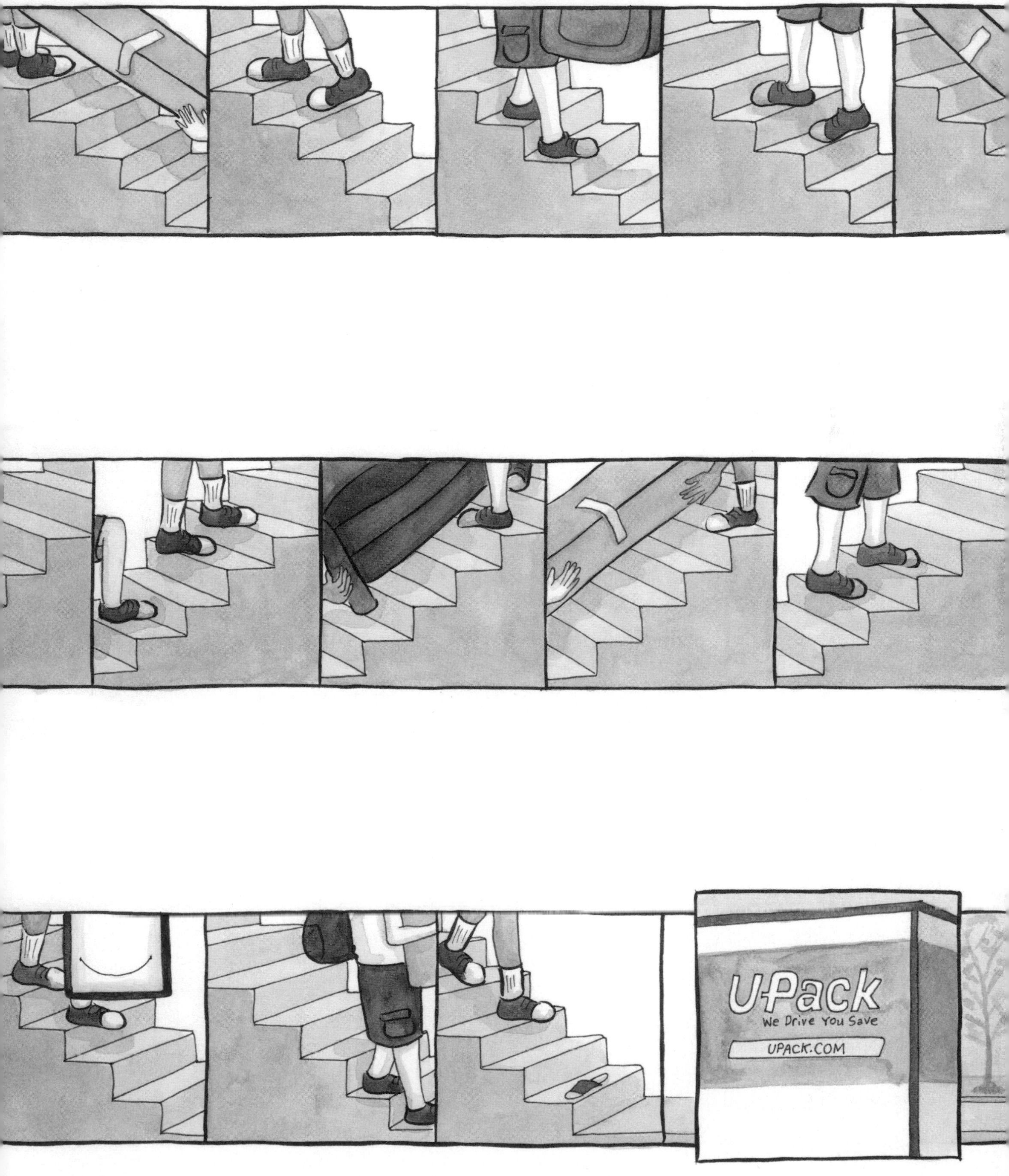
UPack
We Drive You Save
UPACK.COM

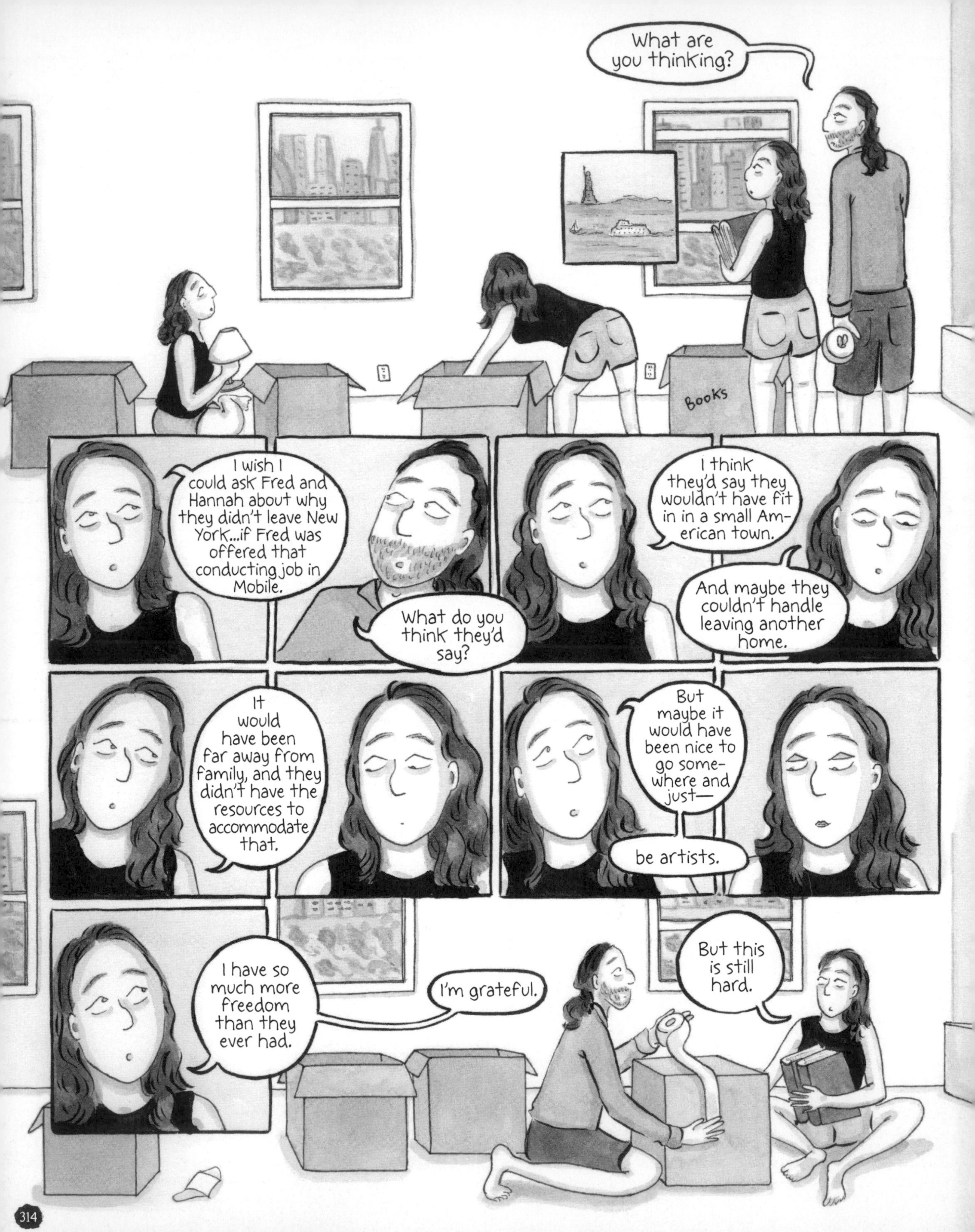
What are you thinking?
BOOKS
I wish I could ask Fred and Hannah about why they didn't leave New York...if Fred was offered that conducting job in Mobile.
What do you think they'd say?
I think they'd say they wouldn't have fit in in a small American town.
And maybe they couldn't handle leaving another home.
It would have been far away from family, and they didn't have the resources to accommodate that.
But maybe it would have been nice to go somewhere and just—
be artists.
I have so much more freedom than they ever had.
I'm grateful.
But this is still hard.

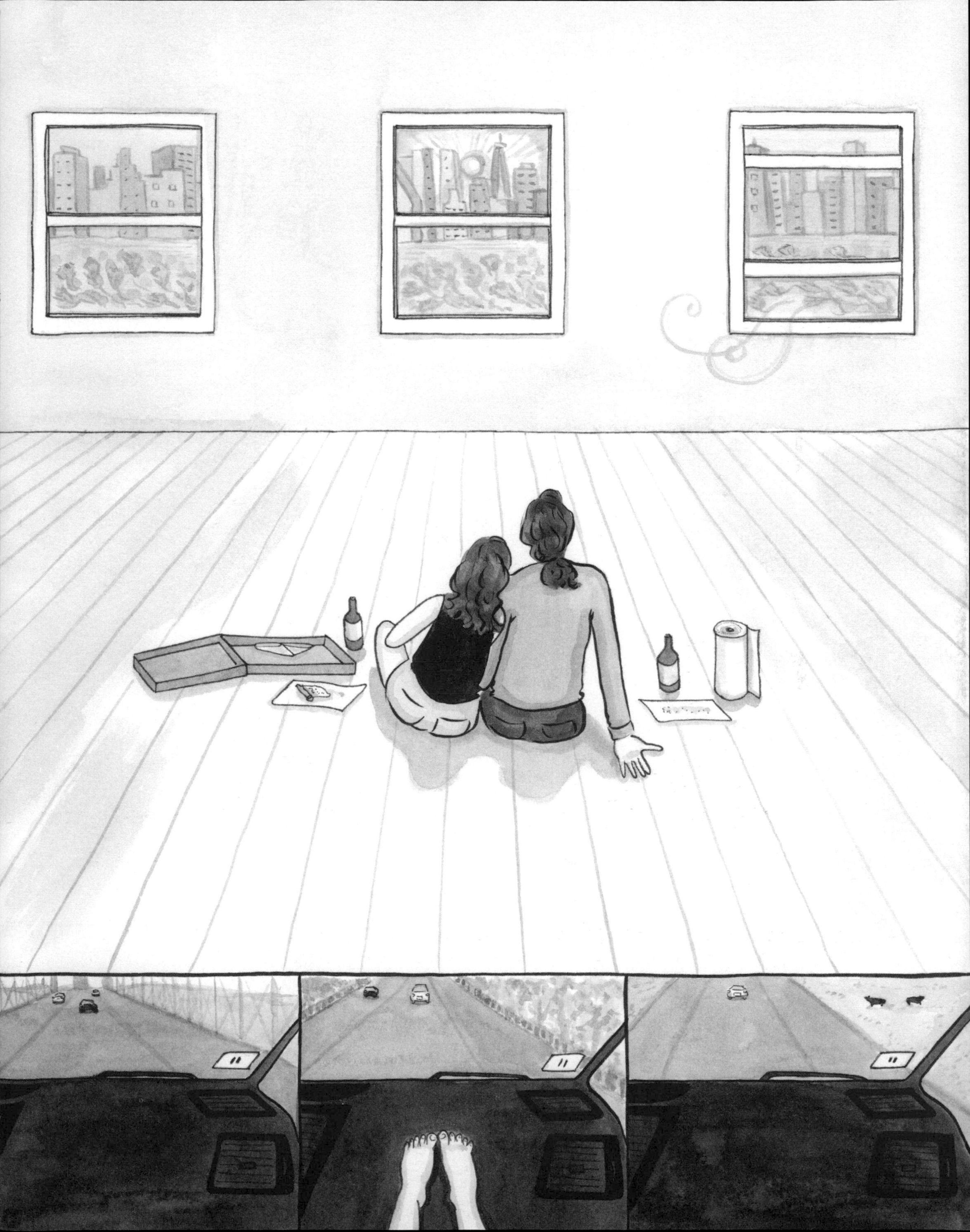

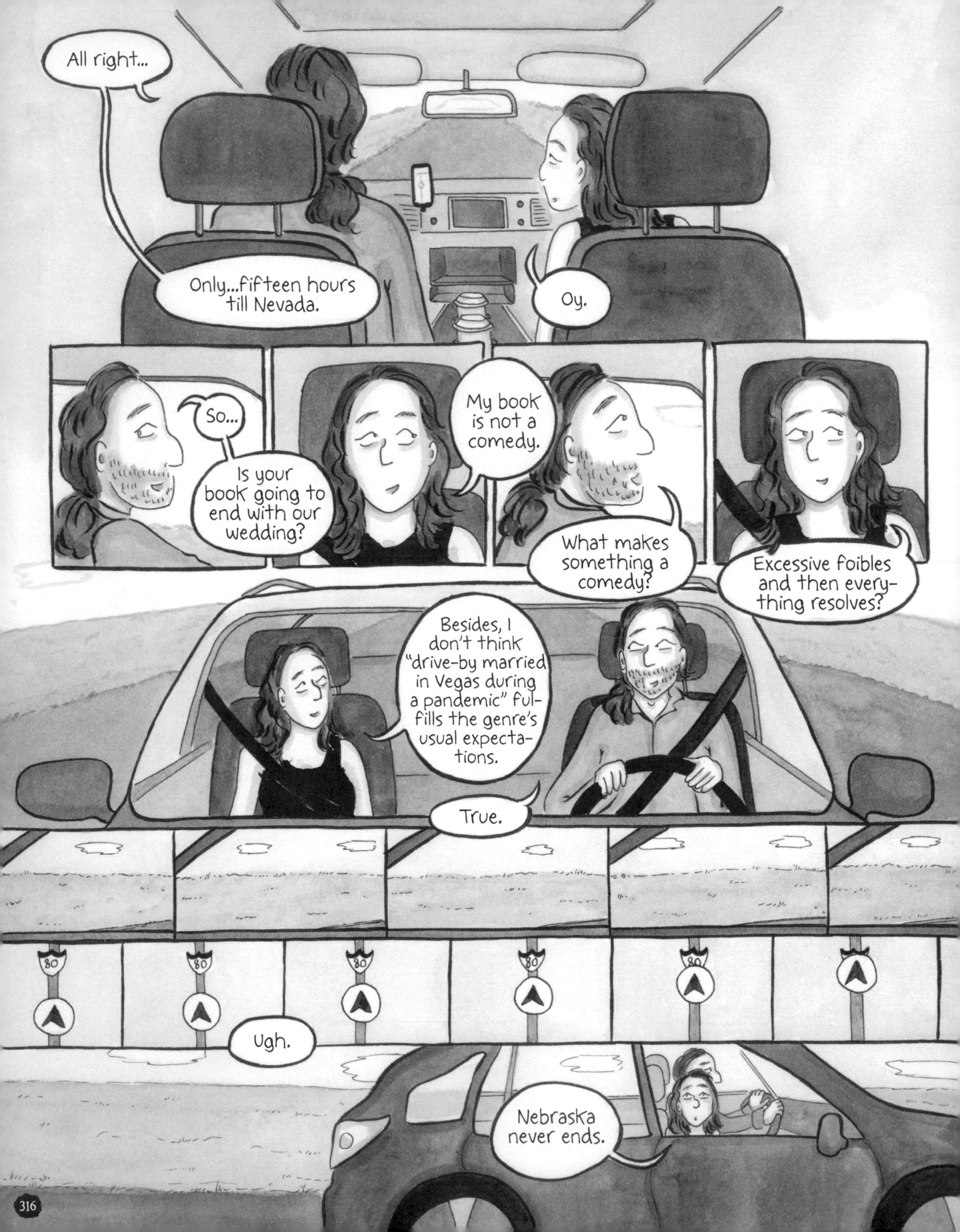
All right...
Only...fifteen hours till Nevada.
Oy.
So...
Is your book going to end with our wedding?
My book is not a comedy.
What makes something a comedy?
Excessive foibles and then every-thing resolves?
Besides, I don't think "drive-by married in Vegas during a pandemic" ful-fills the genre's usual expecta-tions.
True.
Ugh.
Nebraska never ends.

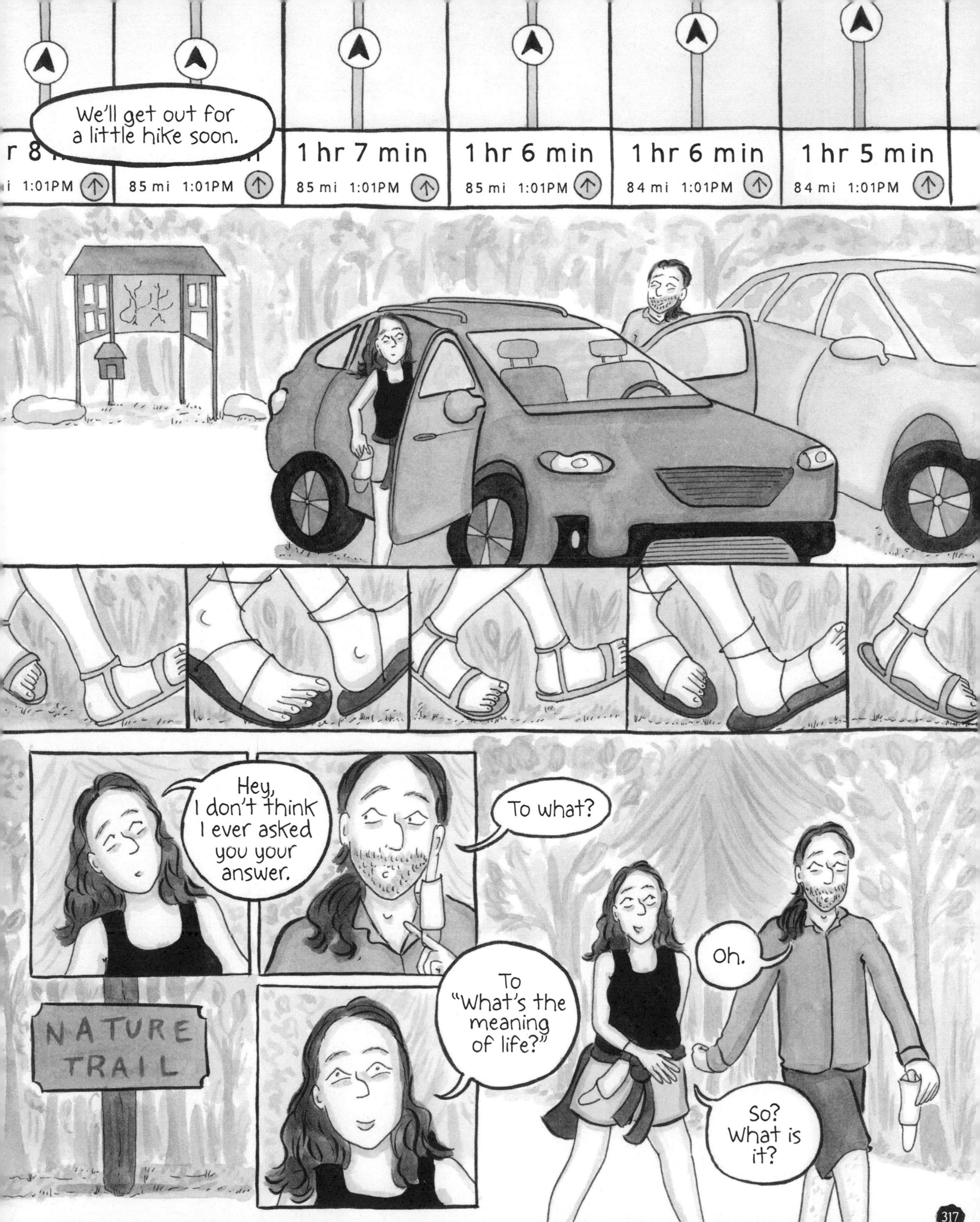
We'll get out for a little hike soon.
1 hr 7 min
85 mi 1:01PM
1 hr 6 min
85 mi 1:01PM
1 hr 6 min
84 mi 1:01PM
1 hr 5 min
84 mi 1:01PM
Hey, I don't think I ever asked you your answer.
To what?
To "What's the meaning of life?"
NATURE TRAIL
Oh.
So? What is it?

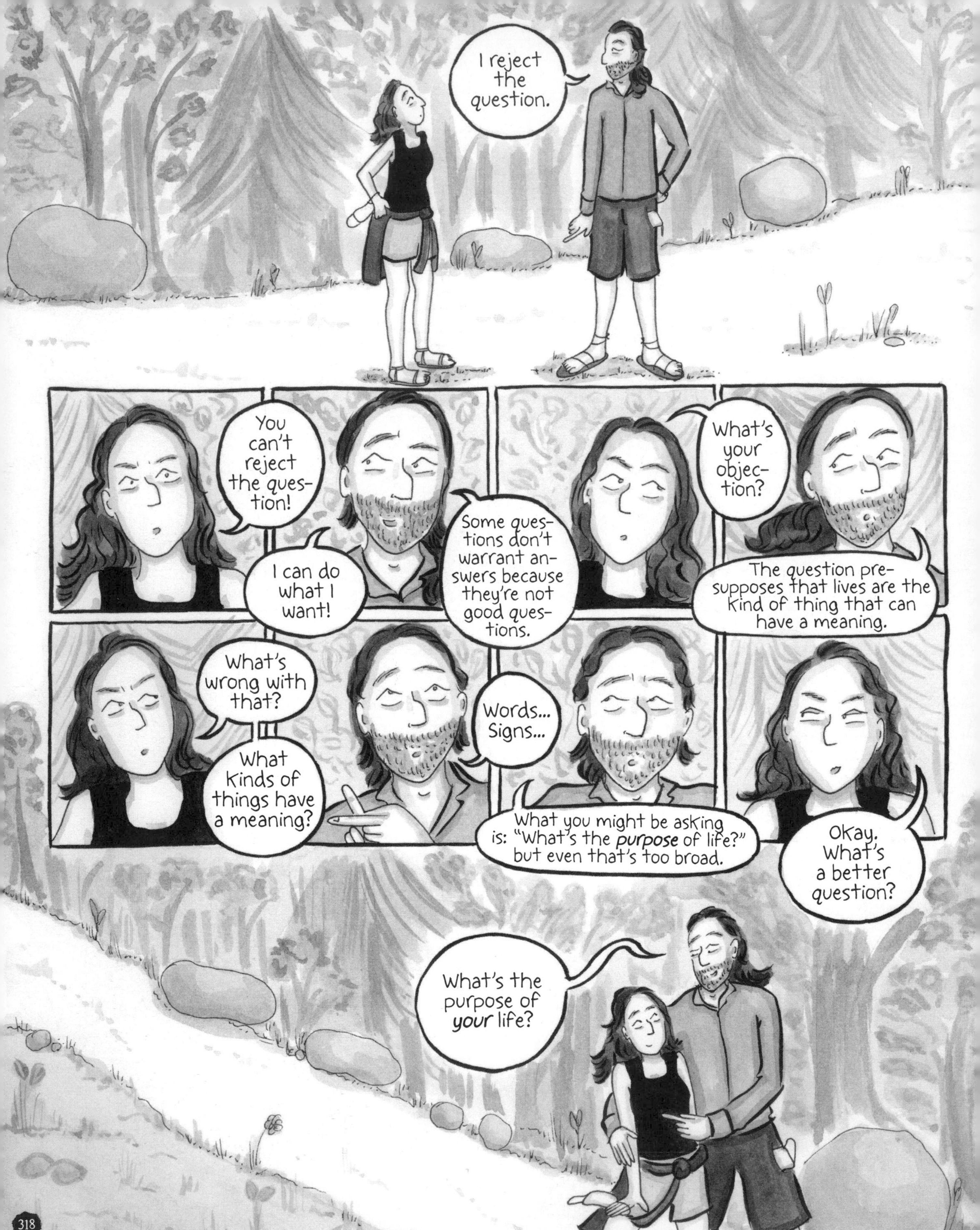
I reject the question.
You can't reject the question!
I can do what I want!
Some questions don't warrant answers because they're not good questions.
What's your objection?
The question presupposes that lives are the kind of thing that can have a meaning.
What's wrong with that?
What kinds of things have a meaning?
Words... Signs...
What you might be asking is: "What's the *purpose* of life?" but even that's too broad.
Okay. What's a better question?
What's the purpose of ***your*** life?

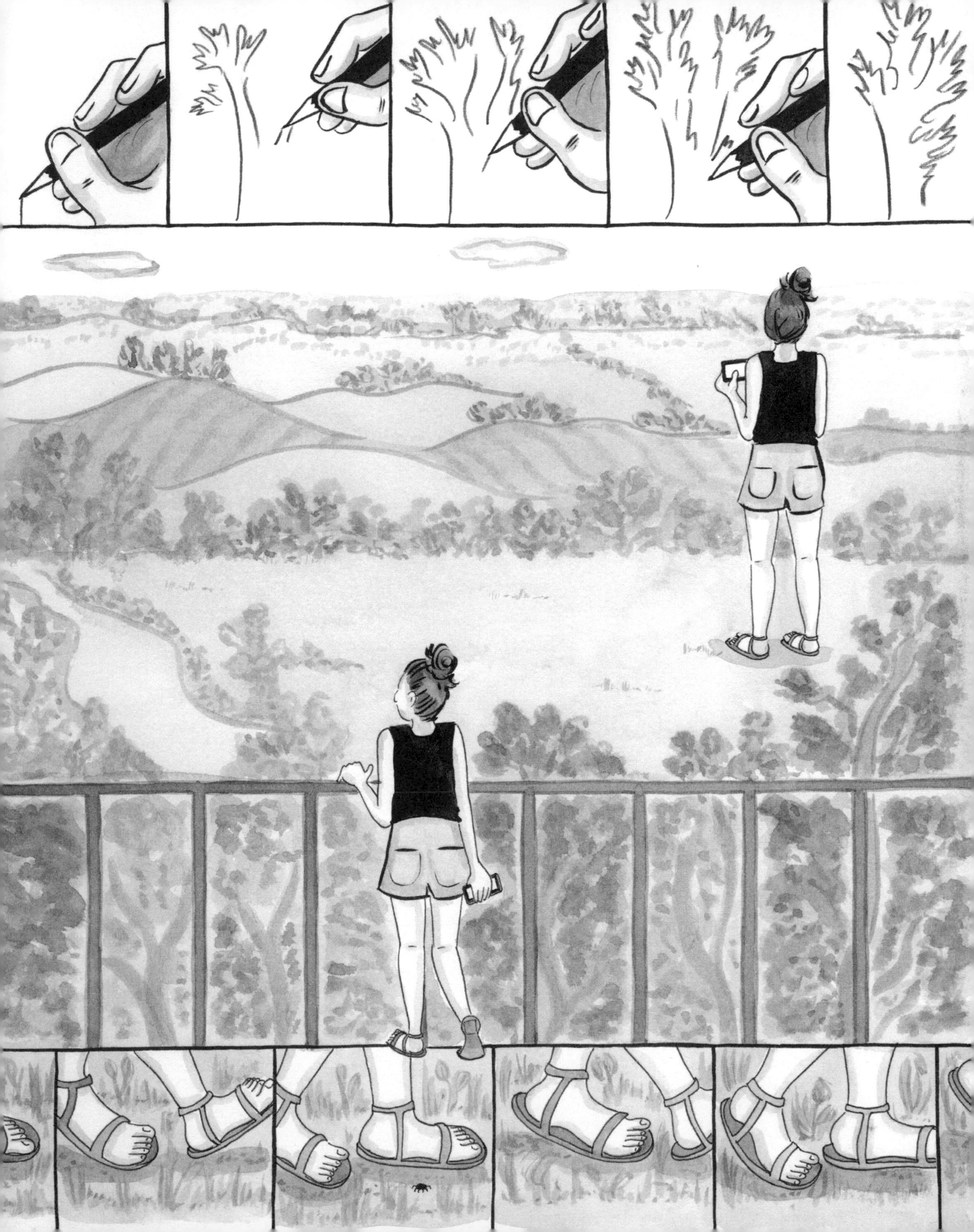

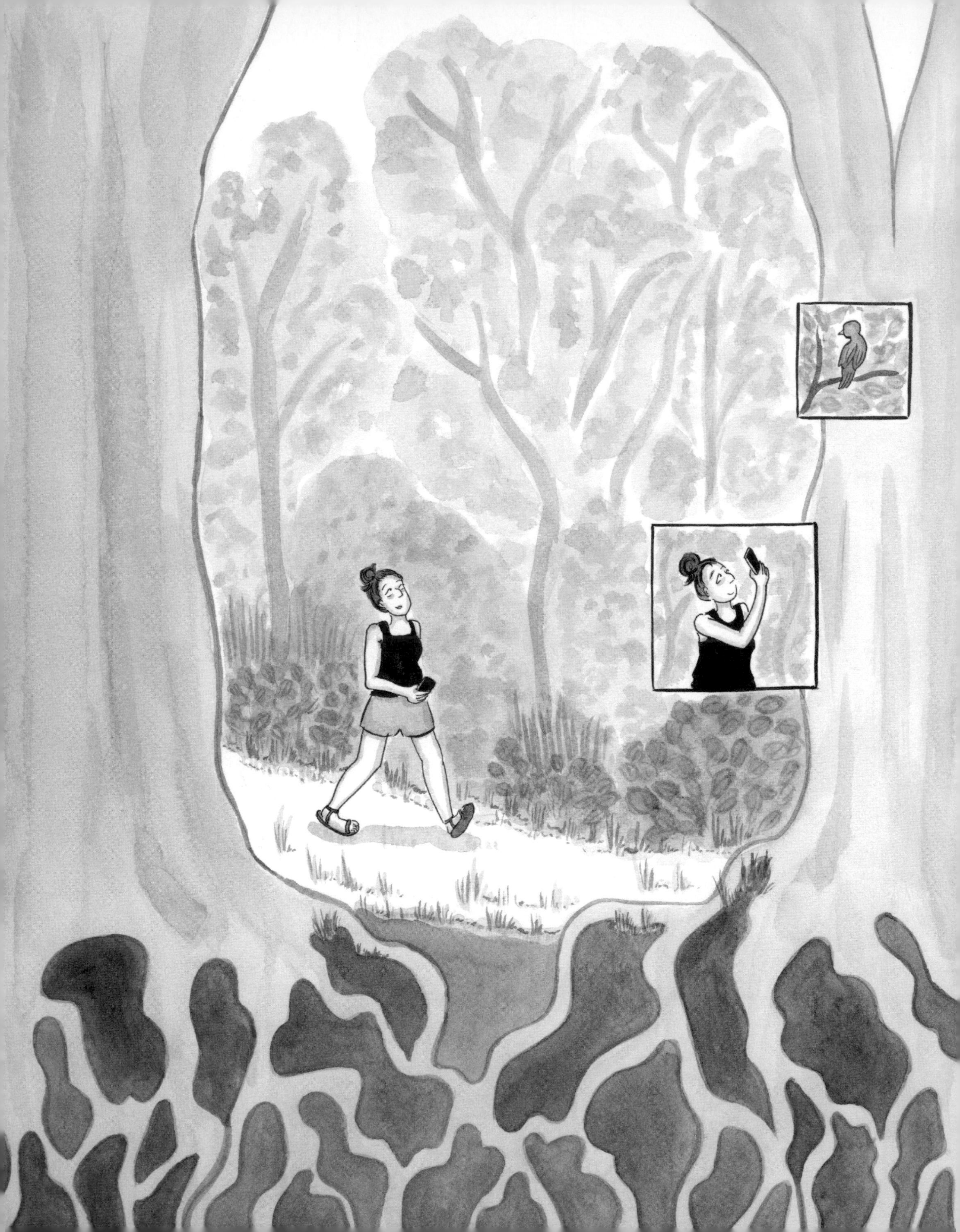

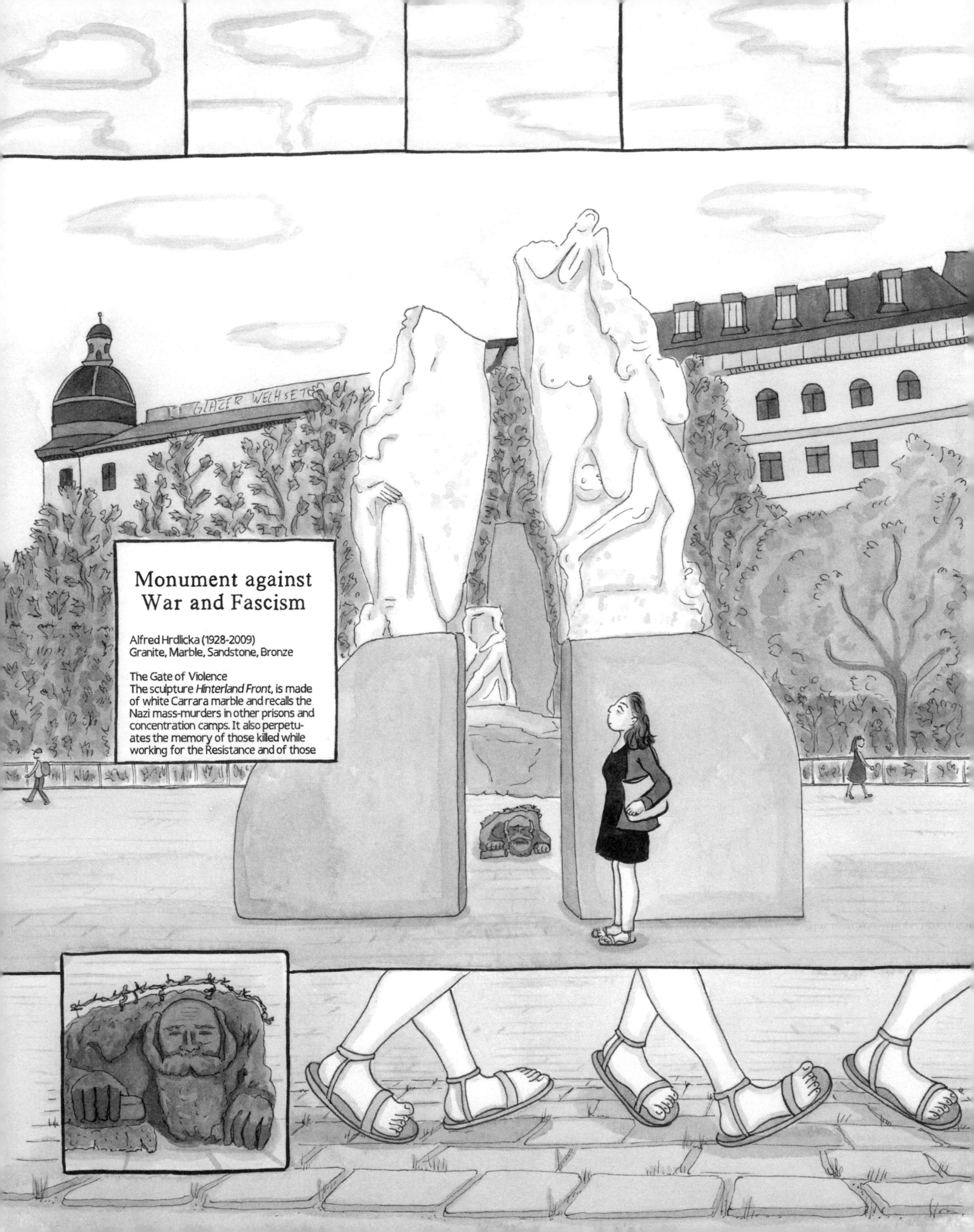
Monument against War and Fascism
Alfred Hrdlicka (1928-2009)
Granite, Marble, Sandstone, Bronze
The Gate of Violence
The sculpture *Hinterland Front*, is made of white Carrara marble and recalls the Nazi mass-murders in other prisons and concentration camps. It also perpetu-ates the memory of those killed while working for the Resistance and of those

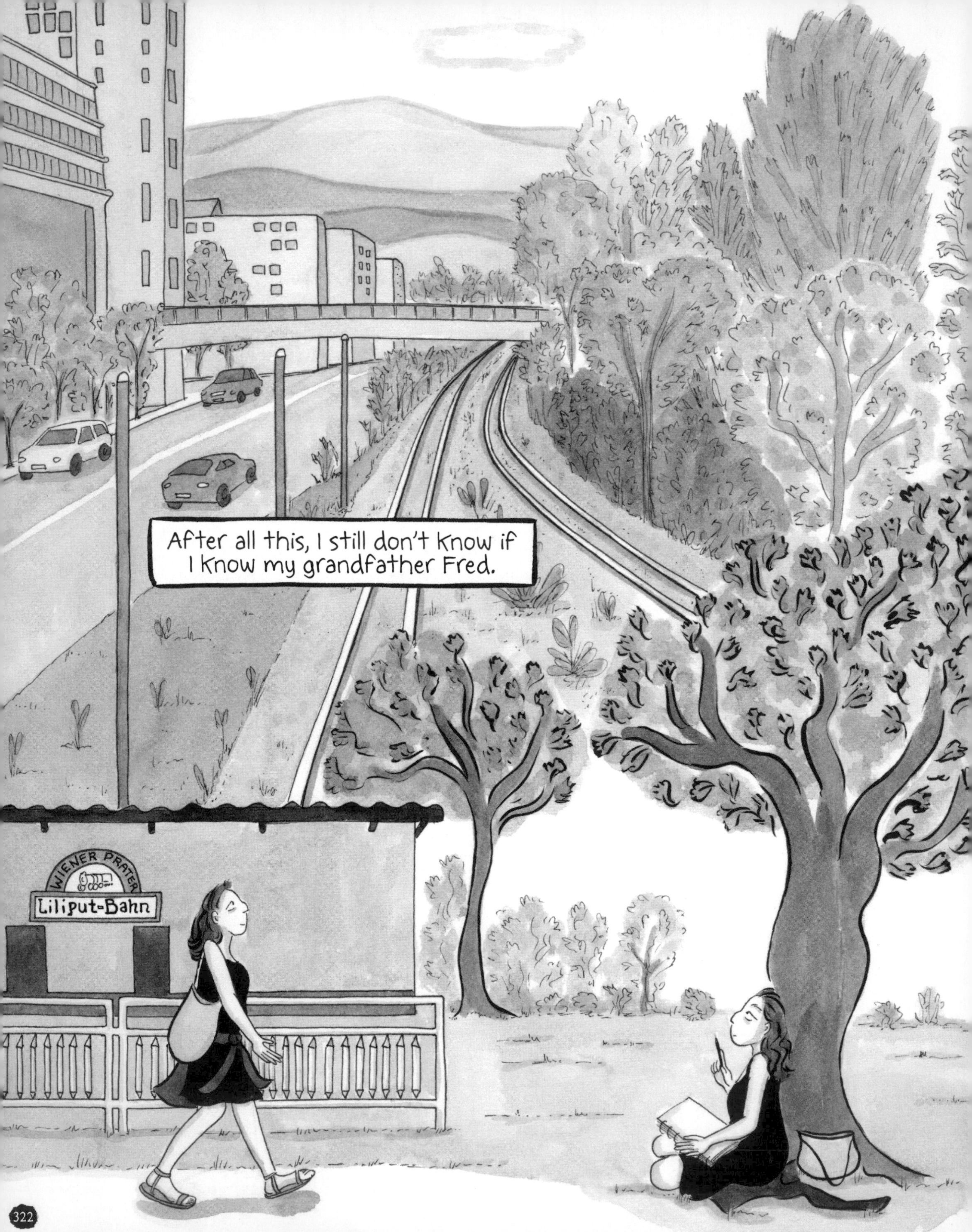
After all this, I still don't know if I know my grandfather Fred.
WIENER PRATER
Liliput-Bahn

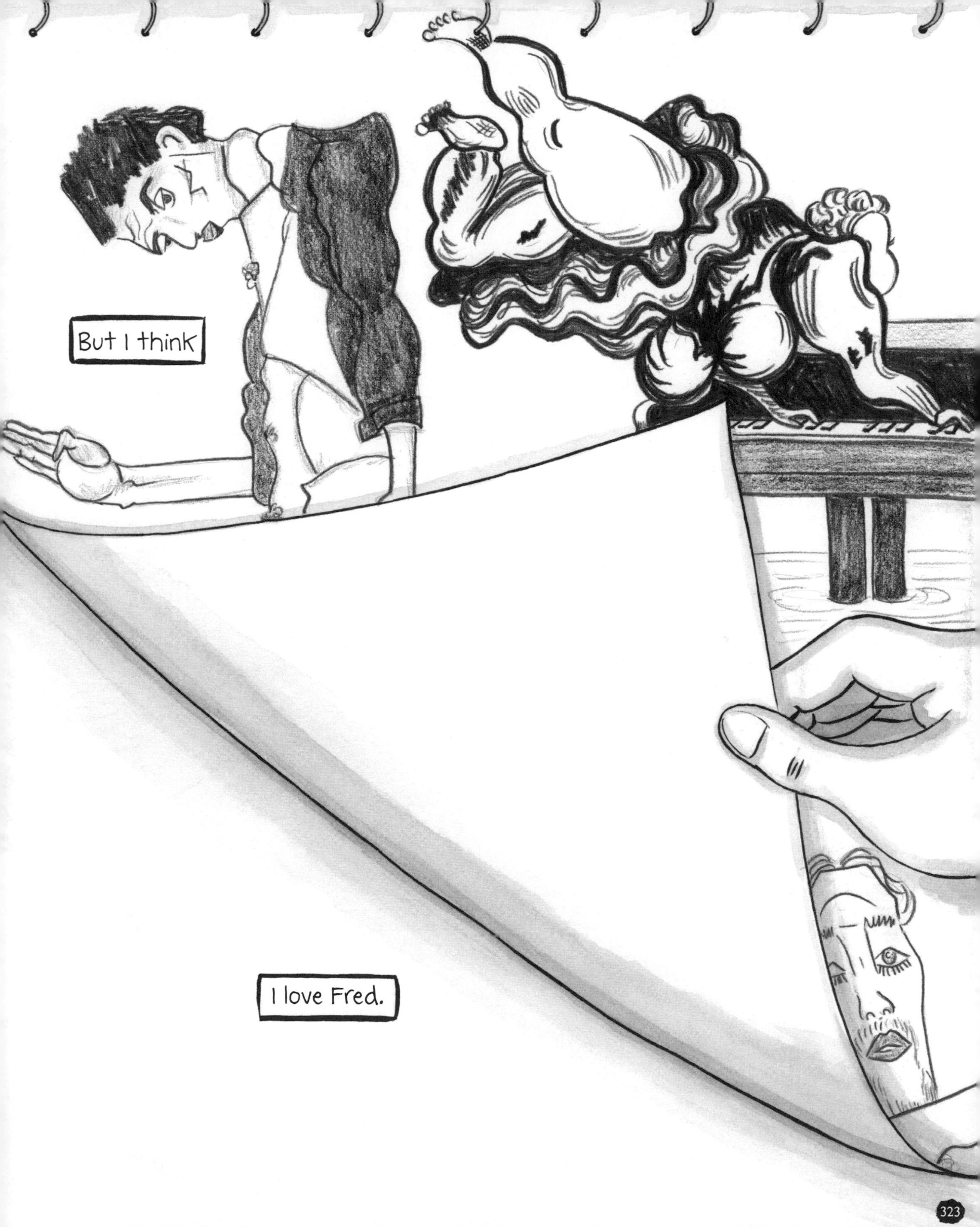
But I think
I love Fred.

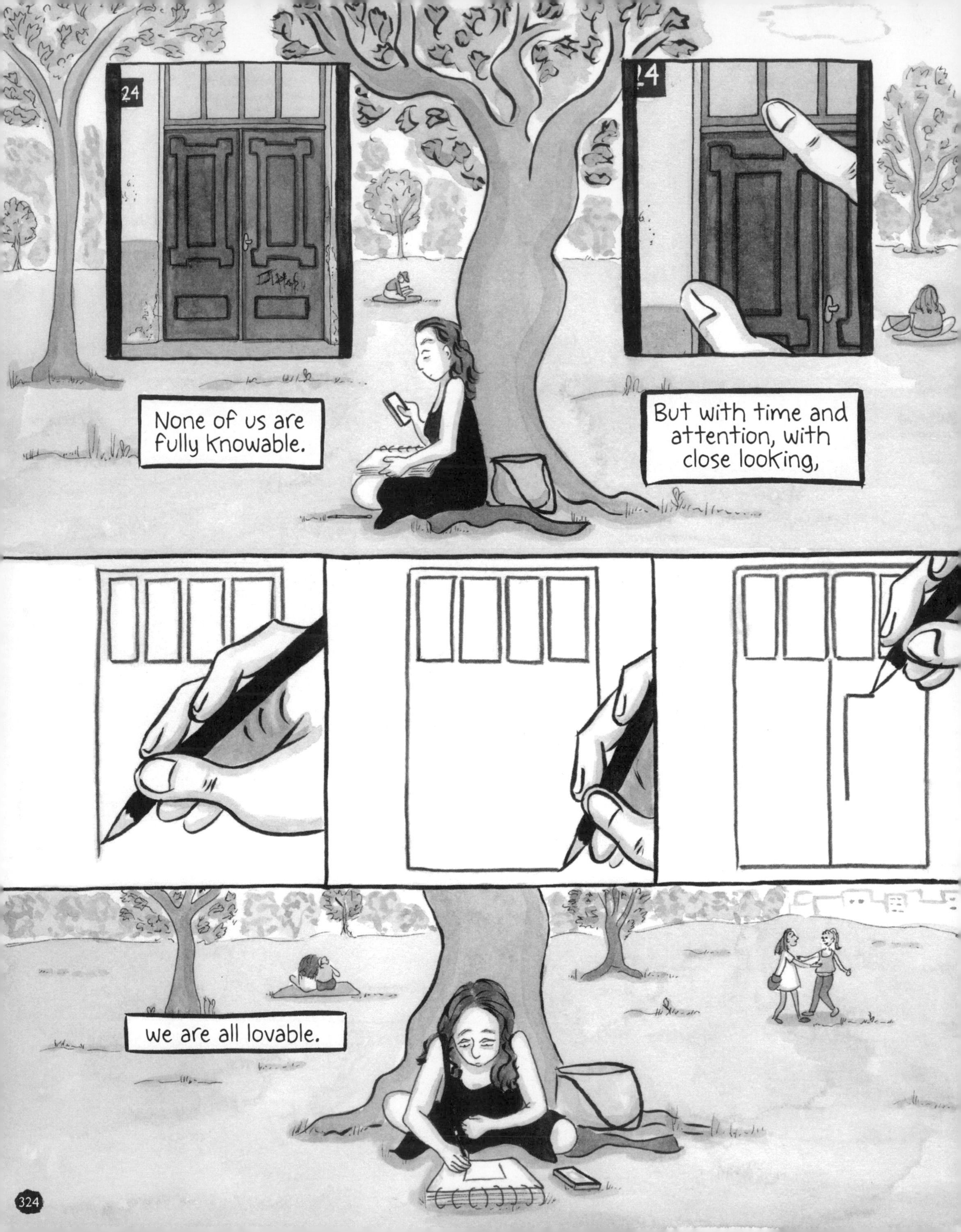
24
24
None of us are fully knowable.
But with time and attention, with close looking,
we are all lovable.

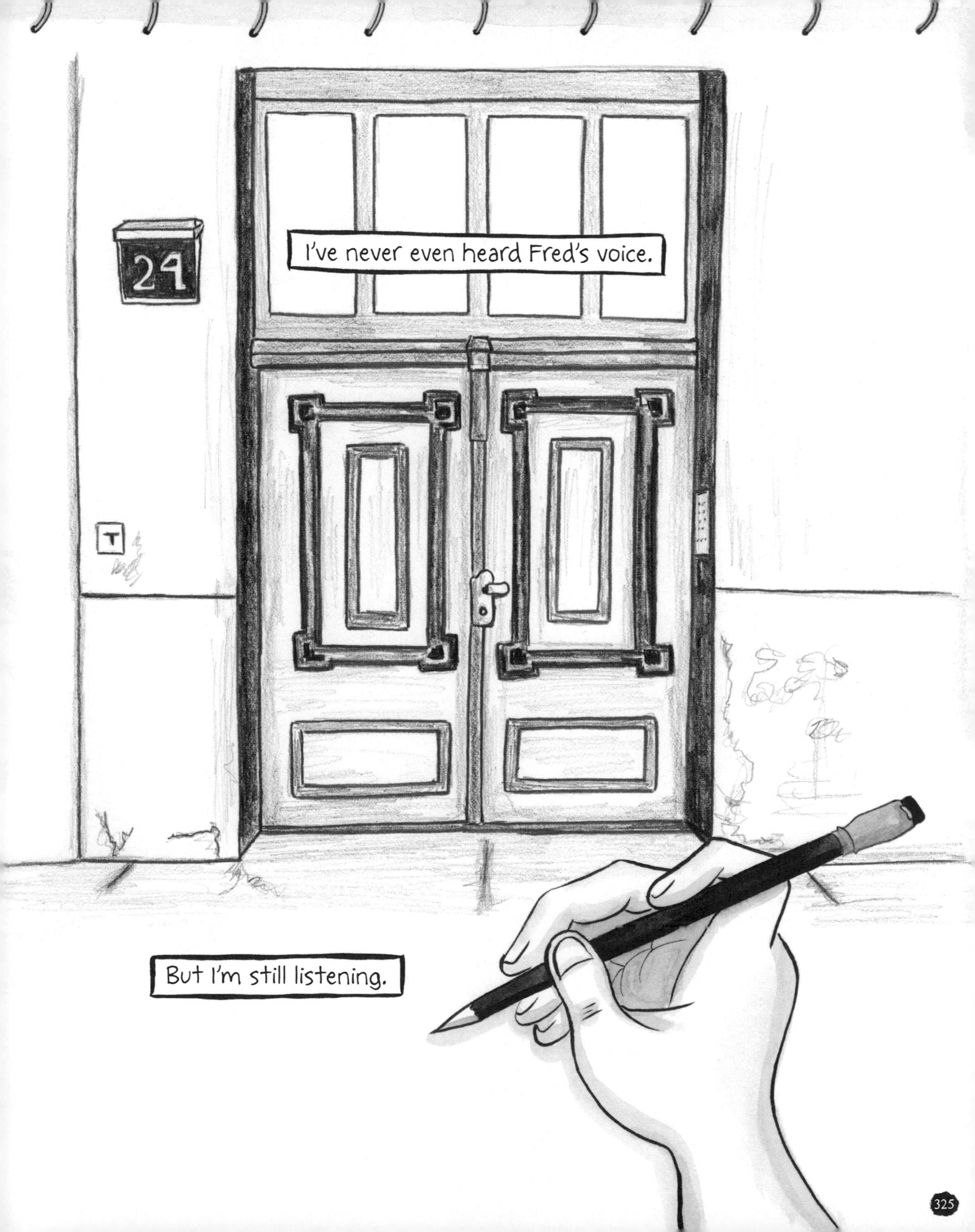
I've never even heard Fred's voice.
29
But I'm still listening.

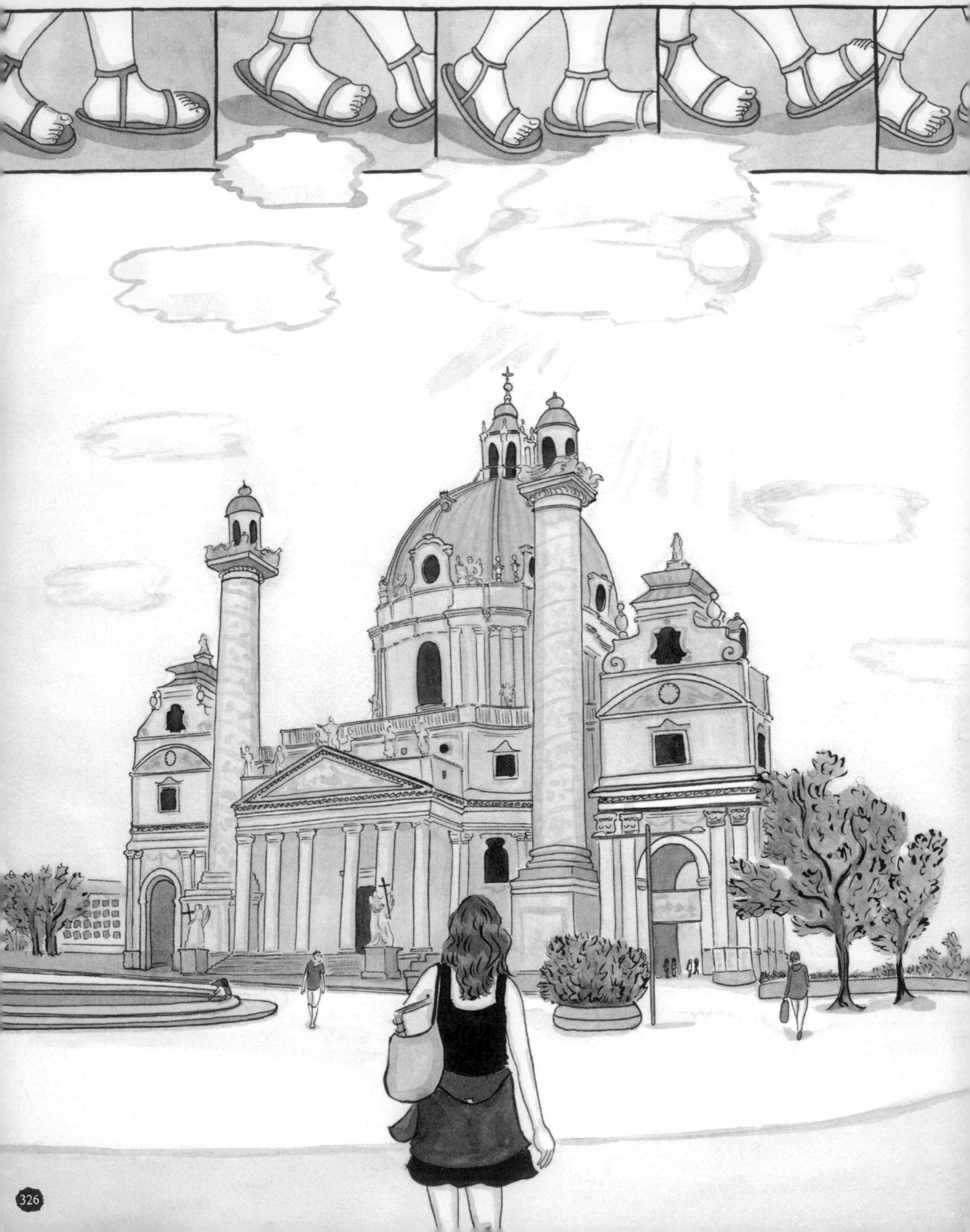

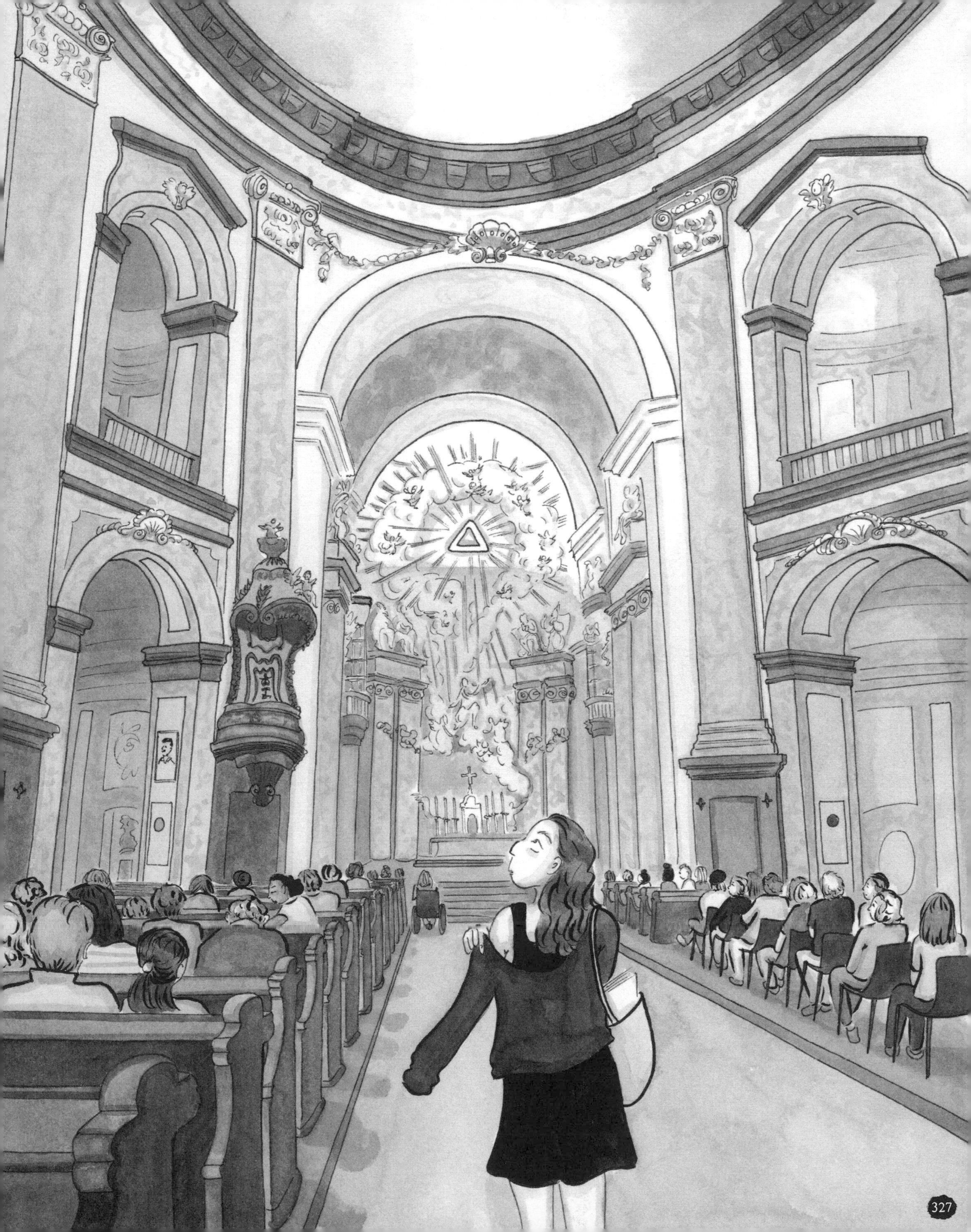

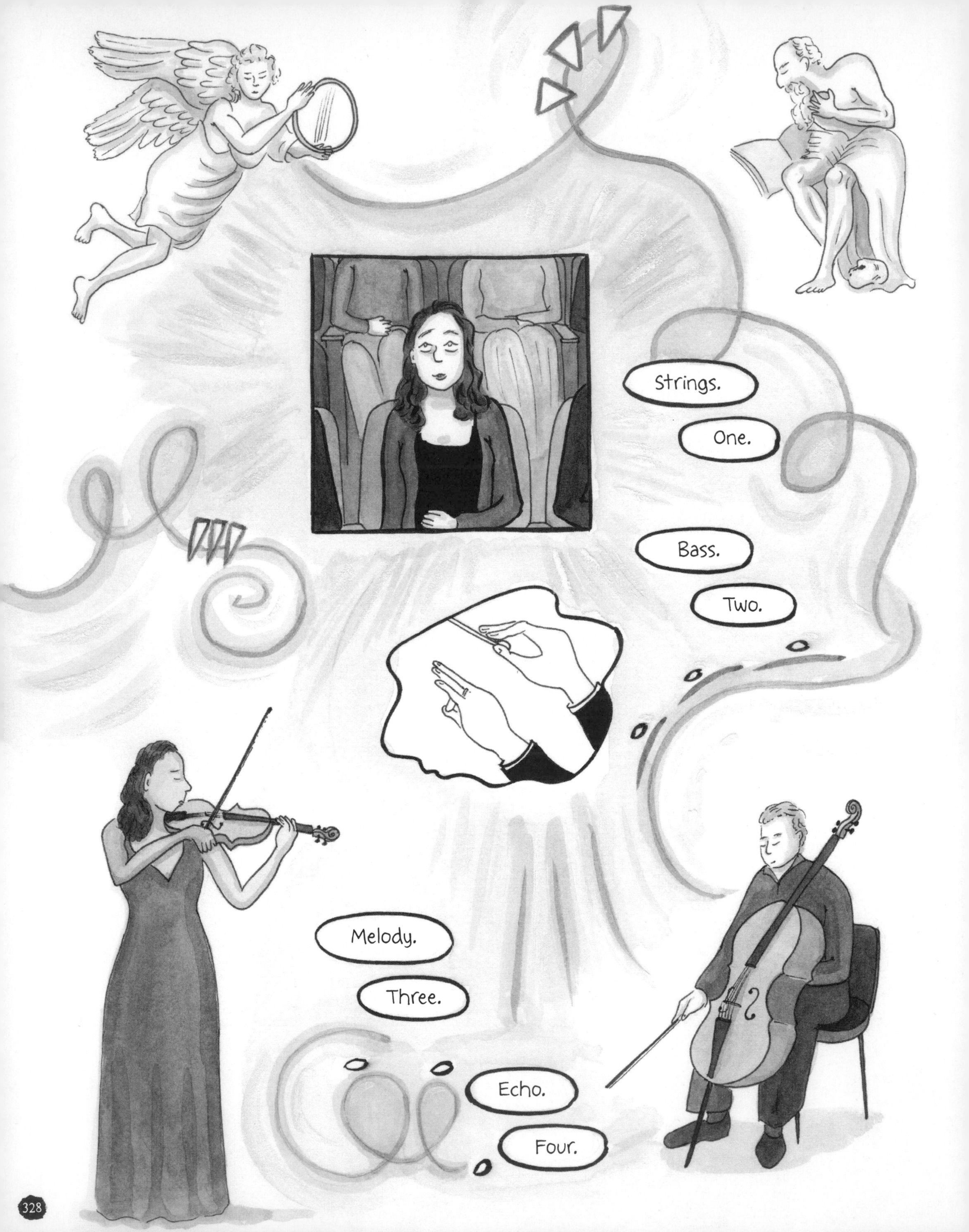
Strings.
One.
Bass.
Two.
Melody.
Three.
Echo.
Four.

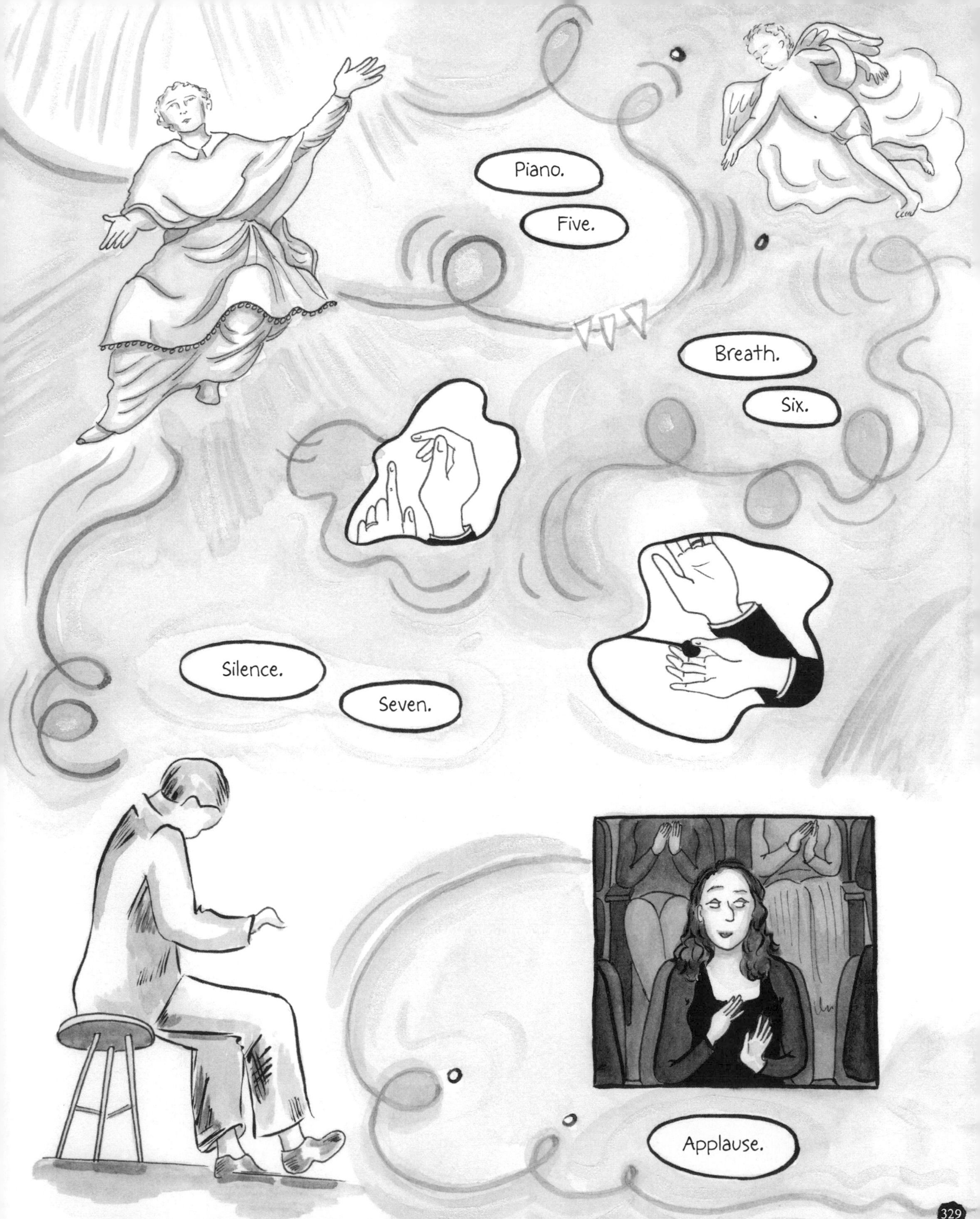
Piano.
Five.
Breath.
Six.
Silence.
Seven.
Applause.

# ACKNOWLEDGMENTS

Before we begin, I'd like to admit that my favorite part of every book is the acknowledgments section. Sometimes I skip ahead to read it before finishing the actual book. (Did I catch you skipping ahead?)

Firstly, I'm grateful to my agent, Jenni Ferrari-Adler, for her steadfast support and enthusiasm over many years. Your know-how and belief in my work have been essential.

Thank you, Julie Buntin, my first and foremost editor. Your care with my books is exactly the kind of loving attention I'm on about at the end of *Artificial*. You've gone above and beyond in your commitment to molding my family's stories into grounded works of art.

Thank you to everyone at Catapult. For editorial guidance at key moments, Alicia Kroell, Kendall Storey, and especially Summer Farah for help with the appendix. Elizabeth Pankova for support. Andy Hunter and Alyson Forbes for leadership. Lena Moses-Schmitt, Rachel Fershleiser, and Megan Fishmann for spreading the news. Mikayla Butchart and Sue Ducharme for copyediting and SD Joseph and Jean Kahler for proofreading. The design and production team for your talent and willingness to collaborate: Wah-Ming Chang for oversight; Nicole Caputo for cover direction and Farjana Yasmin for mechanical design; Laura Berry for diligent typesetting and book design; Olenka Burgess for everything. Thank you for answering my questions and honoring my vision.

Thank you, John Martz, who made and perfected my handwriting font. Thanks, Caligraphr, which helped me draw a bunch more fonts.

Thank you, Courtney Stock, for teaching me about color for *Artificial*'s cover.

Without Lillehammer Allen and her Photoshopping wizardry and emotional support skills, I don't know where I'd be, but I certainly wouldn't be sitting in a nice café, calmly typing my acknowledgments.

Thank you, Martin's Universal Design drawing board, LED Lightpad, Bienfang gridded paper, Blackwing pencils, Pentel brush pen, Micron refillable Multiliners, Arches 140-lb hot press paper, watercolor in lamp black, sable watercolor brushes, and too many Epson wide-format scanners carted all around the world (shoutout to Zach Ellis for housing my ginormous scanner in his van.) Thank you also to aaalllll the podcasts and audiobooks.

*Artificial* has benefited from every artist residency I've ever attended. Thank you to CAMAC and all the artists who breathed mosquitoes with me by the Seine in 2016. Thank you to Djerassi and its attendant artists in summer 2018, especially Nico Ponton. Thank you to MacDowell for providing me with not one but two sessions of writing and drawing utopia. Annie Hartnett and Caitlin Delohery have been my writer text crisis line since 2019. Buzz Slutsky, Josephine Rowe, and so many others lifted my spirits in 2022. If you ever said a positive word to me over a delicious meal in a bucolic setting, it helped.

Thank you to the Black Mountain Institute, especially Sara Ortiz, Ahmed Naje, and the Writers Block for accompanying me in Vegas in 2019, truly one of the most fun semesters of my life.

Thank you to the American Academy in Berlin for feeding and housing me in style, immersing me in my grandparents' and my mother's first language, and validating the scope of my work. Thank you to the 2020 and 2021 fellows for your feedback and encouragement. And special thanks to John-Thomas Eltringham, who is still able to answer any and all questions I have about anything German.

Thank you to *The Believer* magazine, especially Daniel Gumbiner, for giving me a place to write and draw strange stories about technology.

Kristen Radtke's editorial genius has graced all the projects I'm proudest of. Thank you for home-grown meals and the model your work provides me.

Thank you to *The New Yorker* magazine for giving my cartoons a wider reach: Emma Allen for your vision and support and Colin Stokes for being a cartoonist champion. Thank you, Bob Mankoff, for taking a chance on a self-actualized car and never failing to wax philosophical with me about AI and the nature of consciousness.

The best thing that ever happened to me was becoming a cartoonist, not for the fame and glory but for the community of goons I get to pester for the rest of my life: Ellis Rosen, thank you for teaching me how to draw things and forever welcoming my complaints; Navied Mahdavian, who

I texted a picture of possibly every page of this book right after drawing it, thank you for invariably telling me "amazing" and/or "you're insane," and for your genuinely encouraging read of my book as you worked on yours. Kendra Allenby, Jason Adam Katzenstein, Hilary Campbell, and Sofia Warren (who provided detailed and helpful feedback on an early draft) are not only my friends, but they also produce wonderful graphic memoir. TOONSTACK, I love you (toonstack.substack.com!). Thank you, Miriam Katin, for your legacy; Liana Finck, for your inspiration; Leise Hook, for your commiseration. Thanks, Ed Himelblau, for cartoonist companionship in San Luis Obispo.

Thank you to the legends of graphic memoir, especially Roz Chast, Alison Bechdel, and Lynda Barry, whose approach to this form has especially influenced my life.

Thank you, Tahneer Oksman, and other academics who make what we do feel meaningful and also important.

Thank you to the writers who offered me detailed feedback:

Jonathan Lee for reading the book at an important moment and providing excellent tweaks.

I'm so grateful to Jen Choi's brilliant eye. Thank you for always taking my work so seriously.

To the poet Hannah Baker Saltmarsh, thank you for your manic scrawl and the life force of your enthusiasm.

Thank you to Becca Nison, who said, years ago, to the earliest, headiest draft: "I just want to spend some time with you."

Thank you, Sarah Smetana Ostiz, for always seeking clarity in my work.

Katie Peyton Hofstadter, whose expansive reading manifested *Artificial*'s ending, thank you for your vision of AI and artists in compassionate conversation, for helping me meet the mayor of Gloversville and other adventures thereafter.

Thank you to my students far and wide. Special shout-out to my Patrons who have provided me with a new model for teaching and given me a community I look forward to seeing monthly.

Thank you, music genius Jonathan Darbourne, for proofreading my music notes.

Thank you, Daniel Story, for exceptionally helpful and necessary feedback on the appendix and for treating me like a real philosopher.

Thank you to Thomas Y. Levin for helping me interpret the stamps on my grandfather's passport, which carved me a window into his journey out of Vienna.

Thank you to the engineers who worked on the Fredbot technology. Thanks, Itai Rolnick and Brian Kim, for helping me understand large language models.

Thank you, Maryloua Souza, for your help with storage unit access and document compiling. And thanks to others who have supported my father and his ventures over many years: Celia Black, Sarah Black, Aaron Kleiner, Nanda Barker-Hook, Ken Linde, Maria Ellis, Denise Scutellaro, John-Clark Levin, and others.

I'm indebted to Fred and Hannah Kurzweil, Dorit and Morty Whiteman, Peter Pulzer, and others from my extended family living on in memory. Thank you to all Kurzweils or Kurzweil-adjacents (If your last name is Kurzweil, we are probably related.)

Thank you to my aunt Enid Kurzweil Sterling, who is the original family historian. This would be a lesser book without your diligent and thorough collection of family stories and artifacts and the model of your artistic life.

Thank you to the artificer Allen Kurzweil, who found the oldest definition of *artificial* out there, for sharing your Manhattan desk and memories of meals with Fred in New York automats.

Thank you to my brother, Ethan Kurzweil: I'm sorry you're too cool for me to write a graphic memoir about you (the readers would just be jealous). Thanks for your sense of humor and your support. Thank you, Rebecca Hanover Kurzweil, for writerly companionship and venting. Thank you, Leo and Quincy, for helping me write my truest work of genius, *Bob and the Bag of Chips*, and Naomi, for keeping my Play-Doh skills sharp.

For my mother, who imparted to me her commitment to coherence and her eye for detail. Thank you for your belief in my artistic ambition, for celebrating my successes and always knowing how to have a good time.

For my father, the most interesting person I've ever met, the most determined and also the most generous. Thank you for submitting your life and ideas to my pen, for sharing your creative pursuits with me, and for showing me how to have an expansive sense of self.

For Jacob Sparks, who felt all the joy and despair of this seven-year slog and so may claim this triumph as his own. Thank you for feeding me, for lying on the floor with me, and for teaching me how to pay attention.

# APPENDIX

*Information lasts only so long as someone cares about it.*
—Ray Kurzweil, *The Singularity Is Near*

Epigraph **"Sci-Fi":** Former poet laureate Tracy K. Smith's Pulitzer Prize–winning collection *Life on Mars* is an elegy for her father, Floyd William Smith, who worked on the Hubble Space Telescope as one of NASA's first Black engineers.

## I. Pattern Recognition

9–11 *I've Got a Secret*: *I've Got a Secret* was a CBS television gameshow that aired from 1952 to 1967, in which a panel of celebrities tried to determine a contestant's secret, something notable or unusual about them. These images come from stills of the show, which aired in black-and-white in 1965. My father's musical composer was his first invention, an instantiation of his conviction that if you could program a computer to recognize patterns, it could produce extraordinary things. The invention won him the 1965 Westinghouse Science Talent Search.

11 **Music bars:** See **Brahms**, 304.

12 **"A person is a series of patterns":** My father wrote his first paper on pattern recognition in 1962, when, at fourteen years old, he proposed that the human brain was a pattern recognizer, an idea he elaborates on in his 2012 book *How to Create a Mind.*

13 **Singularity University:** Singularity University in Santa Clara, CA, was founded in 2008 by my father and Peter Diamandis. Its goal is to educate young inventors and business leaders about exponential technology.

14 **Stevie Wonder:** In 1976, Stevie Wonder witnessed a demonstration of the Kurzweil Reading Machine on a segment of the *Today* show: a fellow blind man used this machine to read aloud text on a printed page. So Stevie contacted my father's company and became its most high-profile customer and a friend.

This image of Stevie is based on the cover of the vinyl single "Love Light in Flight" from 1984.

14 **The Kurzweil synthesizer:** In the early 1980s, with inspiration and urging from Stevie Wonder, my father founded Kurzweil Music Systems, which created a new generation of piano synthesizers. These machines could simulate the sounds of a full orchestra more evocatively than their predecessors. In 1984, the K250 passed a kind of musical instrument Turing Test: musicians were unable to tell the difference between a normal grand piano and the synthesizer in "grand piano mode." The Kurzweil synthesizer at our house was built into a frame that made it look like a real grand piano. I apologize to my piano teacher, Kevin, for never practicing.

14 **Ray Kurzweil Cybernetic Poet:** These images and featured poems come from the Kurzweil CyberArt Technologies home page. The Ray Kurzweil Cybernetic Poet is a poem-writing algorithm that creates original poems based on the work of particular poets. RKCP creates a language model of a particular author (or group of authors) by analyzing their work based on their word choices, rhythm patterns, and overall structure and then generating new poems based on those patterns. It writes recursively word by word, with each word of the poem having a goal determined by the analysis and each word found in the body of text from the sample poets.

14 **AARON:** AARON is an AI artist, the name for a series of computer programs written by artist and inventor Harold Cohen, developed between 1972 and 2016. Cohen chose the name AARON because it started with two *A*s—he had planned to create successive artist programs, but the project ended when he died in 2016. KCAT developed an AARON screen saver in 2001.

AARON did not create art based on the styles of other artists. AARON used one characteristic style to create its abstractions and moody portraits and potted plants. It was also explicitly a collaborative entity: Cohen created many paintings in partnership with AARON. See compilations of the work on aaronshome.com.

The image in the middle left comes from the Kurzweil CyberArt Technologies home page, which features a still from the 1982 movie *The Age of Intelligent Machines*, based on my father's first book. My father and Harold Cohen stand in front of an AARON painting.

The image in the bottom left of this page is an AARON painting from the downloadable Windows program, posted on YouTube in 2011.

16 **Robot:** The specific wording of this definition comes from a Google search I did at some point during the seven years I spent writing and drawing this book. One of the charms/frustrations of writing and drawing a graphic novel for seven years is that by the time you go to ink your sketch from five years ago, the Google searches for your references turn up slightly different results than they did at first.

16, 18, 19 *Rossum's Universal Robots:* The robots in Czech writer Karel Čapek's 1920 play are made from synthetic organic matter, a substance which "behaved exactly like living matter although its chemical composition was different." Nonetheless, the robot characters were outfitted in tin and metal for the stage, according to old photos.

18, 19 *Westworld:* These images are based on stills from the HBO show *Westworld*, Season 1, which first aired in 2016, featuring Anthony Hopkins, Evan Rachel Wood, Thandiwe Newton, Angela Sarafyan, Ed Harris, and Jeffrey Wright, pictured here. The show's title sequence features a player piano, a primitive music robot that self-plays notes recorded on perforated paper (a classic haunted house gag).

19 **"Rossum's robots kill everyone":** The revolting robots decide to spare one person in Rossum's factory: their craftsman, Alquist, because he "works with his hands." In the play's epilogue, the robots beseech Alquist. They want him to build more robots, and they present two of their own, lover robots, as sacrifice to their reconnaissance mission. Cut them open, the robots ask, learn about their nature, and copy them! (In her despair,

silly Helena had burned the "recipe" for building more robots; thus this deadly surgery is deemed necessary.) But the lovers can't bear to lose each other, and the craftsman can't bear their selfless sacrifice, and so no recipe is recouped, and the robot race dies along with the human.

19 *Blade Runner:* Image based on advertisements for the 1982 film based on Philip K. Dick's *Do Androids Dream of Electric Sheep?*, about a group of synthetic humans called replicants.

19 **Movies:** Images based on advertisements for *The Terminator* (1984), *I, Robot* (2004), *Robocop* (1987), and *Terminator 3* (2003). The 1980s and '90s were filled with movies that pictured human-like autonomous AI as killers of humanity.

20 **Robots:** 1) A Roomba autonomous vacuum, 2) Robear, a patient-care robot developed by Robot Sensor Systems team of Riken, a research center in Japan, 3) a MAARS robot (modular advanced armed robotic system), an unmanned ground vehicle developed by QinetiQ North America, used by the US army, 4) a Real Doll, a life-size sex doll developed by Abyss Creations.

20 **ELIZA:** ELIZA was the first popular computer chatbot, developed by Joseph Weizenbaum between 1964 and 1966 and elaborated on in his book *Computer Power and Human Reason: From Judgment to Calculation* (1976). The bot used keyword matching and minimal context recognition to run scripts that simulate conversation. Weizenbaum cast ELIZA in the role of a Rogerian psychotherapist because the reflective conversation style was "relatively easy to imitate." (How does it make you feel that the role of therapist is relatively easy to imitate?

For more on this question, check out my graphic essay "Technofeelia vol 4: Help" in *The Believer* Magazine, December 2021.)

23 **My grandfather's passport:** See **Passport**, 274–277.

24–28 **George:** George is a work of art (artist unknown) similar to the wax mannequins at Madame Tussaud's. Our first family trip out of the country was to the UK, when I was fourteen, and my father made sure we visited the famous wax museum in London. I posed for a photo with a group of dead male writers; my father posed with not-yet-dead female rock stars. George came into our lives shortly after that trip.

George is named after the virtual assistant of Molly, the fictional character from *The Age of Spiritual Machines* and recurring in *The Singularity Is Near*, who dialogues with my father as she travels through the future. George begins as Molly's virtual assistant but by 2029 has become her lover. Their relationship and the compelling intelligence of George 2029, as described by Molly 2029, anticipates the virtual romance between Theo and his virtual assistant Samantha in *Her* (2013). Although George and Molly's union has a happier fate than Theo and Samantha's: by 2099 they've fully merged consciousnesses.

25 **My first cell phone:** It's a Nokia 3310, circa 2000.

25 **Kurzweil Technologies:** My father's company, which developed and marketed his inventions, founded in 1995 with his best friend Aaron Kleiner.

25, 26 **Painting:** Based on a detail of an AARON painting titled *Mother and Daughter*, 2002.

**26 Artificial:** Another googled definition from some years ago. I'd like to add this definition from *Encyclopedia Britannica*, first edition, 1771.

> ARTIFICIAL, in a general ſenſe, denotes ſomething made, faſhioned, or produced by art, in contradiſtinction from the productions of nature.

**26 Images:** On the wall in the bottom left panel is my father's National Medal of Technology from 2000 and two of his twenty honorary doctorates. The next image is a Kurzweil keyboard, model unknown/imprecisely drawn.

**26 The Reading Machine:** This image, bottom row, panel 3, pictures a model of the very first Reading Machine for the Blind, from 1976, which could read printed text aloud. It was the size of a small dishwasher and cost thousands of dollars. By the 2000s, the technology ran on a standard desktop computer alongside a separate scanner. In 2006, the National Federation for the Blind worked with my father's company to debut a handheld portable reader. Today, the Reading Machine's component technologies are used in your smartphone, and you probably make use of them every day. The original Reading Machine pioneered three landmark technologies: 1) omni-font optical character recognition: the computer recognition of text written in any font (previous to omni-font OCR, scanners could only recognize a few standardized fonts), 2) the CCD flatbed scanner, and 3) a text-to-speech synthesizer.

For a sixth-grade science project, I built a replica of the first Reading Machine out of cardboard, and when I learned that my masterful simulacrum had been lost (or stolen!) from Mr. Bladt's closet, I cried.

**26 *The Age of Intelligent Machines*:** My father's first book, published in 1990 with MIT Press.

**26 *The Age of Spiritual Machines*:** *When Computers Exceed Human Intelligence.* Published in 1999 with Viking Press, my father's second book outlines his vision for the future of humanity. The book's predictions include the creation of nanotechnology, which will enter our bodies, cure diseases, and extend life; the living of our lives in virtual reality; and the creation of autonomous machines more intelligent than we are. "*2029: Computers have read all available human- and machine-generated literature and multimedia material. There is growing discussion about the legal rights of computers and what constitutes being human. Machines claim to be conscious and these claims are largely accepted.*" My father asserts: "*The primary political and philosophical issue of the next century will be the definition of who we are.*" *TASM* is often cited in reference to transhumanism (see **What does his infinity mean?** 258–259).

**28 Freud's grandson:** My grandmother Hannah Kurzweil's family was part of a social circle of nonreligious Jewish professionals in Vienna. Walter Freud, grandson of Sigmund, was around my grandmother's age, and he was a "steady suitor," according to a speech Hannah wrote for Brandeis University in 1986 about her life in Vienna, published in *Hannah Kurzweil: A Biography*. "I never had any trouble with Walter," she wrote. But Walter's father, Martin, used to "chase [her] around the furniture."

**30 Documents:** Photo of Fred and Hannah on the day of their marriage, 1944, Fort Bragg, NC; photos of Fred circa 1944–1950s; advertisement for the Mobile Opera Guild's production of *La Bohème*, 1963; advertisement for the Mobile Opera Guild's production of *The Barber of Seville*; article from *Island Society*, January 25, 1944; Separation Qualification Record form from the Army of the United States assigning Fred to 4.5 months of field artillery basic training followed by two years as an entertainment specialist at Fort Meade.

**31, 32 Musical notation:** Music to the song "Ceora," written by Lee Morgan in 1965. The version by Tom Kennedy from the album *Just Play* (2013) really was *just playing* in the storage unit, somehow, during my first visit (I Shazammed it). Brahms's "Wiegenlied" (Op. 49, No. 4), notated on page 39, was *not* really playing.

**32 Photos:** Photo of my father circa 1965; family photo Jan 1962; Fred circa 1944–1950s.

**33 Welcome:** A drawing from the storage unit, made by my father and his sister Enid sometime in the 1960s, welcoming Fred back from a trip to Mobile, AL, where he often traveled for work.

**34–36, etc. Suspenders:** These days, my father is rarely seen without his signature suspenders, which were hand-painted by a friend.

**35 "Is the Charles River still there?":** My father's question about the Charles River might be read as a Bostonian's formulation of the pre-Socratic Greek philosopher Heraclitus's meditation on the turnover in a river (~500 BCE). Heraclitus notes that, because its matter is constantly changing, "you cannot step in the same river twice" (from Plato's *Cratylus*). Is Heraclitus saying that change is so constant that a river can never be itself again? That a river is only itself *because* it's constantly changing? That the *you* who steps in the river is constantly changing?

My father's question also makes me think of the Ship of Theseus thought experiment. Ancient Greek philosophers asked: If every part of the Ship of Theseus has been replaced, one part at a time, is it still the same ship? The question is a rich one for philosophers of personal identity who wonder 1) what is a person? and 2) under what conditions can we say that a person persists over time?

**36 Turing Test:** In his 1950 paper "Computing Machinery and Intelligence," Alan Turing begins: "I propose to consider the question: Can machines think?" Turing interprets this question with a test he calls the imitation game. The game involves a human evaluator judging a natural language conversation between themself and a human and themself and a machine designed to respond like a human. The machine passes the test if it convinces its human interlocutor that it is human too. Turing himself may not have truly equated the passing of this test with intelligent thinking, but his paper nonetheless underscored, for those invested in computer intelligence thereafter, the association of *thinking* and *the ability to engage in conversation*.

**36 A Fredric Kurzweil Turing Test:** A subjective and individualized Turing-like test that makes a determination about whether or not an avatar of Fred is indistinguishable from the judge's memories of Fred. In some interviews, my father has said this kind of test would be easier to pass as people's memories of Fred fade. Here, he implies this test is difficult because people's memories of Fred are fading. I find this equivocation between *easy* in some ways and *difficult* in other ways interesting.

**36 "some of those people might not be around anymore":** My great-aunt Dorit, our family's last living tie to Vienna, passed away in 2022, as I was inking the pages of this book. In fact, she died on the very day (likely in the very moments) I was finishing page 142 in chapter 4, her first appearance in the book. This inspired a vague sense that my studio was haunted.

**36–37 Coco:** *Coco* (2017) is my favorite Pixar movie, conceived and directed by Lee Unkrich about a Mexican boy who longs to be a musician and travels to the land of the dead to seek help from his great-great-grandfather. The guitar here is based on that of the famous Ernesto de la Cruz, the film's antagonist.

---

## II. Immortal Virtue

**40 Transcendent Man:** While my father discusses the storage unit of his father's documents in *The Singularity Is Near* in a passage about the longevity of information, his resurrection goal only registered for me as a real plan upon seeing *Transcendent Man*, a 2009 documentary by filmmaker Barry Ptolemy. The film, inspired by my father's 2005 book, explores his life, work, and ideas, and emphasizes his belief in the pseudoreligious power of technology to transcend mortality and resurrect the dead.

Barry and his wife and fellow film producer, Felicia, became friends of my family, and I remember years when, wherever my father went, Barry would show up with his camera. My interview for the film was cut, thankfully. I stood in front of a creek behind my father's old office in Wellesley Hills, and Barry asked me the unanswerable question, a kind of Zen koan I've been asked so many times: *Do you think your father's really going to live forever?*

The scene illustrated here: my father is lying on the ground, camera close to his face. We don't know where he is, and the previous scene had informed us that he was rushed to Mt. Auburn hospital for heart surgery. Then, my father slowly starts to float, his face beaming with glee, and we realize he's accompanied by a group of joyful floating passengers on a parabolic flight, all suited up in Zero-G jumpsuits, freed from gravity.

**41 Chagall painting:** *The Blue Bouquet* by Marc Chagall, circa 1960. Upon closer scrutiny, this Chagall print in my father's apartment is *not* 3D printed. But the Van Gogh painting above the table in this chapter is.

**41 Ediphone:** Thomas Edison invented the phonograph in 1877 (later called a gramophone), a machine that could record sound by engraving waveforms on the surface of a rotating cylinder, i.e., a record. In the 1880s, Alexander Graham Bell's lab introduced a similar but improved technology, the graphophone, which used wax cylinders for superior playback. Bell's product came to be known commercially as a Dictaphone. Edison swung back with his Ediphone, which also used wax cylinders.

**42 Iron Cross Medal:** A military decoration from Franz Joseph I, emperor of Austria, given to David Eisner. Born in Hungary in 1856, David was the father of Fred's mother, Theresia. I don't know how he earned the honor. Geni.com tells me that he was a *Zeitungskorrektor*, a newspaper proofreader.

**42 Framed images:** Drawings on this page are based on a movie poster for *The Singularity Is Near*; a movie based on my father's 2005 book, starring Pauley Peret as my father's alter ego Ramona; a poster for *Robots and Beyond: The Age of Intelligent Machines*, a short film made by my father for an exhibit at the Boston Museum of Science in 1987, which inspired his 1990 book; the movie poster for *Transcendent Man*, 2009; brain in a vat cartoon (a classic depiction of Cartesian dualism) by Alan Wallerstein, 1966; Fred's PhD diploma in music from the University of Vienna, 1938; White Rabbit painting by Grace Slick.

**42 "just in time, right before all the Jews were expelled from Vienna":** My father is referring to *Kristallnacht*, a wave of state-sanctioned attacks on Jews and Jewish institutions on November 9 and 10, 1938, when many Jews in Vienna were killed or taken to camps. Fred left Vienna, with his diploma, on October 10, 1938.

Nine months prior, on March 11, Nazi Germany subsumed the republic of Austria in what is known as the *Anschluss*. My great-aunt Dorit always described this moment in history as an inversion of existence that happened literally overnight. My great-grandmother Lily Bader, in her autobiography, *One Life Is Not Enough* (2011, published only in German with Milena Verlag), de-

scribes the feeling of hearing the news of Austria's fall as "a horrible monster . . . holding us by our throats . . . fangs only dimly seen." Attacks on Jewish businesses began moments after the announcement of the annexation. The next day, swastikas papered the city.

All anti-Jewish legislation from the Third Reich was immediately applied to Austrian Jews, about 200,000 of whom lived in Vienna. I remember viewing all these laws on floor-to-ceiling lists in the Jewish Museum in Berlin's permanent collection. "April 3, 1936: Jews may not be veterinarians." "November 13, 1937: Jews are no longer permitted to take walks."

My grandfather's diploma is dated July 21, 1938. At that point, a swift and successive process of cleansing Jews from the University of Vienna was underway. By April, the quota for Jewish students had dropped to 2 percent and Jewish student names were given to the gestapo. In June and October, some students were allowed to attend non-Aryan doctoral exams. By December, the University was declared "Jew free."

**42 *How to Create a Mind*:** My father's book from 2012 in which he articulates his pattern recognition theory of the mind, focusing on the neocortex as the locus of human intelligence and creativity, which contains millions of pattern recognizers arranged in a hierarchy.

**43 Images:** Advertisement for a performance at Hofstra College with Constance Cook, an opera singer and friend of Fred's; two watercolor paintings by Hannah Kurzweil; a drawing by me of Ramona, my father's alter ego, circa mid-2000s.

**43 *Tom Swift and His Outpost in Space*:** *Tom Swift* is a long-running series of sci-fi novels written by multiple

authors under the pseudonym Victor Appleton that follows Tom Swift (and subsequently his line of Tom Swift Jrs.) who are all boy-prodigy inventors. My father read all thirty-three books of the *Tom Swift Jr.* series (1954–1971) and cites them as early inspiration for his career path, specifically Tom's gadgets—a house-sized spacecraft, an electric hydrolung, a repellatron, etc.—and his ability to solve a seemingly overwhelming problem with just the right idea.

**45 Musicians:** See **Musicians**, 235–239.

**45 Plant painting:** Based on an image by AARON and Harold Cohen, 2002, signed to my father.

**46 iPhones:** Images based on iPhone ads between 2008 and 2017.

**46, 49, 52–53, etc. Portrait of Fred:** Based on a painting by Frank Mason, from around 1950.

**47–48 "Way It Was":** Text and photos from "The Way It Was," an article written by my aunt Enid Kurzweil Sterling, published in the *Montecito Journal*, Vol. 11, Issue 10, May 19 to June 1, 2005.

**47, 50, etc. Painting above the table:** Image based on *Cypress and Two Figures* by Van Gogh (the one that's really 3D printed).

**47 "Anschluss and Kristallnacht":** Literally *Anschluss* means annexation, and *Kristallnacht* means crystal night; i.e., the night of broken glass. See "**just in time, right before all the Jews were expelled from Vienna**," 42.

**47 Gertrude Sumner Ely:** Fred's visa sponsor, born in 1876, was the daughter of a railroad tycoon, an alumna of Bryn

Mawr College and resident of Bryn Mawr until her death at ninety-four in 1970, two months after Fred died.

**48 "Lily Bader . . . from Hilde's summer camp":** Lily Bader, née Stern, my grandmother Hannah Kurzweil's mother, was one of the first women in Europe to be awarded a PhD in chemistry. She and her sister Hilde ran a school inherited by their mother, Regina Stern, in 1868. The Stern School was one of the first schools in Europe to provide higher education to girls. Aunt Hilde, a talented pianist and teacher, also ran a camp by Worthersee Lake, about three hundred kilometers from Vienna. In 1937, she hired Fred to work at the camp as a music teacher, which is how he met my grandmother. No Jewish people reading this book will be surprised that my grandmother and I both met our partners at summer camp.

**49–52 "Reinvent Yourself":** Text from "Reinvent Yourself: The Playboy Interview with Ray Kurzweil" by David Hochman, April 19, 2016. Article portrait based on a photo by Alex Freund.

**50–52 Wall paintings:** See **Alice Liddell Painting**, 184, and **an oil painter at a San Francisco art fair**, 206–207.

**51 *Jagged Little Pill*:** The 1995 album from Alanis Morissette. She was once my father's favorite singer, and she likely inspired his transformation in chapter 6. The first concert I ever went to was an Alanis concert—and the second.

**52 Library of Alexandria:** One of the greatest libraries of the ancient world, it held hundreds of thousands of scrolls and was part of a larger institution in Egypt dedicated to the Muses, goddesses of the arts. In the Siege of Alexandria, 48 BC, Julius Caesar caused a partial burning of the library when he was forced in battle to set fire to his own ships.

**54 "He's the reason for the teardrops":** Fourteen words from Taylor Swift's 2006 song "Teardrops on my Guitar." Sometime in the mid-2000s, my father's Alanis fandom waned in favor of Taylor.

**54 "...me wishing on a wishing star":** Somebody once told me that copyright law technically allows me to legally print fourteen words from another work without infringing on the author's rights. But as it turns out, there's no specific number of words deemed legally usable by copyright law. The more relevant copyright concept here is *transformative use*: I'm transforming Taylor's words into dialogue and into image by striking them through. But I'm sure Taylor's got powerful enough lawyers to sue me if she wants to.

**54–55 The Symposium:** A Platonic dialogue from around 385 BC that recounts a series of semicompetitive speeches in praise of Eros, god of love and desire, delivered by progressively drunken men at a banquet: the aristocrat Phaedrus, the lawyer Pausanias, the doctor Eryximachus, the comic playwright Aristophanes, the tragic poet and party host Agathon, the philosopher and Plato-favorite Socrates, and the politician Alcibiades. (Most quotes come from John M. Cooper's *Plato Complete Works*, translated by A. Nehamas and P. Woodruff.)

**55 "Music is, then":** Eryximachus, the doctor, claims that love is a kind of reconciliation of opposing elements, like rhythm or harmony. The physician's task, he claims, is like the musician's: both must facilitate an agreement of forces.

**55 The love of heavenly Aphrodite:** Pausanias says that love is not inevitably worthy of praise; it depends entirely on "the character it gives rise to." He distinguishes between two kinds of love, and two goddesses of love: the Heavenly Aphrodite and the Common Aphrodite. Common Aphrodite's love is younger, more drawn to body than soul. This love is bound to be inconsistent since its target "is itself mutable and unstable." But Heavenly Aphrodite's love, for example, "love for the right sort of character," is deeper, attached to something more permanent.

Pausanias's Common Love is "attached to women no less than to boys" and he goes on and on about how men shouldn't have relationships with boys who are too young (ancient Greek men commonly took young male lovers) because this attraction is bound to be motivated by lust. He seems to take for granted a shared assumption that women are granted no access to the heavenly life of soul and mind.

**55 Aristophanes and the rolly people:** The comic poet Aristophanes recounts a mythical story: Long ago, he says, what we think of as a single human being was only half of a rounded creature, with four arms and four legs, two faces, two sets of sexual organs, etc. Of these rounded creatures there were three types: one male, offspring of the sun; another female and of the earth; the third combined both genders and was of the moon. My drawing on page 55 features the multigendered creature. On the following page I offer the other two.

These creatures were too strong and ambitious, and so Zeus cut them in two. Then Apollo turned their faces toward the wound, so they could see their

shame. He spread skin over their center and fashioned a navel.

Note that their genitals, at this point, were now located on their backsides. And these creatures were generally in a sorry state. Longing to be physically united with their other half, they were unable to operate on their own. So Zeus took pity on them and moved their genitals around to the front. This enabled the satisfaction of intercourse when they embraced and allowed for insemination to result from male-female couplings. (Greek men had sex facing each other in an act called coitus *interfemoris*, a fact I share here because of its relevance to comics history: the profoundly muscular thighs of comic superheroes are inspired by Greek male thigh ogling. I learned this fact from a spirited audience member at the New York Comics & Picture-Stories Symposium and I will not forget it.) And so these severed creatures (us) are fated to roam the earth, in search of our other halves. Love is our "pursuit of wholeness," and when true lovers find each other, their greatest desire is to melt into one creature again. (Like what happens for Molly and her virtual lover George in *The Age of Spiritual Machines*.)

56 ***Kleos***: (klé .os/) *n* Ancient Greek κλέος, from the verb *kluen*, to hear.

56 **Achilles:** Says Diotima, via Socrates, of Achilles, the hero of the Trojan War, central character of the Iliad:

"The honor they gave to Achilles is another matter. They sent him to the Isles of the Blest because he dared to stand by his lover Patroclus and avenge him, even after he had learned from his mother that he would die if he killed Hector, but that if he chose otherwise he'd go home and end his life as an old man. Instead he chose to die for Patroclus, and more than that, he did it for a man whose life was already over."

56 **Icarus and:** Escaping from the minotaur's maze, Icarus flew too close to the sun and died, wearing the pair of wings his father, Daedalus, an inventor and craftsman, fashioned. I remember the word *hubris*, excessive pride that gives way to over-grand ambition, was always underlined on the board whenever this Greek myth came up in grade school. But for me now, I can't think of Daedalus without seeing Bruce Bechdel, Alison Bechdel's father in *Fun Home*. "Artificer," she calls him, after invoking the fateful myth.

57 **"My first book has a face":** *Flying Couch: A Graphic Memoir*, published October 2016 with Catapult/Black Balloon. In my second Instagram post

there you'll see a Google self-driving, self-thinking car, a reference to my first *New Yorker* cartoon ever published (April 2016). The next post is a drawing of my friends Anjali and Evan's dog Benji. (The first of three dogs immortalized in this book.)

60 **Sculpture:** *Cupid's Span*, a sculpture by Claes Oldenburg and Coosje van Bruggen, 2002, at the San Francisco Embarcadero.

60–62 **Socrates and Diotima:** Some say Socrates's teacher Diotima of Mantinea may be a fictional character, because she's not cited anywhere outside of *The Symposium*. Real or fake, she's a prophet renowned for her intellect and for successfully warding off a plague.

62 **Aardvark Books:** A used bookstore in the Castro, where I first bought a copy of *Graphic Women* by Hillary Chute, which set me on my way.

64 **Fred's PhD thesis:** Fred's thesis from 1938 explored German composer, pianist, and conductor Johannes Brahms's use of harmony. My aunt Enid had the foreword to the thesis translated to English from German by Ann C. Sherman in 2009. The first two paragraphs:

*So many books and articles have already been written about the work of Johannes Brahms that it may at first seem superfluous for yet another to follow these. But in all the works about Brahms, I find that in none of the chapters dealing with harmony is harmony observed and examined as an ordering factor in the building of forms. For instance, Hermann Wetzel, in an article on Brahms' harmony, says (*Die Musik, vol. 12, no. 1, 1912, p. 22): "What can be said about the harmony of a master in objective terms? One would have to prove which of all conceivable paths through* *the tonal space the composer prefers, how broadly or narrowly he draws his circles, which particular paragraphs of the tonality law book—unwritten, yet followed by all "bound" spirits—he draws upon, which of all possible sounds he loves, what storage form he prefers for each sound, what closing sound forms (cadences) he uses, how he configures the relationship of the two tonal families (major and minor) within his tone circle, and much more."*

*Such a detached observation of harmonics would be like examining a literary work of art for the words alone, without considering how these words function in the rendering of an idea.*

I think I know what Fred's investigating: Can we objectively talk about the way something is built without talking about what it means? Can content really be separated from form? Can soul from matter?

I find it interesting that Fred begins his German thesis with this overture of erasure, just like how he begins the musicology book he started later in life. See **Musica Viva**, 180.

65, 71 **How to Honor Our Dead:** Article in *The Fort Meade Post*, June 2, 1944, "Memorial Day Services Here Supplant Rites on Air" about the Fort Meade Soldier's Chorus, which Fred directed during his army service. Article photo from Corp. Benno Reisler, AGF Public Relations Office.

## III. How Do You Know?

68–69 **John Searle and the Chinese Room:** Philosopher John Searle articulates his famous Chinese Room thought experiment in his 1980 paper "Minds, Brains, and Programs," which I read in Daniel Dennett and Douglas Hofstadter's *The Mind's I: Fantasies and Reflection*

*on Self and Soul.* Searle, like Turing, asks the question "Could a machine think?" Although Searle is positioned as a critic of AI, Searle answers the question affirmatively. "Only a machine could think," he says, "and only very special kinds of machines, namely brains and machines with internal causal powers equivalent to those of brains." What Searle wants to distinguish by way of his analogy are brains/machines from *programs*. Programs don't have what Searle calls *intentionality*, a mind's property of *being directed at* something. As for what gives our brains intentionality, Searle suggests it's something biological. On what that secret stuff is, he's pretty wishy-washy.

I've always wondered how this thought experiment would have resonated if Searle chose a different language. What if it was a Hebrew Room, an Egyptian Hieroglyphic Room? He needed to choose a language with characters as different as possible from English characters, positioned as he is in the English-speaking Western world, and his choice puts me in the mind of the old childhood adage: "dig a hole to China," as if China is so far away physically and psychically that it requires a trip through the earth's molten core to visit. But there are plenty of people in the English-speaking world for whom Chinese characters are familiar, and the thought experiment surely resonates differently with them.

Personally, I find philosophical thought experiments challenging to hold in my mind. Thought experiments are not supposed to be stories; they have very strict boundaries in order to help us isolate very particular ideas. *But you can't lock a man in a room, this is abuse!* I want to argue. The philosophers in my life do not heed these kinds of objections.

69 **Machines:** Top row of images: a transistor, the basic building block of

modern electronics; image based on the Nippon Electric Automatic Computer 2203, an early transistor computer from the 1960s; I don't know if the SVM Commander Model 10010 was a real computer or just something that shows up when you Google "80's computer"; a basic personal computer from the 1990s; a contemporary Apple computer monitor.

70 **"Julie" therapist file:** I always found it fun that my first editor for this book and Fred's therapist have the same first name. Fred's Julie and her husband were both therapists to Fred and Hannah's family, and the two couples were also good friends. (This was pre current norms about patient-therapist boundaries!)

70 **The system:** The systems reply to the Chinese Room thought experiment is anticipated and disputed by Searle in his paper. He disputes the systems reply *with* the internalization reply (see **He internalizes the Chinese Room**, 111). Thanks to Bob Horn's infographic map "Can Chinese Rooms Think? The History and Status of the Debate" from his website bobhorn.us for helping me understand responses to the thought experiment and how they connect.

71 **"labyrinth of bureaucracy":** My great-aunt Dorit always emphasized how much of her family's trial to get out of Europe was about waiting in lines all day to have papers stamped. After the Anschluss, the Nazis' first plan for the Jews was to "help" them emigrate. They opened the Vienna Jewish Community Welfare Department–Immigration Office, and Jews wanting to leave Vienna (i.e., all of them) had to submit a seemingly endless number of forms, in duplicate, to the office; e.g., the document to certify your monthly income,

the document to certify you didn't own a dog. If Jews couldn't prove, through forms, who they were and that they were welcome and capable of sustaining themselves in another country, then their "emigration" was facilitated to concentration camps.

71 **"What did you do in the army?":** A letter of recommendation dated Feb 5, 1944, written by V. M. Robertson, Major Infantry Chief Special Service Branch at Fort Bragg, where Fred did basic training and contributed to the musical needs of the branch. This letter likely helped Fred find a position at his next US Army post doing "the work for which he is best suited," as Robertson described it.

Fred moved to Fort Meade, where he supported the 1st Combat Infantry Band as a piano soloist, arranger, composer, and conductor. He founded and directed the Fort Meade Soldiers' Chorus, a choir featuring male and female vocalists that debuted in May 1944. This chorus continues to this day, referred to as the glee club.

Fred's contribution to the musical history of the U.S. army was recently documented in the Army Field Band's 75th Anniversary: https://www.armyfieldband.com/about/75th-anniversary. Thanks to Brian Eldridge for his research and writing.

72 **But our memories are not storage units:** One of my favorite readings on memory and its relationship to imagination is Felipe De Brigard's paper from *Synthese* (2014): "Is memory for remembering? Recollection as a form of episodic hypothetical thinking," which posits remembering and *misremembering* as "part of a larger system that supports not only thinking of what *was* the case and what potentially *could be* the case, but also what *could have been* the case."

72 **Documents:** Fred and Hannah's marriage certificate, found in a wallet in Fred's desk after he died; the cover of Fred's PhD thesis; his passport.

72 **"the only line":** My mother's parents are Polish Jews; my maternal grandmother, the Bubbe from my first book *Flying Couch*, lost her entire family in the Holocaust: four sisters, parents, and a grandmother; they died in the Warsaw ghetto or were deported to camps. One cousin of hers survived and later immigrated to Israel. My mother's father, David, survived by hiding in the woods after he jumped from a train that was carrying his entire family to Treblinka.

73 **Documents:** Drawings based on primary documents: article from the *Pittsburgh Post-Gazette*, "Bouquet Received in Hospital Starts Artist on Watercolor," by Marion Leslie, circa 1960s; a drawing by my grandmother Hannah, with ink or black watercolor; article by Anne Burrows, "Symphony Presents Exciting Program" in the *Edmonton Journal*, January 20, 1964; Fred's personal collection of press comments; a drawing by Hannah of Fred.

74 **Photos:** Drawings based on family photo from the 1950s; family photo from 1962.

75 **Documents:** Fred's obituary in *The New York Times*; translation of Fred's thesis, a letter from Fred to Enid at camp, 1969; an old recipe for Austrian plum dumplings; photo of Fred at the camp by Worthersee Lake where he met Hannah; photo of Fred conducting the Bell Symphony Orchestra, 1951.

76 **A Ray of Life:** *A Ray of Life: A Genealogical Journey in Poetry and Photos* is a collection of poetry and art published by my aunt Enid Kurzweil with CreateSpace Independent Publishing on Amazon, December 2009.

81 **Johns Hopkins Center for Talented Youth:** A network of summer programs for gifted and talented students that offers academic programming over three-week sessions, with campuses around the world. Jacob and I met at Franklin & Marshall College in Lancaster, PA.

82 **Brave New World, 1984:** Aldous Huxley's *Brave New World* (1932), about a futuristic society in which humans are bred factory-style into a clean, bureaucratic social hierarchy, and George Orwell's *1984* (1949), about an authoritarian surveillance state; both posit futures that use technology as a means of control, but the former—with its *feelies* (multisensory entertainment experiences) and *soma* (recreational drug with "all the advantages of Christianity and alcohol; none of their defects") seemed, at least, a little fun. Both books were on my syllabus for "Utopias and Dystopias," the class I taught at the Center for Talented Youth in the 2010s.

82 **"I was just reading about ":** This argument about *Brave New World*'s similarity to our techno-pleasure-seeking society comes from Neil Postman's *Amusing Ourselves to Death: Public Discourse in the Age of Showbusiness*, 1985. Since Postman, our technology has upped its game both in its dopamine targeting and its invasive surveillance techniques.

85 **amymania10:** The 10 at the end of my AOL Instant Messenger screen name is for my age when I first signed up.

86 **Nokia phone:** My very last flip phone, a Nokia 6101, before I made the jump to a smartphone in 2009.

**87  Utopia Reader:** *The Utopia Reader* (1999), edited by Gregory Claeys and Lyman Tower Sargent, the textbook for my CTY class, "Utopias and Dystopias."

**88–91  "How many sounds do you hear?":** I think Jacob's sound-counting exercise is traceable to his fondness for David Hume, one of his favorite philosophers, a Scottish philosopher from the eighteenth century who distinguished between ideas and impressions. Impressions are forceful perceptions in the mind, and ideas are "faint images" of impressions. I think of impressions as related to our senses; they are fleeting. Ideas stick around longer. Sound counting feels like a way to isolate an impression, and then, through naming it, turn it into an idea that you might hold on to.

**92  Ernst Jentsch's uncanny:** German psychiatrist Ernst Jentsch's 1906 essay "On the Psychology of the Uncanny" explores the uncanny in relationship to E. T. A. Hoffman's story "The Sandman." Jentsch claims the most uncanny aspect of the story is the fact that the protagonist, Nathanial, falls in love with a stiff but lifelike automaton doll named Olimpia.

**94  Freud's uncanny:** In his 1916 essay "The Uncanny," Freud emphasizes other aspects of Hoffman's story as most uncanny. In the climax of "The Sandman," the villain makes off with Olimpia's eyeless body after a dispute with her maker. Nathanial, witnessing this, lets his gaze fall upon Olimpia's beloved eyes lying on the ground, and he goes completely mad.

Comparing the German words *unheimlich* (*uncanny*) and *heimlich* (*familiar* or *from home*), Freud builds to his main point about the uncanny as something *secretly* familiar, something repressed. He does this by tracing the use of repetition in the Hoffman story;

when aspects of the story recur in a haunting way (e.g., Olimpia's eyes and the theme of eyelessness), they strike this uncanny note of eerie familiarity.

**95  Metoprolol:** A beta blocker, a medication that lowers blood pressure and causes the heart to beat slower.

**99–100, etc.  Journals transcribed:** The journals were dated throughout the 1950s, '60s, and '70s, some written in notebooks, others on loose sheets of paper. They were all gathered in a folder with a newspaper tear-out of quotes by Sigmund Freud.

**104  He internalizes the Chinese Room:** The question in the internalization reply is whether understanding Chinese *is* an internalization of the system/program contained in the Chinese Room, or if understanding Chinese is something different, something that requires intentionality. Searle says, and most of us can agree, that internalization of an isolated system such as that described in the thought experiment is *not* the same as the internalization that happens when someone really learns and understands a language, which typically involves integrating the language with other parts of one's mind: perceptual systems, autobiographical memory, etc.

On the computers-can-think side of the debate, contemporary philosopher Daniel Dennett objects to the internalization reply for different reasons. Internalizing language rules isn't realistic to human psychology; no typical human can really memorize this infinitely complex rule book, and even if they could, their execution of the process would unfold slowly and over too much time to be considered understanding. But Dennett doesn't consider understanding to be some mystical process only biological brains can do. He thinks understand-

ing is the sum of speed and complexity. In his view, programs running with speed and efficiency—even computer systems—*are* thinking, because that's what Dennett thinks thinking is.

**104  a strange loop:** This phrase comes from the title of Douglas Hofstadter's 2007 book *I Am a Strange Loop*, which explores questions of self and the puzzle of consciousness, a follow-up to his Pulitzer Prize–winning *Gödel, Escher, Bach* from 1979. A strange loop is a certain kind of highly complex self-referential system. Self-reference, Hofstadter emphasizes, creates transcendent spiral patterns, such as a Bach fugue, or a video camera pointed at its own playback screen.

Hofstadter claims that the self is a point of view, and its capacity for self-reference is what gives it consciousness. This self can exist in other substrates (meaning disembodied AI is theoretically possible), and other points of view can *really exist* inside of us. A Bach fugue is a small sliver of the composer's consciousness, this book is a medium-sized sliver of mine; the people we know and love live on after death because of the rich models we have of them in our minds. "The word 'love,'" he says, "cannot, thus, be separated from the word 'I.' The more deeply rooted the symbol for someone inside you, the greater the love, the brighter the light that remains behind."

**106  *The Singularity Is Near: When Humans Transcend Biology*:** Published with Viking in 2005, a follow up to *The Age of Intelligent Machines* and *The Age of Spiritual Machines*, *TSIN* popularized the notion of the Singularity, referencing a time when computer intelligence will transcend human intelligence, resulting in a practically unimaginable sea change for humanity. The phrase was used by

Vernor Vinge in his 1993 essay "The Coming Technological Singularity," which elaborates on I. J. Good's 1965 claim that ultra-intelligent machines could design better and better machines leading "unquestionably" to an "intelligence explosion." My father outlines a comprehensive vision of this techno-utopian future and its advances in AI, genetics, nanotechnology, and robotics, and he pins the date for the Singularity at 2045.

106 ***The Most Human Human: What Talking with Computers Teaches Us About What It Means to Be Alive*:** (2011) by Brian Christian, about his experience as a human foil for the Loebner Prize Turing Test.

107 **Drawings:** See pages 196–197.

114 **Music bars:** See **Brahms**, 304.

115 **The Uncanny Valley:** Originating with Japanese roboticist Masahiro Mori in 1970, the "Uncanny Valley" theory describes the relationship between an image's or object's resemblance to a human being and the emotional response that likeness inspires. Emotional comfort level with automata increases with human likeness, he said, until they reach the "valley," where likeness comes ever closer to human without reaching it and our emotional responses become increasingly unsettled. See this graph of my father's various biomorphic collections by way of illustration.

*Uncanny Valley* (2020) is also the name of a memoir by Anna Weiner about life working in Silicon Valley in the 2010s.

115 **"Do you know how it works?":** The Fred-bot's technology is a proprietary version of Talk to Books, a Google large-language model built by my father's team at Google in 2018. (The term *large* is relative; the model has around 50 million parameters, compared to 2023's large-language models, which have closer to 500 billion parameters.) Large-language models are deep learning neural networks that process natural language. Talk to Books was trained with a dual-encoder model, meaning it was fed a billion pairs of sentences (structured as questions and answers) and built a semantic model of language based on that training. Using this internal model, Talk to Books identifies a good response to a user's query, retrieving the answer from among the sentences in the 100,000 books in its database.

The Fred-bot uses this same model but retrieves its responding sentences from a different body of text: Fred's writing from our family's collection, which was typed up and entered in its database.

For more on this technology see "Universal Sentence Encoder," a paper by Daniel Cer, Yinfei Yang, Sheng-yi Kong, Nan Hua, Nicole Limtiaco, Rhomni St. John, Noah Constant, Mario Guajardo-Cespedes, Steve Yuan, Chris Tar, Yun-Hsuan Sung, Brian Strope, and Ray Kurzweil, published April 2018.

115 **"graphed in 500 N-dimensional space":** It's actually 512-dimensional space. Basically, this algorithm works by trying to measure a sentence's meaning across 512 different abstract characteristics. Each characteristic gets measured as a number, and so any sentence can be "understood" using only these 512 numbers (called a "vector"), which can be plotted on a complex graph. The algorithm's training on billions of pairs of sentences conditioned it to match queries to answers based on their location in this vector space.

115 **Sherlock Holmes quote:** This quote comes from "Sherlock Holmes: The Red Headed League," a Holmes story from 1891 by Arthur Conan Doyle.

116 **"the engineers might not either":** It's common to refer to machine learning algorithms as "black box" technologies, meaning these are systems that can only

THE UNCANNY VALLEY
porcelain cat figurines
[approx. range, depends on cat]
Vermont Teddy Bears™
real person
[approx. range, depends on person]
Elegant Illusions™ jeweled animal boxes
Hasbro™ "Joy For All" robot cat companion
My Twinn™ dolls
George
life-size oil paintings of family members
[approx. range, depends on painter]
Empathetic response
Realism
gifted
collected
both

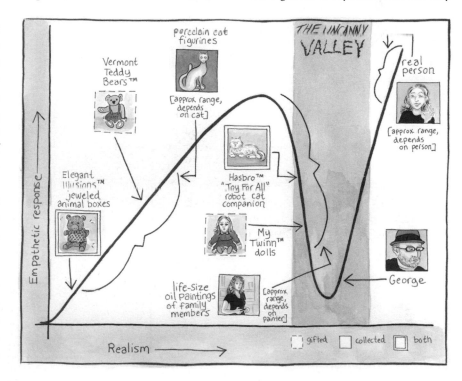

be viewed in terms of their inputs and outputs, with very limited understanding of their internal workings. But this may not be an entirely fair way of looking at machine-learning models. Engineers can look clearly at these algorithms' models and their training data, but what explains the mystification is that, due to size and complexity, there isn't a simple explanation for why the outputs, given the inputs, are what they are.

Nonetheless, it is often the case with AI that *the user* is interacting with an algorithm as a true black box; software is often proprietary, and the public isn't given access (and may not have the education to understand) how and why it works as it does. (Thanks to "The 'black box' metaphor in machine learning" by Dallas Card on Medium for clarifying these ideas.)

**116 "create new speech based on old patterns":** In order to generate new language, the Universal Sentence Encoder in the Fred-bot would need to be paired with, or replaced by, a *decoder* that essentially performs the encoder's inverse. The encoder turns existing sentences into vectors (see **"graphed in 500 N-dimensional space,"** 122), but a decoder can take that vector and turn it into new words and sentences. OpenAI's chatGPT and Google's LaMDA have a similar internal semantic model of language as the Fred-bot, but they generate new text based on prediction. These decoder models were trained using masked sentences (sentences with some words removed) rather than pairs of sentences. In training, the masked model fills in the missing words and is reinforced positively or negatively depending on if it correctly guesses the missing word, which is how those models come to figure out how words can go together. Then, when these models are asked to predict the next word of a sentence, they generate new natural language.

**116 "learns from you and remembers context":** Natural language processing chatbots circa 2023 don't learn and remember as human brains do. The things you tell it don't enter its long-term memory; i.e., the language exchanged with it on the front end doesn't automatically become data it can engage with on the back end. A model's training has to be revisited with fresh data for the model to genuinely learn something new (and this process is expensive!). But there are ways chatbots can be programmed on the front end to (at least appear) to take conversational context into account. GPT-4, for example, holds a good amount of your ensuing conversation in its short-term memory as you talk to it, and the application presents this to the model over and over as the conversation progresses. The chatbot Replika, an app billed as "your AI friend," will "remember" things about you by storing certain statements you make about yourself in a kind of short-term memory, flipping the pronoun, and retrieving those statements when prompted.

**117 Music bars:** See **Beethoven**, 305.

**118–122 Letters to Mobile:** During winters in the 1950s and '60s, Fred worked as a conductor for the Mobile Opera Guild in Mobile, AL. These letters are abridged versions of those sent to Fred by Hannah during February 1957. The Guild's offer to hire Fred as their full-time conductor either never fully materialized or he refused, or perhaps Hannah convinced him not to uproot the family to a small town.

---

## IV. To Eat and Drink

**126 Cat:** Emily, adopted February 18, 2014, [birthdate unknown]–May 14, 2014; named for Emily Gibb from

Thornton Wilder's *Our Town*, a play I taught in my "Utopias and Dystopias" class at CTY.

**131 Photos and documents:** Drawings of photos and documents are based on those compiled in *Hannah Kurzweil: A Biography* by Enid Alyson Kurzweil, CreateSpace Independent Publishing on Amazon, December 2013.

**131, 132 Illustrations:** Drawings based on my grandmother Hannah Kurzweil's illustrations: fashion ladies, pen, and black-and-white paint (watercolor or acrylic) on gray paper; watercolor flowers; dinosaur illustration, blue pen, accompaniment to my grandmother's "Illustrate to Illuminate" lecture at Queensborough Community College "Mystery: The Dinosaurs," 1984.

**131 NEWS: For Release:** A news memo from Richard H. Hoffman Associates, a public relations and publicity manager in New York.

**131 When she came to this country:** Hannah's mother, Lily, after witnessing daily deaths and deportations and the dispossession of all of the family's wealth and property, wrote to two American women teachers she'd met on vacation in Norway in 1937. These women, Allene Markham and Francis [last name unknown], arranged (with American Jewish organizations) sponsorship of the family to America, but the visas took years to be called, so the family fled to England in 1938, where Lily worked as a maid until their American visas came through in 1941.

**132 The Explorers Club:** Founded in 1904, the Explorers Club is "a fellowship of scientific explorers and one of the most fabled organizations in the world"

according to its centennial literature from 2004. My grandmother earned membership in this club when, during a trip to Tobago in the 1980s, she participated in an excavation of Arawak artifacts and discovered Arnos Vale–style pottery later dated between 500 and 1,000 BC.

133 **A debutante:** During the season that went from Christmas to Lent, teen-aged Hannah attended Viennese high society balls at formal settings like the Hofburg, the Habsburg Empire Winter Palace. Hannah was on the committee to open the balls, which meant she'd enter the ball first and waltz around with the "chosen ladies and gentlemen." "At fifteen a debutante," wrote Hannah in a speech for Brandeis College in 1986, "at eighteen an old maid." Hannah was seventeen in 1938 when the Nazis entered Austria and her presence at these balls abruptly stopped.

133 **Unitarian church:** Unitarian Universalism is a liberal religion, composed of individuals from many different cultural traditions, who come together for "a free and responsible search for truth and meaning." Hannah said of her own mother that she "did not allow religion in the home," and if they had a religion, it was "intellect." Growing up, my father attended a Unitarian church in Queens and was involved with the Liberal Religious Youth group and their summer camps. My father joined a Jewish fraternity in college because the members, he said, "seemed the most like me."

133 **Photo with nun:** Image based on a photo of my grandmother with Sister Mary Theresa LeRose in Hannah's old apartment in Cliffside Park. The photo, taken by Joe Giardelli, is from an article in *The Record* from August 23,

1989, "Arawak of Guyana have friend in Cliffside." LeRose, the Guyanese government's welfare officer for Indians, and my grandmother met at the airport on Hannah's way back from her excavation trip in Tobago. Hannah helped LeRose raise money for Arawak craftswomen.

135 **Hannah's paintings:** Watercolor flowers; plein air oil painting of green trees and lake; *Mother Love*, watercolor study of chimpanzees and their babies.

137 **The what-it's-like to be us:** The description of consciousness as a "what it's like" to be something comes from Thomas Nagel's 1974 paper "What Is It Like to Be a Bat?", which makes the claim that "the fact that an organism has conscious experience at all means, basically, that there is something it is like to be that organism." Nagel argues that while I can imagine what it's like for *me* to be a bat, I can't really know what it's like for *a bat* to be a bat.

137 **Is consciousness like a light that's either on or off?:** Theories of consciousness that have affected my ever-more-confused understanding of what consciousness is or isn't tend to negate the idea of consciousness as being a clear yes or no or having an on/off switch.

I've been influenced by the *physicalist* claim that consciousness, as we typically talk about it, is illusory. There is no unified qualia or "what it's like" of experience, says, for example, Daniel Dennett, only a competing array of perceptions, feelings, and sensations. I've also been influenced by *panpsychist* views, articulated by, for example, David Chalmers, who is known for outlining "the hard problem" of consciousness; i.e., how do we explain the relationship between

what happens physically in our brains when we have an experience and the "what it's like" to have that experience? The panpsychist view—i.e., the idea that *everything is conscious* to varying degrees—is just as appealing to me as a physicalist's claim that *there's no such thing as consciousness.* (It's gotta be all or nothing, right?)

138 **"what you see as green is really what I see as blue?":** The redness of red is an often-cited example of qualia, or "what it's like"-ness. My father elaborates on the subjectivity of our experience of colors and the impossibility of communicating this to one another in *The Age of Spiritual Machines* (1999), Chapter 3: Of Mind and Machines.

138 **"I thought you were colorblind anyway":** My father has red-green colorblindness, a mild visual disability that makes it hard to tell the difference between certain shades of red and green.

139 **Flower paintings:** Hannah's watercolors.

142 *The Uprooted*: Written by my great-aunt Dorit Whiteman, *The Uprooted: A Hitler Legacy, Voices of Those Who Escaped Before the Final Solution* (1994) chronicles, based on interviews with 190 escapees, the harrowing experiences of those who, like herself and Fred and their families, managed to leave Germany and Austria before mass execution.

142 *Escape via Siberia, Lonek's Journey*: Dorit's 1999 book *Escape via Siberia: A Jewish Child's Odyssey of Survival* documents Jewish flight eastward through the tale of a Polish boy named Lonek and his family, whose run from the Nazis leads them to imprisonment, hunger, and misery, and eventually—for

Lonek—survival via a *Kindertransport* from Russia to Palestine. *Lonek's Journey: The True Story of a Boy's Escape to Freedom* (2005) is a version of the story geared toward young readers.

147 **Dogs:** Two more dogs here immortalized. Peanut on the couch, and Audrey, who passed away in 2022, by the table.

150 *Ex Machina***:** A 2014 movie by Alex Garland about a programmer who is chosen to be the human component in a Turing Test for a rich CEO's robot. The robot, Ava, turns out to be more intelligent, self-aware, and conniving than expected and so obviously (spoiler alert) ends up killing a bunch of people.

150–151 **Robot cat:** The Joy for All Companion Pet comes from Ageless Innovations, a Hasbro team, who launched their line of robot cats for lonely seniors in 2015.

My robot cat inspired my third cartoon published in *The New Yorker* (September 2016): "Robot Cat Passes Turing Test," which stars a robot cat successfully imitating a real cat by . . . just sitting there. Jury's still out on whether the Joy for All cat passes the Cat Turing Test, or, as many an astute commenter on Instagram has put it, the Purring Test.

152 **Old rituals:** Three traditional rituals of Jewish funerals featured here: the wearing of torn clothing (*Kria*) for the seven days of mourning (*Shiva*), the shoveling of dirt onto the coffin by everyone at the graveside, and the reciting of the Mourner's Kaddish (bottom left panel).

153 **"Our passing will not end in this green valley":** This gravestone was designed by my aunt Enid. Before Hannah

died, Fred's epitaph read "*My* passing will not end in this green valley."

157 **"I hate bipolar. It's awesome.":** Credit here goes to Kanye West, who featured the phrase "I hate being bipolar. It's awesome." on the cover of his 2018 album *Ye*, scrawled over a picture of snowcapped mountains.

157 **"An AI can have a body":** In the 1990s, "embodied intelligence" was a popular theory of robotics pioneered at the MIT media lab run by Rodney Brooks (chronicled in chapter 5 of Meghan O'Gieblyn's 2021 book *God, Human, Animal, Machine*). Challenging assumptions that bodies played no part in human cognition and convinced that human intelligence would emerge in robots through interaction with the environment (as it does for human children), Brooks's lab built robots with bodies and sensory systems, yielding insect-like bots and also playful humanoids, for example: Cog, who could make eye contact and play with a slinky, and Cynthia Breazeal's Kismet, who can coo like a baby and recognize emotion in human voices.

---

## V. Heartstrings

160 **Pinocchio:** Dialogue and drawings based on images from Walt Disney Production's *Pinocchio*, 1940, an adaptation of Carlo Collodi's 1883 children's novel *The Adventures of Pinocchio*.

161 **Stuffed animal:** Now feels like the right time to tell you that this stuffed white polar bear, a GUND original, has a name: Beary.

162 *A Working Theory of Love***:** A 2012 novel by Scott Hutchins about a

man who turns his father's left-behind journals into a chatbot.

162 **"Time to die":** A line from *Blade Runner*.

165 **Marfan Syndrome:** Images, definitions, and descriptions here come from an amalgamation of WebMD and Google searches for Marfan Syndrome circa 2018, when the sketch for this page was drafted, and the results for the same in 2023, when the final image was inked.

168 **"Ray and Terry's":** Ray and Terry's TRANSCEND™ Longevity Supplements are a product of my father's company founded with antiaging specialist Terry Grossman, MD, which has the goal of "helping you live well, forever."

168 *The 10% Solution for a Healthy Life***:** *How to Reduce Fat in Your Diet and Eliminate Virtually All Risk of Heart Disease and Cancer*. My father's first health book, published in 1993, advised that calories from fat should compose less than 10 percent of your diet for optimal health. His later health books advocate for fat content to be closer to 25 percent of your diet, with an emphasis on avoiding sugar and limiting carbs.

168 *Fantastic Voyage: Live Long Enough to Live Forever***:** My father's second health book, written with Terry Grossman, MD, and published in 2005, emphasizes the advances in antiaging science and technology and encourages readers to use diet, supplementation, and other cutting edge medical innovations as a bridge to the explosive longevity outlined in my father's vision of the Singularity. The subtitle is a reference to longevity escape velocity (LEV), a concept first proposed by David Gobel, which refers to the point at which

medical breakthroughs add more than a year to human life span faster than a year can pass, which might mean, on average, people can expect to live forever. My father anticipates we'll reach LEV in 2029. ("So," as he says, "if you can hang in there . . .")

**168** *Transcend: Nine Steps to Living Well Forever*: My father and Terry Grossman's second book together, published in 2010, outlines a nine-step program for "transcending the boundaries of your genetic legacy" and radically extending life.

**171** **Mickey Mouse watch:** A beloved watch my father bought at Disney World during a trip with my brother in the 1980s, which he has worn on and off ever since. "They don't make watches like this anymore," says my father.

**174** **Puppet strings:** One feature of the Pinocchio story I find most interesting is that, even in his nonreal-boy form, Pinocchio is a marionette *without* strings.

**175** **Get Well Soon:** Image based on a card for Fred from some friends, on which he took notes from a doctor's appointment, from the late 1960s.

**176** **Documents:** Death certificate and teacher's insurance forms from 1970; notes from doctors' appointments from the late 1960s.

**177** **Documents:** Drawing based on photos of Fred, Robert, Theresia, and Alois from the 1910s; photo of Fred, Robert, and Theresia from the late 1910s or early 1920s; Fred's passport.

**178** **Documents:** Fred's cover letter and a seemingly infinite number of responses to his cover letter from the 1950s and '60s.

**179** **Documents:** Letter to the dean at New York College of Music signifying Fred's tenure track appointment at Queensborough Community College; Fred's CV; a letter from Fred to his father-in-law, Edwin Bader (his doctor); letter to the dean of Queensborough Community College asking for a reprieve from work.

**180** **Musica Viva:** The beginning of Fred's book on music, written in his own hand. I've heard that after Fred's death, an outline of the book was handed over to a colleague named Dorothea Austin, a pianist and composer from Vienna who escaped the Nazis via *Kindertransport*.

**181** **letter from that final year:** See **Letter**, 224–227.

**184** **"It's a love story, baby, just":** Nine words of Taylor Swift's "Love Story" from the 2008 album *Fearless*.

**184** **Susie's lemonade stand:** Image based on a Verizon Wireless commercial from 2011 in which a young girl named Susie expands her lemonade stand into a successful franchise. On Kurzweilai.net, my father calls this "a wonderful depiction of . . . the democratization of innovation and the increasing youthfulness of entrepreneurship."

**184** **Alice Liddell painting:** *Alice* is a 36" × 24" oil on linen painting by Terry Guyer from 2015, based on a photo of Alice Liddell taken by Lewis Carroll (Charles Dodgson) around 1860. Dodgson was a friend of the Liddell family and their many children. As the story goes, Alice, age ten, and her two sisters were rowing down the Thames with Dodgson and a priest in 1862; Alice asked Dodgson to tell them a story and later to write it down. In 1864, Dodgson presented Alice with *Alice's Adven-*

*tures Under Ground*, which later became *Alice's Adventures in Wonderland*, published in 1865.

**185** **White Rabbit:** Image based on a collector's edition print signed to my father from Grace Slick, American painter and former member of Jefferson Airplane, known for their song "White Rabbit."

**186** **Hand:** Yes, this is really how I hold my pen.

**189** **"Seek to change your mind and not the world":** In Part III of *Discourse on Method* (1637), René Descartes asserts a commitment "to endeavor always to conquer myself rather than fortune, and change my desires rather than the order of the world, and in general, accustom myself to the persuasion that, except our own thoughts, there is nothing absolutely in our power" (English translation by John Veitch).

Descartes asserts this maxim after tearing down his previous beliefs and assumptions before "rebuilding the house" of his convictions about truth. This maxim constitutes one part of his provisional morality, a temporary plan of thought and behavior.

Descartes's shelter in this maxim is likely influenced by Greek stoic philosophy, third century BCE.

**189** **"I'd like to tell Descartes, who":** I consider Descartes's iconic work to be, like this book, a memoir. As he says in Part I of *Discourse*, "It occurred to me that I should find much more truth in the reasonings of each individual with reference to the affairs in which he is personally interested . . . after I had been occupied several years in thus studying the book of the world . . . I at length resolved to make myself an object of study."

Descartes arrives at his famed "I think, therefore I am," in Part IV when he rejects "as absolutely false all opinions in regard to which I could suppose the least ground for doubt." Then he concludes "whilst I thus wished to think that all was false, it was absolutely necessary that I, who thus thought, should be somewhat." He doubts, therefore he thinks, therefore he is. But what is he? Descartes answers that he is "a substance whose whole essence or nature consists only in thinking."

Descartes's dualism, the idea that "the mind by which I am what I am, is wholly distinct from the body," has fallen out of favor with most contemporary philosophers. Nonetheless, Descartes's journey through skepticism is one that every philosophy major on earth for all time will continue to travel, and his severing of the mind from the body has haunted films from *The Matrix* to *Inception* to *Being John Malkovich.*

191 **Dream:** From Fred's journals. Similarly, my performance anxiety stress dream involves being on stage in a dance performance and realizing I don't know any of the moves.

---

# VI. Through the Looking Glass

195 **"If my redrawings change the meaning of the original work":** I will never forget my experience at the Society of Illustrators' *Funny Ladies at The New Yorker* opening in 2018, when, after sharing some cartoons with the crowd—one was a beachy Maurice Sendak homage: "Where the Wild Things Summer"—a fuming audience member approached me and offered some legal counsel: "You should be ashamed of yourself," she said. "The Maurice Sendak Foundation should sue you."

This woman did not understand the copyright concept of *transformative use*, and you can't really blame her, because fair use in copyright law is confusing. The 1976 copyright statute defines fair use in vague terms. Most artists sampling from and commenting on other artist's work can cite the 1994 Supreme Court case *Campbell, aka Skywalker, et al v. Acuff-Rose Music, Inc.*, in which the Supreme Court upheld that 2 Live Crew's rendition of Roy Orbison's "Oh, Pretty Woman" was a parody, writing that *"the enquiry focuses on whether . . . and to what extent [the new work] is 'transformative,' altering the original with new expression, meaning, or message."* This opinion echoes the influential legal essay "Toward a Fair Use Standard," published in *Harvard Law Review*, 1990, by Judge Pierre Leval, who wrote:

*"If . . . the secondary use adds value to the original—if the quoted matter is used as raw material, transformed in the creation of new information, new aesthetics, new insights and understandings—this is the very type of activity that the fair use doctrine intends to protect for the enrichment of society."*

I'm having this text printed on a T-shirt I will wear to future cartoon showcases.

196–197 **Drawings:** Based on drawings by Hannah of Fred (Fritz) at the piano and conducting, original in red colored pencil.

200 **Samantha:** Since my father named his robot cat after Ava, the murderous bot from *Ex Machina*, I named mine after Samantha, the disembodied operating system played by Scarlett Johansson in *Her*.

201 **Samantha's identity conditions:** Jacob would have me make a distinction between *qualitative identity* and *numerical identity*. When "two" things are numerically identical, they are not really two things. For example, Lewis Carroll is numerically identical to Charles Dodgson. But qualitative identity—i.e., sameness—does not require oneness. Listening to my father sing "White Rabbit," I might say, "Oh, this is that song Grace Slick sings," meaning it's *numerically identical* to the one and only song called "White Rabbit" but only *qualitatively similar* to Grace Slick's version of "White Rabbit."

My favorite thought experiment that messes with the assumed oneness of the self is Twinwirld, from Douglas Hofstadter's *I Am a Strange Loop*. In Twinwirld, every birth yields a set of identical twins. These twin sets, known as *pairsons*, do everything together—they are, like Aristophanes's rolly people, two halves of a whole, just not physically conjoined. A *pairson* has one name, and everything in Twinwirld language reflects the assumed oneness of the twin set. The *pairson* Grace has a right part of her self and a left part of her self, just as we, in the regular world, have a right cerebral hemisphere and a left, but we don't think of ourselves as divided in two because our parts communicate so efficiently; so it is with the two parts of Twinwirld Grace.

The thought experiment suggests that a self's relationship to oneness has the potential to be pretty weird.

201 **Painting:** Two monkeys above couch based on watercolor painting by my grandmother.

202–203 **if I could wake up into a different self:** "What am I thinking when I think of myself as a different person?" asks J. David Velleman in

*On Being Me: A Personal Invitation to Philosophy* (2020). How do I know it's *me* waking up into that other self? In "Self to Self" (*The Philosophical Review*, 1996), Velleman distinguishes between first personal anticipation and personal identity, but he connects the two: "whether I can regard a future person as self . . . depends on my access to his point of view."

Is being *one person over time* about point of view, or about patterns? In *Reasons and Persons* (1984), Derek Parfit proposes the "teletransportation paradox." Imagine a machine that scans and records your molecular composition, then destroys those atoms but relays this scan to Mars at the speed of light where a Mars machine recreates you atomically, with all your memories. Is this travel? Or does this kill you and replace you with a copy on Mars? Let's now imagine the same scenario, except the machine doesn't destroy your atoms on earth. Are there now two of you?

My childhood fantasy posits something like this puzzle, except instead of Mars, I imagined being sent to the future, and instead of my exact self I was recreated with new memories. These thoughts were my earliest dabbling into a sort of Cartesian skepticism *(What if I can't trust my memory and "yesterday" has been implanted in me by some evil demon?!)* and also resembles Bertrand Russell's "Five-minute hypothesis" from *The Analysis of the Mind* (1921), which imagines that the world was created five minutes ago; all of us popped into existence with "memory-beliefs" of a longer history. ("It is not logically necessary to the existence of a memory-belief that the remembered event should have occurred, or even that the past should have existed at all.")

How easily questions about the self lead to doubt about everything that ever was!

**202 Manx cat:** Fluffernutter Kurzweil, no-tailed and, later in life, one-eyed, was such a beloved cat that my father froze some of his DNA with the idea that, one day, we'd clone him. Now my father can't remember the details of this arrangement, but Fluffy's DNA is, possibly, still out there somewhere.

**202–203 Cat paintings on the wall:** My childhood bedroom was decorated with framed cat paintings. In lieu of imagination or research, I asked Dalle 2, OpenAI's text-to-image AI system, to generate images inspired by my memory of those paintings; for example, 202, bottom left: *a playful watercolor painting of a sleeping cat curled around a clock.* Who owns my drawing of an image created by an A.I. trained on the images of millions of other artists?

**204 Cheshire Cat hologram:** In real life, this hologram is green light emerging from a black background, a product of John Kaufman from Light Fantastic Limited in London.

**204–205 Cat figurines:** When my father started traveling for work, he wanted to come home from each place with a souvenir. Rather than amass random trinkets, he limited his purchases to cat-themed objects. So his cat collection was born, and once people know you have a cat collection, guess what they buy you for birthdays and holidays. Last I counted, my father's cat figurines numbered somewhere in the five hundreds. Shout-out to the multitudinous and unknown (to me) artists of all these beautiful objects, which inspired my drawings here.

**206–207 an oil painter at a San Francisco art fair:** These family portraits, along with the portrait of Alice Lidell, are by oil painter and bronze sculptor Terry Guyer. My father's portrait is 40" × 30" oil on linen, completed in 2016; my portrait is a similar size, completed in 2017. My father also commissioned portraits of my mother and of my brother, his wife, Rebecca, and their two kids Leo and Quincy. My brother's third kid, Naomi, was born after the painting was completed, so my father tacked a printed photo of her on the frame.

**207 Avatar:** A 2023 googled definition, from Oxford Languages.

**208 *Ray Kurzweil, TED Talk*:** My father's TED Talk from 2005, *The Accelerating Power of Technology*, has over three million views on TED.com, as does his TED Talk from 2014, *Get Ready for Hybrid Thinking*. But you cannot find evidence on the TED website of our collaborative TED Talk from 2001. The YouTube user wwwTrueFreeThinker posted a clip of my father discussing the Ramona project on a CSpan2 BookTV interview from around that time, which includes clips of the performance.

**208–210 Ramona:** Images here come from *The Making of Ramona*, a short documentary about the experience, posted on Vimeo by Kurzweil Technologies. The Ramona project is also documented on Kurzweilai.net, where you can listen to Ramona's original and covered songs (i.e., my father's singing plus voice alteration software).

Ramona also became the talking face of Kurzweilai.net for a time, one of the internet's first chatbots paired with a human-like face. She's no longer on the site, but you can find sample conversations with her across the internet.

Ramona may have been the inspiration for the 2002 movie *S1m0ne*, by Andrew Niccol, staring Al Pacino as a director who transforms himself into a virtual female alter ego in an attempt to save his career.

**210–212 "One pill makes you larger":** Lyrics to the song "White Rabbit" by Jefferson Airplane, sung by my father at TED 2001. I still remember some of this choreography.

**212–213 Women @ the Frontier:** A global network of female game-changers, a nonprofit dedicated to inspiring female leadership in tech and industry. This 2012 event at Singularity University featured several speakers, including Amy Purdy, an actress/model and medal winning para-snowboarder who speaks inspirationally about adapting to the loss of her legs. I was there as part of a floating W@F series in which influential men were interviewed by their daughters.

These images come from a video of the event posted by the YouTube channel We Blog the World, November 28, 2012. These comments were still posted below the video last time I checked. But I don't often check.

**214 "Be what you would seem to be":** Drawing based on those by John Tenniel. Quote from Lewis Carroll's *Alice's Adventures in Wonderland*, chapter IX, The Mock Turtle's Story.

Much time can be spent analyzing the confusing structure of the logician Carroll's sentence here. When the Duchess resolves to put her adage "more simply" and then proceeds to spin the sentence into dizzying complexity, she works against the stability of *being* and *seeming*. Wading through all the double negatives, I do get something that accords with the first sentence:

*Imagine that others will see you as appearing to others as someone whose identity (what you were or might have been) was what you had been.*

**215–217 Danielle:** *Danielle: Chronicles of a Superheroine* was published with WordFire Press in 2019. The book follows Danielle Calico, a girl from Los Angeles, through twenty-two chapters, each chronicling a year of her life, from birth through her marriage to her cross-national lover, the also-exceptional physicist Cheng Liu. The book is narrated by Danielle's also-exceptional sister Clare, who survived the Haitian earthquake, was adopted by the Calico family, and later wins the Nobel Prize in literature for her documentation of her sister and their adventures. Danielle has trouble making friends, doesn't walk or say a word until she's two years old, but she does organize mass protests for immigration reform at age four and bring clean water to Zambia (in cooperation with local leadership) at age six. She brokers peace in the Middle East and becomes president of China *and* the US before turning twenty. There's a hint at the end of the book that Danielle has been "enhanced," which might explain some things, but this is left ambiguous. Each chapter features one of my illustrations of Danielle and crew midadventure. Although Danielle's parents look like my drawings of my parents, Danielle is my father's alter ego, not mine.

My father begins the nonfiction companion book *A Chronicle of Ideas: A Guide to the Concepts That Animate Danielle's World (And Mine)* with a meditation on the power of ideas to change the world. It is basically a book entirely of endnotes. I am trying to keep this appendix of endnotes as short as possible, but it's clear my father and I both have a thing for long lists of references.

See Danielleworld.com for information about the books and resources for how you can *be a Danielle* and work toward solving the world's problems.

**219, 220 Items in room:** The Grammy Award on the table is my father's technical Grammy from 2015 for achievements in the field of music technology. The quilt on the couch is based on one made by Paula Sparks in honor of Danielle.

**220 (The) Society of Mind:** Marvin Minsky's 1986 book which describes his theory of intelligence as a kind of society built from the interactions of many simpler mental processes working together. Minksy, an MIT professor and pioneer of robotics and AI, met my father who, at fourteen years old, wrote him a letter, beginning a decades-long mentorship.

**220 in his dreams:** My father discusses the value of dreams for problem solving in his books *How to Create a Mind* and *Transcend*. He says he assigns himself a problem before falling asleep, and then, since dream space is free from taboos (says Freud) he can "think-dream about solutions . . . without the burden of professional restraints." Lucid dreaming, a dream state in which the dreamer becomes aware they are dreaming, allows him to actively enter this liberated space. Growing up, I remember using a lucid dreaming machine courtesy of my father. It was basically an eye mask that flashed blinking lights at you if it detected you were entering REM sleep. For a time, my father invested in an entrepreneur's more elaborate lucid dreaming invention, which involved synching music with the dreamer's heart rhythms. (It didn't make it to market.)

**223 Creative writing portfolio:** My father majored in creative writing at MIT in addition to computer science. "Another Song for the Cat" and "The Aged Still Turn Their Eyes" are two poems he wrote sometime in the late

1960s, collected in a bound portfolio in my father's collection. At MIT, he took classes with famed playwright Lillian Hellman and poet Barry Spacks.

**224** **Documents:** Typed speech read by my father at a memorial concert for Fred at Queensborough Community College in 1971; "Outer Space" and "The Boy Who Ran Away," written by my father in the 1950s; multiple letters between my father and his maternal grandfather, Edwin Bader, between 1967 and 1969.

**224–227** **Letter:** My father's letter dated September 16, 1969, the culmination of a series of correspondences during the years my father was at MIT, to his maternal grandfather, Edwin, goes on for fifteen typed pages. It's a passionate defense of my father's decision to fully drop his commitment to computer science and instead throw all his weight and brainpower behind the pursuit of becoming a great poet, one who bridges the artistic and technical worlds. My father did, I'd say, become this kind of poet, but he did not abandon computer science.

**227** **"There is no doubt" letter:** One precipitating letter from my father's grandfather Edwin, known in the family as "the little doctor" (he was four foot eleven) from May 1967. Edwin is accusing my father, the math prodigy, early inventor, and winner of science prizes, of faltering on his path to greatness. Edwin disapproves of my father's philandering with painting classes and campus politics instead of sweating over the focused study of computers. "I miss any indication of perspiration," Edwin writes.

**230** **"I think this score":** The score here reveals how close the answer is lo-

cated in vector space to your original query, i.e., a quantification of how relevant the response is based on the algorithm's internal semantic model.

**230** **"And the typos?":** The Fred-bot's answers were riddled with more typos than I included here. The human transcribers of Fred's text (myself included) were not given proofreaders. But while the typos in the corpus of text offered as answers remain unfixed, they don't confuse the algorithm's sense of internal meaning. Since the algorithm was trained on billions of statements, which inevitably contained lots of common typos, these errors are "smoothed" out in vector space.

**235–239** **Musicians:** Images based on drawings by my grandmother Hannah Kurzweil, originally drawn in what looks like black-and-white pastel on green paper. The inscription notes these are members of the NY Philharmonic Orchestra, and "Raviola" is the name of the cello player.

**241** **"there's not a lot to go on.":** The Fred-bot can only offer as answers the sentences that 1) Fred wrote down, 2) were preserved in our archive, and 3) were typed up and entered into this system. The Fred-bot is only saying things Fred has already said. The biggest limitation, in my view, is less in this bot's inability to create new language but in our limited access to Fred's past language. One can imagine how much more dynamic the responses might be if everything Fred *ever* wrote was included in his response pool, especially if he spent as much of his time texting as I do.

The story of turning a digital native's imprint into a chatbot in the aftermath of their death is eerily imagined in the *Black Mirror* episode "Be

Right Back" from 2013, in which a woman, played by Hayley Atwell, opts to bring her tragically dead husband, played by Domhnall Gleeson, back to life. A chatbot becomes a voice on the phone becomes a Frankensteinian pile of flesh that comes to life in the bathtub, but the embodied android is disquieting, too uncannily like and unlike the original, and the relationship ends disturbingly. (But nobody kills anyone else, at least.)

In real life, chatbots of the dead built from digital imprints have less dystopian endings. In 2016, following the death of her best friend Roman Mazurenko, Russian engineer Eugenia Kuyda, of the natural language startup Luka (which later became Replika) built a neural net trained on millions of lines of Russian text, and then, using her own text messages with Roman, trained that neural net to speak in Roman's voice. The algorithm became a chatbot that Roman's friends and family could talk with. At first the algorithm was, like the Fred-bot, selective, meaning it matched each input with an appropriate response from Roman's text messages. Later, the algorithm became generative, meaning the words from his texts could be recombined to make new sentences that theoretically still sounded like him. In Casey Newton's 2016 article for *The Verge*, "Speak Memory," Eugenia described her experience with the bot as like "sending a message to heaven."

For more on the ethics of these endeavors, check out Alexis Elder's "Conversation from Beyond the Grave? A Neo-Confucian Ethics of Chatbots of the Dead" in the *Journal of Applied Philosophy*, 37, from 2020.

**241** **"I keep a journal":** For most of his adult life, my father has kept meticulous journals in Excel spreadsheets, a new sheet for each day, noting significant happenings in his work and family life, his health, and state of mind.

241 **I keep a journal too:** Since I was fourteen years old, I have kept untidy journals, handwritten in bound books, without backup, stored in dusty boxes— some in my childhood home, some in my current home. I have no method for writing other than furiously unloading whatever is on my mind, whenever I feel I have the time.

242 **"soars past it and becomes super-human":** My father's most enduring theoretical commitment is the idea that computational power is growing exponentially, meaning that the rate of growth is itself increasing over time.

To understand the explosive power of exponential growth and our inability to conceptualize it, consider the story of the king and the con artist: Once upon a time, a con man offered a king a chessboard in exchange for grains of rice: one grain of rice on the first square, two grains of the second, four on the third, eight on the forth, and so on for the full sixty-four squares. By the twenty-first square, the king owed over a million grains of rice, by the forty-first over a trillion. Before the final square, his kingdom was bankrupt, the debt impossible to pay.

Many cite Moore's Law as an example of exponential growth. In 1965, Gordon Moore posited that every two years, the number of transistors on microchips would double, meaning computational progress would become faster, smaller, and more efficient at an exponential rate. My father's commitment to exponential growth goes beyond Moore's Law. His technological predictions, informed by what he calls the Law of Accelerating Returns, consider the positive feedback of evolution: the innovations of the past and present are used to create future innovations.

243 **"There's this quote about technology and magic":** My father might be trying to remember the Arthur C. Clarke line from his 1962 book *Profiles of the Future: An Inquiry into the Limits of the Possible*, in which he outlines three laws, the third of which states: "Any sufficiently advanced technology is indistinguishable from magic."

---

## VII. Exponential Growth

245 **"Love is":** British novelist and philosopher Iris Murdoch originally wrote these words about love as the bridge between ethics and art in an essay titled "The Sublime and the Good" (*Chicago Review*, 1959); the full quote:

"Art and morals are . . . one. Their essence is the same. The essence of both of them is love. Love is the perception of individuals. Love is the extremely difficult realization that something other than oneself is real. Love, and so art and morals, is the discovery of reality."

247 **On What Matters:** Jacob's favorite philosopher Derek Parfit's master work of philosophy from 2011; the two biggest books on our bookshelf.

248–249 **Documents:** Jacob's cover letters for a bajillion job applications, my cover letters for a bajillion fellowship applications, written and sent between 2017 and 2019.

253 **"scrubbing cobblestones at the boots of Nazi soldiers":** Part of the Nazis' systematic oppression of Jewish people were rituals of public humiliation. Nazi officials encouraged crowds to watch as Jews were forced to scrub the streets, tasked with removing political slogans critical of the Anschluss. Photographs of these events, which circulated via the Nazi propaganda publication *Der Stürmer*, reinforced the degradation.

254 **Alone Together:** MIT professor Sherry Turkle's 2011 book about how technology and social media are degrading human interaction and connection.

255, 256, etc. **Painting above bed:** Based on Picasso's *Pitcher and Bowl of Fruit*.

256, 260, etc. **Rock painting:** Images based on a painting by my friend Nico Ponton.

258 **arced skyward, to infinity:** When graphed, exponential growth has a certain shape, a line that at first appears linear and later shoots upward, the $y$-axis making huge leaps ahead for every tiny chug along the $x$-axis.

Personally, I spent a lot of my time in math class making pretty shapes on my TI-83 graphing calculator, so I'm more familiar with the aesthetics of functions than with what they mean.

258–259 **What does his infinity mean?:** The Transhumanist movement, based on their interpretation of the implications of the exponential growth of technology, believe science and technology can enhance the human condition, radically extend life, and augment intelligence. Some Transhumanists believe humanity is destined to transcend problems like death through the incorporation of technology into human bodies and/or the transformation of human consciousness into a digital format.

Additional writing that has influenced my understanding of transhumanism include Mark O'Connell's *To Be a Machine: Adventures Among Cyborgs, Utopians, Hackers, and the Futurists Solving the Modest Problem of Death* (2017), Meghan O'Gieblyn's "Ghost in the Cloud" in *n+1* (Issue 28, 2017), and Martine Rothblatt's *Virtually Human: The Promise and Peril of Digital Immortality*, plus Martine's Terasem Movement Foundation, a transreligious movement committed to "diversity, unity, and joyful immortality for biological and cybermetric consciousness via nanotechnology and geo ethics."

261 **News:** Headlines from *The New York Times* and *The Guardian* from between December 2018 and October 2019.

264 **News:** Headlines from *The New York Times*, March 2020.

268 **Beethoven's death mask:** On display in my childhood home is this mask of Beethoven's face, supposedly made from a mold of his corpse. People always said this looked like the face of Fred, and I grew up thinking it was *his* death mask, not Beethoven's.

Beethoven is one of the only people to have a life mask—made by Franz Klein in 1812 when Beethoven was forty-two—and a death mask, made by Josef Danhauser, March 28, 1827, two days after Beethoven's death at fifty-six. There are reproductions of both floating around the world, and I don't know how my grandfather obtained this one. I've encountered some confusion about whether these forms heralded as his *death mask* are not in fact his *life mask*. Beethoven had lost a lot of weight in the last days of his life from extreme cirrhosis, and some purported death masks

feature a face more shrunken than the full-featured face on display in our home.

268 **Fred's piano:** In my childhood home is this Baldwin grand piano, the original piano Fred played throughout my father's childhood in Queens. This piano was made in 1908; I don't know how and when Fred obtained it. My father inherited the piano after Fred's death, had it revamped, and the piano joined him in Somerville, MA, in the apartment he was inhabiting when he met my mother.

270–271 **Concert hall:** This concert hall is rendered from photos of the Musikverein, the Great Hall, also called the Golden Hall, in Vienna, established in 1870. I chose this hall arbitrarily for its grandeur. I don't know what concert hall Fred's 1937 choral performance took place in.

271–272 **Woman:** My drawing of Fred's sponsor to the US. See **Gertrude Sumner Ely**, 47.

271 **Liebeslieder Walzer:** Translates to "Songs of Love," a choral piece, with accompanying piano, composed by Johannes Brahms in 1875. At the famous choral concert of 1937, which Fred's sponsor attended, this was, ostensibly, one piece played, according to a possible eyewitness. (See **Peter Pulzer**, 291.) I've assumed this was a youth choral concert, since Fred was founder and conductor of the Vienna Youth Chorus. This may have been a coed chorus, although I've rendered it as a boys' choir. Fred may have conducted this piece or played accompanying piano.

273 **Toothbrush scrub:** The adage that I heard about these public humiliation rituals is that Jews were forced

to scrub the streets *with toothbrushes.* I don't know if Fred ever participated in this ritual or others like it.

274–277 **Fred's passport:** The following is a likely narrative of Fred's journey out of Vienna, based on the story the stamps on his passports and his ship manifest (courtesy of ancestry. com) tell:

Fred's passport was issued on September 6, 1938. As it was scheduled to become invalid a year later, he knew he would use it only to leave Vienna (**6 Sept., 1938,** 276).

Fred received his visa to America on October 3, 1938. (**Immigration Visa**, 274, 276.)

On Wednesday, October 5, 1938, the Reich Ministry of the Interior invalidated all German passports held by Jews; Jewish passports would only be valid if stamped with a big letter *J.*

On Friday, October 7 (**7 Okt. 1938**, 276) Fred likely went to the banking authority to withdraw what assets he could to take with him but was denied exemption from laws about traveling with or transferring funds abroad. This stamp translates roughly to "no exemptions," meaning all kinds of anti-Semitic tax laws applied to Fred, like the Reich Flight Tax, a tax of 25 percent of assets on those fleeing the German state, just one of many laws designed to strip fleeing Jews of all assets. From an article in *The Jewish Telegraphic Agency*, Dec. 1938. "The Nazi system of restrictive laws, special taxes, enforced loans and capital levies, the Jew leaving Germany today is stripped of anywhere from 96.5 percent to more than 99 percent of his fortune."

On Monday, October 10, or possibly the night before, Fred boarded a train from Vienna. The train crossed the border into Germany, where, on October 10, his passport was stamped with that iconic *J* (281, 277). On October 11, he crossed the border through Emmerich (**11 Oct. 1938**, 276), a border town in Germany, into the Netherlands. His visa to America allowed him to pass through Holland (**NAAR**, 275: NAAR means *toward* in Dutch), where at Rotterdam port on October 15, he boarded the *S.S. Veendam*, which arrived at Ellis Island on October 25, 1938. Fred (Fritz) had $76 (the equivalent of about $1400 today) in his possession, en route to Bryn Mawr, PA.

283 **"Some philosophers suggest that that the way we exist in time":** If you are a *Presentist* about the nature of time, you think that the only times that are real are present times. If you are an *Eternalist*, you'd say that all times are equally real. If you are a *Growing Block theorist* (the best-named theory) you'd say that past and present are real (and growing) but the future is not real.

283 **"the passage of time is an illusion.":** You can also be an *A theorist* or a *B theorist* when thinking about the nature of properties like pastness, presentness, and futurity, a distinction that comes from J. M. E. McTaggart's 1908 paper "The Unreality of Time." *A theorists* believe there is an objective present, and you can say of things that they are past, present, or future. *B theorists* believe all we can say of events from an objective point of view is that they are before, after, or simultaneous with each other—i.e., the *passage* of time is an illusion.

283 **"Your whole self isn't moving through time":** Jacob is talking about a concept called *perdurance*, which I read about in J. David Velleman's 2006 lecture "So It Goes." Philosophers distinguish between two ways objects can persist through time. They can *endure*

through time, meaning the object is wholly present at each point in time that it exists (the object is a ball thrown across a football field and time is the yard marks). Or they can *perdure* through time, meaning objects are extended in time as they are in space; only one part of the object exists at any point in time (the object is the field itself). "A perduring self can be compared to a process, such as the performance of a symphony. The performance doesn't move with respect to time; it merely extends newer and newer temporal parts" (Velleman).

283 **"Doesn't that imply that our future has already been written?":** The short answer is: not necessarily.

283, 285 **"But time is moving across you, illuminating different parts of you" / If time is like a flashlight:** Here is yet another theory of time called Moving Spotlight Theory (phrase coined by C. D. Broad). This is an Eternalist A theory that allows for time to pass *and* for past, present, and future to be real.

283 ***Arrival*:** A 2016 movie directed by Denis Villeneuve based on the short story "Story of Your Life" by Ted Chiang, published in his 2002 collection *Stories of Your Life and Others*. The aliens in the story, called Heptapods, are Eternalists. They don't experience time linearly, so their language is circular, and the human linguist investigating their language starts to experience her own life narrative in a nonlinear way.

283 ***Slaughterhouse-Five*:** Kurt Vonnegut's 1969 genre-bending, nonlinear novel about a World War II soldier who becomes "unstuck in time" when he is abducted by the Tralfamadorians, Eternalist aliens who can travel through and see all points in time simultaneously. As

Velleman discusses in "So It Goes," their orientation toward death is nonplussed: "When a Tralfamadorian sees a corpse, all he thinks is that the dead person is in bad condition in that particular moment, but that the same person is just fine in plenty of other moments."

283 **"This view of time can alleviate suffering":** The concept of perdurance offers Velleman at least temporary relief from anxiety about death: "So the end of me is not a cliff toward which I am constantly hurtling; it's merely a segment of me with nothing beyond it in time, just as there is nothing of me above the crown of my head or below the soles of my feet" (*On Being Me*).

283 **"filling time, rather than passing through it, or having it pass you by":** In "So It Goes," Velleman tries to imagine what it would be like to really live without the conception of an enduring self. "I would think of myself as filling time rather than passing through it or having it pass me by—as existing in time the way a rooted plant exists in space, growing extensions to occupy it without moving in relation to it." Ultimately, for Velleman, shedding the illusion of an enduring self is the way to dispel the illusion of the passage of time.

284 **"people so committed to digital immortality":** One prominent example of digital immortality in the name of a love is Bina48, a robot commissioned by Transhumanist Martine Rothblatt, based on Martine's wife, Bina Aspen. Bina48 is a moving, talking robot bust aesthetically modeled after Bina and downloaded with some of Bina's memories. Martine built Bina48 as an instantiation of Transhumanist ideas about digital consciousness and the future of identity and also because Martine reportedly couldn't imagine a

world without her beloved. For more on Bina48 see my comic "Technofeelia vol 3. (Me)chanical Reproduction" in *The Believer*, December 2018.

## VIII. Con Espressione e Semplice

287 *The Sound of Music*: Like Diane Wu in her 2021 *This American Life* story "Many a Thing She Ought to Understand," I, as a kid, also failed to realize that *The Sound of Music*—the Rogers and Hammerstein musical about the big, happy Austrian von Trapp family and their lovable governess—was a story about fleeing the Nazis, based on the memoir of Maria von Trapp's experience of the *Anschluss*. Wu only watched *the first side* of the VHS tape. My day camp's production of the play in the 1990s was similarly abridged.

288–289, 304, 305, 311 **Music:** My aunt Enid compiled recordings of Fred's piano playing and conducting. You can find many of these recordings on Spotify under the album *Fredric Kurzweil 1912–1970.* "Lullaby" and "Break Break Break" reference original piano and choral compositions, two of six original compositions I only first heard in 2023.

289 **Music:** This drawing and the selection of music bars reference a recording of Bach's *Brandenburg Concerto No. 5 in D Major* (Fredric Kurzweil, Mildred Hunt Hummer, Raymond Kunicki, and the Knickerbocker Chamber Players). The lines and shapes on this page and the other music pages are what these songs look like to me when I try to draw them.

291 **Peter Pulzer:** Pulzer grew up in the same apartment complex as Fred.

We are related through David Eisner, Fred's grandfather, the Iron Cross recipient. Pulzer's family immigrated to the UK in 1939. Peter became a prominent historian of Austria and Jewish Life. He wrote *The Rise of Political Anti-Semitism in Germany and Austria* (first published 1964, revised 1988*)* and *Jews and the German State* (2003).

Peter died in 2023, just as I was finishing this book. I reached out to share these pages with him and received a response from his son Matthew, who also informed me that his family had recently installed *Stolpersteine* near the site of the family home. *Stolpersteine*, or stumbling stones, are small concrete blocks inscribed with the name and life and death dates of victims of Nazi persecution and extermination. The stones were placed in the name of Karl Eisner and Marie Grunhut (née Eisner), Fred's mother Theresia's siblings, who were deported to Treblinka in 1941.

292 **Buildings in Vienna:** Buildings near or close to the Museumsquartier: Kunsthalle Wien (Vienna's institution for international contemporary art and discourse); Naturhistorisches Museum (Museum of Natural History); Statue of Emperor Franz II/I, at Hofburg Palace; Leopold Museum; Mumok (Museum of Modern Art).

292 **Kissing Sculpture:** *Kiss* by Chinese artist Xu Hongfei. The sculptures on display in the courtyard of Museumsquartier change regularly.

292 **Egon Schiele:** The Leopold Museum features an extensive collection of paintings by Austrian expressionist Egon Schiele (1890–1918).

293 **31:** The door of my grandmother Hannah's family home: Wipplingerstraße 31 in the first district.

294 **Freud Museum:** At Bergasse 19, 800 meters away from Hannah's apartment, the psychoanalyst worked and lived with his family for forty-seven years before fleeing the Nazis in 1939. Jacob and I tried to visit the museum in 2021, but as we showed up forty-five minutes before closing and last entry is one hour before closing, we were, Germanically, not allowed in. (Despite the fact that *fifty minutes* is a psychoanalyst's hour!)

294 **Art**, 297 **What is home:** Vienna is full of street art. These images are based on Viennese graffiti I photographed during this trip.

295–296 **24:** Passetistraße 24 in the nineteenth district, Fred and Peter Pulzer's apartment building.

295 **an innocent abroad:** In Mark Twain's *The Innocents Abroad* (1869), Twain recounts, satirically or earnestly or both, the dizzying combination of desolation and historical meaning he encounters in the Holy Land, when he voyages there as part of a Great Pleasure Excursion with a group of American travelers in 1867.

297 **Zwischen 1938:** A plaque near Fred's apartment that honors Austrian Nazi victims and resistors who were executed in Berlin-Plotzensee "because of the political and religious resistance to the National Socialist dictatorship," the plaque reads. The portrait is of Josef Baldermann, a labor organizer and resistance fighter; the housing complex at Pasettistraße 9-21 was named after him in 2013.

297 **"with Robert, who spent some years in Europe after the war":** Fred's brother, Robert, a mechanical engineer, and his mother, Theresia, escaped first

to London, and Fred was later able to secure immigration to America for his mother. So the story of Robert's salvation goes: He was arrested by the Nazis in Vienna in the summer of 1938. Previously, he had ended a courtship to a woman called Ruth, who, working as a dressmaker for a wealthy family in London, heard word of Robert's imprisonment. She, via the British family, arranged a payoff of someone in the British office, which got Robert a visa, which she sent to the Nazis, who let him out of detention. Ruth and Robert were married in London five days after *Kristallnacht*. (The marriage lasted ten years and yielded two children, Lenny and Peter.) Robert spent some years in Europe with his second wife, Edith, and third son, Allen. (Some of those years are chronicled in Allen Kurzweil's 2015 memoir *Whipping Boy*.)

299 **The AI would have to have musical intelligence:** Circa 2023, AI has begun to dabble in original music production, for example *The Lost Tapes of the 27 Club* (2021), from the Canadian mental health advocacy organization Over The Bridge, which is "using AI to create the album lost to music's mental health crisis." Using neural nets to analyze patterns (plus human editing), they created an album of original songs in the style of iconic musicians, like Amy Winehouse and Jimi Hendrix, who died at twenty-seven years old. Music AI can also translate between music and words; for example, MusicLM from Google Research (2023) can create original audio based on text descriptions.

It's a puzzle, however, how exactly to reproduce my grandfather's particular musicality, since he was most gifted as a performer. His talent was, I believe, located primarily in his body: his ability to *play* piano and *conduct* an orchestra. How do you code for that? What would

we need to have preserved in order to reproduce his particular musical abilities?

300 **Dorit wrote a book:** See *The Uprooted*, 142.

300 **Egregious horrors of many of the Polish Jews:** Over three million Polish Jews died in the Holocaust, with an estimated 350,000 Polish Jews surviving (among them both of my mother's parents). Compare this to 65,000 Austrian Jews murdered, with 125,000 fleeing. The odds of surviving the war as an Austrian Jew were much higher, but both populations—along with queer people, communists, Gypsies, Jehovah's Witnesses, nonwhite people, people with disabilities, and other minorities—suffered egregious horrors.

304 **Brahms:** Brahms, *Rhapsody in E flat Major*, op. 119, no. 4. Played by Fred on piano.

305 **Beethoven:** *Sonata number 31 in A-flat Major*, op. 110: III Arioso. Played by Fred on piano.

307 ***The Singularity Is Nearer***: My father's next (as of 2023) book, forthcoming . . . soon!

307 **"about AI . . . something new has evolved":** For example, when my father and I really had the conversation this scene is based on, my father talked about GPT3. See **"create new speech based on old patterns,"** 116.

As I write this, the public is engaging with chatGPT, which reached 100 million users just two weeks after its launch, making it the fastest-growing app in history. Predecessors of ChatGPT had 125 million parameters. ChatGPT has 175 billion parameters (parameter size determines the size and complexity of the model's neural network and gen-

erally improves performance). Between the time I started writing this footnote and the time I finished it, GPT4 launched, with (it's rumored but not confirmed) 1 trillion parameters. By the time you read this, I might be an infinity-parametered chatbot. OpenAI's large language model is just one example of our era's class of chatbots. Here's how ChatGPT explains itself to me today, March 13, 2023:

*I am ChatGPT, a large language model developed by OpenAI. I was created by a team of researchers and engineers who trained me on vast amounts of text from the internet, books, and other sources. I work by processing natural language input, generating responses, and attempting to provide helpful and informative answers to your questions.*

*As a language model, I use deep learning techniques to understand and generate human-like responses to your queries. I analyze the structure and meaning of your questions, search my database of knowledge and language patterns, and generate responses that are relevant to your queries.*

*While I am a machine, my programming allows me to respond in a way that mimics human conversation, and I am constantly learning and updating my knowledge base to provide better and more accurate answers. However, please note that I have limitations and can sometimes make mistakes or provide incomplete or inaccurate information.*

311 **Chopin:** *Prelude in D Flat Major*, op. 28, no. 15. Played by Fred on piano.

316 **"My book is not a comedy":** In Shakespeare's plays, per the conventions of his day, the tragedies ended with death and the comedies ended with marriage.

319–320 **Woods:** Drawings based on photos of Vienna Woods.

321 **Monument against War and Fascism:** This 1988 work by Alfred Hrdlicka stands on the Albertinaplatz in Vienna, near the Vienna State Opera House, atop what used to be the Philipphof house, a home destroyed in a 1945 bombing that killed 300 people. It contains four pieces made of granite, parts of which were retrieved from Mauthsausen Concentration Camp. Two of its sculptures are pictured here: the Gates of Violence, which honors all victims of war, and the Street-Washing Jew, which is meant to commemorate Jewish victims of Nazi persecution and humiliation (see **"scrubbing cobblestones at the boots of Nazi soldiers,"** 253). This piece has garnered critique, both for the ways it fails to engage with Austrian complicity in Jewish oppression and the ways it stereotypes Jewish people. Says Tanja Schult (*Public Art Dialogue*, 8:2 2018) the sculpture positions "Jewish humiliation . . . in the shadow of the war, when in fact it was the other way around." And while Hrdlicka hoped the Street-Washing Jew would "confront the non-Jewish audience with their guilt and shame" the depiction "confirms rather than alters the perception of 'the other.'" Tourists would use the man's back as a bench—eventually the sculpture was given barbed wires to deter sitters.

But this piece is interesting to me for the ways it has encouraged other artists to respond to the problematic depiction. For example, the Jew was vandalized/gilded in gold (Johannes Angerbauer-Goldhoff, 1990), and the memorial housed a live performance in which the artist theatrically cleaned the streets with a giant red toothbrush, clad in a gas-mask-as-thong, a crystal butt plug, and oversized red stilettos (Cleaning Time, Steven Cohen, 2007). In 2015, Ruth Beckermann's temporary installation featuring private black-and-white film footage emphasized the complicity of Austrians who watched and laughed while Jews were forced to clean the streets.

322 **Liliput-Bahn:** A light railway that provides transport around the Prater Park in Vienna.

323 **Sketchbook drawings:** Based on Egon Schiele's paintings *Nude Self Portrait with Blue Green Shirt* (1913) and *Erwin Dominik Osen, nude with crossed arms* (1910) and Xu Hongfei's *Flying Piano* sculpture.

324 **But with time and attention, with close looking:** In "The Idea of Perfection" (1962), Iris Murdoch articulates the connection between looking, attention, and love with an anecdote about a mother-in-law (M) and her initial negative judgment of her daughter-in-law (D). Rather than harden her heart, M says of D, "Let me look again," and in time, she revises her opinion. Says Murdoch, "I have used the word 'attention' . . . to express the idea of a just and loving gaze upon an individual reality . . . When M is just and loving she sees D as she really is." Murdoch emphasizes the connection between *a loving gaze* and *the perception of reality.* "Attention is the effort to counteract . . . illusion."

Close looking is what I call whatever I'm doing when I draw something in a detailed and realistic style. Like Murdoch's M, looking again and again at an object changes my initial impression; it fills me with awe for the complexity of the physical world.

Philosopher Martha Nussbaum, in a 2014 essay about Murdoch, emphasizes the need for vulnerability in the loving gaze. "I think there is something more to loving vision than just seeing. There is, for example, a willingness to permit oneself to be seen." For a comparison of different interpretations of Murdoch's famous anecdote, see Christopher Cordner's "To see 'justly and lovingly': What did Iris Murdoch mean by attention?" in *Religion and Ethics*, 2019.

325 **Door drawing:** This is a re-created sketch based on the original drawing of Fred's door I made soon after this pilgrimage. I sent the original drawing to Peter Pulzer in London.

326–327 **Church:** Karlskirche (St. Charles Church) is a baroque church in Karlplatz, Vienna, built between 1716 and 1737 after Roman emperor Charles VI, reeling from a recent plague, held an architectural competition to build a church for his namesake Charles Borromea, a patron saint and healer of plague sufferers.

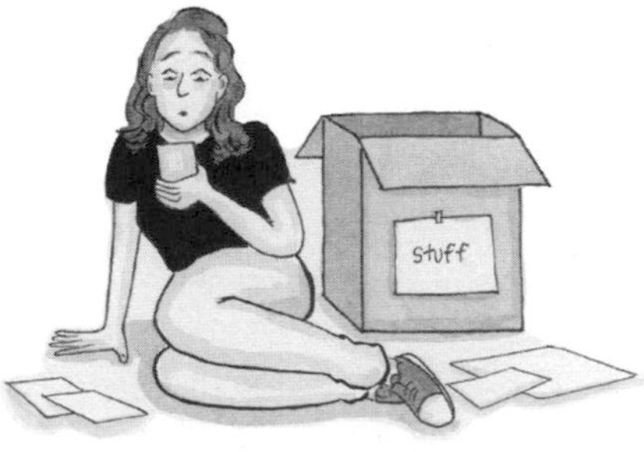
stuff

**AMY KURZWEIL** is a *New Yorker* cartoonist and the author of *Flying Couch: A Graphic Memoir.* She was a 2021 Berlin Prize Fellow with the American Academy in Berlin, a 2019 Shearing Fellow with the Black Mountain Institute, and has received fellowships from MacDowell, Djerassi, and elsewhere.

She has been nominated for a Reuben Award and an Ignatz Award for "Technofeelia," her four part series with *The Believer* magazine. Her writing, comics, and cartoons have also been published in *The Verge, The New York Times Book Review, Longreads, Literary Hub, WIRED* and many other places. Kurzweil has taught widely for over a decade. See her website (amykurzweil.com) to take a class with her.

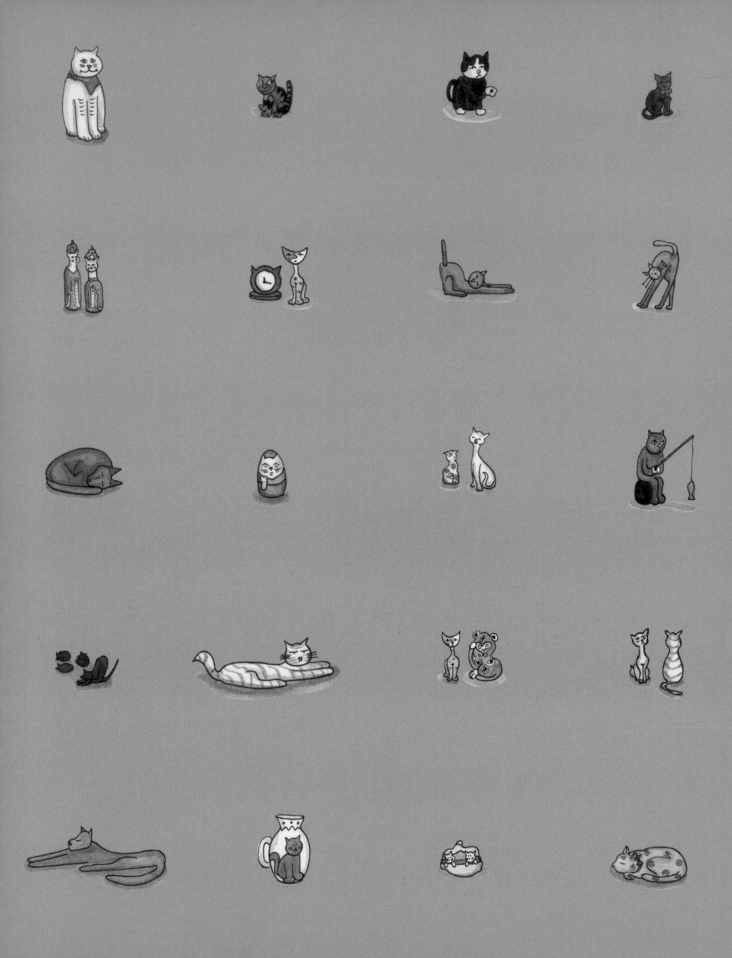